Jobs and Fairness

Jobs and Fairness

THE LOGIC AND EXPERIENCE
OF EMPLOYEE OWNERSHIP

―――――――

Robert Oakeshott

MICHAEL RUSSELL

To ANNE AND WILLIE CHARLTON
for their friendship and support over many years;
and to MARGARET ELLIOTT
for her friendship and support
over nearly as many years
and for her stunning leadership
of employee-owned ventures

© Robert Oakeshott 2000

The right of Robert Oakeshott to be identified
as the author of this work has been asserted by him
in accordance with the Copyright, Designs
and Patents Act, 1988

First published in Great Britain 2000
by Michael Russell (Publishing) Ltd
Wilby Hall, Wilby, Norwich NR16 2 JP

Typeset in Sabon by The Typesetting Bureau
Allen House, East Borough, Wimborne, Dorset
Printed and bound in Great Britain
by Biddles Ltd, Guildford and King's Lynn

Contents

Acknowledgements

Easily my biggest debts are to the three successive Chairmen of Job Ownership Ltd (JOL). The late Jo Grimond, as he still was when JOL was incorporated in 1979, came first. He was succeeded by Philip Baxendale in 1986. David Erdal took over from Philip ten years later. Without Jo's support JOL could never have got off the ground. Without that of his two successors as its Chairman, it could not have been sustained. If there had been no JOL, it would not have been possible for me to enjoy paid work in this somewhat specialised field. Without the paid work, it need hardly be said, neither the case studies nor this book would have been possible.

But my debts to JOL's first three Chairmen are personal as well as ontological. In their different ways all three have offered me both friendship and inspiration. Philip and David have starring roles in the case studies of the Baxi Partnership and Tullis Russell respectively. Jo supplied the political key which unlocked the door to the ownership transfer at Baxi, and thus perhaps indirectly to much that has since happened.

If I have been very lucky in the quality of the Chairmen that I have worked for, I have also been most fortunate in the quality of those who over the years have been ready to serve as members of JOL's unpaid board. I hope it will not seem unfriendly to the others if I single out James Cornford for special thanks.

I must also acknowledge a most substantial debt to those who have served unpaid on the board of JOL's younger half-sister, Partnership Research Ltd (PRL), and especially to its current Chairman, Willie Coupar. Willie has a starring role in the case study of Chesterfield Transport.

JOL and PRL are both not-for-profit undertakings. But PRL, which employs no one, also enjoys charitable status. One of its main functions has been to commission case studies. Most, though not all, of the case studies in this book were originally commissioned by PRL and published by it. I must acknowledge and thank its Chairman and board members for permission to use that material.

My intellectual debts in relation to this book are far too many to acknowledge in full. But I want to single out six people for special mention. The first is Professor Ronald Dore, among other things for his outstanding and outstandingly clear insights into the secrets of Japanese business success. The second, Professor David Ellerman, is also an academic, or rather he was, before moving first to Slovenia as a freelance consultant in 1990, and then on to the staff of the World Bank. For me, David's signal contribution is in his analysis of property rights. I follow him much, though not all the way, in my early chapters. I also want to take this opportunity to acknowledge his important role in the debate in Slovenia which preceded the country's employee-ownership-friendly privatisation laws in the early 1990s. Since the 1970s, David has been one of the intellectual dynamos behind the spread of employee ownership in the US.

Jeff Gates is the second American to whom I owe a great intellectual – and indeed a political – debt. For many years he was chief of staff to Senator Russell Long when the latter was Chairman of the Senate's Finance Committee in the American Congress. It has been through the filter of Jeff, rather than directly from the late Louis Kelso, that I have come to understand the inner logic and the enormous potential of the latter's famous ESOP mechanism, which surely could become one of the most consequential social inventions of this century. What I owe most of all to Jeff is my understanding of why and how, because of the way new investments are typically financed, our conventional capitalist system leads to the concentration of more and more wealth into fewer and fewer hands. I should point the attention of readers to his important new book, *The Ownership Solution: Towards a Shared Capitalism for the 21st Century*.

My political debt to Jeff is that he persuaded Russell Long to come over to Britain at the end of 1986, just before his retirement from Senate. I have little doubt that the Senator's meeting during that visit with Norman Lamont, the then Financial Secretary to the Treasury and later Chancellor, was one of the decisive steps which later resulted in the enactment of more-or-less effective ESOP legislation here in Britain.

The fourth intellectual debt which I must record is also to an American – the late James Smith, for many years a special assistant to successive Presidents of the United Steelworkers of America

(USWA). With Lynn Williams, the last of the Union's Presidents that he served, Jim was the joint architect of a conditionally positive policy towards employee ownership which was developed by USWA from the mid-1980s onwards. Both have starring roles in the book's union case study. My intellectual debt to Jim relates to a key insight which others have pointed to but none so clearly: about the essentially psychological and psycho-political obstacles in the mind-sets of typical middle managers and typical shop stewards which make employee ownership something that they cannot easily accept.

My fifth intellectual debt is to Patrick Dolan, a member of PRL's unpaid board and a working colleague on various JOL projects in former Communist countries in Central and Eastern Europe. Patrick's professional background is many years in management with ICI. More recently – and more relevant to what I owe him – he founded the British Deming Association in the late 1980s. I owe him all I know about Deming's approach to management: maybe not that much, but enough to be sure that it is the only management approach at all suited to employee-owned businesses.

My final intellectual debt is more diffuse: to a very old friend, Antony Martin. After a brave fight starting in the summer of 1996, Antony was defeated by a horrible cancer at the end of February 1997. He had been a member of JOL's unpaid board since the 1980s and more recently, like Patrick Dolan, a working colleague in Central and Eastern Europe. Whatever the issue, Antony's commitment was to get to the bottom of it and to do so with the interests of the less privileged members of society especially in mind. He has left behind important memorials in Eastern Europe, in the shape of Employee Ownership 'handbooks' and 'good practice' guides in four countries: Hungary, Romania, Bulgaria and Slovenia. On some of these he worked jointly with Patrick Dolan. Others were his work alone. His support for the whole employee ownership project was a source of continuing reassurance to me. Had he doubted its validity, or seen it mainly as a personal hobby horse of mine, his backing would, I know, have been withheld.

I must also put on record my thanks to Antony for having had a first go at editing this book for me. If an editor's task may be likened to that of a forester, then Antony's contribution in this case was to do the first thinning out exercise.

In each of the case studies particular people are mentioned. My debts to them are as obvious as they are substantial. But as there isn't space here to list them and thank them individually, I hope they will accept a kind of collective thanks, for the trouble they have been prepared to go to in supplying information and for having made my own – and later Mary Campbell's – research work as rewarding and enjoyable as these things can be. As well as for her research, Mary Campbell must be thanked for an extended stint of editing work which ended in the summer of 1997. But I must make one exception to that collective expression of gratitude and offer special thanks to Fred Freundlich of Ownership Associates in Bilbao for help over the Mondragon material.

Those who helped me with the case study of the Herend Porcelain Manufactory in Hungary are mentioned in the text. I would like to thank them here. But there are others in other former Communist countries to whom I would like to say thank you. They have given a great deal of time and effort to employee ownership in recent years, and have greatly helped my thinking about it. In many cases they have already become friends. The people I have specially in mind are: in Bulgaria, Eugenie and Fanny Kostourkov; in Macedonia, Jursit Rifat and Elizabeta Krkaceva; in Romania, Dan Ghitescu and Serban Stanescu; in Slovakia, Eugene Skultety and Vladimir Borza; in Slovenia, Aleksandra Kanjuo-Mrcela and Nadja Cvek

My thanks are also due to my last four assistants in the JOL office who have helped me in one way or another with a book which I must have by now been working on for about eight years. They are Thecla Mallinson; Paul Johnson; Rachel Sloan; Isabella Tree, more recently Burrell. And for the formidable task of preparing the index I must thank a new and unusually congenial friend, Marina Johnston, and, from June 1998, my assistant in the JOL office.

For the book itself I must thank my publisher, Michael Russell. Like JOL's first Chairman, Jo Grimond, he is one of those people with whom it is a pleasure to work as well as to have lunch.

In conclusion two points of clarification. First, it has not been possible to work the same 'final revise' date for all the case studies and other chapters in this book. Most went through a final revision in 1996 or 1997. But in one case, that of Republic Engineered Steels Inc (RESI), it seemed right to introduce a 'stop press update' which takes the story down to July 1998. Second, in the belief that for literary projects, titles awarded in the recent past are extinguished on death, I have referred to 'Jo' rather than 'Lord Grimond' and, for example, to 'Isaiah' rather than 'Sir Isaiah' Berlin.

Preface

The chief aim of this book is to bring together empirical evidence about the experience and performance of selected businesses which are substantially owned neither by absentee shareholders nor by the state but by those who actually work in them. Behind the aim are two hypotheses. The first is that their successful performance – one of the criteria for their selection in the first place – is in most cases really rather good, better than readers might expect and probably good enough to justify some further modest measures of government support. Conversely, considerable space is devoted to cases of failure and the reasons for that failure.

The second hypothesis is that there is a common ingredient in the performance of these firms. That ingredient is a higher than average level of commitment by rank-and-file employees to the goals of business success. That commitment, in turn, or so I believe, rests on a combination of ownership arrangements which are judged to be more or less fair and reasonable and systems of employee involvement in corporate government which are both effective and compatible with the highest standards of professional management.

One of my motives for undertaking this task is quasi-scientific. Over the last twenty-five years or so I have consistently argued that we have much to learn from the sorts of firms described in this book. I believe that the empirical evidence marshalled here shows that employee ownership should no longer be dismissed as inescapably and fatally flawed because it is liable (a) to favour higher wages at the expense of investment and (b) to reject opportunities for expansion on the grounds that this would dilute the value of an individual's ownership stake. Anyone in touch with the relevant theoretical work by professional economists will know that those two arguments are still very much alive and well. Particularly influential in this respect over the last decade have been *Agathotopia* by the late Nobel Prize-winning economist James Meade, and *The Share Economy* by Harvard's Martin Weizman.

What is the response of theorists when new empirical evidence seems to undermine their theories? At least in the short term, it is to ignore the new evidence – or demand yet more empirical research – and reiterate the old theoretical objections. The history of the physical sciences abounds with examples of this kind. How much more, then, in economics where quite enormous financial and other vested interests as well as scholarly egos are involved?

Of course, I have my own biases and my own ego, and I make no claim to be an academic scholar. I also have my own financial interests, even if they are comfortable rather than enormous. But I am now fairly sure that the balance of the relevant empirical evidence points to conclusions which are the opposite of what the theoretical objections to employee ownership suggest. In other words I think this evidence suggests that where the employees are substantially the owners, and thus share in the financial returns, and where rank and file employees have an appropriate voice, the firms involved invest more and generate more rapid employment growth than their conventionally owned competitors. What is more, because of a greater acceptance by their employee owners of downward flexibility in their financial compensation, including even wages, these firms enjoy a further advantage: of being better able to save jobs when times are hard. Hence the 'jobs' in my title. This book highlights examples of this phenomenon, which hits at the heart of the theoretical economic objections to employee ownership: the US steel industry cases and Mondragon are the most notable. The employee ownership itself and the associated involvement of rank and file employees in corporate government underpin its 'fairness'.

There is also rather specific recent evidence from the Republic of Slovenia where the privatisation laws enacted by the country's first post-Communist governments were remarkably friendly to employee ownership. The particular evidence from Slovenia suggests that we may need to replace the 'cash now' stereotype of the rank and file employee with a new one: the 'cash now' stereotype of the absentee shareholder and rentier and of those intermediaries in the financial services sector who act on their behalf.

The experience of Slovenia has not been as widely reported as it should have been. But readers should note that in Slovenia in 1996 there were striking cases of challenges by outside minority shareholders to the size of the dividends which businesses with majority 'internal' ownership had decided to pay out: challenges that the dividends were too low rather than too high. In at least one case towards the end of 1996, so-called 'investment funds' representing minority outside rentiers went so far as to launch a court case against the 'insiders'. This complements recent work by a Dutch economist, Professor de Jong, which seems to suggest that an important cause of the relatively poor performance of Britain's top companies over the last twenty years has been a combination of 'too high' returns to capital at the expense of labour and the readiness of directors to pay excessively high dividends.

Mention of Slovenia invites me to say something about the geographical and national spread of the employee-owned companies selected for study. With one exception they all come from what I hope may still be called, simply, the West: from Britain and the United States and from four countries in mainland Western Europe – France, Italy and Germany and the Basque provinces of Spain. The one exception is a Hungarian business, the Herend Porcelain Manufactory, which became substantially (75%) owned by its 1,500 strong workforce in a successful privatisation by employee buy-out in 1994.

All over the ex-Communist world there were, from the early 1990s onwards, examples of businesses that had emerged from the privatisation process substantially owned by those who worked in them, often with their ex-employees involved in a slightly wider 'internal ownership' as well. Including those in Russia, the total number of these businesses was almost certainly numbered in tens of thousands when this was written in the spring of 1997. On the other hand, the situation both inside and outside these firms was still then too fluid and the available information about them too uncertain to allow for the inclusion of their experience in what attempts to be a reasonably stable body of empirical evidence.

I have allowed myself to make a special case of Herend for a number of reasons. These include its long, stable and vivid history, going back to the 1820s and including its leap to fame in 1851, when it sold one of its hand-painted porcelain dinner services to Queen Victoria at the Great Exhibition. In 1997 Herend was still making and selling the same hand-painted porcelain under its post-privatisation arrangements as it had been for all or almost all of the intervening years. Second, I had exceptional access opportunities since Job

Ownership Ltd, the company which employs me, was an adviser to Herend on its privatisation. I take this opportunity to acknowledge financial support from the British Government's Know How Fund.

My case study of the Herend Porcelain Manufactory, as it likes to call itself in English, is similar in one respect to all the others. I have not stinted myself on the history of these undertakings. In the large majority of cases they did not start their corporate lives as employee-owned businesses and a good deal of space has been devoted to their pre-employee-ownership years. Herend in Hungary, the Tullis Russell Group in Scotland and the Baxi Partnership in England were businesses already well beyond their 100th birthday when employee ownership started.

I make no apology for going long on the history. It has both intrinsic and explanatory interest. Most important, it is in their pre-employee ownership history that the sources of their employee ownership will in many cases be found. It cannot be emphasised too strongly that we are dealing here with contingent, not pre-determined, developments.

I also make no apology for going long on performance detail. For the busy or selective reader introductory 'overviews' have been provided in each case and the detail can be skipped. But for those with a serious interest there is really no substitute for a proper look at the details on an individual company basis. For without that, in my opinion, it is impossible to make an informed judgement about the *quality* of today's employee ownership experience and thus about its potential for the future.

In this respect my approach is different from that of my main US counterparts. Theirs may be symbolised by the publication of tables with headings like the 'top thousand employee-owned companies'. It is only on close inspection that the reader discovers the great range in the percentages of employee ownership which the 'top thousand' embrace: maybe from 100% to 4%. Moreover what readers may not discover at all is that among those American cases where the employee ownership is really substantial, only in a tiny minority will it be sustained for more than ten or twenty years.

Not that sustainability is everything. The number of good and substantial examples of employee-owned businesses would be much fewer if employee ownership had to satisfy a sustainability condition to qualify. That will remain the case until laws are passed which are not only 'employee ownership friendly' but also 'sustainable employee ownership friendly'. John Major's British Government, through changes in the law in 1994, moved some way in the direction of sustainability. Neither President Clinton nor the American Congress has made any similar move. Indeed, there may be an insufficient acknowledgement in the US that it would desirable to do so.

Because sustainability is not everything, this book includes five case studies where the employee ownership proved to be no more than temporary. Three are UK examples: of employee ownership which emerged from privatisation. The two others are the two steel companies in the US: Weirton and Republic Engineered Steels Inc.

For those businesses where their employee ownership has been designed to continue indefinitely, my hope is that the case studies provide a sufficiently sound base to enable anyone so inclined to re-visit them in the future. It must be more than a racing certainty that they will continue to be both successful and employee-owned at the end of the first decade of the next century. In fact I would myself be prepared to make a bet that they will continue to enjoy a combination of reasonable prosperity and employee ownership at the end of the first half of the next century. Unfortuately, I shall not be around to collect what I foresee would be my winnings.

I would like to conclude this preface by recalling a question put to me once by the first Chairman of Job Ownership Ltd, the late Jo Grimond. It was after we had visited the Mondragon group of mainly manufacturing co-operatives in the Basque provinces of Spain. Jo's question was 'Is there a danger that the Mondragon system and its values make for working lives which are altogether too Cromwellian for our more easy-going fellow countrymen?' In rather different language, a 1996 television programme on the John Lewis Partnership expressed the same reservation when it characterised the Partnership's philosophy as 'goody goody'. A short response is that so long as the Partnership continues to pay annual bonuses which average two months' salary, uneasiness about its 'goody goody' ethos will not be the only thought in the minds of John Lewis partners. They may also welcome a set of rules which ensures that they are treated fairly, and in a real sense as partners rather than just as wage employees. Simone Weil makes the point that human needs include both security and risk taking; and Abraham Maslow writes about those human needs that wages cannot reach.

I am writing this on Bank Holiday Monday, 5 May 1997, just a heady days after the truly stunning victory of Mr Blair's New Labour in the British General Election of 1 May. One of Mr Blair's ideas is that of the 'stake-holder'. Another, first made famous for me by Nelson Mandela, is the idea of 'inclusion'. I will claim no more than that employee ownership seems strikingly congruent with both.

Introduction

The root of the matter is the straining of Spirit of Man to be free. *William Straker, Durham Miners' Agent, in evidence to the Sankey Commission on the Coal Mines, 1919*

The root of the matter is that the relationship of master and servant, on which the organisation of industry has rested during so many centuries, has become untenable in a democratic age. *'Britain's Industrial Future'. Report of Liberal Party Inquiry 1928*

As is clear from the post-war economic record of Japan, a business is likely to outperform the competition when, other things being equal, both shop floor and management are committed to business success. Moreover, progress towards the achievement of these conditions in a country's businesses has a better chance than any readily available alternative of overcoming the familiar, understandable and largely justified discontents of ordinary people with the conventional capitalist system whether those discontents are seen in more or less bread and butter terms, as being about, say, unacceptable levels of employment security or unacceptably large income differentials; or whether they are formulated in the rather more high-flown and over-arching terms of the two epigraphs above.

Leaving out Japan, and with one qualification, that in essence was what I argued in *The Case for Workers' Co-ops*, first published in 1978.

The qualification was embodied in the book's title. Although I insisted that I was not using the word 'co-op' in its narrowest legal sense, I claimed, in effect, that the necessary commitment to business success could best be achieved when enterprises were owned and controlled, not by faraway shareholders or the state, but by the people working in them. I allowed that those conditions might be satisfied just as well by a business registered under company law, like Britain's John Lewis Partnership, as by an enterprise registered as a production co-operative under different legislation. But I did not allow for the fact that what the Continental Europeans call the two social partners – employers and employees – *can* work together in ways which achieve the necessary commitment, without the introduction of employee ownership and ultimate control. In other words, outside Japan, my argument ignored, in part for polemical reasons, the many sustained successes of conventional capitalism, private and public.

More important, my earlier book ignored the success of the co-determination legislation, pioneered in what was then West Germany, in overcoming the divisions between capital and labour and achieving a consensus, within the enterprise, in favour of business success.

In this book I continue to recommend that businesses be owned and controlled by the people working in them. This is the most promising way of securing the desired joint commitment to business success. But there are two important modifications compared with the earlier book. First I wish to make clear throughout that employee ownership (which will normally entail ultimate employee control) will not *automatically* generate the necessary commitment. Of itself, it does no more than provide the best possible setting in which the desired commitment can be worked for. Second, I want to acknowledge from the outset that, so long as it is significant in its size, partial employee ownership is not at all to be despised. The designers of an ideal world should no doubt be encouraged to favour majority rather than minority employee ownership. But after what has happened in this century, there are overwhelming arguments for *not* insisting on the ideal.

At this point I need to anticipate an objection: that these modifications to the argument are not sufficient to justify a second book beating out the same old tune. The justification for this second book is that the central arguments of the first have been immensely strengthened since it was published. The empirical support for them is much greater than it was towards the end of the 1970s. Moreover, the central arguments now rest on more solid theoretical foundations and a propitious legal environment – an array of measures to encourage employee ownership which have been enacted since the middle 1970s by the American Congress. Conceptually derivative, but in some ways superior, legislation is now on the UK statute book. Most recently, the first tentative signs of interest by the European Union have become evident.

As with its predecessor, the largest part of this book is taken up with the empirical evidence: case studies of the performance of employee-owned businesses. But the quantity of experience from which the case study material is drawn is far greater now than it was in the later 1970s. Twenty years ago there were perhaps fifteen substantial employee-owned businesses world-wide. Now, that figure is probably over a thousand. It is clear that the international population of these businesses has grown by between 50 and 100 times since the mid-seventies.

More important for my argument than the great increase in the total population of these businesses is that there are now many more top quality successes to point to. In *The Case for Workers' Co-ops* I managed to find only one substantial example of truly unqualified success: the group of mainly industrial co-operatives centred on the small town of Mondragon in the Basque Provinces of Spain. True, that low score was partly due to ignorance and partly to more or less conscious prejudice. As an example of my then ignorance I will simply mention the omission of the famous German optical apparatus undertaking, Carl Zeiss, which completed its first *century* of ownership by an employee trust (or '*Stiftung*') in 1991. An example of my then prejudice is the John Lewis Partnership (JLP), where employee-trust ownership has now lasted nearly seventy years. It is true that the Partnership does indeed figure in *The Case for Workers' Co-ops*. But its outstanding record was neither properly studied nor evaluated. That inadequate treatment is partly explained, I suspect, by an earlier prejudice on my part against the non-working-class provenance of JLP – and perhaps also by a quite unwarranted prejudice against shop-keeping as a business activity.

But ignorance and prejudice on my part are not the main explanations for the contrast between the one truly top-class success story I put forward at the end of the 1970s and the many available to me now. Using shorthand, I would suggest that employee-owned businesses (EOBs) are best understood as the right-of-centre counterparts of workers' production co-operatives. Those who typically work in them, whether on the shop floor or otherwise, have no real reservations about business success, or about using well-tried practices to achieve it. They may well see this success mainly as a means – for ensuring long-term enterprise survival and perhaps for achieving more ambitious goals as well – rather than as an end in itself. But they are not typically preoccupied with different and competing agendas – to reform the world or to strengthen the working class or whatever else may have been suggested as appropriate by people like Mr Tony Benn. They are typically therefore more single-minded than the members of a workers' co-op in their pursuit of business success. And in principle they have no hang-ups about the key role of professional managers in achieving that. By contrast one of the chief negative findings of *The Case for Workers' Co-ops* concerned the widespread management weakness of these ventures – and the ambiguous feelings which many of their members have typically had about the importance of the management function.

Some counter-examples could also be cited: of workers' co-ops which show extraordinary single-mindedness in their pursuit of business success and are in no doubt at all about the key importance of the contribution of professional managers. We shall even find grounds for the hypothesis that, other things being equal, including quality of management and single-mindedness of commitment, the very best of the co-operatives are likely to outperform their EOB counterparts, essentially because industrial relations ceases to be a problem. But despite that qualification, the main distinction between the culture of the typical workers' co-op and that of the typical EOB still stands. And it creates a distinctly higher presumption of success for the EOBs. This is especially so because employee ownership is normally introduced into existing businesses, whereas most workers' co-ops now start from scratch. The fact that the number of high quality and substantial success stories is now much greater than twenty years ago is largely attributable to EOBs and not workers' co-ops.

This increase in the empirical support for the central arguments is matched by the strengthening of the theoretical considerations which underpin them. There are two rather different groups of points. The first group are those associated with the collapse of the state-controlled economies. As recently as Britain's celebrated miners' strike in the early 1980s, many in the West still looked East for the most eligible way of addressing the age-old and continuing discontents with conventional capitalism. The discontents and frustrations have largely survived. But the collapse of the East European monolith has left an ideological gap. This book argues that employee ownership is the most persuasive candidate for filling that gap.

As for the theoretical economic foundations beneath the arguments for employee owmnership, these have been greatly strengthened by the work of Professor Ronald Dore, and especially by his work on the secrets of Japanese business success. In the past the main economic case for employee ownership tended to rest on two common-sense propositions of an almost excessively simple character:

– that most people will work better if they are working mainly for themselves;

– that most people will work better for an organisation if they have a say in its policies and how it is run.

Dore's. work has not undermined these foundations. But it has improved their sophistication and given them a new elegance. The key necessary condition for the success of Japanese businesses, according to Dore, is that they are, and are seen by their employees to be, fundamentally fair in the way they are organised. It is that, Dore argues, which ultimately explains their exceptional performance over the last thirty-five years, their sustained high rates of productivity growth, and their outstanding levels of what he calls, following the Harvard economist Harvey Liebenstein, 'X' efficiency – 'efficiency inside the business' (in contrast to allocative efficiency: a feature of national economies as a whole and one which depends mainly on the intensity of the competition prevailing between the businesses which make up these economies). We can now argue theoretically for EOBs by saying that their structure makes them well placed to achieve high levels of 'X' efficiency because they are well placed to satisfy Dore's fairness test. Using more traditional language, we can say that they are well placed to overcome – or at least ameliorate – the celebrated 'alienation' of typical employees in conventional capitalist or state-owned businesses.

We can now summarise the main arguments for employee ownership which are at the centre of this book:

– that a joint commitment by management and shop floor to business success is perhaps the single most important factor, other things being equal, for achieving business success;

– that employee ownership, though it does not automatically result in that joint commitment, is unquestionably one of the best available settings in which to work for it; especially when the employee owners have no hang-ups about business success and no hidden agendas;

– that employee ownership is the best available way to overcome people's discontent and frustration with their working lives and their alienation at work.

At the centre of the arguments for promoting the spread of employee ownership should be its potential for improving business performance. For even in the affluent democracies of the West the dominant political imperative is still economic growth, which in turn depends above all on increasing productivity.

But this emphasis should not obscure the fact that there are important subsidiary arguments which point in the same direction. One of the most persuasive and least problematic of these is the effect of employee ownership on the distribution of wealth. The headline facts in the USA, where the issue has been most widely studied and thought about, are easily summarised:

– ignoring ownership by institutions, one per cent of the American people own approximately 50% of its corporate wealth;

– in the absence of employee ownership, and if the compulsory redistribution of existing assets is ruled out, the ownership of this US corporate wealth will inexorably become more concentrated because of the ways in which new investment is typically financed.

Though there may be differences in the actual numbers, both these points apply throughout the developed world and anywhere else where something like conventional private capitalism is the main feature of the economy. As the late Louis Kelso first pointed out, new investment in these countries is normally financed out of depreciation allowances, ploughed back profits and/or bank debt – in ways which further enrich the existing owners of corporate wealth rather than in ways which generate new owners.

This same Louis Kelso, a Californian lawyer and investment banker who died in 1989, is the intellectual progenitor of today's employee ownership in the Anglo-Saxon world. His analysis of the consequences for wealth distribution of the normal ways of financing new investment is only one of his key insights. He also has to his credit a 'social invention' of enormous potential consequence: the Employee Stock Ownership Plan or ESOP. About the ESOP and its children we shall have much more to say later on. Here it is enough to assert bluntly that without it employee ownership would almost certainly be sentenced for ever to a life on the sidelines.

Among the alternative ways of improving business performance by securing a consensus commitment to it inside the enterprise, employee ownership therefore has one extra advantage – wider distribution of corporate wealth. By contrast neither the Japanese approach nor the co-determination arrangements of Continental

Western Europe can produce that extra benefit, or anyway not to the same extent.

As compared, again, with both the Japanese way and with the co-determination approach, we can speculate that employee ownership may even have non-financial benefits outside the factory gates. For example, to the extent that it is structured democratically, it may result in enhanced citizen commitment to democratic arrangements in the wider community. It is also possible that employee owners may outperform other members of the community in a number of measurable ways in their non-working lives. But that is a subject for future research.

Finally there are advocates of employee ownership who argue for it on the grounds of political, economic and natural justice. Foremost among these is David Ellerman, formerly of the American employee ownership agency, the ICA Group, and Tufts University; and more recently a World Bank specialist adviser on privatisation. Ellerman's views were published in *The Democratic Worker Owned Firm* in 1990. We will discuss them shortly.

I

Moral and Legal Issues

Whatsoever then he removes out of the state that nature hath provided, and left it in, he hath mixed his labour with, and joined to it something that is his own, and thereby makes it his property. *John Locke, in 'Two Treatises on Government', 1824*

It is the essence of capitalism that one man works for another's profit. The worker makes the effort now, and it is tiring and boring effort: always in the marginal hour and nearly always in the intra-marginal hours too ... The capitalist merely saved some money in the past – abstinence has disutility, but not very much; and took a decision to invest money, also in the past. What disutilities does he currently bear? Merely those of risk. *Peter Wiles, in 'Schumpeter's Vision', 1981*

From their different standpoints John Locke and Peter Wiles supply the central moral argument for a presumptive link between labour and a property right in its output: that labour is the key to added value. Peter Wiles adds that it has a manifest, and morally compelling, disutility.

Yet both writers go on to qualify these pronouncements. Locke does so in a way which at least on one interpretation turns a labour theory of property rights upside down. For in the very next paragraph he writes that: '... the grass my horse has bit; *the turfs my servant has cut*; and the ore I have digged in any place, where I have a right to them in common with others; *become my* property.' (Emphasis added.)

In other words Locke's presumptive link between labour and a property right in its output is not to be interpreted as undermining what he would no doubt see as a natural right for one man to hire the labour of another and to enjoy the fruits of the latter's labour. For Wiles, on the other hand, the main grounds for ignoring any implied moral injunction against conventional private capitalist property rights are explicitly those of expediency. It is worth quoting further from his essay on Schumpeter, from the point where the epigraph breaks off:

All this [the disutility of the capitalist] is very trivial compared with the pain of labour, especially the pain of the last hour. The monetary rewards are not commensurate. Marx grasped this simple point, and so do Western proletariats down to the present day. The Soviet proletariat also grasps it. Indeed how could it not? – since it is about the only valid point in the whole of Soviet propaganda. The 'exploitation of man by man' under capitalism is reiterated in the USSR, and essentially by every Western union too ad nauseam. In fact, it is only one consideration among many. It may be expedient – it *is* [emphasis original] expedient – for workers to forget it. They should – many of them have – accumulate enough to become 'exploiters' in turn. Political freedom and some aspects of economic efficiency (but not all) are better served in this way.

It was Professor David Ellerman who first drew my attention to the fact that the apparent thrust of the famous Locke passage quoted in the epigraph is in some sense overturned by what he writes about his servant further down the page. In writings of over twenty years down to 1990, Ellerman emerged as the most forthright and unequivocal advocate of a labour theory of property in today's world. More precisely, what he has put forward is a labour theory of *business* ownership. He has proposed an elegant and intellectually convincing analysis of the main separate components of ownership in the case when what is being owned is a business undertaking. Moreover, by grounding his theory in 'jurisprudential' considerations, he argues, in effect, that his proposition is what natural justice or 'natural law' demands.

Ellerman's theory, or perhaps more accurately his 'doctrine' of the 'labour ownership of the firm', together with his complementary doctrine of the 'democratic right' of employees to control the managers who manage them, are so important in this discussion that they need to be treated at some length. Ellerman developed his position in a long series of published papers which stretch back to the early 1980s and which culminated in *The Democratic Worker Owned Firm*. That last is the source for what follows.

I start with a crude summary of Ellerman's main conclusions and then explain how he came to them. They are essentially two:

– People have an inalienable right to enjoy the full fruits of their labour. That right is violated by the conventional employment contract. It can only be satisfied if labour (management as well as non-management) becomes the legal owner of all businesses.

– The government of such labour-owned businesses should be democratic.

The language of natural, or inalienable, rights and of natural law, is less fashionable now than it was even fifty years ago: when William Temple, for example, in his *Christianity and Social Order* relied extensively on arguments from natural law. Yet that is the language which Ellerman has chosen. And any proper account of his views must follow it.

'Labour', Ellerman asserts towards the end of his book (p. 208) is the '*natural* [emphasis added] foundation for private property appropriation.' Earlier (p. 42) he summarises the basis of his theory or doctrine as: '. . . an application to the employment contract of the *de facto theory of inalienable rights* [emphasis original] that descends from the history of anti-slavery and democratic thought . . .'

If we leave the issue of democratic business government on one side for a moment, Ellerman's argument that the employment contract is objectionable – or as he claims 'inherently invalid' – rests on two related points. First, he asserts a 'similarity' between a contract of self-sale (i.e. into slavery) and a contract of self-renting (i.e. the conventional employment contract). In his view the law which rules that contracts of self-sale are inadmissible should do the same for contracts of self-renting, and on the same grounds. The nature of those grounds is thus at the very heart of Ellerman's argument.

The essentials are easy to grasp. They are that human beings are 'inalienably responsible', and to treat them otherwise – as, he contends, the employment contract inescapably does – is for the law to seek to alienate what is inalienable. The comparison with the invalidity of the self-enslavement contract is made quite explicit: 'The natural-law invalidity of the voluntary self-enslavement contract (to sell one's labour) is already legally recognised; the invalidity of the contract to rent or hire human beings should be similarly legally recognised.'

For me, Ellerman is most persuasive when he draws his readers' attention to an important asymmetry: between the law's failure to insist on a labour contract based on human responsibility, on the one hand; and its insistence, on the other hand, that the employee (or slave) becomes completely responsible – and liable to punishment

– when there is any question of criminal or otherwise unlawful actions. He quotes (p. 40) a key passage to that effect from Francis Batt's *The Law of Master and Servant*: 'All who participate in a crime with guilty intent are liable to punishment. A master and servant who so participate in a crime are liable criminally, not because they are master and servant but because they jointly carried out a criminal venture and are both criminous.'

Here, Ellerman is saying that in this respect the law is having it both ways and should not be allowed to go on doing so. He neglects to notice that in relation to torts, or civil injuries, the position of a servant is apparently not the same as it is when an actual crime has been committed. We will return to this set of related questions shortly. But before that we should review the second pillar of his doctrine: namely the requirement that his labour-owned firms should be democratically governed. We also need to look at his disaggregation of the ownership rights in these undertakings.

In arguing for democratic government inside firms, Ellerman's first step is to distinguish between those whose actions are effectively governed by a business organisation (or, more precisely, by its managers) and those whose lives are merely affected by it. Into the first category he puts its workers; to the second he assigns what it has become fashionable to describe as its other 'stakeholders' – viz. its shareholders, suppliers, customers and local residents. He then goes on (p. 48) to pronounce: 'THE DEMOCRATIC PRINCIPLE [capital letters original]. The direct control rights over an organisation should be assigned to the people who are governed by the organisation so that they will be self-governing.'

The final step in relation to this second pillar of his theory is a simple assertion: that the prescribed self-government should take place 'within a democratic framework'. What he is talking about here is full-blooded 'one person/one vote democracy'. A watered-down arrangement of democratic voting – with votes, say, proportionate to worker shareholdings – would not be acceptable to him.

Altogether, Ellerman has come up with a radical prescription. But before commenting on it we need to go briefly through his persuasive disaggregation of 'ownership' inside his democratic worker-owned firms.

Ellerman is on familiar ground when he suggests that the ownership of a business undertaking should be broken down into three separate sets of rights:

– the rights to the net income of the business: i.e. to its profits or losses;

– the right to have a democratic vote in selecting the government of the business (i.e. its directors or top managers); and more generally perhaps in controlling its affairs;

– the right to an appropriate share in any net assets accumulated by the business; with a corresponding share in the liability for any net losses.

Starting from this threefold breakdown, he then goes on to propose that only the third of these constituent elements should be treated as a property right. The other two should, in his language, be treated as 'personal rights'. These should be attached to the function of working in the firm in such a way that their enjoyment is a more or less automatic consequence of starting to work in it; and conversely is subject to a more or less automatic extinction when working in it is stopped. A suggested analogy is the personal right of voting in a local authority election, and its link to residence in a defined neighbourhood. Like the personal rights of voting in local (and indeed general) elections, neither of Ellerman's two personal rights of ownership in his democratic worker-owned firm can be bought or sold. For these personal rights are not pieces of property. Nor indeed is Ellerman's firm itself. Rather it is essentially, at least in these respects, a social institution.

Ellerman underlines the *social* character of the type of firm which he prescribes by distinguishing it sharply from cases of what he calls 'worker capitalism'. It is an analytically persuasive distinction.

Essentially the distinction is that in a worker-capitalist firm all three components into which Ellerman suggests that the rights of ownership be broken down remain property rights. In a worker-capitalist firm, as in a conventional capitalist one, there are no personal rights; only property ones. In respect of ownership there is indeed only one important difference between a worker-capitalist firm and a conventional capitalist one: in the former, but not in the latter, it is the workers who are the (essentially capitalist) shareholders.

The distinction may be brought out more clearly if it is put in a different way. In Ellerman's democratic worker-owned firm, it is by virtue of their character as workers that those involved participate in the control of the business (voting rights) and in the annual results of the business (sharing in profits and losses). In a worker-capitalist firm, on the other hand, at least according to Ellerman's account of it, it is by virtue of owning capitalist shares that those involved participate in control. And it is by virtue of the same criterion that they share in the annual results of the business: its profits or losses.

As we shall see later from the case studies, some real undertakings 'out there in the real world' do bear quite striking resemblances to Ellerman's two types: the democratic worker-owned firm and the worker-capitalist firm. His semi-ideal types are not just the offspring of Platonic armchair theorising. The arrangements which have been developed at Mondragon correspond quite closely with his type of the democratic worker-owned firm; and the plywood co-ops of America's Pacific north-west coincide, more or less, with his worker-capitalist model. Their differences are what are highlighted, for good reasons, by Ellerman. Here we will simply notice one rule which, perhaps surprisingly, is common to most of America's plywood co-ops as well as those of Mondragon: voting in both is on a democratic basis and *not* proportionate to shareholding size.

Two particularly notable points in this Ellerman thinking are its unusually radical character and an unapologetic prescriptiveness which is quite exceptional in today's writing about these kinds of issues.

By virtue of its democratic and 'bottom upwards' set of control arrangements, Ellerman's democratic worker-owned firm is, of course, a radical departure from the conventional capitalist or state-owned enterprise. That is not in itself so new. Theories of democratic and worker-centric business arrangements have been widely developed and canvassed. Perhaps the most famous post-war contributions to the subject, is Jaroslav Vanek's *The General Theory of Labour Managed Market Economies* (1970). But it is far from being the only one.

The real originality of Ellerman's work lies not so much in his prescription of bottom-upwards democracy for business organisations but more in his critique of the employment contract (on the grounds that it is against natural justice and thus 'inherently invalid') and in his proposal, or his prescription, that two of the three component elements into which the ownership rights in a business undertaking are conventionally analysed should be transformed from property into personal rights. Here he has taken as his model arrangements which actually operate in the Mondragon co-operatives. For in those remarkable businesses it is by virtue of their position as workers, and not as shareholders, that the worker-shareholder-members participate in control, and in the distribution of annual results – whether profits or losses.

As we shall see in more detail later, there are important progressive trends in today's conventional capitalism which may be seen as being in line with a shift in business towards the 'primacy of labour' which Ellerman is seeking to promote. The co-determination laws in Germany and Holland are one example of those trends. So is the whole 'social project' of the European Commission: a movement with which Britain's new Labour Government decided to become associated in 1997. The gradual spread, not only of employee ownership itself, but also of less radical schemes of profit-sharing, can reasonably be seen as shifts in the same direction: towards assigning a greater priority to labour in the distribution of the fruits of enterprise. What distinguishes Ellerman's thought is not its direction but the fact that he has adopted a position at the logical limit of the possible and is prescribing what he recommends in the name of natural justice.

In commenting on Ellerman's critique of the employment contract we may start by acknowledging that the survival, under conventional private capitalism, of something which is more like than unlike the old 'master-servant' relationship is almost bound to make sensitive people rather uneasy. The late Professor Anthony Andrewes, when Wykeham Professor of Ancient History in Oxford, wrote convincingly about the uneasiness felt by those who love Athens when the question of Athenian slavery comes up. Sensitive admirers of the achievements of conventional private capitalism are likely to feel similarly uneasy about the 'master-servant' relationship.

The legal position has frequently been studied and discussed. An accessible example is in the work of Professor (now Lord) Wedderburn. In the chapter on 'The Contract of Employment' in *The Worker and the Law* (1965), he poses the question 'Who is a "Servant"?' and goes on (p. 33):

> The common lawyer has for centuries referred to the parties [to an employment contract] as 'master' and 'servant'; and though modern usage has gradually replaced these terms with the more egalitarian 'employer and employee', the latter's contract is usually referred to as a contract of 'service'. As such, it is distinguished from other contracts, such as one of partnership,

or one in which an employer has work done by an 'independent contractor'.

Lawyers with whom I have discussed the issue tend to highlight the distinction between a contract *of* service and a contract *for* (the supply of) services; and that same distinction is also emphasised in the article on employment law in the latest edition of *Encyclopaedia Britannica*. The former implies a 'master-servant' relationship in which, as in Roman law, the master is invested with *imperium*; and can thus give orders. The latter implies a sub-contracting relationship: in which the sub-contractor enjoys a discretion about *how* he will carry out what he has contracted to undertake.

As we saw earlier, one of Ellerman's most specific objections to the law's interpretation of the employment contract is that, having denied 'responsibility' to the employee in the performance of his normal duties, it goes on to assert that he or she becomes fully responsible if and when any question of criminality arises. The position in relation to a tort is perhaps, to repeat, some mitigation of the obvious charge that the law seeks to have it both ways. For as Wedderburn points out: 'A master is "vicariously" liable to a person injured by the tort of his servant acting in the course of employment, e.g. a delivery man who carelessly knocks you down driving his van on the delivery round.'

On the other hand the position about a tort is not of that much help to those who wish to defend the logic of the law's interpretation of the master-servant relationship; because, as Wedderburn also points out, the servant 'wrongdoer' *is* liable for the tort. It is simply that his master is vicariously liable as well.

So in the end it looks as if, at least in his own terms, Ellerman has the better of this argument. There *is* an anomaly between the law's denial of responsibility when a servant is discharging his normal duties, on the one hand, and its insistence that he or she is still a responsible human being from the moment there is any question of a possible criminal action or a tort. Ellerman is surely right to focus on responsibility as a key issue, a point to which I will return at the end.

But to return to torts and criminal actions, no doubt a lawyer might reply that they are too important for questions about reponsibility for them to be settled as it were by analogy. But it would probably be a mistake to pursue the point further in this way.

Given the basically prescriptive character of Ellerman's position on each of his two central points – about the 'invalidity' of the employment contract and of the non-democratic firm – the main question is, surely, whether his prescriptions will win acceptance – political acceptance.

I suspect that if the public, plus labour and management, are to be convinced that Ellerman's objectives are desirable, then a good deal more will be needed than just his prescriptions. The case for *The Democratic Worker Owned Firm* needs to be argued on the basis of what actually happens in those firms – their comparative economic, social and perhaps psychological efficiency.

In fairness to Ellerman I should make clear that he has deliberately and explicitly eschewed '. . . emphasising the efficiency arguments customarily used in favour of the democratic firm'. (p. 210).

And on the next page he explains this self-denial:

> Real social change, when it comes, is driven by ideas and principles, not simply by "efficiency considerations". Absolute government as well as slavery sagged after centuries of inefficiency, but it was their legitimacy in the light of first principles that drove the democratic revolutions and the abolition of slavery in the eighteenth and nineteenth centuries. Thus we have focused on the basic principles that drive towards economic democracy.

Ellerman has performed some notable intellectual services. Perhaps most notable is his critique of the employment contract and his proposed disaggregration of business ownership into a combination of personal as well as property rights. In doing so he has also put into circulation what might be called a platonic model of the democratic worker-owned firm.

Some of us working in the same field as Ellerman have chosen to adopt a more piecemeal and pragmatic approach. It is an approach we feel more comfortable with. We believe that there is room for a great deal of variety, and that efficiency arguments *are* important. They are important too in social and perhaps psychological terms as well as by the familiar test of economic performance. We now move on to look at other theoretical arguments for employee ownership, and at how they have started to find expression at least on the margins of politics. Those who prefer this more piecemeal approach will want to acknowledge their debt to David Ellerman's thinking. But they may also be inclined to note two sentences from the work of the sceptical and humane, if also conservative, political philosopher Michael Oakeshott. Both are from his *The Tower of Babel* (1948): 'The project of finding a short cut to heaven is as old as the human race.' But also: 'The pursuit of happiness as the crow flies is an activity both impious and unavoidable in human life.'

Ellerman might welcome a characterisation of his work as 'impious'. But it would be unfair not to conclude this discussion with a rather more positive comment on *The Democratic Worker Owned Firm*.

In his book *The Just Enterprise* (1986), George Goyder (p. 8) rightly drew his readers' attention to a critique of the conventional capitalist company, as enshrined in the law, from the unlikely pen of Lord Eustace Percy. Lord Eustace coupled up this critique with a call for the legal recognition of a quite new form of economic organisation, namely 'the human association which in fact produces and distributes wealth . . .' The short passage, which is from his Riddell Lecture for 1944, entitled *The Unknown State*, is worth quoting in full. Ellerman's democratic worker-owned firm may reasonably be seen as a radical answer to Lord Eustace's call:

Here is the most important challenge to political invention ever offered to the jurist or the statesman. The human association which in fact produces and distributes wealth, the association of workmen, managers, technicians, and directors is not an association recognised by the law. The association which the law does recognise – the association of shareholders, creditors and directors – is incapable of producing and distributing and is not expected to perform these functions. We have to give law to the real association and withdraw meaningless privilege from the imaginary one.

And yet . . . formal constitutions are all very well. But the empirical observation of what is actually going on in a business suggests to me that the most emancipated business constitution, however great its potential benefits, may be neither a necessary nor a suffcient condition for either a successful economic performance or a satisfied workforce. Both of the latter are likely to depend on what may be called the 'sociology' or 'culture' of the business and on how that is perceived by those who work for it. These are matters which Ellerman's treatment of the subject cannot reach. We will turn to them in a moment and approach them via the teaching of Professor Ronald

Dore about the secrets of business success in Japan. But before that, sticking to the same issues of employee ownership and democratic business which Ellerman has addressed, we must look briefly at some more pragmatic considerations.

2

A More Pragmatic Approach

Like Papal Bulls, Professor Ellerman's prescriptions risk deterring many who are in principle on his side. Public opinion in the world's democracies is still far from convinced that the relationship between master and servant is sufficiently similar to that between master and slave for the employment contract to be at variance with natural justice. On the contrary most people at whatever level on the social scale might regard it as reasonable for the tunes to be called by those who pay the pipers. And yet there are good pragmatic arguments for encouraging both a shift to labour in the ownership of what it produces, and a shift to more accountable business government. One aim of this book is to convince its readers that there is a pragmatic variant of the extreme Ellerman position. As I hope the case studies will show, businesses *can* work very nicely thank you when they *are* employee-owned and when management *is* democratically accountable to those who are managed by it. But public opinion needs to be nudged, charmed and eased in the desired direction. It will be inclined to back away if it is summoned by a series of secular *Fatwas* pronounced by a secular Ayatollah in the name of natural justice. In any case, as Isaiah Berlin has most eloquently reminded readers, in the current age there is a higher order imperative which enjoins institutional pluralism: within limits (which no doubt exclude the owner/slave relationship), people should be free to build corporate entities, corporate ownership arrangements and corporate governments as they think fit.

So what are the more pragmatic arguments, aside from the actual empirical evidence, for moving in the suggested direction? A good starting point is a discussion of questions of ownership and property by the famous historian and critic of capitalism, R. H. Tawney. A key passage comes from *The Acquisitive Society*, first published in 1921. I will quote it in a moment. The general heading of the discussion under which it appears is 'The Divorce of Ownership and Work'.

Tawney's main concern here is to contrast the effects of business property rights in pre-industrial societies with those in modern times; and more especially with those which arose as a result of the Companies Acts and limited liability legislation around the middle of the last century. In the earlier period what was being chiefly protected was the property of peasant and yeoman farmers, of craftsmen and small masters: in other words, property rights which secured for those who did most of the work both their ownership of its output and their ownership of the means of production. By contrast, in the modern world, Tawney suggested, property rights typically protected something very different: the rights to unearned income of the rentier: the almost functionless absentee shareholder in limited liability companies. Moreover in the modern conditions, Tawney argued, the rules of shareholder capitalism also resulted in a further change: power and control was shifted away from those who did the actual work to the agents of the absentee shareholders. He offers (p. 57) a memorable single sentence summary of the contrast between old and new:

> The characteristic fact which differentiates most modern property from that of the pre-industrial age, and which turns against it the very reasoning by which formerly it was supported, is that in modern economic conditions ownership is not active but passive, not a means of work but an instrument for the acquisition of gain or the exercise of power, and that there is no guarantee that gain bears any relation to service, or power to responsibility.

Analytically, there are two quite separate aspects to the ownership part of the pragmatic case for employee ownership: the effects of that ownership *outside* as well as *inside* the factory gates. In the passage just quoted, Tawney mainly has in mind the latter – the effects of ownership on the performance of productive work. But he is equally aware of the importance of the former. For earlier in the same chapter (p. 54) he quotes with obvious endorsement Francis Bacon's famous epigram, offered to King Henry VII on the issue of protecting the rights of tenant farmers: 'Wealth is like muck. It is not good but if it be spread.'

The possibilities and constraints of the property-owning democracy are a topic beloved by politicians of the centre-right. Easily the most important recent contribution has come from the

United States. We must now look a little more closely at what the late Louis Kelso had to say about conventional capitalism and its tendency to concentrate business wealth in the hands of those who already have it.

This tendency, according to Kelso, essentially reflects the ways in which new business investment is typically financed. It is a complete myth that the process involves new (and small) investors subscribing to new share issues on stock exchanges. Indeed, over a number of ten-year periods during the 1970s and 1980s and the first half of the 1990s, Wall Street saw net equity buy-backs as much as net new issues of stocks and shares. That means the concentration of business wealth is intensified.

However those net buy-backs of stocks and shares are not the main cause of ever-greater concentration. New business investment is typically financed without any contribution from stock markets at all. What finances new business investment, at least if we are talking about new investments by *existing* businesses (far the largest part of total investment), is typically a mixture of retained profits, depreciation allowances and bank borrowings. And the beneficial owners of those new investments are not *new* shareholders: they are the existing shareholders. Excluding institutions, existing shareholders are concentrated among a very small percentage of the citizenry, so there are clearly dangers if the process continues unchecked. For unless the relevant processes of financing investment can be changed, or the numbers of existing shareholders be substantially increased, wealth which is already highly concentrated will become even more so. Jeffrey Gates, who was effectively chief of staff to Senator Russell Long when the latter was engineering the passage through the US Congress of successive pieces of ESOP legislation in the 1970s and 1980s, put this point particularly well when he explained that unless there were substantial changes, much of the extra business wealth created in the USA over the next decade would belong to people who are already billionaires. The well-known American academic economist Lester Thurow made the same point in a book which was widely noticed in 1995. He claimed that 64% of all new big business wealth of the 1980s went to the richest 1% of the population.

Jeffrey Gates has also developed a serviceable shorthand for the key feature of these conventional financing arrangements. He calls them a 'closed loop system', one which operates in the interests of those already inside and lets no one else in. He then presents employee ownership as the most eligible alternative system; and the ESOP as the most effective mechanism for getting there.

Next I should recall a second key insight of Louis Kelso: that ordinary employees have neither the savings nor the access to individual credit necessary to buy the businesses for which they work. The ESOP elegantly cuts through those difficulties: by enabling ordinary employees to acquire that ownership by using what amounts to collective credit and by using the assets of the business to guarantee it.

It is easy to grasp the likely negative social consequences, in the world outside the factory gates, of the concentration of private wealth in fewer and fewer hands. It is a process which seems almost designed to increase the incidence of crimes against property. Some have also argued persuasively that inequality *per se* damages the health of the poor.

By spreading out the wealth, employee ownership may generate other more directly positive benefits in the world of the community outside the factory gates. Is it plausible to suppose that these benefits might go beyond, as it were, those associated with avoiding the negative consequences of increased inequality? Intuitively, the short answer to that question is 'yes'. Adam Smith certainly argued to that effect in *The Theory of Moral Sentiments* (1759). His key passage is quoted as an epigraph to my final chapter. For a more comprehensive and systematic answer we shall have to wait for the results of research studies of which, so far as I know, the first only got under way in 1997.

Crime rates are lower among home owners. Are they are likely to be lower among employee owners as well? Like home owners, employee owners have 'more of a stake' in society, more to lose. Is it also plausible to suppose that the behaviour of employee owners outside the factory gates will be affected by more than just the fact that they have more to lose: by the higher levels of responsibility and the greater opportunities for personal development which are already a feature of the best employee-owned businesses in Britain and elsewhere? That brings us back to the second set of potential benefits of employee ownership which was distinguished earlier – benefits at the place of work.

The main arguments for the reality of this second set of potential benefits are, of course, empirical. Readers will be persuaded to believe in them – or otherwise – by the case study material. However, the case study evidence can be supported by a number of other arguments.

We can start with an obvious point: many people work better when they are working wholly or mainly for themselves. When we are working for ourselves we are typically quite confident that we, and not someone else, will be the main beneficiaries of what is done and it is we who are mainly in control of the work process. So if that process is flawed or misconceived we will have no one to blame except ourselves.

These conditions may normally be satisfied when we are working for ourselves. The problem is how to ensure that they are met when the work needs a whole organisation, including managers and support workers.

Following Professor Dore, the key requirement here is a sense of 'fairness'; a sense that the organisation in which I work is fair both in its system of ownership and rewards and in its system of government; and in particular that in relation neither to rewards nor to governing power the organisation is not unfairly or unreasonably biased, whether in favour of management or non-management or towards particular cliques. If this analysis is right, then employee ownership is neither a necessary nor a sufficient condition for achieving the key requirement. I also think that Dore is right in his contention that Japanese businesses probably come closer than any other to perceived, even if not fully real, organisational fairness; and that they do so without introducing employee ownership. On the other hand, at least in the conditions of today's Western societies, I believe that employee ownership is the most promising approach to meeting the fairness requirement.

Dore's analysis is persuasive not only in highlighting organisational fairness – or perhaps perceived organisational fairness – as the key requirement. It is also persuasive because of what he expects to result from meeting that requirement: namely, higher levels of 'X' efficiency, the concept first identified or invented by the Harvard economist Harvey Liebenstein.

Harvey Liebenstein has compared 'X' efficiency with morale as, for example, in the performance of a conquering army. It is something quite distinct from 'allocative efficiency'. The latter is supposedly maximised in a national economy exposed to the full forces of competition both externally and through the elimination of anything which prevents the smooth operation of competitive forces in the home market. As I wrote when reviewing two of Dore's most recent books on Japan:

'X' efficiency is something quite else ... Crudely speaking ... [it] is maximised where workers and managers use their time 'on the job' to maximum effect. Put more generally, an economy will succeed in maximising 'X' efficiency to the extent that the best contemporary practices in any branch of economic activity are most closely matched by the largest number of firms in that same branch. Conversely the outbreak of strike action counts as a case, par excellence, of zero 'X' efficiency during its duration. [*Political Quarterly*, April-June 1988.]

Dore has himself offered a series of memorable examples. 'X' efficiency, he wrote in *Taking Japan Seriously*, is

the efficiency which comes from paying attention to the work you are doing and not boring holes in the wrong place and having to scrap an expensive workpiece; from calculating just how many machining blanks you have in the stock pile to avoid having the machinists run out of work to do; from the conscientiousness that sees to it that deliveries to keep up that stock pile arrive on time. It is the efficiency which ensures that a small businessman's loan application is processed by the bank in three days not three weeks, that hospitals do not get patients' papers mixed up and amputate the leg of an appendicitis case. It comes from making the right decisions because you have done your home work ... It comes from caring about the quality of the work you produce and the service you give to your customers and from giving thought to how you can improve them.

Anyone who thinks that Dore's hospital example is far-fetched has not been reading the newspapers. I remember in particular a picture in *The Times* in the second half of 1991: of a little girl who was reported to be smiling 'bravely'. She certainly needed courage. The photograph showed that she had a bandaged stump where her right hand should have been. Her hand had been amputated. But that operation should never have been performed. She had been brought to hospital to have a cyst removed from her eye.

The little girl's mistakenly amputated hand is just one striking example of what can happen when 'X' efficiency is at low or zero levels. It is easy to see that such mistakes multiplied across an economy can constitute a serious drag on performance, even on that of an economy in which the intensity of competition, and thus the level of allocative efficiency, is notably high. Dore himself attributes the whole of Japan's post-war economic success to the high levels of 'X' efficiency which its businesses have managed to achieve. More precisely, he argues that its levels of 'X' efficiency have been so high that it has been able to accept relatively low levels of allocative efficiency, and still outperform the international competition. For, as he reminds his readers, the Japanese economy is 'riddled with misallocations'.

But for our purposes here it is not so much the results of high levels of 'X' efficiency as the conditions necessary for its inception and growth which are chiefly important. On that issue Dore is quite unambiguous: 'X' efficiency, he tells us, springs from 'a sense of fairness which enables people to work co-operatively, conscientiously and with a will'. But he is equally clear about what is incompatible with achieving it:

> That sense of fairness cannot be achieved in the rough and tumble which results when each actor in the market is encouraged to maximise his own short term benefits, unconstrained by anything except the hard reality of market forces – not at any rate in modern societies with modern concepts of citizenship and the accompanying rights to be respected and consulted and to receive a minimum level of income and security.

On the other hand the key hypotheses behind this book are that you *can*, within an employee-owned firm, create that 'sense of fairness' and, second, that you *can* achieve high levels of 'X' efficiency. Neither will happen automatically but each can be worked at.

The feeling on the part of the non-management workforce that the business is organised in ways that are basically fair and reasonable is one point of convergence between Japanese companies and employee-owned companies. There is another: profit sharing. Though the language commonly used to describe it may be rather different – in Japan it will typically be described as the thirteenth and sometimes the thirteenth and fourteenth month's pay – a high proportion of Japanese employees' annual pay is directly related to profit. Apart from the obvious potential benefit of improved incentives, this link with profits provides an important cushion against redundancies.

There are two other potential advantages of the employee-owned business which I would like to suggest. But once again I am *not* saying that these advantages will arise automatically. Nor am I saying that they are available only in employee-owned businesses. All I want to claim is that employee ownership should provide a promising environment in which they can be worked for.

The first is connected with what we may think of as the extra 'space' which should be available in an employee-owned business provided that it manages to satisfy Dore's fairness requirement. There will be the potential for more 'space' at work in the sense that it should not be necessary to spend every minute of paid time on the repetitive routines of productive work. Time can be devoted to identifying ways of improving output and cutting costs and to personal development through training and education.

Making the potential extra space real, and then using it in these or similar ways, should go some way towards satisfying at work the higher personal needs first identified in this context by the American psychologist Abraham Maslow. Maslow's central suggestion was that what people needed from their work could be structured in a series of hierarchical steps. At the most elementary level, work, or more exactly the income derived from it, was needed to satisfy the basic survival requirements – for food, clothing, shelter and so on – of the worker and his or her family. Once these immediate needs had been satisfied, new ones opened up at a higher level – especially for income security. Once these in turn had been satisfied, the process shifted a further stage upwards: workers started looking for the satisfaction at work of their 'higher' personal needs – to be engaged in creative and/or problem-solving activities; to be provided with opportunities for personal development and stretching; and to enjoy recognition and positive feedback when the quality of their achievements made them appropriate.

The work of professionals and managers is typically of a kind which can and does cater for these higher personal needs; whereas for blue collar workers the opposite is true. In today's world this applies nearly as much in employee-owned as conventional businesses. On the other hand, the most progressive of the employee-owned businesses are now changing: they are starting to provide for the higher personal needs of their blue collar workforce. To be fair, this is also happening in progressive undertakings which are conventionally owned. My argument is simply that these things are both more likely to happen and more likely to be sustained when a business is employee-owned and its management is accountable, not to faraway shareholders or the state, but to the workforce.

Though expressed in rather different language, work arrangements which go some way towards satisfying Maslow's higher personal needs overlap with those which cater for the requirement of much greater employee *autonomy*. Some of the most eloquent and persuasive advocacy of the latter is to be found in the writings of the remarkable French philosopher Simone Weil; in particular in the volume of her writings first published in France in 1955, eleven years after her death, with the title *Oppression et Liberté* (later reversed as *Liberty and Oppression* in the English translation.)

This most original French woman wrote on the subject of work not only as a philosopher but from actual experience. During the 1930s she had a spell on an assembly line in one of France's Renault works, as well as another in a small machine shop in Lyons. She found the experience mentally and physically excruciating. What she argued for was a manufacturing system such that the individual worker would take responsibility for a substantial number of production steps: both thinking out how best to proceed and then carrying the work through. No doubt her proposed alternative was utopian at the time; and no doubt the need for it has been partially superseded by the introduction of robots. Nevertheless, apart from its heroic origin, there is something most persuasive and attractive about her central philosophical idea: that people are free at the highest level only when they take responsibility for both thinking through a project and carrying it out. Transposed into Maslow's language, the opportunity to do that would be said to satisfy one of the highest human needs. There is likely to be more 'space' for these things to happen, and an environment more conducive to them happening, when a business is employee-owned.

Finally, a word about a rather different possibility, and with it a possible comparative advantage, for those employee-owned businesses which satisfy Dore's fairness test. It seems to me entirely on the cards that employee-owned businesses of this kind should, if they work at it, evoke positive sentiments and loyalties from their workforce of employee owners, or anyway from some of them. Institutions in which people spend their working lives *can* evoke such responses. Some colleges at Oxford and Cambridge do it. So do schools and regiments and churches. Though Dore does not say so in as many words, I imagine that a number of Japanese companies do it. I imagine further that it is not too problematic to suggest that when institutions evoke such sentiments, and all other variables are held constant, they will enjoy some comparative advantage.

Many of us mocked the school song in our youth. A typical British reaction to a Japanese company song is likely to be one of derisory laughter. But the sentiment may be admirable and positive, even if any particular expression of it is open to objection on the grounds of good taste. Followers of Mrs Thatcher who pride themselves on their exemplary 'dryness' doubtless include people who want to reject all sentiment in a business context. But if their chief concern is with economic growth and performance, then the Japanese, at least since the middle 1950s, have probably had the last laugh.

More generally, EOBs which satisfy a fairness test are among the most eligible candidates in a secular age for satisfying the widespread need for an institution intermediate between the family and the state in which an individual can feel at home. Moral and religious thinkers have often spoken persuasively about the need for such intermediate institutions. William Temple (1942) put the argument explicitly. Those on the right of centre who are disposed to criticise working people for loyalty to their trade unions tend to forget a key point: that these are among the very few intermediate institutions in which blue collar workers with non-BBC accents can feel thoroughly at home. 'One nation' Tories are no doubt less likely to make that particular mistake. They will be familiar with the importance attached by Edmund Burke to feelings of affection for the 'little platoon'. But then 'one nation' Tories were not exactly in the ascendant in Britain's Conservative Party during Mrs Thatcher's long reign.

There is also what might be called a 'Herderian' point. In a an interview published in the autumn of 1991 in the *New York Review of Books*, Isaiah Berlin remarked that Johann Gottfried Herder, the late eighteenth-century German writer and thinker, 'invented belonging'. The subject matter of the interview was the post-Communist reawakening of nationalism in Eastern Europe and in the territories of the former Soviet Union. The 'belonging' which, according to Isaiah Berlin, was invented by Herder, was belonging-to-a-nation or belonging-to-a-tribe. Herder's implicit suggestion is that most people have a psychological need to belong to a nation or tribe: that is, to a group characterised by a common culture and a common history. Many people may also have a psychological need to 'belong' to groups which are smaller than the nation or tribe but larger than the family. This line of thought clearly brings us back to William Temple's 'intermediate' institutions. What I am suggesting here is, first, that membership of such an institution may answer to some 'Herderian' psychological need to belong; and, second, that those employee-owned businesses which satisfy a fairness test may be well placed to *be* such institutions.

Almost by definition an employee-owned firm is a locally owned firm. It is almost impossible for an employee owner to be an absentee employee owner. Such a firm should thus be well placed to evoke and then draw strength from feelings of local pride and loyalty of a kind more usually associated with football teams.

Towards the end of *Tess of the D'Urbervilles* (1891), Hardy intrudes a brief passage of reflection into his narrative. It is prompted by the parlous state of the village of Flintcomb Ash, where Tess has been harvesting mangelwurzels. Hardy remarks that there are three kinds of village: the kind which is cared for by its lord, the kind which is cared for by itself, and the kind for which no one cares because its owner is an absentee. Most of us did not have depend on Hardy to be familiar with the iniquities of absentee landowners. But somehow the same critique has never been so widely applied to the owners of companies.

An employee-owned business is well placed, applying Hardy's village typology, to 'care for itself'. Moreover its success in so doing may well be strengthened by feelings of loyalty and affection which its members have for their locality. Feelings of that kind are no doubt attenuated almost to the point of non-existence in the more anonymous of today's conurbations. But our case studies will show that local loyalties of that kind are part of the background to a number of striking employee-owned business successes: most notably those of the Mondragon group in the Basque provinces of Spain and those of two remarkable industrial co-ops in the small Italian town of Imola, some thirty miles south east of Bologna.

Before turning to the political expression of the arguments for employee ownership in the West, especially in the UK and the USA, it may be helpful to summarise the ground covered in this discussion so far.

To begin with there was Professor Ellerman's prescription from natural law: the argument that the employer/employee relationship of conventional capitalism should be seen as a system of 'renting' human beings and should be judged to be incompatible with 'natural law' in the same way as, even if not to the same extent as, the institution of slavery. Public opinion has not so far been persuaded that wage employment is sufficiently like slavery to be ruled unacceptable.

On the other hand there is at least *potential* political mileage in the other main arguments for employee ownership. For convenience it makes sense to tabulate them here. For the purposes of this summary table the employee ownership will be of the kind which satisfies a fairness test.

Arguments for Employee-Ownership (EO)

A Inside the Factory Gates
– By reducing the prevalent levels of alienation at work, EO may result in significantly higher levels of 'X' efficiency.

– By making possible a greater degree of the individual autonomy which was so prized by Simone Weil, EO can lead to the satisfaction of those higher human needs first clearly identified by Abraham Maslow. Similarly EO may be associated with higher levels of democratic participation at work than is normal under systems of conventional capitalism. To that extent it can also offer to ordinary employees a greater measure of control over their working lives.

– By becoming the object of positive sentiments and feelings of loyalty, the employee owned business (EOB) may help to satisfy a 'Herderian' need 'to belong'.

B In the Outside World
– By breaking the 'closed loop' of business ownership in conventional capitalist societies, EO can be an effective mechanism for spreading business wealth.

– By encouraging employees to use more of their talents at work, EO may improve their performance – as citizens, for example, and as parents – in the non-work parts of their daily lives.

Those with a taste for 'reduction' might be inclined to argue that, if we ignore the 'X' efficiency arguments, there are just two major arguments for employee ownership: that it increases democratic participation at work and that it spreads more equitably the wealth created by work.

And yet . . . I am sure, to repeat, that for practical purposes we must reject David Ellerman's argument that the employment contract is as objectionable as the condition of slavery. But we can and I think should acknowledge the moral force of his emphasis on the link between employee ownership and personal responsibility. If it makes sense to encourage the diffusion of responsibility at the place of work, then employee ownership is the most promising way to achieve that.

We must now ask how far employee ownership has found expression in the political record of the last 200 years.

3

The British Political Record

The year 1978 has come to be seen, at least in retrospect, as marking a turning point in the record of employee ownership in Britain. For with one minor and notably ephemeral qualification which I ignore, it was in 1978 that for the first time ever a British Government introduced and passed through Parliament a set of tax reliefs designed to encourage broadly based, so-called all-employee share schemes, allowing companies to allocate free shares to employees and pay for them out of pre-tax profits. These measures, which were introduced as part of the 1978 Finance Act, came during Britain's so-called Lib-Lab pact, a temporary but important arrangement under which the Parliamentary Liberal Party, under David Steel, agreed to support the Callaghan Labour Government. The tax reliefs for broadly based employee share schemes were part of the price which the Liberals extracted from the Labour Government in return for their support. Without the insistence of the Liberals there would not have been those tax reliefs.

It is also almost equally certain that, without the precedent in the 1978 Act, the incoming Tory Government of Mrs Thatcher in 1979 would not have chosen to build on those tax reliefs in the long subsequent period of Conservative rule.

For the 100 years before 1978, the employee ownership record in Britain is best explained by the fact that neither of the two main political interests in the country, neither capital (normally represented by the Conservatives) nor labour (represented in this century by the Labour Party and to some extent, earlier, by the Liberals) showed any real enthusiasm for it. Employee ownership simply did not figure on the agendas of either of the two politically towering interest groups in the land.

Going back to an earlier period, however, to the pre-Marxist world that followed the start of Britain's industrial revolution, we find a genuine overlap between the ideas and values of Robert

Owen and the other advocates of co-operative enterprise and those of today's employee-ownership movement. Today we can see the dominance of Marxist thinking on the British left as an essentially temporary phenomenon – lasting for the century or so which separated the translation into English of *Das Kapital* in 1886 and the fall of the Berlin Wall. What should be more natural than that an earlier critique of capitalism should re-surface now that the period of Marxist prescriptive dominance has come to an end.

Attitudes and Objectives of the Labour Movement For the last century at least, the agenda of those who have spoken up for working people has been dominated by two objectives: to secure legal recognition for trade unions and strengthen their legal rights; and to bring the dominant sectors of the economy into Government ownership and state control, an objective partially achieved by the post-1945 Attlee Governments and discussed continuously for decades before and since. For the British Labour Party, its manifesto for the 1992 election was probably the first in which its championship of trade unions and their rights became qualified and cautious. It was also, incidentally, the party's first manifesto to include a reference to employee share ownership.

Since 1992, and particularly since Tony Blair has replaced 'old' Labour with 'new' Labour, the old twin objectives have been almost wholly jettisoned. As we now know, the new Labour Government voted into power in 1997 will not repeal the main restrictions on earlier trade union freedoms which are among the most important legacies of Mrs Thatcher's successive Governments. What is perhaps symbolically more important, New Labour has thrown out the famous Clause IV of the Party's 1918 Constitution, under which it was committed to achieve the 'common' ownership of the means of production, distribution and exchange.

That commitment had a long innings stretching way back before Clause IV into the last century. Britain's Trade Union Congress (TUC) first passed a resolution calling for the nationalisation of land in 1888. In 1893 it went further, with a resolution which called for political support to be confined to candidates who promised to advocate widespread nationalisation. In effect the Labour Movement's overriding commitment to public ownership lasted just over 100 years.

The dominance of these two objectives left little room for

employee ownership. But it was not just a matter of space. Employee ownership conflicted with state ownership and with the goal of strengthening the unions – because of the not altogether unfounded belief that employees who are also owners may be less dependent than their more conventional counterparts on union protection and support.

Given the lack of interest or outright hostility implied by those very different objectives, any support for employee ownership in Britain's Labour Party down to the 1992 manifesto was marginal. What there was came mainly from those associated with co-operative ventures of one kind and another. But even this was a mixed blessing. For it is the *consumer* co-ops which have effectively dominated British co-operation through most of its history from the Rochdale Pioneers in the 1840s onwards. What is more, by rejecting a policy of sharing profits with their own workers, as they did at a famous conference in Dewsbury in the 1880s, the British consumer co-ops more or less parted company from the much smaller group of production co-ops in the UK. Unlike Italy and France, Britain has never really had production co-ops in any numbers.

One of the few to survive to the 1990s, Equity Shoes of Leicester, was founded as long ago as 1896. It was apparently founded as a result of a strike by skilled boot and shoe makers working in and for a Leicester factory owned and controlled by none other than the Co-operative Wholesale Society (CWS). As reported by Equity's own historian, the grounds for the strike were the repeated refusals by the CWS to offer a share of profits to their skilled boot and shoe makers. We look at Equity's long history in one of the case studies which deal with production co-ops.

To be fair, the rule books of a number of the country's most influential trade unions enjoin their members to support, and even to form, production co-ops. Though they have been dead letters for most of their history, these injunctions might help to legitimise a shift of union policy in a more favourable direction in the future. There were, too, the Labour Government's experiments with the so-called 'Wedgwood Benn rescue co-ops' in the 1970s. There have also been exceptional individuals in Britain's Labour Movement who dared to speak out against state ownership well before it ceased to be a dogma. Easily the most eloquent of these in the contemporary world has been Walter Kendall: 'If all that is required for socialism is production according to plan, for use and not for profit, under the supervision of an authoritarian command structure, then the prison workshop is the proper prototype of a socialist community.' (Oakeshott, 1978.)

The Conservatives before Mrs Thatcher Tory rhetoric in favour of a property-owning democracy has been persistent. But before Mrs Thatcher took over the leadership in the middle 1970s, the British Conservative Party was, and had been for most of the previous two centuries, the voice of special interests: first of the landed and aristocratic interest; and later, from the repeal of the Corn Laws in 1846 and more strongly since Balfour ceased to be leader in 1911, of the kind of managerial and paternalist capitalism represented by people like Neville Chamberlain, Stanley Baldwin and Bonar Law.

It is striking that, in contrast to the USA, the interests of what might be called the 'small operator' have found no consistent or influential political expression in the UK. Margaret Thatcher, the daughter of a Grantham mayor and shopkeeper, regarded herself as a champion of small business and of the enterprise culture. But she is an exception. For most of the last two centuries the Tories have had other priorities. Populism, meaning the non-socialist espousal of the interests of the small man, has always had a more pejorative ring in the UK than in the USA. Britain's Conservatives have rarely campaigned with any sustained vigour against monopolies or in favour of tough anti-trust legislation. A few mavericks apart, they have notably failed to embrace what might be called the *yeoman* values of William Cobbett.

I have been able to find only one significant example of right of centre support for employee ownership:– the now largely forgotten 'distributist' movement associated with Hilaire Belloc and G. K. Chesterton between the two World Wars. Though you have to dig for it, there is much good sense in some of the distributist writing, especially Belloc's emphasis on 'the moral effect of economic independence' – with its echoes of Cobbett. In its commitment to a combination of 'small and green is beautiful', distributism was also ahead of its time. On the other hand, outside the world of a few romantic and eccentric artist craftsmen, like Eric Gill, its impact was effectively zero. Indeed it should probably be seen more as a literary movement than one of 'political economy'.

The Liberals, Predecessors of Today's Liberal Democrats The Liberal

Party's 1928 report on Britain's industrial future, the so-called *Yellow Book*, identifies the 'master-servant relationship' as one of the key sources of Britain's industrial unrest and poor industrial performance. Elsewhere the authors of the report put their finger on the second main source of discontent, then as now, with conventional capitalism: its division of society into two quite different classes – those who earn their living by working and those whose income comes mainly from the profits of that work.

It is, of course, precisely these two sources of discontent with conventional capitalism that employee ownership is designed to address. That it should have been Britain's Liberals, already then (as still now) essentially *social* Liberals – and in this respect like their counterparts in the USA rather than Continental Europe – who were responsible for these judgements should occasion no surprise. They were able to see clearly on this issue because their vision was not clouded by vested interests in the *status quo*; whether of capitalist owners or trade unions.

Various policies and pronouncements are associated with prominent Liberals stretching at least as far back as John Stuart Mill in the third quarter of the nineteenth century. Most famously perhaps, there is Lloyd George's call for a policy which offered 'three acres and a cow' to those willing and able to take advantage of them. Such a policy may be seen as the smallholder equivalent of employee ownership. Moreover the non-conformists were an important influence on the Liberal Party as well as on the production co-ops. And so were the classic non-conformist virtues, like thrift.

John Stuart Mill never used the actual language of employee ownership. But, and well known as they are, it is still worth quoting his two most famous pronouncements on the subject: 'The relationship of masters and workpeople will gradually be superseded by partnership in one of two forms: in some cases, associations of the labourers with the capitalists; in others and perhaps finally in all, associations of labourers among themselves.'

Later in life he went further, and associated what he foresaw would follow from a switch to employee ownership with what would be made possible by the emancipation of women: 'The emancipation of women and co-operative production are, I fully believe, the two great changes which will regenerate society.'

Mill also made two practical contributions. First, he was prepared to put his hand in his pocket in support of these beliefs. For example, he provided substantial money backing for what amounted to a co-operative of locksmiths. Second he was one of the influential figures behind the co-operative legislation of the 1840s, and the associated granting of limited liability to co-operative ventures.

In his lobbying activities he joined forces with a middle-class pressure group who called themselves Christian Socialists and included a number of prominent clergymen, writers and lawyers – the names of F. D. Maurice, Charles Kingsley and Thomas Hughes (the author of *Tom Brown's Schooldays*) are probably best known. They stand at the beginning of an enduring strand of middle-class Christian support for co-operative production and employee ownership. That tradition is not Liberal with a big political 'L'; but it has certainly been social liberal, with a small 's' and a small 'l', from the beginning.

The Liberal Party has included supporters of employee ownership from the days of John Stuart Mill all the way down to the introduction of those all-employee share scheme tax reliefs, at the insistence of the Liberals, in the Finance Act of 1978. It was no accident that the late Jo Grimond, the leader of the Liberal Party between 1956 and 1967, agreed to become the first Chairman of Job Ownership Ltd.

But if we ignore the brief period of the Lib-Lab pact, and the coalitions of the 1920s and the Second World War, Britain's Parliamentary Liberal Party has been remote from power since the fall of Lloyd George in 1922. So Liberal support for employee ownership did not count for much, anyway down to the 1978 Finance Act.

After 1978: A Low-Priority Consensus After 1978 the record becomes rather different. Throughout Mrs Thatcher's long reign, as since, employee ownership was a rare consensus issue among the main political groupings in the British Parliament. It was a low level consensus. Its achievements were quite modest. But they were sequential and after 1994 it became possible to argue that Britain's employee ownership legislation, though conceptually derived from the American original, was in many ways superior to it.

There were important differences in the reasons behind the support given by the different parties. For the Tories, the key argument was strengthening the property ownership component in the country's democracy. For Labour, the priority was to give ordinary working people a say and higher status at their places of work. The Liberals simply reminded everyone of their prescient *Yellow Book*.

The legislative starting point, as we have seen, was the 1978 Finance Act during the Lib-Lab Pact and what were effectively the first ever all-employee tax reliefs enacted by it. A key aim of such schemes is to create solidarity between shop floor and management in a business organisation. By contrast, the aim of the 'discretionary' schemes is to tie, or as the Americans say to 'glue', senior executives to the business which employs them. Even the Tories seem to have become partly disillusioned by such schemes – or worried by their negative political impact. In his third budget, in November 1995, the Tory Chancellor Kenneth Clarke clamped a ceiling of £20,000 – later £30,000 – on tax-assisted options and thereby effectively limited the discretionary tax break for management level employees.

The 'all employee' principle is one of a number which are common to all the pieces of non-discretionary employee ownership legislation so far introduced in Britain. The phrase 'all employee', indicating commitment to a democratic principle, must be placed in quotation marks because what it prescribes is, in fact, qualified. A pre-eligibility period of up to five years' length of service is deemed to be compatible with it.

The legislation also lays down what is in effect a fairness test. When a company distributes shares to its employees under a scheme which attracts tax relief, then the distribution of those shares, as between individual employees, must satisfy what is called a 'similar terms' condition. That condition will be satisfied if the shares are distributed equally. But it will also be satisfied if the distribution is proportionate to relevant, objective and measurable criteria – like rates of pay and length of service, or a combination of these .

A more general principle of the UK legislation, and indeed in its US counterpart, is that companies can choose whether to take advantage of it, or to say, in effect, 'no thank you'. Here it differs from some otherwise quite similar French legislation; and from the famous 'co-determination' laws which first appeared in early post-war Western Germany towards the end of the 1940s and have since spread further afield. It needs hardly be said that Britain's post-war Conservative Party attaches great importance to what it calls the 'voluntary principle' in industrial relations.

The two other key principles of UK legislation are a retention condition and a limitation to individual employees. Tax reliefs are normally available only if the employee retains the shares – or saves against the acquisition of them under a Save as You Earn (SAYE)

Scheme – for some years. They are also available only if the shares associated with them end up in the hands of *individual* employees. They are not available, for example, if a company decides to transfer shares into a permanent employee benefit trust.

In mid-1996 three basic categories of scheme could benefit from employee ownership tax reliefs. The first were the so-called profit-sharing employee share ownership schemes first made eligible for tax reliefs way back in 1978. Subject to certain conditions and up to specified annual limits, they allowed companies to distribute to their employees shares which might be paid for out of pre-tax profits and were not subject to income tax in the hands of the employees so long as they were not sold for a specified number of years.

The annual limits in 1996 were £1,500 per employee or 10% of salary (with a cap at £6,000). As well as the general conditions and principles which, as we have just seen, these schemes must satisfy, there are two further requirements. The company must establish an approved 'profit-sharing trust' and all shares distributed to employees must pass through it. Second, all these shares must be 'ordinary' shares.

These arrangements may sound, and indeed are, fairly complex. But they are not problematic. According to the official statistics in 1994:

– Around 1,100 UK companies were operating such schemes.

– Over 1.5m employees probably participated in them: the statistics show shares were allocated to just under 800,000 in each of the five years to 1993/4 – what we don't know is the overlap between the recipients in individual years

– The initial value of the shares appropriated under these schemes was around £3.4bn and had probably become worth over £5bn by mid-1996.

– The cumulative cost of the tax reliefs for the fifteen years between 1979/80 and 1993/4 was £865m, an annual average of £60m. It was running at £90m per annum in the first half of the 1990s.

The second category were the so-called Save As You Earn (SAYE) schemes. They were essentially all-employee share schemes which required participating employees to make regular monthly savings out of their pay for at least three years to cover the initial price of the shares under option. At the end of three years the employees may choose between taking the accumulated savings, which are deposited in a bank or building society, plus tax-free interest, in cash; or, using the same money to convert the options into shares in their employers' company, at the price of those shares, not on the date of the conversion, but on the date on which the savings commitment was first entered into.

In effect, under these schemes, an employee makes a tax assisted 'no lose' bet on the price of the employing company's shares being higher at the end of the savings commitment period than at the start of it. The scale of take-up may be judged from some recent official statistics, again mid-1994: roughly 1,250 companies were operating SAYE schemes, of which roughly 250 were expected not to continue – in the sense that no new shares would be appropriated under them.

Over the fourteen years between 1980/1 and 1993/4 the initial value of the shares over which SAYE options had been granted was £10.8bn. More than 1m employees held options. In the four years to 1993/4 over 500,000 per annum were granted options. But again, we cannot measure the overlap. The cumulative cost to the Revenue of the tax relief had reached £560m by 1993/4, and had been running at nearly £100m per annum since 1989/90

The third and last category of scheme which needs to be mentioned here is the one which, without any real doubt, has the greatest potential – if we are talking about majority employee ownership. First introduced in 1989, but not really operational until 1994, these schemes are generally referred to – not altogether correctly – as 'statutory ESOPs'.

In fact ESOPs in the UK go way back before 1989 to the country's even more opaquely described 'case law ESOPs'. As their name implies, these are employee share ownership plans – or, more precisely, employee share ownership *trusts* – which are not recognised by statute but have evolved as a result of 'case law' instead. They are the offspring of individual company initiatives to establish trusts for the benefit of their employees, sometimes called employee benefit trusts (EBTs), and then to make payments to them. Of course there is nothing in company or tax law to prevent such initiatives. Companies can borrow money and use it to purchase shares on behalf of their employees. The problem is whether payments from companies to these EBTs are tax deductible. More than once over the last thirty years the Inland Revenue has mounted court challenges on this point. But in all cases which have so far come before the courts, the ruling has been that, provided certain not very onerous conditions are met, companies which pass money to EBTs to pay off those borrowings may take a tax deduction for doing so.

At least in part to eliminate the uncertainty involved in relying on case law, the Tory Government in 1989 enacted the provisions which first established the new statutory – as opposed to case law – ESOPs. These are employee share ownership *trusts* of a rather special kind. They are indeed sometimes referred to in the press and elsewhere as 'Qualifying Employee Share Ownership Trusts' or QUESTS. Like case law ESOPs they may borrow money and apply those borrowings to the purchase of shares on behalf of employees in their employer's company's equity: in principle right up to 100%. Like case law ESOPs too, they may pay off the debt using contributions made to them by the employer's company out of pre-tax profits. The advantage that they have over case law ESOPs is that, subject to various conditions, shareholders from whom they buy these shares are eligible for rollover relief – though this applies only if not less than 10% of the share capital of the business has been sold to the trust in what must essentially be a single transaction.

Given this 10% rule, statutory ESOPs will normally also be leveraged, i.e. the money they use to buy the shares will be borrowed. Companies are not often willing and able to finance such large sums from profits or cash reserves.

The importance of rollover relief is that it offers to principal shareholders in private non-quoted companies the same tax treatment as if those shareholders had sold to a quoted company and taken its shares in payment. When this rollover relief was introduced into the previously existing body of American ESOP legislation, there was a sharp rise in new leveraged ESOPs.

During the first five years after 1989, two crippling restrictions prevented the take-up of the new ESOP legislation. Eased in March 1994, these were a requirement that (a) a majority of trustees who controlled the ESOP had to be elected by the company's employees and that (b) the shares acquired by the ESOP had to be 'got out' to individual employees within seven years on pain of claw-back of the tax reliefs. The first problem has been eased by permitting alternatives, most notably a 'paritarian' trust – one in which there are equal numbers of shop-floor-elected and management-appointed trustees, with the balance held by one or more agreed independents. The seven-year limit was extended in 1994 to twenty years.

There is also a postscript to this story of Britain since 1978. It concerns employee ownership in relation to privatisation. The case studies include three examples of companies which became majority employee owned as a result of privatisation. But only in a tiny minority of Mrs Thatcher's privatisations was employee ownership of any real importance: in less than 2% of all cases and substantially less than half of 1% by value.

It is true that in all or almost all other cases employees were offered a small package of free and discounted shares and other 'goodies' like priority allocation. But those packages are best seen as 'sweeteners'. They confirm the view that Conservative Party support for employee ownership, though real, is at a rather low level of intensity.

What of the future? By mid-1997 there were *some* quite specific grounds for optimism. Mr Blair for 'New' Labour seemed committed to a 'stakeholder' economy. Whatever else that may turn out to mean, it would be perverse to suppose that it excludes some strengthening of the position of employees as shareholders. As for the Tories, to the surprise of many and at their conference in October 1997, the newly elected party leader, Mr William Hague, seemed to endorse an important basic principle: of inclusion. That too looks like a starting point which could favour strengthening the position of employees.

However, with the possible exception of the Institute of Directors – the voice of Britain's unquoted companies – it would be foolish to pretend that any really big power centres had been converted when this was written to the employee ownership cause. Whether at the Confederation of British Industry or the Trades Union Congress, whether among top managers, among bankers and others in the City of London, the prevailing attitude remained sceptical, and often downright condescending.

4

Catholic Social Teaching, Profit Sharing and Co-Determination in Continental Western Europe

La participation. Voilà la grande réforme de ce siècle. *President de Gaulle, on the introduction of compulsory financial participation in France, August 1967*

In the Federal Republic of Germany many of those we met saw a strong and direct connection between the success of the West German economy since World War II and the presence of employee representatives on supervisory boards. *[Bullock] 'Report of the Committee of Inquiry on Industrial Democracy'. Cmd. 6706. January 1977*

Works councils and profit sharing, we might say, are 'staging posts' on the road to employee ownership. Works councils give employees a voice in the control of the businesses for which they work; profit sharing includes elements of financial ownership.

If we exclude the production co-ops, there is not yet anything in Continental Western Europe which may be compared with the recent development of employee ownership in Britain and, above all, in the USA. On the other hand, particularly in France and what used to be West Germany, these staging posts are part of the system: statutory works councils and indeed statutory co-determination in Germany; and profit-sharing, and indeed the statutory participation by employees in the fruits of enterprise growth ('participation des salariés aux fruits de l'expansion de l'entreprise') in France. They need to be more fully understood by the employee ownership community in the UK and the USA.

The Pre-1945 Background At least from the fourth quarter of the nineteenth century the priorities of the labour movements in Continental Western Europe did not really include – any more than they did in Britain – the serious promotion of employee ownership. Instead, these labour movements mainly sought to strengthen the trade unions as the key instruments of the movement's power in the business and industrial world and to press for the state take-over of big businesses. The programme of nationalisation by France's President Mitterrand in the early 1980s, even if subsequently reversed, is evidence of the strong survival of that second thrust.

This assessment of the labour movements in Continental Western Europe is not seriously modified by the relative strength of the production co-op tradition in two of them, France and Italy, over the last 100 years. One perverse reason which may explain this relative strength is the relative weakness of the *consumer* co-ops in those countries. By attracting most of the limited amounts of available management talent, and in other ways, Britain's uniquely strong consumer co-ops almost certainly operated to the disadvantage of ventures in co-operative *production*.

But the single most distinctive difference in the background to employee ownership in Continental Europe is the tradition of progressive social teaching in the Roman Catholic Church. Admittedly it is scarcely more that 100 years old. Its origin can be clearly pinpointed to the publication by Pope Leo XIII in 1881 of his famous encyclical on social and industrial questions: *Rerum Novarum*. The main message of that encyclical is that industrial capitalism must have regard to social justice in its treatment of working people.

No doubt its perceived progressiveness partly reflects the degree to which it contrasts with what the Church had been saying earlier. And yet this progressive social teaching has been almost continuously renewed by Leo XIII's successors on the throne of St Peter. Some of the later papal pronouncements have even been almost specific in their endorsement of moves towards profit and power sharing in conventional capitalist businesses. The most recent, the encyclical *Laborem Exercens* issued by the present Polish Pope in 1983, has even been cited in the US Congress as a papal endorsement of employee ownership. It certainly comes close to the assertion of the primacy of labour over capital in productive activity.

The thinking embodied in this tradition of progressive social teaching in the Roman Catholic church was hugely important in what has been easily the greatest co-operative success story of this century. For it was a key influence on the thinking of Fr José Maria Arizmendiarrieta. Fr José Maria, who died in 1976, was the Catholic priest who was both the inspiration and the prime mover behind what is now the Mondragon group of mainly industrial co-operatives in the Basque provinces of Spain.

The Catholic tradition also had a seminal influence on the thinking of France's President de Gaulle. For his commitment to the 'participation des salariés aux fruits de l'expansion de l'entreprise', that tradition is now thought to have been the single most important source.

The one other feature of the background which has no real counterpart in the USA or UK is a feature of German company law which, like *Rerum Novarum*, dates back over a hundred years. It helps us to understand why Germany has developed its almost unique system of co-determination: or, strictly interpreted, of the *dual* control of private business undertakings by capital and labour jointly.

The key and historic point of German company law, since it was first developed to meet what were seen as the needs of large undertakings in the 1870s, is that it lays down an institutional separation between responsibility for day-to-day management, and responsibility for the oversight of that management. The former is the function of the *Vorstand* or management board, the latter of the *Aufsichtsrat* or supervisory board. Germany's system of *co-determination*, that is of the dual control of a business by capital and labour, is widely thought to be a post-Second World War phenomenon – at least that is the popular view in the USA and the UK. In fact employee representation, by two elected employee directors, on the *Aufsichtsrat* of the normal large German company, was made obligatory by a law of the Weimar Republic enacted in 1922. Co-determination at a lower level and in the form of a works council had become obligatory two years earlier. The development of co-determination after 1945 in what was then West Germany was built on these foundations. The separation in German company law of the management board from the supervisory board, the *Vorstand* from the *Aufsichtstrat*, predisposed the country towards co-determination. Institutional and legal furniture can be an important source of 'real' developments.

Germany since 1945: Co-Determination But having two elected employee directors on a supervisory board hardly counts as co-determination. The essential meaning of that term is surely paritarian – in the sense of implying a parity in the control of a business as between capital and labour. Gradually and with important qualifications, a more or less properly paritarian form of co-determination was achieved in the thirty-odd years after the Second World War. The process culminated in the Co-determination Act passed by the Parliament of the Federal Republic in 1976. It had begun in 1947 when, at the request of the recently reborn trade union movement, the military administration in the British zone of Germany agreed to the introduction of a (properly paritarian) form of co-determination in the zone's steel industry.

There is an invaluable discussion of how this came about in *Bismarck to Bullock* published in London by the Anglo-German Foundation in 1983. *Bismarck to Bullock* is mainly the edited record of a series of conversations between a German academic, Professor Wolfgang Hirsch-Weber, and a progressive British industrialist, Wilfred Brown. *Bismarck to Bullock* is out of print and it seems worth quoting at some length the passage about what happened to the steel industry in the British zone in 1947. The speaker is Professor Hirsch-Weber:

> Co-determination was not, as is commonly believed, instituted by the British – they just gave it their blessing. One has to recognise that there was something like a revolutionary situation: the Nazis had lost the war, quite a number of big industrialists who had collaborated with the Nazis had gone into hiding, industry was destroyed and there was not enough to eat. The workers began to re-build industry on very low wages. There was a lot of talk about the need to institute a non-capitalist economy and almost everybody accepted the need for socialisation (public control – not necessarily nationalisation in the British way); even the Christian Democrats had it in their party programme. But the Americans would not permit socialisation and vetoed the socialisation clauses the Länder wanted to put in their constitutions. The British went along with the Americans. Only in Hesse did you get such a clause in the state constitution.
>
> But everybody agreed that the workers who rebuilt industry had to be given more rights than before. A version of the old works councils was put into effect, with quite a lot of powers, though less than in the Weimar Republic. Then, in 1947, co-determination was instituted in the steel industry in the British

Zone, by agreement between the unions, the steel industry and the North German Iron and Steel Control, with *parity of representation of workers and employers on the supervisory boards (Aufsichtstrate) of the companies.* [Emphasis added.]

The system was subsequently instituted throughout the coal iron and steel industries. . . .'

(Anglo-German Foundation 1983, p. 53.)

That happened by act of Parliament in 1951. So, if we ignore the slightly earlier works councils, the road to co-determination in postwar West Germany started in the steel industry in 1947 and was extended to iron and coal in 1951. At the level of the supervisory boards of the companies in those industries it was co-determination in almost its most authentic and paritarian possible form. The shareholders and the employees of these companies elect equal numbers of directors to represent them on the supervisory boards. Moreover these are presided over by independent chairmen.

With interesting exceptions – for example of so-called 'committed' companies engaged in newspaper work and other not exclusively commercial activities – the 1976 law applied to all businesses which employed more than 2,000 people. It required them to move to equality of representation – as between the representatives of shareholders and employees – on their supervisory boards. Under an earlier law of 1952, *all* public companies, i.e. not only those with a workforce in excess of 2,000, had been required to have at least one third of their supervisory board directors elected by employees. So the 1976 law was a real step towards a more properly paritarian form of co-determination; and was indeed vigorously opposed for years by West Germany's employers' organisations.

On the other hand, in two key respects, the rules laid down by the 1976 Act are not quite as faithful to paritarian principles as those which apply in the iron, steel and coal industries. First, under the 1976 Act, the Chairman of the Supervisory Board is always one of the shareholders' representatives and enjoys a casting vote in the event of tied voting. Second the law requires that one of the directors on the employees' side must be drawn from the ranks of 'higher' management: that is, management below the level of the management board (the *Vorstand*) but not all that much below it. There are no prizes for correctly identifying the nature of the main trade union objection to this provision: it seems to have been the subject of an

almost interminable series of test cases before West Germany's industrial courts.

Two final points are worth making. The first is that the German system by which the management of a business and a management board (*Vorstand*) are distinguished from the supervision of that
management and a supervisory board (*Aufsichtsrat*) seems to *lend
itself* to co-determination. Or perhaps the point becomes clearer if
we say that co-determination, understood as a genuine sharing of
power over the enterprise between capital and labour, is likely to be
much less problematic and controversial if it takes place on the top
tier of a two-tier board than if it is located in a single board. The
Germans themselves seem quite clear about this point: they say that
it is important that the membership of the management board (the
Vorstand) should be homogeneous.

The second point is that the German works councils have come to
set the pattern throughout Western Europe. Works councils became
compulsory in many member states of the European Union (EU) as
early as the 1980s. In 1996 they became the subject of an EU directive
which was accepted by Mr Tony Blair's new Labour Government in
1997.

France since 1945: Profit Sharing While the West Germans are
chiefly notable for their co-determination, the highlight in the French
postwar record has been legislation providing for employee financial
participation. It is President de Gaulle – with his characteristic
rhetorical flourish quoted in the first of the two epigraphs – who
should be given the main credit for that policy, under the influence of
the Roman Catholic Church.

Strictly speaking, French Government support for employee
financial participation predates President de Gaulle's two main 1967
measures by a number of years. What a recent European Commission report calls 'the first general law on profit sharing in France'
dates back to the Prime Ministership of M. Antoine Pinay, and was
embodied in a decree dated 7 January 1959. The tax reliefs provided
by the decree were significant. Unlike the more important of de
Gaulle's two measures, its provisions were also voluntary. Quite
likely it is the 'first general law on profit sharing' not only in France
but in Western Europe as a whole. Up to a maximum of 20% of an
employee's pay, the employer was relieved of company tax on
payments out of profits to employees. For the employee the relief

was that such profit-sharing payments were exempted from social security contributions.

De Gaulle's two main measures were embodied in two decrees, both issued on the same day, 17 August 1967. The most important was and is mandatory on all companies with a workforce of over 100 people; a figure which was reduced to 50 in 1991. Britain's Tories, and the Confederation of British Industry, with their almost interminable insistence on the importance of voluntarism in these matters, would express nothing less than full-blown shock and horror if a British Government was to suggest anything of the kind. And yet it would be difficult to present de Gaulle's ideology as other than right of centre; hard too to argue that the measure has had negative effects on the performance of French industry.

The main decree required that above a minimum threshold of a 5% return on capital, a company must agree to assign to its employees a proportion of the balance of its profits up to a maximum of 50%; that it must negotiate what that proportion is to be with either the trade unions, if it recognises any, or with its statutory works council; and that the resulting sums, so negotiated, must be placed in a Réserve Spéciale de Participation (RSP) wherein they remain locked for five years. This is the famous 'participation des salariés aux fruits de l'expansion de l'entreprise'. Provided these conditions are met, then the employee receives relief of income tax (and social security contributions) and the employer receives relief from company tax.

The second de Gaulle decree of 17 August 1967 essentially offers tax reliefs to encourage employee savings through the mechanism of an 'enterprise savings plan' ('un plan dépargne d'entreprise' or PEE). It is voluntary in the sense that no employee can be required to save in this way. It is compulsory in the sense that if employees wish to save through such plans, employers are bound to introduce them. Its key feature is that these savings must be invested in the company: either in its shares or as loans to its cash flow. As in the case of the provisions of the first de Gaulle decree, there is a lock-in period of five years. Subject to that, and up to specified limits, there are company tax reliefs for the employing company if it chooses to 'top up' the employee's saving with a bounty; and there are income tax reliefs for the employee on any interest and dividend payments which result. These PEE schemes in France are both like and unlike the SAYE schemes in Britain. The chief difference is that in France the employee savings must be put to work in the company from the outset. In Britain they may *not* be invested in the company for at least three years. The French arrangement was clearly more likely to encourage feelings and behaviour appropriate to an employee owner.

Quite rightly, this French Government support for employee financial participation in the company sector is also available to France's production co-ops. That is a detail. But it may point to the potential importance of an event which took place at Imola in Italy at the end of October 1996. At the initiative of the Italian and French industrial co-ops, the event brought together with them people from the employee ownership worlds of the UK and the USA, from the world of 'employee financial participation' in France and from Germany's co-determination community. Senior officials from the European Commission in Brussels also attended. So far as I know it is the first event of its kind ever. Retrospectively, it could turn out to be an important new beginning of a new Europe-wide project.

5

A Special Propensity to Fail?

In the first nine months of our life [as The Society for Promoting Working Men's Associations] we set up three sets of shoemakers in association, supplying in two instances the whole of the funds, in the other all but £5. None of the men were picked; we accepted them just as they came to us. We gave them absolute self-government, merely reserving to ourselves certain rights of interference in cases of dispute or mismanagement while any capital remained to us. Each one of these associations quarrelled with and turned out its original manager within six months; one, the West End Bootmakers, went to pieces altogether before nine months had gone. The other two struggled on until the beginning of the next year, never paying their way and continually quarrelling ... Working men in general are not fit for association. They come into it with the idea that it is to fill their pockets and lighten their work at once, and that every man in an association is to be his own master. They found their mistake in the first month or two and then set to quarrelling with everybody connected with the association but more especially with the manager; and after much blood has been raised the association breaks up insolvent. *'Report of the Society for Promoting Working Men's Associations', 1851. Quoted by Ben Jones in 'Co-operative Production', Oxford [1894], vol 1.1, p. 121 and variously since then*

... I have increasingly come to believe that one of the worst things that Tony Benn ever did was to give co-operatives a bad name. He linked co-operatives in the public mind with left-wing politics, loss-making production and endless taxpayers' subsidy. *Kenneth Clarke MP, then Paymaster General in Mrs Thatcher's second Government. Speech to Tory Reform Group, delivered in Manchester in 1986 shortly after an official visit to the Mondragon Co-operatives*

In a competitive market environment, businesses of all kinds are subject to failure. They always have been and they always will be. What we have to examine in this chapter is evidence about any special propensity to fail inherent in the nature of employee ownership but not in conventional capitalist businesses.

Beatrice Webb, the British Fabian socialist and sociologist, was the original source of the profoundly negative view that these ventures were almost bound to fail. She was of course writing about production co-ops – employee-owned businesses in the modern sense did not exist, at any rate in Britain when she did her original research in the 1890s. According to Mrs Webb, their inevitable failure would be either as businesses – by going bankrupt – or as co-operatives. Failure as a co-operative was a 'degeneration', or backsliding from a democratic co-operative business into a more or less conventional capitalist one.

The classic statement of this view comes from a joint book written by Beatrice and her husband Sidney Webb, and published in 1921 as *A Constitution for the Socialist Commonwealth of Great Britain*:

> Democracies of producers, as all experience shows ... have hitherto failed, with almost complete uniformity, whenever they have themselves sought to win and organise the instruments of production. In the relatively few instances in which such enterprises have not succumbed as business concerns, they have ceased to be democracies of producers managing their own work, and become in effect associations of capitalists ... making profits for themselves by the employment at wages of workers outside the association.

Accepting for the moment Beatrice Webb's definition of failure, we should distinguish sharply between production co-ops and employee-owned businesses (EOBs). Unlike many of the production co-ops and especially perhaps those of earlier times, today's EOBs rarely have any major reservations about their commitment to business success. Moreover, the EOBs of the late twentieth century have been well placed to learn from the mistakes of the co-ops of earlier times, and many have done so.

There have been some spectacular examples of business disaster among production co-ops. Two are reflected in the two epigraphs. But they are not the only British examples; nor is Britain the only country where they have occurred.

In my earlier book, *The Case for Workers' Co-ops*, I deal at some length with the almost uniformly disastrous results of the efforts of Britain's earliest, and self-styled, Christian Socialists, led by F. D. Maurice, to promote co-operative production; efforts which started after the collapse of Chartism in 1848. Ventures promoted in the 'hands off' way described in the epigraph – with no effort to select suitable participants, no insistence on any financial commitment by the participants, and nothing secure about the authority of management – are bound to fail.

There was a wave of similar failures in France following the revolution of 1848. The main difference was in the source of the capital. In France the money came from government sources rather than from Christian philanthropists. In other respects they were much the same. In both countries there have been further examples of similarly explained failures since then.

Other examples of more or less spectacular failure in Britain include the Benn Co-ops and, among single ventures, that of the Ouseburn Co-operative Engineering Works in Newcastle upon Tyne in the 1870s. Beatrice Webb estimated that the trade unions lost £60,000 (about £2.5m today) when it collapsed in 1875. Substantially greater were the losses associated with the almost total failure of the so-called building guilds – building co-ops by another name – which mushroomed across the country and then rapidly went into liquidation in the early 1920s.

In ascending order of the length of their survival as businesses, Britain's three 'Benn' Co-ops were a Glasgow-based newspaper, the *Scottish Daily News*; a Merseyside manufacturing conglomerate called Kirkby Manufacturing and Engineering (KME); and Meriden Motorcycles, in the small Midlands town of Meriden, not far out of Coventry. Tony Benn, the Secretary of State for Industry in Harold Wilson's final Government, was the prime mover, against the advice of his top civil servants but with at least the reluctant concurrence of the Cabinet, in securing for all three of these ventures an injection of public funds. All three were born from failed capitalist businesses.

When my earlier book was written, the most short-lived of the three, the *Scottish Daily News*, had already gone into liquidation after barely six months of commercial existence in 1974. All I would now add with hindsight is that I wish I had used less-guarded language in characterising the late Robert Maxwell's involvement with the newspaper as a mixed blessing.

KME went into liquidation on 27 March 1979. Perhaps the date was an omen. For, on the very next day the Callaghan Labour Government finally went down to defeat in the House of Commons, thus precipitating the May election which the Tories won. Meriden Motorcycles just managed to soldier on into the Thatcher era but eventually succumbed to the recession in 1981.

Writing about those two ventures in the late 1970s, I probably put too much emphasis on their success in improving productivity over their previous conventional capitalist days. Those successes were real; they were achieved mainly by the classic method of changing earlier established working practices; and they still look as if they were of some significance. But at KME they were vitiated by the behaviour of the co-op's two leaders – Jack Spriggs and Dick Jenkins, who combined the roles of directors and trade union convenors of the business – making it impossible for its professional managers to play any real part in managing at all. KME is an unforgettable story of human frailty and folly, and of organisational incoherence and management failure (Eccles, 1981).

As for the Meriden Motorcycles co-op, for which I retain real respect, I now think I underestimated the degree to which the business taken over by the co-op had been starved of investment by its former capitalist owners. It had thus been severely and perhaps mortally damaged before ever the co-op took over.

More generally, I failed to emphasise sufficiently the importance of a real commitment to long-term business success; a readiness to take what may be painful steps to achieve it; and a readiness to drop left-wing and other attitudes and behaviour patterns which are almost bound to be incompatible with it. If we compare the behaviour of Messrs Spriggs and Jenkins with that of the United Steel Workers of America (USWA), we can see the essential difference. USWA's attitude to employee ownership is not uncritical. But when it deals with genuine examples of employee-owned businesses, it seeks to lay aside the adversarial attitudes and behaviour which have evolved in its dealings with conventional capitalism.

Some very similar ventures in the 'socialist' France of President Mitterrand in the 1980s also failed. An example is Manufrance, a substantial engineering business, employing several thousand people, which had gone bankrupt as a capitalist undertaking but was later revived as a so-called co-operative with government intervention and financial assistance. Like the Benn co-ops these French examples would be more correctly classified as examples of government-funded syndicalism. In all, or so I understand, there were as many as thirty of them. Only two managed to survive into the early 1990s.

Because of their political genesis, the 1970s Benn Co-ops in the UK and their slightly later counterparts in France were businesses of a special kind. Their leaders were at least substantially relieved of the necessity of convincing steely bankers of their credit-worthiness, and of the reality of their business plans. It seems probable that businesses born in this way *do* have a special propensity to fail.

But there are many examples of more ordinary co-ops which have failed for more ordinary business reasons: for example, their inability to go on competing in rapidly changing and increasingly competitive markets, or because they have been insufficiently capitalised, or for a combination of these reasons. Two French examples which failed in the 1980s were earlier ranked, by employment numbers, first and fifth among that country's production co-ops. They were also among the oldest, having both been established before 1900. The larger, the Association des Ouvriers en Instruments de Précision (AOIP), manufactured equipment for telephone exchanges and employed around 4,000 people in the late 1970s. The smaller, La Verrerie Ouvrière d'Albi, manufactured glass bottles, especially wine bottles, and employed about 500 people in the late 1970s. Each at that time was rather similarly placed in its respective market – among the country's top five suppliers, but also much smaller and less financially strong than their two largest competitors. By the end of the 1980s both had effectively gone under, though some members of Albi's famous co-operative glassworks had managed to keep their jobs by agreeing to the sale of the business to a conventional capitalist competitor. As for AOIP, the particular circumstance of its end was an inability to make a technological transition – from essentially mechanical telephone exchange manufacture to making the new electronic models.

Of course many conventional capitalist businesses have failed in similar circumstances to those which undid AOIP and the venerable Albi Glassworks. On the other hand to the extent that as co-ops they were less financially strong than their capitalist counterparts – and, in the case of AOIP, perhaps also less able to re-structure their workforce rapidly – we can take them as illustrations of a special propensity to fail on the part of production co-ops. There is also evidence towards the end of the co-op's life in Albi that its main Communist-led trade union had ceased to be on speaking terms with the professional management.

We come next to a rather different kind of propensity. Because of the provisions of UK (though not French) co-operative law, Britain's production co-ops have what might be called a special propensity, not to failure, but to voluntary liquidation. This propensity arises because of a peculiar feature of co-operative shares under British law: only in a liquidation can they reflect the market value of the net worth of the business which underpins them. If the shares change hands in any other circumstances, they are supposed to do so only at their nominal value.

The consequence has sometimes been an extreme imbalance between the true, market, value of these co-op shares and their nominal value. It is scarcely surprising that such imbalances have precipitated liquidations. One example is Bristol Printers which went into voluntary liquidation in the early 1980s. Its shares, which had previously been worth no more than a nominal £5, were suddenly, following the decision to liquidate, worth between £2,000 and £3,000.

I know of no research on the subject but I feel sure that this explains the near-disappearance since 1974 of Britain's old production co-ops – the 'cloth-cap co-ops'. In 1974 Britain's then Department of Industry published a list of sixteen of the country's 'old' production co-ops which were still in existence. Fifteen of them, including Bristol Printers, had then survived for at least sixty years. I understand that the corresponding figure in 1993 was just three: Equity Shoes of Leicester, the subject of one of my case studies in this book; a second shoe-making venture, NPS of Wollaston, which is briefly mentioned in the Equity story; and a clothing manufacturing co-op called Queen Eleanor, also in Britain's East Midlands, at Kettering.

Although the circumstances of these British co-ops are particular to them, there is a common factor in their demise with the demise of employee ownership at an increasing number of EOBs today: the employees' entirely understandable wish to convert their 'shares' in the business into hard cash.

This brings me to the failures of these production co-ops in the Webbs' second sense: degeneration into conventional capitalist undertakings. In some of her earliest work, before she married Sidney, Beatrice Potter – as she then was – identified a small string of examples; including a co-operative, or association, of working hatters. But the fact of their 'degeneration' is not in my view especially noteworthy. For, at least in the light of current evidence, it is no longer tenable to argue, as did the future Mrs Webb, that such a degeneration was more or less universal.

Even in Britain, where numbers this century have been much fewer than in France and Italy, a higher proportion have either soldiered on as co-ops, like Equity Shoes, or gone into voluntary liquidation like Bristol Printers, than have failed through bankruptcy or degeneration. Moreover, if we were to examine the record in France and Italy, the number of 'continuing co-ops' would far outweigh the number of 'degenerators'. One important reason is that the relevant French and Italian co-operative laws provide that member shareholders may not benefit from the net worth of the business in a liquidation.

So subsequent evidence has conclusively disproved the Webbs' claim to have established a near universal 'law of degeneration' for those production co-ops which survived as businesses. It was an egregious and arrogant error with profound political consequences over a long period. At the same time, it is worth exploring the reasons why they came to make it, and the senses in which their analysis points towards a truth.

Whether through innocence or guile, the founders of some of the earliest production co-ops framed their rules in ways which allowed for take-over by outsiders. The classic example is the case of the highly successful co-operative textile manufacturing business founded by no less prestigious a group of early co-operators than the Rochdale Pioneers. It is a splendid story of business success; but as a co-operative it ended in tears. The explanation is simple. Such was the co-op's early success as a business, that it decided to raise capital for expansion and do so from non-worker outsiders. The latter soon took over. But I should emphasise that that was not a necessary outcome. Had the founder working members played their cards more skilfully, they could surely have retained control: others have done so at other places and other times. A simple rule is readily available – only workers should hold voting shares. However, although not relevant to this particular case, the issue of capital adequacy can pose special problems for employee-owned businesses, including co-ops, especially in capital-intensive industries, or where, as at Meriden, investment has been badly neglected before employee ownership started.

On another score the Webbs correctly identified a problem with which all employee-owned businesses – whether co-operative or otherwise – have to contend. The problem is that of managers being ultimately answerable to and dismissible by those whom they manage. The case studies in this book are good evidence of both the problem's difficulty and of the fact that it can be solved.

Third, there are numerous examples of what the Webbs might

want to claim as 'partial degeneration': cases where co-op member-ship is unreasonably restricted to a group of privileged workers. In making judgements about such cases there are difficulties about where to draw the line: when membership of a production co-op falls below 50% of the workforce perhaps? Probationary periods are entirely respectable but permanent exclusion of people who are expected to continue working indefinitely for the co-op is some-thing else. The two otherwise admirable Italian co-ops, Sacmi and La Ceramica, are open to criticism on precisely this ground. There are now elements of this at Mondragon too.

An obvious question which the Webbs never raised is the relative failure rates of co-operatives and conventional capitalist businesses. In 1963 Professor Derek Jones (Coates 1976) compared the average ages of the surviving British producer co-operatives with those for a sample of small British conventional companies:

UK: Small Companies v. Producer Co-ops

Average Age by Quartile

	Oldest	Median	Youngest
Small companies	55	22	10
Co-ops	75	66	52

The population of those co-ops has shrunk drastically since then and it may also be argued that in the early 1960s Britain's consumer co-ops provided protected markets for those ventures. However, together with Professor Saul Estrin, Professor Jones later revisited this question. In a so far unpublished paper which they have kindly allowed me to see, they have used the much larger population of France's production co-ops to provide the co-operative leg of the data. Once again this evidence seems to point to a superior perfor-mance by the co-ops. If we add these two pieces of aggregate evidence to the case study evidence accumulated in these pages, the negative claims of the Webbs have simply been blown to bits, at least in the universal terms in which they were pronounced.

The Employee-Owned Businesses of Today When we move from the older production co-ops to today's world of non-co-operative employee-owned businesses (EOBs), my fundamental argument is made by the case studies in this book. These also point to the opposite of what was claimed by the Webbs. But special cases may make for bad generalisations. Here I look for specific evidence of failure among the large populations of EOBs which have grown up since the time that the Webbs condemned employee ownership – and effectively put it on the back burner of the public policy debate, at least in Britain, for two generations.

An area often quoted in connection with the failure of employee ownership is the former Yugoslavia. The whole focus of this book is on the experience of EOBs in economies where the dominant forces are those of the *market*. Strictly speaking therefore the experience of the self-managed and socially owned firms in the former Yugoslavia fall outside our limits. For market forces were never really more than marginal in that economy. In its essentials it was a command system and the decisions which drove it were taken by officials of one kind and another of the Government, the Communist Party and the banking institutions.

Nevertheless, and especially in the context of ongoing privatisation programmes in the mid-1990s of the former Yugoslavia, a few words about the experience of Marshal Tito's socially owned and self-managed firms are in order. It should first be acknowledged that there were some real successes. However, the scholarly consensus is that they were a rather small minority. According to the same scholarly sources, this system of Marshal Tito gradually became the single most important source of an accelerating inflation of prices which became the main negative feature of the country's economy in Yugoslavia's later years.

What is more, the link between the system, taken together with the absence of a properly functioning bankruptcy process, and the country's accelerating inflation is remarkably easy to grasp. The individual employees in Yugoslavia's socially owned and self-managed firms did not own any shares in them. They thus had no financial ownership in the long-term success of their businesses. Given the absence of a properly functioning bankruptcy process, and a resulting almost total employment security, it was a corporate framework which was almost bound to encourage irresponsible wage increases. Self-management, by virtue of which the voice of the shop floor was often decisive in matters like wages and salaries, administered an extra push in the same inflationary direction.

Those with an ideological or other hostility to the spread of employee ownership in the quite different conditions of the market economies have a tendency to cite this Yugoslav experience as evidence that it will not work. It is nothing of the kind. The Yugoslav evidence applies most directly to self-managed and socially owned firms in a command economy, though it also applies to some extent to state-owned and state-controlled firms in other command economies. The distinguished Hungarian economist Janos Kornai has coined a persuasive phrase to explain the cause of the widespread failure of businesses in those command economies. He has attributed it to the absence of any hard budget constraint.

In other words the firms were typically free to take irresponsible business decisions. By contrast, if employee-owners in market economies make similarly irresponsible decisions, they will themselves have to face the consequences.

In the market economies, only one country, the United States, really offers an adequate sample of failures. The population of employee-owned businesses in Britain is not yet large enough. We therefore move on to look at the evidence of failure among the much larger population of ESOP companies in the USA.

To begin with, let me make clear what this discussion excludes. It does not take in the experience of American companies in which the employees own only a small minority of the shares. This book is concerned with businesses where the employee ownership is substantial: at a minimum, say, the figure of just over 20% maintained at Polaroid.

I know of no systematic research which has so far been undertaken on this subject: which would surely have attracted considerable attention if the numbers of failures were really high. In its absence, we are left with no more than a few examples of largely individual business failures which happen to have come to my attention.

In every one of my cases of failure, the context was difficult, even very difficult, market conditions: whether for special reasons, as with Hyatt Clark (see below), or more simply because of the recession phase of the business cycle. Against that background the questions that need to be asked are:

Did their employee ownership, considered quite separately from the market situation, act as a contributory cause of failure?

If so, was that more-or-less inevitable or could there have been a different outcome if the problems had been tackled differently.

Hyatt Clark Industries: Motor Components: 1,500 Employees The specialised nature of its product was unquestionably the most important factor behind the failure of Hyatt Clark (HCI). Its life as an EOB lasted for little more than five years, between 1982 and 1987, when it went into liquidation. The business was just profitable in two of those years. Its workforce numbers reached their high of around 1,500 in 1984. The sales and profit and loss figures between 1982 and 1986 were as follows:

Year	Sales $m	Profit (Loss) $m
1982	65.96	(5.56)
1983	81.41	0.77
1984	97.55	0.83
1985	81.5	(4.80)
1986	57.0	(6.80)

Before the buy-out General Motors (GM) was HCI's owner and only customer. Furthermore, HCI was substantially a one-product business: highly specific motor car components called tapered bearings which are extensively used in rear axle engines but scarcely at all in front axle engines. In the late 1970s GM began to switch from rear to front axle engines for almost half of its total output. Declining to make the new investment needed to re-tool the business, GM announced an impending closure in August 1980. The subsequent employee buy-out reflected a determination by the Clark workforce, including the local management, not to accept the closure.

Little progress was made during the five-year life of the business either in developing new products or finding new markets. In the absence of a major injection of new capital and/or heroic downsizing of the business and higher labour productivity, it is doubtful whether *any* workforce-and-management team, employee owners or otherwise, could have overcome those challenges.

The likelihood of failure was almost certainly increased by the state of the industrial relations in the former GM subsidiary before ever the buy-out took place. The union branch with which the business was in contract, Local 736 of the United Automobile Workers, had a reputation for militancy, as appears from a feasibility study by consultants Arthur D Little before the buy-out:

The situation in Hyatt is typical of what we have found in many US manufacturing plants. Over a period of time management has made concessions to the union and the workforce which result in inefficient work practices. All concerned have come to accept this situation as normal, and, in fact, this situation exists to some degree in most plants.

But we still have to ask whether problems specifically related to its employee ownership *contributed* to the failure at HCI or at least brought that failure forward in time. In situations of this kind it is impossible to identify causes and effects with any certainty. However, while employee ownership was a necessary condition of the venture continuing to trade, it was also in some ways unhelpful. A report prepared by a team from Cornell University in 1985 shows that management and union had totally failed to develop an appropriate new relationship or, indeed, any successful working relationship at all: 'Management and union must realise that feed-back from the employees interviewed says they are tired and frustrated by the constant fighting between the two sides.'

From my researches at HCI while it was still just in business, I also found that the company was confronted with one of those specific difficulties that arise in employee-owned firms where the workforce has accepted a wage cut and wage freeze as part of their employee buy-out package. Faced with a sudden increase in the turnover of its key personnel, the management offered some upward adjustments in rates as an inducement to persuade others in that category to stay on. Under the terms of the buy-out package those offers fell entirely within the management's discretion because they were made only to non-union personnel. Nevertheless 'this issue became an important one in the struggle between the union and the management at HCI' [Oakeshott, 1987].

Seymour Specialty Wire (SSW): Brass Products: 250 Employees

Early in 1984 workers at the Seymour Manufacturing Company, a century-old brass mill with 250 employees [in the small town of Seymour in the Naugatuck valley of Connecticut] learned that the company's owner, National Distillers and Chemical Corporation was planning to divest its metals division. . .

Ultimately a purchase price was negotiated [by an employee-owned company, Seymour Specialty Wire, formed by former employees of Seymour Manufacturing], a bank supplied financing, the state [of Connecticut] provided a loan guarantee, and, after a job search, the current plant manager was hired to be company president. More than a year after the effort had begun ... Seymour Specialty Wire, an employee-owned company, took over the assets. . .

By 1989 the company was in crisis, and in a dramatic confrontation the board decided to 'fire the boss'. A new president began a major turnaround effort, with new financing, reduced workforce, and a partially new management team. But after a few hopeful months the company was losing money and went into bankruptcy. Early in 1993 its assets were auctioned off for the benefit of its creditors.

Employee Ownership at SSW succeeded for seven years in preventing the company from being sold, moved, or shut down. The experience also showed the limits of employee ownership as an unsupplemented strategy. [Brecher 1994.]

I must gratefully acknowledge at once the kind permission of Jeremy Brecher to quote from his study. I should also make clear that his account of SSW covers no more than a quarter of the whole of his 1994 study; and that the author's main interest is in the possibility of a new and radically different community-based economics, rather than with employee ownership *per se*.

Why did SSW fail? Or, to put the same question rather differently, why did it survive, in its new employee-owned form, for no more than seven years? We may begin with what Mr Brecher has to say about the markets for its brass products: 'Like the rest of industry in the [Naugatuck] Valley and like the rest of the wire industry nationally, it was buffeted by international competition and declining markets for its products due to recession in its customers' markets.'

In addition to these difficulties, there were also serious internal difficulties which were closely linked to the employee ownership and strikingly similar to those at HCI. At the centre was a failure to develop new relationships between management, union, and rank and file. Mr Brecher tells us that 'work roles remained largely the same and workers continued to refer to management as 'upstairs' and the mill as downstairs'. He also refers to 'evidence of sabotage' – as clear an indicator of conflict and low morale and industrial relations failure as can be imagined.

To some extent the reality of that failure was obscured by the existence of a democratically elected board:

> Employees initially elected a majority white-collar board of directors who rarely challenged the company president; even when subsequently a blue-collar majority was elected, the board often felt inadequate to overrule what it regarded as the superior business knowledge of top managers, who were often reluctant to share full knowledge of the company's situation and workings with the employee owners. When union members of the board did challenge management decisions, management sometimes charged them with conflict of interest and violation of their fiduciary responsibility to maximise stockholders' profits.

In addition the same specific problem cropped up at SSW as at HCI: 'Much internal conflict arose at SSW from efforts to raise the salaries of managers and high-skilled workers.'

Turning to another area of conflict, Mr Brecher remarks that 'the necessity of paying off loans on schedule gave the company little choice but to treat profit maximisation as its basic criterion of decision-making.'

He then adds in a footnote: 'This criterion was contested. Some union officials maintained that "saving jobs" had been the original purpose of the buyout and that avoiding layoffs was a proper criterion for decisions as long as it did not undermine the company's viability.'

If we are talking about the achievement of necessary cost savings through agreed wage reductions – as at Mondragon – rather than forced redundancies, the line attributed to 'some union officials' seems eminently reasonable. Mr Brecher himself appears to want to go rather further: to a world in which employee-owned or at least community-owned businesses would not be required to make more than moderate profits and perhaps only a modestly positive cash flow. At least an important minority of employee-owned businesses would probably go along with that view.

We may conclude this discussion of the failure at SSW by suggesting that it was probably pre-determined by exceptionally difficult market conditions. But on top of that it seems that management and labour at SSW failed to resolve problems of the relationship between them which are at least partly specific to employee-owned businesses.

O&O Stores: Supermarket Retail: 200-odd Employees at Peak In March 1982 the American retail chain A&P announced that because of market conditions it would shortly close all twenty of its supermarket stores in and around Philadelphia, a network of shops employing together, including part-timers, some 2,000 people. The decision was challenged by the employees' union in the shape of Local 1357 of the United Food and Commercial Workers (UFCW).

As a result of some skilful and determined bargaining, Local 1357 managed, in May 1982, to secure a modification – almost a reversal – of the closure decision. Two key points in the agreement reached between the company and the UFCW's Local 1357 were:

that in return for wage concessions A&P would reopen, as a new 'Superfresh Division', most of those supermarkets previously closed down;

that in the case of two of its supermarkets, those serving the Roslyn and Parkwood Manor neighbourhoods, it would agree to a sale of these businesses to employees through an ESOP.

With remarkable speed, in autumn 1982 the Roslyn and Parkwood Manor stores started trading as employee-owned undertakings, named O[wned] and O[perated] Supermarkets. Both enjoyed initial success. By late 1986 there were a total of six employee-owned O&O supermarkets in and around Philadelphia. When they peaked, the value of their annual sales was over $30m. They even attracted interested attention from the *Wall Street Journal*.

Yet between 1987 and 1989, all but one of the six O&O supermarkets failed. Only Parkwood Manor survived.

Before looking into the reasons for the five failures, we need to introduce a key corporate actor in this O&O drama by the name of PACE, originally spelled out as the Philadelphia Association for Co-operative Enterprise.

First established in 1976 as the local chapter of America's then Federation for Economic Democracy, what later became PACE offered a range of services connected with the setting up of EOBs. Already, in 1981, it had been in discussion with the UFCW's Local 1357. 'Technical assistance' and 'shadow management' are two phrases used in one account of the PACE contribution to the O&O story (Lamas). They may understate the importance of PACE's contribution. It may even be that in PACE's absence there would have been no employee-owned O&O supermarkets. But it is almost certain that its contribution was both a necessary and a sufficient condition of three of the later supermarkets. For the two pioneering ventures, Roslyn and Parkwood Manor, Lamas tells us that PACE facilitated 'a highly participatory business creation and education process'. Later he tells us that the association 'was able to expand its staff and diversify its program'. And he goes on: 'At its peak, PACE (and its subsidiaries and affiliates including a revolving loan fund and a law office) had a budget of more than $500,000.'

Turning to the causes of the failure of five out of the six O&O supermarkets, market conditions were especially tough for businesses of this kind – fairly small supermarket-type retail outlets. The original A&P closedown decision tells us that. From say 1986 onwards, Lamas notes that

> ... significant technological changes, major corporate reorganisations and other developments in the supermarket industry generated increasingly unfavourable conditions for independent retailers across the nation. In Philadelphia, keen competition by new and remodelled chain stores decreased each O&O's margin for error while intensifying the struggle to gain and maintain market share.

Poor management is mentioned by Mr Lamas as a factor which in some cases contributed to failure, but that again is not peculiar to employee ownership. The same applies to what he calls 'operational deficiencies in various departments'. We are closer to the employee-ownership specific when he cites 'factional disputes'. And that seems to be true again when he writes, in relation to one case of failure, that: '... the failure of various stakeholders (including a local community organisation, the worker owners, and various providers of technical assistance and finance capital) to agree on and accept the limits of their respective roles and responsibilities, [which] rapidly paralysed the supermarket's management and governance systems.'

The same sort of failure appears in an extended account of the 'woes' at an O&O store called Strawberry Mansion:

> When the city administration agreed to help finance the new market, it insisted that half the employees be hired from the market's neighbourhood and that they be recruited through the Strawberry Mansions Citizens Participation Council. The city

gave the chairperson of that group a permanent seat on the Strawberry Mansion O&O's board of directors, enabling him to dominate that body. Worse, board interference soon exacerbated problems of poor management. For example the board paid little heed to PACE's recommendation that the number of workers be cut and a new manager hired ... PACE reluctantly withdrew from its advisory role. Not long thereafter, the Strawberry Mansion O&O filed for bankruptcy. [Lindenfield 1992.]

It need scarcely be said that if you want business success it is probably a mistake to select half of your staff and the dominant person on the board by essentially political criteria. Of course we find similar phenomena when ownership is vested not in employees but in the state. There may be a lesson here for advocates of employee ownership: be wary of accepting 'favours' from politicians.

There may be a more general lesson from the O&O saga in Philadelphia about the dangers of EOB top management being other than totally committed to business success. Perhaps promotional agencies like PACE need to be especially wary when new employee-owned undertakings are being started from scratch, as with the Strawberry Mansion O&O. While the entrepreneurial initiative and drive, and the will to succeed, will be strong in the promotional agency, it may be less strong where the more immediate responsibility lies: with the chief executive of the new EOB.

As for Mr Lamas's contention about the failure of various stakeholders to agree on their roles, thus paralysing both management and the system of corporate government, this can be seen as one aspect of a recurrent difficulty of adapting traditional relationships to the changed realities of employee ownership: and especially the relationships between labour and capital, shopfloor and management.

Identifying the Threats to Success The best way of thinking about the failure of EOBs is to distinguish between those sources of failure which are common to all businesses – poor management, inadequate capital, the list is potentially endless – and those that are peculiar to firms which are employee-owned. A high proportion of the EOB failures I have reviewed in this discussion would also have failed if they had been in capitalist ownership. Indeed, many of them had already done so and the Co-op or EOB represented a last attempt to save the business and the jobs. This applies to all three of the Benn Co-ops, to Hyatt Clark Industries, and to at least the initial two of the six O&O supermarkets. Indeed, if it were not for employee ownership, the only O&O supermarket still open at the time of writing would have been closed down in 1982: at the very least EOB status bought it fifteen years' extra life. The very fact that all these companies thought they had more chance of survival as EOBs than as conventional capitalist companies is itself indicative.

However, the evidence brought together in this chapter also indicates specific grounds on which EOBs may have a special propensity to fail and poses the question of whether different behaviour on the part of management and shopfloor and unions, or different financial and organisational structures, might have ensured the continuation of some of those which *did* fail. After all, many conventional companies which face atrocious market conditions survive, just as many others fail. 'Good' structures and practice will at least increase EOBs' chances of survival.

In answer to the question how best may EOBs maximise their chances of survival and prosperity I begin by listing four difficulties specific to employee ownership which the sample of failures has identified:

– Keeping non-business issues off the agenda
– Raising capital without giving up employee ownership
– Adjusting relationships between management and employee owners
– Pressures to increase management and professional salaries against the background of a generally accepted wage reduction or standstill.

In the mid-1990s the need to keep non-business issues off the agenda needs little comment: the examples in this introduction speak for themselves.

The issue of capital is simple. The work of Louis Kelso and others has shown that most investment is financed internally from profits. However, if for any reason this is not possible, a conventional capitalist company can, by selling equity shares, offer capital growth as the prize to investors. In other words, it can raise money free of an obligation to pay interest, year on year, and to repay the loan. For EOBs and Co-ops this is not an option or was not yet widely an option at the time of writing: either the individual employees have to be sufficiently rich to fund investment out of their private savings; or they have to borrow the money at market interest rates from a bank; or they have to give up part or all of their ownership. This poses particular problems for EOBs in three specific instances. First, where the business is capital-intensive – for example, the steel industry; second, where investment has been neglected for a long period before the employees took over and profits, even if they exist at all, are inadequate to make up the backlog; and third, where the business needs to expand fast. Expanding slowly may not always be an option: in some areas of business, if the competition has the capital resources to expand faster, the survival of the slow-expander may be threatened. Elements of these specifically employee-ownership difficulties with capital can be seen in several of the examples earlier in this chapter; we will meet them again in the case studies, for example at Weirton and Republic Steel. If and when it happens, the much-heralded placing in London of what we may loosely call non-voting Mondragon shares would be something of a counter-example. (Though intimated in 1995, that had still not happened at the end of 1997.)

Of the four difficulties listed above, achieving the necessary reform in the relationship between capital and labour is the most difficult to define. Relationships between management and labour are problematic in all other forms of business organisation – whether conventional capitalist or state-owned. However, there is, it seems to me, a reasonable *a priori* expectation that most employee-owned businesses will face distinctive problems in this area, especially in the period immediately following a switch from conventional to employee ownership, and before an employee-ownership culture has got properly bedded down.

Let us take first the most obvious of these special difficulties: the behaviour of employees, unions and management. Once they have become the owners, employees or union leaders may behave as if they had no further need of management, or at least as if they are now free to throw their weight about without restraint. On the other side, conventional managers, rightly believing that there is still a need for professional management, may make the mistake of failing to adapt their behaviour to the new conditions. If such mistakes are identified early, they need not prove fatal. But if not, they may well do so. One of Britain's Benn co-ops, KME, is a good example of how the belief that management can be dispensed with can lead to disaster.

The changed relationship between shop-floor, unions and management gives rise to expectations on the part of union and rank-and-file employees which, unless they are met, may become a source of real difficulty. Put bluntly, employee ownership creates a demand on the part of the shop-floor and the union for a constitutional voice in the policy-making of the business at all levels. What surfaces is a demand for meaningful 'participation' which may have no direct counterpart in a conventional capitalist business. When such a demand does surface and is not then met, the chances of trouble are high.

Or take a more specific type of difficulty: the proper response when an employee-owned business is faced with a reduction in demand or must for other reasons cut back on total hours worked. In a conventional capitalist undertaking the response will normally include a measure of forced redundancy. That must always be painful. But since it is what is expected it will not be fundamentally problematic. Things are more complicated when an EOB is faced with the same imperative. That is because, even when they have been specifically advised to the contrary from the outset, employee owners have a tendency to feel that their employee ownership is tantamount to an employment guarantee. In a very few cases, for example in the Mondragon Group, that may be nearly true. More normally it is not.

My fourth employee ownership specific difficulty relates to extended periods of wage freeze, forming part of the package which made employee ownership possible in the first place – and even sometimes the survival of the business in any form. The specific difficulty arises if, as at HCI, local labour market conditions require a differential increase in the wage and salary rates paid to key personnel. It is easy to see that such relaxations can undermine the legitimacy of the continuing wage freeze necessary for the bulk of the workforce.

Finally, we turn to failure in the second of the two senses identified by the Webbs: failure represented not by business disaster but by a backsliding into conventional capitalist arrangements. Two cases from America's mining industry illustrate this: a copper mine in Minnesota and an asbestos mine in Vermont. The asbestos mine was bought by its employees in the 1970s and the copper mine in the 1980s; they were both sold on to more or less conventional capitalist owners some years later. In each case the employees sold their shares for more than forty times what they had originally paid for them. One can only speculate about the grounds the Webbs would have found for condemning employee ownership in that situation.

6

Selected Examples of Success

We now turn from the failures to the whole wide range of practice. We focus specially here on the variety, across several dimensions, of businesses which are substantially employee-owned – and on the evidence for their success.

The most persuasive evidence consists of case study material about the experience of individual employee-owned businesses, or business groups, from around the Western world. Outside America no attempt has yet been made, so far as I know, to compare the performance of large numbers of these businesses either with matching numbers of conventionally owned firms or with their own performance under an earlier regime of conventional ownership. Even the American research is not perhaps fully conclusive. Given the range of variables which affect business experience, I rather wonder whether absolute certainty will ever be possible.

So I am not claiming a demonstrable, scientific objectivity for the judgement that the 'selected top twenty-two' employee-owned businesses which I am about to present as successes, or at least successes during their employee-owned years in cases where these are now over, are indeed just that. I am not in a position to compare their performance with that of twenty-two other conventionally owned firms engaged in the same branches of activity: and then show with statistics that the record of the employee-owned businesses (EOBs) is superior. Nevertheless what my evidence does show is that, so long as substantial employee ownership is coupled with genuine and effective systems of non-financial involvement and participation by employees – as it is or at least was for a significant time in almost all my twenty-two examples of success – then their performance is often impressive. If I was working in a conventionally owned business, I would be relieved *not* to have to face competition from one of these EOBs in my main markets.

But as the previous chapter has shown, I do not wish to imply for a moment that the record of EOBs, including the record of production co-ops, has been free from failure over the last 150-odd years. On the contrary the record has been littered with failure. Indeed until quite recently it has been sufficiently unexciting to justify the typical attitude of classical economists towards these ventures: 'sympathetic pessimism', in the words of Professor Derek Jones.

But there is a respectable reason for not assigning to the early production co-op failures an amount of attention commensurate with their numbers. It is that they mostly failed because of a set of similar, and in principle avoidable, inadequacies: poor management, insufficient capital, flawed structures, and a lack of commitment to orthodox business goals. Against that background it seems increasingly plausible to accept a judgement about the co-operative predecessors of today's EOBs made by the great Cambridge economist Alfred Marshall more than a hundred years ago. To the assertion that these ventures had been tried and failed, Marshall responded with a telling rejoinder. 'Not so'; in effect; 'what has been tried is not the genuine article but broken-backed versions of it.' If the real thing was tried, he concluded, '*it could not but succeed*.' (Emphasis added.)

The Great Variety of EOB Success Marshall's prediction seems to be born out by the success – anyway during their period in employee ownership – of the following twenty-two individual EOBs or EOB groups, drawn from seven countries with mixed market economies: from the USA and the UK, and from Italy, France, Germany, Hungary and the Basque provinces of Spain. Partly in the hope that it will help their names to be remembered, I first list them together with their countries of origin and main business activity and then repeat their names more than once in subsequent tables in this chapter. All have been at least 20% employee-owned and most are, or have been, either majority-owned by their employees as individuals, or by a trust body on their behalf, or by a combination of the two. The three British examples of post-privatisation employee ownership had returned to conventional capitalist ownership by the time this was written. All three had been privatised, in the jargon, by management-led employee buy-outs (MEBOs). Similarly by the time this book came to be finally revised, the employee ownership at each of the two big American steel companies, Weirton and Republic Engineered Steels Inc., had been effectively superseded by conventional capitalist arrangements.

The Great Variety of EOB Success

Selected Top Twenty-Two EOBs

ACOME	France	cable-making
Allied Plywood	USA	plywood wholesale
Baxi Partnership	UK	home boilers
Carl Zeiss Stiftung	Germany	optics
La Ceramica	Italy	wall tiles
Chesterfield Transport	UK	bus service
CHCA	USA	home care
Equity Shoes	UK	shoe-making
Herend Porcelain	Hungary	hand-made porcelain
John Lewis Partnership	UK	retail trade
Mondragon Group	Spain	wide range of manufacture
NFC	UK	road haulage
Oregon Plywood	USA	plywood manufacture
Peoples Provincial	UK	bus service
Polaroid Corporation	USA	camera & film
RESI	USA	steel bar
Scott Bader	UK	chemicals
Sacmi	Italy	tile-making machinery
SAIC	USA	research
Tullis Russell	UK	paper-making
Weirton Steel	USA	sheet steel
United Airlines	USA	airline

One of the most eye-catching features of the list is their variety: variety by country, or by 'national industrial culture'; and variety by main activity. The two UK bus companies were offspring of Mrs Thatcher's privatisation programme as indeed was the other road transport undertaking in the list – NFC, formerly the National Freight Consortium. A special explanation – the industry's severe difficulties during the 1980s – also lies behind the inclusion in the list of two American steel companies.

It is true that compared with the national economies in which they operate, the businesses in my list are biased towards manufacturing, which accounts for some two thirds of the total. But that may be partly explained by the fact that their origins in some cases go back over a hundred years, to a time when manufacturing's share of total output was much greater than it is today.

The dates when these businesses started to be employee-owned range from 1874 to 1994. They also vary greatly in size. It is often asserted that employee-ownership arrangements can only work, or only work well, in small undertakings. It is true that we have no examples here to match the seven-digit employment numbers of Britain's health service, or the six-digit numbers of companies like British Telecom in the UK and General Motors in the USA. Still the list unquestionably contains large businesses:

Employment Numbers and Dates of EO Origin

United Airlines	80 000	1994
Carl Zeiss Stiftung	32,000	1891
John Lewis Partnership	41,000*	1929
Mondragon Group	26,000	1955
NFC	26,000	1982
SAIC	22,000	1969
Polaroid Corporation	12,000	1989
Weirton Steel	5,500	1984
RESI	4,600	1989
Herend Porcelain	1,500	1994
Baxi Partnership	1,450	1983
Sacmi	1,200	1920
ACOME	1,000	1942
La Ceramica	900	1874
Tullis Russell	850	1987
Scott Bader	600	1952
People's Provincial Bus	300	1988
Oregon Plywood	250	1934
Equity Shoes	200	1886
CHCA	200	1984
Allied Plywood	150	1978
Chesterfield Transport	250	1989

*Including part-timers

For businesses which started their lives as employee-owned, the date in the table's right-hand column coincides with the date when they started trading. That applies to hardly more than a quarter: Sacmi, the Italian industrial co-operative which is now the world's leading manufacturer of the equipment needed to make ceramic wall tiles, is one example; as are most of the 100-odd industrial and service co-ops which make up the Mondragon Group. In the USA the same applies to three very different undertakings: CHCA, Oregon

Plywood and SAIC. CHCA is a homecare provider in New York and SAIC a high-tech research and scientific applications business based in California which was started with a workforce of just five scientists in 1969. Overall, not more than a third of the twenty-two EOBs in the table started their trading lives as employee-owned.

It is true, on the other hand, that there are some odd special cases. For example, the UK's Equity Shoes was formed in 1886 by a group of former boot and shoe-making employees of Britain's Co-operative Wholesale Society (CWS). Its establishment followed a strike in which the men had demonstrated their dissatisfaction with their CWS owners and managers. (The latter subsequently retrieved some of their lost honour by agreeing to buy from the new co-operative venture.) Another exceptional beginning was that of ACOME, the French low-voltage cable-making business, now the flagship of the country's industrial co-ops. Its origin can perhaps best be described as marsupial: it began as the subsidiary of a conventional private company before splitting off as an independent co-operative in the early 1940s. There are examples too, among the listed twenty-two, of businesses which were successively private, then state-owned, then employee-owned and then again privately owned in a conventional way. The two British bus companies fall into that category; as does NFC. More recently, their ownership has reverted back to a more conventional form.

In the USA the ESOP buy-outs from the private sector include the two US steel companies in the list: Weirton Steel Corporation of Weirton, West Virginia, and Republic Engineered Steels Inc (RESI), based on the twin towns of Canton and Massillon in north-eastern Ohio. Because of the union leadership of its buy-out, the case of United Airlines is in a category of its own. The employee ownership in the other American examples has also involved using ESOPs. But Polaroid is rather different because its employee ownership has never been more than a significant minority shareholding. The origin of the employee ownership at Allied Plywood should probably also be classified rather differently. The company's former private owners used an ESOP when they sold the undertaking to their employees but there was a substantial element of philanthropy in that sale. As for United Airlines, it became majority (55%) employee-owned in 1994 as a result of a quite exceptional union-led buy-out.

We are now in a position to classify our twenty-two businesses by the origin of their employee ownership. There are five main categories of source: private philanthropy; privatisation in the UK and Hungary; and ESOP buy-outs in the USA; and self-starting origins; and sale to employees on commercial terms.

The next table shows that private philanthropy accounts for the origin of the employee ownership in the largest number of the twenty-two employee-owned or formerly employee-owned businesses under consideration. The table also indicates whether the businesses are companies or co-operatives in their legal form.

ACOME	Co-op	Special
Allied Plywood	Company	Sale to employees
Baxi Partnership	Company	Private philanthropy
Carl Zeiss Stiftung	Company	Private philanthropy
La Ceramica	Co-op	Private philanthropy
CHCA	Hybrid	Special
Chesterfield Transport	Company	Privatisation
Equity Shoes	Co-op	Special
Herend Porcelain	Company	Privatisation
John Lewis	Company	Private philanthropy
Mondragon Group	Co-ops	Mainly self-started
NFC	Company	Privatisation
Oregon Plywood	Co-op	Self-started
Peoples Provincial Bus	Company	Privatisation
Polaroid Corporation	Company	Special
RESI	Company	ESOP buy-out
Scott Bader	Company	Private philanthropy
Sacmi	Co-op	Self-started
SAIC	Company	Self-started
Tullis Russell	Company	Sale to employees
Weirton Steel	Company	ESOP buy-out in USA
United Airlines	Company	Union-led ESOP buy-out

In the cases attributable to private philanthropy, the employee ownership has come about because the former private capitalist owners have decided: a) to transfer the ownership of their businesses to their employees either directly – to the employees as individuals – or indirectly – through the mechanism of some trust-like entity; b) to effect the ownership transfer either as a gift, or at a price significantly discounted compared with what the business could have fetched in a more conventional transaction. There is obviously a rather grey line between transactions which involve discounts big enough to qualify as philanthropy and those which are full-blooded arm's length commercial sales or nearly so.

The element of bounty or discount in the philanthropic sale of these businesses to their employees has varied considerably – up to 100% – but in all the examples included in our selected 'top twenty-two' it has been significant. Most of those cases share a further common feature – solving an ownership succession problem in a private company. The French have commended this solution to a problem which is faced by large numbers of private business owners when they approach retirement: they call it 'Une Belle Sortie', a phrase later imaginatively translated by a *Financial Times* headline writer as 'A Neat Exit'.

These particular cases, where employee ownership owes its existence at least partly to private philanthropy, are especially interesting. Their former owners have frequently chosen to spell out the reasons which prompted their actions. They have often also taken special responsibility for the design of the ownership and government arrangements in the successor undertakings – the constitutions of which therefore are especially worth studying. They are interesting too because they include a number of businesses which are of the very highest class by top international standards. It is not indeed the quality but the quantity of these businesses which disappoints. A discerning and articulate Frenchman put his finger on the reason for their small numbers when he told me in the 1970s: 'You can't expect that more than one really successful French businessman in ten years will want to go to heaven sufficiently strongly to make the sacrifice of giving the business to its employees or of transferring it to them with a large discount.'

Of course there are humanist agnostics, as well as believing Christians, among those really successful businessmen who *have* chosen to make the sacrifice. However, if one looks to the future rather than at the past, the ESOP legislation in the USA has done much to limit the constraint identified by the Frenchman. As a result, American owners of family or other private businesses are no longer required to make a quite exceptional sacrifice – or to expose themselves to unacceptable levels of risk – if they decide to sell the undertaking to their employees. In 1994 new legislation changed the situation in Britain too. In America, by the middle 1990s, the results were already striking: there was an explosion of such sales in the USA once the relevant new law had been enacted. Who knows, perhaps we shall one day start seeing something of the sort in the UK.

This discussion of private philanthropy is something of a digression. It is included here because, if only the constraints could be removed elsewhere as they now have been in the USA and the UK, it is from the conversion of private businesses that the main future growth of employee ownership will come. That is true at any rate in the predominantly capitalist West, as one of the later case studies, Tullis Russell, highlights.

Let us now examine how the same 'selected top twenty-two' differ along two final sets of dimensions: the related ones of ownership arrangements and enterprise government; and the less definable dimension of ideology and political orientation.

Varieties of Ownership The ownership arrangements in my 'selected top twenty-two' are probably best classified in a linear spectrum: with fully collective ownership (by a trust type body or, in a co-operative, by the co-operative itself) at one end; and fully individual employee ownership at the other.

Ownership Arrangements

ACOME	Co-op members & Co-op itself
Allied Plywood	Individual employees & ESOP
Baxi Partnership	Individual employees & trust
Carl Zeiss	*Stiftung,* or trust
La Ceramica	Co-op members & Co-op itself
Chesterfield Transport*	Individual employees, ESOP & trust
CHCA	Individual employees and Charity
Equity Shoes	Co-op members and Co-op itself
Herend	Individual employees, ESOP trust and Hungarian State (25%)
John Lewis Partnership	Trust
Mondragon Group	Co-ops' members & Co-ops themselves
NFC*	Individual employees & outsiders
Oregon Plywood	Co-op's members
Peoples Provincial*	Individual employees & ESOP
Polaroid Corporation	Individual employees, ESOP & outsiders
RESI*	Individual employees, ESOP and outsiders
Scott Bader	Charity
Sacmi	Co-op members & Co-op itself
SAIC	Individual employees & ESOP
Tullis Russell	Individual employees, ESOP trust & charity

Weirton Steel*	Individual employees, ESOP & outsiders
United Airlines	Individual employees and ESOP Trust (55%),
	public shareholders (45%)

* During its period of employee ownership

Among the owners in the right-hand column, what is meant by individual employees is clear enough. The category of co-op members is slightly less straightforward. In some cases, but not in all, membership is restricted to people working in the business, as in the Mondragon group. But in Equity Shoes, membership can and does include ex-workers (now retired), the relatives and offspring of ex-workers, and corporate bodies – like other co-operative societies and trade union branches. Equity Shoes does impose a rule to the effect that all permanent workers must become member shareholders. But the required minimum shareholding – five shares of £1, or the equivalent of little more than one hour's wages in the money of the early 1990s – is no more than nominal. Arrangements such as those at Equity may involve some risk of control moving out from the hands of the actual working group; and they may offer a less than optimum identification between the interests of the individual employees and the long-term success of the business as a whole.

To include the co-ops themselves among their owners, as I have done in the table, is to use shorthand. A more precise description would be to say that much of the wealth of these undertakings is often vested in permanent reserves; and in reserves which may either be indivisible in all circumstances – the rule which normally applies in the co-operative law of France and Italy – or divisible only in special situations. In the UK's co-operative law, for example, such reserves are only divisible among the membership, as noted earlier, in the event of liquidation. The relative importance of the wealth accumulated in such reserves can be graphically illustrated with an example. In the end-1990 balance sheet of Equity Shoes, the balance in the general reserve is shown to be almost 550 times that of the share capital:

Equity Shoes: Share Capital vs General Reserve

Balance Sheet 2 December 1995

| Share Capital | £8,273 |
| General Reserve | £4,502,000 |

A further word of clarification is needed to explain the inclusion of ESOPs among the owners of some of these ventures in the table's right-hand column. In the sense in which it is used there, ESOP ownership is quite distinct from trust ownership. Frequently the ESOP is no more (but also no less) than a transitional ownership mechanism which will fade away once it has fulfilled its essential function of effecting a transfer of ownership to the individual employees of a business. In other cases it may be kept in existence as a convenient way of warehousing shares which are otherwise temporarily surplus to individual employees' requirements; perhaps also as a mechanism for facilitating a share market. By contrast the trusts which figure in the table's right-hand column are permanent entities; and in a number of cases they have august and indeed sovereign functions. In John Lewis and Carl Zeiss, for example, their permanent trusts own 100% of the share capital of the business and thus also enjoy the controlling last word. Moreover the trust in the Baxi Partnership is only slightly less pivotal and powerful. For it owns a majority, even if not 100%, of the share capital.

Particular explanations may underlie the particular ownership arrangements adopted by each of our selected top twenty-two employee-owned businesses. These will become clear in the individual case study chapters of this book. However three final points deserve to be highlighted. The first is about the reasons for choosing anything other than individual ownership in the first place. Perhaps the key one is the hypothesis that collective ownership (whether vested in a permanent trust or in the indivisible reserves of the Continental co-operatives) is the surest way of protecting the long-term independence of the business; and thus its survival in an employee-owned form. We shall have something more to say about that shortly.

There is another important reason which helps to explain why at least a measure of collective employee ownership has found favour. It is that employee ownership in this form has the effect of eliminating (when it is 100%) and reducing (when it is less than that) what in shorthand may be called the company's buy-back liability. If individual employee ownership is to be sustained over more than one working generation, then the shareholdings of employees who leave must clearly be bought back. They must equally find their way somehow into the hands of new employees who join. But since the latter will not normally have sufficient savings, or access to sufficient credit, to be outright buyers of the shareholdings of the leaving employees, the bulk of the purchase money will have to come from the company's profits. Of course, if the profits of the business are used in this way, they will not be available for other, and perhaps more productive, uses.

It is these considerations, rather than any ideological predilection for collective forms of ownership, which explain why, in one way or another, most of the top twenty-two employee-owned businesses in the table have chosen *not* to favour 100% individual employee ownership. In the case of the co-operatives, they have overcome the problem of a buy-back liability in a rather different way: by using a special type of co-operative share. Unlike conventional capitalist shares, shares in a co-operative do not normally move up and down in value in line with the fortunes of the business. So in the case of the co-operatives, the buy-back liability is normally not much more than nominal. The figure for the total share capital of Equity Shoes is an excellent illustration of this point. The arrangements in the co-operative Mondragon group are rather different. But for most of the traditional production co-ops – other than those in the UK in the special circumstances of a liquidation, and other than in the plywood co-ops of America's Pacific North West (which are a law unto themselves) – the value of employee shareholdings are typically nominal; and so is the buy-back liability.

The choice between individual and collective ownership, including the choice of mixed arrangements, may also have important consequences for what happens to profits. This can be put simply by saying that when employee ownership is collective, then the individual employee owners may share in distributed but not in ploughed back profits (or, to put it rather differently, in asset growth); but when, by contrast, employee ownership is individual, then the individual employee owners may share in profits of both kinds – those ploughed back as well as those distributed. This important difference between these two types of employee ownership is often supposed to create a theoretical presumption in favour of the individual variety on the grounds that where the employee ownership is collective, the incentive to plough back and to invest will be inadequate. We shall have to see, when we look at the records of the businesses which are collectively owned – the John Lewis Partnership, for example, and the Carl-Zeiss-Stiftung – to what extent this objection is valid.

A more complex point about the ownership of profits in EOBs where ownership is at least partly individualised concerns profit allocation as between the individual employee owners. A particular question is whether this allocation should be proportionate to the shareholdings of the individual employee owners, to annual 'work contributions' or according to some mixed and/or more complex formula. Put differently, the question is whether these allocations should follow the logic of being 'dividends on shareholdings', or the very different logic of being 'returns on work'. There are ideological aspects to the system of allocation which may be chosen: the ideology of 'the business as a piece of property' points in one direction; that of 'the business as a working community' points in the other. This issue is central to employee ownership and pervades the discussion in this book. Here we will confine ourselves to making just two points about it. The first is that what looks like a fairly theoretical choice can result in strikingly different outcomes. Employee ownership at NFC was the midwife of perhaps a dozen millionaires. That of the Mondragon Group has not yet produced one; and it is as certain as anything can be that it never will. Second, it would be a mistake to imply that we are confronted here with a crude 'either/or' type choice; profit allocations as between individual employee owners in employee-owned businesses may be based on a mixed formula: one which reflects both the work contribution and the antecedent shareholding of the individual employees.

A final point arises from the fact that it is becoming increasingly common among employee-owned businesses in the West for a significant part of employees' pay to be linked to profits and thus to performance. Allied Plywood, just outside Washington DC, is an extreme case. But the same link is also an important feature of the remuneration arrangements at ACOME in France, where in a good recent year just over one third of a typical employee's 'remuneration package' (including deferred as well as cash income) was profit-related. The odds are that there will be more of this in the future. To the extent that that happens the non basic wage rewards for employment in these undertakings will shift more towards being 'returns to work' and there will be correspondingly less room for 'dividends from property'.

To conclude this discussion of ownership arrangements I emphasise, once again, their great variety. As we have seen, our selected top twenty-two employee-owned businesses exhibit an astonishing diversity across a wide range of dimensions, but clearly ownership is one of the key ones. Under most systems of business enterprise which have been tried in modern history, ownership is the starting point from which the rest follows. In this sense ownership is logically prior to control, which we go on to discuss in a moment.

These selected top twenty-two employee-owned businesses have proved on the whole and, at least during their periods of significant employee ownership, notably successful, despite their great variety. This means that we need to identify the common ingredients which explain what is happening. One obvious common ingredient is that in all these businesses the employees are working substantially for themselves; another is that, to a greater or lesser extent, they all have some 'voice' in what goes on. There is clearly a close link between 'voice' and control. We now move on to look at the way these businesses differ under those two headings.

7
Company Government, Control and Power

In the table on the next page I attempt a crude classification of our selected top twenty-two EOBs on the basis of their corporate government: their control arrangements, the participation of employees and the extent of trade union power. It is sometimes believed that employee ownership and significant trade union power are incompatible. The table shows that, whatever may happen in the long run, the two were successfully co-habiting in many of our selected top twenty-two EOBs in the early 1990s. There is a conventional, and formally recognised, trade union presence in a majority of these twenty-two undertakings. It is not even the case that the trade unions are restricted to those businesses among our top twenty-two which enjoyed a conventional capitalist past. True, they figure in proportionately fewer of the businesses which started their lives as employee-owned. But they are represented even there. Moreover, in the case of Carl Zeiss, though there is no actual union, there is an elected and active Workers' Committee which behaves very much as if it were one.

The classification of our twenty-two businesses by the presence or absence of recognised trade unions is fairly straightforward with the proviso that in three American cases I have had to describe the union role as 'co-determinational'. To do the same job in relation to the control and the rights of participation enjoyed by employee owners is less easy. For this purpose, our twenty-two employee-owned undertakings are classified under two headings:

– by whether or not the employees enjoy ultimate control;

– by whether each of the qualifying employee owners enjoys one vote; or whether the votes are proportionate to numbers of shares held.

It may be objected that the resulting table exhibits a rather bewildering variety of arrangements. But that is a straightforward reflection of what is happening 'out there'.

Control and Related Features: Top Twenty-Two EOBs

	Where Final Power Lies	System of Voting	Trade Union Role
ACOME	With employees	D	Nil
Al'd Ply	With trustees	S	Nil
Baxi	With trustees	S	Conventional
Carl Zeiss	With top management	NA	Nil
La Ceramica	With employees	D	Conventional
Chest'ld Tpt*	Shared	S	Conventional
CHCA	With employees	D	Nil
Equity Shoes	With employees	D	Conventional
Herend	Shared	S	Conventional
John Lewis	With employees	D	Nil
Mondragon	With employees	D	Nil
NFC*	With employees	S	Conventional
Oregon Ply	With employees	D	Nil
Polaroid	With capital	S	Nil
People's P'v'l*	Shared	S	Conventional
RESI*	Shared	D	Co-determinational
Scott Bader	Shared	D	Conventional
Sacmi	With employees	D	Conventional
SAIC	With top employees	S	Not important
T. Russell	With trustees	S	Conventional
Weirton*	With employees	D	Co-determinational
United Airlines	Shared	S	Co-determinational

*During period when employee-owned

Notes In the second headed column 'S' means voting by shares, 'D' means one shareholder one vote. In the same column the democratic voting in the two Italian co-ops needs to be qualified by the fact that only a minority of employees are members; and in the case of Equity Shoes by the fact that about half of the shareholder members are non-employees

In a conventional business, ultimate control rests with the shareholders who enjoy voting power in proportion to the size of their shareholdings. So in a business where the employees are the shareholders we should expect that control would rest with them – with votes either proportionate to shareholding size or distributed on a more democratic basis. Yet the table shows that that is not always the case. What explains the exceptions?

To begin with, the ultimate control in three of the table's businesses is shown as resting with trustees: in Allied Plywood, Baxi and Tullis Russell. In the last two of these there are permanent trusts which either already hold on behalf of employees a majority of the shares (Baxi) or will hold them when the process of ownership transfer is complete (Tullis Russell). The cases of John Lewis and, when it was employee-owned, Chesterfield Transport, also reflect trust ownership; but with the difference that the employees enjoy either an ultimate control over the trust (John Lewis) or used to share in that control (Chesterfield). By contrast, at Baxi and Tullis the permanent trusts are, in effect, self-perpetuating oligarchies. At Allied Plywood, the ultimate control rests with an ESOP trust; and that in turn is controlled, in line with what is permitted under US law, by the company's management.

The constitutional arrangements at Scott Bader are a law unto themselves. No attempt is made to unravel them here (for further details, see Hoe). In the two remaining businesses where the table indicates a sharing of ultimate control – Peoples Provincial and RESI – those arrangements were essentially transitional and reflect the same current constraints: both companies in the early 1990s were in the process of paying off the substantial loans which they took out to achieve the employee buy-outs. One of the conditions stipulated by those who lent the money was that the employees should share ultimate control – and share it with both management representatives and outsiders – until the paying off of the borrowings was complete. In July of 1998 the employee ownership of RESI, as that of Chesterfield Transport before it, became a matter of history.

As a business in which the stake of the employees, though substantial, has never been close to a majority, Polaroid is in a category of its own. Ultimate control rests 'with capital', as it does in a conventional capitalist business. So it does too in Scientific Applications International Inc (SAIC) of Palo Alto in Calfornia. But since well over 80% of SAIC's share capital is held by its individual employees under close company arrangements, it seemed right, in the table, to assign control to those employees. Finally, in the case of Britain's NFC, from the time of its management-led employee buy-out until the flotation of its shares on the Stock Exchange, voting power rested with its rank-and-file employee shareholders.

Ever since the Rochdale Pioneers, it has been a key distinguishing feature of the governing arrangements for co-ops of almost all kinds that the voting should be democratic – on the basis of one shareholder, rather than one share, one vote. The table shows that this system of voting is used in a majority of our selected top twenty-two EOBs; and in all those that are legally registered as co-ops, including all of the businesses within the Mondragon Group. Moreover it is easy to see in a general way that if a shift to employee ownership entails movement from business as a piece of property to business as a working community, then democratic voting will often be an important distinguishing feature of it. On the other hand the democracy in a number of the table's co-ops is of a rather qualified character: in the two Italian co-ops less than 50% of employees enjoy the right to vote; and at Equity Shoes there are outsiders as well as insiders among the voting members.

But at this point it makes sense to stand back for a moment from the detail of the arrangements shown in the table and ask what considerations lie behind the differences of detail. More precisely, we need to ask whether there is a general explanation for the fact that the employee owners as a democratic body enjoy complete control in only a minority of the table's businesses. Why?

The answer to that question is clear. There *are* general explanations; and, put crudely, the most important one is that those responsible for devising these arrangements have frequently put a higher value on the independent survival of the undertakings than on the need for them to satisfy the most stringent conditions of one employee/one vote democracy. Different language has been used by different people. Spedan Lewis, the philanthropic architect of the John Lewis Partnership, wrote of the maximum democracy compatible with business success. Philip Baxendale, Lewis's counterpart at the Baxi Partnership, has often spoken of the need to avoid a situation in which Baxi's employee owners were faced with 'an offer for the business which they could not refuse'. His insistence that management should be 'accountable' rather than elected is also worth noting in this context. Ernest Abbe, the man who in 1891 gave a controlling share in the Carl Zeiss business to the Foundation which he established for that purpose, used rather different language again. But he too was concerned to make a settlement which would secure the business against takeover by conventional capitalists as well as make for optimum business success as he defined it.

But it should not be thought that the overriding concern to protect the business against outside takeover, and the sometimes associated emphasis on the importance of good management, is reflected in the government arrangements only of those of our top twenty-two employee-owned businesses which stem from an initial act of philanthropy. These considerations are also behind details in most other cases; and especially in most of the co-ops.

In France and Italy, the production co-ops on our list – ACOME, La Ceramica and Sacmi among our top twenty-two – are substantially protected against takeover by statute law. The law requires that in the event of liquidation any net assets remaining after the debts have been paid off – and the co-op's own shares redeemed at their nominal value – must go to another co-operative, or be put to a charitable purpose. They may not be pocketed by the shareholder members of the business. These arrangements go a long way to rule out one of the possibilities that worried Mr Baxendale: that the employee owners might be faced with an offer for the business which they 'could not refuse'.

On the important issue of what happens to net assets in the event of the liquidation, the co-operative laws in Spain and the UK are, in effect, the opposite of what they are in France and Italy. It should therefore come as no surprise that in Britain between the late 1970s and the late 1980s there were a number of liquidations among the country's few surviving production co-ops. With the prospect of considerable capital gains if they sold out, the members in at least half of these ventures which were still in business in the late 1970s had decided to call it a day by 1990. A striking exception is Equity Shoes whose shareholders would enjoy an enormous premium on the nominal value of their shares if they were to decide to sell out. It is a most notable tribute to what one might call their 'inter-generational long-termism' that they have so far chosen *not* to do so.

A similar decision of self-denial, with similar potential benefits for the next generation, has been taken by the members of the individual co-operatives which make up the Mondragon group. There is nothing in Spanish law to prevent the members of these businesses from taking steps which would allow them to enjoy the full benefit of the capital gains which their work has created. They would simply have to disaffiliate from the group and then sell out to the highest bidder. Yet, over the group's first forty years, only a very few chose to do so. As with Equity Shoes this looks suspiciously like an example of 'self-denying long-termism' in the interests of the next generation.

Before leaving the co-ops we should say a word about departures from two rules or principles: the democratic rule that all co-op members should have an equal vote; and the identity principle – that there should be as near as possible an identity between those who work in the business and those who own and control it. We have already seen that our democratic principle is *not* honoured by either of the two Italian co-ops, Sacmi and La Ceramica. At Equity Shoes, on the other hand, the democratic principle applies (because after a short period of probation all those who work there have full membership rights), but not the identity principle (because about half the share capital is held by outsiders of various kinds). It is in fact only at ACOME, among the co-ops on the list, that both the rule and the principle apply in full.

Deviations from the identity principle are best understood as reflecting the realities of an earlier age, when the chief feature of these ventures was their working-class rather than their co-operative character. In France they were indeed simply 'les enterprises *ouvrières*' in the early days; it was not until the 1880s that they became co-ops; and even then their official description referred to their working-class character. For they were designated 'les sociétés co-operatives *ouvrières* de production'.

Deviations from the democratic principle in the government of these co-ops may often reflect a nervousness on the part of the founders and/or the elders among their workforces about the possibility of 'irresponsible' decisions if the vote is extended to include everyone. In other words the democracy is limited on partly prudential grounds. Essentially we are back to Spedan Lewis's precept – as much democracy as is compatible with business success.

At Mondragon, management is enabled to get on with the task of managing without too much 'interference' by the democracy because the powers of the elected directors have been defined so that they resemble those of a supervisory and not a management board. Those elected directors in turn have responsibility for the appointment of the chief executive. These arrangements are surely best understood as a kind of self-imposed restriction on freedom, something familiar in Western literature ever since the encounter of Odysseus with the sirens. They may also, surely, be taken as evidence of maturity. In the popular stereotype these co-operatives fail because everyone wants to have a share in management. Actual practice in the Mondragon group could scarcely be more removed than it is from that stereotype. Not only do rank-and-file employees *not* manage; they are not even directly responsible for the choice of the chief executive.

It is true that some other and less respectable reasons may lie behind the deviations from the democratic principle in any particular co-op. The most familiar and important of these is the desire of an initial membership body to restrict the (financial and other) privileges of membership to themselves. Sidney and Beatrice Webb made a tremendous breakfast of this unfortunate, if all too human, tendency. Indeed they elevated it to the status of an iron law. Any production co-op which managed to avoid 'failure through incompetence' was bound, they argued, to deteriorate into a nasty little oligarchy of co-op members who then more or less lived, as rentiers, off the toil of their disenfranchised brothers in the workforce. Of course, that can happen. But to suggest that it is 'inevitable' is absurd.

We need to look at one final dimension of variety among our top twenty EOBs: their position along the familiar left/right dimension of Western politics. The chief difference here lies in the class character of the leadership of the business as that is perceived by the rank and file of its employee owners. Where that leadership is seen as 'essentially working class', or perhaps, in the less class-conscious environment of the Mondragon co-ops, as 'on the same side as the shop-floor', then we have one category of these ventures. Where, on the other hand, that leadership is seen as 'middle class', or 'management oriented', or even as 'representing capital' – even when capitalist shareholders no longer exist – then we have a second category. Broadly speaking, the co-ops in our top group fall into the first category; broadly speaking, all the others fall into the second.

Where the difference probably shows up most of all is in the field of industrial relations. To over-simplify, it may be said that industrial relations in the first category are now normally problem-free – in rather the same way as in Japan, or, say, among the fellows of an Oxford college. By contrast the industrial relations of those businesses which fall into the second category often have as many problems as the UK's conventional capitalist undertakings. Nor should this surprise us. For, in all those cases, the businesses had a conventional capitalist experience (whether in the state sector or the private sector or both) before becoming employee-owned. Most of them are still grappling with the industrial relations legacy of that past.

In the last few years one of the most interesting and exciting developments is the way in which a number of the undertakings in the second category have started to tackle this problem of industrial relations head on: by greater employee involvement and participation, by much greater emphasis on communications, and by restructuring exercises designed to make possible a greater say by rank and file employees in the decisions which most directly affect them. The objective of these changes, when taken together, is sometimes described as being to achieve an 'ownership culture'.

In the case studies we will devote considerable attention to these programmes – essentially because that is where the action is. Meanwhile we should be aware that contrary to what some doctrines might lead people to expect, there is no invariable link between the degree of democracy in corporate government arrangements and the degree to which they are making progress in overcoming the industrial relations problems inherited from their past.

8

Co-operatives: the Ideal Type of Employee Ownership

In my opinion, ... the secret of success of Co-operatives in Imola lies in the special type of relationship between man and company, based on self-management: on conscious and responsible participation of the co-operator in the life of his company; on the equilibrium between common and individual interest; on the achieved awareness of the connection between one's own individual behaviour and the economic results of the co-operative concern; on the consciousness that there is no contradiction between the interests of the co-operative and the ones of the co-operator; and finally on the fact that the worker is not *against* the company, but *sides with* the company. *Benito Benati, Administrative Director of the Sacmi Co-operative in Imola. Speech at International Employee Ownership Conference, Oxford, 1992*

If democracy is the most advanced, most adult, form of government, then the worker-led co-operative may reasonably claim to be the most advanced, most adult, form of business enterprise. In other words the worker-led co-operative can be thought of as representing the ideal 'platonic type' of employee-owned business.

By a worker-led co-operative I mean a production co-op in which, whatever arrangements there may be for the conduct of management, final control rests with a body representative of and elected by the workforce; and which is, of course, owned by those, *all* those and *only* those, who work in it. In practice, few of the business ventures which are legally formed as co-operatives or nominally called 'co-operatives' actually fulfil these conditions. At the two Italian co-ops described in this section, only a minority of the permanent workforce are members ('socii') of the co-op: most of the employees are merely employees, working for a wage. At Equity Shoes, my example of an English co-op, many of the co-operative members are not employees – they are retired employees, or the widows of employees. Of the three case studies in this section, the one whose structure comes closest to a co-op as strictly defined above is ACOME, where all employees are required to become members after a three-year probationary period of employment. But, like Mondragon, ACOME illustrates another potential threat to co-operative purism: as it has expanded it has acquired subsidiary and affiliated companies whose employees do not qualify for membership of the parent co-operative.

What this illustrates is that the practical application of co-operative definitions, like those of employee ownership generally, form a spectrum. Moreover, the extent to which the formal arrangements affect the essence of co-operation – 'us and us' as it might be expressed – can vary under the influence of other factors – factors which in turn can vary over time. Measuring every feature of every 'co-operative' against every feature of the ideal co-operative structure can become otiose and irrelevant. On the other hand, wholesale abandonment of all such features would simply mean that the co-op has become a conventional business. The extent to which co-ops can or do retain the essence of co-operation, despite their failure to stick to the co-operative business form, strictly defined, is one of the themes of this section.

Workers have, of course, been starting worker-led production co-ops for the last 150 years or more – at least since the 1850s' launch of a textile mill by the Rochdale pioneers in the wake of the early success of their shopping venture in Toad Lane. We should probably exclude, as something else, the hundreds and even thousands of micro-production co-ops which have been springing up all over the place in the last fifteen years. But even without these, records show that several hundred production co-ops were started in the USA and the UK before the First World War; that thousands of them have been started – and are still being started – in France; and that in Italy where, as in France, the movement is still very much alive, the corresponding numbers have run into tens of thousands.

Yet despite this record of energy by worker entrepreneurs, only a few have both reached a substantial size and prospered for any length of time in the world's competitive markets. Outside Mondragon (which can be characterised as a group of manager-led rather than worker-led co-ops), the number is certainly less than 100 over the entire period since the Rochdale textile mill. As for those which are still flourishing, and of a fair size in the early 1990s, the number is far smaller again: certainly less than twenty.

While all of the production co-ops I am talking about here have been worker-led, not quite all of them have been worker-founded. In both Italy and France there are examples today of worker-led co-operatives which started their lives as more or less conventional capitalist undertakings, usually family-owned. The successful wall tile co-operative, La Ceramica – one of the two ventures located in the small Italian town of Imola which we look at in a moment – is a case in point. On the other hand, despite this exceptional origin, La Ceramica has been part of Italy's movement of production co-ops since the late 19th century. Despite its origin it has, without question, belonged for many years to the culture of what the French used to call 'Les Entreprises Ouvrières'.

The two main reasons for failure among production co-ops have probably been poor management and inadequate capital. These ventures have often also been hampered by structures of ownership and control which have been ill-suited to their needs. And they have frequently been the scene of fierce clashes of personality. But there is also an optimistic point which emerges from a review of the evidence. It is that most of the causes of failure have been contingent and at least in principle avoidable. This is in pleasingly flat contradiction to the conclusion reached about these ventures by Sidney and Beatrice Webb when they argued that they were bound to fail, either as businesses, or as co-operatives, or both.

One reason advanced for their judgement by the Webbs was what they saw as the impossibility of successful management within a co-operative setting: when managers are constitutionally subordinate to an elected worker leadership. A more popular negative view is that a worker leadership will have a fatal propensity to consume profit and thus to limit investment for the future. Each of these myths is splendidly confounded by the case study examples which follow.

Before moving on to these case studies, it is worth glancing at the common social and political origins of these ventures in the last quarter of the nineteenth century; and at why their numbers have been greatest in Italy and smallest in Britain with France falling somewhere between the two.

In Britain and France, and probably also in Italy, the earliest of the worker-led production co-ops date from the 1850s or even earlier. The starting date for Rochdale's co-operative textile mill was 1854. The first recorded example in France, an artisanal jewellery manufacturing operation in Paris, L'Association Ouvrière des Bijoutiers en Doré, dates from as far back at 1834. However, despite individual forerunners and even short-lived waves of these ventures, in 1848 and then later under Napoleon III in France, it was not really before the 1870s and 1880s that they started to be formed both in significant numbers, and on foundations strong enough to give a real chance of indefinite survival. In Britain the numbers were sufficient for them to establish their own semi-autonomous Co-operative Production Federation in 1882. In Italy the first federation of co-ops of all types (including those which the Italians classify under the heading of 'Produzione e Lavoro') was founded in 1887. In France, it was in the 1880s that these ventures first set up a central organisation: the Conféderation des Societés Co-operatives Ouvrières de Production (or the Conféderation des Scops) in Paris, which continues to this day.

Apart from the existence of legislation under which they could be established, the main factor behind the development of these co-ops was probably industrial. New factory-system methods were spreading into areas of business previously characterised by workshop production and dominated by skilled craftsmen: printing and boot and shoe making for example. Italy, because of the early prevalence there of the so-called navvying co-ops, was partly a special case. In each of these three countries a significant number of the new worker-led co-ops, and one of the four which are the subject of our case studies, were founded by groups of skilled working men following a strike or lock-out.

Registered Production Co-ops: UK, France & Italy

UK (1893)	Italy (1897)	France (1901)
113	152	119

Thus far, the numbers of production co-ops in each country were not that different. But subsequently there is an astonishing divergence in the statistics: especially between Britain and Italy. According to the best available evidence, the number of these ventures in the UK never exceeded the total of 113 achieved in 1893, though it climbed back as high as 112 in 1903. After 1914 hardly a single new venture of this kind was established in Britain at all. In Italy, by contrast, the numbers had climbed to 1,500 by 1915, and were edging towards 3,000 when Mussolini came to power in the early 1920s. He banned the main co-operative grouping, the Lega, in 1925.

What happened in France falls between these two extremes. Claude Viennay (1966) calculated that between the middle 1880s and 1960 a total of some 2,250 worker-led production co-ops were established there. On the other hand, he has also calculated that of the annual average of thirty new start ups, only seven were to be long-term survivors. The Paris records show that the 1901 figure of 119 had roughly doubled by 1914 to 251, and reached a post-Second World War peak of 703 in 1947.

The reasons behind the differences in these numbers are essentially political. Britain's labour movement has been much more monolithic than its French and Italian counterparts. It is true that Britain's co-operatives continued after 1893 to belong, any way in some sense, to the country's labour movement. However, so isolated from the rest of the labour and even the co-operative movement were these ventures that it must have taken exceptional energy and courage to attempt to play the co-operative production entrepreneur in Britain from the 1890s onwards. It is thus scarcely surprising that their numbers never again exceeded the total of 113 reached in 1893.

Neither in the 1890s nor since has there been any comparable hostility on their own (left) side of politics to the co-operative entrepreneurs of France and Italy. Moreover, in the 1880s and 1890s governments in both France and Italy passed a number of measures which offered modest advantages to these ventures as compared with conventional capitalist undertakings. For example, in certain conditions and up to certain limits, they were allowed to negotiate prices for government contracts outside the framework of the normal processes of competitive tendering. Similarly, and again on certain conditions and within limits, they were exempted from the requirement to provide performance bonds to cover their work on government contracts. These concessions were probably of special importance because in both countries large numbers of the production co-ops were engaged in building and civil engineering work. And they were almost certainly of disproportionate importance in Italy because of the large numbers, at least before the First

World War, of 'navvying' co-ops in that country. Typically these ventures were engaged by the Italian goverment, or by the local authorities, to undertake large-scale drainage works. So far as I know they are the only major examples of production co-ops, in Europe or elsewhere, whose members have largely consisted of unskilled labourers.

The Italian word for navvies is '*braccianti*', literally people who work with their arms. The number of these unique '*braccianti*' co-ops in Italy may perhaps be insufficient by itself to explain why the Italian totals are so much greater than those in France – but they are a large part of the explanation. For the rest, the age-old Italian tradition of travelling craftsmen, the famous '*artigiani*', may have something to do with it. Such men may well have exhibited an almost natural propensity to join co-operative ventures. It also seems plausible to suppose that down to the seizure of power by Mussolini in 1921, the Italian authorities were more generous than their French counterparts in applying the concessions to which these ventures were entitled under the law.

During the Mussolini period, some of the Italian production co-operatives folded, while others were put under the fascist Ente Nazionale delle Co-operativa. But the majority managed in some sense to survive. According to Sr Benati, by 1995 the Italian co-ops had over 300,000 members and combined turnover of over lire 18,000bn (over $10bn). Probably, they were even bigger in the 1970s. For though the numbers in the service industries have grown, this has been offset by a decade and more of decline in the traditional areas of building and civil engineering. The construction industry co-ops were hard-hit by the fall-out from the complicated scandals which sharply cut public spending on building works – and were not all themselves entirely free from involvement in those public works contract scandals.

Apart from sheer numbers, the other distinctive feature of Italy's production co-ops is their division along political lines. Until 1919, they were formed into a single national grouping with broad allegiance to the 'left', the Lega Nazionale delle Co-operativa e Mutue ('the Lega'), founded in 1886. But shock-waves from the Bolshevik Revolution in Russia caused about a third of the Lega membership to leave it and form their own Catholic-inclined grouping, the Confederazione Co-operative Italiane (the 'Confederation'). The Lega then developed formal links with the

Italian Communist Party. In 1952, at the height of the Cold War, a minority of Lega members broke away and formed a third grouping with Social Democrat and Republican political orientation; but this remains very small. The political division produced at least one major benefit for Italy's co-ops in the post-war world: cross-party political support. This lasted at least until the mid-1990s when Prime Minister Berlusconi tried to introduce legislation which would have damaged co-ops. In the event his government fell before anything came of his proposals. However, the issue will no doubt rumble on – Italy's conventional businesses argue that the tax and other privileges enjoyed by co-ops are unfair on conventional capitalist businesses. One answer to this is that the Italian state offers advantages to conventional capitalist businesses which, in their aggregate effect, are at least as important as those which it offers to the co-ops (Earle). One particular privilege may however be singled out as especially beneficial: a relief of corporation tax, subject to various conditions and limits, when profits are transferred to inalienable reserves. It has a virtually identical counterpart in France.

That then is the historical background to the case study examples to which we now move. It is the two Italian examples which we consider first; both of them located in the small town of Imola, roughly 35 kilometres south east of Bologna.

9

Two Imola Co-ops: Sacmi and La Ceramica

INTRODUCTORY OVERVIEW

Italian firms were by far the world leaders in the production and export of ceramic tiles, a $10bn industry in 1987. Italian producers accounted for about 30 percent of world production and almost 60 percent of world exports ... Italian tiles were known throughout the world for superior mechanical and aesthetic qualities. Yet Italy's success had been as much, if not more, a function of production technology than design. *Michael E. Porter, 'The Competitive Advantage of Nations'*

According to Benito Benati, Administrative Director of Sacmi, around half of the production of the small town of Imola is by co-operatives. This propensity to co-operate dates back to the late nineteenth century. 'The Imolesi point to the figure and influence of their fellow citizen, Andrea Costa, and his followers,' writes John Earle, the historian of the Italian co-op movement to whom I am indebted for much of what follows:

> Originally a hot-blooded anarchist, Costa founded the Socialist Revolutionary party of Romagna in 1881 ... and soon after succeeded in getting elected to parliament as the first socialist deputy.
>
> Costa's supporters were artisans, craftsmen and labourers who never became submerged into a faceless proletariat by the factories that were springing up in the industrial regions of Lombardy and Piedmont. These people were accustomed to fending for themselves, to exercising a spirit of initia- tive, unlike the factory workers whose energies soon became absorbed in claims and conflicts with capitalist management. This, the visitor is told, helps to explain the co-operative

mentality [emphasis added] in Emilia-Romagna; and nowhere more so than in Imola.

In Italy, as elsewhere in the West, employment in manufacturing industry has been in steady decline for the last generation. But whether or not it is because their Imolese environment is conducive to their co-operative form, two medium-sized manufacturing ventures which have been able to buck this trend are Sacmi and La Ceramica. They are active in adjacent fields of business. La Ceramica manufactures ceramics, mainly tiles. Sacmi ('Societa Anonima Co-operativa Meccanica d'Imola') makes the machines which are used in the production of those tiles.

Employment more than doubled in each of these businesses between the late-1970s and mid-1996 when this chapter was finally revised. Sacmi's workforce, which numbered 359 in 1979, had climbed to 823 by the end of 1995. At La Ceramica the numbers employed reached 903 in 1995, up from just over 400 in 1980. These figures understate the rate of growth, however, since both businesses have also acquired and set up subsidiary companies, abroad as well as in Italy.

Production also multiplied, as did exports. La Ceramica is now the third largest ceramic supplier in Italy, which in turn is the world leader in this business. As for Sacmi, it is probably the world leader in manufacture of the machines for making these tiles. It exported 80% of its total output in 1995 and claims a 45% share of the world market.

Sacmi and La Ceramica have also been successful financially. And their workforces are well paid. With the possible exception of the top management at Sacmi, there is nothing behind these successes of what union officials call self-exploitation. Indeed in almost all respects the business success of these two ventures has been exemplary. If they can be criticised at all, it is on a rather different ground: that only a minority of their workers enjoy actual co-operative membership. Since a new law in 1992, it has been possible for Italian co-ops to offer non-members a bigger financial stake than before; but that does not alter the basic issue of an open democracy – a key point which we shall look at later.

Sacmi was started from scratch as a co-operative in 1919. La Ceramica can trace its history back to the Renaissance and became a co-op when acquired from its capitalist owner as long ago as

1874. Yet in different ways, at different times, and with rather differently orientated leadership, both firms have successfully negotiated the difficult transition from a more or less traditional workshop operation to a modern professionally managed business. Outside the Mondragon group, only a microscopic minority of industrial co-operatives have managed to do that. And if we are allowed the phrase in today's world, the leadership which brought them through that transition came from the working class. However, as Sr Benati put it in a speech in St Petersburg in 1995: 'One should notice how the Co-operatives, at first almost entirely composed of workers, have gradually opened up as they developed to engineers, technicians, university graduates, and, in general to an intellectual manpower with a high degree of schooling and professional training.'

Given its population of about 60,000 there is probably more co-operative business in Imola than anywhere outside Mondragon. To that extent both Sacmi and La Ceramica have benefited from a positive climate of local community feeling. The fact that the municipal council has been controlled by the left without interruption since the war must also surely have been good for the morale of these two essentially 'workers'' enterprises.

Yet there has long been a big divergence in both the political orientation and the leadership arrangements of the two co-ops. In 1979, in what amounted more or less to a change of government, the members of La Ceramica elected Alberto Cicognani as their president. To British readers, the political attitudes of the late Sr Cicognani, who died in the early 1990s, could be called those of a Thatcherite working class Tory. This found some expression in the co-op's external relations. Following his election to the presidency, La Ceramica affiliated itself to Italy's Christian Democrat co-operative grouping, the Confederation, a move which would have been dismissed as unthinkable before his presidency. (Admittedly, La Ceramica also maintained its affiliation to the left-affiliated Lega.) The pre-Cicognani leadership at La Ceramica had been Lega-approved, and thus, in effect, Communist Party approved. As much as anything else, his election marked a rejection of any Lega overlordship. At Sacmi, there have been no such changes of leadership or external affiliation. And though its current leadership is to a large extent depoliticised (or 'laicised' in the current Italian usage) Sacmi's basic orientation has remained left of centre.

The difference in the position of the leadership is as follows. At La Ceramica the top managers are simply hired hands and are excluded from taking up membership while those at Sacmi are encouraged to apply for membership, and generally do so successfully. To the obvious question – which of these two systems works better? – the fairest answer in Imola in the summer of 1996 was that both seemed to be working well: Sacmi's arrangements suit Sacmi and La Ceramica's suit La Ceramica.

Sacmi

Early History For Sacmi's early history I am once more indebted to John Earle:

> The workmen who set up Sacmi in the difficult times after the First World War did so with the help of a loan from a small local co-operative bank and the use of an empty gymnasium provided by the socialist ruled municipality. The mechanics' ideological commitment was clear from the start: 25 per cent of profits were to be devoted to backing the struggle of the working class, while 50 would go to reserve, 20 to the members, and the remaining 5 to promoting the co-operative ideal. The nine founding members agreed to pay themselves less than the minimum union wage scales. Their ambitions were limited to repair and maintenance work, and their first job was to repair the steam engines driving the threshing machines of an agricultural co-operative.
>
> The co-op survived when fascism took over the country in 1922. Its members were anything but fascist sympathisers, and there were incidents in which they were beaten up, imprisoned, and sent to internal exile; but, chameleon-like, Sacmi was one of those bodies that managed to preserve an anti-fascist spirit after the Lega was disbanded in 1925 . . .
>
> However, the municipality – now under the fascists – evicted the co-op from the former gymnasium and the future looked dark. But, as at their birth, the spirit of co-operative solidarity came to their help, and La Ceramica first rented, then sold them, a building. It was in the same spirit that, in the aftermath of the great depression of 1929-1930, a retail co-operative

allowed Sacmi's members – who were working an extra hour
a day without pay – credit notes for their food purchases.

By 1933 Sacmi felt confident enough to launch into
production on its own. Three years before, a citrus farmer in
Sicily had told members of his dissatisfaction with a Spanish
machine for cleaning and selecting oranges. Sacmi succeeded
in developing a variant of their own. By 1940 it was
manufacturing other pieces of machinery too. In all these years,
however, it remained a very small operation – there were
seldom more than 13 members up to 1944, while wage earning
workers rose to a peak of 66 in 1940, sinking back to 21 in 1944.

By then the war was entering its last year . . . Three of the
staff were killed fighting as partisans . . . The decision was
taken to dismantle the plant and hide the machinery from the
Germans in hayricks and barns.

This proved invaluable for the work of post-war reconstruction, which got under way in 1947 when, with 26 members and
42 wage earners, Sacmi undertook to equip the plant of La
Ceramica, which had been destroyed in the war. It was thus
able to repay its debt of solidarity. Sacmi was by now involved
in designing and manufacturing its own equipment for the
ceramics industry. Soon afterwards, in 1949, at the request of
a Bologna businessman, it began studies on the machinery for
making metal caps for bottles, and branched out into what has
become its second principal line of production.

At least until the late 1940s, Sacmi was still essentially a small
local business, with a workforce well below 100, and selling its
products chiefly in local and regional markets. By the late 1970s it
employed between 300 and 400 people and exported roughly two
thirds of its production: 65% in 1977 and 72% in 1978. Behind this
growth was the fact that the 1950s and 1960s were the years of
Italy's economic miracle, which included a rapid increase in building activity and thus in Sacmi's main market.

Though the year-by-year statistics show what looks like incremental change, a number of important discontinuities were
clearly involved in the rapid rise in production: from mainly
manual to mainly automated production, and from management by
generalists to management by specialists, as John Earle helpfully
suggests. Some kind of culture shift must surely have been necessary

too: from that of an artisanal workshop to that of a modern plant, with a corresponding shift in the balance between blue collar and white collar staff.

Benito Benati, Sacmi's longstanding 'chief administrator' (finance director), and one of the top members of its management team, attributes the co-op's remarkable development to two things. First, top quality leadership and, secondly, being in the right market with a good product. For special praise as a leader, Sr Benati singles out an engineer, Sr Aldo Villa, the elected head of Sacmi's board of directors for more than a decade before his death in the mid-1980s. As an engineer Sr Villa was, in Benati's words, 'a very valuable technician and manager'. He was also a

> man of the working class because he started his career as a worker and trade-union representative . . . Just because he was a left union man, he was dismissed by the company where he worked previously (a state body governed by the right); for this reason he was beloved and held in very high esteem by the workers, who regarded him as 'one of them'.

Sr Benati has also supplied a valuable insight into what one might call the processes of change at Sacmi over the years. Perhaps the key point to emerge is that, at least among the co-op's membership, change has been accompanied by continuous discussion: 'Discussions were very inflamed and deep but we came to a unitary conclusion.'

And how was it, given the inflamed character of the discussion, that unitary conclusions were arrived at? Apart from Villa's outstanding contribution Benati offers four more general explanations:
– the working class of Imola is really of top quality; here the left has been governing for many decades exemplarily
– the members' will was never overpowered
– much was made to convince, nothing was made to force, the members.
– the alliance and co-operation . . . of white collars and blue collars.

Sacmi since 1980 In 1990, by virtue of decisions taken by its members (employee shareholders), the Sacmi co-operative in Imola invested some lire 27bn (about £12m at the then exchange rate), all of it financed from its own financial resources. This was the highest annual investment in the history of the business, though the average figures for the three subsequent years were not far behind: lire 22bn. Those subsequent investment expenditures were also self-financed.

Sacmi was able to make these investments from its own resources because over the previous ten years, as well as investing at a respectable annual rate, it had managed to build up a substantial cash mountain. The key statistics of Sacmi's business record are set out in the table. As between 1978 and 1993, there is employment growth of over 100% from 352 to 728. After allowing for inflation the growth of turnover is that much greater, indicating significant improvement in labour productivity. The export percentage is seen first to fluctuate at a notably high level and then to go even higher: to 92% and 90% in the years 1992 and 1993 respectively.

*Sacmi since 1978: Key Statistics**

	Turnover Lire bn	Exports %	Cash flow %	Profit Lire bn	Employees Nos	Investment Lire bn
1978	25.4	72	15	3.0	352	0.7
1979	34.6	56	17	4.5	359	1.5
1980	53.5	50	21	9.3	393	1.3
1981	75.9	64	21	11.0	424	1.6
1982	72.7	78	29	12.2	411	2.8
1983	79.8	75	22	11.6	410	4.9
1984	127.1	59	27	19.0	434	6.1
1985	130.7	78	22	14.8	442	7.0
1986	126.0	85	16	14.0	449	6.3
1987	179.7	83	15	18.9	484	7.3
1988	262.0	77	16	32.7	526	18.4
1989	289.5	79	17	40.7	586	12.4
1990	311.9	83	21	44.0	634	27.1
1991	339.0	86	17	39.5	651	22.0
1992	458.9	92	17	62.3	701	18.0
1993	653.8	90	18	100.9	728	25.7
1994	666.1	83	18	103.3	754	39.0
1995	803.0	80	9	50.0	823	34.0

*all lire at current price

As against a healthy underlying upward trend of profits, the year-on-year results show falls in some years – if allowance were made for inflation they would be rather sharper. These are largely explained by the economic cycle in Sacmi's main business of supplying machinery for the manufacture of ceramic wall tiles. However despite these fluctuations, the overall financial results are quite exceptional. Even after investment, Sacmi was able to go on adding to its reserves of cash.

Moreover, it is not as if Sacmi's main successes have been won merely in cosy domestic markets. The fact that it characteristically exports over 80% of its sales is itself remarkable. Even more so is the spread across the world. For example, from the start of the 1990s the Chinese market for Sacmi's main product rapidly expanded to some 30% of sales. The Mexican market began to become important; and demand even grew from those who cater for the large, even if slow-growing, middle class in India. By the mid-1990s Sacmi had ten affiliated or subsidiary companies outside Italy, from Shanghai to the USA and Germany.

It is the potential of those markets which have previously been thought of as almost in the third world – China, Mexico, and India for example – which offer the best assurance of continued success in the future. For it must surely be a fair bet that expenditure on housing in those countries is going to rise disproportionately fast over the next generation; and so, with it, the demand for the ceramic tile machinery. By a mixture of good luck – the character of the output of its main product line – and bold investment in expanding capacity and improving quality, Sacmi as a business seems well positioned for a success over the first decades of the next century similar to what it has enjoyed over the last decades of this one.

Is there a weakness in Sacmi's recent business record? In the late 1980s, expenditure on R&D, then no more than 1.5%, might have caused concern. The position was radically changed in the early 1990s. In this period Sacmi built itself a research and development laboratory focussed on the products of its customers. Its own staff in that laboratory work on improvements in the materials and processes used in the making of ceramic tiles. In this way the co-operative aims to keep ahead of the competition. There has been a significant increase in its employment of graduates, and Sacmi's R&D expenditures are now understood to be well up to the levels expected in a business of this quality.

Notwithstanding the long existence of its metal bottle-cap machinery business, it has also been suggested that Sacmi is dangerously dependent on a single market – ceramic tile machinery. In the early 1990s Sacmi has taken some steps towards diversifying into adjacent products. For example, in 1991 it made its first sales of the machinery needed to make ceramic sanitary ware and refractory bricks.

Some businesses are criticised for being too dependent on a single market; others are praised for concentrating on the niche market which they know best. In Sacmi's case it is probably a fair hypothesis that its steps towards diversification into adjacent product lines would be more advanced had it not been for the surging growth in the demand for its staple product: ceramic tile-making machinery. Between 1990 and 1995, a period when inflation was only modest, sales more than doubled: from lire 300bn to nearly lire 800bn. In effect the whole of the increase was in sales of Sacmi's main products.

So demand for its main product seems buoyant. But Benito Benati is one of those fairly rare top managers in co-operative ventures, who forcefully expresses his strong and confident belief that the business also enjoys substantial supply side advantages by virtue of its co-operative structures. He is inclined to highlight two of those. First he is convinced that the substantial linkage between the earnings of the workforce and the success of Sacmi is a source of significant comparative advantage. Second he argues persuasively about the advantage which stems from the altered relationship in a co-operative between capital and labour. He put the point simply in a newspaper interview (Keegan 1990): 'In a co-operative the partner/worker is on the side of the co-operative and not against it. That is a great advantage.'

It is to Sacmi's record as a co-operative, its management and control processes, that we now turn.

Sacmi as a Co-operative To start with, we should remind ourselves that the co-op's pioneer founding fathers in the 1920s 'agreed to pay themselves less than the union wage scale'. Have Sacmi's outstanding financial results involved sacrifice on the part of its employees? Is this perhaps a case, at least for those who are members of the co-op, of what it is fashionable in some British left-wing circles to call 'self-exploitation'? The answer is a resounding 'no'. Employees who are not co-op members are paid market rates. Under Italian co-op law Sacmi's members (its employee shareholders) can be paid an additional bonus up to a further 20% of their pay – and that has been paid at Sacmi for many years.

Sacmi's top managers, however, do *not* enjoy a margin of extra remuneration compared with their conventional capitalist counterparts. In the mid-1980s, John Earle reported that the co-op's top management salaries were '40% less' than in conventional capitalist business. It seems that there has been an improvement in that relative position since then, and top managers in the 1990s are being paid roughly the same as – though certainly no more than – their counterparts in the more directly capitalist competition. Unlike at La Ceramica, the managers are eligible for co-op membership, and thus for the 20% bonus – and their applications for co-op membership usually succeed.

We have noted that just over a third of Sacmi's workforce are members of the co-op:

	Employees	Members	%
1988	537	242	45
1993	728	250	34
1994	754	274	36
1995	823	284	35

This low proportion is, of course, entirely within the provisions of Italian co-operative law. Moreover, analytically as well as historically, the law partly reflects a world and an era – Italy in the 1880s – when fluctuations of employment in any particular business were a good deal sharper than in Imola today.

However, that is not the whole story. At Sacmi, as in Italy's other industrial co-ops, new recruits have always had to complete a probationary period successfully before being allowed to apply for membership. Initially this was a year at Sacmi, but in the 1960s it was increased to five years and a minimum age threshold was imposed: of 24. It is important to be clear that admission to membership, which is by decision of the co-op's elected board, is by no means automatic. Successful applicants have to satisfy the directors on a number of counts: John Earle cites 'professional skills and moral conduct' as well as 'loyalty towards the co-operative'. Some applicants fail.

It would be naive not to suppose that in making judgements about applications for membership the directors are sometimes influenced, if only subconsciously, by the reflection that there is a cost to the co-op in extending membership. This is because with a larger workforce percentage as members, the larger (other things being equal) will be the disbursement to cover the members' bonus. At 20% of pay, the sums involved, though not enormous, are also not negligible.

It is in this context that the offer of so-called 'financial shares' to non-members in 1995 should be seen: high-yielding short-term bonds would be a better description. This followed a change in Italian law in 1992 under which co-operatives were for the first time allowed to issue 'financial shares' to non-members. The main purpose of this measure was to improve the capacity of co-ops to raise capital – perhaps by issuing these so-called 'shares' to financial investors. The law requires that the co-op prepare an investment plan and that any capital raised be linked to this investment.

However, at Sacmi and La Ceramica, the law has opened up a way of giving non-member employees a quasi-stake in the co-op without giving them votes or control. The 'shares' are to be reimbursed after three years and offer a 'dividend' two percentage points higher than the rate paid on the ordinary membership shares (i.e. the voting shares). This is likely to be 16% – several percentage points higher than rates paid by banks. The new 'financial shares' do not carry votes or any membership rights. The formula under which they were issued is complicated: the essential points are that (a) co-op members as well as non-member employees could subscribe, (b) the amount to which anyone could subscribe was related to length of service, and (c) almost anybody who was eligible applied. At Sacmi the total value of the issue was about lire 18.5bn. The money was used to finance two new workshops and three tooling machines at lire 2-3bn each.

Could there be a conflict between members and non-members, that is between employee shareholders and employees who are not shareholders? According to Benito Benati, the straightforward answer has two parts. The first is that so long as the status of employee non-shareholders is only temporary, i.e. for the duration of a period of probation, then serious conflict will be avoided. But the second is that that is not the situation at Sacmi in the 1990s. So a potential problem is probably still there. Union membership, though fairly general, is higher among Sacmi's employees who are not shareholders. In the case of non-members and non-shareholding employees, the union is in fact the only representative body which speaks for them. For, as non-members, they have no voice in the election of the co-op's board of directors, which consists of five members who hold office for two-year terms but may be re-elected without limit.

Defenders of the co-op membership system at Sacmi sometimes argue that there has been a greater propensity to fail among those of the country's industrial co-ops which follow a policy of open membership. My first response would be 'maybe', though I doubt whether it would be possible to demonstrate such a link statistically: other factors – poor management and/or market difficulties – seem more likely to be the main causes of failure in any particular case. More confidently I would argue that at Sacmi in the 1990s the risks that a move towards a more open membership policy might provoke a slide towards failure are surely minimal. That is because of the prestige and dominance of the present membership group. It seems as certain as these things can be that that group would continue to set the 'culture' of the business even after the membership had been significantly opened up.

For the rest, dealing with Sacmi as a co-op, and rather as in the case of a club, those who secure membership must make a subscription. This takes the form of a purchase of what are rather misleadingly called capital shares in the business. The amount to be subscribed was increased in 1983 from lire 4m to lire 19m and has been raised steadily ever since: it now stands at the legal maximum, lire 120m per share. The increase had nothing to do with the co-op's financial needs. Rather members considered that investing money in Sacmi would be to their advantage and would bring in a fair return. The same applies in relation to the loans which members are permitted to make to the co-op. In both cases, though only fixed interest may be paid as a return, the percentage rate is significantly higher than members could normally expect on deposit accounts with a bank.

One final question may be raised about the financial relationship between its members and Sacmi. Both the Lega (of which Sacmi is a member) and Italy's other two co-op groupings have been pressing the government since 1989 to change the law so that co-operative shares became more like equity: by linking their value to 50% of the co-op's indivisible reserves. Would Sacmi's members favour such a change? Given Italy's glacially slow movement in relation to legal changes of this kind, the question may be dismissed as academic. The formal answer is that the question has not yet been put, but when it is, smart money will surely bet on an affirmative answer. Moreover it seems reasonable to argue that Sacmi's members should have *some* equity interest in the higher capital values which their work creates.

What of control? For an English-speaking audience, the single most important point may be that though Sacmi is management-managed, it is unquestionably worker-led. The major decisions, whether about investment or otherwise, are taken by a combination of Sacmi's membership and the board of directors which it elects. It is true that, unlike the position at nearby La Ceramica, Sacmi's top managers enjoy membership of the co-op. Nevertheless the overwhelmingly predominant voice at meetings of both the membership as a whole and the board of directors is *not* that of the top management. It is in this sense that Sacmi is worker-led.

That the kind of business success which Sacmi has been enjoying is compatible with worker leadership is at variance with much conventional thinking. For, according to the latter, a workforce is almost incapable of taking a long-term view and will nearly always prefer higher consumption (rates of pay and cash bonuses) to capital investment. That view is wholly confounded by the Sacmi experience – and indeed that of La Ceramica – which has now extended over a long period. The membership's decision to back sustained high levels of investment is all the more remarkable if we take account of the fact that under Italy's existing and long established co-operative law, shares in a co-op can never do better than retain their nominal value: unless and until that law is changed Sacmi's members have no real capital stake in the new investments which have been approved.

La Ceramica

Early History In that it has a successful private family business as its ancestor, La Ceramica belongs to a small minority of Italy's industrial co-ops. The family's name was Bucci. According to John Earle, the Bucci family had bought . . . [the business] early in the nineteenth century; through previous owners the firm could trace its roots to the Renaissance. In 1874, when social conditions in the region were still unsettled after the unification of Italy, Guiseppe Bucci handed over the firm to his 32 workers as a co-operative. He decided to do so partly because his health was not good, and partly because he was a convinced follower of the Republican leader Mazzini. He was also one of those rare idealists who put their convictions into practice. Bucci himself drafted the statute; and suggested a trial period of two years, at the end of which he offered to take the firm back without payment for wear and tear of the equipment; if the experiment did not prove a success. Such was nearly the case. Before the ownership passed to them as a co-op definitely in 1877, the workers found it necessary to sign a 'pact of brotherhood', in which they pledged to put aside the 'personal rancours' and 'reciprocal offences' that had arisen among them.

Till 1913 production was limited to kitchen and tableware – about 700,000 pieces of crockery a year with a workforce of around 60. It was still little more than an enlarged artisan workshop. The leap forward to an industrial firm took place after the First World War, with the acquisition of a modern factory, together with a railway siding for the speedy despatch of goods. Production began of floor and wall tiles, which in the 1920s began to be exported, notably to the United States. The co-op continued to exist under fascism; but in the Second World War nine tenths of its plant were destroyed. This at least provided the opportunity to acquire modern plant, supplied by a fellow co-op, Sacmi.

La Ceramica's early postwar growth, once its plant had been rebuilt by Sacmi, seems to have been more steady than dynamic. By the 1920s La Ceramica had already effected the transition from an artisanal workshop to an industrial firm. In this respect it was well ahead of Sacmi in the late 1940s and early 1950s. Perhaps the most important development during this period was the commissioning of a well-known artist, Gio Ponti, to design a new line in tableware: the now famous 'Blue Carnation' design. Though tableware (and the related kitchenware) accounts for only a tiny percentage of La Ceramica's output, it has a vital marketing role. The Chinese artist

Hsiao Chin was commissioned in the late 1980s and, according to John Earle, designed a total of 278 new pieces.

The period of rather more than thirty years, from the opening of its new plant soon after the war to the election of Sr Cicognani in 1979, seems to have been one of steady rather than spectacular growth. An impression of relative immobility, and thus of missed opportunity, may well have been one of the considerations which spurred Sr Cicognani and his friends to start campaigning against the old regime, as they did from the middle 1970s onwards. Evidence of immobility and lack of management grip is certainly suggested by the high absenteeism figure recorded in the year in which Sr Cicognani first took office as President. It was as high as 18%, or three times the rate to which it had come down by the time of Sr Cicognani's last full year in the top position.

The Cicognani Years Alberto Cicognani was elected President of the Board of Directors at the comparatively young age of forty-one. Rising from the blue collar ranks of the co-op's workforce, he had already been a board member for four years. But his promotion was not simply a change of face at the top. For as a board member he had already been campaigning for changes of direction and emphasis, especially for a reduction in the influence of the Italian Communist Party, resulting from La Ceramica's affiliation to the Lega. He also wanted a more professional and single-minded approach to business management. His election to the presidency was in fact an endorsement of the changes he had been calling for; and a rejection of the rather different policies of the previous regime.

To demonstrate its enhanced commitment to business values, the new board gradually replaced the old management team with tougher and more single-minded men. Moreover, it introduced a new statute which laid down that from then on managers were debarred from membership of the co-op and from election to the board. To demonstrate its independence from the Lega, the co-op decided to affiliate to the rival Christian Democrat-orientated grouping of Italy's co-ops – the Confederazione. The Lega affiliation was not dropped, but notice was clearly served on the officials of that organisation to keep their distance.

Cicognani stepped down from the presidency and from the co-op's board of directors in May 1989. He had been continuously re-elected during the intervening period and would certainly have been voted in again had he chosen to stand. The decision was apparently all his own. It may well have been largely explained by exhaustion. For though he was retained as a consultant to the co-op, he died in his middle fifties in 1993. A young engineer from the Co-op's white collar technical department, Gianpiero Mondini, had been elected to succeed Cicognani.

Cicognani had left school and joined La Ceramica at what now seems to be the unbelievably early age of fourteen. He was first elected to the board of the co-op – more precisely its Council of Administration – in 1975, and to the Presidency, as we have seen, in 1979. There is no evidence that La Ceramica was actually losing money at that time. But it is clear from what subsequently happened that it was underperforming partly because of the influence of the Lega. Cicognani's achievement was to lead La Ceramica from underperformance to high performance. During the ten years of his presidency the numbers employed in the co-op increased by more than 50%, from just over 400 to 675. Measured in square metres, its output of ceramic tiles more than tripled: from just over 3m in 1979 to just under 10m in 1989.

A steadily declining rate of absenteeism, complemented by a steadily improving rate of hourly physical output on the part of La Ceramica's blue collar workers, are among the best illustrations of improving performance and tighter management grip during the Cicognani years.

Labour	Productivity*	Absenteeism†
1979	5.5	18
1980	5.7	16
1981	6.4	15
1982	8.9	13
1983	9.3	11
1984	11.4	10
1985	11.5	8
1986	11.9	7
1987	12.2	6
1988	13.5	6

*M2 of ceramic tiles per man/hour †% of normal working hours lost

The improved productivity of the blue collar workforce is no doubt due only in part to extra personal effort or what is now called, in the jargon, 'X' efficiency. It must also be explained by the sustained investment programme which was one of the outstanding features of this period. In aggregate the co-op made cumulative investments costing nearly Lire 70bn (about £30m) in the ten years from 1979 to 1988.

This investment programme chiefly consisted of two large new kilns, together with twelve new small ones. In some cases the new kilns simply increased capacity, in others they speeded up production, and sometimes both. Particularly important for speeding up production were a pair of rapid and 'double colour' kilns which were installed at Imola in 1987 and 1988. It was this investment programme which of course made possible the more than three-fold increase in La Ceramica's output of ceramic tiles between 1979 and 1989. Exports rose to 72% of total sales in 1988 from 35% in 1979.

With this sort of achievement, La Ceramica out-performed most of the competition – all of it conventional capitalist businesses – for a fairly long time. According to Marino Callegati, who was elected to be La Ceramica's Vice President in 1991, the co-op ranked twentieth among Italy's manufacturers of ceramic tiles at the start of the 1970s. By 1989 it had climbed to fifth place and was indeed, by then, the fifteenth largest manufacturer of these products in the world.

We turn now to the financial record of La Ceramica during the ten years of Sr Cicognani's presidency. It may be recalled that over the same ten years to end 1988 Sacmi was able to finance its entire lire 40bn investment programme from its own resources and build up substantial reserves of cash. La Ceramica, admittedly with a larger investment programme, did not match that financial result. The total of its post-tax profits for the period 1979 to 1988 fell well below its investment spending. Nevertheless, despite the relationship between its profits and investments, it managed to improve, over the ten years to 1988, the ratio of its capital to its sales. The former, technically its 'social capital and reserves', increased by over nine times at current prices: from just over lire 4bn to just over lire 38bn. The corresponding increase in its sales was more like seven times: from lire 13.5bn to lire 94bn. A part of this improvement is explained by increases in the capital which members were required to put in. The figure was raised to lire 9m (from a mere lire 2.9m) in 1981 and then again to 10m in 1986. (By 1996, it had been raised to lire 120m, the maximum allowed by Italian law.)

La Ceramica: Statistical Record

	Profit	Sales	Exports	Investments	Employed	Members
	Lire bn	Lire bn	%	Lire bn	Nos	Nos
1980	3.0	19.7	36	2.0	412	153
1981	2.1	24.9	39	8.1	471	157
1982	0.6	31.3	55	5.6	461	155
1983	2.2	43.5	69	5.7	527	140
1984	4.7	56.7	72	4.7	561	142
1985	4.6	64.6	72	3.9	565	143
1986	6.0	67.7	71	1.8	593	148
1987	9.2	76.6	71	3.9	609	152
1988	9.7	94.0	72	28.8	649	149
1989	12.7	117.3	72	12.1	675	148
1990	11.4	129.8	69	19.9	707	147
1991	14.6	149.0	68	26.3	763	148
1992	19.9	177.6	67	14.1	774	139
1993	31.6	222.0	67	14.0	807	132
1994	50.9	259.5	69	19.3	845	152
1995	48.0	273	70	41.0	903	155

From Strength to Strength: 1989 to 1995 Following the election to the presidency of Sr Mondini, La Ceramica continued to go from strength to strength. The years 1989-95 saw historically low inflation in Italy. Ignoring changes in the value of money, sales by the parent business more than doubled. Measured in square metres, output of ceramic tiles rose more than 50%, to nearly 14m in 1994, up from under 10m in 1989. The growth of employment in the parent business between those two dates was about 15%: from 675 to 845. It follows that labour productivity improved rather sharply. So did profits. After tax, they climbed from lire 13bn in 1989 to lire 48bn in 1995. As is shown in the table, post tax profits were sufficient over this period for La Ceramica to finance the whole of a massive investment programme from its own internal resources.

These gains and achievements were made possible because, over this period, as during Sr Cicognani's presidency, La Ceramica managed to increase its market share both in Italy and abroad. True, exports declined slightly as a share of total sales. But given the huge increases in both sales values and sales volumes, the absolute export numbers went up sharply. Its biggest foreign market used to be Germany, but by the mid-1990s had shifted to Scandinavia and Eastern Europe. The co-operative moved from fifth place to third place in the league table of Italy's manufacturers of ceramic tiles.

However, in one key respect the five years from 1989 to 1993 were not simply an extension of Sr Cicognani's success. In the early 1990s La Ceramica successively acquired two small, failing, ceramic tile manufacturers in its own Emilia Romagna region. One, at nearby Faenza, ten miles further south east from Imola, is called Nuove Ceramiche La Faenza. The second, rather further from Imola, is called Leonardo 1502 Ceramica. By 1995 the co-op also had other small subsidiaries or affiliates both at home and abroad, including a joint venture in Poland. Nearly a third of the 1,292 group employees were outside the core Imola business.

The first two acquisitions represented a new departure for La Ceramica. Their availability for purchase was a necessary condition for the acquisitions to have taken place at all. But the two deals also reflected a combination of La Ceramica's financial strength and the business confidence of its leaders. At the time when this was written, there were no plans to bring them or their employees into the co-operative structure. They were simply owned and controlled, as subsidiary businesses by La Ceramica, the Co-operative. The financial strength of La Ceramica was such that its profit and loss account for 1993 shows net annual financial costs as low as lire 3bn, or some 1.5% of total costs. That was after the two acquisition deals had been completed. Heavy borrowings had evidently not been necessary.

La Ceramica as a Co-operative As at Sacmi, we must dispose of one possible explanation for this success story: in theory it could have been achieved at the expense of La Ceramica's employees, whether members or not, through short-changing their wage and salary payments. Leaving its hired top managers on one side for a moment, the entire workforce was for many years paid at rates significantly above market levels – perhaps 20%, though this has apparently now stopped. On top of that, for the minority of the workforce who are also members of the co-op, there is the extra 20% in wages and salaries which Italy's co-operative law permits and which La Ceramica has now been paying out for as long as anyone can remember. Third, the co-op's elected board members receive a total remuneration package which is about 50% above what they would receive if they were doing the same jobs in a conventional capitalist business, while for the elected president the corresponding figure is around 100%. Of the elected board only the president is engaged on board business full time.

The position of the top management team, as hired hands debarred from co-op membership and election to the board, is, of course, different from that of their counterparts at Sacmi. There are four top management posts of this kind, managing respectively Finance and administration; sales; production; the factory.

Typically, these top managers at La Ceramica are paid more (probably by about 25% on average) than their counterparts at Sacmi. The policy is to 'go for the best', and so high salaries must inescapably be paid. On the other hand, the turnover of these positions, at least in the early years after the introduction of the new statute, was quite high. The hired top managers were then typically staying with La Ceramica for less than four years. However, according to Sr Callegati, the situation started to become more stable from 1990 onwards.

Some may well be sceptical in principle about a formula which assigns the leading role to the elected workers and puts them in charge of hired professional managers. But it is hard to argue with the facts of La Ceramica's success. Class divisions are no doubt less pronounced in Italy than in Britain. So professional Italian managers are no doubt less unwilling to be subordinate to 'worker' bosses than British managers would be. But the key points suggested by the extraordinary success of Sr Cicognani's ten-year reign may well be rather different. One is a hypothesis about the potential of working class business leadership, a potential which is almost totally unused in Britain. The second is a more specific hypothesis to the effect that worker leaders may be more successful than middle-class professionals at 'getting the best out of the lads', by reducing absenteeism for example. It is as if the successful regimental sergeant-major were to take over command of the regiment from the colonel. Who is to know whether that might not produce rather good results?

We turn now to the crucial issue of membership. Actual membership of the co-op is enjoyed by only a minority of its workforce, and the percentage has been falling. La Ceramica begins to look less like a co-operative and more like what the French used to call 'une entreprise ouvrière'. By the mid-1990s less than 1 in 5 in the workforce enjoyed membership.

Members as a Percentage of La Ceramica's Workforce

1979	40	1987	25
1980	37	1988	23
1981	33	1989	22
1982	28	1990	20
1983	26	1991	19
1984	27	1992	18
1985	27	1993	17
1986	25		

Apart from the exclusion from membership of La Ceramica's top management, the forces which explain the decline, and the mechanics of dealing with applications, are precisely the same as at Sacmi. The single most important general point is that the existing members have an interest in restricting new admissions. As for the procedures, a minimum of five years' probation is required in both businesses; there is a similar list of eligibility criteria; there is the same absolute discretion on the part of the elected board: to admit to membership or to withhold it. Following the decision at Sacmi in 1995, La Ceramica in 1996 introduced a similar system of 'financial shares' for non-member employees.

Again there are no major differences, as between La Ceramica and Sacmi, in the main other areas of co-operative machinery. For example, in both businesses, elected board members serve for three years and are eligible for re-election.

Yet these similarities and identities mask what seems to be a major difference in political orientation and culture. At Sacmi the prevailing values seem to be those of a left of centre social democracy. At La Ceramica, at least since 1979 and the first election of Sr Cicognani to the Presidency, the values seem much more like those of Mrs Thatcher's working-class Tories.

10
ACOME

The worker-owned and worker-led businesses, or *entreprises ouvrières*, which we consider in this chapter, have always typically been urban phenomena. ACOME ('Association Co-opérative Ouvrière en Matériel Electrique'), the flagship of France's industrial co-ops in the 1990s, is unusual in this respect. Though it started life between the two World Wars, in the Paris suburb of Argenteuil, it has been located since 1943 in the little town of Mortain, deep in rural lower Normandy.

ACOME is also exceptional in a characteristic which must surely be related to its rural setting: like the Mondragon group of co-operatives in the Basque Provinces of Spain, it is union free. Had it remained in Paris, there would doubtless be an important union presence today, as there was at its birth.

Moreover, its rural setting and the absence of the trade unions are that much more striking in the light of its size, and of the blue collar character of the majority of its workers. Total numbers employed were over 1,000 in the mid-1990s.

ACOME's record as a business in post-Second World War France has been exemplary. It has some notable technical innovations to its credit. It has built up a strong position in its main market: for low voltage electric cable. Particularly over the 1980s it showed excellent rates of return on capital, and similarly excellent rates of improvement in the productivity of its labour. Indeed the latter have been such that ACOME has been forced to diversify into new product lines, since otherwise it would have been obliged to reduce employment. It now has offices, subsidiaries or affiliates across France and elsewhere in the EU. It has expanded from its core business of cables, especially into PVC windows. Much of its business is now abroad. In short, it has a business record of which any conventional capitalist would be rightly proud.

ACOME's success as a business has not been at the expense of its success as a co-operative. For example, there is no 'democratic deficit' at ACOME of the kind which we found at La Ceramica and Sacmi. After a probation period, all who work in the business are required by its rules to take up membership.

The income differentials at ACOME seem to reflect a strong commitment by the co-operative to a kind of social idealism; or at least to something which is quite distinct from a mere acceptance of market forces. Broadly speaking the 'total compensation packages' at the lower levels of the workforce are well above market rates: whereas the opposite is true in respect of top management. That was until recently the position at Sacmi. It is also still in the mid-1990s the position in the Mondragon group. So far as I know, among the famous 'principles of co-operation'. there is none which specifies that pay differentials should be narrower than those prevailing in the market. Nevertheless that has often been the position in practice.

The clumsy phrase 'total compensation package' (rather than the simple word 'pay'), was not used in the previous paragraph by accident. Those who work at ACOME typically qualify for substantial financial benefits over and above their pay packets: some benefits in cash but also some others which are 'locked in' for a number of years under French law. These 'non-pay' financial benefits may amount to as much as one third of a typical 'total compensation package'. They are strongly profit related and therefore tend to align the interests of individuals in the workforce with the success of the co-operative as a whole.

The importance of its 'profit-related compensation', and the narrowness of its income differentials, stand out at ACOME with almost as much force as the absence of trade unions and the co-op's rural setting. All are surely related to one further characteristic of the business which needs to be noted at the outset: its unproblematic and almost totally trouble-free industrial relations.

In what follows we will first briefly review the French co-operative and local background; and features of French law which affect ACOME's business performance and behaviour. We will then go on to look at ACOME's business record. But before getting on to that it makes sense to offer a selection of 1994 key statistics:

Employment numbers	1,029
Turnover	Ffr 1,043m
Operating profits	Ffr 144m
Net profit	Ffr 78m

The Co-operative and Local Setting Unlike their Italian counterparts, the French co-operatives have never been organised into rival groupings, with different political affiliations. Unlike in Italy, there are separate organisations for each separate sector: agricultural co-ops, consumer co-ops and industrial – or as the French say *production* – co-ops. The full title of the national organisation of this last grouping was for many years the Confédération Générale des Sociétes Co-opératives Ouvrières de Production. Since the middle 1980s it has been simply the Confédération Générale des SCOPs, or the CGS.

For the production co-ops which form its membership, the CGS offers a range of services of a more or less technical character. For a well-established and strong business like ACOME, its main importance is a lobbying body In this respect it exists essentially to persuade successive French governments to retain and, where possible, extend legal and tax arrangements of benefit to its member businesses. The French production co-ops have in fact enjoyed a number of privileges, especially on contracts for government work, since the end of the last century.

Provisions of France's Co-operative law of 1978 may be seen as one of the results of a sustained and successful lobbying exercise by the CGS. Easily the most important provision is one which, in effect, exempts these French co-ops from corporate tax on profits transferred to inalienable reserves. The exemption is allowed to a limit equal to the sum allocated by the co-op out of these same profits to its members and/or employees on a locked in basis. When full advantage is taken of this provision, the whole of any corporate tax liability falls away. ACOME has benefited substantially from this tax provision.

As with a similar provision in Italy's co-operative tax arrangements, this relief is regularly attacked as unfair by the stalwarts of France's conventional capitalism. And as in Italy too, it is robustly defended by the CGS, the organisation's supporters and members. This is partly on the grounds of different favours and reliefs granted through the tax system to conventional capitalist undertakings; and partly on the grounds that the relief is justified by the inalienable character of the reserves to which the tax relieved profits are transferred.

ACOME also takes advantage of the reliefs available to all French private businesses, whether co-operative or conventional.

These can be traced back to a decree on cash profit sharing first introduced by the Government of Antoine Pinay in 1959. The two most important are designed to encourage employee financial participation and were introduced, under President de Gaulle, in 1967.

CGS thinking has also had a progressive influence in France's production co-ops. The relevant French law now requires that a 'substantial' proportion of a production co-op's employees must be members. The adjective is given no precise definition. The existing members of a French production co-op still retain the same right of veto over applications for membership as their Italian counterparts. All the same there is now only a small minority of French production co-ops in which membership is as restricted as at Sacmi and La Ceramica; or where the associated 'democratic deficit' is as substantial as it is in those two Imola ventures. The more democratic climate of the French production co-ops needs to be acknowledged, even though the rules and policies at ACOME itself might well be the same even if that climate had been rather different. The absence of any communist influence no doubt partly explains it. The periodic recurrence of Catholic social teaching in the discussions of these French production co-ops has probably also played a part.

Its co-operative structure and the framework of law and discussion in which it has operated has helped to shape ACOME's postwar record and its remarkable success as a business. But its setting in the country, deep in rural lower Normandy and just southwest of the base of the Cherbourg peninsula, has been of equal, or greater, importance. Apart from the absence of unions, there is at least anecdotal evidence that recruits to industry from peasant households may, if the conditions are right, be predisposed to align themselves with the success of the businesses into which they are recruited. For eliciting that response the conditions at ACOME could scarcely have been more favourable.

ACOME's Record as a Business The business was registered as a production co-op, with a capital of 500 shares valued at 100 francs each, and premises in the Paris suburb of Argentuil, in April 1932. Its birth was in some sense marsupial. For it was very much helped into existence by a conventional capitalist undertaking called Electrocable. The latter made available rented accommodation to the infant co-op. More important it supplied ACOME with work in the form of orders – mainly for electric cable for the French telephone system. In effect ACOME seems to have started its life as a labour-only subcontractor to Electrocable.

By its tenth birthday, in 1942, ACOME was already employing about 80 people of whom as many as 30 were apparently engaged in office work and selling. In other words it had already by then progressed some way beyond its origins as an artisanal labour only subcontractor, operating on a small workshop scale in rented premises. But in that same year, 1942, both ACOME and its half parent, Electrocable, suffered a formidable blow. Their premises in Argentuil were completely destroyed in an Allied bombing raid. But the subsequent fate of the two undertakings was very different. Electrocable, the capitalist half parent, went into liquidation. By contrast ACOME, the production co-op, managed in 1943 to shift its entire operation to Mortain, deep in rural lower Normandy. Their respective corporate responses to being bombed out in Paris were the reverse of what the text books would suggest: for it is capital rather than labour which is supposed to enjoy an advantage of mobility. But in any event it was ACOME which moved and survived. And it survived again in 1944 when the little town of Mortain was largely destroyed in the Battle of Normandy. ACOME's factory was one of the few buildings which escaped more or less undamaged. The co-op's survival twice over in quick succession is a splendid illustration of the contingent in business history.

Already in the 1950s and 1960s the business had started to become known as something of a pioneer and technical innovator. For example, ACOME was the first French manufacturer of low voltage cable to switch to plastic coatings for the cable wires. It was also responsible for introducing a special kind of wire with a special advantage for use in motor car circuits: eliminating engine interference with car radios.

By the late 1960s, ACOME had become essentially what it is today: a good medium-sized manufacturing business with a strong and respected position in its main market for low voltage cable. By 1976 its workforce had climbed to almost 700; and by the measure of employment it had come to rank fourth among France's production co-ops. By the more qualitative measure of value added per employee, it was already by that year in the top position.

During the 1980s, when detailed statistics first become readily available, ACOME's business of manufacturing low voltage electric cable reached maturity. More recently, productivity improvements started to outpace the growth of demand in ACOME's main markets. The business responded to the new situation by launching a number of diversification initiatives. Had it not done so, the co-op would have been obliged to cut back on numbers employed. As it was, ACOME managed to achieve a significant if unspectacular employment growth of 15% during the 1980s.

ACOME also achieved very respectable rates of return on capital in the 1980s; as well as those improvements in labour productivity which drove it towards diversification. Return on capital averaged 19.6% during the period 1982 to 1989. It reached a significantly higher figure of 22.8% in the second half of the decade, from 1985 to 1989. As for labour productivity it showed an increase in real terms, after allowing for inflation, of 45% between 1981 and 1989. Moreover, that measure includes work associated with the co-op's main diversification initiative. If the labour productivity of its electric cable manufacture was measured separately, the increase would be that much greater.

ACOME's financial and investment record for the 1980s is also strikingly impressive, especially during the second half. The actual figures are worth putting on the record:

ACOME: Net Profits and Investments (FFrs m): 1985–1989

	Net Profits	Investments
1985	59.4	50.0
1986	67.1	53.1
1987	69.9	55.9
1988	88.1	56.0
1989	106.1	69.0

In other words, during this period, as we earlier saw happened in the case of Sacmi, the co-op was able to finance a significant investment programme entirely from its own resources; and build up something of a cash mountain at the same time. Here again the contrast with the stereotype of the workers' co-op is instructive: the stereotype of the 'lads' consuming all the profits in higher wages, and no doubt – as sometimes happened in what used to be Yugoslavia – *more* than the profits.

It is difficult to see what serious fault the financial analysts of

Wall Street and the City of London could find with this sort of record – beyond perhaps calling for the co-operative equivalent of more generous dividends. And the same is true when we turn from the recent financial record to what has lately been happening in ACOME's real economy: and especially to its various diversification initiatives.

In effect, ACOME has been diversifying out of the supply of cable to the French and international telecommunications industry, its traditional and core business, in three different ways: first, by finding new customers for its core product of cables and coated wires; second, into new materials for those core products – plastic fibre optics; third, into entirely new products, especially extruded plastic pipe and window frames.

By 1990 the proportion of total turnover accounted for by ACOME's traditional core business – sales of cable to the telecommunications industry at home and abroad – was below 60%. The biggest success among its three diversification initiatives was in the sale of its core cable products to new customers: to makers of railway signalling equipment, for example, and builders of rapid mass transport systems. Altogether sales of its traditional products to new customers accounted for over 30% of total turnover in 1990. Sales of the co-op's new building material products, its plastic pipes and plastic window frames, had already climbed to over 10% of turnover. Sales of plastic fibre optics in 1990 were still tiny, great though their future prospects were widely taken to be. Meanwhile ACOME continued over the 1980s to sustain its reputation for innovative technical work.

The 1990s have not presented ACOME with easy market conditions and this shows up in the record of the business. Employment in the parent company has barely changed, while cash flow, turnover and profit have all declined. Investment, however, has continued apace with new factories at Mortain for optical cable (1992) and wiring for automobiles (1994).

With the French market depressed, especially for public sector telecommunications, exports accounted for 16% of turnover by 1994. This was up from 13% the previous year. By 1995 ACOME had offices in Spain, Portugal and Germany, as well as in several other regions of France itself. By the time this chapter was finally revised, ACOME was fulfilling export orders on a worldwide basis.

Product diversification has also continued. Building products – mainly PVC windows – accounted for 16% of turnover in 1994, a sharp rise on the 1990 figure.

Key Statistics: 1991–1995

	1991	1992	1993	1994	1995
Turnover (Ffrsbn)[1]	1.10	1.17	1.09	1.05	1.09
Net profit (Ffrsm)[2]	94	98	85	78	71
Cash flow (Ffrsm)[3]	174	187	170	145	110
Investment (Ffrsm)[2]	60	77	75	76	87
Employees[2]	1,021	1,021	1,030	1,029	n.a.

[1] Corrected for a constant commodity base price

[2] Parent business only

[3] From operations and investments

Finally, we look at some characteristics of ACOME's manpower and at human resources policy and experience: and thus approach the final section of this case study in which we will look at the enterprise not so much as a business, but as a co-op.

To begin with ACOME seems to operate at remarkably low rates of absenteeism, both in absolute and relative terms. It may be recalled that following Sr Cicognani's election to the presidency of La Ceramica, the absenteeism rate there gradually declined to a figure of around 6%. I remember hearing an estimate from someone concerned with these matters in the Mondragon Group to the effect that if absenteeism was kept down to only those cases which were fully justified, the figure should be around 2%. ACOME's figures fall between those achieved at La Ceramica by the time Sr Cicognani resigned and the minimum postulated to me in a conversation at Mondragon:

ACOME: Absenteeism

1987	3.44%	1992	3.53%
1988	4.02%	1993	3.61%
1989	3.36%	1994	3.41%

Rates of absenteeism are often the best available measure of workforce morale. ACOME's comparative success may perhaps owe something to its rural setting: convalescence after illness tends to be more rapid in the countryside. Yet these figures must be seen as evidence of unusually good relationships between shop-floor and management at ACOME, and of unusual shop-floor commitment to business success.

Two important features of ACOME's manpower policy were mentioned at the outset. The first is the extent to which the 'total compensation package' of the workforce consists not of basic wages and salaries but of other financial emoluments, in cash and/or otherwise, with a direct link to business performance. An excellent illustration of this is provided by the relevant data for the year 1989.

Pay and Other Financial Benefits in 1989

Total Expenditures & Allocations

A	Wages and salaries	FFrm 138.937
B	Locked in profit shares	FFrm 52.132
C	Cash profit shares	FFrm 17.446
D	Dividends on ACOME shares	FFrm 0.206

BCD as a percentage of A: 50%

The second feature of ACOME's manpower policy arrangements is the relative narrowness of its income differentials. The position is clearly illustrated if we look at data for the end of the 1980s. If we exclude the marginally different arrangements for those working on shift, there are just four different pay scales at ACOME, those for: executives; other managers; technicians; unskilled workers.

For the three years to 1989, those on the top scale were paid only slightly more than double those on the bottom scale. Although the figures had changed by the mid-1990s, the relationship was almost the same:

Salary (FFrs per month) and Wage Scales 1987-9

	Executives	Other Mgrs	Technicians	Unskilled
1987	19,761	12,643	10,682	8,641
1988	19,649	13,469	11,482	9,183
1989	20,419	14,066	11,835	10,097

Because of the rules governing financial benefits at ACOME other than basic pay, these numbers in fact understate the degree of compression between the highest and the lowest 'total compensation package' at ACOME. There is a limit to the extent that top salaries can be kept down if the services of top people are to be retained. Nevertheless, if only in contrast to what is typical of conventional capitalist industry in the west, these ACOME differentials suggest that if you want to develop solidarity between shop floor and management then a narrowing of differentials is probably a useful first step.

ACOME as a Co-operative Under French law those who work in production co-ops are substantially protected against abuse by narrow oligarchies which, according to the Webbs, are bound to destroy them, either as businesses or as genuine co-operatives. ACOME's statutes, as well as internal agreements negotiated between the elected board of directors and the elected Enterprise Committee, go even further.

This is most easily shown by comparing what is provided by French law and what is provided at ACOME, in respect of three most sensitive issues: membership, elections to the board of directors (or more exactly the Conseil d'Administration), and the distribution of profits.

Taking membership first, French law provides *some* protection against the exclusion of newcomers by an existing minority of members. It does so in two ways. First, as noted earlier, it lays down, without offering any definition, that membership must be substantial. Second it lays down a procedure such that, having completed a qualifying period of probation, newcomers must have the right to apply for membership. But it remains possible under the law for the existing members to reject such applications.

ACOME's statutes are much more robust about the rights to membership of those who work in the co-op. Indeed they turn that right into a duty. The relevant Article 12 of ACOME's statutes is quite unambiguous about the matter: 'Tout travailleur . . . employé dans l'entreprise depuis trois ans *doit* [emphasis added] présenter sa candidature au titre d'associé. Au défaut de présentation de sa candidature . . . l'interéssé sera réputé démissionaire de son emploi . . .'

In other words there is a normally an *obligation* to take up membership – on pain of ceasing to be employed in case of not doing so.

This is broadly the same rule, apart from the length of the probationary period, as that which applies in the Mondragon group.

In the case of rules governing election to the Conseil d'Administration, ACOME's statutes do no more than repeat what is required by French law. Article 16 simply lays down that at least two-thirds of the board members must be employees: 'Les deux tiers au moins des administrateurs doivent être employés de la Société.'

More interesting is what happens at ACOME in relation to the third of these highly sensitive issues: the distribution of any net profits. To begin with Article 31 simply follows what is required by the law: that as a first charge not less than 15% of any net profits must go to the legal reserve; that dividends must be paid on the co-operative shares at a fixed rate of interest (8.5%); and that an allocation of 25% of the same net profits must go 'à tous les travailleurs, associés ou non, employés dans la co-opérative'.

But then, and this is the point of particular significance, the article goes on to allow for the possibility that the co-op's board and the enterprise committee will reach agreements which will serve to increase from 25% to 50% the proportion of any net profits which go to *all* those employed; whether they are members of the co-op or not. And that is what has happened at ACOME

In short the co-operative arrangements at ACOME are such as to prevent either the political or the economic exploitation of 'outsiders' by a body of existing members. This is done by preventing the exclusion of outsiders and by providing that, with the small exception of dividends, entitlement to a share in profits must be equal for members and non-members alike. The specifics of ACOME's social idealism could hardly be more rigorous.

It is worth emphasising, since it is very different from what is provided in UK co-operative law, what happens in the event of a liquidation. The short answer is that the co-op's shareholders can take out no more than the nominal value on their share certificates; any balance left over, for example in those inalienable reserves, must go to some good cause or another. Finally, the entry cost for membership of the co-op is no more than nominal. The cost of the compulsory share to which co-op members must subscribe is 500 French francs, though the Articles provide that the figure could be dramatically increased to the equivalent of one year's salary should the Conseil d'Administration judge that to be necessary.

11

Leicester's Equity Shoes

Equity Shoes opened for business in July 1887, as the Leicester Co-operative Boot and Shoe Manufacturing Society Ltd, with a starting workforce of twenty-one and in rented premises on Friars Causeway. Growth in the early days came fast. By 1889 it had to move into a larger rented factory, on Leicester's Bede Street. By 1892 the profits and prospects of the business were thought to be sufficiently favourable to justify the purchase of a piece of land where the co-op's own factory could be built – on Western Road. The building was completed in 1895.

The business was still on the Western Road site when this case study was finally revised in mid-1996, though the original building has been extended, both horizontally and upwards. In 1964 the Western Road site was extended by the purchase of the next-door property, an old iron foundry – replaced by a warehouse and offices. To cope with increased demand during the Second World War, a second factory was acquired which was operational down to 1962. But what followed was the consolidation of manufacture back into the Western Road premises and the sale of the second factory.

More generally, and after that explosive beginning, it is the enduring and barely changing continuity of the business which has been its chief characteristic. The century old stability of its place of work has been matched, more or less, by an underlying stability in the numbers employed: at around 200. True employment climbed above 300 in the early years of this century and again in the mid-1930s; and seems to have briefly exceeded 400 during the period of the two factories after the Second World War. And it fell as low as 150 in the specially difficult trading conditions of the middle 1920s. In 1994 and 1995 the figures were 193 and 187 respectively.

The record of the co-op's first century exhibits a third stability: of product. At the very beginning, in the late 1880s, a decision was made to specialise in boots and shoes for women. And with the exception of the two World Wars, it has done so virtually ever since. In the late twentieth century Equity's output has become somewhat more specialised still: it has come to concentrate on boots and shoes in the middle market price range, and in the sizes designed for women with broader feet. This is said to be a market where changes of fashion come only rather slowly.

This stability makes Equity an example of a rather unusual economic phenomenon: of a business which has survived over a long period, and survived with considerable financial success as we shall see shortly, and with little or no change in its overall size. Perhaps indeed it provides us with a possible model for business success in a no growth world of the future.

Of course there have been *some* changes: in the technology of manufacture and, to a greater extent and over a crucial period, in the actual markets for women's shoes that have been supplied. In 1986, the centenary year, Mr S. W. Pepper, who had already been with the business for more than fifty years and was then its President, wrote a short history called *100 Years of Equity*. He was rightly keen to emphasise the achievement of technological modernisation and improvement. Comparing the mid-1980s with the period during and after the Second War when the business was operating two factories he wrote: 'Having kept abreast, and even ahead, of modern technology the factory is now producing one third more output with half the workforce . . .'

In other words labour productivity more than doubled over the forty years following the Second War. Though I have been unable to obtain statistics for a precise measurement, it seems likely that labour productivity has improved at least fivefold over the whole life of the business. By the standards of less artisanal branches of industry, the pace of technology change implied by those numbers is no doubt rather low. But the point to emphasise is that Equity managed to keep up with the pace of technology change at least well enough to stay in business. All but one of Britain's other boot and shoe making co-ops had gone out of business by the end of the 1980s; and so had the great majority of the smaller private independents of a conventional capitalist form. Equity's survival has been even more notable than its stability.

A key feature of the period since the late 1950s and without question its greatest business achievement, is to have detached itself from a near total sales dependence on the retail co-operative societies. This has meant moving from inside the protection of the co-operative movement as a whole, and successfully entering new markets at home and abroad. This switch of market direction was why, in the late 1950s, the corporate name of Equity Shoes was adopted in place of the original Leicester Co-operative Boot and Shoe Manufacturing Society. It was a major change, and not only in marketing terms, despite the fact that the co-op had used 'Equity' as a trade name since early days.

Already by the late 1950s demand from the retail co-ops had started a steady decline as the latter lost market share to conventional private capitalist competitors. A switch away from heavy dependence on their custom was a necessary condition of Equity's survival. In the late 1950s not more than 15% of total output was sold outside the co-operative movement; whereas in the early and middle 1990s less than 15% of the total was being sold to the retail co-ops.

Most surprising was Equity's export success. By the end of the 1960s the switch to new customers in the home market had already gone some distance. But as late as 1969, as much of 60% of total output was still being sold within the co-op movement. A little before the mid-1970s, Equity launched a big export drive. From just 1% of sales in 1972, exports rose to over 50% in 1980. It was an astonishing achievement; without question the greatest triumph in the whole most successful exercise of changing market direction. It was apparently very much attributable to one man: Frank Dean. He was appointed general manager in 1969 and died, quite suddenly and quite young, while still holding that position, in 1980. His success in switching to export markets deserves to be on the record:

Equity Shoes: Exports as a % of Sales 1972 to 1980

1972	1	1977	40
1973	n.a.	1978	40
1974	10	1979	49
1975	17	1980	52
1976	22		

Partly, no doubt, because of Mr Dean's death, but also because Equity by then had a strong customer base outside the co-op movement in the more profitable domestic market, the export percentage declined significantly during the 1980s. In the four years to 1990 exports averaged just 20% of total sales, though they had bounced back to about 25% by the mid-1990s.

Equity's export success in the 1970s may well have been the single most important factor in ensuring its survival. What is certain is that by the end of the 1980s it was one of only two surviving enterprises, among Britain's boot and shoe manufacturing businesses, which was registered, despite its changed name, as a co-operative production society. According to G. D. H. Cole there were as many as twenty of these ventures in the late 1890s; and as many as nine at the outbreak of the Second World War. According to the then Ministry of Labour, four were still trading, Equity Shoes and three others, in 1973. (The other large survivor in the mid-1990s was NPS Shoes, which built its continued success on the fashion for Doc Martens.)

In 1997 Equity Shoes was comfortably into the twelfth decade of its corporate life. The number of people who worked there, 185 according to the 1998 annual accounts, was close to what it had been one hundred years before. On the other hand, because of intensifying 'global market' competition, the going was much tougher over the six years following 1990 than it had been over the previous six. A good measure of the harsher competitive climate is supplied by the amount of profit distributed annually to employees. We shall look at some exact numbers in the second half of this case study. But in round figures, close to £350,000 was distributed to employees in 1990. The corresponding figure in 1996 was barely over £50,000. True, the biggest single fall was between 1990 and 1991, when the profit distribution was only marginally above £200,000. But the downward trend was continuous right through to 1996.

The Co-operative and Local Setting The British co-operative environment, into which the business which later became Equity Shoes launched itself in the late 1880s, differed in one major respect from the counterparts in Italy and France. In Britain the consumer co-ops and the Co-operative Wholesale Society (CWS), which they owned, were overwhelmingly dominant. In 1903, when the number of Britain's production co-ops was just over 100 and around its all time peak, the corresponding number of consumer societies was peaking at 1,455 (Cole). In both France and Italy the relative numbers were much less unequal; and the relative influence of the production co-ops in those countries was therefore significantly greater. We may imagine that even by the turn of the century the national institutions in France and Italy could offer useful support services to individual production societies. And we may suppose that that was true notwithstanding the difference between the relevant national institutions in those two countries. In France the production co-ops could look for help to their own organisation: the Confédération des SCOPs; whereas in Italy the National body, the Lega, was, of course, responsible for supplying support to co-operatives of all kinds.

It is true that in 1882 Britain's production co-ops established their own representative and support institution: the Co-operative Productive Federation (CPF). It is also true that the Leicester Co-operative Boot and Shoe Manufacturing Society became a CPF member very early. But it is rather doubtful whether either then or later the CPF could offer any substantial resources. In terms of what might be called supportive political institutions, the new co-operative venture in Leicester must have been pretty much on its own when it opened for business in 1887. And the same has probably been true, if only more so, since then. Indeed, given its relative strength and enduring survival, what became Equity Shoes had probably given more to the CPF than anything it had received when the latter finally folded up. It was 'absorbed' into Britain's central co-operative body, the Co-operative Union, at the end of the 1970s. For many years before it succumbed, Mr S. W. Pepper, the former Equity President, held the part-time post of the CPF's general secretary.

There is also the point that when the future Equity opened for business, there was a real disagreement of substance between Britain's consumer societies and the CPF. The former insisted on consumer co-operation to the point of rejecting any worker, or more precisely any employee, membership in their co-operative societies. Neither in the retail societies nor in the CWS, which they owned, was any employee membership permitted. Furthermore, inside the latter, employee membership, and with it any employee participation in either control or profits, was comprehensively forbidden. This applied not only in respect of its wholesaling but also of its production activities, which had already become important.

This key disagreement of co-operative doctrine, however fiercely debated in the 1870s and 1880s, may seem rather remote from the world of the late twentieth century. I have argued elsewhere that that is not so. But however that may be, the disagreement is highly germane to the story of what later became Equity Shoes. For, according to Mr Pepper's history, it was the occasion of the strike which in turn led directly to the establishment of the co-op. He puts it in the very first paragraph of his account:

> In 1886 the workers in a Leicester Shoe Factory thought they would receive a fair share of the profit they had helped to create, and that this share would be an incentive to make them redouble their efforts and work with renewed energy. The Management, however, thought otherwise, and there was much bitterness resulting in a strike.

I have quoted Mr Pepper verbatim because a different source offers something rather different as the cause of that 1886 strike. Mavis Kirkham included Equity Shoes as one of three case studies in a dissertation called *Industrial Producer Co-operation in Great Britain* which she submitted to Sheffield University for her MA in 1973:

> In 1886 the boot trade in Leicester was very depressed, and many disputes were in progress. Most of these disputes were over piecework rates, and they generally resulted in the disputed work being put out at lower rates either to outworkers or to country factories ... This was the cause of the CWS strike, which led to a long and unfruitful dispute.

Even if Ms Kirkham's account is correct, Mr Pepper's serves to remind us of the disagreement between the production and consumer co-ops about employee membership and thus about employee profit-sharing and participation in control.

Whichever account is preferred, the environment into which the new boot and shoe co-op was born in Leicester in the late 1880s was not very supportive. On the contrary, because of the ideological disagreement, and because of the relative weakness of the production co-ops as a whole, the new venture was very much on its own. However, any ideological hostility to the new venture of the retail consumer co-operatives was far outweighed by what they could and did offer to it: access to their semi-protected markets. As we saw earlier, what became Equity Shoes was almost totally dependent on those markets – if we exclude government contract work making army boots during two World Wars – for its first seventy years. Some would argue that Equity Shoes might be stronger today if it had started to reduce its dependence on those co-operative markets rather earlier than it did. But early on, the new venture enjoyed enormous benefits as a result of having access to those markets: both at the start of its life and for many years thereafter.

Indeed, G. D. H. Cole made this point generally about the experience of Britain's industrial co-ops up to that time. He also put it in harsher terms which call into question the genuineness of the independence which these ventures enjoyed: 'In effect', he wrote in 1945, 'Industrial Co-operation among producers exists in Great Britain only as an adjunct to the Consumers' Movement, on which it entirely depends.'

We can conclude this discussion with two final points about the local and cultural environment.

The first is about geography. Leicester in one of the main towns of Britain's East Midlands. It was in this region that a majority of Britain's new production co-ops, those which sprang up in the last quarter of the nineteenth century, were concentrated. At least since the middle of the last century much of Britain's boot and shoe manufacture has also been centred in the area.

Thus the Leicester Co-operative Boot and Shoe Manufacturing Society Ltd would have found in its neighbourhood a number of co-operatives already active in the same line of business when it started to trade in 1887. Given that all were supplying the same market – the retail co-ops – that may seem to have had disadvantages as well as benefits. But any competitive disadvantage was almost certainly outweighed by the psychological gain of knowing that others were engaged in similar pioneering endeavours. It seems too that there was often at least token financial support between these boot and shoe co-ops, through the mechanism of small cross shareholdings. Mavis Kirkham cites more than one example.

I am also indebted to Ms Kirkham for the second and final point about this East Midlands environment. She reminds us that it was something of a centre of working class non-conformists. Wesley was born not far away in Lincolnshire; and the centre of Bunyan's activities, in Bedford, is not far away either. There were almost certainly advantages for the new co-op in having a high proportion of non-conformists among its workforce. For they are well known for a combination of hard work, abstinence from alcohol, and thrift.

Equity as a Business since 1980 Equity's chief business virtue both down to the late 1950s and subsequently was probably thrift. True, there are a few years in the record when the business showed a loss. But for the rest, after providing for any necessary investment, a large part of annual profits have invariably been put to reserve. According to Ms Kirkham, the co-op's reserves on deposit with what was then the bank of the CWS had reached nearly £30,000 by 1921: some £1.5m in today's money. By 1995, its reserves had trisen to £4.5m. If a business maintains a policy of continuous thrift, as this has, then accumulated reserves are bound to go on rising.

The main pay-off of this policy of thrift was to strengthen Equity's capacity to survive. It has provided the resources for Equity to keep abreast of technology and, when the time came, to switch away from customers in the protected world of the retail co-operative societies, and gain access to new markets, especially export markets, from the late 1950s onwards.

Perhaps the most eye-catching feature of the business record during the 1980s was Equity's ability to combine a significant profit share for its workforce and a continuation of its old habits of thrift with a consequent steady build up in its general reserve.

Equity Shoes: Profit Shares and Reserves

	Profit Share % *	General Reserve £m
1982	15	1.67
1983	22	1.87
1984	25	2.09
1985	25	2.35
1986	23	2.57
1987	15	2.92
1988	23	3.28
1989	21	3.59
1990	21	3.93
1991	12	4.14
1995	6	4.50
1996 [estimated]	3	n. a.

*% of wages and salaries

Averaged over the ten years down to 1991, the annual bonus amounted to just over 20% on top of wages and salaries, which were not less than current market rates. This is slightly higher than the average for the annual partners' bonus at John Lewis over the same ten years. In the light of the steady and uninterrupted increase over the same period in Equity's General Reserve, the rate of profit share can scarcely be criticised as extravagant. It is also worth emphasising a point made earlier: the sharp reduction in 1991, a year when profits fell.

Expressed as a percentage of Equity's value added, the profit shares of the ten years to 1991 are probably more or less in line with the average dividend payouts to their shareholders by the quoted companies over the same period. Looked at in that way we see the essential character of these profit shares at Equity Shoes: as the main mechanism for distributing the capital income of the business. Interest on the shares by contrast was low.

Equity Shoes: Profit Distribution

	1996	1995	1991	1990
	£	£	£	£
Share of profit to employees	50,271	100,690	200,916	338,840
National Insurance on above	5,128	10,271	20,892	35,409
Interest on shares at 5%	316	312	337	337
Interest on shares at 2 ½%	154	155	167	167

As we have just seen these profit distributions have gone along in step with an ever-increasing accumulation of Equity's general reserve. And we can reinforce that point by setting out the figures for the profits which were retained in the business in 1990 and 1991 after providing for tax:

Equity Shoes: Retained Profit

1991	1990
£203,206	£343,943

So the charge that Equity Shoes has been recklessly consuming its profits, eating its seed corn, simply cannot be sustained – whatever may be true of, for example, self-managed businesses in the former Yugoslavia. Any lingering doubts about Equity on that score can be finally demolished by a look at the balance sheet. For that shows that, far from eating its seed corn, the business has been building up a mountain of cash:

Equity Shoes: Balance Sheet Summary

£	1996	1995	1991
Fixed Assets	881,426	865,796	940,588
Current Assets	4,388,813	4,315,288	3,955,328
Current Liabilities	(650,961)	(580,768)	(646,806)
Net Current Assets	3,737,852	3,734,502	3,308,522
Provisions	(55,800)	(73,400)	(58,047)
Total Net Assets	4,563,488	4,526,898	4,191,063

The total of cash in Equity's current assets was £1.4m in 1991 and £1.25m in 1995. Both figures had fallen in the previous twelve months as a result of an increase in stocks and work in progress. At least on the margin, the business was coping with difficult trading conditions by increasing its inventory of finished goods: to be sold when trade starts to pick up. For unlike many of its competitors in the shoe trade there is no serious doubt that Equity can survive recessions without redundancies. Essentially, it is able to do that because of the great strength of its balance sheet. The 1995 Annual Report has this to say about the enduring reality of recession and Equity's ability to cope: 'Although the shoe industry is very depressed, we the Board of Management, feel that we can maintain our market share in both home and export markets.'

For what it is worth, the 1996 report also expresses cautious optimism about the future despite a continuation of manifestly difficult trading conditions. The harshness of the market situation is perhaps best shown by the sharp decline between 1995 and 1996 in the share of profits distributed to employees as shown in the earlier table, thus continuing a trend which had started as early as 1991. Compared with the position in the 1980s, market conditions for the five years down to the end of 1996 seem indeed to have been so different, and to have gone on for so long, that readers may doubt whether it makes sense to see the industry as just 'very depressed', in the words of the 1995 annual report. Are we also perhaps dealing with the effects of a truly global competition?

Be that as it may, its strong balance sheet confers a specific trading advantage on Equity Shoes in the highly competitive market for women's footwear. Its financial strength enables it to carry a complete range of stock at all times: small boot and shoe retailers can pick up the phone, place a small order, and expect immediate delivery.

Against the view that worker-led businesses tend to consume their seed corn, some academic economists have recently argued that they have a tendency to build up cash reserves (see e.g. Estrin & Jones, *1995*). The argument is that these businesses prefer security to expansion and tend to settle for zero growth. That seems to be a fair way of looking at Equity's record, both over a century and over the decade to the early 1990s. The business has shown remarkable thrift: derived perhaps in part from the old non-conformist culture of working people in the East Midlands. But the fruits of that thrift have mainly been used not to build a larger business but to ensure the survival of the one which exists. Moreover, given the state of the balance sheet what may need explaining is not why Equity has chosen not to expand; but why it has eschewed liquidation. We will look again at that point in the final section on Equity as a co-operative.

But before doing that it is surely worth pointing to the contrast between the policies of stability which have characterised the business record of Equity shoes, and the policies of expansion at the Italian and French worker-led enterprises which we looked at earlier. If the academics are claiming that there is an almost inescapable link between no growth policies and worker-led enterprises, the evidence from mainland Europe suggests that they are surely wrong. What happens in any particular case will typically depend on an array of contingent factors: on the personalities of the leaders, on the corporate culture, and on the objective opportunities for expansion.

Equity Shoes as a Co-operative With one major proviso, the co-operative arrangements as they have evolved over the years at Equity Shoes are in line with good, if not best, practice and seem to be working well. The business is governed by an elected board which appoints and overseas the top management, but does not normally interfere with day-to-day managerial activity. On the financial side, as we saw a moment ago, such profits as are distributed go overwhelmingly to Equity's employees. Third, there is no 'democratic deficit': all permanent and full-time employees are required to become members and do so by subscribing for five £1 shares.

But the proviso is important – or at least potentially so. Because of a combination of Britain's co-operative law and the strength of its balance sheet, Equity is vulnerable to a move by its own shareholders to put it into liquidation. Moreover Equity has non-employee as well as employee shareholders. In a decision on whether or not to go into liquidation the votes of the former would be counted alongside those of the latter. The balance of voting strength as between employee and non-employee members is, of course, subject to continuous change on the margin; and information about it is rightly kept close. But it is known that the total weight of the non-employee vote is considerable.

Given Equity's remarkably strong balance sheet, Britain's co-operative law supplies a powerful motive for a decision to liquidate: especially but not exclusively to its non-employee members. That is because the law provides that only in a liquidation do shares in a co-operative enjoy a value related to its net balance sheet assets. In all other circumstances co-operative shares have no more than the nominal value for which they were originally purchased: in the case of Equity's shares, just £1.

Using Equity's 1995 balance sheet at the end of November 1991, it seems likely that each of its 8,500 £1 shares then in issue would have value of about £450 in the event of liquidation. By 1995 the value was close on £550. And that calculation assumes no premium over book values. It is easy to see that the prospect of such capital gains might well test the commitment of even the most dedicated of Equity's co-operative shareholders, and not only that of its non-employee shareholders. The financial incentive to vote for a liquidation is almost as clear cut for employee shareholders who are approaching retirement as it is for their non-employee counterparts. A significant proportion of Britain's former production co-operatives which have gone out of business since the Second World War have gone into voluntary liquidation precisely for the reasons which apply to Equity – i.e. that the co-operative shareholders can then take a real equity value rather than simply a nominal value out of the business.

Because of the way that this provision of British co-operative law operates, the more successful a business like Equity becomes, the greater is the incentive to choose self liquidation. And that is even more so when the business, again like Equity, has consistently followed a prudent and 'nonconformist' policy of thrift. The relevant provisions of co-operative law in France and Italy are quite different. In those two countries the shareholders in successful co-operatives are not faced with the same dilemma. For in the event of liquidation they still receive no more than the nominal value of their shares. I return to this question briefly at the end.

It remains to spell out the co-operative arrangements which have evolved at Equity. In the early 1970s when she did her research, Mavis Kirkham found that there were two 'ways up' in Equity. One was by election to the board; and the second by appointment to a junior position of management. By convention, though not apparently by rule, board members who accepted managerial appointments resigned their board membership.

Elected by the co-op's shareholder members, the 'board' was called the 'committee' before 1962. Including an elected president, it has nine members who serve for two years and retire annually by rotation.

The board appoints, and may dismiss, the chief executive of Equity who is called simply the manager. Its essential duty is to oversee the manager and the subordinate members of the management team, and the life and prospects of the business. Compared with the board of a conventional company the main differences are two. Equity's board is a wholly non-executive or 'lay' board; and only employees, and among them non-management employees, are eligible for election to it.

Within reasonable limits the manager and his team are left to run the company and manage it on a day to day basis. In effect, though not in law, the board functions like a supervisory board in Germany rather than like an executive board in the UK.

In recent times this arrangement seems to have worked well, at least in part because of an enlightened self-denial on the part of the elected board: in effect it has adopted a policy of non-interference with day to day management. But, as Mavis Kirkham makes clear, the system has not always worked smoothly. Indeed she reported that from the starting date in 1887 down to the early 1970s only one of Equity's managers had left office on speaking terms with its elected board. The co-op's founders and their successors were pioneers in the whole project of self-governing businesses. Even when Mavis Kirkham wrote her thesis in the early 1970s the distinction between a supervisory board and an executive management was not well known. In effect the men and women at Equity Shoes have found their own way to that distinction, with little help from anyone outside. With hindsight it may be easy to see

that there must be two separate power centres in a democratic
and self-governing business. These two centres must have separate
functions (or they will quarrel); and those separate functions must
be those of management and supervision, including supervision of
management, respectively. But these are 'musts' of best practice,
not 'musts' either of manifest logic or of Mosaic law – and not
evident to anyone in the 1880s when the Leicester Co-operative
Boot and Shoe Manufacturing Society was established. So for many
years there were quarrels. What is more notable is how the costs of
these quarrels were contained, and how responsibilities eventually
came to be divided between board and management as they are
today, and how that came to be accepted as reasonable.

What may still be below modern best practice at Equity is
employee participation *below* the level of the elected board and top
management: at levels of their own jobs where, through their
specialised knowledge, employees can almost certainly contribute
most to improved performance. On the other hand, given its
co-operative form of government, and the economic incentives of
its workforce, the business is specially well placed to achieve
substantial performance improvements in this way.

Like other aspects of Equity's life as a co-operative the financial
incentives have also evolved. When the business first started to
trade, a 20% share of profits went to the retail co-operatives stores
through which all, or most, of its output was sold. Later that figure
was increased to 40%. At various times percentages of profits have
been earmarked otherwise than for the employees of the business as
a whole. For example, the allocations at the beginning included
12% to the committee of management (now the board) and 5% to
education.

However, in the early and middle 1990s, and for many years
before that, virtually all the profits distributed by the business have
gone to its employees and have been divided in proportion to their
rates of pay. Here too it may be said what has evolved at Equity is
very much in line with best practice: essentially identical with the
arrangements which have evolved at the John Lewis Partnership.
Indeed, these annual profit distributions of 20% or more in buoyant
market conditions give those shareholders who are also employees
at least some incentive not to liquidate the business.

And yet ... It is impossible to rule out the risk that, in the
absence of appropriate change in the ownership arrangements,

Equity's shareholders will be faced sooner or later with an offer they cannot refuse. It is not clear to me that existing co-operative law in the UK offers any reliable protection against that happening. On the other hand, if the ownership of the main balance sheet assets could be transferred, without excessive tax penalties, to an employee trust, that might perhaps offer a stronger protection against a collective decision to liquidate.

I2

Employee Ownership by Benefaction

A minority of conventional capitalists have long chosen to conduct their affairs in what may be called worker friendly ways: at least since Robert Owen pioneered humane employment methods at his textile mills in New Lanark early in the last century. Of course they have been able to do that only within the limits imposed by the need to survive in a competitive market. And of course, at the other end of the scale, even the most worker unfriendly among the captains of business have had to consider employee welfare at least to the minimum point of being able to recruit hands to work for them. Still, the difference of regime as between the two extremes has been wide. Moreover, some differences have persisted notwithstanding the advances in the welfare of working people achieved by progressive governments and trade unions. The good employer has simply kept ahead of the field.

To avoid any misunderstanding, I should make clear that the adjective 'good' in the phrase 'good employer' does not necessarily imply any attribution of moral or selfless purpose. Those captains of business who have introduced enlightened policies for employee welfare may have done so with the main aim of increasing profit. Given what we now know about 'X' efficiency, such a strategy may well have been far from wrong-headed. On the other hand, enlightened captains of business have been influenced by a wide range of considerations. At least that seems to be a plausible inference from the numbers of Quakers among them in Britain: the chocolate-making Rowntrees, Cadburys and Frys in the nineteenth and twentieth centuries; the Darby family and their progressive ironworks in the eighteenth; and indeed Ernest Bader in our own times.

Within this enlightened minority, a much smaller group has chosen to go a stage further: to relinquish conventional capitalist ownership and replace it with something else. That 'something else' has taken a variety of forms. Strictly, it is not true to claim that what has replaced conventional capitalist ownership in these cases has always been employee ownership of one kind or another. For example, in the case of the Carl-Zeiss-Stiftung, the German optical instrument and scientific glass-making business, its leaders have always insisted that what they have is a form of impersonal ownership. Readers will have to decide for themselves whether the differences at Carl Zeiss are sufficient for it to constitute a separate species. For the rough-and-ready purposes of this book it seems reasonable to classify it alongside Britain's John Lewis and Baxi Partnerships. For in all three the control of the business is fundamentally collective: exercised by an employee trust in the two British cases and by an endowed Foundation, or '*Stiftung*', in the case of Carl Zeiss.

Whether or not these three can properly be classified as examples of employee ownership, there can be no dispute about the benefaction or bounty element in the transition from their original to their present ownership. The *Stiftung* paid nothing for the Carl Zeiss optical business. In 1891 the firm was simply passed over as a gift by Dr Ernst Abbe, who had become its sole owner on the death of the founder three years before. In the case of both John Lewis and Baxi their former owners received a consideration when ownership was acquired by the two employee trusts; but in each case the payment was well below what would have been a market price, especially in the case of Baxi.

These three are not the only examples. La Ceramica was given to its employees by the Bucci family as long ago as 1873, a pattern which can be traced elsewhere among Italy's relatively large population of workers' co-ops. Among the workers' co-ops in today's France there may well be more than a hundred small businesses which started their lives as conventional private capitalist companies and were later sold to their employees at a discount by the retiring former owners. I have left these French and Italian co-ops out of this section partly because of their different legal form and partly because, notwithstanding their capitalist origins, they have typically assimilated a co-operative culture.

Left out for reasons of space are other cases in Britain and elsewhere. The Scott Bader Commonwealth is a good medium-sized undertaking, which employed over 600 people in 1994 manufacturing chemical resins near Northampton. It was given to the

Commonwealth, a charity set up to receive it, for little more than a nominal sum in a two-stage transaction starting in the early 1950s. The donor was its former private capitalist owner, Ernest Bader. The Commonwealth is essentially an employee trust by another name. It is a successful business in a highly competitive market. A number of smaller British undertakings have followed Ernest Bader's example over the last generation: their total may even have reached double figures by the early 1990s.

But the key point is that there are not all that many examples of 'employee ownership by benefaction'. The reason is obvious: only a rather small minority of successful private businessmen have been prepared to make the financial sacrifice which employee ownership by benefaction necessarily requires. And some of those who might have been tempted had they been sole owners have been prevented from doing so by the – perfectly reasonable – opposition of fellow shareholders.

Within these restricted numbers, the three selected for inclusion here are both the most substantial and among the most successful. I do not apologise for that choice. For it is a main aim of this book to put the case, which is still less than halfway accepted by Western governments, that it is in the public interest for these numbers to be increased. Taken together, the records of John Lewis, Zeiss and Baxi, are persuasive evidence to that effect. Moreover, we now know how the numbers may be increased: by introducing an appropriate set of tax reliefs. That has partly been done by the British government since the writing of this book was started. On the other hand neither the British nor the US government has yet introduced a set of tax reliefs tailored to the need to sustain employee ownership over time.

The records of John Lewis, Zeiss and Baxi are impressive. Like all other human institutions they are capable of indefinite improvement. Even without their other benefits, and especially the way in which they achieve a spread of wealth more equitable than that under conventional capitalism, I believe that their performance is very good.

Including their time as conventional capitalist undertakings, they have together racked up, as the Americans say, more than 400 business years; and nearly half of that is accounted for by their post-conventional capitalist existence. The age of Britain's now more·or less defunct 1945 generation of nationalised industries will soon look like the twinkling of an eye by comparison.

Looking at them together, rather than separately, it is also worth emphasising the way in which each pursued enlightened employee welfare policies from a date many years before their ownership change. The latter, when it came, can be seen as no more, but also no less, than a continuation and extension of earlier well-tried policies.

We said that good employers are motivated by a mixture of reasons. Can we also detect a mixture of reasons behind the decisions by their three owners to make what was not only an extension of previous policies but also a leap into the unknown world of non-conventional ownership? Defensive motives were certainly common to each: to protect the businesses against the risk that enlightened policies would be reversed by a new capitalist owner and, more basically, to protect the business, and its independence, against predatory attack and possible asset-stripping. Beyond that, though there was unquestionably *some* overlap of aim and vision, a number of separate motives and objectives were at work.

Can we detect, finally, any significant common features in their corporate government arrangements? The basic answer is 'yes'. In each of the three businesses the professional management is to some degree accountable either to a separate body representing interests other than its own, or to such representatives sitting together with executive directors in what amounts to a joint decision-making body, or both. At both Baxi and John Lewis the power of the professional management is partly checked in each of these two ways. The arrangements at Carl Zeiss are in many ways a special case. The fundamental form of its corporate government is best seen as a self-perpetuating oligarchy of top management. Yet the Zeiss management is also subject, under the well-known provisions of German corporate law, to a supervisory board.

The similarities between them can also be highlighted by comparing them with those in the co-operative category which we looked at in the first group of case studies. Despite checks on the power of top management, Zeiss, John Lewis and Baxi are unquestionably management-led. In this respect their employee ownership should be clearly distinguished from that of, say, Sacmi or Equity Shoes. For this reason, too, what is most distinctively problematic about them is unlikely to be the same as in the worker-led co-operatives. In the former it is the relationship between management and shopfloor which is most distinctively problematic. In the latter it is probably the quality of management and the availability of capital.

A NOTE ON SOURCES

With the exception of the pre-1939 Carl-Zeiss-Stiftung, and unless otherwise stated, all the business data comes originally from company records. For the Zeiss narrative I have relied heavily on a study, *The Carl-Zeiss-Stiftung: its First Hundred Years of Impersonal Ownership*, published by Partnership Research Ltd (PRL) in 1990. That in turn relies heavily, for its treatment of the early years of the Zeiss business, on an English translation of a German study by Felix Auerbach, published at the turn of the century. The Auerbach study was later translated into English by Siegfreid Paul and Frederic Cheshire under the title *The Zeiss Works and the Carl-Zeiss-Stiftung in Jena*. Its scope is well indicated by its subtitle: *Their Scientific, Technical and Sociological Development and Importance Described*. In relation to the early years, I have also been lucky enough to find a second source: a pamphlet written in German and published in Jena in 1919. Its title is *Das Arbeitsverhaltnis im Jenaer Zeisswerk*. I shall refer to it simply as the Jena pamphlet. For the details of the Stiftung's constitutional arrangements, I have been able to take advantage of versions in English published since the Second War by George Goyder.

For Baxi, I have been lucky enough to enjoy easy access to Philip Baxendale, the Baxi Partnership's president and a key member of its trustee body, former principal family shareholder and prime mover behind its 1983 move to employee ownership. Mr Baxendale was also, for ten years until 1995, the Chairman of Job Ownership Ltd (JOL), my own employer.

But in Baxi's case there is a further key point about my sources. I have relied heavily, and indeed partly followed word for word, a case study which I wrote for Partnership Research Ltd and which was published in 1993 with the title *The Winding Road to 'X' Efficiency: the First Ten Partnership Years at Baxi*.

The John Lewis Partnership has given rise to a substantial literature, including a number of books by its architect, and first Chairman, John Spedan Lewis. Among his writings, I have mainly relied on *Fairer Shares*. But the Partnership has also been the subject of two PRL studies, both written by Professor Keith Bradley and Professor Saul Estrin, and published in 1986 and 1988 respectively.

The second, *Does Employee Ownership Improve Company Performance ? The Case of the John Lewis Partnership*, differs mainly from the first in separating the results of the Partnership's Waitrose supermarkets from those of its department stores. About Bradley, who was Chairman of PRL until he resigned early in 1989, I should perhaps add that, together with Simon Taylor, he published a full-length book about John Lewis in 1992. *Business Performance in the Retail Sector: the Experience of the John Lewis Partnership* (Clarendon Press).

I must also declare an interest: in 1992, both JLP and Baxi had been giving financial support to my own employer, JOL, for a number of years, and Baxi was still doing so in 1998.

13

The Carl-Zeiss-Stiftung

INTRODUCTORY OVERVIEW

There are few who do not know the name of Zeiss, and many are those who, at the end of the war, acquired a pair of field glasses made in his works. These works are probably unique, and the system on which they are run almost ideal. Many thousands of hands are employed, and large profits are earned; yet not a penny goes to either owner or shareholder, for the simple reason that neither exists. They were abolished about thirty years ago, not by the modern method of strike and revolution, but by the sagacity and public spirit of a single man. The tale is worth telling and I am able to tell it in part as I had the good fortune two years ago to visit the beautiful, sleepy University town of Jena, which is the home of the works. *Malcolm Darling in the 'Irish Economist', July 1923**

Because of a combination of legend and drama, the history of Germany's Carl Zeiss optical instrument and glass works is one of a kind. The dramatic highlight was perhaps the forced removal to the West in June 1945 by the American military of key company personnel from their homes in Jena. What followed was the rebirth in West Germany of a new Zeiss optical works and a new Schott glass works in the second half of the 1940s. But at the same time the original businesses were also revived, albeit as state-owned undertakings, by the Soviet authorities in Jena. From then on, down to German reunification, there were in effect two rival 'Zeiss' groups: one with its headquarters at Oberkochen in what was then West Germany and the other in the German Democratic Republic. The two finally came together again in November 1991, when, with the agreement of all the interested parties, including the German privatisation agency (the 'Treuhand'), the West German group acquired what was in effect a controlling interest in the former East German Jena entities.

Since the reunification of the two companies in 1991,

*Later Sir Malcom, he had a notable career, mainly between the wars, in the Indian Civil Service.

developments have been dominated by restructuring. At Jena, the post-reunification Zeiss employed less than 5% of the pre-unification numbers. In the former West Germany too, at least in the optical parts of Zeiss, the workforce fell sharply. Between 1992 and 1996, several thousand jobs were lost there – over 20% of the workforce in the most affected division, where, according to one report, virtually everyone over fifty-five went into early retirement. Important steps were taken to re-integrate Jena into the larger Zeiss business. Altogether, during this period, the importance of employee ownership was dwarfed by other factors. (Summaries of developments at Jena since 1945 and in the whole group since 1991 are set out in appendices at the end of this chapter.)

And yet ... someone, some day, will surely think it worth writing a comparative history of the two Zeisses during that long period of more than four decades after the Second War when they existed separately – but in some sense side-by-side. I can think of nothing remotely similar in business history, let alone the history of employee ownership. The world of the two rival Zeiss Groups is vaguely reminiscent of that bygone political oddity, the Kingdom of the Two Sicilies; but the analogy cannot be pressed very far.

The formal reason for including Zeiss in this category of case studies is the origin of its ownership arrangements, which had survived for well over a century when this was written. They arose from an act of benefaction. But there are also persuasive other reasons for paying special attention to Zeiss. And here we come to the legend. For two decades or so before the First World War, and during the interwar period until the rise of Hitler overshadowed almost everything in Germany, excellent or otherwise, the Carl Zeiss works were looked upon and pointed to as a model both of business virtue and business success. Over those two periods its hold on the imagination of people of an earlier generation who thought seriously about reforming industry was similar to that exercised by Robert Owen's cotton mills at New Lanark in the early years of the nineteenth century, and by the Mondragon group in recent years. In all these three cases what has fascinated thinking people has been the same combination – of business success and a quite exceptional degree of workforce emancipation and welfare.

The Zeiss group has had two separate long periods of business growth and success: the first, based in Jena, ended in 1945 and the second followed the rebirth of the *Stiftung* in West Germany.

The most obvious measures of these successes are the numbers employed. At Jena, in 1945, admittedly swollen by wartime military demand for optical instruments, the total numbers appear to have been at least 15,000. In what had previously been West Germany the group numbers in September 1991 – i.e. just before the two Zeiss's came together – were a little over 32,000. As an indicator of its comparative performance in a set of highly competive world markets, the then West German Zeiss claimed in 1989 to be the world's second most important producer of optical instruments and the fourth most important of spectacle lenses. In retrospect, the position in 1991 may well be seen as the top of the employment curve. The sharp falls in the subsequent years arose from the business requirement to concentrate on products with the highest added value.

Similar forces explain the one major pre-1990s exception to the postwar success of Zeiss in the West: its camera-manufacturing business, Zeiss Ikon. This had first been pulled together by the group between the wars. It eventually resurfaced after the move to the West – but had to be closed down with heavy redundancies and at huge financial cost in 1981. Poor management and fierce Japanese competition are the main explanations for that disaster. Whether the dangers would have been spotted earlier, and a survival strategy attempted, if the business had been a conventional capitalist one are questions which cannot be objectively answered. We can only report that the disaster was contained. Its main indirect result was probably a growth rate in the seventies which was slower than it otherwise would have been: scarce resources had to be diverted to paying off borrowings associated with the Zeiss Ikon redundancies.

What about the Zeiss reputation for business virtue? Its foundation was laid in the last quarter of the nineteenth century. The business was years in advance of its time in the introduction of employee welfare schemes: for sick pay and holiday pay and, most striking of all, a scheme for relatively generous compensation in the event of forced redundancies. But that was not all. The 1890s saw the constitutional recognition of an elected works council with a right of access to top management. Moreover it was as early as 1891 that the two most momentous and irreversible steps were taken: ownership was transferred by Dr Ernst Abbe to the *Stiftung*, for which Dr Abbe supplied a written constitution. Embedded in that constitution are many of the social welfare and participative arrangements which Zeiss had earlier pioneered. It also commits the business to what may be called a 'scientific vocation'. With minor exceptions all the main provisions were still intact and in force 100 years later.

How far did the Zeiss which was reborn in the West after 1945 manage to recreate and sustain the earlier commitment to these enlightened policies? In the area of welfare its postwar practice inescapably became less unusual than it had been earlier. Other businesses caught up with policies and practices first introduced by Zeiss more than fifty years before.

More in question, anyway at the end of the 1980s, was top management's commitment to promote employee participation as a source of business strength. Between the start of 1987 and the middle of 1989, Zeiss was taken to an industrial tribunal by the employees' side of the business's top level consultative board on no less than five occasions. Each time the company lost.

Those conflicts hint at two points which apply as much to Zeiss Jena before 1945 as to the Zeiss which was later reborn in the west. The first is that, despite his pioneering recognition of a works council, the constitution written by Dr Abbe for the *Stiftung* is only minimally democratic: essentially the business is governed by a self-selecting oligarchy of top management. There is no democratic reserve power, as there is for example at John Lewis where a weighted majority of elected workforce representatives may in extreme circumstances remove the chief executive. Instead, in the case of the Carl-Zeiss-Stiftung there is a public official appointed by the *Land* (state government) and designated as the 'deputy' – a kind of constitutional monarch. Whatever else he believed in, Dr Abbe was no kind of industrial democrat.

That apart, Dr Abbe's constitutional arrangements have a number of exemplary features. One is the scientific vocation to which the business is committed. A second is a requirement to have regard to the welfare of the local community. And a third is a set of maximum income differentials – which have the consequence that Zeiss's top managers are probably paid some 20% less than they would be if working for a competitor. All these seem to be symptoms of enlightenment. They lie behind the judgement of George Goyder that the constitution and rules of the Carl-Zeiss-Stiftung could well be adopted as a model for company government in Britain and elsewhere in the advanced capitalist world. What he particularly liked was the commitment to objects which go beyond the obviously necessary one of making profits. For a business with the *Stiftung*'s objects, Goyder would have been inclined to say, profits are essentially a means and not an end.

Business Performance: Origins to 1945 Carl Zeiss's father owned a toyshop. But he was also blessed with a mechanical aptitude. At one time he acted as an instructor in fitting and turning to the Grand Duke Ferdinand I of Saxony. His son Carl evidently inherited these talents. After secondary school he served an apprenticeship in the mechanical and engineering trades; and spent time in Weimar, Stuttgart and Vienna. Carl Zeiss never enjoyed a university education: his formal training never went beyond that of a skilled journeyman, or '*meister*'.

In 1846 he opened, in the university town of Jena, what cannot have amounted to much more than a jobbing optical workshop. The translators of Felix Auerbach's study describe its output as having originally consisted of 'optical and other *philosophical* instruments' (emphasis added). In fact easily the most important products, from the start and for many years thereafter, were microscopes. The flourishing biology department at Jena University was an important source of demand. One of its most distinguished scientists, Jacob Schleiden, supplied Carl Zeiss with a testimonial to the quality of his products in 1857: 'Mr Zeiss has asked me for a recommendation; I really do not know why. My testimony can only be valuable for his optical instruments, and these no longer require a recommendation from anyone.'

A diagram at the back of the translation of Felix Auerbach's study records the number of 'microscope stands' sold annually. For 1847, the first full year of business, the number appears to be about twenty. It is no higher eleven years later in 1858. But thereafter there is a significant increase in each year down to 1866 when more than 200 were sold. In retrospect, that year was a milestone for a rather different reason. It marked the recruitment of Dr Ernst Abbe. At the time Dr Abbe had no special knowledge of optics. The subject matter of his doctoral thesis had been the mechanical equivalent of heat; and his lecturing at Jena University had covered mathematics, physics, and astronomy. But he could contribute a key intellectual asset to the business: his scientific training.

Some years before, Carl Zeiss had seen the need to put the production of his optical lenses on a more scientific basis and to rely less on trial and error. He had not himself the necessary theoretical knowledge and training to achieve that shift. What he had was a combination of the vision to see what was needed and the determination to persevere in the face of setbacks.

In 1868, two years after his appointment, Abbe introduced 'his method of microscope construction consisting in the complete theoretical determination beforehand of the required data': a manifest shift away from trial and error. About the same time the senior foreman at the works, August Lober, introduced a new and more successful method of testing lenses. In effect the optical works had been put on a firm scientific footing.

A gradual acceleration in the rate of growth of the business is reflected by some milestones in the production of its microscopes. Number 1,000 was produced in 1866, after the business had been trading for twenty years. Number 2,000 followed just seven years later, in September 1873, and only a further three years were needed before number 3,000 appeared. The benefits of Dr Abbe's presence were starting to work through.

But despite the gradual increase in the pace of growth, the progress of the business was held back throughout the 1870s by a technical and commercial obstacle: the existing manufacturers of optical glass were not interested in improving the quality of their products to meet the more exacting needs of the optical instrument makers. The technical requirements were already well known, but the manufacturers believed that an improvement in the quality of their output would turn out to be unprofitable. It was Ernst Abbe who saw the problem most clearly and felt about it most strongly. So much so that, as the translators of Felix Auerbach's study tell us:

> in a report on the state of microscopic optics, written ... in 1876, on the occasion of an exhibition of scientific apparatus in London ... he loudly bewailed the fact that the practical optician had at his disposal a fully developed theory and a thoroughly tested practice – everything in fact except suitable glasses for the construction of the necessary lenses.

It was this lament which eventually elicited a response from Otto Schott, who was to become the third pillar in the triumvirate on which Jena's linked optical and glass works were constructed. For his doctorate in Leipzig Schott had written his thesis on window glass. But in 1881, having read Abbe's paper on the non-existence of good quality optical glass, Schott took the crucial step of writing to him. A programme of experimental work, to their joint design, started soon afterwards. Schott moved to Jena in 1882, and the glass works which has carried his name ever since started trading in 1886. In the task of putting it into commission he was greatly assisted by Roderich Zeiss, Carl's son. The project further benefited from a substantial cash grant from the Education Ministry of the Prussian State.

In the same year, 1886, when the Schott works opened for business, microscope production by the optical works already exceeded 1,400 units annually – or 40% more in one year than the total output of the firm's first twenty years. It was about this time that the business made the transition from artisanal workshop operations to modern factory production: '. . . everything changed at once. The workshops became a factory which, instead of producing microscopical apparatus only, soon embraced the whole field of practical optics, constantly extending its operations in new directions.' (Auerbach)

The various new departments which sprang up alongside the original manufacture of microscopes included:
– the optical projection and photomicrographic department
– the photographic department
– the astronomical department
– the terrestrial telescope department
– the measuring instrument department

In effect over the last twenty years of the nineteenth century the business developed from being little more than an artisanal microscope maker's workshop into an integrated manufacturer of optical instruments and measuring equipment. With few exceptions, it produced in 1900, as in the early 1990s, a full range of the more sophisticated optical products of the day. For readers in the UK, the name Zeiss is most closely associated with binoculars – or double eye-piece field glasses. By the time Felix Auerbach wrote his study, in 1901, the numbers of binoculars manufactured and sold annually had already climbed to 10,000.

But the growth of the business, from the beginning of the last quarter of the nineteenth century down to the end of the First

World War, is probably best reflected in the employment statistics. The Jena pamphlet supplies a valuable series:

Zeiss Employment: 1877–1918

1877	36	1906	1610
1880	82	1908	2104
1885	240	1909	2576
1888	300	1910	2884
1890	440	1911	3476
1891	500	1912	4383
1895	615	1913	5141
1896	800	1915	6025
1898	923	1916	8430
1900	1114	1917	11043
1902	1333	1918	6540

The founder of the business, Carl Zeiss, died in 1888. As early as 1875 he had associated Dr Abbe in its ownership as co-proprietor. And his son, Dr Roderich Zeiss, had been brought in as a third financial partner. However, within a year of his father's death, Roderich decided to withdraw from the business leaving Dr Abbe as sole proprietor. The translators of Felix Auerbach's study allow themselves at this point an extended purple passage:

> Abbe was now sole proprietor ... The fruits of ... [his] short period of autocratic power are not great in number. They consisted of a single act only, but this was an act of such surprising grandeur, that nobody could have expected it to ripen under the leaden sky of modern industrial life. It was an act not only great in itself, but rich and fruitful to generations yet unborn, which will reap benefits derived from it. Abbe's achievement was the creation of the Carl-Zeiss-Stiftung, which he named after his late colleague, and to which, in 1891, he ceded all his proprietary rights, both in the Optical Works and in the Glass Works.

Otto Schott retained during his lifetime his part proprietary interest in the Glass Works; but that too passed not to his heirs but to the *Stiftung* on his death in the 1920s.

The table suggests that the new collective ownership arrangements did not inhibit business growth. The annual average increase in employment was more than twice as great in the ten years following the switch to *Stiftung* ownership as in the final ten years before it.

It remains to say a word about the business between the wars. Already, less than two months after the 1918 armistice, the workforce had been cut by almost half compared with 1917. It would be interesting to know whether those made redundant enjoyed the generous compensation terms laid down in the *Stiftung*'s statutes; or whether, because of *force majeure*, these had to be suspended: I have not been able to discover the answer.

There were, however, a number of British visitors to Jena between the wars just as there had been before 1914. The epigraph is quoted from one of them.

For the *Stiftung* during the depression we have a glimpse of Jena in 1931 in a note contributed by a British visitor to the journal *Co-Partnership*. He found that the optical and glass works were suffering less than conventionally-owned capitalist firms; and for a specific reason. They had saved cash flow by eliminating profit-related bonuses and were thus able to limit redundancies to below what they would otherwise have been. This is a defence mechanism widely used by employee-owned enterprises during downturns in the business cycle, at Mondragon for example, and indeed at John Lewis.

We may imagine that numbers started to increase again after Hitler came to power in 1933 and Germany started to re-arm. Goyder supplies valuable information about the effect of the Nazi regime on the *Stiftung* and its statutes:

> The changes introduced by the Nazis were of limited extent, but the independent and tolerant attitude of the [*Stiftung*] ... was undermined by the appointment of a Nazi deputy to supervise the company and by small significant changes in the articles. Article 56 which expressly forbids discrimination in making appointments ... was amended to make discrimination possible, and subsequently one of the company's managers with Jewish connections was dismissed. Appointments were in future to depend on 'a sense of duty in service' which might mean anything a Nazi Government wanted it to mean.

It is probably safe to assume that the numbers employed continued to go up during the 1930s and during the second war, as they had in the first. What happened next is mainly explained by the geography of Jena in relation to the position of the allied armies when Germany surrendered in the first week of May in 1945.

Second Period: 1945 to Reunification in 1991 The American army controlled the town of Jena when Grand Admiral Doenitz announced Germany's surrender in the first week of May 1945. On the other hand, according to the boundaries of the zones of occupation into which post-war Germany was initially divided, it fell some way inside the Russian Zone. As a result there was a brief interregnum of American occupation before the synchronised entry into Jena by the Russians, and the American withdrawal, which happened on 21 June.

Acting, presumably, on orders from higher up, an American air-force colonel set in motion an exodus to the West of key personnel from the optical and the glass works during the night of 18 June, just seventy-two hours before the Russian army was due to move in. Altogether a total of 127 people, including the four top managers and most of the top engineers and technicians, were moved westwards out of Jena in US trucks. The convoy carried with it much of the *Stiftung*'s intellectual capital, embodied in patents and drawings, as well as in the heads of those key personnel. There is no reason to believe that those who were moved to the West were given the opportunity of saying 'No thank you.' The piratical character of the whole set of events is also reflected in the final destination of many of the key papers: they ended up in the USA.

On arrival in the American zone of what was later to become West Germany, the refugees from Jena made an early start with the tasks of building up a new optical and glass works. The production of optical instruments began again at the small country town of Oberkochen, in the hills east of Stuttgart, as early as 1946. In the same year the manufacture of special glass was resumed on a site in the town of Zwiesel. In what follows we shall be mainly concerned with the rebuilding and growth in the west of the optical instrument side of the business. Yet the successful rebuilding of the optical glass works was an equally remarkable achievement, perhaps even more so. For only 40 of the 127 people who left Jena on the night of 18 June 1945 were glass works personnel. Moreover, because of its special raw material needs, the initial glass works site in Zwiesel proved to be less than fully satisfactory. The glass works only started production in what became its permanent home in the West, the town of Mainz, in 1952.

We get a glimpse of the reconstructed optical instrument operation at Oberkochen in the year 1950, when it was briefly visited by George Goyder. A former industrialist himself, Mr Goyder spent much of his later life thinking and writing about the best arrangements for the ownership and government of business. Until his death in January 1997 he was for many years an indefatigable admirer and advocate of all things Zeiss.

At the time of his 1950 visit, Goyder found that about 700 people were employed in the manufacture of optical instruments in Oberkochen. In other words the business was successfully re-established in its new home, and had already grown back to be of good medium size. A striking feature noted by Goyder was the age of two out of three in the top management team. Dr Bauersfeld, who combined the posts of Chairman and Director of Research and Development, was in his seventy-second year; and Dr Heinrichs, the Sales Director was in his seventieth. Both had been working with Zeiss since before the First World War. Only the third member of the top team was still relatively youthful – Dr Kuppenbender, whose responsibilities covered finance as well as production, was in his fiftieth year.

Goyder was told that there had never been a serious discussion of the case for rebuilding the business in a conventional capitalist form, or indeed on any other basis than that of the 'impersonal' ownership of the *Stiftung*. It seems that at least among those at Oberkochen who had come from Jena, there was an almost complete consensus that the original Stiftung statutes should be followed as closely as possible. Had they been abrogated, Goyder was told, many of the best workers would have left.

Perhaps there would have been a different outcome if the *Stiftung* had had trouble negotiating loans. But from Goyder's account that had not been the case. It seems that some time earlier Dr Kuppenbender had succeeded in negotiating a series of substantial loans from Dr Hermann Abs of West Germany's reconstituted central bank.

The 1950 figure of 700 employees had exploded to above 4,000 by 1957/58. It was an astonishing achievement of reconstruction. Even if it tells us nothing directly positive about the ownership and control arrangements of the *Stiftung*, it certainly appears to rule out a negative: that 'impersonal ownership' was incompatible with a renaissance in a new environment.

Employment at Oberkochen doubled again between 1957/58 and the late 1960s to around 8,000. It then fell to a low of around 7,000 at the end of the 1970s, before recovering in the later 1980s and rising to a peak of 8,144 in 1991. However, to put these numbers into perspective we need to introduce an important organisational distinction.

What is now called the Carl-Zeiss-Stiftung *Group* consists of businesses in two categories. There is an inner core of key businesses, directly owned by the *Stiftung* and subject, anyway in theory, to the whole array of its statutes and privileges. There is also what amounts to an 'outer circle' of more peripheral businesses. The latter are owned only indirectly by the *Stiftung*, and their ownership by it may be only partial. They are not normally subject to the statutes of the *Stiftung* nor do they enjoy its privileges. As between businesses of the inner core and outer circle there is a further important difference: at least in theory the position of the former is permanent and will continue, according to the Stiftung's statutes, for ever. By contrast the businesses in the outer circle come and go, through sale, acquisition or closure. About these latter there is a further point of detail that needs to be noted – they are associated either with the Carl Zeiss optical instrument business or the Schott optical glass business, rather than directly with the Carl-Zeiss-Stiftung Group as a whole. So, within the group as a whole, there is a Zeiss sub-group and a Schott sub-group.

The main businesses in the inner core are, of course, the Zeiss optical instrument business and the Schott optical glass undertaking. There is also a third smaller corporate entity inside the inner core of the Zeiss optical works: a specialised microscope-making business which was 'bequeathed' to the Stiftung by its former family owners between the wars and is located in Gottingen, about fifty miles from Hanover. In the post-war division of Germany, Gottingen found itself just to the west of the Russian zone. So there was no need for it to be transplanted.

The relevance of these organisational arrangements to the

postwar history of the group will become clear in a moment. Here, for the record, are the broken down employment numbers at the end of September 1991, i.e. just before the resumed involvement with Zeiss Jena in November 1991.

Entity	Employment
Zeiss Oberkochen inner core*	8,144
Zeiss sub group	14,624
(of which outside Germany)	2,958
Schott Mainz inner core	6,315
Schott sub group	17,758
(of which outside Germany	5,065
Grand Total: *Stiftung* group world wide	32,382

* Includes Gottingen microscope business

The distinction between the inner core and the outer circle is allowed for in Abbe's original statutes and had already become operational between the wars. It was used in the 1920s and 1930s when Zeiss pulled together a group of German camera manufacturers and merged them into a single entity as Zeiss Ikon. Zeiss Ikon was never brought into the inner core or directly owned by the *Stiftung*. It was always a subsidiary or outer circle business. It was kept at arm's length in this way mainly because of the potential costs of extending to its employees all the privileges enjoyed by those employed in the inner core undertakings; and, most important, so as not to have to face very high compensation costs in the event of redundancy.

Zeiss Ikon was closed in 1971 when, in the face of fierce competition from Japan, a decision was taken to withdraw from the manufacture of cameras for the mass consumer market. This was the most serious setback in the whole history of the group and its scale was enormous in both human and financial terms. Approximately 4,400 were made redundant and the total closure costs were over DM 300m in the money of that time. It is true that, with the exception of Polaroid, the manufacture of cameras for the mass consumer market has scarcely survived on any scale elsewhere in the West. Whether the problems could have been identified earlier and some kind of survival strategy devised is something we shall never know for sure.

One point about the episode which is not in doubt is that the costs of the disaster would have been much greater, perhaps fatally so, if Zeiss Ikon had been admitted into the inner core of businesses owned directly by the *Stiftung* and subject to its statutes and privileges. For in that case the compensation payable to those made redundant would have been much higher.

A second point is that the banks were persuaded without too much difficulty to lend the money necessary to cover the close-down costs. (Whether they also insisted on changes at the level of top management, I do not know.) The loans were later repaid out of the profits of the group over the following decade. The downturn of employment in the 1970s was no doubt partly caused by the shock of oil price increases and the resulting slow down of international economic growth. But the need to repay those borrowings was certainly also a factor.

That the banks were prepared to lend that money should come as no surprise. For whatever the problems of Zeiss Ikon, the banks were bound to acknowledge that by the end of the 1960s the two core businesses in the group were among the world's leaders in their respective branches of activity. Their growth over the 1950s and 1960s was sufficient evidence of their strength. The quality of their work is probably best attested by a stream of new products and processes for which Zeiss and Schott were responsible during those same two decades:

1950 – Zeiss automatic level
1951 – Schott immersion coating process
1953 – Zeiss surgical microscope
1955 – Zeiss photomicroscope with automatic exposure unit.
1956 – Zeiss/Schott anti-glare driving mirror
1957 – Zeiss light coagulator
1958 – Schott sintered glass to metal seals.
1960 – Zeiss aerial survey camera lens with correction for visible & infra red light
1961 – Zeiss electron microscope for the production of ortho-photographic maps
     – Schott development of sol-gel process for production of liquid glass.
1964   – Schott special glass fibre for fibre optic light guides.
1967   – Schott production of transplant glass ceramic with zero expansion

1968   – Schott 'Zerodur' glass ceramic with zero expansion: for telescope mirrors etc.

1969   – Zeiss scanning microscope photometer for cell research

Even to the layman this looks like a rather impressive list. Moreover, it seems strong in areas – medical technology, fibre-optics, glass ceramics, and photographic mapping for example – which were almost bound to increase in relative importance in the years ahead. They are also excellent evidence that the two core businesses remained faithful to the scientific vocation enjoined upon them by Ernest Abbe.

This stream of new products and processes continued with apparently no appreciable falling off during the difficult 1970s and on down into the last decade of the century. At the end of the 1980s, it was the proud claim of the top management of Oberkochen that 30% of sales consisted of products which had been brought to the market for the first time only in the previous three years. Behind all this has been a sustained high level of expenditure on research and development (R&D). Between 1973/74 and 1984/85 the R&D expenditure incurred by Zeiss in Oberkochen and Gottingen, taken together, never amounted to less than 8% of total sales and reached a peak of just over 10% at the end of the 1970s and in the early 1980s.

	Sales DMmil	R&D Expenditure DMmil	R&D as % of Sales
1973/74	422.9	40.7	9.6
1974/75	506.3	40.5	8.0
1975/76	516.4	43.6	8.5
1976/77	568.6	49.5	8.9
1977/78	600.3	56.1	9.3
1978/79	638.6	64.1	10.0
1979/80	716.6	73.0	10.2
1980/81	776.3	79.0	10.2
1981/82	837.8	80.5	9.6
1982/83	959.0	89.1	9.3
1983/84	1,041.9	100.8	9.7
1984/85	1,142.8	111.8	9.8

That there was no significant falling off in this R&D effort in the second half of the 1980s or early 1990s is suggested by the figure quoted in the annual report for 1990/91: expenditure on R&D for the twelve months to end-September 1991 was as high as 11% of sales. Though it is always possible to have too much of a good thing, it is hard to resist the hypothesis that expenditure in R&D was one of the keys, and perhaps the single most important one, to the sustained success of the Zeiss business down to the early 1990s. Corresponding R&D expenditures for Schott are typically less than half of those at Zeiss, probably because a substantial part of the output of Schott's essentially process work is sold not to third parties but to Zeiss. Schott's R&D expenditure in 1991/92 was 4.2% of sales.

Zeiss's R&D expenditures promote the improvement of its performance partly through the constant stream of new products to which they give rise. But they must also lie behind a rather different benefit: a continuous improvement in the labour productivity of the whole group of businesses associated with the Carl-Zeiss-Stiftung. This improvement is most clearly seen if we compare total employment in the group with sales expressed in constant (1987) prices:

Carl-Zeiss-Stiftung Group: Employment and Sales 1976/87

	Employment Nos	Sales in DMm
1976	28,123	2,458
1977	28,228	2,621
1978	29,272	2,742
1979	29,690	2,818
1980	30,651	3,001
1981	30,385	2,911
1982	29,724	2,999
1983	28,500	3,122
1984	29,606	3,477
1985	31,123	3,593
1986	31,649	3,718
1987	31,725	3,782

For the group as a whole and in round numbers the table shows a roughly 12% increase in employment against a roughly 50% increase in sales (at constant prices) over the eleven years down to 1987. The growth of labour productivity therefore averaged slightly more than 3% annually. That rate of improvement looks as if it was probably ahead of – and certainly not below – that of the average for West German manufacture at about that time. According to estimates of the OECD, the latter improved by an average of 2.7% annually between 1973 and 1985.

Turning to financial results, the first and most general point to highlight is that at least down to the early 1990s profits were not seen by management to be an appropriate measure of the group's financial performance. Indeed, before the problems of the middle and late 1990s, the management aim was *not* to maximise profits. In part that was because there are no shareholders demanding a return in the shape of dividends. But it also and more specifically reflects the fact that in the special circumstances of the group it used to be more rational to maximise, not profits, but net cash flow. That is because the only element within the cash flow which is liable to tax is the profit element. Of course it is important to avoid making a loss. But so long as that objective can be achieved, then the managers used to be content that profits should be scarcely more than nominal: they hardly averaged more than 1% of sales between 1981 and 1987.

We may contrast that figure with the evidently vigorous cash flow record of the business between the same two dates. Between 1981 and 1987 cash flow was in fact sufficient to cover all the group's investments and to add to its financial resources.

Group as a Whole: Cash Flow and Investment

	Cash Flow DMm	Investment DMm	Increased Financial Resources DMm
1982	172.2	152.0	20.2
1983	248.4	125.0	123.4
1984	297.5	207.0	90.5
1985	297.5	253.0	44.5
1986	273.8	262.0	11.8
1987	317.8	282.0	35.8

Given that profits were then no more than nominal, the two main elements in the positive cash flow are first, of course, depreciation and second – what may come as some surprise to UK readers – contributions to the group's private pension fund. This is clearly not the place for an extended digression either on

Germany's private pension funds in general or on those of Zeiss group in particular. But two key points are worth highlighting. The first is that under German law there is nothing to prevent a company from investing its entire pension fund in its own balance sheet and broadly speaking that has been the practice at Zeiss. Second and partly because, with only nominal profits, there has been no significant employee profit-sharing, the Zeiss workforce, including the management, has tended to take its 'partners' bonus' in the form of higher private pensions. So much so in fact that in the late 1980s and early 1990s there were apparently people who retired from the business and went on to draw more in total pension – adding the money from Zeiss to Germany's relatively generous state pension benefits – than in their final salaries. However it is understood that because of the tougher conditions faced by the company from 1992 onwards, the rules have since been modified and the levels of the Zeiss pensions somewhat reduced. We will come back to those changes briefly at the end.

Standing back from the detail, and using strictly business criteria, how should this record be judged?

The group seems to have made just one bad mistake: the Zeiss Ikon disaster. On the positive side, its sustained commitment to its scientific vocation seems to be the outstanding feature of this period. That commitment is reflected in the very high levels of R&D expenditure, in particular by the optical instrument side of the business. For it is this which was then seen as the key condition of the constant improvement of labour productivity, and the constant flow of new products and processes which stand out in this postwar record.

There is one qualification: the absence, or apparent absence, of human resource management policies of the kind designed to maximise shop-floor participation, and thus the contribution of the blue collar workforce to the process of continuous improvement. The absence of these policies may be linked to the evidence for some industrial relations conflict towards the end of the 1980s. These are discussed in the next section.

Self-Government, Welfare and Industrial Relations The eloquent tribute to the old (pre-1945) Zeiss works in the article by Malcolm Darling quoted in the epigraph had an arresting title: *The Zeiss Works, or What a Factory Should Be.*

In his review of the progressive features which he found in Jena, Darling singled out the compensation payments which the business was required to pay when its employees were involuntarily made redundant through no fault of their own:

A hundred years hence, when the history of the present factory system is finally written, the historian will assuredly speak of wage earners' almost universal liability to dismissal without compensation as a barbarity of an otherwise civilised age. All honour then to Ernst Abbe that he was one of the first to remedy the evil.

A tribute to Zeiss by William Temple, when Archbishop of York during the Second World War, is also worth rescuing from its oblivion in an out-of-print appendix. Temple, along with his friend from Rugby and Balliol, R. H. Tawney, spent some months in Jena before the First World War and the Zeiss and Schott works clearly made an impression upon him. For he remembered them in an appendix to his *Christianity and Social Order* which was first published in 1942. He is arguing for the proposition that 'every citizen should have a voice in the conduct of the business or industry [in which he or she works]', and he goes on:

The lack of any participation by labour in the conduct of the actual work of production is a manifest sign of the broken fellowship of our economic life. The ideal arrangement would be a revival of something like the medieval guilds on the basis of national charters. An alluring illustration of this was afforded by the Zeiss glass-works at Jena before 1914; I do not know what became of this admirable scheme and I hope it is flourishing still.

We can accept the Archbishop's use of the adjective 'admirable' without having to agree that there are very close similarities between the then arrangements at the Zeiss works and a medieval guild. But the main point of these Darling and Temple quotations is to show the impact which Jena's optical and glass works made on enlightened English visitors of an earlier generation.

In what follows the discussion will be confined to four topics:

1 The long series of progressive measures relating to employee welfare and employee participation introduced into the Zeiss works. Included in the series are some of the statutes of the *Stiftung*

which came into force in 1896. But the first measures date from much earlier: 1875.

2 The constitutional provisions of the *Stiftung* itself, especially those dealing with its aims and objects, its corporate government and the allocation of any profits or surplus.

3 The apparent thinking of Ernst Abbe which lies behind the *Stiftung* and its central provisions.

4 The human and industrial relations record of the Carl-Zeiss-Stiftung which was reborn in the West after 1945.

The first major measure of employee welfare was the introduction of a sickness scheme. It happened early – in 1875, when the business was still quite small, with a workforce of no more than 60. The main benefits were three: free medicine, free treatment by the employee's own doctor; and sick pay – at full rates for the first six weeks and half rates for the second six. The level of these rates was apparently fixed annually.

These sickness benefits were revised from time to time over the next thirty years, and no doubt also thereafter. Except to the extent that the scheme became partially contributory, the direction of change was towards making the arrangements more generous.

The first sickness schemes at Zeiss pre-date by more than a decade Bismarck's famous compulsory employee sickness insurance enacted in 1887. On the other hand, the first provisions at Zeiss for employee pensions seem to have coincided with the first Bismarckian legislation on this, also enacted in 1887.

A provision which is perhaps more like a constitutional liberty than a piece of employee welfare was introduced when Abbe codified a set of workshop rules for the first time in 1893. It was laid down that overtime could not be imposed by management but could only be voluntary. In the late 1980s employee representatives challenged the Zeiss management with breaking this rule. The challenge was upheld by the industrial court.

Apart from smaller benefits – like the introduction of medical inspections for apprentices and the opening of employee baths – there are a number of other significant welfare reforms contained in the detailed statutes of the Carl-Zeiss-Stiftung. These came into force in 1896. The most eye-catching and the one most in advance of its time was a provision that those made involuntarily redundant for economic (as opposed to disciplinary) reasons must be compensated with at least six months' pay.

A year later Abbe introduced another reform which, on paper at any rate, was as far ahead of its time as the provision for compensation in the event of forced redundancy: he extended constitutional recognition to a Permanent Workmen's Committee at the optical works and provided for its unimpeded access to top management. Unfortunately we know little or nothing about how this worked in practice. What we do know is that in the late 1980s top management was challenged in the industrial court about this provision too – and lost again.

We move on now from Zeiss's early welfare provisions – some pre-dating the *Stiftung* and its statutes, some actually embodied in the latter and some subsequent to it – to the Stiftung (the endowed foundation) itself. There were two separate stages in what happened after Ernst Abbe became sole owner of the optical instrument works and part owner, with Otto Schott, of the glass works in 1889. In that year he established the foundation and endowed it with limited financial resources from his own fortune. However at this first stage it had only a restricted role which was confined to the provision of support for Jena University. Only at a second stage, in 1891, did Abbe take his truly revolutionary step: the transfer to the Stiftung of his 100% ownership interest in the Zeiss works and his partial interest in Otto Schott's glass works.

Third, five years later in 1896, he laid down the statutes which were to govern the working of the *Stiftung* and provide it with a constitution. In the dry language of UK company law, the statutes may be seen as the memorandum and articles of association of the *Stiftung* itself and the businesses which it had come to own and control.

The control or government arrangements which Abbe provided for the Stiftung and the businesses under it are, and remained in 1996, those of a self-perpetuating oligarchy. The top management boards of the optical works and the glass works are the governments of those businesses and they choose their successors. The only qualification is that the state, originally the Grand Duchy of Saxony, and after the *Stiftung*'s rebirth in the west, the *Land* of Baden-Württemberg, appoints a kind of constitutional monarch, called the *Stiftungkommissar* or 'deputy'. The two top management boards must consult the 'deputy' on all important matters; and he or she is also required to ensure that the statutes of the *Stiftung* are obeyed. The two boards are linked by a provision of the statutes which lays down that one member of the management of the glass works must always be a member of the board of the optical works.

The 'deputy' chairs a so-called advisory council in both the Zeiss business and the Schott business. These can be seen as the Stiftung's counterparts to the supervisory boards which all German businesses of any size are required to establish. The employee representatives on these advisory boards are drawn in turn from the successor bodies to the 'permanent workmen's committee', first recognised by Dr Abbe in 1897.

But neither the office of the 'deputy' nor the existence of the advisory boards seriously modify the basic character of these arrangements of corporate government: that of a self-perpetuating oligarchy. There can be little doubt that that is what Abbe intended them to be.

What, then, are the aims and objects which the *Stiftung* and its governing boards of management are required to pursue? The answer is that, though Abbe recognised the need for economic success as a precondition of anything else, he laid the greatest emphasis on the *Stiftung*'s *scientific vocation* and, to an only slightly lesser degree, on its obligations to the local community of Jena. The language used about these objectives in the statutes is specific. The *Stiftung* is enjoined:

> To promote the general interests of the [optical and glass] branches of precise technical industry not only within the works . . . but outside it.
>
> To take part in organisations and measures designed for the public good of the working population of Jena and its immediate neighbourhood.
>
> To promote study in the natural and mathematical sciences both as regards research and teaching.

When it comes to the economic objectives of the *Stiftung*'s businesses the language of the statutes emphasises that neither the highest possible increase in 'net profits' nor 'working surpluses' should be seen as the main criterion of success: 'The *Stiftung*'s . . . business activity shall have as its object not so much the highest possible increase in net profits or working surpluses of its undertakings, as the increase in the economic net result which these undertakings are capable of undertaking for the employees of the

Stiftung, for the Stiftung itself as entrepreneur and with a view to its further development.' Moreover, under an earlier provision the Stiftung is required: 'To pay permanent regard to the economic security of the ... [optical and glass works] ... as well as the conservation and further development of their industrial labour organisation – as a source of subsistence for a large number of people and as an efficient member in the service of scientific and practical interests.'

How are resources to be allocated as between, for example, the 'economic security' of the business and the honouring of its commitments to its scientific vocation and the local community? The statutes supply extended and detailed guidance by specifying levels of reserves which must be achieved and maintained before substantial expenditures are made outside the business. In practice, anyway since its rebirth in the West, the *Stiftung* has honoured its commitment to its scientific vocation mainly, as we have seen, through its expenditures on research and development, and thus in ways which do not involve spending money outside the business. As for the commitment to the local community, this seems to have counted for less in Oberkochen and Mainz since the Second War than it did during the years at Jena which came before.

On the other hand the injunction in the statutes to pay attention to the 'economic net result' of the business rather than to the increase of profits or 'working surpluses' seems to have been followed fairly closely by the Zeiss management in the West since the war. As we saw earlier, attention was for many years focused more on aggregate cash flow than on the profit component within it; and that for the excellent reason that only the latter is subject to tax. It is also worth noting that more than once in his writings Dr Abbe expressed a marked lack of enthusiasm for profit-sharing schemes. His argument against them is a familiar one: that more or less regular profit shares come to be regarded by employees as part of their regular wage, and so there is a risk of resentment when they are not paid. (Though the argument is familiar so is the remedy: a programme of employee education.)

However, the fact is that in the post-war reincarnations of the Stiftung's businesses in the West, profit-sharing has not been an important feature: far, far less important than at either the John Lewis or the Baxi Partnerships, for example. However, generous pensions in the *Stiftung*'s core businesses partially compensate.

Even in 1990 and 1991, after some reductions in the 1980s, these could amount to 75% of final salary.

Nevertheless the contrast, and the absence of a strong profit-sharing tradition at Zeiss, is a matter of some importance. In choosing *not* to favour profit sharing, Zeiss may be denying itself the benefits of a valuable incentive. But that is what the founder intended.

One last and special provision of the *Stiftung*'s statutes must be noted. A maximum difference is specified between the remuneration of the top management and that, in effect, of a qualified man. The limit is set at a multiple of ten. In the West, since the Second War, its operational effect has been slightly loosened by applying it after rather than before tax. Its logic is obvious enough: to strengthen solidarity between management and non-management. There is a similar provision at John Lewis. At the end of the 1980s, top managers at Zeiss were apparently being paid about about 20% less than what they might have received elsewhere in Germany – not counting the possible benefits of arrangements like share options which would not have been available to them.

What sort of sense are we to make of Abbe's whole project: both the project of the *Stiftung* itself, with what he called its 'impersonal title of ownership', and the array of statutes with which he buttressed it? The best starting point is to recall the more defensive of his motives. Two passages from his writings give a clue. The first is from a letter to all employees in 1896, when the statutes of the *Stiftung* were being specified. Of the *Stiftung* itself he wrote of 'its guarantee of the continuance of the principles which have animated the firm since its inception'.

Five years before in a letter which set out to explain why the ownership of the business had been transferred to the Stiftung he used rather different language. But the main point is very much the same. He had made the ownership transfer. 'To enable me better to ensure that the present economic condition, and satisfactory administration ... shall, even in the distant future, be maintained more effectually than can in the long run be expected under private proprietorship, I have ... [transferred ownership to the *Stiftung*].'

However, it seems clear that, as well as these defensive motives, he had at least two more positive motives as well. Put crudely, one of these, surely, was to neutralise, by seeing off, what he had come to look upon as the objectionable powers of private capital.

Conversely he seems to have sought to confer on its employees something like genuine partners' rights in the business, but only in ways which would not destabilise management, and would not allow for the financial diminution or disposal of the undertaking.

Combining the two objectives we might say that the overarching aim of the whole project was to achieve the emancipation of the workforce and to do so mainly by neutralising much of the power of capital. That Dr Abbe was thinking on these lines is confirmed by a remark of his which was quoted to George Goyder on his visit to Oberkochen in 1950. As recalled by Dr Bauersfield, the then Chairman of the optical works, what Abbe had said was: 'The cock only crows when there is something to crow at.'

The interpretation offered by Dr Bauersfield of this somewhat oracular pronouncement was simple: he saw it as pointing to the need for 'removing the economic causes of differences between classes'; and thus as a way 'to get rid of the class war'. Looked at in this way the *Stiftung* may be rather more than just a device for protecting the business from the frailties and follies of personal proprietors in the future.

Finally, we need to emphasise what the *Stiftung* is not. It is not a device for distributing either ownership or power to employees. The power of capital may have been neutralised. But the capital itself is not distributed among the workforce nor are workers given the power to select their managers, still less to manage themselves. Felix Auerbach's study is emphatic about the way that the Zeiss arrangements differ from those of a co-op:

> In a productive co-operative society the usual practice is to attend to management matters . . . through the medium of an elected board, or committee; a mode of procedure which has been shown by experience to be extremely defective. This fortunately is not the case at the Optical Works; we say fortunately because, if it had been, none of the steps which during the last quarter of a century have made the business great would have been taken . . . The board of management of such a concern, if it is to be successful, must be independent of the will of the individual members of the society; it must be responsible only to the whole of them collectively. To correctly define the character of the Stiftung, the following limitation must therefore be introduced:

The Optical works is a production co-operative society only with respect to its economic interests, and not with regard to its administration and management.

It remains to discuss briefly the evidence for some industrial relations disharmony at Zeiss Oberkochen towards the end of the 1980s. But it should be made clear that the employees there appear to have no quarrel with either the fairness or the welfare rules of the business. The focus of disharmony has been rather different: on employees rights and liberties and issues of 'industrial democracy'.

The theoretical issue is between those who emphasise the management prerogatives of the Stiftung's statutes and the constitutional legitimacy of its self-perpetuating management oligarchy, and those who stress the rather different provisions which prescribe a measure of downward accountability, for example by virtue of Abbe's early recognition of the permanent workmen's committee, and indeed by virtue of Germany's co-determination laws.

Between 1987 and 1989 the Zeiss management was several times taken to an industrial tribunal by the employees' side of its top-level advisory council. The employee side won on each occasion. This gives some weight to criticism of top management by one of the advisory board's senior elected employee representatives that management's behaviour is at variance at least with the spirit of the industrial relations provisions of the constitution. In defence of its record, the management pointed out at the time that there had never been a strike at Zeiss – which was still true in 1996.

A more general point seems worth repeating in conclusion. Unlike what happens in the best employee-owned companies elsewhere, the Zeiss management has never tried to turn its workforce into genuine business partners or to make itself as accountable to the managed as is consistent with successful business. No doubt there are powerful historical factors which explain why this is so.

APPENDIX A: ZEISS JENA 1945 TO 1991

When George Goyder visited the Zeiss optical works at Oberkochen in 1950, his hosts supplied him with some brief items of intelligence about what had been happening in Jena since that American-organised exodus of key personnel in June 1945. He recorded the following points at the time:

The Russians, following the American example, had removed and transported off in an eastern direction 250 of the Stiftung's remaining key men in Jena.

They had also removed up to 95% of the actual physical 'works' from Jena, that is 95% of both the optical 'works' and the glass 'works'.

In 1950, i.e. at the time of Mr Goyder's Oberkochen visit, there were still 6,000 ex-*Stiftung* employees in Jena.

It is not clear at what date or in what stages, starting from the 5% of the optical and glass works *not* removed by the Russians, the plants in Jena were rebuilt and started trading again. What we know is that on 30 November 1948 there was a formal, legal change in the status of the former *Stiftung* business in Jena. The old entry in the town's commercial register was cancelled and the works were officially designated as the 'property of the people'. Twelve months later a new entry appeared in the register and the works became a *Volkseigner Betrieb* or 'People's Enterprise'.

From these early and not altogether promising beginnings, the former *Stiftung* business in Jena had become, by the end of the 1980s, the biggest and most famous state corporation in the GDR. Measured by employment numbers, they were also by the late 1980s far larger than the rival *Stiftung* group of Zeiss and Schott in the West. In 1988 Zeiss Jena was employing 69,000 people as against slightly less than 32,000 in the West. Moreover, it was exporting a higher proportion of its output (65% v. 51%) and the percentage of expenditure it devoted to R&D was also slightly ahead (12% v. just over 10%). But, as need hardly be said, when sales per employee were compared, the West German businesses were far ahead. At the free market exchange rate for the late 1980s, the output of the Western Zeiss was between four and five times more valuable than that of Zeiss Jena and thus the value of its output per employee was roughly ten times higher.

An article in the *Wall Street Journal* dated 12 January 1989 is the source for all the end-1980s statistics that I have just quoted. Of course the fall of the Berlin Wall was still some little way ahead in time, and the 1991 coming together of the two Zeisses was further away still. It is only with the benefit of hindsight that we can now fully appreciate the irony of a rather specific political judgement offered to the correspondent of the *Wall Street Journal* by the

GDR's Zeiss state corporation's general manager, Wolfgang Bierman: 'There is not need for *Perestroika* here.'

However, the duty of balance requires me to quote finally a point about the improving quality of the Zeiss Jena's product made by the same *Wall Street Journal* correspondent, Thomas F. O'Boyle, in the same article. He cited the opinion of a Zeiss microscope dealer in the USA who told him about the Jena microscopes: 'Ten years ago they weren't competitive. Now they are.'

APPENDIX B: AFTER REUNIFICATION: 1992–1996

Zeiss and Schott in Jena As against its final workforce numbers of 69,000 – admittedly spread all round the country – in the last days of the old GDR regime, the annual report of the *Stiftung* for the year to end-March 1995 gives a figure of just 2,237 people as being employed at Zeiss Jena. If the numbers at the Schott group's Jena operation, Janaer Glaswerk, are added in, then the total would still have been less than 3,000. And there were further declines over the period down to the summer of 1996 (when this chapter was finally revised). Altogether, the numbers employed by mid-1996 were less than two-thirds of the 4,000-strong workforce for which the *Stiftung* took main responsibility when the East-West coming together was agreed towards the end of 1991. Of that greatly reduced total, about three-quarters were working in the optical group and the balance in glass-related activity with Schott as parent.

For the citizenry of Jena the loss of jobs must have been painful. However, in May 1995 the parent undertaking appeared to increase its commitment to Zeiss Jena when it acquired the 49% of the Jena business's share capital previously owned by Jenoptik.

Moreover, the real content of this commitment had apparently been confirmed rather earlier. Responsibility for the entire microscope division of the business was shifted from Oberkochen to Jena in October 1994, a move which was followed in the autumn of 1995 by a similar shift of responsibility to Jena in respect of two sub-divisions, namely those of opthalmology and surveying. With these moves, the leadership was surely signalling that it was serious about what it had promised to Jena.

However, that is not the whole story. After the shift of responsibility for the microscope-making business, a number of buses started to head eastword from Oberkochen early each Monday morning. A similar bus convoy left Jena and headed westward each Friday at lunchtime. It is understood that more than 100 former Oberkochen employees had become weekly commuters to Jena in this way by the summer of 1996.

Huge contributions to the cost of the whole restructuring exercise at Jena were made by the German public authorities, especially by the Treuhand – which had the most direct responsibility for privatisation until it closed its doors at the end of 1995. On the other hand, the accounts for the year to end-March 1995 state clearly that the losses at Zeiss Jena have had to be taken into the results of the parent business. And this is understood to have been the case for the following twelve months as well.

Despite the huge infusions of government cash, it is as certain as anything can be that sentiment rather than commercial calculation lay behind the *Stiftung*'s 1991 decision to make a commitment to Carl Zeiss's old home town of Jena. Had the ownership of the business in the former West Germany been of the conventional capitalist type, would its shareholders have accepted a similar obligation to its original home town?

Zeiss and Schott in the former West Germany 1992–1996 The 1991-5 reduction from 69,000 to more than 3,000 in Zeiss employees inside the former GDR is a case of 'restructuring' on a colossal scale. Over the same period, the experience of the *Stiftung*'s businesses in the former West Germany was also dominated by restructuring. Of course, fewer people lost their jobs in the West than in the former GDR. All the same, especially in the case of the optical businesses centred on Oberkochen, the numbers were large – thousands, not hundreds. By all accounts, restructuring had not fully run in its course when this was written.

Successive annual reports down to 1994-5 show that employment in the *Stiftung*'s optical group in the former West Germany fell from 11,666 to 8,720 between the last year before the coming together of the two Zeisses and 1994/5. Admittedly, the reduction was much smaller in the case of Schott. Even so, the total workforce there fell by some 2,000 to slightly more than 10,500. However, in the Schott glass group, there was a small increase in numbers employed outside Germany (West and East): between 1990/1 and 1994/5, such employment rose from 5,065 to 5,861, as some of Schott's production was moved to lower wage countries, for example Hungary. At the optical group, extra-German employment fell, from 2,958 to 2,534.

The relative strength of the Schott group also appears from the cash flow figures. By 1994/5, cash flow of the optical businesses managed to reach DM24m or 1% of sales after a period in the red. At Schott, 1994/5 cash flow was DM396m, 15% of sales, after continuously improving.

What of the Stiftung ownership and government arrangements over the five years from 1991?

I repeat that it was essentially sentiment – grounded in the Stiftung's century-long ownership – which after the fall of the Berlin Wall persuaded Zeiss that it had an obligation to the citizens of its old home town of Jena. By taking steps to enhance work and responsibility at Jena, top management has shown that it is seriously committed to the move, despite costs being much higher than expected and restructuring deeper. This may be presented as an exemplary case of corporate social responsibility. Alternatively, we can say that top management chose to make a virtue of enormous political pressure. But the key point is that it was *able* to do so partly because there were no private and Anglo-Saxon shareholders pressing for a very different set of policies. Whether German private shareholders would have accepted an obligation to move back to Jena is an interesting but clearly unanswerable question.

As for the loss of jobs in the restructuring, even the fiercest critics of Zeiss – and they spoke up during this time both inside and outside the undertaking – will concede that the problems faced between 1992 and 1996 by the *Stiftung*'s business in the former West Germany were largely the same as those that have confronted their conventionally owned counterparts: the problems of wages and social charges, including those for state pensions, which are among the highest in the world. These problems are not specific to Zeiss; nor either were the difficulties caused by the government's need to increase taxes to pay the historic once-and-for-all cost of raising those regions which were formerly part of the GDR to the standards of the former West Germany. The *Stiftung*'s ownership and government arrangements have certainly been tested by these uniquely demanding circumstances – but have proved at least as robust as arrangements in other German companies.

14
The John Lewis Partnership

INTRODUCTORY OVERVIEW

The Partnership's supreme purpose is to secure the fairest possible sharing by all its members of the advantages of ownership – gain, knowledge, and power; that is to say, their happiness in the broadest sense of that word so far as happiness depends on gainful occupation. *Spedan Lewis, Founder of the Partnership at John Lewis (JLP)*

... If in any six months period a Partner has had more than three separate periods of absence of one day or more, whether recorded as sick absence or as unauthorised absence, the Staff Manager, or equivalent authority, shall be notified by the Registrar in case there may be circumstances requiring consultation with the Medical Department; consideration of the Partner's suitability for his job; or consideration of his continued membership of the Partnership. *Constitution of the JLP – Regulations, Terms and Conditions of Employment, Regulation 186*

If there was ever a competition to select a flagship undertaking from among employee-owned businesses worldwide, the John Lewis Partnership (JLP) would quite possibly be the favourite. For a start it is large – including part-timers, the total workforce averaged 41,100 in the year to January 1996. What is more, the employee ownership dates back as far as 1929. But I suspect that JLP would also be rated strongly in relation to business quality: an elusive and multi-dimensional concept, to be sure, but not one to be ignored. Perhaps above all it would score well because of the good sense and sophistication of its institutions, which are the basis of a relationship of widespread consent between the management of the business and those whom JLP calls the rank and file.

The John Lewis Partnership is a retailing operation, though it also includes a few manufacturing businesses and a farm. Well over 95% of the partners are employed either in one of JLP's department stores, of which there were a total of 23 in mid-1996, or in the growing chain of Waitrose supermarkets which had by then reached a total of 113.

The business is owned by a trust – to which it was sold in 1929 by Spedan Lewis, the son of the founder. Since then, we can say that those who work in John Lewis have owned its capital income as individuals and its accumulated capital collectively. As in the Carl-Zeiss *Stiftung*, there are no individualised partners' shareholdings.

The Partnership has long been successful. It has not stopped growing for any appreciable period over the last sixty-five years and seems certain to go on doing so. One measure of this is employment growth:

Employment: Selected Years 1928 to 1992

1928	1,500
1948	12,000
1972	20,000
1975	22,000
1978	26,000
1983	28,000
1988	37,000
1992	40,200
1993	39,300
1994	38,800
1996	41,400

Note: Actual numbers, not weighted for part-timers

As for recent relative performance, for the years until 1987 at least, the research evidence is unambiguous. Over the period 1971-87 the annual growth of sales was well ahead of the increase in employment, over 6% in real terms (Bradley and Estrin, 1988).

Thus, its performance was characterised by a more and more efficient use of labour – a key indicator of business success. The same two academics, Bradley and Estrin, also compared JLP's capital productivity with selected competitors (Great Universal Stores, Marks and Spencer, Sainsbury and Tesco). Their conclusion was striking:

Thus, the John Lewis Partnership outperforms its main competitors in terms of factor productivity. The [annual average] growth of the Partnership's nominal capital productivity over the period is 2.1%. This compares with

0.3% for Marks and Spencer, *minus* 4.7% for Sainsbury, and *minus* 3.1% for Tesco. Comparable figures for the [annual average] growth of nominal labour productivity are 14.4% [JLP], 13.2% [Marks and Spencer], 13.6% [Sainsbury] and 12.8% [Tesco]. Because employment in GUS is falling, the growth of [its] labour productivity is comparable to the John Lewis Partnership at 14.6%, but [its] nominal capital productivity is declining over the period at a rate of 3.9% per annum. In summary, *the Partnership achieves the fastest sales growth from given additions to both capital and labour* [emphasis added].

This research evidence supports the judgement that, at the very least, JLP's performance is not inferior to that of the main competition. It should follow therefore that if, as will be shown in a moment, the Partnership is also able to spread to the lower paid a larger share than the competition in the fruits of its enterprise, then it must be in the interests of public policy that more partnerships of this kind come into being. The key question, about the sources of John Lewis's business success, can be put, if rather cumbersomely, as follows: 'Assuming that the Partnership is able to recruit managers of a quality at least comparable to the competition's, and assuming that Bradley and Estrin are right in concluding that it has the edge over its competitors, is the source of that edge to be found in the special – constitutional and other – arrangements of the Partnership, including its employee ownership?'

To complete this introductory overview, a few words are necessary about those arrangements. The best starting point is a sentence already quoted in the first epigraph: 'The Partnership's supreme purpose is to secure the fairest possible sharing by all its members of the advantages of ownership – gain, knowledge and power . . . '

How do JLP's arrangements implement the sharing of gain, knowledge and power?

Gain-Sharing Bradley and Estrin showed that, for lower-paid partners at least, wages, salaries and associated conditions were as good or better than those of its competitors. So the first point to highlight about gain-sharing at John Lewis is that it is in addition to, and not at the expense of, basic pay and conditions. The next point is about the form which the gain sharing takes. Though it had earlier incarnations, for example as non-voting preference shares, it has mostly taken the form of the so-called Partnership Bonus. This is paid annually and in cash. In principle it is the whole of the 'free profit' earned by the Partnership in the preceding year: that is, what is left of profit after making adequate provision for investment and reserve needs – and after allowing for tax. Within that framework, the actual amount is decided each year by the John Lewis directors and then expressed as a percentage of the partners' wages and salaries – which are seen as the best measure of the relative contribution of each partner to business success.

Over the ten years to 1991, this cash bonus averaged 19% of wages and salaries. That may be seen as the distributed capital income of the business – what in a conventional private company would be paid by way of dividends to (largely absentee) shareholders. In other words over a forty-year period a partner might expect to receive annual bonuses equal in total to about five times his or her annual salary. True, in the recession years after 1991, the bonus fell sharply. But even if we allow for stretches of lean years, experience since 1970 suggests that the total of annual bonuses would be unlikely to amount to less than three years' salary over a working life of forty years. For the record, we may note that the annual partners' bonus had climbed back to 20% in 1996/7.

Knowledge-Sharing Spedan Lewis more than once expressed the view that public opinion was sovereign in the Partnership. Whatever the validity of that rather compressed judgement, JLP's journalism and its whole communications effort are exemplary. The most eye-catching features are three. First is *The Gazette*, published weekly, which among its many virtues supplies the latest business results no more than one week in arrears to all partners. Second is the system of 'Committees for Communication'. These were Spedan Lewis's first major innovation – they can be traced back to 1912 and have survived, virtually unchanged, ever since. They are local bodies in each store or branch which are elected by the so-called rank and file and from the membership of which all the branch's 'managerial' partners are excluded. Their sessions are chaired by a representative of the Chairman of the Partnership.

The third striking feature in this area of 'knowledge-sharing' and public opinion is a right to anonymity for partners voicing complaints and criticisms – and a duty laid on management to reply. Other than in defined exceptional circumstances, *The Gazette* is required to publish all anonymous as well as all signed letters. Moreover the duty of reply, which is imposed on the relevant manager and must be put into effect within three weeks, applies to anonymous and signed letters alike. In the case of the Committees of Communication the anonymity rule goes much further. Minutes of their proceedings are prepared and widely circulated, but the identity of who said what is not disclosed. In the case of questions raised at these meetings, a similar duty of reply is imposed on the relevant manager.

Power-Sharing The Committees for Communication could be presented, without doing too much violence to language, as part of the power-sharing arrangements – especially if management accountability is deemed to be a *kind* of power-sharing. The same is true, but more so, of the JLP's other representative institutions – its largely elected branch councils and its largely elected Central Council.

Even the fiercest of John Lewis's outside critics are inclined to accept that it could not do much better than it does in relation to gain-sharing and knowledge-sharing. But there is no such consensus about its power-sharing arrangements. Many outside critics would probably assert that the power sharing was more apparent than real; or they might use stronger language.

Among these critics there may still be a few 'dictatorship-of-the-proletariat zealots' who condemn the way that the Partnership is governed on straight ideological grounds: because the management is not directly and systematically subordinate to 'worker' political direction, whether that direction is located within or outside the business itself. I hope it is not unreasonable to ignore that criticism – on the grounds that what it proposes would almost certainly be incompatible with anything like the level of business success which JLP has achieved.

More generally, JLP's critics tend to object to two features in its corporate government arrangements. The first of these is that at John Lewis there is no formal recognition of any trade union. The second is that for the partners to remove the chairman, and thus in effect vote for a change of top management, requires a weighted and not a simple majority among their elected representatives. We

shall consider these matters in more detail later and confine ourselves here to one point: at least in Britain, the trade unions have
always been relatively weak in the retail trade.

THE BUSINESS RECORD

Phase One: To the Retirement of the Partnership's Founder in 1955
Spedan Lewis's father, John, after whom the Partnership is named,
died in 1928 at the age of ninety-two. He had started in business on
his own more than sixty years before in a small shop in Oxford
Street, on the site which the business still occupies today. John
Lewis never retired. Only after his death could his son put into
effect those 'Partnership' plans for the business which he had
worked out in his twenties, and which were virtually complete and
clear in his mind as early as 1910.

Young (John) Spedan Lewis entered the business straight from
school, aged nineteen, in 1904. Following his twenty-first birthday,
his father gave him a quarter share. In 1906 a second retail undertaking was purchased – Peter Jones in Sloane Square. In January
1914, John Lewis effectively handed Peter Jones over to Spedan,
both to manage and to own. Already by the end of 1912, Spedan
had embarked on his first institutional experiment: the so-called
Committees for Communication. Between 1914 and the death of his
father in 1928, it was at Peter Jones that most of the other 'Partnership' reforms were first tried.

Indeed, if we exclude the matter of actual ownership, it is not too
much to say that at Peter Jones a 'Partnership' more or less got into
full swing during and after the First World War. For example, it
was there that the forerunner of today's Partnership Bonus was first
distributed to the workforce out of profits in 1920. It was there too
that *The Gazette* was first published. These innovations also coincided with a turn-around in the results of the business. Helped by
what seem to have been the rather easy trading conditions of the
First World War, Peter Jones moved from a loss of £8,000 in 1914 to
a profit of £20,000 in 1920.

When Spedan took full control in 1928, the business was in good
enough shape to provide a firm base for an extended experiment in
'industrial democracy', or at least in 'industrial partnership'. Taken
together the two stores already added up to a fair-sized business.
They employed around 1,500 people, and had a turnover of some
£1.25m in the money of 1928. They had two first-class sites and a

reputation for quality and fair dealing. Moreover, despite Spedan Lewis's manifest frustration over his father's refusal to retire, it is not as if the business had been standing still. When he joined John Lewis in 1904, admittedly before the acquisition of Peter Jones, not more than a few hundred people appear to have been employed.

Spedan is wonderfully ambivalent about his father's business achievement. On the first page of his 1948 book *Partnership for All* he writes:

> At home we had regarded him as a superman, virtually infallible in matters of business. I had not expected in the very least to find that his business was in fact no more than a second-rate success achieved in a first-rate opportunity. But that is what I did find.
>
> [And again, near the end of the first chapter] Like a man who builds a boat so heavy that he cannot handle it properly, he added to his earlier smaller business of which his management was brilliantly successful, a great deal of further space and capital. To do justice to this, he needed to be able to share profit and power to an extent that his temperament did not allow. The team he had built up was utterly inadequate to the possibilities of his business . . . But, when all is said and done, from a very small beginning long ago my father had made a great fortune.
>
> From first to last throughout the whole of a long career my father held steadily to a simple policy of genuine and solid service. He took immense pains to have constantly in stock the greatest possible choice in goods of certain kinds. He took equal pains to give really good value and to win in all other ways a first rate reputation for general trustworthiness . . . It was his success, as it seemed to me, in those aims that made me feel that it would be good for the Partnership to bear his name.

Whatever his son's assessment, we can be confident that John Lewis the father would no more have contemplated turning the business into a Partnership than turning himself into a Buddhist monk.

When his father at long last died, Spedan lost no time in implementing the Partnership project in law as well as in practical fact. In 1929, in what was called the First Settlement, he sold – for just £1m – what was effectively a 100% interest in the combined business of John Lewis and Peter Jones. The buyer would today be called an employee trust. Following the transaction, the seller lent back most of the purchase price, at zero interest, to the trust. Spedan himself, as chairman of the trustees and of the business, remained in complete control. It was only in the Second Settlement, dated 1950, that a mechanism was introduced under which these top positions became constitutionally subordinate to a weighted majority of the partners' elected representatives.

The quarter century or so between the formal establishment of the Partnership and the retirement of its founder in 1955 can be divided into two parts. The first of these, down to 1940, saw vigorous growth, essentially by acquisition. The second, from 1941 to 1955, was the period when JLP was least successful as a business. One reason for that was bad luck: the main John Lewis store in Oxford Street was destroyed by a direct hit in a wartime bombing raid. But there is probably also something in the view that the founder's energies and business talents were not quite as strong as earlier. At any rate, anecdotal evidence in the 1990s from the Partnership's folk memory points in this direction.

There were five main acquisitions or groups of acquisitions, the first in 1928, just before the establishment of the Partnership, and the rest between then and 1940:

T. J. Harries & Co: contiguous business in Oxford Street.
D. H. Evans: site only. Contiguous in Oxford Street.
Four provincial stores: In Nottingham, Southsea, Southampton and
    Weston-super-Mare.
Selfridge Provincial Stores: 15 department stores, of which 6 in the
    provinces and 9 in London.
Waitrose Ltd: Parent of 113 supermarkets in the food trade by 1996.

The Waitrose acquisition, which took place in 1937, was seminal. But many years passed before the Partnership decided to try its hand at major development in the food trade. So the sowing of the Waitrose winter wheat was still in the future when the founder wrote his first book.

As for the acquisitions of T. J. Harries and the D. H. Evans site, Spedan Lewis makes it clear that these were opportunities which the Partnership simply could not afford to pass up. It was indeed an astonishing coincidence that the two sites, on either side of the original John Lewis, should come on to the market, one after another, within five years: 'Both the T. J. Harries chance and the D. H. Evans chance might easily never have occurred in the whole of a long lifetime.'

But Spedan Lewis also makes clear that there were strategic objectives behind this policy of expansion by acquisition. At the margin, acquisitions outside London during the 1930s were seen by him as a sort of insurance policy – to offset the vulnerability of JLP's assets in London in the event of war. More generally, he believed that in a case like that of the Partnership, in marked contrast to his views about the matter when the business was his father's, size meant security. Having discussed what might have happened if T. J. Harries and D. H. Evans had *not* been acquired he goes on: 'But in that case the business would have been standing on a much narrower base. Both its buying and its employing power would have been much smaller. In quality the team might have been first rate but the smaller quantity of its major key posts must have made it much less stable and secure.'

And, writing quite soon after the end of the war, in early 1948, he goes on: 'If such losses, as in these last few years the Partnership's team has chanced to suffer by death and illness, had fallen on a much smaller organisation, the consequences would have been far more serious unless in the filling of these gaps the Partnership had had such luck as would, I think, have been hardly possible.'

Finally, the need to provide enough space for internal management ladder promotions was by itself an independent justification for a policy of significant expansion: 'Fairly substantial growth will obviously be necessary if all those of the younger Partners, who are qualified for important responsibility, are not to have to wait for dead men's shoes . . . '

On the other hand, in the early postwar years which coincided with the last decade of the founder's direct control, we move into a period when good profits were hard to make and when expansion came to a virtual standstill. In effect, expansion was not resumed until the decision was taken to develop a chain of food supermarkets under the name of the Waitrose food store which had been acquired in 1937. But that decision was taken in the chairmanship of Sir Bernard Miller, the founder's successor.

In fact, trading profits fell in real terms between 1945 and 1954, the last full year of the founder's chairmanship. The year 1953 seems to have been notably unsuccessful, apparently due to the impact of the end of the Korean War when JLP was obliged to take heavy markdowns in order to clear stock. Trading profits for the years from 1947 to 1954 (under the founder's chairmanship) compare as follows with those for 1955 to 1960 (under Sir Bernard Miller):

JLP Trading Profits: Years Ending January 1947 to 1954

Year	£
1947	1,091,469
1948	1,073,160
1949	1,052,514
1950	1,083,766
1951	1,062,181
1952	1,040,343
1953	461,863
1954	1,137,753
And then:	
1955	1,500,168
1956	1,578,075
1957	1,610,194
1958	1,694,978
1959	1,652,578
1960	2,136,058

Developments between 1955 and 1960 point up the contrast between what was happening in the last years of the founder's control and the first ones of his successor. Bradley and Taylor describe the 1949-54 annual profit record of John Lewis as 'lacklustre' by comparison with some of the quoted department store businesses for which data is available. However, they acknowledge the effect of the terrible destruction inflicted on the Partnership's flagship store in Oxford Street by German bombers. The task of rebuilding and repair absorbed enormous resources – of top management time as well as of cash.

It is also true that in this period the Partnership had to digest the new department store businesses bought from Selfridge's in 1940 and scattered across the London suburbs and the provinces. These newly acquired undertakings had to be integrated not only into the business but into the whole 'partnership system'.

In *Partnership for All* in 1948, Spedan Lewis expresses unqualified confidence in the good sense of the Partnership system, and a
recurrent belief in its potential comparative advantage. But he also
expresses considerable impatience at the fact that the full benefits of
the system had not yet materialised. He is quite clear what the most
specific benefit would be: an annual Partnership Bonus (as it is now
called) averaging 8% of pay roll. This would equal not less than the
equivalent of four weeks' wages and salaries – on top of conditions
on pay, pensions, etc at least as good as those of the competition. He even speculates that an annual average bonus of twice
that figure is well within the realms of possibility. But he is im-
patient because the business is still, in the early postwar years, a
long way from achieving that result. For no partners' bonus was
paid during the war years and the record thenceforward was both
modest and patchy for more than the next ten years. Not altogether
unreasonably Spedan Lewis pins most of the blame on the war and
on his father – for insisting on soldiering on till his death at ninety-
two, instead of gracefully retiring at, say, seventy-five.

We saw earlier that Spedan Lewis's Partnership system *can*
deliver the benefits in the way of partnership bonus, on top of a
competitive array of pay and other conditions. Over the ten years
to 1991/92, the bonus averaged 19%. The passage in which the
founder of the Partnership system sets out what he foresees as its
potential benefits runs as follows:

> . . . it seems reasonable to hope that the Partnership will be
> able in the fairly near future and thenceforward to give, in the
> first place to all its members, as much as it is doing already and
> indeed rather more pay than on the whole they would be
> really likely to get for equivalent work in any comparable
> business, and in the second place, as it is likewise doing
> already, the pension-prospect that is described in this book
> and, in the third place, rather liberal help in cases of excep-
> tional need and rather liberal collective amenities in the way of
> sports clubs, music, adult education and, in the fourth place,
> yearly Partnership Benefit that will probably not be less than
> about eight per cent upon the total pay-sheet of the recipients,
> that is to say about four weeks' additional pay upon a full
> year's work and proportionately for newcomers.

The Business Record from 1955 to 1996 When Sir Bernard Miller took over as chairman in 1955, the Partnership employed around 12,000 people and made trading profits of £1.5m. When he retired in 1972, those figures were approximately 21,000 and £11m. In round numbers the Partnership thus achieved under his steward-ship a growth of roughly 50% in those employed. After allowing for inflation, trading profit roughly tripled.

Sir Bernard was succeeded by a nephew of Spedan, Peter Lewis, who remained as chairman until January 1993. Between 1972 and 1993, employment in the Partnership roughly doubled to 40,000 while trading profits again tripled in real terms to a peak of £139.4m in 1989. The deep recession which followed on the great Lawson boom scythed those profits down to just over £77m in 1992 though they recovered, at current prices, to £172.8m in the year to end-January 1996 and to a record £238.9 in 1996/97..

The success of the Partnership, measured by the key performance indicators of labour and capital productivity growth and its posi-tion in the top rank of British retailers, was the main achievement of the successive chairmanships of Sir Bernard Miller and Peter Lewis. In fact its business had become divided into two rather different activities – its traditional department store business, and up-market food retailing, through the successful development of its Waitrose chain of supermarkets. Each of these activities is highly competitive. It was by no means a foregone conclusion, when Sir Bernard Miller took over from the founder in 1955, that the Partnership was going to be one of the top businesses in both fields.

The single most important development of Sir Bernard's reign was the gradual build-up of the Waitrose chain of food retailing supermarkets. It will be recalled that a single grocery store, which had formerly belonged to a Mr Waite and a Mr Rose, was one of the Partnership's acquisitions in the 1930s. More than fifteen years elapsed between that acquisition and the decision to expand into food retailing on the basis of the Waitrose bridgehead.

In the 1930s, the department store expansion took place through acquisition. By contrast in the second half of the 1950s and there-after, and in its food retailing business, the Partnership's method of expansion was organic growth. All, or almost all, of the Waitrose chain of supermarkets are new businesses which have been started from scratch. Organic growth takes longer and is typically also more expensive than growth by acquisition but, once established from scratch, the new businesses of an organic growth process may well have stronger roots than those associated with growth by acquisition.

By 1959 the growth of the Waitrose chain had already gone so far as to justify the creation of a new post on the Partnership's main board: Director of Trading (Food). In 1970, for the first time, the Waitrose chain accounted for more than 25% of the Partnership's total turnover. By the time of Sir Bernard Miller's retirement in 1972 the Waitrose share of total sales had reached nearly 30%. This growth continued to the time of writing and looked set to go on. The milestone 100th supermarket was opened, in the Medway towns area of Kent, in October 1992. By 1991 total Waitrose sales had reached close to the same level as those of the department stores: at a little over £1bn each. From then down to 1996/97 sales of each of the two divisions were never far apart but with the department stores' total remaining in the lead.

Sir Bernard Miller's reign is important for reasons which go beyond successful growth and the improved performance. Spedan Lewis expressed the view more than once that no final verdict could sensibly be pronounced on the 'Partnership system' until it had stood the test of at least two successive helmsmen after his own withdrawal from the bridge. Well, it not only survived Sir Bernard's stewardship: as we have seen, it grew stronger as well as larger under it.

I shall return at the end to a considered verdict on the success or otherwise of the Partnership system, independent of the capacities and qualities of its helmsmen. However, it is worth recalling an observation of Sir Bernard Miller, taken from the Scott Bader Common Ownership lecture which he delivered in 1976, a few years after his retirement. Sir Bernard discussed, among other things, the percentage of John Lewis's more or less permanent workforce who could be regarded as 'committed' to the Partnership system. He estimated that the correct figure was 'about one third' but he went on to say in effect that that was quite enough because behaviour patterns in the business were quite largely set by that third. The consensus view of top management in the early 1990s would perhaps be that Sir Bernard's estimate of the committed percentage was on the high side; but that there was no doubt that the majority of the rank and file is significantly influenced by this minority.

In this review of the Partnership's record as a business, we come on now to the period starting from Sir Bernard Miller's retirement, the twenty-one years until 1993 during which the post of chairman was held by the founder's nephew, Peter Lewis.

We should note a financial 'rite of passage' which was negotiated in the early 1970s. Up to that time and apparently since anyone there then could remember, almost the whole of the company's pension fund had been lent back to the business. The accounts for 1972-3 record the repayment to the pension fund's trustees of a loan of rather more than £6m on which an interest rate of 8% was being paid. They also record the issue of a £5m debenture stock, and other bank loans are shown as having been negotiated.

The following tables track the Partnership's record over the sixteen years to 1996/97 and set it against the general evolution of business in the two sectors of activity in which it is chiefly engaged:

Food Retailing: Waitrose Record: 1981/82 to 1991/92

	Sales £m	Index No.	National Food Retailers' Index
81/82	359.3	100	100
82/83	411.6	115	108
83/84	487.6	131	116
84/85	553.7	154	126
85/86	634.1	176	136
86/87	725.8	202	142
87/88	796.7	222	148
88/89	884.5	246	157
89/90	960.2	267	167
90/91	1036.6	289	179
91/92	1117.9	311	189
92/93	1151.2	100	100
93/94	1150.2	100	105
94/95	1229.0	107	110
95/96	1384.0	120	117
96/97	1539.8	134	123

Note: from 92/93 to 96/97 the 'National Food Retailers' Index' is replaced by that for 'Predominantly Food Stores'. The hiccup in Waitrose relative performance between '92 and '95 is partly explained by the fact that, unlike many of its competitors, it did not start trading on Sundays until that was permitted by law.

The corresponding series for the Department stores shows a slightly lower margin by which the Partnership's sales growth outperformed the industry average during this period.

Non-Food Retailing
Department Stores Record: 1981/82 to 1991/92

	Sales £m	Index No	National Non-Food Index
81/82	440.4	100	100
82/83	500.1	114	109
83/84	572.4	130	118
84/85	638.1	145	129
85/86	718.5	163	139
86/87	822.6	187	149
87/88	906.1	206	159
88/89	995.2	226	172
89/90	1040.7	236	179
90/91	1080.5	245	186
91/92	1125.1	255	191
92/93	1206.2	100	100
93/94	1269.8	105	106
94/95	1346.5	112	109
95/96	1431.7	110	113
96/97	1620.7	134	122

Note: from 92/93 to 96/97, the National Non-Food Index is replaced by that of the 'Non-Specialised Stores'. As with Waitrose, none of the department stores opened for trading on Sundays until that was permitted under the law.

If sales growth is a good measure of success, over the sixteen years down to early 1997, the Partnership's comparative performance was not too bad. True, its comparative success was that much greater in the food league, in which Waitrose competes, than among the non-food retailers. I suspect that further research would show that this difference correlated quite closely with the comparative new investment in the Partnership's department stores and in its Waitrose chain.

We must look next at how, under the Partnership system, the fruits of this success were shared. A good starting point is Bradley and Estrin's 1988 study. They began by dividing the retail trade into three different strata: major, minor and locals:

The John Lewis Partnership pays well by the standards of the retail sector, even before the bonus and other benefits have been taken into account. For example, if we consider the checkout staff, the average pay per hour in the Majors is £3.00, in the Minors £2.60 and in the Locals £2.50. The Majors also expected fewer hours of work per day: 6 hours as against 7 in the other two groups, and fewer days worked per week: 5 as against 5.5 and 6 respectively. The figures for the Partnership were £3.20 per hour, 5.75 hours per day and 6 days per week. A weekly income for checkout staff in the John Lewis Partnership amounts to £110.40 as against £105.00 for comparable work in the Majors, £104.00 in the Minors, and £105.00 in the Locals. The John Lewis Partnership is not quite the best payer of checkout staff in the sample: some groups, particularly those undertaking rapid expansion, were offering slightly more per hour. But the Partnership's basic pay was virtually the highest on offer. These findings apply to the other types of job considered.

Bradley and Estrin's findings apply '*even before the bonus and other benefits have been taken into account* [emphasis added]'. Among 'other' benefits, Bradley and Estrin highlight the staff discount and the 'subsidised meals, paid holidays, and sick pay'. The staff discount figures increased to 12% and 25% respectively in 1989. But the comparative advantage enjoyed by the John Lewis partners in these respects is dwarfed by the importance of their annual bonus. It is to that that we must now turn.

We may recall that Spedan Lewis had foreseen that the annual bonus, which he called the Partnership Benefit, 'will probably not be less than about eight per cent upon the total pay-sheet of the recipients, that is to say about four weeks additional pay upon a full year's work and proportionately for newcomers.'

Indeed he ventured a further and more ambitious prediction. For he goes on, in the very next paragraph: 'There seems to be a real possibility that in the most profitable years the rate of Benefit may be about twice as high as this.'

How do these predictions stand up to the actual experience of recent years?

As we have seen, over the ten years to 1991, the partners' bonus at John Lewis averaged 19.1% of payroll. The annual numbers from 1982 to 1991 were:

Partners' Bonus as % of Payroll: 1982-1991

1982	16	1987	24
1983	16	1988	24
1984	21	1989	22
1985	19	1990	17
1986	20	1991	12

So it is not only that the *average* partner's bonus for the ten years to end 1991 was comfortably ahead of what Spedan Lewis foresaw as no more than a possibility for the 'most profitable' years. In two of the years of the 'Lawson boom', the bonus was equivalent to close on three months of the partners' wages and salaries. As for what happened to the bonus in the years of the recession and recovery in the years from 1992 to 1997 the record is shown in the table below:

Partners' Bonus as % of Payroll: 1992-97

1992	9	1995	12
1993	8	1996	15
1994	10	1997	20

In Bradley and Estrin's words, and not counting the bonus, 'the John Lewis Partnership pays well by the standards of the retail sector'. This was probably still true in 1997.

The JLP's record of growth was substantially ahead of the national averages in its two main branches of activity. So it is not as if the partners have been eating their own seed corn. Taking all this together it is hard to resist the conclusion that the Partnership performs rather successfully.

One last point thrown up by the Bradley and Estrin researches into the record of JLP during the 1970s and 1980s is that downward fluctuations in its employment have been significantly less than at the competition – essentially because the bonus provided an invaluable cushion. On the face of it, that too, from the viewpoint of public policy, looks like an important comparative advantage.

I shall conclude this account of the business record at JLP with a question: how precisely, if at all, is its business success to be explained by what we may call the Partnership System? In the final section of this case study we first describe that system and then return to that key question.

THE PARTNERSHIP SYSTEM

Genesis and Main Features A good place to begin is an index entry in *Partnership for All*. The general entry refers to the founder's father, John Lewis. The particular sub-entry of interest here is 'John Lewis *Wealth*', and, under that, the following double reference, to one of the book's numbered paragraphs: Excess of, 44; Unreasonableness of, 44.

If we turn up the reference, we find a passage where the son, Spedan Lewis, is reflecting about the wealth of his father and contrasting it with the 'so meagre' livings of his staff.

> The more I considered all this the more utterly unreasonable did it seem to be. There on the one side was my father and on the other side his staff – my father with over a hundred separate pieces of property that he never saw and that were nothing but a bother to him, and with an income so far larger than the cost of his very comfortable way of living that the surplus was constantly obliging him to make more and more of those investments: the staff with an employment that was extremely insecure and that gave them a living so meagre that they were very far less happy than they perfectly well could have been, a happiness that would have increased very greatly both the soundness of the business and the real happiness of my father's own life.

And Spedan Lewis goes on, in the next numbered paragraph (45):

> All this led me to the notion that people who control businesses should not take for their own work more than they would think it reasonable to pay someone else to do that same work or, if their abilities are in their view so exceptional that they cannot be said to have a definite market-value, then to their personal revenues they should set merely arbitrarily a limit which has some relation to a reasonable standard of living. They should not take beyond that limit a margin that will accumulate into a great mass of capital that will be no real good to them and that their heirs, if their own earning power is good, will not need and, unless their own earning power is good, ought not to have at their disposal.

Spedan Lewis is quite unequivocal about the starting point for the reforms of his father's business which he was later to introduce. It was the extreme imbalance, as he saw it, between the very high income enjoyed by his father (and to some extent by his brother and himself) and the bare subsistence wage paid to the great majority of the staff.

On the title page of *Partnership for All*, the business is referred to as a '34-year-old experiment in industrial democracy'. A critical book-length study written in 1968 by three academics uses the same phrase for its title: *Experiment in Industrial Democracy*. As we shall see, the phrase is often the source of a tiresome and essentially linguistic discussion though, of course, it need not be so.

It seems to me especially salutary, therefore, to begin this discussion of the Partnership system at John Lewis, by giving proper emphasis to what might crudely be called its financial bottom line: the fact that the Partners *own* the business in at least two senses. The first is that no one else owns it and the second is that, in so far as the imperatives of growth and investment permit, the capital income of the business is distributed annually to the Partners in the form of an often large bonus – a bonus which has been paid in cash since the middle 1960s.

When first introduced at Peter Jones after Spedan Lewis had taken over the business there in 1914, these bonuses were paid, not in cash but in what amounted to the managing director's IOUs. For many years after the Partnership was formally established in 1929, they were paid in preference shares – to protect the cash flow of the business. However, what is important is not this historical detail but the fact that since 1929 the Partnership has rested on a solid foundation of employee ownership. Arguably, this means that the Partnership has substantially transcended the 'exploitation' of conventional capitalism, though even in the 1990s, some of those on the left would doubtless decline to go that far. But the reality of the other elements in the Partnership system would be greatly attenuated if they did not rest on the solid rock of employee ownership.

What are those other elements? The most general answer is that they are about what it has become fashionable to call corporate *governance*. I am myself happier with the more muscular phrase corporate *government* and I propose to stick to it here as elsewhere in this book. The other elements in the Partnership system are about securing for the partners a voice in the business to complement their ownership of it. Put one way, they are about the 'participation' component in the duality of employee ownership and participation. Alternatively, we can use language about these other features in the Partnership system which is particularly favoured by the John Lewis management; or language that was particularly favoured by the founder, Spedan Lewis himself. He liked to say that these other parts of the system were designed to make 'public opinion sovereign' in its affairs. He also emphasised a distinction, to which we will have to return, between the Partnership's executive side and what he called its critical side. Among the managers of the business, a favourite phrase is that the arrangements are designed to ensure that management is *accountable* to the Partnership's rank and file: that is to those of the partners who have no management powers whatsoever. Finally, this whole partnership system is embodied in a constitution, or more precisely in various constitutional documents. At least in theory we are dealing with the rule of law, rather than with the rule of men.

Committees of Communication A good way into the specifics is through Spedan Lewis' notion of public opinion. In fact the oldest of the partnership institutions which he introduced was not those 'partnership bonus IOUs' which he started at Peter Jones in 1914. Even earlier, in the original shop in Oxford Street in 1912, he persuaded his father to introduce the Committees for Communication. They have survived essentially unchanged to this day. If anything in the history of employee participation has stood the test of time it is these committees.

The most unusual feature of these committees is that only the so-called rank-and-file partners, and not even the most lowly ranks of junior management, have a vote in the election of their members and are eligible to stand for membership. That reflects what the founder saw as their logic. He made their role and function abundantly clear in *Partnership for All*: The idea was and is to bridge the gulf that in large scale business develops between, on the one side, the workers, the 'rank and file', as the Partnership calls them, the people who have little or no authority over others, and, on the other side, the Principal Management, the people who have on the contrary the ultimate authority, the real control of the whole business.

In other words, though their members are elected – and elected in secret ballots – these Committees for Communication should not be seen as essentially 'representative institutions'. The latter are otherwise institutionalised in the Partnership system – in the shape of the Central Council and branch councils – and we shall come on to them separately later. The Committees for Communication should rather be seen as a mixture of a two-way communications mechanism (top down and bottom up) and as rather unusual units for grievance transmission: rather unusual partly because they are both democratically elected and constitutionally approved as a component of the partnership system. They are also unusual because their proceedings are covered by a rule of anonymity, to protect the identity of the individual rank-and-file partners from their departmental superiors, and a duty to respond on the part of the relevant principal director.

Meetings are held at least six times a year and are chaired by a person appointed by one of JLP's 'principal management' (in turn accountable only to the JLP chairman) and attended by the members elected by the rank and file. Minutes must be written up and made available with a minimum of delay. They are written up in a way which conceals the identities of the individual committee members: the anonymity rule. If questions or grievances have been raised at the meeting, then the relevant principal director must reply to them with the minimum of delay: the duty to respond.

These Committees for Communication have been around for so long that it is hard not to conclude that they play an important part in the system. Moreover, in a survey of sample Partnership opinion in the 1960s, it was found that they were valued more highly by the rank and file than were either the branch councils or the Central Council. Two hypotheses, which are not mutually exclusive, are perhaps worth putting forward. The first is that the rank-and-file partners may attach particular value to an institution which they see as exclusively 'theirs'. Second we may perhaps see the Committees' members as performing some of the functions of elected shop stewards; and shop stewards who are also, as it were, fully licensed by the Partnership's constitution.

'The Gazette' Clearly, on the other hand, the main function of these bodies is what their name implies: to permit (two-way) communication. Accordingly they must be seen as having their

part to play in what Spedan Lewis took to be of the first importance: namely the formation of a public opinion in the business, which would be as well-informed as possible. That can also be seen as one of the chief objectives behind the launch of an in-house weekly journal – *The Gazette*. The first issue came out on 16 March 1918 and it has been coming out without a break ever since.

The Gazette and the branch *Chronicles*, which first started to appear in addition to it during the Second World War, are exemplary models of in-house business journalism which other employee-owned companies and co-operatives should seek to emulate. Perhaps the statistics of the retail trade give the editors of *The Gazette* an advantage when it comes to publishing results with a minimum of delay after they have happened. But the consequence is most striking; information about how the Partnership, and how the individual branches are doing is made available to all partners within a week of the results which are recorded in it.

The Gazette has many other functions beside that of recording the latest results. For example, it provides very full reports of the proceedings of the (mainly elected) Central Council. But I have space here to mention no more than one other feature: its generally lively letters column and the fact that, as with the Committees for Communication, an anonymity rule, and a duty of reply, are associated with it.

At this point in our discussion of the non-financial components of the Partnership system, a sceptical reader might well feel entitled to ask what all the fuss is about. 'After all,' he might say, 'don't almost all businesses make special efforts these days to communicate with their employees?' 'OK,' he might add, 'I grant that John Lewis was something of a pioneer in this and that there may be some unusual points of detail, but please don't pretend that there is anything in this stuff to get all that excited about.'

It is true that many, perhaps most, companies do now make serious efforts to communicate with their employees. Yet the rule of anonymity and the duty of response are still genuinely distinctive features of both *The Gazette* and Committees for Communication. Moreover, at John Lewis these institutions of communication are not just *ad hoc* arrangements but part of an overall Partnership system which is constitutionally underpinned.

Registrar and Partners' Counsellor The next two institutions of the Partnership system of which we need to take account are the Chief Registrar (and branch registrars) and the Partners' Counsellor. To a greater or lesser extent both perform functions of what might be called 'industrial welfare' which are also performed in conventional capitalist companies. Yet both also have duties in relation to the constitution: for example to advise partners, especially rank-and-file partners, of their rights under it. It is these 'constitutional' duties which make these functionaries unusual. Again, they are components of the overall Partnership system which is constitutionally underpinned.

Another way of looking at all these institutions of the Partnership system is to adopt Spedan Lewis's own language and describe them as features of the Partnership's 'critical side', which he distinguishes from its executive side. At least in part they function as watchdogs: they are part of the founder's answer to the familiar question, often put in its Latin form, which all constitutionally-based organisations must answer: Quis custodiet ipsos custodes? Who will watch the watchdogs?

Central and Branch Councils We come on next to the representative institutions of the Partnership system – the Central Council, at the level of the Partnership as a whole, and the Branch Councils at the level of individual branches or small groups of them. Both are mainly elected bodies: Branch Councils have mainly single member constituencies but Central Council constituencies range from single to four or five seats. Each also includes some members *ex officio* and some appointed by the Partnership's chairman. One of the reasons originally put forward for including non-elected members was the need to ensure a proper representation of people working in middle management positions. In the words of Spedan Lewis: 'The original aim of this *ex-officio* membership was to ensure the presence of everyone who ought to be available there as a source of information and to bring into the Council particular partners who were likely to be specially useful there.'

In fact, since only 45% of those elected to the Central Council are typically rank-and-file partners, that particular argument has at least partly fallen away.

The sceptical critic is likely to argue that the Central and Branch councils are little more than glorified works councils. Any votes which are taken inside them usually – though not always - go the way that management wants them to go. Of course, these representative institutions are not *ad hoc* bodies operating in a void: they are components of an overall Partnership system which hangs together and is constitutionally underpinned. Moreover, they are mechanisms for overseeing the so-called executive side, and in relation to this function of oversight or superintendence the Central Council enjoys an important and radical fall-back power.

To understand this power we must say a word about the office of chairman. It is not an overstatement to say that in all normal circumstances, and at least insofar as the executive side of the business is concerned, the chairman has almost unlimited power within the organisation. He does so first through his control of the main executive board of the business: of that board's twelve members he appoints six; and together with these six he is always in a position to outvote the remaining five, who hold their positions through election by and from the Central Council. Second, he holds *ex officio* the forty 'A' shares in John Lewis Partnership Trust Ltd, the trust company which controls the principal holding company in the Partnership, John Lewis Partnership Plc. In normal circumstances, only these forty 'A' shares are enfranchised; the sixty 'B' shares are vested in three trustees, appointed annually by the Central Council. But the voting powers of those sixty 'B' shares (and therefore the power of Central Council to dismiss the chairman) crystallise only following confirmation of a 'Resolution on the Constitution' – the fall-back position described below.

Furthermore, and this makes him in a sense more powerful in relation to his fellow directors than the Pope is in relation to members of the College of Cardinals, the chairman appoints, again in all normal times, his own successor.

However, against this enormous concentration of power in the hands of the chairman, the constitution offers a fall-back provision. In effect, if a two-thirds majority of the members of the Central Council so decide, they can remove the chairman from office. Moreover, they need not specify their reasons, although such a 'Resolution on the Constitution', as it is somewhat quaintly called, comes into effect only if the decision has not been rescinded during the period of a month.

It should go without saying that very few works councils have a fall-back power of this kind. Of course, the Partnership's critics are apt to dismiss it as mere window dressing – and to point to the fact that it has so far never been used. But they have misunderstood what is essentially a twofold logic behind the provision. It is there, in the first place, to highlight the fact that even the all-powerful chairman is subordinate to the Partnership's constitution. Second, the provision is so framed that it will not be lightly or frequently used. The provisions of the American Constitution which relate to the impeachment of the President may offer some kind of parallel. It seems likely too that well before any resolution under this provision was actually introduced into the Central Council, the chairman's top management colleagues would have quietly persuaded him to stand down.

There seem to me to be two final points to underline about this whole, undoubtedly complex, Partnership system. The first is that it should be seen as a set of linked components. It is not clear how it would work and whether it would work as well as it apparently does if one of the components – say, the Committees for Communication or *The Gazette* – was removed. Second, the system is validated and legitimised by a constitution to which all partners, including the all powerful chairman, subscribe.

A point of detail from the constitution of particular relevance to public debate in the early 1990s is the limit it sets on the top salary which may be paid to anyone working in the Partnership. It figures as clause 10 of the settlement made by Spedan Lewis dated 10 October 1950:

> The total return by the Partnership to any one of its members for services rendered to it by him in the course of any year shall not exceed, after taxation in both cases, twenty five times the concurrent minimum for a year's service rendered to it by a married man resident in the County of London and having four dependent children and shall in no case exceed the equivalent of five thousand pounds in 1900.

The latter limit, it may be noted, is calculated after tax and gave a maximum in 1996 of about £300,000.

Whatever else, Spedan Lewis was evidently determined to avoid what he had regarded as the 'utterly unreasonable' income of his father when he had himself joined the business at the beginning of the century. In this respect, as perhaps in some other ways, the founder of the Partnership accepted the moral force of the famous injunction of the Ancient Greeks: μηδὲν ἄγαν – 'nothing to real excess'.

CONCLUSIONS

The Big Questions In their 1988 study, Bradley and Estrin showed beyond reasonable doubt that the Partnership, at least for the period from the early 1970s to the late 1980s, was among the best in the highly competitive business of the retail trade. Indeed what they showed went rather beyond that in two ways. First, for the performance of JLP as a whole, they showed that, measured by the key indicators of capital and labour productivity growth, John Lewis had actually outperformed the competition of Great Universal Stores, Marks and Spencer, Sainsbury and Tesco. Second, they showed that JLP was among the best in both of its two main lines of activity – in its Waitrose chain of food retailing supermarkets and in its department stores. Moreover their researches also showed that these comparative successes had not been achieved by short-changing the partners: by the standards of the retail trade the basic pay and conditions enjoyed by the partners were close to the very top, and way above this if partnership bonus was thrown in.

I should make clear that these findings do not in my view entail anything for certain about the future. Particularly in food retailing, it may be that the sheer size of the major players will sooner or later undermine the success of a relatively modest operation like Waitrose. For the size differences are enormous. In the mid-1990s Sainsbury, Tesco and Marks and Spencer had investment programmes which dwarfed those of JLP. Still, up to the time of writing, one may say 'So far so good.'

But it is important to introduce that disclaimer because it underlines the proposition that the findings of Bradley and Estrin do not depend on what happens in the future. It is enough for the purposes of this book that over a longish period and on a relatively level playing field the business performance of the Partnership was at least as successful as the competition, and probably rather better. It is also true that the benefits of this success were shared more equitably with the rank and file of employees.

That is the main point of this case study. I return now to the question of whether there is any link between the Partnership system and the success of the business.

Sir Bernard Miller, the second chairman, had no doubt of this. In his 1975 Ernest Bader lecture, he identified four consequences of it which were positive for that success:

First the knowledge that all workers are recognised as full partners, or members, or co-owners in their enterprise, with the sanction of legal authority behind the recognition. Second, confidence, born of this recognition, that the enterprise is being operated in the interests of all who work in it. Third, willingness, born of this confidence, *to give management the authority to manage subject to full accountability to the managed* [emphasis added]. Fourth, the acceptance of mutual responsibility by management and managed for the safety and success of their business and a willingness to subordinate personal or sectional interests to the needs of the whole community of workers.

The fact that there is little if any direct empirical evidence for the hypothesis that the rank-and-file partners 'give management the authority to manage subject to full accountability to the managed', and for the benefit to business performance, is largely because such a hypothesis is virtually impossible to test. Nevertheless there are some nuggets of evidence which suggest that the Partnership system may indeed contribute measurable commercial benefit to the profit and loss account. There is also evidence that one of the keys may be that the rank-and-file partners 'give management the authority to manage' to an extent which goes beyond what is to be found in similar businesses of a conventional capitalist character.

One is the low rate of absenteeism. In the mid-1990s the figure was running at around 3.5%. That is low by most standards and perhaps particularly so in a business in which part-timers make up about one-third of the total workforce.

Second, it seems probable that if a systematic and comparative study could be made, JLP would show up rather well by the measure of what is called the stock shrinkage per cent. The shrinkage we are concerned with will result from various different causes, of which shoplifting and staff pilfering are perhaps the most obvious but not the only ones. The Partnership has always declined to disclose its stock shrinkage figures but there is recurrent anecdotal evidence that by this measure it is way ahead of its main competitors.

Finally, 1989 research supplies some evidence that labour turn-over rates at the Partnership are low – 7.1% in 1984/85, compared with over 30% in the retail sector as a whole (Bradley and Estrin, 1989). At Sainsbury, annual turnover of weekly-paid staff was 45% in 1989, and 40% in 1990, though it fell sharply later.

These pieces of evidence clearly reflect worker attitudes to the business. I suspect too that a research study into comparative discipline as between John Lewis and its competitors might disclose some interesting differences. My hypothesis would be twofold: first that the incidence of disciplinary cases would be proportionately lower at John Lewis than among the competition; and second, on the other hand, that the penalties imposed by the Partnership in cases of serious indiscipline would be systematically tougher than those of its competitors. Feeling stronger about the legitimacy of its own position and that of the 'system', the Partnership management can afford to treat indiscipline with greater toughness.

That, incidentally, seems to me to be the way to interpret the surprisingly tough 'Regulation 186', of the Partnership's terms and conditions of employment, the regulation about absenteeism, quoted as the second epigraph to this case study. I see its toughness, in other words, as reflecting a greater confidence on management's part in its own legitimacy.

Moreover, it seems that that toughness may extend to the not directly work-related behaviour of partners. For example, Regulation 262 provides that 'membership may be closed for any serious failure in courtesy either in the Partnership's business or in its social life, and particularly for any disgusting and outrageous language and any deliberate effort, especially if persistent, to cause pain or make mischief'. In other words, the Partnership will not just look the other way when confronted with unacceptably loutish behaviour. It seems too that if partners are convicted of serious crimes in the courts of law, they may put their position in the Partnership at risk.

In a Britain confronted with the consequences of a growing 'redneck' culture, it may well be that the Partnership's insistence on some minimum standards of behaviour has a benefit which spins out into the community at large. The Partnership's ethos of 'fair dealing and fair shares' has an influence on the behaviour of a significant number of partners. The indirect social benefits back up the public policy case for stronger tax reliefs to promote partnership of this kind.

15

The Baxi Partnership

The end of March 1996 marked the thirteenth birthday as the Baxi Partnership of what had previously been the family-owned business, Richard Baxendale & Sons. Founded in 1866, Baxi's history goes back almost as long as that of John Lewis and Carl Zeiss. The big difference is that the whole of Baxi's experience of employee ownership has taken place in today's world. American (and French) evidence suggests that, given an appropriate tax and legal environment, sale to their employees, probably through some mechanism similar to an employee trust, can offer an attractive exit route to family business and other private company owners as they approach retirement. That was the source of the ownership changes at Baxi. Unlike what happened later at Tullis Russell, the Baxi transaction took place *without* the benefit of specific employee ownership tax reliefs. Nevertheless, Baxi's experience as an employee ownership pioneer in today's Britain – and its long struggle to gain commercial advantage from its employee ownership – make it exceptionally interesting to any family businesses which might consider following its example. Incidentally, its struggle to get its employee owners onto a single side – that of the business itself – was still far from finished when this research was largely revised in mid-1996. Of course, in some sense it never will be.

The Partnership is engaged in manufacture. From the late 1960s it held its place as one of Britain's top manufacturers of domestic gas-fired boilers supplying hot water for washing and central heating. Its market share over the ten years to the end of 1992 varied between about 20% and 24% – tending to increase, but, since the later 1980s, as a gently rising share of a sharply declining market.

In the two following years, 1993 and 1994, the business continued to register strong cash flow and retained a leading position in the market. But its market share fell away somewhat. And then in the year to 31 March 1995, while the cash flow remained positive, for almost the first time its accounts showed a pre-tax loss: of £2.5m. Helped in part by the fruits of some diversification and by a small upturn in its share of the main market, the results bounced back into a respectable profit in the following twelve months and exceeded £9m in both 1997 and 1998. In retrospect, as we shall see later, the experience of moving into the red may even have been salutary: in the specific sense of making easier a key adjustment to levels of pay which could well otherwise have been more intractable.

The difficulties of the mid-1990s should not be allowed to conceal what had become by that time, as a result of a long run of profitable years and zero dividends, an unusually strong balance sheet. By the end of Baxi's tenth partnership year, the business had in fact built up a cash mountain of over £50m. On the other hand, throughout the period it also stuck pretty closely to its core business of domestic boiler manufacture and its home market.

The only significant exceptions were the acquisition of two small air-heating system businesses in the late 1980s. Yet they were something of a portent. For following a reorganisation of the business on a group-with-subsidiaries basis in 1992, Baxi made its first substantial entry into the market for domestic heating boilers in Continental Western Europe. It bought the leading manufacturer in Denmark, plus linked distributors in France and Sweden. In that same year it also formed a close 'downstream' relationship with France's dominant manufacturer of so-called 'combi' boilers, one of only two significant categories of these domestic boilers which Baxi did not then itself manufacture.

There was a further, and partly different, flurry of entrepreneurial moves in 1994 and in early 1995. Some, it is true, were indirectly linked with the core business of boiler manufacture. But others were not. Where there was no link, the rationale was either employee ownership or local community involvement. For example, Baxi took over an employee-owned sanitary ware business in Scotland and joined in launching an Employee Share Ownership Fund. It also acquired the local football team, Preston North End.

These latest developments were made possible by the combination of the cash mountain and the switch to a group structure. Though important to the future of the Baxi business, they are less central to the experience of its employee ownership which is our main concern, and are not discussed further here.

Baxi's initial success in gas boiler manufacture, which gave it a head start in what was then essentially a new market, can best be seen as a reward for 'solving a problem' – fitting an efficient system of gas heating into the constrained spaces characteristic of many of Britain's homes. Its solution to the problem, a back boiler called the 'Baxi Bermuda', was first brought to the market in the second half of the 1960s.

Baxi's boilers are iron castings made in Baxi's own, modern and, it is claimed, ecologically benign foundry. Much of the balance of the Partnership's work can be colloquially called 'metal bashing'; and would be officially classified as semi-skilled. There was a switch to multi-skilling in the early 1990s which will probably go on. All the same, Baxi is an essentially blue collar manufacturing operation in which most of the production workers look after one or more machines. These workers have *not* passed through a craft apprenticeship.

Both geography and the fact that the blue collar workforce has been 100% unionised since anyone can remember reinforce the company's 'old industrial' identity. The main unions are the Amalgamated Engineers and the Sheet Metal Workers. The geography is that of mid-Lancashire, within biking distance of Orwell's Wigan Pier.

This character of Baxi as an 'old industrial' manufacturer clearly distinguishes it from both John Lewis and Carl Zeiss. A further difference is that Baxi is much smaller. Since 1983 employment has fluctuated between a high of nearly 1,450 (early 1996), and a low of just over 900. Partly because of a contraction in the market for domestic gas boilers in the late 1980s and early 1990s, and partly because of improvements in its own productivity, employment fell in the early 1990s. These reductions have since been more than offset by the numbers employed in the series of businesses acquired by the Partnership since then.

In the case of John Lewis, Spedan Lewis had settled in his mind the main elements of his proposed 'partnership system' while still a young man. By contrast, for Philip Baxendale and the Baxi Partnership, employee ownership was, at least partly, the solution to the linked problems of succession in a substantial family-owned business and its long-term survival. As Mr Baxendale saw it, the problem was to ensure that Baxi, a business in his view with some exceptional features, could continue to enjoy an independent existence. He also wanted to ensure that this was done in such a way that the interests of those who had helped him to build it were secure.

He told his children at an early age that ownership was not going to be passed to them. But the more he thought about both the morality and the likely consequences of either a trade sale to a third party or a stock market flotation, the more uneasy he felt. Given his business philosophy and the participative arrangements which he had developed since taking over from his father as a young man, Mr Baxendale saw employee ownership as an outcome with real positive attractions.

There is an obvious difference between partnership seen as an 'experiment in industrial democracy', and partnership as the solution to a specific problem of ownership succession in a family business. Given the frequency of ownership succession problems, it seems possible that in the long run Baxi may be a more significant model for the future than John Lewis. The number of family business owners who face Philip Baxendale's problem must run to hundreds annually in a country the size of the UK; the number of successful entrepreneurs who are also 'industrial democracy visionaries' is unlikely to exceed one or two per generation.

After the 1983 change of ownership, profitability, as we have seen, went from strength to strength before falling away. Are there obvious explanations for the profit variability?

An important factor was that, with the exception of what happened in the middle years from 1986 to 1989, there was a continuous decline in the market for Baxi's main domestic heating boilers. But there were also problems over the leadership. The top executive position in the business was held for twenty-eight years, until his retirement in the autumn of 1989, by Ian Smith. And the way in which the succession at the top worked out could scarcely have been worse. Including one who had a brief trial before Ian Smith's retirement, three successors were tried and then superseded before Bryan Gray took over in the summer of 1994. Readers with a knowledge of Roman history will remember the famous 'year of the four [sequential] emperors': it can be safely assumed that it was not a good year for Imperial business. Probably the single most important mistake since the ownership transfer was the failure to make smooth arrangements for the succession to Ian Smith.

On the other hand, even though they evidently concealed a

number of errors of omission, especially in new product development and product trials, the higher profits of 1991 and 1992 also reflected some genuine and positive changes. In particular, a real effort began to be made, from just before Ian Smith's retirement onwards, to enable and empower Baxi's rank and file partners to contribute to improved performance, and to create a new 'culture of ownership'. Undoubtedly those efforts had some real results – even if their good effects were swamped in the short term, at least at the bottom line, by other variables.

An obvious question arises: how secure is the Partnership's new 'ownership culture', assuming that it exists at all? There are sceptics, as there are bound to be. What has unquestionably been learnt is that partnership or employee ownership doesn't *automatically* work.

The experience of Baxi's first thirteen years of employee ownership tells us that the potential benefits of these arrangements do not arise spontaneously. No doubt there are necessary conditions if they are to be harvested. But it may be doubted whether any set of conditions will be sufficient to guarantee them. Instead we should probably look at employee ownership, both at Baxi and elsewhere, as a continuing quest for best practice, which is unlikely ever to be fully achieved. At Baxi, the environment in which the quest took place has not made for particularly easy riding.

Before Employee Ownership: 1866 to 1983 The original business, an iron and brass foundry, was started in Chorley in central Lancashire in 1866 by Philip Baxendale's great-grandfather, Richard, and his two sons, George and Thomas. The original legal form was that of a partnership between the father and his two sons.

From the beginning down to the early 1930s it was both a general foundry and a multi-purpose engineering shop with its main customers in Lancashire's cotton textile industry. From the original partners the business was passed on to George Baxendale's two sons, Richard and John, who converted it into a limited company. Richard was Philip Baxendale's uncle and John his father. Philip remembers long periods when they were scarcely on speaking terms.

Whatever their personal relations, the business thrived. The late 1930s saw the first step away from general foundry work and jobbing engineering and towards the present concentration on domestic heating. This happened through the invention by Philip's father, John, of the Baxi patent underfloor draught fire. This fire, later designated the 'Baxi Burnall', is again best understood as the solution to a problem: that of cleaning out a traditional fire grate. The awkwardness of that operation was ameliorated by the device of providing an ash pit below the grate coupled with an easily removable ash can. The new product had the extra advantage of generating a greater draught to the fuel bed and thus more responsive and controllable burning.

During the Second World War most of Baxi's capacity was switched to defence production. But after 1945 Baxi's new patent fire came to dominate the British underfloor draught solid fuel fire market, with an 80% market share in the 1950s and 1960s. In effect, from the late 1930s onwards the company had a national product, and a national market. Driven by growing sales of the patent underfloor fire, employee numbers were steadily increasing. New premises became necessary and in 1961 the company moved from Chorley to its present site at Bamber Bridge outside Preston.

In these postwar years, the Baxi Burnall was increasingly sold not just by itself but together with a back boiler – either a small one to supply domestic hot water; or a larger one sufficient to run several radiators as well. But the popularity of solid fuel for home heating started to decline from the late 1950s onwards. The Burnalls had to contend with the growing unpopularity of coal, as well as with environmental legislation in the shape of clean air laws. All the same, the Baxi Burnall was still making annual sales in the early 1990s running in the low thousands of units and, if the sales of its spare parts are also taken into account, contributing nearly £0.5m to sales.

But from the late 1960s onwards the bulk of the company's business, which then started to increase very fast, came from sales of gas-fired heating appliances. The story of this key development was summarised in a document published to mark the change to employee ownership in 1983 and entitled *From Participation to Partnership*. The relevant paragraphs are these:

> If the Burnall was the first of Baxi's key products, it is the 'Baxi Bermuda' which has had by far the greatest impact on the company's fortunes. It enabled Baxi to enter the new and high-potential gas central heating market and to do so with an unusually innovatory product.
>
> In the late 1960s, any householder who wanted to install

gas central heating had to solve the problem of finding floor space in a rapidly filling kitchen area – an area often with little enough space to cope with a cooker, fridge and washing machine.

With about 70 per cent of the then potential customers ... living in homes with kitchens which had less than 90 square feet of floor space, an alternative to the traditional floor standing boiler (the only type available for gas at that time) was urgently needed.

This was just the opportunity Baxi was seeking. Its experience with the solid fuel back boiler market, coupled by its own research into consumer attitudes, pointed to the ultimate solution – a gas back boiler.

It was an exceptionally neat way out, for it took the boiler out of the kitchen area and put it where it took up no space at all: in the fireplace opening. Not surprisingly the Baxi Bermuda met with an immediate response from both installers and customers.

The growth was phenomenal and by 1973 gas back boilers were accounting for 40 per cent of the total boiler market. But it was not only space saving which accounted for the popularity of the Bermuda. The attraction of a focal point in the living room was important; and the range of available fire fronts quickly expanded to incorporate the now popular wood surround type and more recently the 'live fuel effect'.

Almost since its launch, the Baxi Bermuda has been the company's flagship product. In the early 1990s it still accounted for over 60% of turnover and an even larger share of profits. But it is no longer Baxi's only gas boiler. Since the late 1970s the range has also included both wall-mounted and floor-standing boilers.

The explosive growth of the business can probably best be traced in the employment record. Employees numbered around 60 when Philip Baxendale took over in 1955. Still in the pre-gas era, they had increased to just under 200 by 1960. The explosion came after the mid-1960s – employees numbered 800 by the early 1970s. The oil price rise and other recession-induced factors held down employment growth through the later 1970s. But it then started to grow once again. Baxi was employing some 900 people when it became employee-owned early in 1983.

Meanwhile, turnover increased by more than seven times between 1972 and 1983 at current prices, and at least respectably fast in constant ones:

	£m
1972	4.8
1975	6.3
1978	14.1
1981	22.0
1982	30.6
1983	37.0

Turning from sales to profits, the results for this period were consistently very good – with the exception of 1974 and 1975. Despite those two recession years, profits measured as a return on capital averaged over 26% between 1972 and 1983.

By almost any standards these were golden years. Behind Baxi's success was its commanding position in a market which was taking off, but which could not be expected to sustain the same rate of growth indefinitely. Once the bulk of the country's housing stock had been fitted with hot water and radiator systems, demand was almost bound to level off and be confined to that for replacements and for newly built homes.

Over these prosperous years, as throughout its previous history, the dividends paid to the business's family shareholders were modest. For example they totalled just £77,000 in the last year for which they were paid, 1981/2, when the company earned £5.84m pre-tax. The bulk of the profits were reinvested so that Baxi could remain sharply competitive – or put into a cash profit-sharing scheme which had been introduced by the company in 1965.

The profit-sharing scheme was one reflection of Philip Baxendale's belief in employee participation, which he based on the view that 'people will work better and more happily together if you allow them to participate as much as possible'. The proportion of profit shared is linked to return on capital and paid in proportion to individual wages and salaries. Apart from 1974 and 1975, the annual average of this cash profit sharing in 1965-82 was 6.3% or the equivalent of just over three weeks' pay.

Since even earlier, 1961, there has been a second dimension of participation. That year the then general manager, Ian Smith, set up the Works Council. It brought together elected non-management employees with management appointees. In 1976 the Council's constitution was amended to require unanimous voting for any changes in its rules. The logic behind this was to prevent a minority being coerced into accepting change. Aside from matters to do with wages and conditions of employment – which remained exclusively within the arena of collective bargaining between management and trade unions – the non-management representatives were free to raise any subject.

This 1961 Works Council was eventually superseded by the changes which accompanied and followed employee-ownership. But in the 1960s it was a rare and pioneering departure. Philip Baxendale and Ian Smith had been persuaded of the value of Works Councils largely through the writings of Wilfred Brown. Wilfred Brown was then managing director of Glacier Metals and subsequently, as Lord Brown, a junior minister in one of the Wilson Governments. At Baxi, the Works Council gave a company-wide voice to all employees through their elected representatives and expressed the commitment of the business to company level participation.

From an early date – well before the 1983 ownership changes – Baxi also showed commitment to participation at a different level: the employees' place of work. When a new foundry was commissioned in 1974, *all* workers on *all* shifts were trained to do *all* the various jobs involved: not just one each. Participation at the place of work was later to become one of the company's key mechanisms for improving business performance, and making its 'partnership' more real.

The sceptical reader may ask for direct evidence on the benefits of Baxi's emphasis on employee participation in the years before the ownership change. Arguably, the company's excellent financial results reflected nothing more than the strength of its market position after the introduction of the Baxi Bermuda.

An answer can be found in two unpublished studies of employee attitudes at Baxi, both undertaken before the ownership changes: one by the Tavistock Institute, in 1979; and the second by the London School of Economics in 1983. Both showed an unusually high level of positive feelings about the company.

On the eve of the ownership transfer in 1983, perhaps the three most positive characteristics of the business were:

– The excellence of the financial results over at least the previous decade;

– The underpinning of those results by the strong position of the Baxi Bermuda in its market;

– The apparently excellent attitudes towards the company of a majority of its employees.

The cloud on the horizon was the prospective contraction in demand for Baxi's main products. It is a cloud which was to dominate Baxi throughout its first thirteen years of employee ownership.

How and Why the Family Was Bought Out Following the deaths of John and Richard (Philip's father and uncle) control lay with Philip. Not only had he inherited his father's shareholding, his uncle Richard had passed over a few additional shares in order to give him control. The other big shareholder was his cousin, Mrs Castleton, with only small parcels of shares being held elsewhere.

. The upshot was that, so long as what he proposed was acceptable to Mrs Castleton, decisions lay with Philip. There was not, as there often is in family businesses which survive into the fourth generation, an array of diverse family shareholders. In this respect Philip was in a similar position in relation to Baxi as had been Spedan Lewis to John Lewis and Ernst Abbe to Carl Zeiss.

It was not only Philip Baxendale who made it clear to his children that they would not inherit the business: the same message had been passed to his cousin's children. The temptation to found or extend a dynasty will often prove stronger than a clear-headed judgement of what is likely to be the best for the business, and in many countries, including the UK, tax reliefs favour 'handing on'. Why then did Philip Baxendale decide against?

The short answer is that he judged it to be against the interests of both the business and of those to whom it would have been passed. Philip Baxendale is awash with anecdotes about disasters when substantial family businesses are handed over. Often the person taking over is unsuitable for the job; often, too, the difficulties of a father-son relationship inside the business contribute to the disaster. The end, in Mr Baxendale's experience, has too often been bankruptcy, drink or suicide – or more than one of these. So the risk, in his view, is simply not worth taking.

More generally, he is a sceptic about the success of the hereditary principle as a mechanism for selecting leaders in a competitive world. He is fond of quoting Keynes on the link between celibacy and the great institutional age of the Roman Catholic Church. He also likes to quote Homer's *Odyssey*: 'Few sons indeed are like their fathers; most are worse, only a few, again, are better.' (*Odyssey* 11. 276/77)

But there is also a more positive side to his view of the matter: those in the upcoming generation are free to choose careers or ways of life in keeping with their preferences and talents, and unconstrained by inherited imperatives.

Given his decision not to pass the business to a member of the family, and given that he was not going to live for ever, what choices were there? The two most obvious ones were: a sale to a competitor; or a flotation and associated listing on the Stock Exchange.

In his foreword to *From Participation to Partnership*, Philip Baxendale says of the second that it 'might turn out to be the same as the first because we would then be vulnerable to being taken over'.

He then goes on to explain his reasons for rejecting a sale to a competitor. These were essentially two: his anxiety about the long-term survival of the business and his feeling that it would be wrong – morally not legally – for him to make such a sale:

> I . . . believe that if the Company was bought by a competitor the jobs of our present employees would be at risk and that the unique Company which is Baxi would disappear.
>
> I feel very strongly that I could not sell my share in Baxi to the highest bidder and not care what happened to the Company or the people in it. I also believe that the Company is not mine to sell, certainly not in the sense I would sell a car or a house.

At my request, Philip Baxendale has kindly given me some notes about the possible influence of his Methodist upbringing on his decision including his belief that children should not inherit too much money:

> . . . when I explain why I do not think that it is in children's best interests to inherit a lot of money I tend to say that . . . people get satisfaction from making the best use of the talents they have – that is, their special aptitudes and their money.

And if somebody has too many talents they cannot have the satisfaction of feeling they have made the best use of them.

He also thought it possible that the Methodist boarding school where he spent six years from the age of ten, Woodhouse Grove School, may have had some influence on his thinking. The school motto was 'Bonus et Fidelis' (Good and Faithful) and he noted that:

> The best sermon we got at school was by the headmaster, Clifford Toulson, on the parable of the good and faithful servant. I suppose he gave that sermon about every other year so I probably heard it two or three times.
>
> This idea [about making the best use of your talents] is also reflected in my thinking about family businesses. When I became General Manager at Baxi we employed about sixty people. It was a good profitable business but I can feel I made the best use of my talents in seeing it grow to its present position, not only in terms of its size, employing many hundreds of people, but in its leadership in industrial relations, participation, product design and quality.
>
> *The Company had not been built up by me but by a lot of us working together. I did not feel I was so special that I could take a very large sum of money and leave everybody else's future in the hands of an unknown buyer* [emphasis added].

The school may also have predisposed him towards a democratic approach to business leadership:

> If [the decision] was anything to do with my Methodist School it has . . . to do with the fact that our preachers were ordinary people in ordinary suits. I find it difficult to accept priests in fancy robes as being anybody special. I have never felt that because I [was] the Chairman of the Company that I was somebody special.

Finally, as an afterthought, prompted by his earlier reference to preachers in ordinary suits:

> I think it is something deeper than the suits the preachers wore, but that is all a fundamental part of the Methodist approach. Perhaps this is the reason for my idea of Jesus as a simple ordinary man which perhaps had a greater influence on me than I had realised until I came to write these notes.

If we strip down to the essentials there are similarities as well as dissimilarities in the experience and thinking of Spedan Lewis and Philip Baxendale. Both favour as much democracy as is compatible with the achievement of sustained business success and both find unacceptable rewards to capital which go beyond a reasonable limit and excessive bequests to the next generation. As we shall see, Baxendale sold his family business for about £5.25m in March 1983. This was very nearly the same as the pre-tax profit for the year ended March 1982, £5.8m, but much less than the £8.4m profit the next year. The money was a fraction of what it would have fetched on the stock market. We may also recall in the same context a passage from Spedan Lewis's writing: '... people who control businesses ... should set ... a limit [i.e. to their own rewards] which has some relation to a reasonable standard of living.'

In any event, having rejected the obvious options, an alternative plan was needed:

> I have ... spent a considerable amount of time and effort in the last three years looking for an alternative. With the assistance of Geoff Whittle [then Baxi's Finance Director] we have now come up with a method which enables the company to pay the shareholders a price they are prepared to accept and which the company can afford to pay. The Company will then be owned by an Employee Trust. Ultimately, the majority will be owned by the trustees and up to 49 per cent by the partners as individual employees.

Neither in logic nor in direct money terms was there any serious difficulty about a transaction on these lines. Given how much less than the market value they were prepared to accept, the company was in fact able to pay out the shareholders from its own liquid resources without borrowing a penny. The difficulties were rather different: about how to arrange the deal in such a way as to minimise any resulting tax liabilities. The problem was not one of capital gains tax (CGT). For himself and his family Mr Baxendale made no attempt to get round CGT liability and it did not affect Mrs Castleton and her family, who were resident in the Isle of Man.

Instead the difficulties had to do with Capital Transfer Tax (CTT). They had to be overcome because of the magnitude of the possible liabilities. Mr Baxendale risked ending up as a 'minus millionaire'. CTT (which has since been abolished) was payable at that time at a 40% rate on any difference between a so-called market price for the business and that at which the deal was struck. It was also payable on gifts.

As to the market value of the business, Andreas Whittam Smith, then City Editor of the *Daily Telegraph*, ventured a figure of £40m, noting that Baxi 'has an excellent record with pre-tax profits rising from £419,000 in 1971/72 to £5.84m in 1981/2'. If it was worth anything like that, and some might argue that the figure was low, Mr Baxendale's bank balance might have moved into the red to the tune of £5m or more if he had had to pay CTT.

Nor was this all. A second possible CTT liability was also involved: in getting money from the company to an employee trust, so that the latter could become the new owner of the business once the family shareholders had been bought out.

How the trust could become the owner without incurring quite unacceptable tax liabilities baffled Mr Baxendale and Mr Whittle during much of 1982. Both the answer, and its source, were matters of some surprise when they eventually appeared.

The source of the answer was the Financial Secretary to the Treasury at the time, Nicholas Ridley. He and his advisers pointed out that interesting possibilities had been opened up by some little noticed provisions of the previous (1981) Finance Act. Under these provisions a company was, in principle and in certain circumstances, permitted to buy back its own shares and then cancel them.

The Financial Secretary and his officials went on to outline a solution. Its starting point was a modest employee trust which had already been established by the company in the previous year, and which owned just over 2 per cent of the share capital of Richard Baxendale and Sons. The shareholding amounted to 150 of the 7,000 x £1 ordinary shares then in issue and a further 150 of the 7,000 x £1 preference shares in issue at the time. Using after-tax profits, the company had given the Trust the quite modest means – a sum of £15,000 – which it had needed to buy this small shareholding. Mr Baxendale and Mr Whittle had hoped that the Inland Revenue could be persuaded to allow the company to pass a much larger sum to the trust so that it could acquire a much larger shareholding. But the Revenue's response had been unambiguous: any substantial sum which was given by the company to the trust would be taxable.

At the heart of what Mr Ridley and his officials suggested was a method of 'pumping up' the 2% shareholding already owned by the Employee Trust so that it became not 2% but 100%. Once suggested, it seemed like simplicity itself. The company would buy from Baxendale and his fellow shareholders the whole of the balance of 98% of the company's share capital which they owned, and then cancel them. Hey presto! The Trust's shareholding would have been 'pumped up' from 2 per cent to 100 per cent. Further, Mr Ridley and his officials gave it as their oral opinion that no tax liabilities – other than any for CGT – would be incurred, though that was not put on paper.

For Mr Baxendale, the oral assurance from Mr Ridley and his officials was sufficient and the set of steps which they had put forward was duly implemented at the end of March 1983. Once the various transactions had been completed, the former shareholders in Richard Baxendale and Sons received 'a price which they could accept and which the company could afford to pay'. The Employee Trust became the owner of the entire share capital of the business and neither at the moment of completion nor later was there any demand from the Inland Revenue to the effect that CTT was payable. In a letter dated 21 December 1983, the Share Valuation Division of the Inland Revenue finally put in writing that it was 'able to confirm that the purchase by the company of its own shares has not given rise to any liability to Capital Transfer Tax'.

It may be worth adding a political footnote. In the background was a promise which had been made to Jo Grimond MP by Nigel Lawson MP – Ridley's predecessor as Financial Secretary – during the second reading of the 1982 Finance Bill. The promise was given by Lawson in exchange for the withdrawal by Grimond of an amendment which he had tabled to facilitate the sale of businesses to their employees. The promise was that if an actual business had difficulties in achieving that objective, then his door and that of his successors would always be open to discuss the matter. I should only add that when he spoke on his amendment in that Finance Bill debate, Lord Grimond, as he later became, had declared an interest: that of being the unpaid Chairman of the company which employs me, Job Ownership Ltd.

The Business Record: 1983–1996 In comparison with its main competitors and in its core business of domestic gas boiler manufacture, Baxi's record from early 1983 to early 1993 – its first Partnership decade – was as good as the best and probably rather better. The main factor in this success was the strength of the position which the company inherited from its pre-partnership past.

Detailed data for years eleven and twelve suggest a quite sharp falling off. Aside from the conditions in the market, the single most important factor behind this deterioration has been persuasively identified by Philip Baxendale. It is one for which he accepts a full share of responsibility: a series of different chief executives as the company struggled to find the right successor to Ian Smith who retired from the top post in 1989. Only in 1994, when the reins were taken over by Bryan Gray, was it widely felt that the right answer to the succession problem had been found.

But the costs of failing to solve the problem earlier, or indeed of failing to avoid having a succession problem at all, were clearly considerable. There was some loss of market share in 1993 and 1994. Potentially more damaging, it seems that development expenditure was seriously cut back in the early years of the 1990s after Ian Smith's retirement. And these 'costs of failure over the succession' were highlighted in the year to end – March 1995, when the company posted an actual pre-tax loss of £2.5m.

One other fundamentally important issue during Baxi's first thirteen Partnership years was the reality (or otherwise) of the company's partnership arrangements – the involvement of its employee-owners in running their company. From the late 1980s this issue was the source of important changes. The story of the company's quest for a real partnership is set out later.

To begin with, Baxi remained far and away the market leader in its own flagship line of domestic gas back boilers. For cast iron wall-mounted boilers, its second most important product, the increase in market share over this same period was dramatically greater: a growth of some 50% to nearly a quarter share of that market.

Baxi entered the market for floor-standing boilers, its third boiler line, only in 1983. However, almost immediately it succeeded in grabbing a useful share of above 5% of total deliveries, and then in effect held on to it. Taken altogether, Baxi increased its share of the total British gas boiler market by a little over 10% – from around 21% to a little over 23% – between the beginning and the end of its first Partnership decade. Moreover, there were then two significant gas boiler lines in which Baxi did *not* compete – the so-called 'Combi' boilers and those wall-mounted boilers which are not made of cast iron. Thus its share of the market for those gas boiler products in which it did compete was very substantially more: probably well over 30% by 1993.

More specialised data sets are available. They enable us to bring Baxi's comparative performance over this decade into sharper focus.

A set of market share statistics for 1981 and 1991 offer the clearest picture if we arrange the suppliers into three groups. First, Baxi itself; second, the 'other suppliers among the big five' (Stelrad, Glow-worm, Potterton and Myson) taken together; and third, 'all others'. This last category includes overseas suppliers as well as the smaller UK manufacturers. The comparative breakdown of supply as between 1981 and 1991 shows the following: a sharp squeeze on the aggregate share of the 'other big five'; a big increase in the share of 'all others'; and Baxi rather more than holding its own.

UK Gas Boiler Market: Shares – 1981 and 1991

Baxi	20%	21%
Other big five	74%	61%
All others	6%	18%

This comparative success is the more impressive given that the whole market contracted sharply in the second half of Baxi's first Partnership decade. In round figures the fall was close to 25% between the record of over 900,000 units in 1987, and a total of below 700,000 in 1992. The contraction in the total market was also found in the three main subdivisions in which Baxi was competing – the back boilers, the cast-iron wall-mounted boilers, and the floor-standing boilers.

Comparative statistics from a well-known corporate data base which covers UK manufacturers of cooking and heating appliances offers further evidence of Baxi's performance. The data is for 1992 and covers pay, profit margins and sales per employee.

Measures of Comparative Performance: 1992

	Profit Margin %	Average Remuneration £	Sales Per Employee £
Baxi	15.3	17,581	65,459
Top Industry Q'tile	11.5	11,983	54,762
Median of Industry	7.6	10,932	44,444
Low Industry Q'tile	(2.0)	9,524	26,191

The Baxi 'average remuneration' statistic does *not* include either the partners' cash profit payments or the value of the shares distributed to them under the company's so-called 1978 Act scheme. Taken together, these add just over £2,400 – nearly 14% – to the average of £17,581 which partners received in 1992 as straight pay. On the other hand, in 1995 Baxi decided it would be unwise to sustain these high remuneration levels and pay rates were adjusted downwards, towards those of its competitors in the top quartile. Critics would say that they should never have been allowed to reach the figures reflected in the table.

We can broaden this picture of the first ten years with the statistics of Baxi's annual turnover. Baxi's sales moved mainly in line with the market as a whole:

Annual Sales 1983–1992

£m Constant (92) Prices

1983	65.3	1988	83.6
1984	60.6	1989	81.9
1985	59.5	1990	81.6
1986	69.7	1991	77.0
1987	82.2	1992	73.5

In effect the total market expanded quite sharply in the middle years of the Partnership's first decade. The 1987 annual report records an increase of 12% in the total gas central heating market, just ahead of Baxi's own 11% increase. But later it went into sharp decline: the 1992 annual report discloses a cumulative decline in the central heating market of 25% between 1989 and 1991.

Against that market background, the annual figures for trading profits supply a first measure of the trend of Baxi's own performance; and the statistics for the percentage return on sales give an idea of the changing strength of the competition.

Trading Profit and Return on Sales

	(£m Constant '92 Prices)	(%)
1983	12.7	19.9
1984	11.0	18.5
1985	8.1	14.5
1986	10.8	16.1

1987	13.9	17.3
1988	10.7	13.0
1989	7.0	9.1
1990	5.5	7.7
1991	8.5	11.9
1992	8.7	12.8

So much for the statistics of the first ten Partnership years down to 1992. The record of the mid-1990s is summarised, if rather crudely, by pre-tax profits: a decline into actual loss, followed by a recovery in 1995/6.

Pre-tax Profits (Losses) 1990/91 to 1995/96

£m at current prices

1992/3	7.3
1993/4	5.6
1994/5	(2.5)
1995/6	5.2

Having looked at the statistics, I now turn to the Baxi story and especially that of its leadership and of the new products and investments. During the first seven years of Partnership, from 1983 until his retirement in 1989, Ian Smith was managing director. He had held this position since 1974 when Philip Baxendale became non-executive chairman. Mr Smith is a foundryman by profession. He joined the business in 1958, and as general manager created the Works Council in 1961.

In the foreword to *From Participation to Partnership*, Philip Baxendale paid a warm tribute to Ian Smith's attitude to industry's human dimension: 'I have been extremely lucky in having Ian Smith working with me, who believes as I do, that people will work better and more happily if you allow them to participate as much as possible.'

The biggest single investment between the establishment of the Partnership in 1983 and Mr Smith's retirement in 1989 was Baxi's £7m new foundry – hailed by Mr Smith in the annual report after it had come into production in 1987 as 'the most modern new Foundry complex of its kind in Europe'. I referred earlier to its ecological virtues. The same annual report highlighted its potential for giving Baxi a competitive edge:

This is a most exciting development and gives Baxi the opportunity to design better heating appliances.

The new product strategy revolves around the new Foundry
permitting the manufacture of smaller, cheaper, higher quality,
lower weight heat exchangers ... we can now forge ahead and
turn out products, especially boilers, significantly better than
the competition.

Baxi's 1992 annual report had this to say about the £7m new
foundry investment, and the new product range which it made possible:

Baxi's faith in the future of cast iron heat exchangers [i.e.
boilers] was proved beyond doubt when, in 1987, against
the conventional wisdom of the experts, the company commissioned a £7m state-of-the-art foundry. Through this installation ... Baxi turned the *traditionally unwieldy process
of green sand foundry production into a flexible tool for
the manufacture of light weight monobloc cast iron heat
exchangers. The success of the mould-breaking Solo wall
mounted boiler range is tangible proof of Baxi's ability to
employ innovation for profit* [emphasis added].

In his last annual report (the year to end–March 1989) Ian Smith
foresaw the introduction 'in the coming year' of – 'our new wall
mounted boiler – the Baxi Solo. The Solo is a product that we
believe has 'broken the mould' in boiler design. It is the only 'one
man lift' cast iron boiler on the market and it is smaller than any
fanned flue boiler the competition have to offer.'

The new investment (the new foundry) and new product
introductions (the Baxi Solo) in Mr Smith's last years did not bear
fruit till after his retirement. He was also responsible for a number
of other highly positive developments: for example the 1985
agreement to introduce 'single status'. This brought the elimination
of most of the differences between the conditions of blue collar and
other employees. The best ever trading profits in the year to
end–March 1987 was also a milestone achievement of a kind, even
if mainly explained by the luck of the market. There was too the
launch of a Company Improvement Plan (CIP) in the same year
under the initiative of Simon Carter, to whom we return in a
moment.

However, Mr Smith's last years were not all good. Some 'teething faults' apparently limited the initial success of the Baxi Solo. There has also since been criticism of the growth of a cash mountain during his period of office – or more exactly of the failure to find sufficient opportunities for new investment. The mountain had grown to £19m by the time of his retirement in 1989. By March 1993, it had reached £49m.

As for Ian Smith, I thought it right before completing this case study to ask Mr Baxendale for his considered view of Mr Smith's twenty-eight-year tenure:

I will begin by paying proper tribute to Ian Smith's major role in taking Baxi from being a small manufacturer of solid fuel appliances to being the highly profitable market leader in Gas Domestic Boilers, mainly due to excellent 'marketing' in the full sense of that word.

On the negative side of what was carried forward to the next business period, we have to note that not enough was done about management succession. Partnership cannot be blamed for this. It was the responsibility of Ian Smith acting with the approval of the Trustees . . . A lot of problems would have been avoided if my wish to move to a group structure had been implemented several years before Ian Smith was due to retire. I accept ultimate responsibility for this myself. As Chairman of the trustees I should have insisted on the changes being made.

The other main negative legacy of Ian Smith's last years was a marked deterioration in industrial relations which was most convincingly documented at the time by Simon Carter in a paper entitled *The Partnership Dilemma*. Part of the cause may have been the fact that responsibility for Baxi's industrial relations, which had been convincingly praised by top professionals before the 1983 change of ownership, was delegated by Ian Smith during his last ten years. But the fall in morale may also have reflected his own rather limited belief in the potential of employee ownership. On that crucial issue I now accept that his views were different from mine.

I find Ian Smith's change of heart difficult to understand because, prior to his delegating responsibility for industrial relations, he was very keen on encouraging participation. It was he who established the unanimous voting on the Works Council and introduced training of all workers to do all the jobs when the new foundry was commissioned in 1974. The hard work and enthusiasm he put into encouraging participation was reflected in the excellent attitudes shown in the Tavistock report of 1979. It was this enthusiasm of Ian Smith which led me to the comments I made about Ian Smith in *From Participation to Partnership*, believing as I do in participation.

For the purposes of this book it is clearly the issue of industrial relations which is most important. For the central concern of this case study is with the reality and evolution of the 'practice of partnership'. Other criticisms could just as well apply – or not – if Baxi was a conventional capitalist company. But if you are a 'partnership company' and fail to make – or to try to make – a serious reality of that 'partnership', then you may be open to a rather different specific criticism.

So in what follows I shall be concerned mainly with the industrial relations issue. But I must also reiterate that Philip Baxendale also attaches particular importance to the top management succession problem and sees his own share of responsibility in that case as specially important. In the first place, Mr Baxendale accepts a share of responsibility for the fact that there was no acceptable 'inside' candidate to succeed Smith when he retired. He also accepts a share of responsibility for what followed from that. There was, first, an attempt to bring in an outsider to work initially under Smith and eventually to succeed him. It lasted only a few months. Second, David Dry was designated successor to Smith. He lasted in the top position for just over two years and then bowed to a request that he offer his resignation.

The turning point in the succession saga probably came with what may be seen in retrospect as an 'interregnum' under Simon Carter. He took over the top post when Mr Dry resigned in 1992, but himself resigned in 1994. The appointment of Bryan Gray from outside, first as 'group commercial director' and subsequently to succeed Mr Carter as group chief executive looked at the time of writing as if it had provided a long-term solution to the leadership problem.

But what seems clear beyond any shadow of doubt from the

above evidence is that there was a leadership failure. It seems reasonable to agree with Philip Baxendale that the failure had nothing directly to do with 'partnership'. The sharp deterioration in the results of the business from 1993 to 1995 can – if only indirectly – be ascribed to that failure. As a matter of detail, Mr Baxendale also believes – and he may well be right – that the extent of the deterioration from 1993 onwards partly reflects a degree of 'false' profits in the results for the two previous years.

The Partnership Issue I turn now to the issue of industrial relations: what came to be called at Baxi the issue of 'partnership'. Mr Smith's later years were characterised by a widespread fall in morale and the growth of a disturbing cynicism about the notion of 'partnership'. The reality of that fall in morale is not in dispute. More complex and problematic are the reasons *why* it happened, though the deteriorating market conditions were no doubt part of the explanation.

The problems were analysed by Simon Carter in a seminal report written in 1989 – and the validity of this report was not challenged by Ian Smith or his board. To begin with Carter reminded his readers that life in Baxi's particular market place was not getting any easier and that all might not be for the best inside the business:

> The business is less profitable today than it was a few years ago; the rate of technological development will at some time outdate our existing product base; the market environment is more competitive with our having to fight harder to maintain a stable position let alone increase it; and an ongoing battle to improve our manufacturing capability with a clash between advanced techniques and traditional craft and skill based environments. Add to this the characteristics of an ageing workforce; a narrowly, rather than broadly, developed management competence; inter and intra union conflicts ... and all within a business which calls itself a Partnership, but with an operating environment of 'reality' different from the expectations of a lot of people who work in it.

To establish the non-reality or even the negative reality of 'partnership' Mr Carter cited an array of attitudes and feelings expressed to him in his discussions with partners. Here are a selection from a total of twenty, all negative.

– 'Being a Partner' does not actually mean anything.
– 'Them and us' is stronger now than ever before.
– Management do not listen to us or ask for our views.
– The real power-holders in the Company are the unions.
– The Partnership Council has low credibility.
– Share ownership is contrived and valuations manipulated.
– Partnership is not a topic for discussion in day-to-day terms. It doesn't mean anything, therefore people don't think in Partnership terms. What is the point, we're all here as individuals at the end of the day?

However after the end of this baleful litany, Carter went on: 'Beneath the comments listed above there is a strong feeling that the Partners want it [the Partnership] to be something meaningful and that they have a valuable contribution to make.'

Should that last sentence be dismissed as pious wishful thinking? Early in 1991 the Partnership was visited by William Brenneisen, then the Vice President for Human Resources at the employee-owned Weirton Steel Corporation of West Virginia in the USA. Mr Brenneisen was exposed to various episodes of 'employee owner-ship in action', in particular, to presentations by a number of Continuous Improvement Programme (CIP) work teams who described contributions they had made to improvements in product quality and work practice, and to reductions in costs. Mr Brenneisen later told anyone who was prepared to listen that neither at Weirton nor elsewhere in the United States had he ever seen evidence of such an advanced 'employee ownership culture'. What he was saying was that he had never seen a bunch of employee owners whose be-haviour came so close to that of real owners.

Mr Brenneisen is a top professional in the field and must be assumed to be a good judge of the quality of what he saw. Of course there may have been an element of luck about the par-ticular presentations which he witnessed. Sceptical readers may also want to consider a more general cautionary point: that if attitudes can change as rapidly as they appear to have done between those reported by Mr Carter in *The Partnership Dilemma* in early 1989 and those to which Mr Brenneisen was exposed little more than two years later, they may well not be very strongly established.

But the important questions are not about whether what Mr

Brenneisen saw was the result of real cultural change; nor are they about what part of the improved performance between 1990 and 1992 can be attributed to the same source. The real questions are: first, whether more positive attitudes to the partnership concept have replaced those which Mr Carter found in his seminal study; second, whether whether systems of employee involvement have been introduced which are acceptable to all the main parties – management, unions and rank-and-file employees; and third, whether these systems enable the shop floor to enhance its contribution to the success of the business.

This is a continuing and never-to-be-completed process: hence the metaphor of a continuing quest. Nevertheless, developments since Mr Carter wrote his report, including those which have since been superseded in their turn, have undoubtedly moved the company further down the road. Some changes were explicitly designed to enable ordinary shopfloor workers to become more involved in the decisions and routines which most directly affect them. Others have been spin-offs from changes external to the 'partnership issue' itself – consequences for example of the move to a group structure, or of a redundancy exercise early in 1991.

Analytically, these changes are probably best understood as reflecting a spectrum of opinion about 'partnership' and about employee ownership generally. It is probably fair to identify the views of Ian Smith as being at one end of the spectrum and those of Simon Carter at the other. Put crudely, Mr Smith's view is that partnership and employee ownership are basically ornamental in character and must not be allowed to interfere with the well-established norms of sound business practice. Put equally crudely, Mr Carter's view is that because of its structure as a partnership, Baxi has a duty to maximise almost without limit the 'empowerment' of its rank and file employees. If it does not, it will risk cynicism, disillusion, frustration and disastrously low morale. There is plenty of space for positions intermediate between these two.

The details of what happened will be easy to understand if we think of partnership as potentially operating at different levels: the workplace is at the bottom and the supreme company government at the top, with intermediate levels in between where it may also find expression.

There were two main phases. During the first, which ended when

Mr Carter stepped down as chief executive in 1994, the direction of change was towards greater empowerment at both top and lower levels. In the second phase, the situation was mainly frozen; some would say that empowerment was put into reverse. This happened because a proposal by Mr Carter to introduce a 'partnership' component at the apex of the company's government – by giving elected partners a voice on the group board at least equal to that of management – was effectively turned down. Evidently, Bryan Gray, who succeeded Mr Carter as chief executive, was not ready to accept such an arrangement. He was opposed to it despite the fact that employee directors remain on the boards of subsidiaries and a promise has been made that two elected employee directors will be added to the group board in due course. One was added in 1998. But Baxi moved into the later 1990s with a fairly conventional group structure and a group board controlled by non-executives.

The rest of this section discusses these developments in more detail.

In 1990, while David Dry was chief executive, a whole tier of management was eliminated and the departmental structure completely reorganised. The previous structure, divided by function (production, finance, sales and so on), was replaced by a system of semi-separate business units. Each was in principle responsible for satisfying its own specialised needs. For example, it was required to sell its own output as well as manufacturing it, and to keep a record of its own financial results. The flagship Baxi Bermuda range of boilers became one of these new businesses, the sheet metal workshop another. Members of the board were given 'portfolio' responsibility for one or more of these businesses. Under them each unit had its own business manager. Under these managers was a tier of team leaders, and below them came the actual rank-and-file workers. These were to have no formal management functions at all. Between this rank and file and their responsible director there were thus no more than two intermediaries.

It is surely right to see this reorganisation as a move towards 'empowerment': having fewer middle managers means that those at the bottom are closer to the decision-making level at the top. But the changes clearly also had the aim of making all partners more business-minded, more responsive to their markets – whether inside or outside the firm – and of cutting down the time needed for responses, both to changes in demand and to suggested supply side improvements. The changes were memorably depicted in a wheel-shaped organigram. The chief executive, Mr Dry, was at the centre of the wheel – like the sun in the Copernican diagram of the planetary system. Shop-floor and other non-management partners were at the outer edge. The implied thrusts were both ways: from the centre outwards to the customers beyond the wheel's edge, and from those customers back to the centre.

Linked both in time and logic to this reorganisation was a new company-wide continuous improvement programme (CIP) which found its expression in continuous improvement (work) teams (CITs) for which the new semi-autonomous units became responsible. The hypothesis was that proposals for improvement thrown up by the CITs would be implemented significantly faster than otherwise. Presentations by CITs of their own home-grown improvements were what so impressed Mr Brenneisen when he visited Baxi. There is a stream of anecdotal evidence during the period before Mr Carter's departure about specific improvements originated by them, and the resulting savings. For example, the redesign of a paint-shop was said to have yielded savings of hundreds of thousands for a modest outlay.

To complement these moves towards greater empowerment of Baxi's partners in the actual workplace, Mr Carter later made changes at the top of the business. But before we go on to them, we must consider the redundancies imposed in 1991 and the resignation of Mr Dry in 1992.

In 1991, just under a hundred partners, about 10% of the workforce, were made compulsorily redundant. The fact that those who left were selected by management is at least as important as the number. Under Mr Dry, Mr Carter held special responsibility for industrial relations. He makes no bones about having included among the redundancies a group of partners who had been particularly associated with traditional (and still then essentially adversarial) trade union activity at Baxi. Mr Carter concedes that he and Mr Dry were lucky to have got through this highly charged episode without a strike. An unusually generous redundancy package may have helped; so indeed may the fact of employee ownership. What seems certain is that there had been no serious resurgence of adversarial trade union activism at Baxi up to the time of writing.

As for Mr Dry ... put simply, he was *asked* to resign because his style and methods were judged to be incompatible with what should be the realities of a genuine partnership. We may assume that, at the very least, his departure affected the 'political chemistry' at Baxi. It must surely have indicated that there were people at the top who meant what they said when they talked about making the partnership more real.

Having stepped into Mr Dry's shoes, Mr Carter chose after only two years to return to the consultancy work from which he had joined Baxi in the first place. But a number of the changes he made affected the partnership dimension of the business.

To begin with he sought to make a reality of what had been a key component of Philip Baxendale's original idea of how the partnership should work. That component was the Partnership Council, a hybrid body set up shortly after the ownership transfer. It was composed of representatives (elected by the partners) and appointed trustees (who held the main block of controlling shares in their trust).

Mr Baxendale's original idea had been that the Partnership Council (PC) should operate as a supervisory board to which the top executive management should be answerable and accountable. And indeed, under Mr Smith and Mr Dry, regular meetings between the chief executive and the PC were in some sense *conducted* as if the latter were a supervisory board. But the reality, down to Mr Carter's appointment as chief executive, was very different. He changed all that. It is significant that Mr Smith, who had been appointed a trustee on his retirement as chief executive, chose to make the role of the Partnership Council a resignation issue. His view was that the elected partnership councillors were simply not competent to perform as members of a real supervisory board. Mr Baxendale blames himself for not giving the PC the leadership which would have enabled it to act as a real supervisory board. He originally stated that the executive would be accountable to the PC. The managing director, Ian Smith and later David Dry, accounted to the PC for what they wished. Mr Baxendale feels he should have led the PC to monitor the executive. This would have given the PC a real role and would perhaps have challenged the executive, for example over the growth of overheads from 1985 onwards.

These events, and especially the resignation from the trustee body of Mr Smith, created quite a stir at Baxi. On the other hand, the effect (if not the intention) of a quite different set of changes introduced by Mr Carter shortly afterwards was to alter the Partnership Council and its role.

Those changes included a merging of various employee representative bodies into one council, a switch to a group structure, and the introduction of elected employee directors onto the boards of the new subsidiary companies with a promise that they would later be introduced onto the group board – a promise honoured at least in part when one employee director was included in the main board in the summer of 1998.

The change to one council was something which had been recognised as desirable almost since the partnership was formed. There had been a latent source of conflict with employees having two different representatives, one on the works council and one on the Partnership Council. Mr Carter brought this out into the open, and got people to agree after much discussion. This new council was not really different from the old PC but, as the only council, was much more credible. The change to one council also meant there were changes in handling issues of wages and conditions. Most notably, (a) trade unions lost their traditional right of total responsibility for negotiating wages and conditions; and (b) after the switch to a group with subsidiaries, it was at the level of subsidiaries that decisions about wages and conditions came to be made. At least in Mr Carter's eyes there was a partnership as well as an operational element in these changes. The employee directors at the subsidiary level, taken together with the promise of their early presence on the group board, were essentially seen by him as a kind of 'partnership new deal' – in which the surrender by the trade unions of their exclusive wage bargaining power was also part of the overall settlement.

Since Mr Carter had left Baxi before the whole package was implemented, the vision he had for it is perhaps of little more than academic interest, and also necessarily somewhat speculative. But not in the least bit speculative are the two main developments since the introduction of the group structure. There were a number of acquisitions and a painful but necessary wage adjustment in 1995.

While Mr Carter was chief executive and Bryan Gray commercial director, four significant acquisitions were made: two on mainland Europe, one in Scotland and one in the Midlands. Though Mr Carter, as chief executive, had final responsibility, the deals were actually negotiated by Mr Gray. Baxi itself also moved towards 'new business' with substantial growth potential. The foundry (later Alfar Ltd) and the sheet metal department (later Spartek Ltd) were reorganised as separate companies and encouraged to look outside Baxi for customers. Alfar was soon devoting more of its capacity making castings for outside customers than for Baxi Heating. Spartek makes sheet metal and engineering components for other subsidiary companies and outside customers, as well as for Baxi Heating. Another subidiary has been formed, which is now involved in a joint venture with an Italian company to exploit development of an innovative method of producing aluminium castings.

The logic of these developments was essentially commercial. Others were only partly commercial. Baxi took a minority stake in a specialist employee ownership consultancy called Capital Strategies. With a firm of venture capitalists, it then helped to set up a fund to finance employee buy-outs and the expansion of businesses where employees own a significant stake. Close to home, it bought the local football team – Tom Finney's old club, Preston North End.

As well as reflecting their own potential, these new developments also reflect the continued impact of that cloud which has hovered over the business ever since the ownership changes of 1983: the long-term decline in the market for domestic boilers. This same decline prompted a most painful project of wage 'adjustment' – and in the case of almost all affected individuals – of wage *reductions* in 1995.

Readers may recall the earlier table which showed that wages paid by Baxi in 1992 were way above those paid by other companies in the industry's top quartile, even before allowing for the cash bonus and employee share schemes. In 1993, before its importance began to be diminished by the switch to the group structure, the Partnership Council decided to come up with a 'policy guideline' on pay. Generally this was 'good pay for all employees', and specifically, the aim was that Baxi's rates should coincide with those of the industry's top quartile of firms. Without, it seems, suspecting what the actual comparison would show, the Council authorised management to look into the matter. Given the data in the earlier table, what the management found will come as no surprise.

Moreover, when the related issue of comparative productivity was also examined, Baxi's performance in terms of value-added per employee appeared to be well *below* that of the top quartile. For the rest, it is enough to say that painful remedies of the obvious kind were insisted on by management, though cushioned slightly in the first year. In response, Baxi's unions sought the advice of local full-time officials. The latter predictably urged industrial action. It is perhaps indicative of the unions' dwindling power that Baxi's employee-shareholder partners rejected their unions' advice.

Four rather different points seem to me to have been established beyond all reasonable doubt by Baxi's employee ownership experience over its first thirteen years. Early Christians identified as the 'Pelagian' heresy the view that human effort, as opposed to the grace of the holy spirit, makes the real difference to outcomes in the long run. The first point which Baxi's experience has established is that in employee ownership 'Pelagianism' should be the orthodoxy not the heresy. For that experience shows that employee ownership by itself, and without strenuous human efforts in support, will not generate beneficial results. Mr Carter's seminal partnership report in 1989 in fact suggests a second and tougher point: that if employee ownership is introduced, and nothing else changes, then frustration and cynicism are the most likely results. But thirdly, this Baxi experience perhaps suggests that the realities of the employee ownership may very gradually sink in. That is at least a possible, though not a necessary, inference to draw from the rejection by the workforce of the union officials' advice to go on strike against the wage reductions insisted on by management. Finally – though at least as important as the earlier three conclusions – it must be clear that employee ownership needs strong managerial support if it is to realise its potential.

Ownership and Control As used here the word 'partnership' does not have its formal legal meaning. The employees of Baxi and John Lewis are not partners in the same sense as in a partnership of lawyers. In both Baxi and John Lewis the legal form of the corporate entity is that of a limited company. The word 'partner' is used to express the fact that employees are part-owners of the business in which they work and have a voice in its control. But the details of the ownership and control arrangements in these two Partnerships, Baxi and John Lewis, are far from identical.

On ownership, the main contrast is that at John Lewis the *entire* share capital of the business is owned, in some sense collectively, by an employee trust, while at Baxi part is owned individually. The John Lewis partners may be said to own the capital *income* of the business; but not, or anyway not as individuals, the capital itself. It is true that an Employee Trust became the owner of Baxi's entire share capital in 1983. But as Philip Baxendale wrote at the time: 'Ultimately it will be owned, the majority by the employee trust and up to 49 per cent by the Partners as individual employees.'

In explaining these prospective arrangements and in particular their individual component, he began by recalling the reasons which had persuaded the company to introduce its cash profit-sharing scheme much earlier:

> We started our profit-sharing scheme in 1965 because it seemed to us that you cannot talk to people about the need to make a good profit unless they benefit from it.
>
> Equally it seems to me that it is difficult to convince people of the need to plough back a major proportion of the profit, if they don't have any interest in it once it is ploughed back.

Since that was written, shares in the Baxi Partnership have been got out to individual employees in successive years starting in 1984. Up to 1991 the sole mechanism was a '1978 Act Scheme'. Since then two further channels have been opened up – one linked to the Partnership's cash profit-sharing scheme, and the second a so-called 'Save as You Earn' (SAYE) scheme.

The cumulative result of these schemes by mid-1996 was that 9.6% of Baxi's ordinary share capital was then owned by its individual employees. But that greatly understates the aggregate of shares which have passed into the ownership of employees since 1984. Under various rules Baxi's partners have been permitted or required to sell back their shares. If we add to the shares held by employees in mid-1996 those which *have been* so held but have since been sold back, some 35% of the equity has been individually held.

A basic rule is that those who leave are *required* to sell back their shares: otherwise, there would be a steady outwards leakage of ownership to non-employees. The buyer will normally be one or other of two employee trusts. The first is the main trust which must always own at least 51% of the shares. The other is required by law to figure as part of Baxi's so-called '1978 Act Scheme'.

As well as being required to sell their shares back when they leave, Baxi's partners are permitted to do so in other circumstances. Up to 1995, the retention rules in the tax laws governing employee shares were supplemented by Baxi's own rules. But since the 1995 Budget, partners have been permitted to sell as soon as they are allowed to by the law of the land. For those wanting to avoid tax, the retention period was reduced to three years in the 1995 Budget. This change triggered off a precipitous decline in the percentage of individually held shares between 1994 and 1996.

There is an important distinction between the shares which reach Baxi partners through the SAYE scheme – and through its cash profit-sharing arrangements – and those which reach them through the the 1978 Act Scheme. In the first two cases the partner must make a cash commitment. This can be either in actual money or in money foregone. The commitment is one condition of acquiring employee shares or options on shares. By contrast, no cash is required for partners to enjoy benefits under the 1978 Act Scheme.

Two other points about the individually-owned Baxi shares should also be mentioned. The first is that no dividends have been paid on them, and this is likely to continue. The logic here is that the Partnership's cash profit-sharing scheme – still in good years very much alive and well – may reasonably operate as an appropriate substitute for dividend payments on employee shares. Moreover in the absence of dividends, the partners have a reinforced interest in seeing that the value of their shares goes up, not down.

Second, the Baxi rules do not permit the buying and selling of shares as between individual employees. Here, the logic is that this would risk undermining internal cohesion. For it could result in an unacceptably unequal distribution of shareholdings.

As it is, some have argued that the distribution of shares through the 1978 Act Scheme has been unacceptable in the opposite direction: altogether too equal. That is because, in line with majority opinion at the time, it was decided in 1983 that, after an initial adjustment to take account of length of service, the share distribution under Baxi's 1978 Act scheme would be completely equal. This means that the managing director and the floor sweeper would receive an identical parcel of shares. The danger with such an arrangement is that it may supply an insufficient incentive to spur and retain top management. It is because of this danger that distributions under Baxi's cash profit-sharing scheme are linked to rates of pay.

It is worth noting that the statutory rules which apply to the distribution of shares when a 1978 Act Scheme is used allow for a range of possibilities, always provided that the formula chosen satisfies what might be called a 'fairness test'. The actual phrase used in the legislation is that the distribution must be on 'similar terms'. The condition is satisfied when the distribution is completely equal, but also when it is proportionate or partly proportionate to rates of pay, or length of service, or to a combination of those two. It does not appear that any generally accepted 'best practice' has yet evolved on this issue. Whatever seems best, in the circumstances of a particular business at a particular time, probably *is* best.

Next, we need to ask about the value of accumulated shareholdings. The actual share values are set annually in agreement between the company and the Inland Revenue. As against an original figure of £2.10 set in 1984, those values reached a peak, following two unusually profitable years, of £4.42 in the summer of 1992. But they fell quite sharply in each of the two following years, were down to about £2.50 in the 1994 valuation and down again in 1995. However, they had recovered significantly twelve months later and the 1996 valuation was £3.41 and then higher in 1997 and 1998. For a partner who had been in the scheme from the start, who had sold no shares and had been earning an average wage, the value of his or her shareholding in mid-1998 was roughly £12,000, or equivalent to about nine months' pay for that same year.

But to get a full measure of the financial benefits enjoyed by the partners, we must add in the annual cash bonus. This is a benefit which, as we saw earlier, averaged about the equivalent of three weeks' pay over the decade down to end–March 1983, and only slightly less over the following one. Recently, it has been a different story: a sharp fall in 1993 and 1994, and zero in 1995; what amounted to an *ex gratia* payment of about 3% in mid-1996, followed by bonuses of over 10% in 1997 and 1998.

Following changes in 1996 and 1997 to the already rather bewildering arrangements of the employee share ownership and financial participation at Baxi, a stop press paragraph has to be interpolated. The changes relate to what used to be the fairly uncomplicated system of cash profit-sharing which goes back to the pre-Partnership days. Partners are now enjoined to take their 'profit sharing' in shares not cash; but may be permitted to prefer cash so long as they accept a tax penalty. The benefits flowing from this scheme remain proportionate to rates of pay. But secondly, and following the change to the new 'group-and-subsidiaries' structure, this 'profit sharing' is linked to the results of the particular subsidiary in which individual employees are working. On the other hand, the main elements in the logic of the original '1998 Act employee share Scheme' has not been changed. It continues to be linked to the performance of the (group) business as a whole. And the benefits under it continue to be distributed equally, regardless of pay rates.

To complete this account of Baxi's ownership arrangements, we need to say a word about the shares owned by the original Employee Trust which must always remain a majority. The basic logic is to erect a permanent barrier against the temptation to sell which might assail the individual employee shareholders if faced with a really attractive offer. The acceptance of such an offer would go against the key ground on which sale of the business to a competitor was rejected in the first place.

The trust's permanent majority shareholding also helps to bring within acceptable limits the continuing cost to the company of financing the turnover of the individually held shares. For, of course, the requirement that those who leave must sell back their shares creates an equal and opposite buy-back liability. Without the permanent trust shareholding, this buy-back liability would be that much greater. Thus the business's ability to finance investment internally would be that much less. We can put this point more generally by saying that even in an only moderately capital intensive business like Baxi, its employee ownership can only be permanent if the business substantially 'owns itself'.

Finally, it is worth noting an ingenious device, the brainchild of the 1982 finance director Geoff Whittle. It provides a kind of safety valve against the possibility – which admittedly now seems remote – that the need to distribute additional shares to employees might ever run up against the 49% limit. The device takes the form of a holding by the trust of preferred shares. This holding would permit the company to issue new ordinary shares to the trust – in the form of a dividend on its preferred shares – without doing the same for the employee shareholders. That share issue in turn would serve to increase the number of shares that could be held individually, without breaking the 49% limit.

The trust's majority holding brings us to the question of control: whoever controls the trust controls the company. For under company law, control of a company is vested in its ordinary share capital. Whoever speaks for a majority of the shares has the final say and the power, directly or indirectly, to appoint and dismiss the board of directors and the top management. The managers are essentially agents of the shareholders and their authority derives from that source. Ultimate sovereignty lies with the general assembly of shareholders. As a reflection of the primacy of capital under company law, voting in the assembly is proportionate to shares, not on an individual shareholder basis.

In a conventional company there is rarely felt to be a need for a standing representative institution to reflect the interests of the shareholders. They exercise their final control through their votes – to elect the directors (and thus the management) and otherwise at the general shareholders' meeting.

In an employee-owned company, the control arrangements are normally more complicated. As in a conventional company, the authority of management derives ultimately from the shareholders, whose elected agents the managers are. But there is also felt to be a need to create a representative institution of employee shareholders of one kind or another. Employee shareholders, the argument runs, need a representative institution to express their interests as employee shareholders. Such an institution should carry out duties and exercise responsibilities on their behalf in ways which cannot normally be assigned to management or unions.

Over the Partnership's first thirteen years there have been changes – *de facto* if not *de jure* – in the way the partners have been represented. But the locus of power has not moved or changed. By virtue of its permanent majority shareholding, the power has been with the main employee trust ever since the 1983 ownership transfer. *To that extent*, to use a Marxist phrase, the partnership representative arrangements at Baxi are essentially 'superstructure'. In effect, whoever controls the main trust has the power at Baxi. In the beginning, it was Philip Baxendale who chose the first trustees and took the chair at their meetings. He finally stepped down from the chairmanship in 1994, though remaining a trustee at the time of writing. Though there is a convention of wide consultation before a new trustee is chosen, and though the trustees for the time being must stand for re-election every three years, this body of trustees is essentially a self-perpetuating oligarchy. There are no rights vested in the individual employee shareholders, or enjoyed by their elected representatives, which enable them to change the trustees and thus the top management. In this respect, at least in formal terms, the position at Baxi is sharply different from that at John Lewis. For, as we have seen, given a weighted majority in the John Lewis Central Council (its main representative institution), the trustees and thus the chairman and the top management can be changed.

At least for the ten years from the ownership transfer down to the switch to a group structure in the early 1990s, the main representative institution at Baxi was the Partnership Council. This was so notwithstanding its hybrid character, bringing together the trustees as well as elected representatives of the partners. Indeed it was probably that mixture of elected representatives and trustees that made it possible for Mr Baxendale to see the Council from the beginning as having a role similar to that of a supervisory board in Germany.

In the previous section we noted that until Mr Carter took over as chief executive in 1992, the Partnership Council, even if it 'went through the motions, did not really perform as a supervisory board'. But we noted too that the Council then effectively gave up that role because, with the switch to the group board, the role of supervisory board was inevitably taken over by the group board. There is no way of knowing how stable these new arrangements are going to be. In particular, it cannot be said how the new board will be affected once the second of two employee directors is introduced to it. However it is right to flag Mr Baxendale's optimism about the potential benefits of the new group structure. In a letter to me in August 1996, he underlined his conviction that the change to a group structure had significantly improved employee involvement. He went on:

The members of the subsidiary company councils are better able to make a contribution at the level of their own smaller company than they were as members only of the Partnership Council for the larger company. The members of the group council are now the group board plus the employee directors of the subsidiary companies. We have now reached the stage at group council where the group board is discussing things with the councillors, asking them to discuss with their company councils, so that when we discuss it further the employees will have been much better consulted than they ever were under the Partnership Council.

A few points may be made in conclusion. The first is to highlight the importance of bringing employee directors onto the group board. Best practice in employee-owned companies increasingly points in the direction of having elected workforce representatives on the top decision-making body. Most of the large majority employee-owned companies in America do it. It has now been the practice at John Lewis over many decades. The arguments for it are essentially those of 'democratic transparency': the important decisions must *not* be taken by top managers behind closed doors. Moreover, it is simply wrong to argue that employee directors should never be put in the position of being associated, for example, with a painful redundancy decision. There are already numerous cases where this has happened in Britain – in bus companies for example. That it should be so is surely part of the education-in-reality of employee directors in a market economy.

The same arguments – essentially of 'democratic transparency' – make a persuasive case for bringing a minority of elected employees onto Baxi's main trustee body. Once again, John Lewis provides a valuable precedent. No doubt there are important and relevant differences between the cultures of a largely female workforce of non-unionised shop assistants and a largely male and still largely unionised workforce which includes a high proportion of semi-skilled metal bashers. But, in relation to Baxi's workforce, the policy aim must surely be to develop the culture to the point where the shop floor is as concerned as the management about the long-term future of the business.

Whether Baxi would be well advised to take what might be called the final step down this road, and follow John Lewis in creating a mechanism which would allow a weighted majority of the partners to unseat the chief executive, is more debatable. Quite apart from the cultural differences between the workforces in the two businesses, John Lewis has had about five times as many partnership years as Baxi – nearly seventy against fifteen. The John Lewis top management is almost certainly more confident in its position than Baxi's; and management confidence is an important business asset. The episode of David Dry's forced resignation may also tell us that a formal replacement mechanism is not needed. Public opinion can do the job. The key point, perhaps, is the one made first, I think, by Aristotle: once institutions have stood the test of time you should make it quite difficult but not impossible to change them.

16
Employee Ownership Outcomes of Privatisation

The waves of privatisation in the former Communist countries of Central and Eastern Europe and of the successor states in the territory of the former Soviet Union offered in the early and middle years of the 1990s what may well be a never-to-be-repeated set of opportunities for employee ownership: a kind of 'jubilee season' for employee buy-outs of one kind and another. Less eye-catching but perhaps of potentially equal consequence were the generally slightly later beginnings of moves to privatise so-called 'parastatal' businesses across the Third World, everywhere from Zimbabwe and Ghana to Bolivia and Peru.

For Russia there is a striking estimate which has been widely circulated and was given at least a token of respectability by appearing in the *Financial Times*. It is to the effect that as many as two thirds of all the medium and large Russian businesses that had been privatised down to the end of 1996 emerged from the process internally owned in one way or another. A similarly high percentage has been quoted for Romania. In Slovenia, to take a third example, the main privatisation law is exceptionally friendly towards broadly based employee ownership outcomes and well over half of those Slovenian businesses that had been privatised by early 1997 were majority employee owned – typically to the extent of 60%.

Other books have been and will be written about this experience. Here I confine myself to three summary points:

– With a few notable exceptions, the great majority of Western economists, and some of the most articulate ones, have expressed their near total opposition to employee ownership outcomes.

– However much a broadly based and equitable employee ownership may be specified in the privatisation laws of ex-Communist countries, in the majority of actual cases ownership becomes concentrated quite quickly, and sometimes from the beginning, into a minority of usually management hands. By 1997 that had apparently even started to happen in Slovenia, where the privatisation law is most exemplary in its insistence on a broadly based and equitable distribution of shares. Under more or less formal arrangements of purchase and sale, managers in Slovenia's privatised companies had, by early 1997, started to buy up shares initially distributed to rank-and-file employees

– Notwithstanding the extent of these processes of ownership concentration, in a small minority of cases managers and sometimes managers, unions and rank-and-file employees have sought to preserve and sustain a broadly based and equitable post-privatisation spread of employee shares.

In the case studies which follow there is just one example of an employee ownership outcome in a former Communist country: the case of the Herend Porcelain Manufactory – as it likes to call itself in the English language – in Hungary. In many ways – for the fairness and broad basis of its employee ownership and for its sustainability – the Herend case is exemplary. Moreover we are not talking here of a business on the scale of a William Morris-type craft workshop, still less of a post-1960s' 'drop out enterprise' for the arty children of the professional middle class. We are talking about a business which employs over 1,500 people and one which first sprang to international fame when it sold a handpainted dinner service to Queen Victoria at the Great Exhibition in 1851.

This group of case studies begins, however, with three British examples: of employee ownership outcomes in the pioneering Thatcherite programmes of privatisation. The first two UK privatisation examples of management-led employee buy-outs are both local bus companies, one based in Fareham and the other in Chesterfield. The third example is the road haulage business, later know as NFC by the initials of its former name, the National Freight Consortium. NFC was in fact Britain's MEBO pioneer.

In all three of these British cases, the post-privatisation employee ownership lasted for no more than a few years. Shares in NFC were floated on the London Stock Exchange in 1987, just five years after its pioneering MEBO, and by 1996 the percentage of its employee-owned shares had fallen from an initial level of over 80% to below 10%. Each of the two local bus companies was 'sold on'. To describe what happened in slightly different language, their employee shareholders accepted takeover offers which they felt they could not refuse. In one case that happened after seven years of employee ownership, in the other after just over five.

A compelling contrast emerges from a comparison of these two local bus company MEBOs with the privatisations by Management Buy-Outs (MBOs) which were overwhelmingly more common. In our two cases several hundred employees, including managers, enjoyed capital gains after five or eight years ranging from about £15,000 to rather more than twice that. In the case of the great majority of local bus company MBOs a tiny management group, consisting normally only of men and not normally more than three or four in number, walked away with capital gains in the low single digit millions of pounds, after significantly shorter periods of transitional ownership.

Before getting on to the two case studies of actual local bus company privatisation, of People's Provincial in Fareham and Chesterfield Transport, we need an opening discussion of the privatisation of Britain's local bus industry as a whole. Within the UK's total privatisation experience, there was nothing directly comparable. We shall see why in some detail in a moment. But it is also true that where majority employee ownership was the outcome, it attracted really forthright comments which are worth having on the record. Two examples must suffice. The first is an opinion expressed by James Miller, the Financial Director of Chesterfield Transport at the time of its employee buy-out: 'I saw and still see employee ownership as the least worst of the possible solutions open to us in our privatisation.'

The second is perhaps specially important. For it reflects a mature understanding by an ordinary bus driver of the longer term advantages of employee ownership for rank-and-file employees: 'At least *we* will get the rewards when conditions do improve.'

Within the Great Privatisation Project of successive Tory Governments, under first Mrs Thatcher and then Mr Major, that of Britain's local bus industry stands out for a number of reasons..

With the stated aim of promoting competition, the larger units were compulsorily broken up into local undertakings before privatisation was allowed.

Among those local undertakings a high proportion were privatised through internal buy-outs, mostly by straight management buy-outs but with a significant number of management-led employee buy-outs and a few hybrids.

By end-1995, ten years after the first of the local bus privatisations, most had been 'sold on'.

By then too, partly as a result of those 'sellings on' and partly as a result of aggressive aquisitions or acquisition threats by the largest private undertakings (especially Stagecoach and First Bus – by then quoted companies), the industry had substantially consolidated into a number of big groups. The former state and local authority oligopoly was well on the way to being replaced by a private oligopoly.

In towns and cities where particularly marked competition developed between private bus companies, some negative consequences emerged – excessive pollution and traffic jams. Such negative effects were recognised even by those most ideologically committed to competition's virtues, like the *Economist* newspaper.

This sequence of changes provides the setting for the two case studies in this chapter: of what – for the duration of their employee ownership – were known as Chesterfield Transport and People's Provincial. Each was basically an example of privatisation by management-led employee buy-out (MEBO). However, among the top managers at People's Provincial (PP), only the Managing Director supported the MEBO project. Chesterfield Transport (CT) was a joint management- and union-led employee buy-out.

The two had come from different pre-privatisation stables: PP had been part of the state-owned National Bus Company, while CT had been in the municipal ownership of the Chesterfield local authority. But the ultimate fate of their employee ownership was similar: during 1995 each was 'sold on', PP to First Bus and CT to Stagecoach. It must be emphasised that in neither business was the decision to sell a negative verdict on the employee ownership which was thereby given up: rather it was a rational response to an implied threat of otherwise being destroyed. At PP employee ownership had lasted for eight years and at CT for just over five.

Both cases are important for public policy. Four main lessons emerge:

1 Given appropriate leadership and what are seen as a fair set of buy-out rules, the great majority of rank-and-file employees will choose to participate in MEBOs.

2 Given good management and appropriate levels and systems of rank-and-file employee involvement, the employee ownership will work well and labour will acquire a closer appreciation of business realities.

3 Given the opportunity and depending on the size of capital gains foregone or postponed, a majority of the employees would probably prefer their employee ownership to be sustained.

4 In contrast to what happens following a management buy-out (MBO), in a MEBO the capital gains realised when the business is eventually sold on are widely shared.

The rank-and-file employees who took part in these two buy-outs and held on to their shareholdings to the end – adding to them on the margin at PP where that was allowed – were handsomely rewarded. For a stake which, after adjusting for preference share repayments, was no more than £50, their return was approximately £16,000 in the case of CT and rather more than twice that in the case of PP. Of course, as we have seen, employee ownership lasted longer at PP. But it is also true that PP performed better.

In round figures, the 200-odd employee-punters in each of the two MEBOs enjoyed a capital gain equivalent to about eighteen months' salary at CT and to over three years' salary at PP. Some part of these gains were due to the 'arithmetic working in the punters' favour' – as loans associated with the largely credit financed buy-out were paid off. They also reflected higher market valuations for the bus undertakings when they were sold on.

These are striking figures. They are even more striking when compared with the size and distribution of capital gains in local bus businesses privatised by MBOs rather than MEBOs. The following table shows data on seven businesses privatised by MBOs and sets them alongside PP. Like PP, all the seven were of NBC provenance and were later sold on. In the case of the MBOs, three or four people have often made £millions in capital gains, as against the 200-odd people making gains of tens of thousands at People's Provincial.

NBC Privatisation: Seven MBOS and One MEBO

Name	Year Privatised	Year Sold on	Interval Years	Price B/O	£M S/O	Gain £M Total
Cheltenham & Gloucester	1986	1993	7.0	1.0	13.7	12.7
Maidstone & District	1986	1995	8.5	1.8	16.0	14.2
Midland Red (West)	1986	1988	1.5	1.9	10.5	8.6
Potteries MT	1986	1994	7.2	2.6	23.0	20.4
Eastern Counties	1987	1994	7.4	4.5	6.7	2.2
Provincial	1987	1995	8.4	0.7	4.1	3.4
Crossville (Wales)	1987	1988	0.8	3.0	6.0	3.0
London County (North West)	1988	1990	2	3.7	4.4	0.7

Name	Numbers Employed	Buy-Out Participants	Remarks
Cheltenham & G	560	10 [M. Thomas MD]	PSS or SOS promised
Maidstone	940	5 [S. Trennery MD]	Employees given £200 NVS free
Midland Red W	875	3 & 16 [K. Mills MD]	Promise of 30% of Equity for EP.
Potteries MT	1,000	4 [M. Moors MD]	PSS or SOS promised
Eastern Cs	850	4 [P. Brundle MD]	Promise of 20% of Equity for EP. *
Provincial	220	About 190	Rule of Equal Investment
Crossville Wales	930	3 plus** [I. Reid MD]	Promise of all Employee SO.
London County NW	1,040	4 [D. Ord MD]	Promise of SPS or PSS

* MBO partly financed by immediate sale of depot to Norwich Union.
** Some local managers also took part.
B/O = Buy-Out (ie privatisation); S/O = Sold On; PSS = Profit Sharing Scheme; SOS = Share Option Scheme; NVS = Non-Voting Shares; EP = Employee Purchase; SO = Share Offer; SPS = Share Participation Scheme.
Sources: Data from Centre for Management Buy-Out Research & NBC

It is also worth comparing these MEBOs with an example of a 'hybrid' buy-out. The former Yorkshire Rider was bought out in a 51:49% split between top management and non-management employees (represented by an Employee Share Ownership Trust). According to David Wheatcroft, about whom we will be hearing a good deal when we get on to the Chesterfield case study, the chief executive at Yorkshire Rider walked away with approximately £3.5m when it was sold on to Badgerline. Other members of the management team are understood to have received about £1m each. The average slice of the capital gain for Yorkshire Rider's non-top management was about £5,000.

Capital gains are, of course, an entirely proper feature of systems of private capitalism. An entrepreneur who has been the prime mover behind the creation of a significant and successful business is surely entitled to be rewarded by realising appropriate capital gains: his or her contribution is of a scale and quality similar to that of the inventor of a new and needed machine. But the contribution of those top managers who took part in the MBOs listed in my table does not seem to be of remotely comparable worth. Can one really justify the gains of £3m realised within less than a year by the top three managers of the ex-NBC Crossville bus company in Wales?

The huge gains made by those and other top managers of bus companies in the former NBC stable can be seen as missed opportunities for a much wider distribution of gains. If we ask who could have increased those chances, the most plausible answer is the leaders of the rank-and-file employees, namely the trade unions. True, a minority of union officials at district level eventually realised what was happening. But by that time all or almost all of the seventy-odd ex-NBC businesses had already been privatised with only two MEBOs. In the unions' defence, it may be conceded that the proportion of MEBOs was a good deal higher in the later bus privatisations – in Scotland and among the undertakings formerly owned by local authorities.

But it is also true that had the attitude of the Government been more positive, employee ownership would have spread more widely in the UK's bus industry, and indeed elsewhere. The NBC privatisations are good evidence for this – just two cases of employee ownership out of seventy (People's Provincial and Luton & District). In fact, it is surprising that there were even those two. For it was clear from discussion at the time that those responsible for the selling off of the NBC subsidiaries were at best lukewarm towards employee ownership. Very likely they had not thought the matter through. But that should not obscure the single most important result of their preference for MBOs as against MEBOs: that the capital gains associated with the great majority of successful privatisations were restricted to a handful of managers.

The Government's views started and remained at best lukewarm. What changed the attitude of the main union?

The Transport and General Workers' Union (T&GWU) has not modified its principled stance against privatisation or its commitment to the idea of a local bus operation as more of a social service to the community than a profit-making business. On the other hand when it became clear that resistance to privatisation of any particular bus business was bound to fail, the T&GWU, usually led by its local membership, began to adopt a more pragmatic approach, and to favour one possible privatisation outcome rather than another. For example, in each of our two case study companies, we will find that what amounted to management-led employee buy-outs were strongly supported by both the local T&GWU membership and by the local officials. Indeed in one case the buy-out was led jointly, by the unions as well as the management. It was also the T&GWU which originally pressed for the 51:49% ownership split in the case of the 'hybrid buy-outs' like Yorkshire Rider.

Initially, this pragmatism was *ad hoc*. But from 1992 the thinking of the T&GWU seemed to shift more formally to a position where, if privatisation was regarded as unavoidable, the union in most cases came to see majority employee ownership as the 'least worst' outcome.

That a union should *ever* promote majority employee ownership flies in the face of the traditional hostility to employee ownership of almost all unions in the Western world: a hostility based on the fear that employees who are also owners will become co-opted on the side of capital in the class struggle. On the other hand, a preference for majority over minority employee ownership as the 'least worst' outcome of privatisation makes excellent sense in the light of the sentiment expressed in the first epigraph. For, whether privatisation is effected by MBO or by MEBO, it is likely to involve substantial borrowing. In both cases, paying off that borrowing will depend upon the management and non-management employees working successfully and together. But the resulting benefits, once the borrowings have been paid off, are distributed very differently in the two different cases.

There are parallels between the T&GWU and the evolution of the attitude to employee ownership of the United Steelworkers of America. In both cases, the starting attitude of the union was made up of a mixture of suspicion of employee ownership and an underlying preference for the status quo. In the case of the T&GWU and Britain's bus services, that preference was strengthened by the union's view of them as community rather than profit-oriented. Only when it became apparent that a continuation of the status quo was simply not an option did the attitude of both unions to employee ownership start to become more pragmatic. Both unions – though not necessarily all their members – would have preferred to soldier on with the conventional ownership arrangements to which they were accustomed.

And that brings me to my last two general points. The first is that demand for these bus services in the period before privatisation had been falling sharply and indeed continued to do so at least until 1994. In 1953 as much as 42% of all passenger travel in the UK took place by bus. Thirty years later that figure was well below 10% and still falling. During the 1980s, total passenger journeys taken by bus *and* coach were falling by about 2% annually. Since the number of coach journeys was actually going up, bus journeys were contracting even more sharply. That provides the fundamental context of our two case studies, even if it is also true that there is evidence of a possible change of trend in the 1995 results: with an apparent 1% increase in passenger miles.

The second concerns pre-privatisation restructuring. The local bus undertakings were already under pressure before privatisation to make themselves profitable by shedding labour, increasing prices, and putting more emphasis on profitable routes. Where necessary, as for example in the case of undertakings owned by municipal councils, they were further required to transform themselves into companies limited by shares (with all the shares owned by the municipal authority). The case studies of People's Provincial and Chesterfield Transport reflect these developments and this background.

17

Two Provincial Local Bus Companies
People's Provincial and Chesterfield
Transport

People's Provincial

From May 1987 to October 1995, the local bus company at Fareham in Hampshire was owned not by absentee shareholders nor by a tiny group of top managers but by its staff. It was bought in 1987 by its employees under the leadership of its then managing director, James Freeman. Though the annual results varied, the eight-year experience of employee ownership was judged to be a success by the great majority of the employee owners. An offer which would have given them a return of over twenty times on their equity investment was turned down by a big margin in 1990. Yet by the autumn of 1995 there was almost unanimous acceptance of the advice given by their managing director and finance director that they should sell out to First Bus. That advice was based on a perception that the value of the business could be at risk if competitors chose to adopt methods of operation similar to those which had destroyed local bus undertakings in Warrington and Darlington over the previous two years.

Unlike the other case studies in this book, I was personally involved in the early stages at People's Provincial (PP). In the depth of the winter, during early February 1987, and at an hour well past my normal bedtime, I was lucky enough to be asked to take part in a mass meeting in Fareham that had been called by James Freeman. The meeting was well attended: Mr Freeman estimated that more than 80% of the workforce (200 and more strong) turned out. They then voted overwhelmingly to attempt an employee buy-out under his leadership. What is more, they accepted, again by a huge majority on a show of hands, that it would be reasonable for everyone who took part to subscribe a sum of £750.

Given what happened later, I have felt it reasonable to claim that I was 'present at the creation'. In fact my connection with Mr Freeman and the project had started as early as 1985 when I had been asked by Robert Brook, then Chairman and Managing Director of National Bus Company (NBC), to address the half-yearly meeting of the managing directors of all its subsidiaries. As the then MD of Shamrock and Rambler Coaches, NBC's small Bournemouth subsidiary, Mr Freeman took part in that meeting. Later, before he moved from Bournemouth to take over in Fareham, we had talked about the possibility of a management-led employee buy-out of Shamrock and Rambler.

Together with the two union convenors at the Fareham Bus Company, John Speed and John Early, Mr Freeman visited my office in London on the day before the mass meeting. My feeling at the time – that it was a potentially seminal event – has been reinforced subsequently both the buy-out's success and by the fact that this was the pioneering management-led employee buy-out in the bus industry. The feeling that the Fareham mass meeting was a notable occasion was also reinforced by the subsequent success of the business.

The other point to emphasise is that the buy-out transaction was a high speed affair. It was completed within a few months early in May: in less than a quarter of the time taken at Chesterfield Transport. I was not involved in this process: well over 90% of the associated professional and advisory work was not done by my employer, Job Ownership Ltd, but by a combination of the accountants, Grant Thornton, and the employee ownership specialists, New Bridge Street Consultants.

Geography, Scale, History Look at a map of the south of England. You will find Fareham at the northern end of a densely populated little peninsular which juts out into the Channel between Southampton and Portsmouth. At the Channel end of the peninsular is Gosport with its ferry connection to Portsmouth. The railway passes east and west through Fareham but there is no motorway connection between the two towns.

James Freeman once told me how struck he had been on his first visit to Fareham and Gosport by the number of people who were using the buses at non-peak times. He attributed that largely to the absence of a motorway and of a railway. Whatever the explanation, what he had seen had satisfied him that there were profits to be made from running a local bus service. In fact it later turned out that NBC had long recognised its Fareham bus operation to be potentially among the best along England's South Coast.

Both turnover and numbers employed shot up between the buy-out and when PP was sold on in 1995. Employment increased by well over 40%, from 212 to above 300, while turnover rose by over 75% in nominal terms to £6.54m (by roughly 50% after allowing for inflation).

As with most of the former subsidiaries of NBC as well as Chesterfield Transport (CT), Fareham's bus company has for many years employed its own team of maintenance engineers who service its bus fleet. On the other hand unlike CT, it does not have a spanking modern garage. That may at least partly explain why its employees managed to negotiate a buy-out price which looks as if it was more favourable than that paid in Chesterfield.

As for history, PP can trace its origins back to a private horse tram company established towards the end of the last century. Much later, starting in the 1960s, it spent some twenty years as a subsidiary of NBC. It was not controlled by its local authority. Moreover its spell in the public sector lasted for less than twenty years, from 1970 onwards. By contrast, CT spent almost a century in the public sector and was owned and controlled throughout that period by Chesterfield Borough Council.

Manoeuvrings before the Buy-Out James Freeman took over as managing director of what was then called just the *Provincial* Bus Company in November 1986. The business was already up for sale in the sense that NBC's residual management had put it on the market. Mr Freeman recalls that he was struck by the apparently low morale of the workforce. He also recalls that two prospective buyers had already expressed an interest. One was the redoubtable Stagecoach – which has since gone on to acquire a reputation as one of the toughest of Britain's conventional capitalist bus companies. The second was the existing management group, including – as its prospective chairman – Tom (Paddy) McQuade, the previous MD from whom Mr Freeman had been appointed to take over.

Around New Year 1987 it became public knowledge that the

in-house management group bid had somewhat changed its character. It had come to be backed, and indeed be more or less taken
over, by a second capitalist undertaking in the bus industry: Devon
General. What Mr Freeman next remembers is that for most of
January 1987 Stagecoach and Devon General competed to win the
approval of the Department of Transport (DoT) for their respective
bids. It was a contest which ended in early February when officials
of the DoT advised Mr Freeman that Devon General was likely to
be the bidder recommended to the Secretary of State; and that since
it would not be requiring his services, he should start looking for
work elsewhere.

Devon General's grounds for wanting to dispense with Mr
Freeman were reasonable enough. In the contest to make the winning
bid he had sided with Stagecoach, which had offered him an
alternative job in the group if its bid was not successful. On the other
hand, in the light of what he was advised by the DoT officials in early
February – that Devon General and not Stagecoach would be the
preferred bidder – Mr Freeman was in effect forced to make a choice:
between attempting himself to lead a bid, or accepting that the best
he could hope for was an alternative job from Stagecoach.

He decided to have a go at the first of these and then remembered
his earlier discussion with me about a possible management-led
employee buy-out of Shamrock and Rambler. And he recalled that
government had instructed NBC's residual management team to give
a modest preference to buy-out bids with a major 'in house' component. But, of course, he was in no position to approach his fellow
top managers at Fareham. For they, together with Mr McQuade his
predecessor, were already on the side of the bid from Devon General.

So for support in his prospective initiative, Mr Freeman turned
instead to the two union convenors at the Provincial Bus Company:
John Speed and John Early. He found their reaction cautiously
positive. And so was that of Alex Hodder, district secretary of the
Transport and General Workers Union (T&GWU) in Portsmouth,
and at that time probably the most influential full-time union official for the road transport industry on that part of the South Coast.
Mr Hodder was later carpeted by the top union leadership for his
role in the whole transaction.

On the other hand, encouraging as this union support must clearly
have been, time was rather short. The advice about the likely outcome of the bid contest had reached Mr Freeman in the middle of a

week in early February. He was further advised that that decision would become final and irrevocable at the end of the following week. He and his trade union supporters had to move fast. The details need not concern us. It is enough to say that they succeeded in meeting the deadline. Early on the following Friday afternoon officials of the DoT were presented with a new bid. It was led by Mr Freeman and, following the mass meeting which I had attended, it enjoyed the support of more than 80% of the workforce.

For the record, when the buy-out led by Mr Freeman was eventually completed in early May, all his fellow top managers and fellow directors of the old Provincial Bus Company resigned and left the business.

The Buy-Out and Its Financing Devon General maintained its bid and remained in play for some time after the employees' bid was formulated. But it withdrew a little before the DoT indicated, in March, that Mr Freeman and his buy-out team had replaced it as the preferred bidder. The deal was in fact completed in May, when NBC's residual management formally approved a sale to Mr Freeman and his fellow employees. Devon General's earlier withdrawal was only disclosed much later by its chief executive, Harry Blundred. We shall meet Mr Blundred again later in this story. A possible reason for his decision to withdraw from the fray is that he may have anticipated a far from friendly reception from the employees and the unions if his bid had won against theirs.

The price finally agreed for the Provincial Bus Company was £730,000. It is believed to have been slightly less than Devon General's earlier offer, but within the margin of preference for 'in house' bids authorised by government policy. In relation to subsequent profit levels, the price now looks low. But the transaction took place at a relatively early stage in the privatisation of the local bus industry, when prices were generally lower than they later became.

Mr Freeman and his fellow employees mustered £144,000 which they put up under an agreed equal subscription rule. The rule was that any employee who subscribed should put up precisely £700 for redeemable preference shares and £50 for ordinary shares. It appears that of the 212 employees of the business on the date of the purchase, 192, or 90%, subscribed. For those with limited cash, personal loans were made available on reasonable terms.

The balance of the purchase price came from corporate borrowing, with loans of £540,000 from Barclays and the balance of £40,000 from Unity Trust Bank. That money was lent to a non-statutory ESOP trust set up for the purpose by the new People's Provincial. Loan guarantees were given by PP.

Following the deal's completion, the employees as individuals owned some 20% of the share capital of the new company and the ESOP trust owned the balance. On the eve of the transaction to sell PP in 1995, the ESOP trust still held about 40% of the equity with the balance split between employees as individuals and retired employees or their widows. As early as 1988, little more than one year after the buy-out, all employee owners had £250 worth of their £700 preference shareholdings redeemed.

The Post-Buy-Out Record We noted earlier the sharp rises in employment and turnover between 1987 and 1994, the last full year before PP was sold to First Bus. Underlying these changes was an increase in market share, most notably in the neighbouring territory of Portsmouth and possibly, in the view of the top management team, some actual increase in the size of the market on the company's home turf of Gosport and Fareham.

Turnover 1987–1994	*£000*
1987	3,693
1988	4,413
1989	4,701
1990	4,773
1991	5,172
1992	5,739
1993	6,031
1994	6,539

By contrast with turnover, operating profits fluctuated sharply:

Operating Profits 1986–1994	*£000*
1986	464
1987	76
1988	1
1989	213
1990	343

1991	123
1992	173
1993	340
1994	191

Compared with the last full year in NBC ownership (1986) the main reason for the collapse of operating profit in 1987 and 1988 was apparently an excess of experimentation with new routes – which proved to be inadequately profitable. However, these were also the first post-deregulation years and profit margins in the local bus industry fell right across the country. In 1991 and then again in 1994, the main cause of the downturn was rather different: intensified and specific competition right in PP's backyard. There was competition within PP's 'home' area in Fareham and Gosport, and competition in neighbouring Portsmouth. The chief competitor from early 1991 was the privatised local bus company in Portsmouth, across the ferry from Gosport. The third party buyer who had eventually acquired that Portsmouth business was none other than Harry Blundred, with his company Devon General.

Devon General's subsidiary in Portsmouth apparently sustained quite heavy losses in 1991 and 1992. Mr Blundred is known to have imposed a wage cut on his Portsmouth staff in 1992 – in a message communicated to them on a video. Drivers' wages are believed to have been cut from £4.50 to £3.50 per hour. The morale of the Portsmouth staff was plausibly reported to be low when I enquired about it during the summer of 1993. Whether or not it staged some recovery in 1994, I do not know. What is certain is that PP was again confronted with tougher competition in 1994 and this was reflected in its operating profit for that year.

On the whole, the morale of the staff at Peoples Provincial seems to have been high during its employee ownership years. Their determination at least to hold their own with Devon General was from time to time demonstrated in a most convincing way: by drivers volunteering to take their buses out without payment on their days off – a quite exceptional expression of commitment. More than once in the years before the business was sold on, Piers Marlow (who took over from Mr Freeman as managing director in early 1990) expressed his conviction that its employee ownership gave to PP an enduring competitive edge: because, as he once put it, individual employees will behave in the spirit as well as in the letter of their instructions. His finance director, Jacqui Martin, has put on record judgements about the benefits of employee ownership which are, if anything, even more specific. In a paper presented at a meeting in Pangbourne towards the end of 1995, she looked back on her time with the employee-owned People's Provincial:

> When competition started in February 1991, the advantages of employee ownership became more evident with the commitment of staff to make sure the competition did not damage the business plus volunteering to work additional hours.
>
> Some years we [were] able to give reasonable pay rises. [But] some none at all. This was easier to get accepted by the staff as in good years we always gave what we could afford ... It is much easier to negotiate a nil pay award with a group of people who own the company and who benefit from dividends and the appreciation of share value than if the Company was owned by outside parties or one or two directors who would benefit in relation to the hardship of the employees.

No doubt there were those who foresaw, when the big bus businesses like NBC were broken up as a prelude to privatisation, that the smaller of the resulting units would not survive for ever as independents in the new deregulated market. What may not have been foreseen is the degree of ruthlessness which the bigger groups might be prepared to use to get their way. One example must suffice. In the North-East town of Darlington the local authority, the then owner of the town's local service, announced early in 1994 that Yorkshire Traction, a private company based in Barnsley, was the preferred bidder in the competition to buy the business. Almost within hours of the announcement the Scottish-based Stagecoach, already the country's largest bus business, flooded the town with its vehicles and offered the citizenry free bus rides. Within weeks, the business of the 'preferred bidder' had been destroyed. After the event the matter was referred to the Monopolies and Mergers Commission but Stagecoach suffered nothing and got exactly what it wanted as a result of what was officially described as its 'deplorable' behaviour.

There seems little doubt that fear of suffering a similar fate was the main consideration when, in the autumn of 1995, Mr Marlow and Ms Martin advised the employee shareholders at PP that it would be wise to sell on. Specifically they knew that their chief competitor in neighbouring Portsmouth was up for sale and they feared for the consequences if it was sold to a major group. We shall look at the details of the sale and the distribution of the resulting capital gains in the final section. Here we may simply note that the agreed price was £4.1m, well up from the figure of approximately £750,000 which had been paid for the business eight and a half years before.

But no account of the post-buy-out record of PP would be complete without dealing with the takeover bid made for the business in 1990 by the Isle of Wight bus company, Southern Vectis.

We should remind ourselves that 1989 was one year after the redemption of £250 worth of the preference shares originally acquired by the employee shareholders: when the bid approach was made their original £750 investment in the buy-out of the business had thus been reduced to £500. The final offer for the business of Peoples Provincial made by Mr Batchelor, the managing director of Southern Vectis, was worth just over £11,000 to each of those original employee shareholders. In other words each of them stood to make a capital gain of over twenty times their reduced original stake of £500. The offer was turned down by a margin of 70:30% of the employee shareholders. The trust shares were voted after those held by the individual employees and properly voted in the same proportion. There could scarcely be better evidence of the readiness of employee shareholders to take a long view.

Ownership and Control Arrangements In 1987, just under 51,000 ordinary shares with a nominal value of 1p each had been issued and paid for, with the ESOP trust holding just over 40,000 (80%) and the balance owned by the 190-odd employees who had subscribed. Thus, at this starting point the individual employee shareholders, owned 50 shares each. They paid £1 for each of these shares with the nominal 1p of value. A glance at the 1987 balance sheet tells us that the difference – of some £49,000 if we also include the ordinary shares of the ESOP trust – was credited to a 'share premium' account.

The original plan was that shares should gradually be transferred out of the trust using the tax-efficient mechanism of the special kind of scheme which essentially distributes shares free to qualifying employees and was first introduced under the UK's Finance Act of 1978. The plan was in line with what was then regarded as best practice in situations of this kind and probably still was when the business was finally sold on in 1995. (A similar scheme was in fact used throughout at Chesterfield Transport.)

A few thousand shares were in fact got out free to individual employees using this mechanism in 1988 and 1989. On the other hand, following the rejection of the Southern Vectis offer in early 1990, it was decided that a way must be found to speed up the process of shifting shares out of the ESOP trust to the individual employees. Essentially the individual employees wanted the feel of enjoying direct control more quickly. The scheme under the 1978 Act, or so it was argued, was just not doing the job fast enough. In 1993 the original scheme under the 1978 Finance Act was discontinued: its administrative costs and complexities were said to have fallen out of line with its benefits. In fact it remained unused after 1989.

Instead, two other mechanisms were used to speed the movement of shares to individual employees from the ESOP trust. First, for employees who had subscribed for shares in the original buy-out, it was agreed that the ESOP trust would make them an annual offer of ordinary shares in exchange for the £450 of preferred stock which they were still holding. The price for ordinary shares at which this exchange was to take place would be fixed by their annual valuation. For each £100 of preferred stock the price would be £108 – the original buying price plus £8, to make up for accrued interest.

At the same time a second channel was opened up for those employees who had either chosen not to subscribe in the buy-out or had been recruited since. It was agreed that when the ESOP trust effected its annual exchange of ordinary shares for the preference shares of the original employee shareholders, those who fell outside that group might purchase the same number of shares from the trust for cash. This second channel – to allow the 'outsiders' a limited way in to employee shareholding – may be seen as a modest concession by the 'insiders': those who had bought themselves in at the outset. The 'outsiders' were indeed allowed in; but only on conditions which ensured that the margin of extra shares held by the 'insiders' would not be reduced. The same point may be put rather differently by saying that while the original employee shareholders remained in the workforce – and while the business remained employee-owned – the ownership of shares was heavily skewed in their favour.

Moreover, those who took part in the original buy-out were not only allowed to hold on to their shares indefinitely but also to pass them on to their wives.

By the summer of 1993, these arrangements had resulted in the following distribution of the ordinary shares:

ESOP Trust...40%
Current Employees 50%
Retired Employees & Spouses 10%

In mid-1993 the ordinary shares of PP were valued at £1.33. But this valuation applied *not* to the nominal 1p shares which had been bought at the time of the buy-out; but to each of five nominal 0.2p shares into which the former had been split in 1990. Had that share split not taken place, then the 1993 valuation per share would not have been £1.33, but five times £1.33, viz £6.65.

By mid-1993, the number of issued shares had been increased from the original 51,000 to just under 57,000. Some of the shares issued free to employees under the 1978 scheme were newly issued, rather than coming from the ESOP trust.

Against this background we can now move on to some quite precise shareholding numbers: by mid-1993 an original shareholder held 1,175 nominal 0.2p shares with a further 50 held on his or her behalf in the profit-sharing trust (the latter due to be distributed by April 1994). These original employee shareholders had by then exchanged the entire balance of their preference shares for ordinary shares.

How many of these original employee shareholders were still on the PP payroll in mid-1993? The answer is 96, or exactly half of those who had bought themselves in the first place. If we multiply that figure of 96 by the shareholding number of 1,225 (1,175 plus 50 due from the profit-sharing trust), the resulting total of shares held by this group comes to 117,600. Given the rule that ESOP trust shares must be voted in line with the preferences revealed by the individual employee shareholders, this group continued to have a controlling voice in the business down to the eventual sale in 1995.

What about the 'outsiders' who bought shares for cash after that possibility was first opened up for non-original employee shareholders following the rejection of the Southern Vectis bid in

1989? By mid-1993 there were 54 employees in this category and the total number of shares then held by them was 25,800. This was an average of between 400 and 500 shares each, with a maximum of 845.

There were two final groups of employees: those owning *no* shares; and those holding only those shares which they had received free under the original profit-sharing scheme. In mid-1993, there were 69 of the former – or some 25% of the total workforce – and 41 of the latter. The total number of shares held by this group in 1993 was 1,700, an average of just over 40 shares each with a maximum shareholding of no more than 50.

The table summarises this data about the breakdown of shares held by individual PP employees in mid-1993.

Employee Group	Nos	No of Shares (each or max)	Total
Original buyers	96	1,225 (each)*	117,600
Cash buyers	54	845 (max)*	25,800
Free shares only	41	50 (max)	1,700
No shares	69	n.a.	n.a.

* Includes their free shares.

In addition to these, 24 retired employees and their spouses together held some 14,000 shares, or roughly 10% of the issued total. As noted earlier only original shareholders were allowed to retain their shares into retirement and they could also pass these shares to their spouses. But the shares of any employee who died in service might be retained by his or her spouse.

The picture that emerges of the share ownership as it was among the 260-odd PP employees in mid-1993 is a spectrum. At one end were the 'insiders', the 96 who remained from the original 190 who bought themselves in at the time of the buy-out. They owned over 80% of the individually-held shares. At the other end of the spectrum were 69 employees who owned no shares at all. In between there were two smaller groups: a more dynamic one, which incidentally included in mid-1993 both the then managing and finance directors, consisting of employees who had bought shares for cash since that opportunity was opened up; and a less dynamic one which had done no more than passively accept free shares when they had been on offer.

What stands out most clearly is the dominance of the original 'insider' group. It was a dominance which continued down to the time of the final sale.

In fact, the share distribution at the time of the 1995 sale was not very different from what it had been in the summer of 1993. For example the number of the original shareholders had come down by only from 96 to 92. Those in that group who had also bought additional shares up to the limit when these had been offered for sale realised a total of just over £35,000 in the sale. At the other end of the spectrum, all employees at the time of the sale were given five free shares from the ESOP trust's shareholding with the balance of the latter's shares being distributed pro rata to individual shareholdings.

Some will wish to criticise the 'insiders' who called the shots, first in determining the rules of the share distribution and then by deciding how the trust's shares should be divided up: so there were the lucky 92 – and some at the other extreme with no more than 5 shares apiece from the ESOP trust. But a contrast which would be even more striking is between what actually happened and what would have happened if the business had been privatised by an MBO.

Chesterfield Transport

People's Provincial (PP), as we have seen, was fortunate in the geography of Fareham. The road system in the peninsular over which it mainly operates is relatively *un*friendly to the motor car. By contrast, any Chesterfield bus company is at a relative disadvantage. The neighbourhood in which it operates is certainly *not* motor car unfriendly. Also, there remains a strong social imperative to indicate upward social mobility by a move off the buses and into a private car. In addition, in 1992 and 1993, the then employee-owned Chesterfield Transport (CT) lost business as a result of pit closures in the Derbyshire coalfield.

Employee ownership lasted just over five years at CT, from early 1990 to mid-1995. As at PP, the eventual decision to sell on was taken with great reluctance and in response to a perceived threat. A local competitor was East Midland Buses, which had become a subsidiary of Stagecoach. It is true that I have never heard any complaints from CT about unfair competition from Stagecoach. Still there was the feeling, especially towards the end of its employee-owned life, that CT could only sustain its independence by the grace and favour of Stagecoach, a not altogether comfortable position.

Arguably, however, it was not so much the competition as the underlying relative disadvantages of Chesterfield as against Fareham which explain its lack of success relative to PP. Whatever the reasons, at Chesterfield employment gradually fell and so did turnover: the opposite of the PP experience. At the start of their respective employee ownership periods, the Chesterfield business was significantly the larger. By the time they were both sold on, it was significantly the smaller.

Turnover at CT in the year to 31 March 1990, the final twelve months before it became employee-owned, was just over £6.75m. Its total workforce at that time was around 350 and it had 138 buses, including 13 operating from a semi-detached garage in the small town of Bawtry near Doncaster. Like PP therefore, it was relatively small by the standards of Britain's 130-odd local bus undertakings.

The main operation is run from a large modern garage and set of offices at a site, Stonegravels, on the edge of Chesterfield. Both in 1990 and 1995, the garage maintenance staff accounted for roughly a quarter of the workforce. In the past, and indeed in the first year after the buy-out, these maintenance engineers had a number of local authority contracts to supplement their work on the bus fleet.

The origin of the business can be traced back to a Victorian private company, the Chesterfield and District Tramways Company, established in 1882. However those horse trams were taken over by the town's local authority as long ago as 1897. And the business remained council-owned for a continuous period of more than ninety years until the sale to its employees in 1990.

New Management and Restructuring: 1986 to 1990 Under the provisions of the 1985 Transport Act, local authorities like Chesterfield Borough Council which owned and operated local buses were required to make a number of important changes. In formal legal terms these businesses had to be reconstituted as companies limited by shares – with the local authority itself owning 100% of the share capital. The councils were also in effect required to restructure and re-organise these bus businesses and to make them profitable if they were not so already.

To bring about the necessary changes, a new top management team was brought in at CT. In October 1986 William Coupar came in as managing director and James Miller as finance director. A third executive director, Ian Duff, was brought in to the post of operations director in October 1988. Also about this time the Council made an important and imaginative industrial relations innovation: it created the position of employee director and laid down that it should be filled through an election by the whole workforce; and then held for three years before a further election. David Wheatcroft won the first election to this position. He was still holding it early in 1995, having already been twice re-elected, and following the sale he was indeed asked to stay on by Stagecoach, the buyer.

In the two years after Mr Coupar and Mr Miller took over, an annual loss of some £650,000 was turned into an annual profit of £500,000. The single most important ingredient in this turnaround was a reduction of sixty-five, or just under 20%, in the workforce. In the background was the deregulation of the industry: increasingly competitive conditions led to gradually more competitive pricing.

In parallel with the reduction in employees, the size of the bus fleet was cut by some 15%. Bus routes were revised and higher fares were phased in. And there were significant changes in working practices, too, especially by the bus drivers. Probably most important the amount of non-driving time for which drivers were paid was sharply cut back.

In effect, there was a continuum of restructuring, from the appointment of the new top management team in 1986, down to the 1995 sale. Doubtless it is still continuing. But what is important for our purposes here is that it preceded the employee buy-out of spring 1990 and continued after it. Before he moved to a new job in London in summer 1993, Mr Coupar characterised this change as having to put profits before people. He was referring as much to what happened after the successful management/trade union led employee buy-out of spring 1990 as to what happened before.

The Management/Union-Led Employee Buy-Out As we have seen, PP prepared its employee buy-out in something of a rush. Those responsible for preparing the corresponding transaction in Chesterfield had much more time. As early as autumn 1988 a joint management/trade union working party came together to examine and make decisions about the buy-out itself. Its purpose was also to look at the employee ownership and control structures – and other arrangements – of the prospective successor business.

On this working party, which came to be known as 'the buy-out team', union-linked voices were in the majority. Management had just two representatives: Mr Coupar and Mr Miller. By contrast, each of the three unions recognised by the company were represented by a senior shop steward; and in the case of the T&GWU, to reflect its larger numbers, by two – Haydn Clegg and Tony Huggins. The Amalgamated Engineering Union (AEU) was represented by David Johnson and the white collar workforce, unionised in the National Association of Local Government Officers (NALGO), by Mary Rhodes. The final member of the buy-out team was the employee director, David Wheatcroft, whose recent background was as an active member of the T&GWU.

The union strength on the buy-out team was critically important in two key aspects of the whole process. The most consequential of these was relationships with the prospective seller, Chesterfield's Labour-Party-controlled local authority. The local authority was mainly persuaded to sell by the trade union members of the buy-out team. More generally it was because of this strong union involvement that the Council became sympathetic and indeed positively helpful from a quite early stage. Second, and in a similar way, the union voice in the buy-out team was critical to the success of negotiations over pension arrangements with a different, but still Labour-controlled authority: Derby County Council.

Let it be made clear at once that the Labour councillors, who were then, as before and as later, in a substantial majority on both the borough and county councils, had no love for privatisation. But Chesterfield's Labour councillors formed the view that local authority ownership could almost certainly not survive, at least in the medium-term. If that was so, then, with two major provisos, they saw employee ownership as the 'least worst' outcome of the privatisation process. The provisos were that the employee ownership should be as widely based and as equal as possible. Mr Coupar and most if not all of his working party shared those preferences.

Given this rapport between the (Labour) majority on the

Borough Council and the majority view of Mr Coupar's working party, it is not surprising that a most important and specific advantage was extended to the latter. It was allowed to put in the only bid and thus avoided the competition of rival potential buyers. Britain's Tory Government allowed existing managements and employees of local authority owned bus companies to enjoy this important advantage in the privatisation process down to the end of 1992. It was discontinued, except in cases where the process was already well advanced, after the 1992 general election.

As to the deal itself and how it was financed, in line with what had happened three years earlier at PP, the working party decided that all employees who subscribed for shares would be governed by a rule of equal initial subscription. The total sum to be subscribed by those employees who chose so to do was fixed at £800. That sum, again following the PP example and for the same reasons, was to be split unequally between £750 of £1 preference shares and £50 of 10p ordinary shares. The former were redeemable at a fairly early date and were to pay annual interest of 10% until so redeemed. The balance of the ordinary share capital was to be put up, on the employees' behalf, again as at PP, by an employee trust. This trust was to be, more exactly, an Employee Benefit Trust (EBT) – which was to borrow the money necessary to make that possible. On the other hand, in a notable departure from the PP precedent – and following essentially and explicitly the example of the Baxi Partnership – it was decided that a controlling sharehold-ing of 51% of the equity was to be held in trust indefinitely and if possible for ever.

Judged by the percentage who chose to take it up, the share offer to the CT employees was well designed. An astonishing 86% initially promised to subscribe. Thereafter, there was some modest slippage; and some part-timers took advantage of a concession which allowed them to put up not £800 but £400. The result was a total down payment by the workforce, including managers, of £215,000. This amounted to rather less than 10% of the total price of £2.45m.

The total subscribed by the employees included about £200,000 in preference shares and £15,000 subscribed for 150,000 ordinary shares of 10p each. The balance of the equity – £85,000 worth or 850,000 shares of 10p each – was subscribed on the employees' behalf by an EBT; and money was borrowed to make that possible.

The balance of the purchase price came from two sources: £450,000 from Chesterfield Council in the form of a deferred payment arrangement; and £1.7m in bank borrowings.

A final point of detail needs to be added about this in many ways exemplary buy-out transaction. The purchase and sale agreement included a claw-back clause in relation to the main Stonegravels garage and offices site. The clause provided that were this asset to be sold within a ten-year period then a declining proportion of any profit on such a sale would have to be passed back to the Borough Council. The ten-year duration of the clause has been criticised for being unreasonably long. But it is hard to quarrel with the logic of a claw-back clause when the relevant transaction is an employee buy-out. For such a clause allows the seller to accept a lower price and one which is therefore more within the reach of the buyers and more likely to be compatible with future profits.

I make no apology for referring to this CT buy-out as 'in many ways exemplary'. It was exemplary in the first place as a *process*. The decisions – for example about the equal initial subscription rule – were taken not by an autocratic management team but by a working party representative of the whole 350-strong workforce. And it was exemplary in at least two other respects. First, because of the permanent 51% trust shareholding, it was a buy-out which was at least compatible with the indefinite continuation of employee ownership into the future. Second it was a buy-out remarkable for the enlightenment of the seller, Chesterfield Borough Council. The Council's enlightenment was shown in its agreement to defer part of the purchase price and similarly in its acceptance, in return for a claw-back clause, of a lower than market price for the main fixed asset: the Stonegravels garage and offices. Those features of the deal strengthened the chances of subsequent business success.

The process of privatisation in former socialist countries in Central and Eastern Europe and elsewhere would be smoother, less problematic and more likely to be followed by commercial success, if this Chesterfield buy-out was adopted as a model. For those interested in doing so, it is perhaps worth concluding with a technical or mechanical point: the CT workforce – its management and non-management employees – formed a new company, Chesterfield Transport 1989, when they decided to attempt to buy the business. That new company made the offer to buy the business that was owned by the Borough Council. It was the offer of that new company which was subsequently accepted.

The Post-Buy-Out Record After allowing for inflation, turnover started flat but fell from 1991-2 onwards. Operating profits (before redundancy costs) started with a sustained increase but went into reverse in 1993/94 and moved into actual loss over the twelve months to the end of March 1995.

Turnover and Operating Profits 89/90 to 94/95

Years to to 31 March	Turnover £000	Operating profits £000
89/90	6,783	223
90/91	7,226	381
91/92	7,308	479
92/93	6,930	515
93/94	6,702	457
94/95	7,200	(70)

Crude though it no doubt is, operating profit is probably the best measure of those aspects of business performance over which a bus company like CT has some control. What the two sets of figures suggest is first an improving business performance in increasingly difficult conditions, and then some loss of ground. During their post buy-out honeymoon, the men and women at CT had to cope with the effects of the recession superimposed on top of a continual switch in the town and the surrounding country side away from bus transport and into private cars. Moreover, the maintenance work on the local authority's vehicle fleet was not sustained at pre-buyout levels. CT still had a contract in early 1995 to service the council's refuse collection fleet; but all or almost all the council's other vehicle maintenance work was being done elsewhere.

As for the changing trends of business performance, they should first be understood as a continuation of the process of restructuring originally put in hand by Mr Coupar in 1986. There were redundancies before the buy-out, as we saw earlier, and there were further redundancies after it. From a workforce of approximately 350 in the spring of 1990, numbers had fallen to an average of 318 in the twelve months to end March 1993. They had fallen again to below 300 by early 1995. Numbers increased slightly with the acquisition by CT, in August 1993, of a small coaching business in the town's vicinity, but not enough to offset the generally declining trend.

Real efforts were made throughout the five-year period to mini-mise and cushion the pain of redundancies. As much advantage as possible was taken of natural wastage. Early retirements were also used as a substitute for forced redundancies and, when they took place, the associated payments were above the minimum required by law. During the last twelve months of employee ownership the entire staff accepted a 2.5% wage cut – to save three jobs and what would otherwise have been compulsory redundancies.

But redundancies were not the only feature of the post buy-out restructuring. For example, after the buy-out as well as before it, the drivers' non-working paid time was cut. Cost savings were also achieved by the introduction of a special, lower, hourly rate for newly recruited drivers: at £3.50 against the £4.78 paid to CT's established drivers in both 1992 and 1993. Because of tough busi-ness conditions, there was only one general increase in wages be-tween the buy-out in the spring of 1990 and the late summer of 1993. What is more the workforce agreed in 1993 to surrender two days of annual holiday entitlement, without any compensation, monetary or otherwise. And that was in addition to the across-the-board wage reduction of 2.5%.

Taken together with what amounted to a wage freeze, the post-buy-out restructuring measures significantly improved labour productivity; and that improvement was the main factor which explained the increase in operating profits. Moreover it was an improvement for which the unions at CT are entitled to take considerable credit. In effect the fact of employee ownership meant a greater readiness by the drivers to make concessions: because they acknowledged that these were for the good of their company.

Yet there was clearly an obverse to this improvement in busi-ness efficiency. Redundancies, to the extent that they exceeded the decline in demand, were a part of that. Much of the improvement in efficiency resulted from imposing extra pressures on the drivers – by cutting down the 'waiting time' for which they have tradi-tionally been paid. Bus driving may not be skilled work: but it is clearly associated with stress. Some improvements in labour productivity result from working harder – or more intensively – and others have their source in what the Americans call 'working smarter'. It would, I think, be misleading to put the improvements in the productivity of CT drivers into the second of these two categories.

Shortly before he stepped down as managing director in the summer of 1993, Mr Coupar remarked that the CT employee owners were not yet ready to embrace policies of 'pain sharing', except on the margin. What he meant was that there had been no discussion about the possibility of replacing redundancies with really significant all-round pay cuts. It is a possibility with which a union-led workforce is likely to have particular difficulties. True, there are plenty of examples in America of employee owners accepting 'voluntary' pay cuts when the alternative is plant closure. On the other hand, among the businesses studied in this book there is only one example of an overt scheme to replace redundancies with substantially reduced wages: the scheme developed by the group of Mondragon co-operatives towards the end of the 1970s. Because offset by shares, the big wage cuts agreed at United Airlines are not quite the same.

That is something of a digression. But it serves to highlight a general point which has come up again and again in these case studies. It is that changes of attitude and behaviour – or of what it has become fashionable to call 'business culture' – do not as it were, 'happen spontaneously', following a switch from conventional arrangements to employee ownership. Such changes must be specifically and consciously midwifed if they are to happen. And the fact that desirable changes do not happen spontaneously may be the best explanation of something that did not happen in the three years following the buy-out at Chesterfield: there was no measurable improvement in the rate of absenteeism, usually one of the best available measures of workforce morale.

The extent to which the switch to employee ownership was thought of as a 'good thing' at CT probably depends on the alternative. If the post buy-out years at CT are compared with the earlier days of a 'community bus service' before the arrival of Mr Coupar in 1986, and before any restructuring, then the earlier period was seen as preferable; and indeed looked back upon as something of a golden age. Apart from anything else, working conditions were simply easier in those days.

On the other hand if the post buy-out period is compared with what happened in many other privatisations, for example at the neighbouring East Midlands Bus Company, a former subsidiary of National Bus, then working for the employee owned Chesterfield Transport was surely preferred. (The East Midlands Bus Company was privatised through the mechanism of a Management Buy Out. But it was then rapidly sold on and became a subsidiary of Stagecoach which was to be CT's buyer in 1995.)

A further general point may be taken from a response of Mr Coupar to a question about what he saw, three years after it had happened, as the most positive outcome of the buy-out. His answer was clear: a greater understanding of how businesses operate on the part of Chesterfield's employee owners; and thus a greater realism.

Nevertheless that realism was perhaps only partly converted into what might be called self-sustaining programmes of continuous improvement. Such programmes face particular difficulties in industries like buses where members of the main section of the workforce – the drivers – are engaged in what is essentially individual rather than team working. Still there are good working models for owner-drivers: one needs to look no further than the country's taxi drivers. I suspect that throughout its five years of employee ownership there remained a big gap between the relevant behaviour of a CT 'owner driver' and that of the typical owner driver of a Chesterfield taxi.

Ownership and Control Arrangements On the morrow of the buy-out the share capital of CT was divided between 10p ordinary shares and £1 redeemable preference shares. Beyond noting that the latter paid an annual 10% dividend in two equal six-monthly instalments and that they were due to be redeemed, at the company's discretion, between mid-1995 and 1997, we can ignore the preference shares from now on.

Turning to the ordinary 10p shares, the first point to note is that a total of just less than one million of these were initially subscribed with total payment of just less than £100,000. Approximately 150,000 were subscribed by employees as individuals – for which they paid approximately £15,000 – and the balance by an employee trust. On the morrow of the buy-out, therefore, the ownership of the ordinary capital of the business was divided roughly in the ratio 15:85 as between individual employee and employee trust ownership.

In the years down to the 1995 sale, and in line with policies first decided by the buy-out working party as long before as 1989, ordinary shares were distributed annually out of the trust's holding and into the ownership of employees as individuals. As a result, by summer 1993 employees as individuals held more than 20% of the equity and the trust's ownership stake had declined to below 80%.

With an initial exception to take account of length of service, the annual distribution to individual employees of shares previously held in the employee trust was always as egalitarian as the original share subscription rule: the number of shares distributed to the managing director was the same as those which went to the lowest paid eligible employee.

In the first year the assignment of shares for each year of service was in fact 37. The average number of years for which eligible employees qualified was surprisingly high – no less than eight. So the average employee-shareholder received a total of 296 shares in that first year. In the table below that average figure is included for 1990. For the subsequent years, the distribution was of course equal. Against each year, I also record the price at which the shares were valued.

	Number of Shares	Valuation in pence
1990	296	6
1991	100	45
1992	33	55
1993	35	70

Total: 464

By the summer of 1993, those employees who had bought in at the start and had qualified for the average length of service bonus in the first distribution owned a total of 964 shares – 500 plus 464 – and these were then worth rather less than £700. Those who had not been initial subscribers had accumulated just less than half.

In order to achieve maximum tax effectiveness for these operations it was necessary, at CT as elsewhere, to set up a further employee trust, sometimes called a Profit Sharing Trust (PST). What then happened in each of the four years 1991 to 1994 was that following the approval of the annual accounts and the fixing of the valuation of the shares in agreement with the Inland Revenue, the directors decided on a sum of money to be contributed to the PST out of pre-tax profits. The PST then in turn applied that money to purchase from the original trust the so-called EBT shares which it subsequently distributed to eligible employees. The process was only arrested at the end of 1994/5 because of the negotiations to sell and, of course, the lack of profit in that year.

At least down to the summer of 1994, those CT employees who chose to subscribe for shares in the spring of 1990 enjoyed a not unattractive return. On their £750 of preference shares they received 10% (after tax) annually for four years. They saw the value of the ordinary shares they bought for 10p rise to 70p by mid-1994, and the value of their ordinary shareholding climb, without any additional investment on their part, from £50 to just under £675.

As a footnote to this discussion, it is worth mentioning a debate which first surfaced in 1992, which was then resolved for the time being, but which might well have been reopened had the employee ownership survived. This was about whether the purchase and sale of ordinary shares between individual employee shareholders should be allowed to take place under arrangements of regulated trading. The issue was resolved in 1992 in favour of allowing these transactions to take place so long as that happened in accordance with an established set of rules, including:

– dealings should be permitted only once each year on a designated dealing day and at a price set by the most recent valuation;

– the maximum permitted individual employee shareholding should be limited to 5% of the ordinary share capital;

– when buyers outnumber sellers, priority should be given to those employees with zero or only relatively small shareholdings;

– when sellers outnumber buyers priority should be given first to employees who have left, and second to those with 'compassionate' grounds for wishing to make a sale.

If the success of CT's employee share scheme was measured by the ratio of would-be buyers to sellers, then – on the evidence of the first two dealing days – it may be counted rather a success. On the first dealing day, in 1992, there were more than 150 would-be buyers and less than 10 would be sellers. On the second, in August of 1993, the numbers were only slightly less skewed in the direction of would-be buyers.

So far we have considered the ordinary CT shares simply as units of financial participation in the value of the company's business. But ordinary shares have, of course, a second function. They also confer a voice and a vote in the government of the company's business. We must now turn our attention to how CT was governed during its employee-owned years.

To begin with it cannot be emphasised too strongly that the top management team, grouped together in an executive board, was fully responsible for managing the business on a day-to-day basis and for taking the normal range of management decisions. There is only a minor qualification in this respect compared with what would be normal practice in a conventional private company. As we noted earlier, the executive board included – from a date well before the buy-out – an elected employee director (David Wheatcroft) as well as a managing director and two other executive directors with departmental responsibilities: a finance director and a director of operations. The elected employee director's function on the executive board is probably best understood as communication from top management to rank-and-file employees – and vice versa.

Just as it retained a basically conventional arrangement of executive top management, the employee-owned CT also kept in place conventional machinery for negotiating with the unions which it inherited from the past. There were annual wage negotiations during the employee-owned years in the same way as there had been since anyone could remember. The machinery was not changed; but under employee ownership all the basic information became freely available to both sides.

The big formal change under employee ownership compared to what had happened before the buy-out had to do neither with top management as such nor with management/union relations. It had to do with the *government* of the company, that is with what goes on *above* the level of top management, and with the way that management is held responsible. And that brings us back to the employee benefit trust (EBT) which acquired about 85% of the new company's share capital in 1990 and still owned well over 60% when the business was sold on in 1995. By virtue of this shareholding and down to the date of sale, the EBT ultimately controlled the company and its top management. It is to the trustees of the EBT that the top management of the employee-owned CT used to report.

So a key question under employee ownership was the composition of this trustee body: seven trustees consisting of three elected employee representatives, three outsiders appointed by the buy-out team, and one executive director. The trustees elected by the employees were not permitted to hold positions as union shop stewards as well: they had to choose between one or the other.

Finally the reader may reasonably ask whether, down to the date of sale, it was possible to offer any verdict on these arrangements, whether on those of the employee-owned CT's corporate government or more generally. Because of the recession coming on top of the continuing decline in the demand for local bus services, the new structures were subjected to enormous strain. The fact that they survived, that they remained in place down to the decision to sell is perhaps a significant achievement. At minimum, or so it seems to me, the fair-minded reader must concur with the verdict of Mr Miller, for a number of years the company's finance director. His verdict was that, given that a continuation of the old *status quo* was not on offer, a period of employee ownership was probably the 'least worst' solution.

The end in 1995 came rather quickly. On the other hand, in the absence of what seems in retrospect to have been a perverse ruling by the Monopolies and Mergers Commission (MMC), the Chesterfield bus company might well have come to be a subsidiary, not of Stagecoach but of the then 80% employee-owned Mainline bus undertaking in nearby Sheffield. The details need not concern us. But the key facts can be quickly summarised. By early 1995 CT had realised that if it sought to sustain its independence it risked destroying the value of the business. So it started negotiations with what was taken to be the potentially fraternal, because majority employee-owned, Mainline. For quite other reasons, but at about the same time, the MMC ordered Stagecoach to sell its 20% minority stake in Mainline and ruled against any acquisition of Chesterfield by the latter until that had happened. But Stagecoach was not thereby debarred from itself making a bid for Chesterfield. It did, and both the directors and the trustees advised a sale. Those employees who had bought shares at the beginning and held on saw their shareholdings valued at up to £15,000.

18

The National Freight Consortium

INTRODUCTORY OVERVIEW

We have a once in a lifetime opportunity to buy the business for which we work. Peter Thompson, first chief executive of the National Freight Consortium and architect of its management led employee buy-out, speaking to fellow employees of the business on video, 1981

Of all the substantial British companies which have had large employee stakes, it is the National Freight Consortium (NFC) which has probably attracted closest attention from ex-Socialist countries researching examples of employee ownership in practice. Its core business is a road haulage, distribution and transport undertaking, the largest of its kind in Britain and quite likely in western Europe. The five most notable features of the buy-out by which it became employee-owned in 1982 were:

– the high proportion of borrowed money in the £53.5m paid to the government for the business: approaching 85% of the total;

– the proportion of the workforce, roughly 35% and about 10,000 people, who put money into the buy-out and became employee shareholders: strikingly high in view of the pioneering character of the transaction and the bitter hostility of the main trade union to it;

– the size of the overall business: about 24,500 employees when the deal was done;

– the fact that the agreed price, based on professional estimates of a 'market' price, was way below asset values;

– that all this happened under a Government led not by a social democrat or social liberal but by the Conservative Margaret Thatcher.

On the subsequent performance of the newly employee-owned business, one indicator above all captures the imagination and interest of visitors and is easily memorable: the movement of the share price between the time of the buy-out in February 1982 and the flotation of the shares on the London Stock Exchange seven years later. This price rose just over 100 times. As a Hungarian visitor to NFC remarked in 1991, it is a 'notable statistic, and perhaps potentially the most notable one in the whole great privatisation programme of the Thatcher years'. Moreover, as a result, those individuals who staked the most – the highest figure was just over £40,000 – and who held on till the flotation, became multi-millionaires. Even those who invested the minimum permitted, £100, finished up seven years later with a tidy capital sum.

It is true that there has been criticism of the distribution of the main 'wealth creation' benefits which have resulted from this success. These went disproportionately more to managers than non- managers, and disproportionately more to top managers than middle managers: those who were prepared and able to 'take a punt' on the success of the project at the time of the buy-out. The two thirds of the workforce who chose *not* to make a punt in early 1982, even though most of them later became shareholders, never had a remotely comparable second chance to climb onto what turned out to be a rapid upward escalator of a share price. The unequal distribution of the NFC 'wealth creation benefits' has probably had an important influence on how arrangements have been structured in some subsequent management-led employee buy-outs in Britain, especially in the bus industry: in a number of cases where bus undertakings have faced privatisation, the managers and workers have agreed that all those who subscribe for shares must either invest the same amount – for example seven or eight hundred pounds – or nothing at all.

Whatever the validity of these criticisms, they do not affect the two key judgements which can be made about this NFC experience: that as a form or method of privatisation the management-led employee buy-out seems in principle to have much to commend it; and that this method of privatisation is far from incompatible with subsequent business success. These lessons are of special interest to governments and others involved in the privatisation process in ex-Socialist countries in the 1990s.

Moreover, there are at least limited rejoinders to the implicit criticism of the way the NFC wealth benefits have been distributed: the entire workforce was invited to participate in the buy-out and had a real opportunity to do so. Of course it is true that the richer the employee the easier it was to take advantage of that opportunity. On the other hand, an interest-free loan of £200 was available, at the time of the share offer, to all employees. And there is persuasive evidence that it was the negative influence of the main union, the Transport & General Workers Union, as much as any financial constraints, which explains many of the individual employee decisions *not* to invest. That view is certainly consistent with the size of the average 'punt' – of £700 – by those employees who chose to invest. It seems improbable that £700 was beyond the reach of all but a minority of NFC's employees: the figure was equivalent at the time to between four and six weeks average wages of non-management employees.

Two further related reasons make NFC of potentially outstanding interest to those involved with privatisation programmes in Eastern Europe and elsewhere. Before privatisation, NFC was a notably unglamorous state-owned undertaking. What is more it was the subject of considerable 'restructuring' before the buy-out took place: the workforce was slimmed down, debts from its state owned past were written off, and it was moved from loss making to at least modest profitability. It is doubtful, indeed almost out of the question, that the buy-out could have taken place unless that process of restructuring had gone before.

NFC's core business of road haulage and distribution had been taken into public ownership, alongside Britain's railways, in 1947 as part of the Attlee Government's programme to nationalise the 'commanding heights' of the country's economy. Parts of it were formerly the road service delivery operations which had been owned by the railways themselves. In pursuit of what may now seem to be the chimaera of a rationally-integrated transport policy, the Transport Act of 1947 brought into public ownership virtually all Britain's road haulage business. The exceptions were that private firms remained free to transport their own goods in their own trucks and that small truckers were permitted to carry goods for hire within a radius of twenty-five miles. To be fair to the authors of that legislation a further motive behind the 1947 Act was the welfare of the truckers. There is some evidence that government rules about, for example, the maximum number of hours that drivers were permitted to work without a break, had been quite widely disregarded by private road hauliers in the period between the two world wars.

In 1976, nearly thirty years after the Attlee Government's Transport Act, Peter Thompson was promoted from one of NFC's subsidiaries to become chief executive of the whole. The business then employed some 50,000 people – roughly twice as many as at the time of the buy-out six years later. Moreover, although there had been some improvements in the preceding years, its operations in that year were running at a loss.

Between 1976 and 1982 Peter Thompson and a new top management team which came in with him, restructured the business so that it became eligible for privatisation. There was extensive de-manning. There was a move from loss-making to modest profitability and there was a big change in the style and approach of management to engender a more participative business culture. In the early stages of this process, while a Labour Government remained in power, privatisation was not the goal. In the years between 1976 and 1979 Peter Thompson and his management team were concerned with the more limited objective of making NFC efficient, profitable and able to stand on its own feet without government subsidy and support.

Why was it that this unglamorous road haulage business was selected by the incoming Thatcher Government as one of the first candidates for privatisation? One probable reason was precisely its unglamorous character: so that shifting it into the private sector was unlikely to provoke unacceptable levels of political opposition. A second reason may have been something of an accident – in the late 1970s the Thatcher Government's first Minister of Transport had recommended that NFC be privatised, or partly privatised, and this recommendation had been incorporated into the Tory Party's 1979 election manifesto.

The buy-out was successfully achieved in February 1982. Following it, the ownership of the successor business – the National Freight *Consortium* rather than the National Freight *Corporation* (as it was known before privatisation) – was substantially in the hands of its employees. Together with the pensioners of the business and members of their close families, they owned 82.5% of the Consortium's equity with the balance owned by the banks which loaned the much larger sums which made the deal possible.

Just before he retired in 1991, the chairman, Sir Peter Thompson (as he had by then become), took a valedictory look back to the year 1976 when he first took the reins:

In January 1976 we had just completed a year in which losses of £31m had been recorded. We were losing market share in most of our activities . . . We were state-owned and supported by Government subsidy.

Contrast that with the NFC of 1990. This year's results show that despite a difficult economic climate we have delivered £98m profit before tax, the ninth successive year of profit growth.

What has happened since then? If changes in prices are allowed for, both profits and turnover at NFC had in fact peaked in 1989, the year of the share flotation. After adjusting for inflation, NFC's turnover and profits were lower in each of the three years – 1990, 1991 and 1992 – than they had been in 1989. That this should have been so was, of course, at least partly due to the 'difficult economic climate' to which Sir Peter referred in his final Chairman's Statement. On the other hand, between February 1989, the date of flotation, and early 1993, NFC's share price significantly outperformed the London stock market averages. On the face of it, the still substantially employee-owned business weathered the recession at least as well as the average for corporate Britain. We shall look more closely at that in the final section. We shall also need to highlight the much weaker performance of the company as it moved away from employee ownership after 1993.

From Public Ownership to Privatisation, 1947 to 1981: From the Transport Act of 1947 to the Transport Act of 1980 There are said to be economic advisors who have earned good money explaining to governments how best and why they should take into public ownership some or all of their countries' nationally important enterprises – and then earned good money a generation later advising governments in the same countries how best and why to do the opposite. Governments in the former British colonial territories of Africa received advice of the first kind in the 1960s and 1970s and of the second kind in the early 1990s, sometimes apparently from the same economist.

Civil servants in Britain's transport ministry who were in their early twenties in 1947 would still have been short of retirement age in 1980. In that case their experience may have have been similar to that of the economic advisers. They would have advised their minister how to take most of the country's longer distance road haulage industry into public ownership, through the mechanism of a Transport Act, in 1947; and in 1980 they would have advised their minister how to prepare that same industry for privatisation, through the mechanism of a rather different Transport Act. In between they doubtless advised successive Labour and Tory Governments about how to extend or reduce the amount of the country's road haulage activity owned and controlled by the state; and about how to make that road haulage business more commercially oriented or otherwise. Only in the 1970s did the thrust of Labour Party and Labour Government policy for the road haulage industry begin to change in this last respect: towards greater support for commercial and market success.

The NFC story begins with the 1947 Transport Act. But the genesis of the Act's road haulage provisions was not the general objective of Britain's post-war Labour Government to take under state control the commanding heights of the country's economy. Rather it was two pieces of then recent history: first, the joint and in some sense integrated control which government had exercised over both rail and road transport during the Second World War; second, the conditions which had prevailed, or at least were widely believed in Labour Party and trade union circles to have prevailed, in the country's road haulage industry between the wars. The belief was that there had been a widespread disregard of government regulations, especially safety regulations, by the private owners of road haulage undertakings. (For a full account of NFC before privatisation, see Bradley and Nejad, 1983.)

The trade unions were apparently so convinced of the case for nationalisation at this time that they argued for the inclusion of the country's entire road haulage industry within the scope of the 1947 Act. As it happened, partly because of the huge number of tiny units in the industry, the Act fell short of that. But subject to exceptions for small local operators and in-company haulage, the new state-owned road haulage undertaking enjoyed a monopoly. The new undertaking, which traded as British Road Services (BRS), was itself ultimately controlled by an umbrella organisation, the British Transport Commission (BTC). Because it also controlled the railways, BTC could be given the task of sustaining the integrated transport policy which had operated during the war years.

Despite the exceptions, the task of identifying and then nationalising all those private transport businesses covered by the Act took a long time. Bradley and Nejad tell us that it was not completed until 1951. By then, BRS had acquired over 3,700 firms, which owned some 41,000 vehicles, based upon 1,000 depots, and employed over 75,000 people.

It is to these numbers that we can trace back the size of the undertaking which was eventually privatised in 1982 and the extent of its still very considerable property portfolio. But the year 1951 also saw the return of a Conservative Government which remained in power for thirteen years. So the next question is obvious enough: how far, during that thirteen-year period, did the Conservatives unscramble the near-monopoly nationalisation of road haulage ushered in by the 1947 Act? The short answer is that they ended its monopoly of contract hire outside the twenty-five-mile radius and slimmed down BRS, but left its position as the country's largest road transport undertaking more or less intact. They also eliminated from domestic transport policy any requirement that road and rail services should be integrated. According to Bradley and Nejad, they kept it in public ownership, first, because it proved difficult to find buyers for many of the smaller business units and associated garages and, second, because the retention by BRS of its trunk routes would provide a 'strategic reserve' of road transport capacity, additional to that of the defence services, in the event of an emergency. Perhaps that argument had a special appeal to Sir Anthony Eden's Government.

The Conservatives not only allowed BRS to survive. They also encouraged it to compete and ensured that it had the power to do so by allowing it to make such acquisitions as it thought commercially justified and for which the necessary resources were available. That brings us on to the years between 1964 and 1970 when the country was again governed by the Labour Party. BRS was strongly encouraged by Labour to make the most of the freedom to acquire businesses in competition with it which had been permitted by the previous Conservative regime: 'A spate of takeovers was negotiated, though far more selectively than in the 1940s, in what became known as back door nationalisation [Bradley and Nejad].'

Second, Labour reintroduced the old requirement for an integrated domestic transport policy. However, the monopoly which BRS had enjoyed during the Attlee years was not reintroduced. To that extent the Labour Party, or so we must assume, was gradually coming to accept that there may be some advantages in competition.

It was in yet another Transport Act, that of 1968, that these Labour Party policies were embodied; and in its provisions that arrangements for transport integration were spelled out. The most important of these could not be implemented before the Conservatives were returned again at the 1970 general election: the movement of bulk goods would have been permitted by road only if the railways were unable to do the job. However, under the Act all road transport activities in the public sector, including those previously controlled by British Railways, were brought together into a single corporate body, designated the National Freight Corporation (NFC). When first established, and including large numbers of people formerly with British Railways' road haulage operation, employees totalled as many as 66,000. De-manning stretched over a period of fourteen years with a cumulative reduction of more than 60% of the workforce – to 24,000 by the time of the buy-out in 1982. Given the restructuring challenges faced by the state-owned undertakings in today's ex-Socialist countries, both the numbers of those de-manned and the time scale over which it took place are worth highlighting.

Bradley and Nejad tell us that the operations of BRS had been profitable, with the exception of only one year, over the entire 1947 to 1968 period. But they cite statistics which suggest that it was significantly *less* profitable than its private competitors. They also argue that because the period was marked by a continuous increase in demand, itself partly the result of a continuous shift of traffic from rail to road, profits were relatively easy to make.

Partly because it was obliged under the 1968 Act to take over the highly unprofitable road haulage business of British Railways, the new NFC showed losses for most of its first ten years; and never showed more than a quite modest profit before the 1982 buy-out. The corporation's management during the years between 1968 and 1975 has frequently been criticised and no doubt with some justice. But it must be given some credit for starting the whole process of restructuring and de-manning – already by 1976 the workforce had been reduced from 66,000 to 50,000.

One of the key actors in the subsequent buy-out transaction was Norman Fowler, the Conservative spokesman on Transport during the party's years in opposition down to 1979. In that position he wrote and published in 1977 a pamphlet which discussed the future of the National Freight Corporation. I want here to highlight a remark he made in 1982 after the buy-out about his assessment of the corporation at the time he wrote the pamphlet: 'I came to the conclusion that NFC was a good business trying to get out. There was no need for it to be in the public sector [McLachlan].'

The remark refers to a judgement at the time the Fowler pamphlet was written, i.e. not later than 1977. In his 1977 transport policy pamphlet Fowler suggested that the Corporation might lend itself to an hybrid ownership arrangement similar to that which applied at the time to the oil company, British Petroleum: with both Government and private shareholdings.

Less than three years later, after the Conservatives had won the 1979 election, Fowler was appointed Transport Minister in the first of the three Thatcher Governments. He was thus in a position to do something about what he had proposed in his 1977 pamphlet. His first step, embodied in the Transport Act of 1980, was essentially an enabling one. Under its provisions National Freight Corporation was transformed, without a change of name, into a Companies Act company limited by shares with the Government as the sole shareholder. The step allowed, but did not require, a second step, of actual privatisation, to follow. Such a step was further facilitated by a provision of the Act under which Government assumed a part of NFC's under-funded pension liabilities.

This section began with the Transport Act of 1947. It ends with the very different Transport Act of 1980. Only one further point should be noted. For reasons which no one was very clear about at the time, a commitment to privatise NFC was included in the Conservative Party's manifesto for the 1979 election. It was surprising on a number of grounds; but especially because it was the only specific privatisation commitment in that whole manifesto.

The Buy-Out Itself
[From the Prospectus]

In this Prospectus you are being given the facts and figures on investing in the consortium which is proposing to buy NFC from the Government. On behalf of its Directors I am inviting you to buy shares.

Our motives for proposing the purchase of NFC are the

same today as they were in May, 1981, when we first put the
idea to the Secretary of State for Transport.

First and foremost, we were being defensive. We believed
that everyone in the NFC group would benefit if we could
keep intact, and maintain the management style which has
served the NFC group successfully in recent years.

So, with a letter from Peter Thompson opening 'Dear Colleagues', began the prospectus of the National Freight *Consortium*
which was sent to all employees of the National Freight *Corporation* in January 1982. Peter Thompson closed the letter with an
expression of his own commitment to the project, a reference to
that of his top management staff and a call to the entire workforce
to join them as fellow shareholders:

> I intend to apply for at least 40,000 [£1] shares. My twelve
> senior colleagues who assisted me in establishing the consor-
> tium have decided to apply for at least 300,000 shares be-
> tween them. This shows how confident we are in the future
> of the NFC group. I'd like you to share that confidence. I
> hope you will join us as shareholders in the consortium and
> so help to create the first UK company of our size controlled
> and substantially owned by the people who work in it.

In between the beginning and the last paragraph of the letter, he
set out both negative reasons for supporting the buy-out – to do
with the probable alternatives if it did not happen – and 'four
good reasons why this is a good time to invest in this enterprise'.
The broad philosophy behind the buy-out was openly explained
in Peter Thompson's letter:

> ... we had a vision. We believed, as we do today, that by creat-
> ing a company controlled and owned mainly by employees, we
> were launching a new kind of industrial enterprise. We believe
> that this will help us to get rid of the conflicts between manage-
> ment and workers traditional to British industry – the 'us and
> them' attitude. In its place would be a new attitude of co-opera-
> tion which should lead to improved efficiency, better prospects
> for employment and better profitability.

Two key developments before the buy-out had been the move
from loss to modest profit since 1976 and the fact that the three key

actors were in favour of it: Peter Thompson and the 'twelve senior colleagues' referred to in his prospectus letter, the government (the prospective seller) and a group of banks. The latter, headed by Barclays Merchant Bank, had made a conditional promise to provide the financial assistance necessary for the purchase. The condition was that the employees (including their families) and pensioners of the business should subscribe not less than £4.125m towards the purchase price. I may add that well before the prospectus went out that price had been set at £53.5m.

We noted in the previous section that the workforce was reduced from 50,000 to 24,500 between 1976 and 1981. In line with that reduction, the profit and loss account had shown a considerable improvement, at least up to the onset of the recession in 1979 and 1980:

Pre-Tax Profits, 1976–1981

Years*	£m
1976	(3.5)
1977	2.0
1978	11.1
1979	10.0
1980	0.4
1981	4.3

*1976–79: calendar years; 1980–81: years to September 30
Source: *NFC Prospectus*, 1982

Excluding the parcels operations, trading profit had increased from £8.1m in 1976 to £16.8m in 1981. The success of the (more radical) restructuring programme introduced in 1976 taken together with other factors, was enough to persuade a group of banks to make their conditional offer of support for the proposed buy-out.

The Peter Thompson prospectus letter was forthright about the disadvantages as he saw them of any realistic alternative to the proposed buy-out. Because of the 1980 Transport Act the continuation of the *status quo* was not, the letter argued, a realistic possibility:

> . . . we knew we could not remain in the public sector. The choice was *how* [emphasis original] we would be privatised not whether.

... If we had not taken the initiative, NFC might have been privatised in either of two ways.

The first way was for the Government to float NFC on the stock exchange ... Although the shares would have been sold as widely as possible, there would have been no effective means of protecting NFC from a later takeover bid by a company not of NFC's choosing. Any company could, after our flotation, have made an offer for the shares.

The second way was to sell NFC complete to another company, without going through the Stock Exchange. *The danger in both cases would have been that the purchaser might not have wanted to continue to run the NFC Group as a broad based freight, travel agency and storage business, with a participative management style. Indeed the purchasing company might well have wished to break up the NFC group* [emphasis added].

In other words a key reason adduced by Peter Thompson for his opposition to the alternatives to the proposed buy out was identical with one adduced by Philip Baxendale for opposing any alternative to a sale to an employee trust at Baxi: that the character and culture of the business would be at risk and that it might be broken up. In the case of a successful business which faces ownership change – whether through prospective privatisation or otherwise – this is one of the single most persuasive arguments in favour of an employee ownership solution.

After the 'vision' paragraph which I quoted earlier, the Thompson prospectus letter then goes on to identify 'four good reasons why this is a good time to invest in this enterprise'. The key points put forward in the letter were that NFC had survived the then recession – 'the worst ... since 1945' – in reasonably good shape, that the worst (of the recession) was over, that the group had managed to implement the most important of its investment projects; and that the worst of the redundancy programme was in the past. The prospectus letter went on: 'We are facing the future with lower operating costs, reduced overheads and a smaller but more productive workforce.'

Later in the prospectus, though not in the Thompson letter, there are references to the price at which the government had agreed to sell – £53.5m. – and the conditions which would have to be satisfied to secure the financial assistance of the banks. The most important of the latter was that the NFC workforce should themselves muster not less than £4.125m.

The Thompson letter, perhaps pointedly, did not offer an explicit opinion on whether the £53.5m price was a good one or otherwise – indeed it did not refer to the price at all. On the other hand, if only in the light of the subsequent history of the share price, it has since been widely criticised as too low. How was the price reached?

It seems that as early as 1979, hard on the heels of the Conservative Party's election victory, the Government appointed J. Henry Schroder Wagg, the London merchant bank, to advise NFC on the sensitive issue of its valuation. Schroders apparently came up fairly promptly with a figure, or more exactly – as is normal in these kinds of exercise – with a range of valuations. The Schroders numbers were £57m at the bottom of the range and £90m at the top. Essentially these figures were estimates, or predictions, of what the business would fetch if it was sold on the Stock Exchange. Any relationship between them and, say, the net book value of the undertaking was more fortuitous than otherwise.

Given this range of Schroder valuations in 1979, how did it come about that the government eventually agreed to accept only £53.5m for the business – a figure below the bottom end of the Schroder valuation range? The answer to this question is impeccably proper. Early in 1981 Schroders advised that their earlier valuation needed to be adjusted downwards to a figure close to the bottom of their original range. The bank gave two reasons for this downward adjustment. The first was that because of the recession all stock exchange prices had come down. The second was that, since the original valuation, the business had failed to secure the renewal of an important and rather profitable contract with British Rail; and thus its own profit forecasts – one of the key elements in the original valuation estimates – had had to come down. Schroders further advised, early in 1981, that even on the basis of this lower valuation, a flotation on the stock market might well not succeed before the summer of 1982.

The downward revision of its earlier valuation by Schroders offered the Government almost complete protection against any charge that state property was being sold off, without any process of competitive tendering, at bargain basement prices. It also seems sensible to suppose that the Government saw political attractions in a sale which could be presented as promoting 'popular capitalism'. Given the rather unglamorous character of road haulage they probably also calculated that the sale was unlikely to provoke much of a political fuss. But it is worth adding that the prospective buyers were almost certainly lucky in the identity of the Minister of Transport when the decision to sell at this price – and to allow the National Freight *Consortium* a clear run as the only bidder – was taken. For the Minister, at that time was none other than Norman Fowler, whose political interest in the business went back, as we saw earlier, a number of years.

To conclude this discussion of the price at which the deal was eventually struck a word must be said about the value of the assets transferred to the buyers when the transaction was completed. An indicative balance sheet in the prospectus offers a net asset figure of £89.2m and a value of fixed assets – property, vehicles, plant and equipment but substantially the first – of £96m. I have heard it argued, by Conservative politicians among others, that in the light of these numbers the Schroders valuation was too low. Critics who take such a line simply fail to distinguish between a market-based price and an asset-based price. Those involved in the early 1990s privatisation process in the ex-Socialist countries of Eastern Europe and elsewhere will be all too familiar both with the distinction and with the difficulty of getting it across to politicians and to the public.

Having said that, it should also be conceded that at least in retrospect the promoters of the buy-out may be reckoned to have been extremely fortunate in its timing. For the reasons given earlier, that resulted in a downward adjustment of the market price they had to pay. Moreover, as we now know, property prices were shortly to start on nearly a decade of rapid and uninterrupted growth. The indicative balance sheet figures in the prospectus clearly could not take that into account.

As we shall see, property sales made a significant contribution to the success of NFC, at least in the early years. We must assume too that the prospect of such sales, and the strength of the balance sheet more generally, were important factors in the decision of Barclays Merchant Bank to offer its conditional support to the buy-out. And we must assume that these factors must have had a positive weight for Peter Thompson, his senior managers, and other members of the workforce. What seems odd, at least with the benefit of hindsight a dozen years later, is why Schroders did not offer to support the deal themselves; why they allowed Barclays to move in instead. As it was they limited their role to one of continuing to advise the government on the prospective sale. About Schroders' later advice, it is worth noting one specific point: so far as I know Schroders never suggested that the sale should include a provision which would allow the seller to share in any increase in asset prices if there were asset disposals in the short or medium term. Such provisions have figured quite widely in subsequent privatisations both in the UK and elsewhere.

As for Barclays, the mix of considerations which lay behind its conditionally positive attitude included one other ingredient: the commitment of top management. The late Philip Mayo, who was executive legal director of NFC at that time and one of the key figures in the whole transaction, was fond of telling a story about the first formal meeting on the buy-out between the Corporation and the bank. The former came to the meeting, as can be well imagined, with enormous piles of heavy, detailed, and no doubt not all that easily digestible documents. Imagine their feelings then when the Barclays team suggested that, at least for the time being, these documents should be set on one side. What the bankers then asserted was that as a condition of the discussions making progress at all, Peter Thompson and each of his twelve senior management colleagues must commit not less than £25,000 to the buy-out. As we saw earlier that commitment was forthcoming. The prospective lenders to the buy-out clearly, and rightly, attached exceptional importance to it.

From the Buy-Out in 1982 to the Float in 1989 For those of its employees who were lucky and bold enough to subscribe for a significant number of NFC shares in 1982, and who then held on to them till 1989, what happened to the share price must have seemed like a fairy tale. As early as 1983, there had been a bonus issue of a second £1 share for each one purchased at the time of the buy-out. The £1 shares were progressively divided so that early in 1987 each original shareholder held twenty five-pence shares for each £1 share originally purchased. Between the buy-out and the flotation on the stock exchange in February 1989, they could be traded in an 'internal market' on dealing days which happened every three months. By the first dealing day in 1987, on March 7, the five-pence shares were trading at £1.05 – or at a level equivalent to £42 in terms of the original £1 shares. Two years later, at the time of the float, the corresponding figures were £2.63 and £105.

If we take inflation into account, then the share price increased by roughly 70 times, rather than 105 times, over the seven-year period. After the inflation adjustment, share prices on the London Stock Exchange roughly doubled in price. So we have a thirty-five-fold increase in the NFC share price to explain and understand.

Part of the explanation is that there was a strong increase in the pre-tax profits of the business between 1982 and 1989: over six times, after inflation. Pre-tax profits for the years 1982 to 1992 are set out below, expressed in constant 1992 prices.

Pre-tax Profits 1982 to 1992

Year	£m
1982	17.7
1983	20.0
1984	26.0
1985	41.8
1986	53.8
1987	66.3
1988	87.7
1989	109.4
1990	108.2
1991	98.8
1992	91.1

The figures highlight the spectacular six-fold increase in the success of the business, as measured by inflation adjusted pre-tax profits, between 1982 and 1989. It has sometimes been claimed that these should be largely attributed to a vigorous policy of selling off the considerable property assets acquired as a result of the buy-out. The claim has some justification. But it is easy to exaggerate its importance, anyway after the first two years. Both in 1982 and 1983 profits on sales of fixed assets made a significant contribution to operating results, but were much less important thereafter.

Of much greater consequence was the parallel upward movement of both sales and sales per employee. In constant prices, total sales more than doubled over the seven-year period down to 1989:

Sales 1982 to 1992: 1992 Prices

Year	£m
1982	826.6
1983	842.7
1984	913.5
1985	1,028.4
1986	1,087.6
1987	1,273.3
1988	1,645.6
1989	1,818.5
1990	1,802.7
1991	1,801.0
1992	1,723.8

Employment was also significantly higher at the end of the period: with nearly 32,000 in the workforce as against no more than 24,500 at the time of the buy-out. All the same, between 1982 and 1989, there is still an increase of nearly 70%, after taking inflation fully into account, in sales per employee. When both sales and sales per employee are showing rapid increases in real terms, it is a racing certainty that the increase in profits will be disproportionately rapid.

But it may, of course, still be asked what lies behind the increase in total sales and, more importantly, behind the increase in sales per employee. Apart from the effects of acquisitions, the former can no doubt be substantially explained by improvements in demand, or more exactly by management response to improved market opportunities. It need hardly be said that the explanation for the increase in labour productivity is rather different. Here we are substantially dealing with a supply side phenomenon. Moreover, though I am not in a position to disentangle them, there are probably two separate elements to be distinguished: a shift of employees from lower to higher productivity work; and a productivity improvement by employees who stayed in the same jobs during this period.

Discussion with NFC staff suggests that at least three separate but similar sets of changes were going on during this period, and indeed have, in principle, continued since then. Typically all have involved a shift from less to more specialised transport work; shifts from a general goods or parcels service, to extended contract work for specialised and highly demanding clients in, for example, the retail food trade. The latter work will be significantly more taxing on the driver. He or she will be required to keep to tight delivery schedules. Typically too these latter services involve greater investment in warehouse facilities and more complex co-ordination arrangements. For all these reasons this is significantly higher value added work than a general parcels service. Shifts in this general direction occurred before the buy-out and after the float as well as during the emplyee-owned period in at least three different ways: a) an existing service became more specialised; b) a more specialised service within the UK has replaced a less specialised existing one; c) following the acquisition of a foreign subsidiary, a higher proportion of NFC's total otput was devoted to specialised work.

According to managerial anecdote, one further main source of improved labour productivity was that a significant number of employees were 'working smarter'; and in some cases showed a readiness to stretch themselves rather more than was normal before the buy-out.

Under Peter Thompson's leadership, efforts were made to increase what might be called the content and meaning of NFC's employee ownership. The AGM was built up as an event at which rank-and-file employee shareholders and indeed other shareholders within the families were especially welcome and at which the agenda would be made as interesting as possible. The numbers of employee shareholders who attended these events – which were deliberately held at week ends – ran well into four figures. And they were much livelier, less dry and formal, than is the case in most conventional companies. Furthermore, quarterly meetings of employee shareholders were introduced, a notable innovation. Because of the country-wide dispersion of the employee shareholder body, they were held concurrently in different parts of the country, with each individual board member assigned responsibility for a particular region.

Some may be inclined to dismiss these developments as little more than glorified public relations. However, it would be hard to maintain the same line about two other bits of evidence from this period: evidence of the commitment to the reality of employee ownership by Peter Thompson and his top management group.

The first was a policy of refusing to sell a subsidiary business if a majority of its employees were opposed. A case in point was Waste Management Ltd (WML), a non-core business, but one with considerable potential in its own specialised field, and well established in Britain's North West. As Sir Peter Thompson put it to me in late 1994, NFC was offered a fancy price for WML in the mid-1980s. The majority view on the board was that the financial arguments strongly favoured a sale. On the other hand when the WML workforce, including its managers, were consulted, it turned out that they were almost overwhelmingly opposed. Accordingly, in line with what was then agreed policy, negotiations about a possible sale were simply discontinued. But that wasn't in fact the end of the story. In 1992, by which time Sir Peter had retired from all positions bar that of honorary President, a new fancy offer was made for WML. A sale was again favoured on financial grounds by majority opinion on the Board. And that was backed by the City. This second time round there was no consultation with the WML workforce. A sale simply went ahead.

The second piece of evidence was the introduction, as early as 1983, of what is known in the technical jargon as a 'profit- sharing employee share ownership scheme'. Readers will remember that under such schemes, which are supported by tax reliefs, existing shareholders agree to divert a percentage of pre-tax profits to pay for shares which are then in principle distributed to all employees. In NFC's case, as in other companies with substantial employee ownership, the logic of the scheme was to spread that ownership more widely. From the time of its introduction down to Sir Peter's retirement, allocations out of pre-tax profits were made annually for this purpose. But in the admittedly more difficult years after he stepped down, these allocations were sharply reduced and in 1994 and 1995 were stopped altogether.

I have been making the case that while the leader of NFC's pioneering employee buy-out remained in the chair, the commitment to making that ownership real found specific expression. Moreover, I would argue that over the period we are discussing here, the commitment of Sir Peter makes plausible the hypothesis that employee ownership itself was one of the drivers behind higher productivity. Of course, as always in these cases, it is not possible to quantify an 'employee ownership benefit'. All we can prove is that increased productivity was one of the factors behnd the sharp increase in profits between 1982 and 1989; and that in turn was one of the factors behind the spectacular increase in the share price.

But the upward movement in NFC's profits was not the only

driver behind its rocketing share price between 1982 and 1989. At least two other factors may be identified.

The actual flotation itself in February 1989 was one of these. Before that, as we have seen, trading in the shares was confined to dealings on an internal market, and the price had been fixed quarterly by an independent valuer. Those valuations took into account the restricted character of the then market for the shares; and thus assigned to them a lower price than would have been appropriate if they had been freely tradeable. When the flotation occurred this 'discount' would be eliminated. The share price rose some 30% between the last trading day of the internal market and the flotation.

Even more important than the elimination of the 'restricted market discount' when the shares became freely tradeable was the extent of the gearing in the original buy-out. The business had then been purchased for £53.5m, using borrowed money for all but £7.5m of that total. It is true that, because the purchase was made, as we saw, at a price well below the then asset values, the equity in the business, or what are sometimes called 'shareholders' funds', on the day following the buy-out were substantially in excess of that £7.5m. However, even if a higher figure is substituted for the £7.5m it is still dwarfed by the figure of £327.8m recorded as 'shareholders' funds' in the balance sheet of 1989. Moreover, in the same balance sheet, borrowings with a maturity of a year or more are shown to be quite low (no more than £18.1m); and the same is true of what that balance sheet calls 'provisions' (a figure of £35.3m). In any case the figure of £327.8m of 'shareholders' funds' is net of those liabilities, even if off-balance sheet borrowings are not allowed for.

In other words, over the seven years between 1982 and 1989 NFC managed in effect to pay off the borrowings that had made the buy-out possible *and* to retain a significant proportion of its profits; and to do so after paying quite generous dividends. But what we should perhaps focus on here is the equivalent of the effect of paying off a mortgage on the value of a house to its owner. Quite apart from any improvement in profits, the repayment of borrowings will have acted as an independent engine to push up the share price. And so will NFC's success in retaining profits within the business during this period.

As well as these positive factors, it is likely that there was also a factor which inhibited a decline. The original prospectus records an important stipulation by the banks which had put up the loans (and a minority of the equity) which made the deal possible. It was to the effect that until the shares were floated any 'dilution' of the original equity should be held to a minimum. They stipulated, in other words, that new shares should only be issued in exceptional circumstances. The stipulation was quite strictly honoured. And it was evidently honoured for good business reasons – the rapidly appreciating value of the equity – as well as because of the original provision in the prospectus. Had there been a substantial dilution, that would have tended to put a downward pressure on the share price.

It is true that, as we saw earlier, a year after the buy-out all the then shareholders were issued with a second share to match each one that they then held. But that new issue did not count as a dilution, because the percentage of the equity held by each shareholder was the same after it as before it. Similarly, there was a rights issue, immediately before the flotation. But that again did not offend against the 'no dilution' rule because only existing shareholders enjoyed the relevant rights. And the same applied, though for a rather different reason, to new shares issued by the company in 1986 in part payment for an acquisition: there was no dilution because new assets were acquired to set against the newly issued shares.

In fact the annual accounts show that during the period 1982 to 1989 exceptions were permitted to the banks' stipulation on only two grounds. One was that new shares could be and were issued to new recruits who joined the NFC during this period. As a special concession they were allowed, on joining, to buy newly issued shares at the price at which these had changed hands on the dealing day immediately before their recruitment.

Second, in 1986, the issue of new shares to what amounted to an employee profit sharing scheme was authorised. Both may be seen as examples of exceptional cases provided for in the original bankers' stipulation. But there is a further and equally important point to be made about them. It is that even if we take them together, the degree of dilution which resulted was almost negligible – less than 5% over a period of seven years.

One justification for this extended discussion of the factors behind the upward movement of NFC's share price between 1982 and

1989 is its spectacular character. In the context of privatisation, a general point to emphasise is the possibility of high capital gains when privatisation is effected substantially with borrowed money. For, following such a transaction, significant capital gains are likely to be achieved simply as a result of the borrowing repayments. As long as those repayments can be achieved, there will be a near automatic upward movement in the equity of the business which has been privatised; or in its 'shareholders' funds'. As with the case of the paying off of a house mortgage, it can be almost as if, by itself, the 'arithmetic of reduced indebtedness' works in favour of the new owners. Without wishing for a minute to diminish the achievement of NFC, in, for example, raising its productivity and profits, 'the arithmetic of reduced indebtedness' was also working away in the interests of its new owners. For what it's worth there was also a sharp increase in off balance sheet borrowing over these years: good evidence of a clear understanding of that 'benign arithmetic' by top management.

To conclude the discussion of NFC's experience between the buy-out in 1982 and the flotation on the London Stock Exchange seven years later, just two points remain to be dealt with. First who were the chief beneficiaries of the enormous increase in the value of the business? Second, why did the stock market flotation happen and how was it achieved?

The main beneficiaries of the more than hundredfold increase in the NFC share price were, of course, those who had been in a position to make significant share purchases at the time of the buy-out in February 1982, who were bold enough to seize that opportunity, and then held on until the flotation in February 1989. A very comfortable majority of the shares purchased at the time of the buy-out were still being held at the time of the flotation by the 35% of employees who had bought them in the first place.

Such at any rate seem to be the implications of data about the volume of trading *before* the flotation, when the only permitted dealings were on NFC's internal market. The aggregate of the shares traded on the internal market over the seven-year period amounted to about one third of the total. The percentages traded during each calendar year between 1982 and 1988 were roughly as follows:

Percentage of Issued Shares Traded on Internal Market 1982 – 1988

Year	Approx %
1982	1
1983	5
1984	5
1985	6
1986	6.5
1987	6.5
1988	3.0
Total	33.0

Source: NFC Share Trust

We already know that dilution was almost negligible during this period. We also know that on all but one of the twenty-six internal market 'dealing days', between buy-out and flotation, there were more would-be buyers than sellers; and so the numbers applied for by would be buyers had to be scaled down. It seems to follow that those who missed the boat in February 1982 had the chance of only rather limited subsequent redress. Conversely, the lion's share of the capital gains went to those who had bought themselves in at the outset. Such, of course, is the classic logic of successful capitalism. It was mitigated in NFC's case only marginally by the set of priorities laid down for buyers on the internal market: these assigned the lowest position to large shareholders.

Following the February buy-out, the first dealing day on the internal market was 8 August 1982. The last one before the flotation in February 1989 was 9 November 1988. So far as I know, the progression of the share price between those two dates is not on the public record anywhere else, so I include it here:

Share Prices on the Internal Market 1982–1988*

Date	Price £
August '82	1.65
November '82	2.00
March '83	2.45
May '83	3.20
August '83	3.40
December '83	4.00
March '84	5.20

June '84	6.00
August '84	6.28
December '84	8.60
March '85	10.60
June '85	12.40
September '85	14.00
December '85	16.60
March '86	22.00
June '86	27.00
September '86	31.00
December '86	35.00
March '87	42.00
June '87	46.00
September '87	54.00
December '87	47.00
March '88	56.00
June '88	66.00
September '88	70.00
November '88	74.00

*Actual market prices adjusted as for original £1 shares

The price of £47 in December 1987 was the single exception to the upward movement of the price over the entire seven years. The explanation has nothing to do with any hiccup in the performance of NFC at the time: it is entirely explained by the occurrence of 'Black Monday', the day in October 1987 when stock market values plunged by some 30% almost all around the world.

The key rule which governed dealings on the internal market was designed to spread the employee shares more rather than less widely. So, among buyers, priority was assigned to those with either no shares or only a few; because a significant majority of the shares were never on offer, the extent to which shares were actually spread by this rule was limited. As for priorities between sellers, these were governed essentially by the principle of minimising hardship. So, in the event of supply exceeding demand, priority went, for example, to the representatives of deceased shareholders and to those who could show a special need for cash. Since sellers exceeded buyers only once during the seven years, this is of largely academic interest.

We must turn, finally, to the flotation of February 1989. As was noticed earlier, the flotation carried with it the elimination of the 'discount' which had been applied to share values when dealings could take place only on the internal market. That discount turned out to be quite large. Against an internal market price of £1.85 for each 5p share – or the equivalent of £74 for the original £1 shares – on the last dealing day, in November 1988, the price reached £2.63 – or the equivalent of £105.20 for the original £1 share – on the first day of stock market trading in the following February. In the language of the racecourse those who had taken a punt on NFC seven years earlier had in effect backed a winner at odds of over 105 to 1.

Because they leave out the benefit of a seven-year stream of dividends, the success of the wager is, in fact, understated by those numbers. Moreover, concurrently with the flotation, the then NFC shareholders enjoyed a rights issue at a deeply discounted price. Whether or not those rights were sold – and roughly half were *not* sold – they may be thought of as an extra 'layer of icing' on the benefits which NFC's shareholders had enjoyed. Taking one thing with another, and again in racecourse terms, they must be said to have had a good run for their money.

What of the decision to float? Given the build up of capital gains, there was bound to be pressure for finding a way in which they could be realised at something close to full market values. Values on the internal market involved an inescapable discount compared with those when the shares became fully tradeable on the stock market. The key point is that the business had by this time become so valuable that an attempt to shift the bulk of the ownership on to the next generation of NFC's employees was almost bound to seem unrealistic. What had been bought for not more than £7.5m of equity seven yearsbefore was valued by the market when the business was floated in February 1989 at around £950m. The workforce at that time was just under 32,000. An equity of that size split equally among a new workforce of the same number would involve an average employee stake of some £30,000. Such amounts of average employee equity may indeed be achievable: in 1993, a New York taxi driver has to pay the equivalent of £100,000 simply for the right to practise his profession; and he almost certainly had to find at least £30,000 of that as a down payment. All the same, it must be acknowledged that possibilities along these lines will scarcely have seemed a realistic alternative to flotation when the issue was debated at NFC in 1987.

Given the financing of the original buy-out, and given the sub-sequent success of the business, it is arguable that an eventual flota-tion was inevitable. Might it have been possible to persuade NFC's employee shareholders to soldier on with that discount for a num-ber of years? The late Philip Mayo used to argue that if the numbers who subscribed to the buy-out transaction had been larger – and the spread of shareholding size had been narrower – then it might have been possible to sustain NFC's ownership arrangements in-definitely without recourse to the stock market. The actual num-bers which used to be suggested by Mr Mayo as a possible basis for sustained employee ownership are worth citing: roughly 20,000 – or about twice as many as actually invested – employee subscribers to the buy-out; and a range of shareholding size extending from £100 at the bottom to £20,000 at the top, that is about half the extent of the actual range. In his 'might have been' hypothesis, Mr Mayo then used to put forward plausible assumptions about what the share price would have been in the absence of a flotation; and the rate at which employees would want to sell their shares after retirement. And he used to conclude that in that very different scenario, NFC's employee ownership could well have been sus-tained indefinitely. Maybe. And in the absence of the fierce opposi-tion of the Transport and General Workers Union, might the num-ber of initial employee shareholders have come close to that postu-lated in the late Philip Mayo's hypothesis? Again, maybe.

In the event, a significant majority of NFC's employee share-holders, some 60%, voted in 1988 to authorise the directors to seek a flotation. They also voted that an attempt be made to negotiate special voting rights for employee shareholders and special provi-sions for profit-sharing beyond those normally permitted for flota-tion on the London Stock Exchange.

It was, I think, at least partly because of the rather exceptional negotiating skills of the late Philip Mayo that in pre-flotation bar-gaining discussions with the London Stock Exchange each of those two objectives was achieved. In relation to voting, it was conceded by the Exchange authorities that in the post-flotation world, so long as employees continued to own at least 10% of the equity, each NFC share held by an employee would have two votes – against one vote for shares held by non-employees. Moreover, contrary to and way beyond the guidelines stipulated by the institutional inves-tors' Investment Protection Committees, NFC could feel free to allocate in any year up to 15% of pre-tax profits to profit-sharing by employees. For the Exchange authorities and the Investment Protection Committees, this extra latitude over the allocation of pre-tax profits was probably sweetened by a formula which Philip Mayo devised and we shall look at briefly in the final section. But perhaps, too, as Mr Mayo used to enjoy claiming in private, NFC's bargaining position on these issues of voting and profit sharing was stronger than what at first met the eye: in an international environment marked by the absence of exchange controls, it would have been theoretically possible for NFC, if disappointed by the London authorities, to make an approach to Wall Street. That at least is what Philip Mayo used to like telling his friends. I suspect it was a card which, regardless of the outcome, he would rather have enjoyed being forced to play.

After the Flotation From the flotation onwards – or anyway from the retirement of Sir Peter Thompson some two years later – the NFC story ceases to be mainly an employee ownership story. It becomes more and more the story of an 'ordinary', more or less conventional, quoted company. This shift may be said to have taken place *pari passu* with the decline in the percentage of the equity owned by NFC's employees. At the time of the buy-out that figure, we may recall, was 82.5%. At flotation, which had been preceded by a discreet placement of a parcel of shares with institutions, it was only slightly less. But the figure had fallen to well below 20% by the spring of 1993. With the end-1993 rights issue, about which I will have a little more to say in a moment, it had fallen sharply further.

It is true that most of the workforce still owned some shares even at the end of 1994. It is also true that their employee shares still carried two votes as against only one for those owned by outsiders. Quite likely, if those of ex-employee pensioners are added, the employee shares would still, again at the end of 1994, have represented the biggest concentration of voting power if they had been voted together. But by the end of 1995 the share of NFC equity held by employees had fallen below 10%, and their shares therefore ceased to attract double voting rights. Less than half the employees still then held shares in the company they worked for. Employee ownership was history.

In business terms, down to the end of 1992, what dominated the scene was the recession. In 1992 prices, pre-tax profits peaked at just over £109m in the flotation year of and did not reach this level in the subsequent six years. The table which follows shows key data for the seven years following flotation (in current prices):

	Sales £m	Profit Pre-Tax £m	Shareholders Funds £m	No. of Employees
1989	1,494	78	326	31,763
1990	1,627	82	328	33,761
1991	1,664	65	330	33,861
1992	1,724	90	320	33,850
1993	1,911	105	312	32,955
1994	2,058	106	560	33,989
1995	2,201	37	529	35,575

Year to September 30

Source: NFC Annual Reports

Down to the end of 1992, the price of NFC's shares outperformed the market by a comfortable margin: in other words, its performance was regarded as a creditable effort taking the recession into account.

On the other hand, and whether the market's judgement was right or wrong, the share price significantly *underperformed*, compared with the averages, in 1993 and 1994. In 1994 Peter Sherlock stepped down from the post of chief executive after holding it for scarcely eighteen months, and this was widely taken as evidence that all was not well at the top. Sentiment was not improved by the size of what amounted to his offered leaving present, which later became the subject of litigation. A negative verdict on the success of the leadership in 1993 and 1994 was further reinforced with the announcement, in the autumn of 1994, of the impending retirement of NFC's by then long-serving chairman – Sir Peter Thompson's former colleague and successor, James Watson.

The key point about this period is that, with the retirement of Sir Peter Thompson, the commitment of top management to the employee ownership which he had pioneered seems to have gone into progressive decline. In his valedictory statement, in his last year as chairman, Sir Peter made no bones about the difficulties being experienced as a result of the recession: 'In this my last year as chairman, NFC has faced the difficulties of a harsh economic climate . . . we were slower to react than we should have been.'

The theme of a tough and depressed market environment was echoed by James Watson, who succeeded to the chairmanship, in his annual statements for both 1991 and 1992.

When I spoke to Sir Peter Thompson in late 1994, he emphasised that that, notwithstanding the recession, he had not wavered in his commitment to the special employee-owned character of NFC. In particular there had continued to be allocations out of pre-tax profits to the company's profit-sharing employee share ownership scheme. He had also remained committed to the policy of not selling a subsidiary without the consent of those employed in it. These changed when he left.

We may recall that in its pre-flotation bargaining, NFC had been given a conditional green light to approve allocations to employee profit sharing of up to 15% of pre-tax profits: a figure way beyond the then guideline limit set by the City of London's institutional investors. Conditions associated with that green light required that allocations to employee profitsharing would fall faster in a recession than the fall in the profits themselves. The logic was that the proportion of profit allocated to financing employee shares should strengthen the share price in a recession rather than the opposite. Moreover that seems to be part of the explanation of the fact that the share price outperformed the market until 1992, notwithstanding the recession.

On the other hand, for better or worse, NFC's top management decided during 1992 to reduce sharply, to well below what was allowed by the conditions agreed earlier, the allocations from pre-tax profits for employee profit sharing. In 1994 and 1995 profit sharing was eliminated altogether. This was one of a number of top management or Board decisions which were taken between 1992 and 1995 and which may be interpreted as downgrading NFC's commitment to its special employee-owned character. That at any rate was how they were presented to me by Sir Peter Thompson. Of the others which he identified as having this same character, one – the decision to accept a fancy price for Waste Management Ltd (WML) without consulting its employees – was described earlier. Pickfords was also sold about this time, because it did not fit in with a new 'strategic' plan, again without its workforce being consulted.

The last was the decision to launch a rights issue, without any consultation with employees or indeed any other shareholders, at the end of 1993. This was seen by Sir Peter Thompson as a further indication, given the absence of any employee consultation, of top management's waning commitment to the special character of the business. Sir Peter felt sufficiently opposed to the decision to make a public issue of it at the company's AGM in early 1994. He had chosen to resign from his position as honorary President of NFC before it.

The likely rejoinder by NFC's top management to Sir Peter criticisms is that as the proportion of employee shares fell, so it was both appropriate and natural for the company to pay more attention to its institutional shareholders in the City of London than to its employees.

Top management may indeed have decided, as Sir Peter in effect argues, to say goodbye to the company's special employee-owned character. But at least up to the end of 1994, it had evidently not identified an alternative set of distinctive characteristics. In their absence, and with the continuing performance decline in 1993 and 1994, the prevailing impression given by the company was one of business drift, coupled with an ever-declining percentage of employee-held shares.

Concluding Remarks In conclusion it is probably right to suggest that the NFC experience is better understood as an exemplary case of privatisation through a management-led employee buy-out than as an exemplary case of employee ownership as such. If that is right then the NFC story should mainly be compared with the other two privatisation case studies in this book – those of the two British bus companies, Peoples Provincial and Chesterfield Transport, and that of the Herend Porcelain Manufactory in Hungary. There are striking differences between these three British cases both in terms of the actual buy-out and of the subsequent ownership arrangements.

But finally it seems worth suggesting that, despite its exemplary importance as a privatisation outcome, this case of NFC represents something of a missed opportunity on two grounds. One has already been highlighted: the opportunity, frustrated by the bitter hostility of the Transport and General Workers Union, of achieving really wide employee participation in the original buy-out. The second was suggested by Philip Mayo, who kindly sent it to me in a note written about six months before his untimely death in early 1994. It is his concluding reflection on the whole story:

> If you are right that the NFC buy-out is more an exemplar for privatisation than for employee ownership, then its lessons have largely been lost or misunderstood. It is a sad expression of the dysfunctioning nature of capitalism in this country that the later privatisations took on board our experience in reaching out to ordinary people as investors; but only to use it to create a new sort of gambling chip for 'Sid' to play with. Not, as we hoped, a new sort of ownership for industry.

19
Herend Porcelain Manufactory

INTRODUCTORY OVERVIEW

Hungary's famous and venerable Herend Porcelain Manufactory – as it likes to call itself in English – was privatised using the mechanism of a management-led employee buy-out (MEBO) in 1993. Since then it has been majority employee-owned, with the Government keeping a 25% stake. For the greater part of its long history, it has been both commercially and aesthetically successful; and at least adequately profitable.

The business has been through a bewildering series of ownership changes during the 170-odd years of its mainly illustrious history. However, the current arrangements were specially designed, with a significant measure of collective employee ownership, to be both broadly based and sustainable. They could quite well remain more or less unchanged for the second 170 years of the manufactory's business life and indeed beyond.

The special 'designer quality' of the ownership arrangements is complemented by two linked identities which have underpinned the business since its foundation. The first is between the values added in its manufacturing processes and the special skills of the great majority of its 1,500 strong workforce. The second is between the great majority of the employees and the community of the village of Herend on the low hills at the eastern end of Lake Balaton in which the manufactory is situated. It is a business which depends for its success overwhelmingly on the skills of its workforce, which in turn is the largest group in the the local community. This combination is found only rather rarely in today's world: namely when the local community group and the employee group of a single business are roughly co-terminous and when the contribution of capital to the success of the undertaking is rather limited. True there are plenty of 'company towns' all over

Europe and the United States and no doubt Japan. But all or nearly all of them are dominated by capital. What makes Herend so unusual is that while it is, indeed, a 'company town' – or anyway a company large village – it is one dominated not by capital but by a labour, in the shape of an employee group mainly made up of exceptionally highly skilled people who work with their hands. In these unusual conditions, employee ownership looks like a 'good fit' and an arrangement likely to endure, once it has been established.

The total workforce has remained steady at a little over 1,550 since the early 1990s. Between two thirds and three quarters are highly skilled, and about 60% are women. There are roughly 750 hand painters and some 300 hand potters. A further 50 make by hand the moulds in which cast porcelain is manufactured. So the word 'manufactory' in the preferred title of the business is not a pious archaism: it reflects a living and enduring reality. It is another question whether the skills of the hand painters are adequately reflected in the designations 'craftsman' and 'craftswoman'. When you see them at work, the word 'artist' is just as likely to make a spontaneous appearance in your brain.

Given the expensive and top quality product, management, distribution, marketing and selling have been important since its foundation. An early coup was selling a dinner service to Queen Victoria at London's Great Exhibition of 1851. The company has recently taken steps to bring more of the distribution – which adds significant value on its own account – into its own hands.

What will threaten the business? In the early 1990s one of Britain's leading scholars in the field of fine porcelain, a professor of ceramic art, ventured to predict that Herend would be unable to maintain its ancient tradition of handwork, except at the margin, into the next decade. He argued that the pressure to increase wages to Western levels would price Herend's hand painters and other craftsmen artists out of the market and would do so sooner rather than later. When that happened – and the professor confidently expected big changes before the year 2000 – Herend would have no choice but to follow Wedgwood and Royal Doulton down the road of porcelain made largely by machine and with the design work mechanically applied.

However, when I visited Herend in October 1996, the changes predicted by the professor did not look imminent. It continued to maintain and improve on the profitability it achieved under state ownership during the Communist period. In this respect it is very different from its most obvious competitor and rival, Meissen, in Germany. Morover, it is profitable notwithstanding the fact that it pays wages roughly 50% above Hungary's industrial average and that at least inside the manufactory the potential benefits of employee ownership remain largely untapped. On the other hand it may already benefit from that ownership in a different way. Apart from the Government it has no outside shareholders. Significant dividends have already been paid – but unlike say Wedgwood and Royal Doulton, Herend is *not* under relentless pressure to drive up shareholder value.

The First 163 Years: from 1826 to 1989 Rather as with racehorses and stud farms in today's world, Europe's earliest porcelain making in the eighteenth century was dominated by monarchs – kings, lesser princes and even emperors. The alchemist Johann Friedrich Bottger, the first man in Europe to unpick the secrets of China's age-old porcelain, worked for King Augustus the Strong of Saxony where, in 1710, the porcelain house of Meissen was established outside Dresden. From as early as 1718 there was an imperial porcelain factory in Vienna. In France, where royalty summarised its position in the phrase 'l'Etat, c'est Moi', the porcelain-making business at Sevrès outside Paris seems, in 1859, to have been taken over by the French state rather than the French kings. According to *Encyclopaedia Britannica*, even Frederick the Great was for some time the owner of a porcelain business in Berlin which he bought in 1763. Further north, Royal Copenhagen is evidently still in business today. Perhaps royal family ownership was the eighteenth century's counterpart to state ownership in our own. Perhaps too it offered only limited incentives to good performance on the part of the management and other employees over whom the various royal owners exercised their superintendence. Who knows? But in any case by the late eighteenth century there were already numerous non-royal porcelain houses, especially in the region of what is now south-east Germany. Herend's Manufactory falls into this second, non-royal, category of porcelain house.

The man who founded the business in 1826, Vince Stingl, is normally described as having been a craftsman potter. The man who bought it off him and saved it from bankruptcy in 1838, Mor

Fischer, is normally described as having been an entrepreneur. But he was also one of those notable entrepreneurs – perhaps a minority – who like working with their hands.

The manufactory is unusual in a second respect as well: the German roots of much of its local population. In the village of Herend in the middle and later 1990s, there are still those among the grandparents' generation who speak German as their first language. It seems that for the hundred years or so after the Turks had been forced back out of Hungary in the last quarter of the seventeenth century, there was a substantial migration of Swabians from south Germany eastwards. For the most part these migrants were sturdy peasants and they seem to have been pulled rather than pushed – by the prospect of low cost agricultural land in areas that had become underpopulated following the earlier departure of the Turks. Those with long memories will tell you that Herend was still a predominantly German-speaking village between the wars. It is not known whether the German immigrants brought the porcelain tradition with them.

The 170-year story of Herend's recurring though by no means uninterrupted business and artistic success owes as much or more to these people as to the sequence of men who have directed and managed them: well-trained armies can survive a poor general or two. Among the best of the managers were Mor Fischer and his two grandsons, who pulled the manufactory back to his original 'business plan'. There have also been disasters in the top position.

It is not too much to say that Herend owes neaarly everything to Mor Fischer. He saved the original workshop from otherwise certain bankruptcy in the late 1830s. Then, having made substantial investments in kilns and other manufacturing plant, he had turned it into a successful and much-admired business by the early 1840s. When he founded the business in 1826, Vince Stingl had employed a handful of craftsmen in a small village workshop. Mor Fisher had over 50 people working for him by 1841. In recognition of the quality of his workmanship, and as early as 1842, the local authority gazetted the right of the Herend business to use Hungary's coat of arms.

This is indicative of the key point in what would today be called the business plan which was designed and put in place by Mor Fischer. It was in place by the early 1840s and it was triumphantly still in place in the later 1990s when this was written. The vicissitudes in

Herend's business record have tended to coincide with times when the business departed from this business plan.

His up-market focus goes a long way towards a commercial definition of Mor Fischer's business plan for the manufactory. With only minor qualifications on the margin, the essence of the Fischer business plan is to aim at the very top of the porcelain market. Already before the first world war and then again between the first and second, it was supplying its porcelain to three of London's most prestigious stores: Aspreys, Fortum & Mason, and Harrods. These shops, it may be confidently asserted, are the special favourites of the Royal and the Rich.

By definition the plan does not worry too much about pricing Herend porcelain out of the mass market. No doubt the Sultan of Brunei is in a class of one among Herend's customers. But the manufactory's marketing thrust in today's world – as throughout most of Queen Victoria's reign and for the years in between – has not been in the direction of the man on the Clapham omnibus.

A recent Hungarian study by Jozsef Vadas makes clear that in the crucial Mor Fischer years of the 1850s and 1860s this 'top of the market' focus was not an accident but linked explicitly to eighteenth-century styles, subjects and treatment:

> At a time [mid-1840s onwards] when the great European makers were turning to a broader middle-class market, Herend revived the style of the old princely porcelain factories in splendid pieces executed in a masterly fashion. As Fischer himself put it, 'The factory set out to adhere in its pattern-making exclusively to the antique, or so-called Old Saxon style . . .'
>
> [By way of clarification the author comments:] The greatest influence on Herend was the late Baroque-Rococo Meissen style of tea and coffee services decorated with flowers, fronds, and often birds.

Jozsef Vadas sees Fischer's creations as 'not divorced from the works that inspired them but not identical with them either'. He then writes of the 'restrained elegance of late Hungarian Biedermeir' in such a way as to suggest that we are dealing with pieces designed for upper middle-class rather than royal and other aristocratic markets.

Gallant Huzzar officers and shepherdesses almost proclaim

themselves as being aimed at the aristocratic market. But what about the birds and animal figurines – for example the ducks and speckled owls – which account for a surprisingly large proportion of today's output and sales? And what, for that matter, of the sculptured heads of Stalin which were apparently produced and sold in their hundreds, if not in their thousands, in the late 1940s and early 1950s? There is nothing especially princely – or indeed upper middle class – about the markets in which such pieces may be expected to sell.

At the beginning of his final paragraph, Jozsef Vadas announces to his readers that '. . . Herend turned its back on modernity'. And he goes on: 'Since 1976, the factory has run a master course where special training is given to the most talented painters into how to make virtuoso use of old motifs and style, and there are a great many old-new pieces to show that the objective is a viable one.'

He acknowledges that 'Herend's critics have reproached it for sticking to its traditions . . .' and offers the answer '. . . that history does not run in a straight line'.

And he even suggests that retrospectively Herend may be thought to have had the better of the argument:

> Curiously, the Herend concept is in tune with the times again, as it was once before, towards the end of the last century, when its archaism tied in with the historical revivalism of the day. This is an age of eclecticism and postmodernism. The puritan style has given way to rich treatment of surfaces. Ornamentation is no longer considered to be old-fashioned fussiness. The post-modern decorative ware designed by Laszlo Horvath, Zoltan Takacs and Akos Tamas shows that people have realised that Herend has a worthy place in the world.

By contrast with the success of Mor Fischer's up-market commercial and aesthetic focus, the only serious effort to move down market, in the 1870s, ended in disaster. Partly because of some recession of demand but mainly because of a decision by Mor Fischer's sons to depart from their father's business plan and move down market, the manufactory experienced such serious difficulties that it had to be rescued by goverment. However there was a reasonably benign subsequent outcome. The business was bought back by a private group including Fischer's grandsons. Essentially they reverted to the business plan of their grandfather, taking the manufactory back up market and back to a reasonable level of commercial success.

The manufactory also went through difficult times during both World Wars largely because, while hostilities lasted, it was denied access to some of its most important markets. It also had difficulties of a market-related but more general character during the great inter-war recession. In effect, during each of the two wars and during the slump of the early 1930s between them it was prevented by market difficulties from sticking to Mor Fischer's business plan.

By 1945, when the Second World War ended, there are understood to have been just 180 working in the business and it is thought to have been in mixed state and private ownership. It was taken into full state ownership in 1948. The total workforce then numbered 362. The numbers had reached what was up to then an all-time high of 1,863 in 1989. We must now turn briefly to look at what happened, under Hungary's Communist régime, over the next forty years.

The crude employment numbers tell us a fair part of the story. Between 1949 and 1963 the employment total doubled and nearly doubled again in the subsequent fifteen years to 1,410. But whereas the earlier increase represented just 364 new jobs, the extra ones created in the second fifteen years came to close on 700. Because of higher productivity growth in the second fifteen-year period, that difference probably understates the true improvement in the performance of the manufactory comparing the second of those two periods with the first.

The statistics in Appendix 2 show some further growth of employment in the years down to the fall of the Berlin Wall in 1989. But for the later 1980s, and indeed for 1990, the Herend totals include people employed in a quite separate undertaking: a manufactory with majolica rather than porcelain articles as its output; and one located not at Herend but in a village some three kilometres away. The Herend management had been forced to assume responsibility for the majolica business by the Communist Government in the 1980s. They were permitted to spin it off, before Herend itself was privatised, by the country's first non-Communist Government in 1991. It makes no further appearance in this case study.

The whole Communist period from after the war to 1989 is in fact best broken down into three phases. In the first, ending roughly in the early 1960s, the main task of the manufactory was to re-establish itself in its prewar foreign markets. That was something which could be accomplished only slowly. And local demand inside Hungary, though clearly helped by sales of a political character – whether of sculpted porcelain heads of Stalin or of pieces purchased by Government as gifts for foreign dignitaries – was bound to be severely restricted by almost rock-bottom local incomes. It followed that growth during this period was inescapably rather slow.

The second phase from the early 1960s until the late 1970s saw growth driven by rapidly increasing demand in Herend's traditional Western markets, and particularly in the US and UK. This growth, as in the initial postwar phase, took place within the framework of an only slightly updated and adapted version of Mor Fischer's original business plan. There was the old concentration of sales at the top end of the market, the retention of hand-painting – and indeed hand-potting – from before the war, and the reproduction of old designs from the nineteenth century and before. Apart from those sculpted heads of Stalin – of which the production must surely have been discontinued following the 1956 revolution – Mor Fischer's plan was adapted only to the extent that an increasing percentage of output and sales was accounted for by hand-painted animal figurines.

In the final phase under the communists, over the 1980s, the top management at Herend acquired an increasingly independent control over business decisions. In 1981 the business moved out of the control of the then Goverment's Fine Ceramics Trust and became a state-owned company with a considerable degree of management independence. Later, from 1985 onwards, its management was permitted to take over full responsibility for foreign trading activities – for its foreign purchases and, clearly more important, its foreign sales.

During this final period, we can see the beginnings of a policy of resisting further increases in total sales, or at least of sharply slowing them down. After privatisation was completed in 1993, a policy on these lines was to become the main addition to the time-honoured Mor Fischer business plan. It seeks to intensify the effects of the plan and thus increase the benefits flowing to the manufactory from it. The handwork, the traditional designs, and the concentration of selling effort at the very top of the market all remain in place. But there is one main extra ingredient. Put crudely the extra ingredient is an iron clamp on total physical output. Its logic is to give greater scope for raising prices unilaterally and at rates which go beyond those of inflation in Herend's foreign markets. In the later 1980s the trading operations of the business became highly profitable: at least they did so before the payment to the then top management of enormous bonuses. As we shall see, that turns out to be a crucial piece of contingent background in the run-up to privatisation.

Two other specific developments at Herend during the period of the Communist regime were first, in 1960, the opening of a training school on its own premises and second the designation of top artists as 'master painters'.

A system of apprentice training had apparently been formally instituted as early as 1897. But that consisted entirely of training-on-the-job. From 1939, this was supplemented by some classroom teaching for hand-painters in the village technical school. With the change to teaching in its own special technical school in 1960, off-the-job training was extended to potters and mould makers as well as painters. Trainees entered the school at fourteen for a three-year spell during which roughly half their time was spent learning and practising their craft. Soon after the manufactory was privatised, the age of the students changed to seventeen and eighteen and the length of their course was cut to two years.

Earlier, from Jozsef Vadas's book, I referred to three of Herend's present top painters by name. That would not have happened in Mor Fischer's day and probably not before 1970. From that year on it became the practice of the manufactory to designate selected top artists as master painters. Up to that time these men and women were at least publicly anonymous: identified if at all only by their works – as for example the 'Rothschild birds' painter. The manufactory's master painters numbered twenty-eight at the end of 1996.

Over the Communist years there was a gentle increase in the white collar proportion of the manufactory's workforce. In 1949 the non-blue collar workers were roughly one in seven. And by 1989 they were slightly less than one in six. The numbers suggest a rather notable achievement in the unsung field of overhead containment.

A final point is that since 1970 the manufactory has not insisted that all its employees move into retirement on reaching pensionable age. On the face of it that was a notably liberal concession to more normal practice.

The Run-up to Privatisation and the Buy-Out: 1989–93 At the beginning, I suggested that there is a strikingly good 'fit' between the inner economic realities of the Herend Manufactory and of the local village community on the one hand, and the broadly-based employee ownership with which it emerged from privatisation in 1993 on the other. But for most of us economic determinism had ceased to be a plausible theory long before the Berlin Wall passed into history in 1989. Outcomes, or so it seems to me, are often linked to contingent factors as much or more so than to the underlying realities.

That, I think, is how it was with employee ownership at Herend. There *were* the underlying realities. And those included, as well as the 'congruence' of broadly-based employee ownership, Herend's widely recognised position as a most exceptional component of the country's cultural and artistic heritage. But there were also key contingent factors of personality and circumstance. The most important of those were probably two. The more consequential and less predictable was the availability from 1989 onwards of a top employee ownership specialist who was also a Hungarian: Dr Janos Lukacs, a sociologist by profession but one who had spent several months in 1988 studying employee ownership in America, including a six-week spell in the then employee-owned Weirton Steel in West Virginia, the subject of a later case study. The fact that he was on hand in nearby Budapest, with highly specialised and relevant knowledge and know how, cannot plausibly be seen as the result of economic determinism.

The second key contingent factor was the very high bonuses that were being paid to top managers towards the end of the 1980s. This background circumstance offers a good way in to the privatisation story. In one year, the chief executive was paid in bonus over 6m Hungarian florints (HUF) – or more than forty times the then annual average wage in the manufactory. The number may perhaps be quite modest compared to what widely happens in today's top American companies where multiples of 160 times are evidently common. But it was way above anything that was openly acceptable in the environment in Hungary at the time, and it was between two and three times as high as the multiples prevailing in top Japanese companies in the 1990s.

As well as authorising these unacceptable bonus payments, it was later discovered that the former chief executive had been a party to the establishment of a wholesale intermediary between the manufactory and its retail clients in the UK. This failed to add any real value in the distribution chain and is best seen as a mechanism for diverting part of the manufactory's cash flow into other hands. That at any rate is how it was seen before the company was eventually able, in 1992, to bring the arrangement to an end.

It is apparently true that neither the bonus payments nor the distribution arrangements constituted a breach of the law. On the other hand once known about, they were almost bound to create an uproar in the climate of those times. Hungary was still then, after all, Communist-governed.

Once the bonuses had become widely known, that led on in quick succession to:
– mass defection from the established trade union – on the grounds that its leaders had failed to oppose the payments;
– the successful setting up of a new free standing trade union at Herend;
– the firing by the then sovereign Enterprise Council of the old chief executive and his closest associates and his replacement by a new top team under Jozsef Kovacs, the former commercial director.

For our purposes here the main consequence of these events was to forge a strong degree of solidarity between the new union and management leadership and to encourage a joint assertion by them of the rights of the manufactory as a working community.

The whole subsequent employee buy-out project was described at the outset as a MEBO or management led employee buy-out. However, such was the solidarity which developed during the process that the eventual acquisition of the business might be more correctly described as a 'consensus-led' employee buy-out.

With rather less impact than either of these two main contingent factors in determining the final outcome, but still contributing to it, was the availability of some special 'technical' assistance for employee ownership financed by the British Government's so called Know How Fund. Essentially this British technical support provided a back up to what Dr Lukacs was already making available. But it probably also contributed something of its own under at least two headings.

Here, however, we must return to the late 1980s and to the high bonuses which the current chief executive and his closest colleagues were then paying themselves.

One further piece of background needs to be spelt out before we come on to the process leading up to privatisation and the manufactory's exemplary employee buy-out.

Starting from 1986 the Herend Manufactory had enjoyed the legal form of 'self-governing enterprise' with the power of final decision vested in what was originally a twenth-six-member Enterprise Council of whom just half – thirteen – were elected by the non-management workforce. However, in a key change of law in 1988, the number of the elected non-management members was increased to fourteen, giving them a majority when it came to Council decisions. It was the Enterprise Council, so constituted, that took the decision to replace the top management team in 1990. In effect it held on to the reins until the privatisation buy-out deal was completed.

It was shortly after the formation of the new union and the top management changes of 1990 that Dr Janos Lukacs first appeared in the village of Herend and employee ownership was first presented to those working in the manufactory as a possible privatisation outcome. A number of would be private buyers had already surfaced in the village before Dr Lukacs arrived and indeed continued to do so thereafter. As against what these potential third party buyers were able to offer, Dr Lukacs argued, first, that if private capitalists wanted to buy the business, it must surely have some real value; and, second, that almost all of any value which had been built up in the manufactory was the result of the skills and talents of its artist craftsmen and craftswomen. It followed, according to Dr Lukacs, that any buy-out offer from the workforce should be assigned both an appropriate margin of priority and an appropriate discount compared with what a third party would be required to pay. The second argument was also to be used most effectively later in negotiations with the State Property Agency (SPA) about an appropriate price for the business.

Laszlo Szesztay, the manufactory's commercial director, has kindly supplied me with a chronological framework set out below.

1989 Privatisation began to be discussed and employee ownership was raised for the first time as a possible outcome.

1990-92 Following an Enterprise Council decision to go for employee ownership as the preferred outcome of Privatisation, there were a series of field trips to companies with significant employee ownership including a study visit to UK. That UK study visit happened in the spring of 1991 and followed Herend – and other Hungarian – participation in an international employee ownership conference, held in Oxford in January of the same year.

June 1992 Hungary's ESOP legislation passed by Parliament.

July 1992 Herend became a 'share' company with 100% state share holding.

December 1992 Herend's ESOP Trust was formally established.

June 1993 The SPA approved Herend's ESOP privatisation including the distribution of shares and the buy-out deal conditions. The contract was then completed.

October 1995 Final instalment under agreed buy-out deal paid to the SPA.

Laszlo Szesztay attended the Oxford conference in January 1991 and took part in the study visit to Britain three months later. He likes to compare his hopes for employee ownership at Herend following the Oxford conference and the subsequent study visit with what was actually achieved.

The Employee Buy-out of the Herend Porcelain Manufactory

Mr Szesztay's hopes in 1991	Actual Outcome 1993
Achieve 40%-50% employee s/holding	75%: 25% kept by State
Negotiate reasonable price	Yes. Net asset based deal
Reasonable payment terms	Yes

Mr Szesztay has also recalled that compared with his best expectations in 1991, the enactment by the Hungarian Parliament of the country's 'employee buy-out' or ESOP legislation happened with surprising speed. Mr Szesztay's 1991 expectation had been that it would take two to five years. A great deal of the credit for both the law itself and for its surprisingly rapid enactment must go to Dr Lukacs who was himself responsible for much of the initial drafting and then lobbied tirelessly and effectively for it. But the inclusion of two carefully-chosen Hungarian MPs in the 1991 study group that visited the UK must also have helped. They were Dr Pal Becker of the Democratic Forum which was then the party of Government and Dr Gyula Teller of the Alliance of Free Democrats which then formed the main Parliamentary opposition. The whole visit was in fact financed by the British Government's Know How Fund [KHF], the third and last of the three contingent 'factors' which seem to have contributed to the outcome of Herend's employee ownership project.

This is not the place for a detailed exposition of what has come to be called Hungary's 'ESOP Law'. It is sufficient to identify first what seem to me to be its most essential specific features and second its almost inescapable weakness – if it is taken as some kind of guarantor of genuinely broad based employee buy-outs:

– It conferred statutory recognition on a 'second legal entity' which the employees of a business were required to set up as one necessary condition of achieving an employee buy-out.

– It defined a *fairly* inclusive participation of employees in the process of setting up that second entity and in its subsequent control.

– It permitted these second entities, if properly established by 'due process', to bid for the businesses in which their members worked and indeed – if that was judged to be in the public interest – to be the only bidder.

– It also allowed that any resulting employee buy-outs might take place on credit – or on an instalment plan basis – and that the assets of the employing business might be used as collateral.

For the paying off of any credits or agreed instalments, the ESOP Law also allowed that up to 20% of the employing businesses' profits might be used pre-tax.

From the standpoint of genuine and broadly-based employee ownership its weakness was, and remained at the time that this was written late in 1996, that it imposed no set rules about the distribution of employee shares, nor did it impose a set of rules about how any decisions should be reached. In effect therefore it legitimised as employee buy-outs transactions which, in their essential character, were something very different: namely management buy-outs with a few shares for rank-and-file employees thrown in. A moment ago I suggested that this was a probably inescapable weakness. By that I mean that it would almost certainly not have been possible to persuade the Hungarian Parliament to enact an ESOP law at all if that weakness had been corrected and had the law sought to insist on the 'genuine article'.

This digression about Hungary ESOP Law of 1992 is necessary for a proper understanding of what happened at Herend. It also brings out the exemplary character of the share distribution arrangements which were agreed in this particular case and indeed of the process of decision making which led up to them. Essentially the distribution was fair and the process of decision making was democratic.

In line with widely accepted good practice in the West, it was agreed that share distribution among employees should be mainly proportionate to rates of pay but with a small margin to reflect length of service. There were in fact *two* distributions of employee shares. The first involved issuing company bonds to employees free of charge and later exchanging those for shares. That was a concession which was in principle open to any business that was to be privatised and was permitted up to a limit of 13% of its share capital. The second and larger distribution of employee shares related directly to the employee buy-out. For the first of these distributions, a 1% margin on top of the shares-assigned-pro-rata-with-pay was added for each year of service. For the second, that 1% was increased to 3%.

As for the process by which these share distribution decisions were reached, they were if anything still more exemplary. A number of steps were involved:

– As early as 1989, the establishment by the Enterprise Council of a so-called 'ESOP Foundation'.

– The appointment by the Foundation of a professional consultant with a respected trade union background.

– Starting from the consultant's report, the formulation by a small working party of proposals to be put to a meeting of all prospective employee shareholders. (The three-person working party consisted of the top two elected union officials and the manufactory's finance director.)

– A final decision by a meeting of employee shareholders and taken on a one person one vote basis. (In fact, the proposals of the working party were accepted.)

Both the decisions and the way they were arrived at clearly reflect the relative strength of Herend's non-management employees, above all its painters, potters and mould-makers: their relative strength both in an economic sense (as the creators of most of the manufactory's value added) and in a formal sense (by virtue of their representatives' majority position since 1988 in the Enterprise Council).

The balance of power at Herend is also reflected in two further rules. First, the maximum percentage of the share capital which may be held by any employee shareholder is restricted to 1.6%. In a workforce of 1,600, that puts the top limit at what would be fifty times the *average* employee shareholding. But when pay differentials together with those marginal length of service adjustments are taken into account, the limit does not seem excessive.

The second is more radical. The incoming top management at that time bound itself to limit the differential between top and average pay rates in the manufactory to a ratio of four to one. It was relaxed somewhat in 1995, to allow for the recruitment of an outsider to a new top management position. (She left quite soon afterwards but I am not clear whether the rule later reverted to what it was before.)

Up to this point what has emerged most strongly from this discussion of Herend's 'employee ownership' project is the most notable degree of equity and fairness – as between management and non-management employees – which was built in to its design. It was still a dominant feature at the end of 1996. And it can hardly be emphasised too strongly that in this respect Herend is in a minority – and a small minority – among those of the country's formerly state-owned businesses which have made use of the 1992 ESOP Law. But it is not in a minority of one. Also rather unusual but not unique was the fact that the Hungarian Government, through the State Property Agency (SPA), retained a 25% shareholding plus a veto over certain decisions.

What is, I think, unique is that Herend's employee shareholders decided before the buy-out *not* to hold as individuals all of the 75% of the share capital which they acquired through a combination of exchanging company bonds for shares and the subsequent buy-out transaction. Instead they decided to hold one third of 'their' equity interest – or another 25% of the total share capital – on a collective basis. More precisely they decided that that 25% should be held by the second legal entity which had been set up to effect the buy-out. That second entity was called at Herend – using language which reflects the essentials but is not strictly correct in law – the 'ESOP Trust'. It has a twofold logic: to add an extra protection to Herend's employee ownership and to make it more sustainable.

The idea for this collective Trust ownership came from exposure to examples of employee-owned companies in Britain. That exposure in turn was made possible by the British Government through the KHF. It is a further specific example of the effects of an essentially contingent factor.

As well as deciding before the buy-out to go for 25% of 'collective' ownership, Herend's employee shareholders reached a number of decisions of detail designed to facilitate the indefinite extension in time of the employee ownership – about the rules which would apply when people ceased to employed and about new employees.

Before moving on to the post buy-out world into which the manufactory moved in the summer of 1995, I need to put on record the main facts of the buy-out deal itself.

It is pleasant to begin with an argument about the valuation of the Herend business in which the manufactory came out much more of a winner than a loser. The argument was about the appropriate approach to business valuation in any particular case and most fundamentally about whether the approach should be more-or-less asset-based or more-or-less based on the estimated present value of future profits and cash flow.

Those with a good deal of experience of privatisation sales in former communist countries will know that the state, the seller, normally argues for an asset-based approach to valuation whereas prospective buyers favour a formula linked to future profits. The point to highlight here is that in the case of the Herend Porcelain Manufactory (HPM), the interests of the seller and prospective buyer pointed in the opposite to the normal direction. For Herend, an asset-based valuation was in its best interests. For the seller, the SPA, if it wished to maximise the prospective proceeds of the sale, a valuation linked to future profits was the better bet.

Profits before tax in 1990 were equivalent to roughly 20% of sales. What is more, the pressures of demand were already then such – and remained down to the time of writing – that this margin of profit was confidently expected to continue. So the level of a valuation based on an estimate of future profits was likely to be high. By contrast, given that the value added by the undertaking was overwhelmingly the work of its hand painters, hand potters, and hand mould makers, its physical asset base is rather modest. There is raw material mixing machinery and there are kilns. There are also the works and office buildings. But that is about all. Not surprisingly the the manufactory's valuation advisers, the well-known accountancy firm of Coopers & Lybrand, came up with a valuation that was essentially asset-based.

What was on the face of it rather surprising was that with a fairly modest upward adjustment of 33%, the SPA eventually accepted the Coopers & Lybrand valuation. The officials were apparently impressed by the force of the argument that Dr. Lukacs had suggested long before: that it would be unreasonable to ask hand-painters, hand-potters and hand-mould-makers to pay a really high price for a business when its value was almost entirely attributable to their own talents and work. Consciously or otherwise, the 'politics' of the transaction may also have influenced the SPA's officials. When a government agency is the seller then, whether what is being sold is a porcelain factory near Lake Balaton or a coal mine in South Wales, it is a fair bet that a buyer which includes the rank-and-file employees will succeed in striking a better bargain than either the managers alone or a third party.

On the basis of the Coopers & Lybrand valuation plus 33%, the price for the whole of HPM's equity capital was set at HUF1.66bn. Had the price been based on an estimate of future profits a significantly higher figure would have been expected. In fact the manufactory's employees, including their managers, bought their controlling stake at a price which valued the whole business at just less than three times its 1993 pre-tax profits.

The price having been agreed, what remained to be negotiated were the terms of payment. The starting point was a provision in the Privatisation Law which stipulated a minimum cash down payment of 2%. We need not bother with the detailed arithmetic. The result for Herend's employee shareholder was an individual down payment equivalent to about two weeks wages. For the newly privatised business, it was eventually agreed that the balance of the purchase price could be paid in instalments.

That last was a valuable concession. For it enabled the manufactory to avoid taking out a bank loan and so to avoid meeting the additional charges which the bank would have added to the agreed rate of interest. The agreement allowing payments by instalments was in fact negotiated not with the SPA but with another state entity, State Property Handling PLC, to which the ownership of Herend's shares had by then been transferred.

Readers may remember that Laszlo Szesztay had been anxious since the very earliest stages of the buy-out process that the payment terms associated with any deal would be reasonably benign. The final agreement in fact provided that the payment should be completed over five years in five equal instalments. The interest rate on the outstanding balance was set at just 3% – effectively a negative rate given the then rate of Hungary's price inflation. The company's cash flow was sufficiently buoyant for the instalment payments to be completed in two years not five: the final payment was made in August 1995.

In step with the final instalment payment came the final distribution of shares to the manufactory's individual employees. Together they thus became the owners as individuals of 50% of HPM's share capital: having acquired an initial 13% in exchange for the former company bonds and the balance *in step* with the paying off of the instalment debt.

After the Buy-Out: 1993–96 Between 1992, the last year before Herend's privatisation, and the end of 1995, prices in Hungary more or less doubled. So did the value in current florints of the manufactory's sales. The increase in total costs was a little bit less and that for both personnel costs and net wages even slightly less again. Partly because of this relative success in containing costs, the increase in profits was well ahead of inflation. The numbers employed were effectively unchanged.

The Herend Porcelain Manufactory 1992–95
HUF bn, current prices

	1992	1993	1994	1995
Sales	1.79	2.23	2.77	3.35
Total costs	1.40	1.65	1.93	2.60
Personnel costs	1.00	1.14	1.33	1.75
Net wages	0.63	0.71	0.85	1.05
Profits pre-tax	0.34	0.57	0.85	0.94
Nos employed	1,561	1,571	1,583	1,569

Source: Company Records

The first point to highlight is that, starting from an already comfortable margin of profit, the manufactory managed a significant improvement over this initial post-buy-out period. I noted earlier that already by the second half of the 1980s profit margins had become rather good, and that they had reached 20% of sales by 1990. The table shows that by 1995 this margin had increased to over 25%. The management concedes that in the years immediately before the buy-out the maximisation of profit was not its main priority. So part of the improvement between 1992 and 1995 may be more superficial than real. All the same the move up from a 20% to a 25% profit margin over a six-year period – between 1990 and 1995 – is a solid achievement. Expressed as a return on the HUF1.6bn at which HPM had been valued for the buy-out, the 1995 profits looked notably healthy – even if the intervening inflation explains a good deal of the success. Taking a mid-1995 exchange rate of HUF160 to £1, total 1995 sales were rather over £20m, pre-tax profits were somewhat over £5m and net wage payments about £6m. Dividing by the numbers employed gives an average of after-tax annual earnings of about £1,500, say £125 per month and £30 per week.

This raises the issue of pay. If prices were at British levels, people earning such wages would be living way below the poverty line and might hardly have the energy to get out of bed. On the other hand, in 1995 Herend was paying net wages approximately 50% above the average rates for Hungary's industry. The margin between Herend rates and the industry averages had in fact been much the same for the previous decade.

The level of their wages relative to the country's industrial average does not mean that the typical employee shareholders at Herend were expressing satisfaction with their rates of pay when I visited the manufactory in October 1996. However, during the first half of 1995 the general assembly of all shareholders had decided to declare a dividend on the profits achieved in 1994. During the first half of 1996 they appropriated HUF150m for dividends from the 1995 profits. In line with shareholdings, the State Holding PLC got 25% of these, the so-called ESOP Trust another 25% while the remaining 50% was paid to the manufactory's individual employee shareholders. As we know, the main basis on which the employee shares had been distributed was in proportion to pay: these first two dividend payments made to Herend's individual employee shareholders were equivalent to an average of one month's net pay. What is more, in the hands of the recipients, these payments were taxed at only 10%. Here for the first time was an effective demonstration that there was some real beef in the individually-held employee shares.

It was evident during my October 1996 visit that the managers were well pleased by the decision to pay these substantial dividends. It was also encouraging that the elected leaders of Herend's two unions, Mrs Elisabeth Ughely and Mrs Judit Csendes, expressed to me their complete understanding of the relative tax effectiveness of rewarding employee shareholders with dividend payments rather than higher wages. In fact the two union leaders were prepared in discussion to go a little further. They acknowledged that at least on the margin it made sense to pay dividends rather than higher wages. On the other hand the elected head of Herend's Works Council, Mr Joszef Jilek, who took part in the same discussion, was simply not ready to agree. He thought wages were unacceptably low and that there was an unanswerable case for raising them.

However, on a quite different issue which came up in my discussions with them there was complete unanimity between these three workers' representatives. They were all agreed that there was a most urgent need for more information and more education about the manufactory's employee ownership in general and about the ESOP trust in particular.

During that same visit to Herend those two urgent and overlapping needs – for more education and more information about employee ownership – were echoed and re-echoed at other meetings with top management and with the ESOP Trustees. Already, from after the first dividend payments, the importance of the employee shares had begun to sink in. The shares had not at the time of my visit started to work as incentives to change behaviour. But their real value was beginning to be understood.

The evidence for this concerns an increase in 1996 in the 'unofficial' price at which the manufactory's employee shares changed hands. In line with what has become best practice in similar situations in employee-owned companies in the UK and the US, authorised but regulated trading in employee shares was introduced at Herend in 1994. This takes place in principle on two specified dealing days each year. An official price is set on the basis of an independent valuation. The ESOP trust buys back shares at that price from priority sellers – retired employees, others whose employment has finished and the legal representatives of employees who have died. It also sells shares, at the same price, to new employees who have recently joined and wish to start buying whatever number of shares is fixed for those earning their salaries in the business.

Up to the end of 1996 the ESOP trust had neither been willing nor able to buy back shares in those dealing days from non-priority sellers: that is from employee shareholders who are continuing to work in the manufactory but who find themselves suddenly with an urgent need for cash which demands to be satisfied. So we should readily understand why it is that, with one qualification, Herend's employee shareholders are free to trade shares between themselves on the same specified dealing days. They simply do so at unofficial prices agreed between themselves. Such transactions are allowed to happen on the basis of willing buyers and willing sellers and after the event are duly registered by the ESOP trust. The only proviso that any of these dealings must respect is the rule that no individual employee may own more that 1.6% of the total equity.

What happened following the first dividend payments was a rise, relative to the official dealing day price, of the price at which unofficial deals were done. In the case of the official prices, these kept somewhat ahead of inflation between 1994 and 1996 when measured against the values struck at the time of the buy-out. Their gentle upward movement in real terms over the immediate post buy-out years reflected the improved profitability of the business and a reducing and finally eliminated instalment debt. Against these official prices, unofficial transactions took place before the first dividend payments at discounts of roughly 40%. Thereafter the unofficial prices moved sharply higher on a relative basis and the discount narrowed to approximately 25%.

The evidence that the employees were putting a higher value on their shares two years after the buy-out than before serves as an excellent starting point for a discussion of the manufactory's post buy-out business plan.

What I earlier called Mor Fischer's business plan continued to define the manufactory's key policies in the mid-1990s as it had done 150 years before in the mid-1840s. This meant the old mix of aiming at the very summit of the market, and of aiming at it with hand-painted – and otherwise hand-made – porcelain, and with basically traditional designs and decorative patterns. Equally, in the mid-1990s, just as in the mid-1840s, all market segments except for that at the very top were being systematically ignored and top prices were being charged as an inescapable corollary of these policies. What is more, and in line with what had already started to happen during the later years of the Communist era, employee-owned Herend in the 1990s even intensified the core policies of Mor

Fischer's business plan: by keeping a continuous iron clamp on total physical output. As I explained earlier, the idea behind this new refinement was that, by controlling supply, the manufactory would be better able to raise its prices by more than inflation in its hard currency markets and would thus gradually manage to increase its prices in real terms. That must remain the overriding long-term objective: for without higher prices the scope for higher wages will be necessarily limited. On the other hand, it should go without saying that for this strategy to be successful the manufactory's products must not be subject to serious competition in the foreseeable future.

Within that overall strategy, Herend's employee ownership in the mid-1990s changed some proximate goals and objectives. A good example of a new proximate goal is to increase profits so as to be able to increase the level of dividend payments to employees since they are seen as the most tax effective way of increasing the real annual incomes of the manufactory's employee shareholders.

Given the potentially stronger incentives to change behaviour, the employee ownership of the mid-1990s also offers new opportunities for supply side improvements. One of these was already well underway when I visited Herend in late 1996. It is a child of the stronger incentives on management – rather than on rank-and-file employee shareholders – to improve performance.

What was probably the most important post buy-out initiative was aimed at selling a higher percentage of the manufactory's output through its own retail outlets, especially in sales to the increasing number of foreign tourists who visit the country and indeed the village of Herend. So long as it avoids offending well-established retailers in the world's rich countries – with some of whom Herend has had relationships for close on a century – the initiative makes excellent business sense. A painted dinner plate for which retail buyers will be asked to pay £60 at a London store will have been sold to the store keeper for just £20. Moreover the manufactory will itself have covered the costs of transporting and insuring the plate on its journey to London, costs which may well have reduced the proceeds of sale by 20%. The lion's share in the value of a Herend dinner service which sells for £2,500 in London has been added by the processes of distribution and sale and not by that of manufacture.

What the statistics show is that between 1992 and 1996 the

proportion of total sales achieved through Herend's own outlets within Hungary climbed from just less than one quarter to rather over one third. The actual numbers are worth having on record:

Retail Sales through Herend's Own Hungarian Outlets
as Percentage of Total Sales:

1992	24.5%
1993	25.7%
1994	29.1%
1995	33.1%
1996	35.8%

In line with this same policy and for the same reasons Herend chose not to come to an arrangement with a local retailer when it started selling its porcelain in Singapore in 1995. The Singapore shop opened in December 1996.

Other new supply side opportunities opened up for Herend by its new employee ownership are harder to realise. Essentially they are the familiar opportunities of cost reduction and quality improvement which all businesses may seek to realise but in relation to which employee-owned companies should be well placed to enjoy a comparative advantage.

The obverse of these opportunities are the defect rates of a business and, for example, rates of absenteeism whether or not the absence in any particular case is officially classified as being related to sickness. For reasons which may well be rooted in its experience during the Communist era, Herend went into the privatisation process with what in the West would be judged to be rather high rates of both defects and absenteeism. And neither showed any significant improvement over the first three post-privatisation years.

The top Herend managers are aware of these opportunities and recognise the need for some action. They recognise that need in the same way as they recognise the need for more information and education about employee ownership. Some recognise too that programmes designed to make the workforce more informed and more ownership conscious could well be linked to initiatives aimed at achieving significant supply side improvements. Good practice in relation to programmes of this kind is now reasonably well established in the West and doubtless in Hungary as well. Within the smaller world of employee owned businesses, there is also a growing awareness of the need to build up a positive climate of public opinion among employee shareholders, including a measure of public disapproval when an unacceptable degree of free riding is detected.

There is a particular 'corporate government' problem at Herend with which it is easy to sympathise: a proliferation of power or anyway of influence centres. To begin with there is, of course, the top management with its authority embodied – under Hungarian company law – in the board of directors. Conversely over against what one might call the power centre of top management, is the union power centre: with in this case, for historical reasons, two unions and not just one.

But to these two 'centres' we have to add a further three. Two are imports from German co-determination law. The third is taken in effect from employee-ownership practice in the Anglo-Saxon world. From Germany Herend has imported a supervisory board and a works council, both bodies having an elected membership. Of the supervisory board's five members three are non-employees elected by the general assembly of shareholders. The remaining two are elected by the employees. Its main current function is to prepare an annual report on the management for presentation to the assembly of shareholders. As for the elected works council, the main point to make is that the scope of its interests are wider than those of the trade unions which are mainly, if not exclusively, concerned with wages and conditions.

Turning to the so-called ESOP Trust, this is a seven-person body with five of its members elected by the employee shareholders on a one person one vote basis, and two appointed by management. Of the five elected members, all are managers and two are also directors of the company. Laszlo Winkler, who is chairman of the Trustees, is the manufactory's finance director. Tamas Tanai, the production director, is the second board member who is also a trustee. Let me remark in passing that for the 'lads and lasses' in employee-owned companies to elect 'bosses' to represent them is not altogether uncommon at least where it is not disallowed by company statute. There is a striking recent example at Tullis Russell in Scotland where the new chairman for its Share Council – roughly the equivalent of Mr Winkler's position – elected in the summer of 1996, was James Daglish, the Group's chief executive.

To the extent that Herend's ESOP Trust has power and not just influence, this derives from its 25% shareholding. It is the largest of the manufactory's internal shareholders and how it votes its shares must be expected to influence the voting decisions of the individual employee shareholders.

It is easy to understand the genesis of this 'proliferation of power and influence centres' at Herend. Employee ownership in Hungary is quite new. Insofar as the provisions of Hungary's ESOP Law extend beyond the buy-out transaction itself and allow for the continued existence of a 'second legal entity', they do not sit all that comfortably alongside the requirements of the country's co-determination legislation. The existence of both the ESOP Trust and a supervisory board under Hungary's co-determination laws is, at least on the face of it, somewhat anomalous.

This raises the question of whether this issue of corporate government at Herend should be addressed sooner rather than later. There is an excellent precedent which points to how the problem might be approached. In the run up to the buy-out, highly charged and highly sensitive decisions about the distribution of employee shares had to be taken: the result on that occasion was excellent.

Moreover, it was because of the quality of those decisions about the distribution of employee shares and related issues – decisions taken well before the 1993 buy-out – that the employee ownership at Herend has a better chance than most of surviving for an indefinite future. That is partly because of the rules governing the sale of shares by departing employee shareholders and the purchase of them by new recruits. It was also partly because of the decision to pass 25% of the manufactory's share capital to the 'collective' ownership of an 'employee trust'. By 1996, however, both of these were being questioned.

There are essentially three buy-back subrules:

– Those who leave upon retirement may keep their shares until they die but thereafter they must be sold back by the legal representative of the deceased ex-employee. The price paid will be the one officially fixed for one of the specified dealing days.

– Those who leave voluntarily before retirement are not permitted to retain their shares but must sell them back in six months' time, and they will be paid for at the official price.

– Those who are dismissed from their employment must sell

their shares back immediately. But they will be paid for at only half of the official price fixed for the dealing day next after their dismissal.

Some have argued that it is a mistake to allow retirees to hang on to their shares until death on the grounds that their interests may not coincide with those of the shareholders who continue to be employed. It is true that there may not be a coincidence of interest or at least not a complete one. But both liberal and sentimental principles may count in the opposite direction. If this subrule is mistaken, at least the mistake is not a serious one.

On the purchase of shares by new recruits, there are again three subrules:

– The purchase of shares by new recruits is voluntary. But with only one exception, all new recruits since the 1993 buy-out have decided to buy in.

– New recruits are allocated shares at the official price fixed for the dealing day following their acceptance into permanent employment with a down payment of 2% to 5%. The balance may be paid by instalments.

– The number of shares that a new recruit may buy follows the original share distribution rule: i.e. it is proportionate to salary.

It was the third of these subrules which had become the focus of some criticism when I visited Herend in October of 1996. Critics pointed out that since new recruits typically begin their working life at lower salaries, the rule is biased against new employees compared with the position of those who were working for the manufactory at the time of the buy-out. There was some acknowledgment among the ESOP Trustees to whom I spoke of the force of this criticism. There must be a fair expectation that it will be modified.

By making these rules in relation to the sale of employee shares by those who leave and their purchase by those who join, the working community at Herend was already demonstrating a clear 'sustainability intention.' In this respect their commitment to the concept of employee ownership was well ahead of many others in the field both in Hungary and elsewhere.

But by October 1996 the decision to set aside 25% into collective ownership was being questioned. And there was criticism too of the 25% shareholding which had been retained by State Property Holding PLC (SPH).

The only function of the Government's 25% shareholding which is of potential value to the manufactory and the working community associated with it is as an extra protection against takeover. If the consensus is that the extra protection is superfluous, then it would clearly make sense to approach the SPH and seek to negotiate a purchase. If the price to be paid was not too high and could be readily financed then a net financial gain could appear quickly. For the dividend payments which went to the SPH in 1995 and 1996 could start going to Herend's insider shareholders instead at a reasonably early date.

The case for change in relation to the 25% shareholding of the ESOP Trust seems to me to be much more problematic. That is because the trust's shareholding has two functions. As well as strengthening the defences against a takeover, it limits the proportions of the manufactory's profits and cash flow which are needed to buy back the shares of those employees who leave. By containing the cash outflows associated with those buy-backs, the trust shareholding operates to increase the resources which the business can devote to investment.

Is a 25% trust shareholding more than is strictly necessary to achieve the desired containment of the 'buy-back outflows'? Without a detailed knowledge of the business it is not really possible to offer an informed judgement. But my guess would be not. If anything I would be inclined to think that it would be wiser to increase it somewhat than to reduce it. At the employee-owned Tullis Russell Group in Scotland investment needs must be substantially greater than Herend's and the need to contain their buy-back outflows must be that much greater as well. On the other hand they are aiming at a collective employee shareholding of 70%, not 25%.

But in any case the question of the optimum size of the Employee Trust's shareholding at Herend is surely one which can be quantified. Detailed projections could cover the future values of the Herend shares. Taken together with a set of 'demographic projections', they would make it possible to forecast future buy-back liabilities. Future cash flows and investment expenditures could be estimated. On the basis of such data the employee shareholders at Herend could decide what percentage of collective ownership they would have to keep if they wished their employee ownership to be indefinitely sustainable.

What finally about the 'sustainability' of Mor Fischer's business plan? Can the rich and super-rich be persuaded to pay an increasing premium in real terms for hand-made and above all hand-painted porcelain? And can they be persuaded to increase that premium at a pace and to a degree which allows incomes at Herend to go up sufficiently to keep people working there as they are now? Who can say? The potential supply side improvements, if they can be realised, will make a most useful contribution. But the final answer will depend on the evolving expenditure patterns of the very rich and the nearly very rich. Those patterns in turn will depend in part on the pace, relative to the rest of us, at which the very rich and nearly very rich get even richer. My guess for what it is worth is that Mor Fischer's business plan will continue to bring relative property to Herend over the next 50 years as it has over the last 150. After all, for the very rich or nearly very rich £2,500 is not all *that* much to pay for a traditional hand-painted dinner service from the Herend Porcelain Manufactory.

APPENDIX I

Traditional European Porcelain Manufacturers

Some Data for 1994

	Founded	Employees	Sales DMm
Staatliche Porzellanmanufactur Meissen	1710	1,100	82.0
Wiener Porzellanmanufactur Augarten (Austria)	1718	240	24.4
Staatliche Porzellanmanufactur Nymphenburg (Germany)	1747	100	5.5
Sèvres porcelain (France)	1753	170	1.5
Porzellanmanufactur Ludwigsburg (Germany)	1758	48	3.8
Koenigliche Porzellanmanufactur Berlin KPM (Germany)	1763	391	34.7
Herend Porcelain Manufactory (Hungary)	1826	1,570	43.0

Source *Die Welt* 15 May 1995, p.12

Ownership Position, 1997

Meissen	The state (Land) government of Saxony.
Augarten	The city government of Vienna.
Nymphenburg	Indirectly owned by the state (Land) government of Bavaria, through a caretaker body, the WAF.
Sèvres	The French state.
Ludwigsburg	Indirectly by the state (Land) government of Baden-Württemberg and the city governments of Stuttgart and Ludwigsburg, with the Duke of Württemburg as a fourth indirect owner. It is directly owned by the Old Ludwigsburg Foundation.
KPM	The city government of Berlin.
Herend	Owned 50% by its employees as individuals and 25% on their behalf by an employee trust, with the state having retained a minority 25% shareholding when the manufactory was privatised in 1997.

APPENDIX 2

Herend Employment Numbers 1949–1996

Year	Production Workers	Office and Management	Working Pensioners	Grand Total
1949	313	49	0	362
1950	331	53	0	384
1951	353	62	0	415
1952	333	66	0	399
1953	361	67	0	428
1954	379	72	0	451
1955	396	69	0	465
1956	405	67	0	472
1957	396	61	0	457
1958	451	62	0	513
1959	477	64	0	541
1960	515	70	0	585
1961	557	77	0	634
1962	595	82	0	677
1963	636	91	0	727
1964	678	101	0	779
1965	720	99	0	819
1966	757	99	0	856

1967	830	104	0	934
1968	878	116	0	994
1969	894	125	0	1019
1970	931	139	10	1080
1971	958	149	12	1107
1972	998	152	14	1164
1973	1046	157	18	1221
1974	1131	163	19	1313
1975	1165	170	20	1355
1976	1145	197	22	1364
1977	1166	204	22	1392
1978	1180	208	22	1410
1979	1219	211	21	1451
1980	1226	219	22	1467
1981	1230	224	18	1472
1982	1243	231	19	1493
1983	1260	235	22	1517
1984	1315	247	26	1588
1985	1318	262	28	1608
1986	1333	268	34	1635
1987	1378	268	32	1678
1988	1442	287	33	1762
1989	1521	298	44	1863
1990	1601	303	42	1946
1991	1357	236	5	1598
1992	1324	232	5	1561
1993	1336	230	5	1571
1994	1341	237	5	1583
1995	1280	264	7	1551
1996	1288	276	6	1572

* Majolica factory spin-off.

20

Saving Jobs with ESOPs & Union Help in the US Steel Industry

INTRODUCTION

Of all the benefits delivered by the late Louis Kelso's ESOP over the first twenty years of its legally recognised life, its use as an instrument to save the jobs and incomes in large North American steel plants should most excite the imagination of the thinking public. We are not talking here mainly about just scores or hundreds of jobs in small- and medium-sized forges and foundries, though, as we shall see in the table at the end, some of those too have been saved by the same ESOP instrument. What we are specifically talking about are three integrated steelmakers, each employing a workforce in the middle single digit thousands. In each of these three cases the business was the subject of a successful employee buy-out financed by what was, *de facto* if not *de jure*, a leveraged ESOP. These three integrated steel undertakings are:

Weirton Steel in West Virginia;

Republic Engineered Steels Inc. (RESI) in Ohio;

Algoma Steel in Ontario (Canada).

The first two are the subject of separate case studies in what follows. But the third of those case studies is not about Algoma Steel. Instead, and partly because the trade union role has been a critical one in all or almost all the American steel industry's ESOPs, the third case study is about union attitudes to employee ownership. In turn that third case study is divided into two parts. In part one we look in a general way at the attitudes of English speaking trade unions to employee ownership in both the US and the UK. In the second and longer part we look at the changing attitudes and policies of one particular union: the United Steelworkers of America (USWA).

In both the Weirton and RESI case studies, readers will be left in no doubt that the role of the union was vital in winning the acceptance by the workforce of an ESOP buy-out proposal. But they will also discover that at RESI the union spoke with two voices and it was essentially the voice of the top national leadership which secured a majority 'yes' vote. And they will learn that Weirton Steel is exceptional in many ways including the identity of its union. Weirton's blue collar workforce is organised, and has been since the 1930s, not by USWA but by the Independent Steelworkers' Union.

What emerges from each of the steel company case studies is that after a more or less extended 'honeymoon period', the views of the union leadership, reflecting the attitudes of its membership, quite sharply cooled off. Having moved a long way towards a more co-operative relationship with management at the time of the buy-outs and over the years which immediately followed, both the ISU at Weirton and USWA at RESI effectively 'snapped back' into a traditionally adversarial union role. No attempt is made to minimise that reversion to an older relationship. But it is argued in effect that, disappointing though that change undoubtedly is, the majority of the jobs which the ESOPs at Weirton and RESI saved are till secure, or anyway they still *were* when this was finally revised in late 1997.

An attempt is also made to explore the reasons for the 'snap back'. The RESI case study includes an extended quotation from an important speech made in 1993 by the late James Smith, shortly before his retirement as a top assistant to successive USWA Presidents. In it Mr Smith explains persuasively how many managers and many trade unionists in conventional capitalist businesses have built much of their personal identities behind their traditional adversarial roles.

In the second part of the trade union case study, Mr Smith also emerges as one of the two key figures in the gradual evolution of USWA's policy towards a conditionally positive attitude to the possibilities opened up by ESOPs and employee ownership. That evolution is shown to have taken place quite rapidly in the early and middle years of the 1980s, essentially as a response to the almost unprecedented recession in the steel industry of those years. Two different uses of the ESOP by the steelworkers' union are then distinguished: the so-called 'investment bargaining ESOP' and the ESOP as an instrument for achieving an employee buy-out of a whole undertaking, as in the case of RESI. What USWA achieved with these new policies is carefully recorded and that is shown to have depended above all on a combination of its readiness to give a lead and its exemplarily professional approach.

If we stand back before plunging into the case studies and ask, as a matter of analysis, why it is that Kelso's ESOP can deliver the saving of many thousands of jobs, part of the answer lies in the tax reliefs that the ESOP brings with it. But there are – or anyway there may be – two other parts to the answer. The first is that once they become part owners and especially if their jobs are on the line, the workforce may well be prepared to accept a modification to the so-called wage/effort bargain. They may accept lower pay, as at Weirton, or they may join management in finding ways of cutting costs other than pay and allowances, as at RESI. Second, with the replacement of mixed debt and equity capital by what amounts initially to just debt, they will in most cases be able to reduce their capital costs.

Weirton Steel

INTRODUCTORY OVERVIEW

There is no single element more important to our future than improved relationships – not money, not machines, not materials, but men and women working together.' *Robert Loughhead, Chairman, President and CEO of Weirton Steel Corporation, 1984-1986: from a letter to employee shareholders introducing the 1985 accounts*

The experience of Weirton Steel, bought by its workers in 1984, suggests that the alignment of interests between management and workers may not last. All was harmony during times of plenty. When the company ran into losses, the usual conflicts between the priorities of managers and those of workers reasserted themselves. *'The [London] Economist'*, *25 December 1993*

We don't consider ourselves an ESOP company any more. *Weirton spokesman, John F. McMahon, quoted in 'Business Week,' 18 March 1996*

In a deal completed in early January 1984, the workforce and management at what had previously been the Weirton Division of America's National Steel used the mechanism of a leveraged ESOP to buy it out. At the time, barely ten years after the passing by Congress of the original ESOP laws, it was easily the largest transaction of its kind that had taken place. The money needed to effect the buy-out was rather less than $200m. Including managers and other white collar staff, the workforce numbered nearly 8,000. Over 6,000, or nearly 90% of the unionised blue collar workforce, approved the deal in a ballot. Its key feature, and what made possible the borrowings needed to effect the transaction, was the acceptance of a substantial wage cut, of about 20%, across the board. The name chosen for the new company was simply Weirton Steel. Once the deal had been completed its entire common stock became ESOP-owned.

Twelve years later, in mid-1996, and following the second of two offerings of its common stock to outside investors in early 1995, the original ESOP and two successors owned about 27% of the company's common stock and controlled some 49% of the votes. Both those numbers were set for a steady decline. The numbers and the trend provide the basis for the third epigraph.

The buy-out was essentially a defensive response to a decision by National Steel to discontinue investing in its Weirton subsidiary. National plausibly claimed that returns on the capital invested there were unacceptably low. What followed, after the buy-out and during the twelve years of majority employee ownership, was a massive restructuring exercise. Its two key and linked – though in part sequential – features were huge new investments and a phased rundown of the workforce. Total investment amounted to $0.75 *billion*, with the bulk of the capital spending, some £550m, incurred after 1989. Numbers employed had fallen from a high of about 8,500 in 1985 down to a little more than 5,500 in 1995, with the greater part of the reduction again coming after 1989. Further prospective reductions were announced in early 1996: total numbers were expected to fall to no more than 4,000 before there was much prospect of them stabilising.

By the second half of the 1990s the threat to Weirton from other steel producers was growing, especially from the ever-more sophisticated mini-mills. However, there can be little doubt that this massive restructuring exercise has ensured the survival of Weirton and its associated jobs and incomes, now admittedly reduced in number, well into the next century. Nor can there be any serious doubt that without the ESOP restructuring could not have taken place. Nor, thirdly, can there be any serious debate about what made the ESOP possible: that 20% wage reduction across the board accepted alike by rank and file employees and by the management. It may be possible to challenge the view that the ESOP was a necessary condition of the acceptance of the wage cut: *in extremis,* when their jobs are on the line, people may be persuaded to accept lower wages and salaries *without* the possibility of recouping even part of what they have lost through becoming employee owners. Still the trade-off between wages and ownership, if it can be achieved, makes unarguable good sense, on the grounds of both incentives and equity.

It is also worth spelling out why, at least for the less skilled, less mobile and older members of the workforce, the acceptance of a 20% pay reduction was almost certainly in line with their best interests. That is because any realistic alternative must have been sharply worse. Even after the pay reduction and without counting their non-money entitlements like health care, they remained on an hourly rate above $20. For most of them, unskilled jobs in the service sector would have been the only realistic alternative – at rates well below half that. And because Weirton was a one-company town, if the company had failed, most of the local service jobs would have gone too.

But it is one thing to point out to others that a substantial sacrifice in pay is in line with their realistic best interests. It is quite another to persuade a whole workforce to make that sacrifice and to lead them down that road. It is because of their courage and success in just such a leadership project that the local management, and especially the union at Weirton, must command our respect as well as our attention. Their example raises an obvious question: how much more widely could jobs be saved in America – and indeed elsewhere in the West – in the late twentieth century if unions and local management behaved like those at Weirton in the early 1980s?

The union at Weirton, the pioneer in America in using an ESOP to save jobs on a large scale, is not in fact the United Steelworkers of America (USWA) but essentially a one company operation called the Independent Steelworkers' Union (ISU). We shall see later how and why it came into being.

But here I want to flag the fact that there will be criticisms as well as praise for the ISU in what follows; for the ISU and indeed for the Weirton management. The fact is that despite an exemplary set of corporate government and ESOP arrangements, the ISU and the management at Weirton were not successful, during its years of majority employee ownership, at building a new and mainly non-adversarial relationship. That is to be greatly regretted. But *sub specie aeternitatis,* it surely counts for very little beside the achievement of saving the business, its jobs – or anyway half of them – and its incomes.

Pre-Buy-Out Weirton To start with history and geography: both the business, and the small town of Weirton in which it is located – some thirty miles west of Pittsburgh in West Virginia's panhandle – take their name from an engineer businessman, Ernest Weir. He built Weirton's first steel mill in 1909 and the business has operated there continuously ever since. Weirton is essentially both a steel town and a one-company town. For most of its business life it was part of National Steel, formed in 1929 when Earnest Weir's business joined with Michigan Steel and with the conglomerate M. A. Hanna (iron, coal, steel and transport). Weirton became National's largest component, with 50% of the share capital. Weir himself was appointed chairman and chief executive of the newly merged undertaking, and its headquarters was set up in nearby Pittsburgh. Partly because of the sustained success of the original Weirton business – which is said never to have missed making profits and paying dividends even in the depths of the interwar depression – National grew and prospered. Following the 1929 merger, it was number nine among America's steel companies. Before the Second World War it had moved up to number five and at its zenith in the 1950s it was number three, after US Steel and Bethlehem.

Throughout this period, and as a matter of policy which went back to Weir and his co-founders, National's divisions enjoyed considerable independence and developed their own distinctive cultures. That was still broadly the position down to the time of the employee buy-out in 1984.

During the 1930s, when the blue collar labour in most of America's large and integrated steel works was organised and recruited into membership by what became the United Steelworkers of America (USWA), the Weirton management fought hard and successfully to keep USWA out. Weirton's blue collar workforce was organised into a free-standing union, the Independent Steelworkers' Union (ISU), and that is how it has gone on being organised since then. Though free-standing, the ISU has no members who are not employed in Weirton's steelworks. It has long been a boast of management, though something about which the ISU is understandably more reticent, that there has not been an official strike at Weirton since 1933. The ISU and its early loyalty to the business may partly explain Weirton's astonishing relative success during the years of depression between the two wars.

The old Weirton Steel was decidedly hierarchical. I have even heard it called feudal. A junior manager did not speak to a superior unless spoken to first. On the company's private golf course junior managers would give way to their seniors and 'let them through'.

Weirton was (and remains) very much a company town – the business not only owned much of the town's housing but also had responsibility for things like the fire brigade. For a number of years in the 1930s and 1940s the company's third chief executive, Thomas E. Millsop, was also the mayor. As for the hierarchy and the reality of 'them and us', it used to be even geographical: it is said that the higher up the valley sides in Weirton your home was, the more senior your position in the company. But only up to a point; for unlike almost everybody else, the chief officers themselves do not live in the town at all, while the company's administrative buildings which contain the offices of top management are on a hilltop a mile away from the valley floor plant.

It is perhaps a present legacy of this past that the town still feels as if it is a community on its own – only thirty miles from Pittsburgh but in fact a world away.

The 1984 Buy-Out and the ESOP Itself The deal by which the Weirton Steel Corporation became 100% employee-owned was completed on 11 January 1984. The process leading up to it had begun nearly two years before in February 1982: with a letter to the shareholders of National Steel from that company's then chairman, Mr Howard Love.

In his letter Mr Love gave notice of a plan for downsizing the steel making operations of its business 'to whatever size is required to meet market demand and earn a return to . . . stockholders'. The plan was couched in terms such that it covered National's steel-making operations generally; it was not Weirton specific. Then, less than a week later, the company issued a press release which was exclusively focused on Weirton. The main message was that National had decided, as a minimum, to 'substantially limit' any future investment at Weirton. It went on to say that various more radical alternatives, including a possible sale to the employees, were under consideration. This press release stirred the local management at Weirton, the trade union and to some extent the whole Weirton community into action.

It is not clear whether actual losses had been incurred at Weirton while it was still a subsidiary of National. But we do know that, because of a combination of slower economic growth and tougher competition – from local all-American mini-mills as well as from imports – the conditions faced by integrated steel makers in the US became progressively tougher in the early and middle 1980s. We know too that the steelworks at Weirton was at a significant competitive disadvantage in respect of the rates paid to its hourly and blue collar workforce.

In the years of the American steel industry's greatest prosperity – from the start of the Second World War down to the mid-1970s – it became customary for the ISU and the local management at Weirton to negotiate their wage agreements in the months *after* settlements had been reached between USWA and America's major steel businesses. The Weirton rates came to be typically fixed about 5% above those negotiated by USWA. This may have made them the highest paid blue collar workers in the country: by the early 1980s, according to one estimate, wages in the American steel industry were at a 92% premium compared with the average for the country's manufacturing businesses (Fruhan 1985). No wonder there were no strikes.

According to Fruhan, the management of National Steel anticipated cumulative pre-tax losses of $334m for the five years starting 1984 on the assumptions (a) that the business would remain a National subsidiary and (b) that no new investment and no changes in wage rates would have been made. Fruhan characterised the then 'mind set' of the National management as 'short term'. Whatever the precise figures, it is clear that if it had done nothing about its Weirton subsidiary, National Steel would have sustained damaging losses.

Following Mr Love's letter and the press release, a body called the Joint Study Committee was set up at the steelworks including representatives of non-union employees as well as of local management and the ISU. Next, with money contributed in part by employees, and in part by the local community and local political grandees like West Virginia's Senator Rockefeller, consultants (McKinsey) were commissioned to explore the feasibility of an ESOP-financed employee buy-out. When their study suggested that it would be feasible on certain conditions, Lazard Frères, the New York investment bank, were brought in as financial advisers to the joint committee. McKinseys were paid just over $500,000, as an unconditional fee; Lazard Frères were paid a fee of just over $1m. But the latter was conditional on the successful completion of an actual buy-out transaction – no deal, no fee.

The chief condition judged necessary by both McKinseys and Lazard Frères was a very big reduction in labour costs, including a sharp cut in wages. The eventual numbers, including some downward adjustments already introduced before the deal was completed, were a total labour cost reduction of just over 30%, and 20% wage cuts for all employee groups. Essentially what McKinseys and Lazards advised the joint committee was that if these reductions were agreed by the workforce then money could be borrowed to finance a deal at a price which they, as the employee owners of the successor business, could afford to pay. Of 6,977 union members who were eligible to vote when the time came, as many as 6,203, or just under 89%, voted 'yes'.

This vote to accept the new labour contract cleared the way for the buy-out deal to be completed. The vote was also taken as a positive verdict on the detailed arrangements of the proposed ESOP. The price at which ownership of the business was passed by National to the new Weirton Steel Corporation, which the Joint Study Committee had set up and registered, was a shade below $194m. That reflected payment of full book values for the net short-term assets of the business but no more than 22% of depreciated net book values, or $72m, for the fixed assets.

The costs to National of closing its Weirton Division have been estimated by Fruhan at over $400m. He reckons that at the start of 1984, and on various assumptions of what might have been negotiated in a closedown agreement with the ISU, the pension liabilities would have been $318m and that health care would have added another $100m. As it was, the new Weirton Steel assumed an obligation to cover pensions for all periods of service which postdated the buy-out. In a final gesture of goodwill National agreed that if the new business failed, then it would itself take partial responsibility for meeting pension obligations for post buy-out periods of work. Despite that gesture, however, the liabilities assumed by National under the sale and purchase agreement were significantly less than they would have been had the business been closed down.

ESOP Features Features of the Weirton ESOP and of the company statutes of the new employee-owned successor business have been replicated in progressive ESOPs elsewhere, particularly by those in which USWA and its members have been involved. They have probably come to constitute something close to 'best practice' in this field.

Perhaps the single most important feature is what has come in Britain to be called the 'paritarian' character of the corporate government which was established. Alternatively, using language favoured in postwar West Germany, this feature can be seen as essentially 'co-determinational' but with a group of independents thrown in to hold the balance between the two sides. Specifically, and just as happened at Republic Engineered Steels five years later, the board of directors was drawn from three different groups. There were equal numbers of directors appointed by the top management on the one hand and elected by the ISU on the other. A group of independents, greater in number than either of the other two groups, was then chosen jointly by them. The logic of this arrangement is clear. As long as union and management agree, the function of the independents is to raise the quality of the discussion. If the directors from each of the two sides of the business are unable to agree, then the role of the independents is to have the last word.

The corporate government arrangements put in place at Weirton in 1984 also offered a 'democratic protection' against any hasty or unequally advantageous decision to seek a stock exchange listing or to make some other move which might carry the possibility that its employee ownership could come to an end. This took the form of a provision in the statutes to the effect that after five years there should be a referendum on the future of the business: more precisely on whether, beyond the end of that five-year period, Weirton's shares should continue to be closely held by its employees or whether steps should be taken to make them publicly traded. Furthermore, it was provided that the referendum should be counted on the basis of one employee one vote regardless of shareholding size.

The ownership arrangements associated with Weirton's 1984 ESOP and its corporate statutes were liberal – in the sense of favouring the individual employee's interests to the maximum that the law and business prudence would permit. Four features should be mentioned. The first is that once shares were allocated to employees they immediately became vested. There was no delay – as is permitted by the ESOP legislation – between allocation and vesting. But, second, by the terms of Weirton's original ESOP, the employee shareholders had no way of turning their shares into cash until either a) the net worth of the successor business had reached the figure of $250m or b) the shares came to be quoted on a stock exchange. Third, the basis on which employee shares would be allocated as the buy-out borrowings were paid off was proportionate to rates of pay. Finally, in a notably liberal provision, the ESOP's rules provided that, at least for the first five years of its life, newly recruited employees would take part in the ownership scheme.

As a postscript, it is worth asking what was the intention of those who framed them behind the key provisions about an eventual stock exchange listing. The evidence makes it clear the architects of these arrangements were concerned about the process by which that decision would be reached – namely by a democratic referendum – but were not inclined to make any attempt to pre-judge it. They may have recognised that, in the long run, a listing would probably be inescapable and that, eventually, in the long aftermath of an initial listing, the employee shareholders would lose control. But at the time of the buy-out the overriding priority was to save jobs.

A Good Start for Employee Ownership: 1984–89 The period from 1984 to 1989 was characterised by relatively easy trading conditions, though the going became a little tougher during 1988 and 1989. It was also characterised by growing sales – which measured in dollars peaked in 1988 and in tons in 1987 – and buoyant operating income. There were also positive innovations in labour/management relationships and employee morale was high.

The early 1990s will be discussed in the next section. However, to show the contrast between the earlier and later years, the main numbers are set out in continuous series for the whole period.

Some Key Statistics: 1984–95

Year	Tons Shipped (000)	Net Sales ($m)	Operating Income ($m)	Numbers Employed
1984	2,108	1,075	86.1	7,844
1985	2,357	1,156	83.2	8,131
1986	2,418	1,173	69.0	8,429
1987	2,786	1,329	104.3	8,345
1988	2,729	1,384	93.3	8,094
1989	2,499	1,329	82.8	7,980
1990	2,206	1,191	17.6	7,788
1991	1,938	1,036	(46.4)	6,979
1992	2,102	1,079	(0.4)	6,542
1993	2,431	1,201	(3.4)	6,026
1994	2,606	1,261	48.5*	5,565
1995	2,718	1,352	99.8*	5,627**

* Affected by insurance recoveries in connection with fire.
** There were further job cuts, running well into four figures, between 1996 and 1998.
Source: Annual Reports

As the table makes clear, market conditions after 1989 became ferociously more difficult. In the US steel markets, and to a significant extent for the American economy as a whole, these were years of the worst depression since the prewar slump. Furthermore they coincided with the physical implementation of Weirton's $550m investment plan. So problems of demand were compounded for Weirton by those of supply. There was a relatively high incidence of what in the American steel industry are called 'outages' – the temporary shutting down of facilities for essentially technical and supply side reasons. The results moved from the profits of the earlier years into loss. But all that is to anticipate.

For the earlier period down to end-1989, the growth in the net worth or shareholders' funds suggests that Weirton's performance was better than expected. It had been provided in the labour contract that a huge 50% share of net profits would be allocated to an all-employee cash profit sharing scheme, once net worth exceeded $250m. Surely, those who devised that formula expected more time to be needed to reach the $250m milestone – or they would have tried to set a higher threshold.

There are also more objective measures of the quality of Weirton's business performance in the early post-buy-out years. For example, there was almost continuous improvement in both dollar sales per employee and tons shipped per employee. With only minor setbacks on the way, there was also a big improvement – of more than 25% – between 1983 and 1988 in the annual rate of inventory turnover:

Improvements in Productivity & Inventory Turnover 1983–88

	1983	'84	'85	'86	'87	'88
Shipments/Employee (net tons)	266	280	303	299	347	351
Sales/Employee ($000)	136	143	149	145	166	178
Inventory Turnover	5.8	5.7	6.2	6.1	6.7	7.4

Source: *Prospectus for Common Stock Offering,* 1989

I have not been able to find evidence on whether Weirton's overall performance was superior to the average achieved by the competition – domestic or foreign – during this period. However the corporation sharply increased its share of America's national market for tin mill products – from 19% to 23% – between 1984 and 1985, and then held on to that larger share of a fundamentally static market.

More important, or at least so it seemed at the time, was an array of institutional and similar innovations whose logic was to exploit employee ownership's potential for improvements in management/labour relationships and thus in performance. It was this potential which was highlighted by Robert Loughhead, employee-owned Weirton's first CEO, in that letter to shareholders quoted in the first epigraph.

Perhaps the experience of working together gained by the management and the ISU leaders in the Joint Study Committee provided a good send-off for an improvement of relationships after the buy-out. It has also often been argued that, because of the company's traditional high wage policy and the old Weirton's strike-free record, relationships between the local management and the ISU have normally been quite cosy. On the second of these claims – or at least of its effects on the experience from 1984 onwards – the post buy-out evidence is at best rather ambiguous.

With hindsight, the whole post-buy-out thrust towards greater employee involvement may be seen as partly a *political* initiative (with a small 'p'). Given the switch to employee ownership, it was imperative to recognise the new status of the workforce. One might go further and say that it was as important to be seen to be introducing such programmes as it was to make sure of their success. There was also a widespread and predictably negative reaction by middle management to the new higher status of employees in the early post-buy-out years.

Those are general points. More specifically, all or almost all of the main cultural, communications and related initiatives which date from the early post-buy-out period were joint projects of the top management and the ISU. There may have been an especially strong relationship over the first two post-buy-out years between Robert Loughhead, the then CEO, and Walter Bish, who was the ISU's elected president at that time.

To begin with, as part of a policy of maximum disclosure, two new communications initiatives were promoted soon after the buy-out. The first was a monthly newspaper, *Independent Weirton*; the second a weekly video *News & Views*. Editorial control in both cases was shared betwen the management and the union.

Of potentially greater impact on employee behaviour were initiatives on improved participation which were designed to 'unlock' the knowledge of the workforce and use it to improve performance. The most extensive of the these early initiatives was the establishment of a plant-wide network of employee participation groups (EPGs). These are best understood as fully union-backed quality circles with the main aim of tapping into shopfloor knowledge and ideas. By early 1994 it was claimed that as many as 50% of the then workforce had had experience of EPGs or similar 'participation schemes'.

A second initiative had management behaviour as its target. It was called the Management for Productivity Program and was given a training agenda, with subject matter which included motivation theories, teamwork systems and the so-called Maslow hierarchy of employees' needs. Until 1989 the majority of Weirton's senior, middle and junior managers spent time on this programme. Then, deemed to have served its purpose, it was largely discontinued.

Two other new schemes in this category were introduced quite soon after the buy-out with a specific aim of achieving improvements in productivity and reductions in cost. According to an early published commentary, the first of these, the so-called Operations Improvement Program (OIP)

> puts together teams of employees to solve specific problems relating to quality or productivity. Ideas generated from these teams go to a high level steering committee made up of the chief executive officer, the executive vice president, the head of operations and the chief financial officer. This program has its own staff which assists ... [with] preparing and screening proposals so that only carefully researched proposals reach the steering committee.

Finally, a scheme was established for training selected employees in the techniques of what is called Statistical Process Control. It aimed at improving the ability of shop floor employees to identify variables in production, as a way forward towards achieving consistently higher quality.

In those early days, and even in the early 1990s – ten years after the buy-out – Weirton's management and the ISU agreed that these programmes and others were crucial to the success of the business. Both also argued that it was only through programmes of genuine participation and involvement, and of the fullest possible disclosure that management leadership, within the essentially bottom-upwards structure of an employee-owned business, could be properly legitimised.

There are many employee-involvement schemes in conventional capitalist companies which are at least as radical as any of those introduced at Weirton in the aftermath of the buy-out, especially if we look to Japanese rather than Western examples of conventional capitalist business. By Japanese standards the first Weirton steps were doubtless elementary. What was unusual was the paritarian nature of Weirton's board and the fact that the communications and involvement initiatives were jointly sponsored by management and union.

Having discussed the company's array of what may be called 'participation initiatives', we come on next to a cluster of linked events in 1989 which represent the high water mark of employee ownership at Weirton. These were fundamentally driven by the need to raise new capital for investment in order to modernise casting and hot-rolling capacity. But although the events of 1989 can in part be seen as a financial restructuring of the business following the completion of the repayment of the buy-out debt, they were also a new bargain with labour.

A total of $300m of Weirton bonds – Senior Notes as they are formally described – were sold in America's financial markets and a further $56.3m worth of pollution control bonds were refinanced.

But the most consequential element was rather different. Following the agreement of its employee owners, approved in a referendum, just over a quarter of Weirton's common stock – 4.5m shares – was sold to US investors at a price of $14.50 per share. This valued the business at some 90% of the net current assets accumulated since the buy-out. It is true that restrictions remained on the employees' right to sell their ESOP shares. An individual could not sell more than 35% of his or her holding while still employed at Weirton with a further limit of 5% in any one year. But the corporation's stock 'went public' in the key sense that non-employees were from then on permitted to be shareholders. Despite that momentous change, Weirton's employee owners managed to retain voting control of the business by establishing a second ESOP with special features. These included a restriction on the ownership of the new ESOP's special preference shares to those involved in the first ESOP, and the assigning of ten votes to each of them.

There were two further ingredients in this 1989 financial package. First, for the period to end–September 1995, the employees accepted a cut to 35% from 50% in what was to be allocated to them as a cash bonus from Weirton's net profits. Because it was also agreed that there should be an adjustment for any payment of dividends, the reduction to 35% in some sense understates what the employees agreed to give up. But second, as a once-off 'sweetener' and at a total cost of $5.1m, the entire workforce was paid either one week's holiday (vacation) pay or $500 – whichever was higher.

It is these two points which partly define the 1989 funding exercise as a bargain between capital and labour. In return for keeping a control through the mechanism of the new 1989 ESOP and for the $5.1m once-off 'sweetener', labour agreed that its cash allocation out of pre-tax profits should be scaled down. As for capital, it was ultimately represented in the bargain by the underwriters for the new borrowings and the share issue. As compared with the underwriters on one side and Weirton's workforce on the other, the

Weirton managers can be seen as playing two roles. As members of the workforce and employee shareholders they were involved in the labour side of this labour/capital bargain. But they clearly also played a part in 'brokering' the deal: that is in commending the whole package as reasonable to the ISU membership and the other non-management personnel in Weirton's workforce.

However, in a pointer to the future, these arrangements were not agreed without cost, especially to the internal politics of the ISU. True, Weirton's employee shareholders – about 85% of whom were and are ISU members – approved the whole package by a comfortable majority on the basis of one shareholder one vote. But that was not the whole story.

Mr Walter Bish, the elected President of the ISU when the buy-out took place, had two three-year terms of office between 1982 and 1988. In the summer of 1988 Mr Bish was a candidate for re-election for a third term. The likely need to scale down labour's prospective 50% share of pre-tax earnings loomed over the election and seems to have become the dominant issue. Mr Bish's policy was to encourage realism. He argued that it would be necessary to accept a reduction of the profit share as a precondition for a financial restructuring which in turn was a precondition for raising the capital for the investment plan. His opponent, Mr Virgil Thompson, who had lately returned to the ranks of Weirton's workforce after getting himself a law degree, adopted a more sceptical stance – to the effect that a reduction of the profit share might or might not be necessary. Roughly nine months later, once safely elected, Mr Thompson advised the ISU members to accept a reduction in their cash profit share as part of the overall financial restructuring package and bargain. But the damage had been done: it was clear that the way to get elected to office in the ISU was to oppose 'cuts'.

As a footnote to these transactions it is worth looking a little more closely at the price at which the business was valued when those 4.5m shares in its common stock were offered for sale in the summer of 1989. As we have seen, the selling price of these shares to the public was $14.50. At the time just under 20m had been issued. If we deduct $1 per share for underwriters' commission and discount, we can put the imputed value of the company at some $270m. Between them, at the time of the offering, Weirton's 8,000 odd employees owned roughly 75% of the shares. So, the value at that time of the shareholding of Weirton's average employee was some $30,000 or a little less.

As we move to more recent events, we should not forget the success of this first phase – and the promise it held forth. With a hybrid set of transactions, partly financial restructuring and partly a bargain between capital and labour, Weirton raised the money for an investment programme necessary for it to remain competitive. Moreover it managed to raise that money without its employees having to give up control of the business. At the same time it managed to ease itself at least partially off two hooks on which, by virtue of the profit-sharing and share buy back provisions of the original buy-out deal, it had come to find itself impaled.

The Second Phase: to Mid-1996 The difficulties faced by Weirton in the seven years from 1989 arose partly from the tougher market conditions but were also partly specific to itself. For these were the years of peak investment, especially relating to the new continuous caster and to the modernisation of the hot-rolling mill. There were frequent 'outages' – the temporary closing down of distinct operations – both planned and unplanned. The 1993 results are substantially explained by special factors without which they would have shown an improvement on 1992. The 1994 and 1995 results were distorted by a factory fire. The key statistics are shown in the earlier table. Measured in both tons and dollars, sales as well as operating income reached their low point in 1991. In that year, following payments in 1989 and 1990, the directors decided to pass the dividend. They did so again in each of the two following years. In the three years 1991 to 1993 Weirton's employee owners had to do without both cash profit shares and dividends.

The damage was considerable. In 1992 the company's share price fell relative to other steel companies and its debt was down-rated by both Moodies and Standard & Poors into their sixth lowest grade (out of nine) of corporate bonds. Moody characterises such bonds as 'generally lack[ing] characteristics of the desirable investment', and it goes on 'Assurance of interest and principal payments or of maintenance of other terms of the contract over any long period of time may be small.'

And yet, by the end of the first quarter of 1994, the price of Weirton's shares had recovered more than 75% of its earlier under-performance relative to the steel sector. Moreover during 1994 as a whole the value of Weirton's stock increased by 41%, comfortably outperforming the competition even if from a low base.

Though these were years of 'outages' they were also years, as the CEO – Mr Herbert Elish – never tired of pointing out, when the business was 'positioning itself', through its capital investment programme, to compete more successfully in the future.

In fact, as early as February 1993 Weirton successfully managed a new issue of $140m of loan notes and Mr Herbert Elish was at least partly justified in claiming, in the 1992 Annual Report, that 'this successful offering demonstrated the financial community's confidence in our results and outlook'.

The key business achievements at Weirton during these difficult years were the implementation of the $550m capital spending programme which paid for Weirton's new continuous caster and the modernisation of its hot-rolling mill. Both had been successfully completed by 1993.

The price was lower employment. Given the culture of America's industrial relations, this could be achieved only by a reduction in workforce numbers. The theoretical alternative – a general acceptance of shorter hours and lower pay rates – was probably never a serious possibility. The upshot was that the Weirton workforce was cut from just under 8,000 to 5,565 between 1989 and 1994. Commenting in the 1994 Annual Report that the cost-saving efforts had reduced employment by about 30% since 1988, Mr Elish went on: 'It is a special achievement that virtually all of these personnel reductions took place through voluntary retirements, thereby preserving jobs for our younger employees, who are the future of the company, while giving those ready to retire an opportunity to do so.'

But this rundown of employment numbers provoked a sharp cry of pain and protest from the ISU in November 1992: in the form of a letter from its executive committee to Weirton's board of directors. In it the union called, as if they were alternatives to an important degree, for cost savings to be achieved in ways other than through de-manning. Furthermore – and I quote from the prospectus associated with the $140m issue of loan notes in early 1993 – the letter expressed 'concerns as to the ability of present management to achieve an acceptable level of operating performance and to determine the future course the company should take.'

However that same prospectus goes on to report that

In January 1993, the company and the representatives of the ISU reached a settlement agreement on the subject of enhanced retirements which would enable the company to implement its business strategy of manpower reductions covering represented employees for the duration of the current collective bargaining agreement. On February 5, 1993, the settlement agreement was approved by vote of the union's membership.

It is common ground between the management and union at Weirton that these special programs of higher 'retirement benefits' were entirely initiated by Mr Herbert Elish and his top management team. They were also widely accepted, through voting with their feet, by affected ISU members. The ISU's leadership had little or nothing to do with them. On the other hand, given their widespread acceptance by union members, they could hardly have been formally rejected by the ISU leadership.

All this was to be revisited in 1996 – which brings me to a more general point which was central to the company's position in 1996. More than once between 1990 and 1993, visitors to Weirton – people generally sympathetic to its employee ownership project – came back with reports of difficult relationships between management and the ISU, and between management and the shopfloor. Stories appeared in the American press to that effect. They were reflected in the *Economist* article quoted at the outset.

Objective evidence of continuing mistrust of top management by Weirton's blue collar workforce is provided by the fate of the two incumbent ISU presidents who sought re-election between the buy-out in 1984 and the early 1990s. I have already mentioned the defeat of Mr Walter Bish by Mr Virgil Thompson in 1988. More or less the same pattern repeated itself in the 1991 election for the presidency, when it was Mr Virgil Thompson who was the incumbent and who went down to defeat. It was another outsider, Mr Mark Glyptis, who won. He did so, by all accounts, after conducting an anti-management or at least management-sceptical campaign. Mr Glyptis won again, in an election in which he was unopposed, in 1994. According to some management sources, one of the ways in which Mr Glyptis retains his hold on employees is by being seen to be constantly critical of management.

Further evidence of mutual distrust includes the protracted

process of negotiations – lasting more than six months – which were needed for the management and the ISU to reach their new three-year labour agreement early in 1994, several months after it had been due to take effect.

The mistrust hypothesis is stregthened by other events in 1993 and subsequently. At the May AGM, votes cast in connection with the election of Mr Herbert Elish to the board were 22.5m in favour and 17.3m against. A source of more damaging publicity in the same year was the fate of the first proposal from top management that the capital base of the business should be enlarged and strengthened by offering new shares to the public. The proposal was vigorously opposed by the ISU on various stated grounds, but perhaps most fundamentally because the union's leadership welcomed a trial of strength with the management. When one of Weirton's independent directors, Philip Smith, swung his vote behind the ISU and in opposition to the proposal, management decided to withdraw it.

This and other evidence seemed to suggest that there was still a long way to go before blue-collar workers at Weirton assume anything like an identity of interest with the top management of the business – and vice versa. The continuing two-way mistrust between management and union and management and shopfloor is no doubt the child of the pre-buy-out culture; a culture which is highly resistant to change. We should not be surprised by the evidence of its survival in the shape of that mutual mistrust. Progress made during the 1980s was by the mid-1990s beginning to look like a brief interlude.

We must now look at some details of the new labour contract approved in March 1994. With the encouragement of management and at the expense of the company, the ISU hired its own financial advisers. The thrust of their advice to the union was that a competitive labour contract was essential if the damage done to the credibility of the business by the withdrawal of the original 1993 share offer proposal was to have much chance of being repaired. After who knows how many gulps, the ISU negotiators followed that advice, at least in the later stages of the protracted bargaining process.

Three features in this new labour agreement stand out. The first is its conditional guarantee, to the bulk of the union's membership, of employment security during the contract's three-year life.

The second is that it provided for a three-year wages standstill at the rates agreed in the previous contract. Third, as at least a partial sweetener, it offered unconditional bonus payments on top of wages for each of its three consecutive years: of $1,000 per head in the first year and of $1,250 in each of the subsequent two.

However, for what may be called the professional human resources community in the USA, it was not those features but the provisions to do with health care which made this labour contract truly remarkable and competitive. Mr Brenneisen, then the Vice President, Human Resources, believed that these provisions would yield savings of some $25m over the contract's three-year life.

To understand them, it is first necessary to grasp a distinction – that between managed and non-managed health care. If they accepted 'managed care' under the 1994 labour contract, Weirton employees and their dependants were assigned to an identified group of medical practitioners in their home neighbourhood. If they chose not to accept, then they remained free to take their illness or injury to any doctor or specialist they liked. The costs of treatments by the latter are typically much higher and may involve excessive treatment relative to the nature of the ailment or injury. An example given by Mr Brenneisen is the likely costs of being treated for a stuffed-up nose by a fully qualified ear, nose and throat specialist.

The trick, if what is desired is a high number of employees choosing managed care, is to negotiate an agreement with the union which imposes much higher personal contributions to any medical charges if they choose not to accept managed care. In the 1994 labour contract at Weirton that annual contribution for employees within managed care was fixed at a maximum of $2,500 per employee with a further maximum of $5,000 for covered dependants and a lifetime maximum of $250,000. By contrast, if you opted for non-managed care, the lifetime maximum was $1m. The contract put the personal contributions for managed care at $150 for an individual and $300 for dependants. It is scarcely surprising that 98% of the workforce chose to sign up for managed care. In this case the ISU deserves considerable credit for seeing an identity of interest between the business on the one hand and its members on the other.

Mr Brenneisen offers a telling detail in support of his contention that over-treatment of Weirton employees by local doctors and in local hospitals had been widespread. According to late 1980s' national US data, medical expenditures per head in the West Virginia county in which Weirton falls were the third highest in the whole country – after the County of Miami in Florida and Cook County, Illinois. Mr Brenneisen goes on to assert the general principle that when people become responsible for making a substantial contribution to the costs of their health care they will tend to prefer a system which eschews excessive treatments.

I must now turn to the labour agreement's employment security provisions. These were not incompatible with a continuing rundown of workforce numbers. Indeed already at the time of the agreement Weirton's top management was publicly committed to a further reduction – to a workforce total of around 5,000 by 1998. But the management also believed that that target could be achieved by a combination of attrition and voluntary early retirement.

Once the ISU membership at Weirton had voted strongly in favour of this agreement in March 1994, Mr Brenneisen was prepared to express some optimism about the future. With one proviso, the CEO's introductory remarks to the 1993 Annual Report were also notably optimistic. Mr Elish's caveat was the inadequacy of Weirton's equity base. He had been the prime mover behind the aborted 1993 proposal to increase Weirton's share capital. On the other hand, a similar proposal was supported by the necessary large majority of eligible votes at Weirton's key special shareholders' meeting on 26 May 1994 – and went on to be successfully implemented in August.

The key to the new public share offer proposal was in the numbers. The issue of a total of 20m new shares was authorised. Within that total, 15m were to be offered to the public with the balance of 5m set aside for a new employee stock purchase plan. As for the latter, participation by employees was voluntary and these shares were in principle available at a 15% discount. The 26 May meeting also approved the purpose of the offering: to pay off high cost debt and strengthen the financial base of Weirton's pension scheme. The latter was made necessary by the continuing policy of encouraging early retirements.

In the event, when the actual share offering took place in August, a total of 17m shares were offered and disposed of. However the offer still fell within the authorisations of the earlier AGM –

because 2m of those on offer were not new shares but old ones sold to the public by Weirton's pension plan.

What about the balance of voting power, as between employee and outsider shareholders, once the new shares had been successfully offered and purchased? The detailed numbers are complex. In summary, before the new share offer Weirton's employees held just over 75% of the votes and an aggregate of just over 28m out of a total of rather over 40m issued shares; once the additional 15m shares had been sold, the balance of voting power between insiders and outsiders became much closer. It is true that, in the immediate aftermath of the public offer the insiders still retained a small margin of voting control: just over 51%. However, even at the time the offer was approved, it was easy to see that as Weirton's existing employees sold out either on retirement, or by exercising the limited pre-retirement selling rights which they already enjoyed, the balance of voting power would shift to the outsiders. The new voluntary employee stock purchase plan, for which 5m shares were authorised, might slow down that process but it was unrealistic to suppose that it would ever be reversed. In other words, over a period which could have been slightly shorter or slightly longer, control would inexorably move outside. By early 1996 that had happened.

The same special meeting on 26 May 1994 also approved various additional recommendations proposed by the board of directors. The most important was to increase the number of directors by one, from 13 to 14, by designating a special 'ESOP' director, to be chosen in a way which gives considerable influence to the union. A further change was to redefine the criteria which Weirton's independent directors must satisfy so as to exclude professionals, like lawyers, already under contract to the company. I mention these changes in the rules of Weirton's corporate government chiefly because the ISU thought them important and gave them as one of the reasons for switching its line on the public share offer from rejection in 1993 to support in 1994. It could happen that the appointment of a specially designated 'ESOP director' will turn out to be an important innovation. On the other hand, if the ISU opposed the 1993 offer at least partly because it welcomed the chance to show its strength, then the importance it claimed to attach to the corporate government changes may have been more rhetorical than real.

Nonetheless, Weirton's top management must accept a part of

the blame for the debacle of the 1993 share offer. For example it seems difficult to justify its refusal in 1993 to spell out precisely for what purposes the proceeds of the share offer would be applied. For it was an open secret in early 1994 that those purposes would have been identical to those spelled out when the issue of the share offer resurfaced.

With the share offer successfully over, there seemed in late 1994 to be a case for cautious optimism about an improvement in ISU and shopfloor relations with management at Weirton in the period ahead. It seemed likely that much of the 'aggro' during the economically difficult years had been linked to just those difficulties: when there are no cash bonuses, no dividends and no wage increases, morale is almost bound to be depressed. Second, another part of the earlier 'aggro' between 1990 and 1993 might plausibly have been attributed to the absence of any agreement between the ISU and management about employment security. The employment security provisions of the 1994 labour agreement might reasonably have been expected to remedy that. Finally, the continuing effects of Weirton's various participation and involvement programmes might, after ten years of employee ownership, have become more or less bedded down in the Weirton culture. They figure prominently in Mr Elish's remarks in the Annual Reports.

From the start of the big capital investment programme and of the more difficult times after 1989, there had been a significant shift in how the main programmes operated. It is probably no accident that the phrase 'employee participation groups' had been largely abandoned and replaced by the much more familiar and fashionable 'total quality management'. Behind the change of name was something of a change of substance. It seems that in their early days the EPGs were largely responsible for setting their own agendas; and threw up as a result a variable scatter of tasks and projects. Among these there were doubtless *some* with a high potential for either cost saving or quality improvement. But since there was no consistent method of selection – nothing similar, for example, to the process of functional analysis at Republic Engineered Steels – the likelihood must be that they were a small minority.

After about 1989 management gradually took more of the initiative over the projects and problems to be worked on by the old EPGs. As a result, a higher proportion of what was essentially the same involvement activity started to have direct cost-saving and/or quality improvement potential. It seems, more specifically, that a much larger part of this activity became directly devoted to the objective of reducing the percentage of defects. That work, or so it is widely believed, is not only at the centre of the total quality management (TQM) concept; it is also where shopfloor knowledge is most successful in the generation of improvements.

In his statement introducing the 1993 accounts, Mr Elish claimed a cumulative $35m worth of cost savings had resulted from this (TQM) process. The figure was accepted as realistic even by Weirton's hard-bitten professional accountants who are partly *paid* to be sceptical. In his 1994 report, Mr Elish went further and claimed that:

> Total Quality Management has resulted in lowering annual costs by over $46m since the program's inception in 1992. TQM has been central to our efforts to change the way work is planned and performed and manufacturing processes controlled. The combination of improved analysis and teams of employees throughout the mill identifying opportunities for improvements in costs is making a fundamental difference. *Perhaps most important for the future, the concept of 'continuous improvement' is now embedded in the organisation, meaning that further improvements in quality, cost and service are assured* [emphasis added].

Jumping on from Mr Elish's 1994 Annual Report to 1996, Weirton Steel presented a paradox. On the one hand, it had just been presented with a prize for outstanding service to customers. Its mills 'operated at maximum productivity and efficiency . . . setting records for yields in all product areas . . .' to quote the first annual statement by the new CEO, Richard Riederer, formerly the chief financial officer. Cost of sales per ton continued to fall and, at $434, stood about $100 lower than in 1991. In June 1995 the company refinanced debt with a sale of $125m ten-year notes. The damage done by a serious fire in early 1995 had been made good with remarkable speed. The customer-orientation of the company and its employees looked impressive.

On the other hand, the external market looked ever more competitive. Between 10m and 20m tons of new capacity was said to be coming on stream from mini-mills, which pay a base remuneration of less than half that at Weirton, but couple that up with a truly radical incentive system. In the mini-mills, as Mr Brenneisen puts it, 'if there is a problem at one end of the building everybody dashes to mend it because the incentive stops for everyone whatever the cause of the stoppage.' At the same time, Weirton also faced pressure on its selling prices as a result of consolidation amongst its tin-mill customers. Weirton had a clear strategy to cope with this: concentration on the quality end of the market. But whichever way you turned, the market looked tough.

Perhaps more seriously problematic was the relationship with labour. Indeed, in the run-up to the next labour agreement negotiations, due by late 1996, the labour relations position looked rather unhopeful. The negotiation of the 1993-6 agreement had been hard, and relationships had become worse since then. One cause of this was the issue of merit rises for management. External consultants presented a proposal to the board which recommended that what they saw as low management salaries should be augmented with profit shares and stock options. At the board meeting to adopt the bonus system, a couple of hundred pickets demonstrated against the proposal. The board approved the bonuses and suggested that management meet with the unions and attempt to work out any misunderstanding during the negotiations. Business was good and the company offered a performance bonus system that had the potential to pay $1,500 per union employee. But the union turned the offer down and the negotiations ended.

By this stage, the management had had enough. The company sued the union for damages in connection with a work stoppage. A counter-suit by the union failed. After the management filed the suit in the federal court, relations were reported to be businesslike, if frosty.

This was the background to an announcement by the Weirton management in May 1996 that a further reduction in staff would be necessary to maintain competitiveness. In other words, in the 1996 negotiation further employee reductions would have to be agreed with the union. In total the management was looking for cuts of about 1,000 employees. One interpretation of the change was that management had given up hope of negotiating savings via improved working practices and saw an intensified programme of job cuts as the only feasible way of making the cost savings necessary to stay competitive.

In his annual statements the long-standing CEO Herbert Elish became accustomed to pay lavish tribute to co-operative processes involving the workforce in building the company's future. Apart from the specific case of the recovery from the fire, such a tribute is notably absent from the first annual statement by the new CEO – who confined himself to a terse 'I look forward to working with Weirton employees'.

According to an article in *Business Week* (March 1996), union members had demanded in 1994 that Herbert Elish depart:

> Elish retired last year, but he got his revenge by handpicking his successor ... Riederer seems determined not to let the union treat him the same way ... He has cut much of the communication with union leaders, says Robert J d'Anniballe Jr, a board member and legal counsel for the union. Complains union president Mark Glyptis, 'You would hope that you could sit down and reasonably, discuss issues and resolve them.'

Early in 1996 Mr Brenneisen left the company, opening the way for a new Human Resource Management Director to face the union in the 1996 negotiations. Perhaps symbolically, his replacement has the title 'Executive Vice-President, Human Resources and Corporate Law'.

As we draw to a close, it makes sense to cite again the rather chilling, even if realistic, third epigraph at the beginning of this case study: 'We do not consider ourselves an ESOP company any more' – the comment, offered by a spokesman for the management, John McMahon, in March 1996 and quoted by *Business Week*.

If majority employee ownership is a necessary condition of being an 'ESOP company' then Mr McMahon's comment is simply true by definition – no less but equally no more. And yet ... it is surely not too much to suggest that in making this comment, Mr McMahon thought he was doing something more than simply utter a definitional truth. Surely what he was really saying was that top management had reverted to thinking about its employees and behaving towards its employees – and indeed their union – in the ways traditional across much of conventional capitalist America. Put more sharply, he was saying that management had reverted back to its pre-buy-out adversarial relationship with the union and with Weirton's blue collar workforce.

Given the post-1989 deterioration in management-labour

relationships which we have traced in some detail, it is not surprising that by early 1996 the top Weirton management was thinking in the way suggested by Mr McMahon's comment. On the evidence of its actions the leadership of the ISU had also reverted back to its time-honoured adversarial ways by 1996, and indeed well before. Nor should British readers be altogether surprised that this was so. There were several cases of 'reversions back to time-honoured adversarial relationships' in Britain's local bus industry following the end of majority employee ownership in the early and middle 1990s.

Whether the increasingly adversarial stance adopted by the ISU has helped or hindered its stated aims is also problematic. In his reported comments on the new 1994 labour agreement at Weirton, Mr Mark Glyptis, the ISU president, said in effect that the preservation of steel-making jobs at Weirton was at its heart. He explicitly mentioned the objective of seeking to preserve those jobs for the children of the present workforce. It is possible that that objective would be more readily attainable had it been possible for Weirton to remain at least majority-owned by the employees.

That is speculation. On the other hand, and despite the job cuts, what we know is that employee ownership was notably successful in preserving employment and incomes in West Virginia's panhandle and that it must at the very least be doubtful whether any of those jobs and those incomes could have been preserved under any arrangement of conventional capitalism. And such is the nature of the Weirton community that if Weirton Steel had gone down, more or less the whole town and its environs would have been on the dole. We also know that the labour relations problems became steadily worse at Weirton when majority employee ownership was surrendered.

21

Republic Engineered Steels Inc. (RESI)

We must get 'ownership' of profitability by everyone in our organisation. By structuring the company into appropriate profit centres, we will push control of, and responsibility for, financial results down into the organisation. *Russell Maier, President & C.E.O., Republic Engineered Steels Inc., February 1991*

The company's unique partnership with its employees and the USWA has greatly facilitated the company's ability to achieve cost savings and improve quality. *Prospectus for sale of 7m. shares, Republic Engineered Steels Inc, Common Stock, April 1995*

The 'unique partnership' referred to in the 1995 prospectus is in almost total abeyance. *Author's headline note following a visit to RESI, late 1997*

INTRODUCTORY OVERVIEW

What is now Republic Engineered Steels Inc. (RESI) was bought out by its then 5,000 plus workforce, under the joint leadership of the United Steelworkers of America (USWA) and its management, towards the end of 1989. The mechanism used to effect the purchase was the now familiar one of a leveraged Employee Stock Ownership Plan (ESOP). The seller was LTV Steel Company, the third largest integrated steel business in the US at the time of the buy-out, but from 1986 down to mid-1993 in Chapter 11 bankruptcy. What is now RESI was previously LTV's bar division.

Having survived the ferocious recession of the early 1990s, the employee-owned RESI raised $50m with a share offer and became quoted on America's NASDAQ exchange in 1995. All or most of the proceeds of the common stock sale were used to repurchase preferred stock from employees which could otherwise have become unmanageably expensive to redeem. Following the sale the proportion of the equity owned by employees fell to 59%.

In an earlier financing exercise, RESI had been reasonably

successful in securing new loans for vitally needed investment. The bulk of this credit was used to acquire and install a new, state of the art, cast-roll facility at a total cost of over $150m. After a predictable, and probably inescapable, bout of teething troubles, the facility began to justify itself by delivering significant cost reductions in 1997. On the other hand the advantage of those lower costs were more or less wiped out by lower product prices in RESI's increasingly competitive markets. When first offered for sale in 1995, shares in the common stock had been priced at $8.00. By May 1996 the price had fallen by 50% to around $4.00. By early November 1997 it had fallen further, in fact by more than 50% to just $1 9/16. Over almost the whole period of its employee ownership from late 1989 to the third quarter of 1997, the company's published accounts showed losses.

Nevertheless, for all or nearly all the thirty-one quarters starting from the buy-out in December 1989 and ending on 30 September 1997, RESI enjoyed a positive cash flow. That was because of a combination of ESOP tax reliefs and the surprisingly generous rules governing depreciation charges enjoyed by corporate America.

It is a racing certainty that without the ESOP buy-out the business would not have survived, not at least on the basis of uninterrupted operations. One of its main competitors, the bar division of Bethlehem Steel, was indeed liquidated during the recession of the early 1990s, even though it is also true that bar steel making was restarted on the same site but under different ownership in 1995. Moreover, despite its positive cash flow, and its new cast roll facility, RESI had precious little room for manoeuvre in the autumn of 1997 when this case study was finally revised.

Given the state of the balance sheet, additional borrowings were not really on the cards. On the other hand, all parties were agreed that a new bar mill was a necessary condition of medium-term survival. The resolution when it came was unexpected outside the inner circle of top management and union. As we shall see on pp. 428–9 the business was bought as a going concern in September 1998.

So what of the employee ownership at RESI? It goes without saying that the main achievement was to save the great majority of jobs taken over from LTV in 1989. There were roughly 5,000 jobs at the start. In the autumn of 1998 that number had fallen by about 1,000.

Along with the jobs go the incomes which they generated. Moreover, and unlike what happened at Weirton, RESI's workforce were *not* required to take any pay cuts as a condition of the buy-out deal. It is true that they were required to make an investment of a significant, even if not of a king size, dimension – of roughly $4,000 per head. On the other hand these investments were embodied in the employee preference shares which, as we have seen, were bought back, using the proceeds of the common stock sale, in 1995. They had earned an attractive rate of interest, admittedly in the form of additional shares and not of cash, in the years between.

Altogether it is impossible not to conclude that RESI's employees have done rather well, at least compared with any alternative realistically available to most of them. There cannot be many blue collar manufacturing jobs in the twin towns of Canton and Massillon in North East Ohio – where most of RESI's work is concentrated – which pay as well. As for the employment opportunities in the new fast food and other service industries the popular perception of their pay and conditions is well captured by calling them not jobs but *Mac*jobs.

But if the workforce has been the main beneficiary of the buy-out and the jobs and incomes it sustained, it is also fair to acknowledge that rank-and-file employees have made a real and measurable contribution to survival and one that has gone well beyond what happened before under LTV. The 'unique partnership' highlighted in the second epigraph from the April 1995 prospectus cannot reasonably be dismissed – or anyway could not have been so dismissed at the time – as just a case of sharepushers' rhetoric.

Management's calculations are that changes in working practices of a whole range of different kinds had yielded a cumulative $40m of savings in the period down to the end of 1994 and rather more than a further $20m down to the autumn of 1997. Total costs in 1996/7 were running at around $750m and falling because of the effects of the new cast roller. So an annual saving of $60m amounts to well over 5% of the cost base.

We shall look in some detail later on at the various schemes and programmes which seem to have played a major part in the achievement of these savings. But here, in summary, it is not too much to say that between about 1991 and 1995 RESI was widely regarded in these respects as exemplary for both its efforts and its results. I myself may have had a small part in spreading the company's reputation in this whole critical area of productivity improvement. I wrote and published a first case study in 1991 and updated it in 1994. The subtitle of the first was 'Struggling to Get onto the Same Side'. Of the second it was 'Progress in the Struggle to Get onto the Same Side'. But I must emphasise, especially in the light of what has since happened, that I was not alone in my judgement at the time: that something rather exceptional was going on at RESI, and that its key was an evolving new relationship between management and the United Steelworkers of America (USWA).

As some readers will know and as will become the centre of our attention later, that new relationship was in fact set in motion when the USWA leadership in Pittsburgh announced a bid for LTV's bar division in February 1989. The subsequent buy-out deal itself was then very much a joint project of USWA's leaders and the bar division's top management. Most eyecatching of all, in the mass vote on the deal by USWA's membership the union's top leadership aligned itself with management – against a strong minority of the presidents of its own locals – in calling for a 'yes' vote.

And yet ... it is sufficient to say, in line with the judgement expressed in the third epigraph, that in the autumn of 1997 nothing was apparently left of what I and others had previously seen as a most promising evolution in the relationship between management and and union. Perhaps that was partly due to changes in the top union leadership. Of the two men who had played the key roles in the 1989 buy-out, one, James Smith, was dead, the other, Lynn Williams, had retired. What was certain was that management and union had, in effect, snapped back into their old adversarial relationship.

However, despite that snap back, and even if it proves impossible to reverse, there is still much of interest and much to be learnt from a case study of RESI over its first eight ESOP years. For what may be called the international employee ownership community, the first five or six years of RESI's ESOP life are an object lesson in how to achieve significant reductions in cost and improvements in quality without cutting either pay or jobs. Starting from an actual set of ESOP arrangements which came as close as was realistically possible to establishing a form of management/union co-determination, the two 'sides' at RESI introduced some notably innovative and apparently effective joint programmes. The fact that all or most were in abeyance when I paid my last visit to Canton and Massillon does not destroy their logic or indeed completely undermine their value as examples of good practice.

For policy makers too, this RESI experience must surely merit attention. After all, the jobs were saved and a huge new investment project was successfully financed and implemented. It is regrettable that from about 1995 onwards the strains and pressures became such as to sweep away the fragile new co-operative relationship between management, the union and the blue collar workforce which people on both sides had struggled hard to build. On the other hand, and as the previous case study of Weirton Steel unambiguously confirms, it is possible for businesses which were initially saved by an ESOP to 'win through' and survive despite a prolonged snap back to their old adversarial mode in the relationships between management, the union, and the blue collar workforce.

Historical and Other Background, Products and Markets The plant, facilities, buildings and freeholds of the former bar division of LTV which were acquired by RESI in the employee buy-out of end-November 1989 are spread over five American states: Ohio, Michigan, Pennsylvania, Indiana and Connecticut. But the main facilities purchased (85% of the total) are concentrated in the twin towns of Canton and Massillon in eastern Ohio. Between the buy-out and the autumn of 1997, employee-owned RESI acquired two additional facilities, one in Indiana, the second in Maryland.

The company's head office is at Massillon together with a hot rolling mill and its main cold finishing (bright bar) facility. Canton is where the actual steel making takes place and is also the site for the company's alloy and other special bar manufacture. More than half of RESI's total workforce are employed in the town of Canton. There is a wire mill and smaller hot rolling mill in Chicago and that was still true after the closedown in early 1996 of the eight-inch bar mill at Canton. The facilities at the three remaining sites are on a smaller scale: namely those at Beaver Falls, Pennsylvania; Gary, Indiana; and Willimantic, Connecticut. They have cold drawing capacity but their rationale, especially in the case of Willimantic, is as much a commercial as a production one.

It is with the plants and facilities in the twin Ohio towns of Canton and Massillon, and their history, that we are chiefly concerned from now on. That is where the core business and its headquarters are located. Moreover these plants and facilities in

Canton and Massillon have been part of the same business since the 1920s. Together with a number of other more scattered steel works, they were welded at that time into a single business, Republic Steel, by the well-known Canadian industrialist Cyrus Eaton. But it is Republic's president and chief executive officer during the 1930s, Mr Tom Girdler, who should probably be given 'credit' for the strength of traditional union feelings and attitudes among elected local union officials in Canton and Massillon today. Girdler fought a long rearguard action against the recognition of the union in the 1930s and 1940s. There were two steelworkers among a number of fatal casualties when police opened fire on a crowd in Massillon in 1937. On the same day as many as twelve people were killed when the police opened fire on a memorial holiday crowd in Chicago. Because of Massillon's much smaller size, the impact of its two deaths may well have been greater than that of the twelve in Chicago.

Cyrus Eaton retired to his home at Pugwash in Nova Scotia in the 1950s; and went on to become improbably involved in campaigns for nuclear disarmament. Republic Steel prospered throughout the 1950s and 1960s – and on indeed into the early 1970s. These were years of sustained growth for the American steel industry and ones during which the USWA, with only a short pause for breath during a long strike in 1959, pushed wages and conditions up to around the highest levels in US manufacturing. Republic Steel was then the industry's third largest undertaking – after US Steel and Bethlehem. When the industry's shipments reached their peak of 109.5m tons in 1973, Republic Steel's production was over 10m tons. At that time, as for most of the 1950s and 1960s, over 50% of its output consisted of steel bar. At RESI today the entire production is steel bar. Over 50% of RESI's bar output, like Republic's before it, goes to the automotive industry.

Bar production remained profitable at Republic without the need for much new investment down to the early 1980s. Most of the company's new investment during this period went into its flat rolling activities.

From the early 1980s, competitive conditions became progressively tougher. US steel imports, whether in the form of steel itself, or embodied in finished goods like motor cars, steadily increased. Meanwhile, partly because of high oil prices, partly for other reasons, the American economy was failing to achieve the high growth rates of the first thirty-odd postwar years. US vehicle production reached its all time peak of 12.8m units later than might be expected, in 1978. The figure for 1990 was 9.9m vehicles.

From the early 1980s too, America's large integrated steel businesses began to be confronted with the growth of new so-called mini-mills. Partly because they rely entirely on recycled raw materials, these typically enjoy a considerable advantage in their overhead and manufacturing costs, and more often than not employ non-union labour. The mini-mill competition was particularly strong at the bottom end of the steel bar spectrum, namely in reinforcing bars for concrete, known as 'rebars'.

It was this combination of depressed demand and fierce competition which lay behind the merger of Republic Steel with another integrated producer, Jones & Laughlin, the steel subsidiary of the LTV conglomerate, in June of 1984; the offspring was LTV Steel. At least indirectly, these conditions also lay behind LTV's 1986 decision to seek protection from its creditors under Chapter 11 of the US bankruptcy law. It was also these conditions which set USWA on the road to qualified support for employee ownership.

The immediate cause of LTV's move into Chapter 11 seems to have been its inability to meet ballooning retirement pension liabilities to former employees. Those arose precisely because the company had been forced to close plants in the face of fiercely difficult business conditions.

Some time after the company's move into Chapter 11 in 1986, the LTV management decided to sell off its bar division and began taking steps to bring it into profit as a precondition for a sale. The division losses reached an all time high of $85m in 1986. By 1988 when it was offered for sale, the business had turned around and achieved a modest profit of $25m. Apart from plant closures and some improvement in market conditions, sales and administrative functions were streamlined, and more emphasis was put on the manufacture of special quality bar products.

Mr Maier, the chief executive of the bar division and later of RESI, is a Massillon man. His father was a barber in the town and he himself was born and went to school there. In 1985, shortly after his appointment as head of the bar division, Mr Maier was presciently asked by a local journalist whether he would ever consider being involved, through the mechanism of an ESOP, in a leveraged employee buy-out of the business. His reply was a terse but emphatic negative.

Yet, following the buy-out, Mr Maier's commitment to the whole employee ownership project was little short of total, at least in the early years. He saw it then as the key to RESI's success and survival. The factors which changed his mind must have included the unattractiveness of any possible alternative. He must also have been influenced by the tax advantages which flow from the use of an ESOP.

In the early autumn of 1988, when it had already become clear that its bar division was working at a profit, LTV invited bidders to come forward. It hoped for an offer from one of America's established steel businesses. There were polite inquiries, even plant visits by steel men, but there was no offer, either domestic or foreign.

The deadline for bids was 16 February 1989. By the evening of 15 February there were in fact just two qualified bids but both were essentially from financiers with no real experience of steel making. However, a third if necessarily conditional bid came forward on 16 February. Its source was the New York merchant bank, Lazard Frères. The principal on behalf of which the bank was acting was, of course, the United Steelworkers of America (USWA). The bid did not come out of the blue. Lazard Frères had carried out an extensive feasibility study on behalf of USWA and developed a business plan. An environmental study had established in advance the liabilities for making good past acts of pollution which the successor company would have to assume. Moreover, the USWA deal had special attractions for LTV. USWA proposed that in return for ownership, employees would agree to accept only '75% of the present value' of shut-down benefits otherwise due to them from LTV; if any other bid were to be accepted, USWA would insist on 100%.

The ESOP Deal: Preconditions, Finance, Logic and Politics The provisional bid for what was still then the bar division of LTV Steel, which came in, via Lazard Frères in New York, from the United Steelworkers just in time to meet the deadline of 16 February 1989, may or may not have been anticipated by LTV's top managers. But though the financial package which turned out to be needed was substantially larger than anything with which the union had previously been associated, and though this may have been the first case of an USWA ESOP buy-out initiative, as opposed to a response to a distress call, the bid was not itself a new policy departure for the union. As we shall see when we come on to discuss union policy in the last of this group of three case studies, a conditionally positive policy towards ESOP buy-outs was already in place in the union's head office in Pittsburgh. The union's policy on these buy-outs had evolved to the point that it was prepared to offer its support provided two main conditions could be met:

– the actual ESOP had to be structured in such a way as to avoid various 'flaws' which had been identified as being inimical to USWA members' interests and which we will have to look at in some detail in the union case study;

– any deal would need to be grounded in a feasibility study and business plan which met the highest professional standards.

It goes without saying that the involvement of the New York investment bank Lazard Frères offered a reasonable assurance to the USWA leadership that the second of its two conditions would be met. Indeed it seems likely that, from discussions which must have been going on with the union, the bank staff already had a fairly good idea of what the deal might look like. Otherwise it is hard to see how the necessary work and the necessary negotiations could have been started and finished – as they were – for the deal to be completed less than ten months later, by the end of November.

Including the costs of the transaction itself, the deal which was completed at the end of November involved total borrowing and total spending of some $280m. Easily the largest source of the borrowing was a $190m medium term loan from the Bank of Boston. As was noted earlier, the 5,000-odd employees of the newly formed RESI contributed $4,000 each in one way or another – for a total of some $20m. The balance of the money was put in by the seller, that is by LTV, essentially as a set of credits but with the outside possibility – which never in fact materialised – that up to 50% might eventually be converted into equity.

These dry numbers become a little more real when we look at how the money was spent. More than two thirds, in fact $162m, was used to buy what the Americans call the 'inventory', that is stocks of raw materials and of finished and semi-finished goods. These were purchased at their so-called fair market value. On the other hand the price of $20m paid for the fixed capital of the business – that is for its freeholds, buildings, plant and equipment – was deeply discounted compared with its value in LTV's books, and indeed compared with its so-called fair market value. We shall look at the logic of that discount in a moment. For the rest, and aside from the $10m costs of the transaction itself, virtually the whole of the balance was injected into RESI as the working capital needed to get it started in business on its own account.

In the pro-forma balance sheet with which RESI started its life the 'fair market value' of the fixed capital, which it had bought for just $20m, is put more than seven times higher – precisely, at $148.6m. On the other hand and as at least a partial explanation of the difference between the two numbers, we need also to note from the same balance sheet two numbers on the liabilities side: a liability of $74.6m which RESI assumed for post-retirement benefits and a second liability of $27.1m in respect of prospective environmental clean-up costs. As for the balance between what RESI paid for the fixed capital and its 'fair market value', that can only reflect a fairly determined interest on the part of LTV, the seller, in clinching the deal.

Two final and essentially footnote points about the deal help to explain the degree of that interest. One reflects a concession by USWA. Well in advance of the deal's completion, the union made it clear that if the new employee-owned RESI were indeed the successful buyer then it would forgo on its members' behalf 25% of the benefits to which in those circumstances they would have been entitled. But the union also made clear at the same time that this concession would not be on offer if LTV was to sell the business to a 'third party'.

So LTV had that specific interest in reaching a deal with RESI. Moreover, it also showed the general strength of that interest that it offered a special sweetener to the buyers in the last few months before the deal's completion. This was a time when warning bells about the coming recession were starting to sound more and more loudly. In response to a demand from the buyers that it should itself share in the recession risks, LTV in effect adjusted the numbers by some tens of millions of dollars in the buyer's favour. It was on the basis of that adjustment that the deal eventually went through.

In line with normal practice the buy-out deal, if it was going to be implemented, needed the support in a ballot of a majority of USWA's membership employed in LTV's bar division. Concurrently with their approval or otherwise of the ESOP deal, the union's membership would at the same time give their verdict on a prospective labour agreement between RESI's future management and the union. About the latter it is enough to say here that it provided for a \$1.00 increase in the hourly rates of the blue collar workforce. Other, and in many ways more interesting, provisions in that labour agreement are held over for later discussion.

When it eventually happened, the union members' vote was exceptional and striking in at least three different ways:

– The union's top national leaders and its district leaders called for a 'yes' vote as did the future top management at RESI.

– Four out of nine presidents of USWA Locals, representing a majority of its 4,000-odd members, called for a 'no' vote.

– The ESOP deal and the associated labour agreement was approved by a comfortable 62% of USWA's membership.

Some will doubtless want to ask whether the deal was reasonable and fair. Given the weaknesses in the bargaining position of both sides, that question seems to me to be beside the point, as well as intrinsically unanswerable. The three key facts that seem to me to be worth holding on to are:

– That a comfortable majority of those most effected by the decision, RESI's blue collar workforce, voted in favour.

– That a much larger majority of their jobs and the associated incomes were still in existence all of eight years later.

– The chances that more than a tiny minority of that blue collar workforce could have found jobs with similar rates of pay and conditions elsewhere, had LTV's bar division been simply closed down, are virtually zero.

The Post-Buy-Out Business Record: End 1989 to Mid-1993 Essentially because of the recession in its main markets, the first three employee-owned years at Republic Engineered Steels were unusually tough ones. They were all difficult but the middle calendar year, 1991, was especially so. In the fourth year, however, market conditions substantially improved and by the end of 1993 shipments of steel were taking place at an annual rate of around one million tons, or at roughly their pre-recession levels, albeit at lower prices. The company's success in weathering the recession, taken together with the improved conditions of 1993, provide the background for two most notable events in that year: a new labour agreement with the United Steelworkers of America (USWA) which was signed in August, and a major new \$200 financing exercise which was completed in December. We will postpone the discussion of those two key events of 1993 until later. But here we should already flag the important twin claims of top management at the time of the successful refinancing offer – that RESI had emerged from the recession as America's market leader in the production of special bar quality (SBQ) steel, and with an increased market share.

In the the period of just over three years to the end of 1992, the principal achievement of the newly employee-owned RESI was to have survived without having made any of its blue collar workforce redundant. Not all its established competitors in the bar-making sector of America's steel industry can make the same claim. As noted earlier, there was one major casualty of the recession. Bethlehem Steel, the second largest integrated steel business in the US, shut down the whole of its bar-making division – with annual capacity approximately equal to RESI's – in 1991. There was also a second, if lesser, casualty among America's producers of bar steel during this period: the Western Steel Group stopped trading. Part of its business was in fact acquired by the employee-owned RESI in the summer of 1993.

The achievement of survival and the avoidance of blue collar workforce redundancy are not in doubt. Nor, I think, is the main explanation for that success. It was achieved above all by a set of supply side response measures to what were rapidly deteriorating conditions in the market. In effect these measures resulted in significant cost reductions between the calendar years 1991 and 1992. Put differently, they made it possible between those two years to lower the level of production at which the company could break even. We shall look at the numbers shortly. But we should note already that the achievement of reducing the break even point was at least partially frustrated by a further reduction in prices.

Still, as an improvement in market conditions which had started in 1992 strengthened, in early 1993 RESI was apparently well positioned to take advantage of the upturn.

Here we need to say something about the extent and pattern of the recession and the degree of RESI's success in responding to it. The buy-out took place in November 1989. In the twelve months of that year the total sales of the business were rather less than 1 million tons by weight; and worth approximately $800 million by value. As will be seen in the worst year of the recession, 1991, the tonnage figure was down by approximately 25% and the price by substantially more.

RESI Sales in Tonnage and in Dollars: 1990 to 1992

Year	Tons	$ooo
1990	909,816	642,431
1991	734,725	538,288
1992	853,285	594,882

1990, the first year of both employee ownership and recession, was mainly spent preparing the structural and other changes needed in the light of these worsening conditions. But some white collar redundancies were imposed early in 1990; and work went ahead with the implementation of a number of small investment projects designed either to improve quality or reduce cost. Still, 1990 was basically a year of preparation. The effects of the recession over the period from the buy-out to the end of 1990, though undoubtedly serious, could to some extent be contained. For example, the balance sheet at the end of 1990 showed accumulated negative retained earnings of no more than $13m over the period since the buy-out. Over the same period it showed charges for depreciation of approximately the same amount. For that reason and because its profit and loss account included other non-cash items – payments to the ESOP, for example, and provisions to cover post-retirement health care – the cash flow in 1990 was significantly positive. So indeed it was, for these same reasons and because of a phased run-down of stocks, throughout the recession years.

As 1990 was the year of preparation, so 1991 was largely spent implementing and making fully operational the structural and other changes which began to be prepared in 1990. In 1992 they started to deliver specific benefits. The most readily measurable and important of these were reductions in the direct costs of producing a ton of finished steel products, as between 1992 and 1991. The actual numbers are worth having on the record.

Direct Costs of Production: 1991 & 1992: Average per ton

1991	$678
1992	$628

There were also useful reductions between the two years in the indirect costs of production, i.e. in the administrative overheads and in the costs of selling. On the other hand, these improvements in performance were substantially offset by a fall in prices.

Selling Prices: 1991 & 1992: Average per ton

1991	$733
1992	$697

So, on the side of demand, the main story of RESI's first three years is one of recession, with the volume of demand – but not the level of price – starting to improve in 1992. What we must turn to next is the supply side response of the newly employee-owned business to these conditions. It is essentially because of this response that the first three years of employee ownership at RESI are worth studying.

The Supply Side Response to the Recession A good starting point for the discussion is the original labour agreement signed by the union and RESI's prospective top management – and then approved in a vote by the company's blue collar workforce – in the run-up to the finalising of the ESOP deal in the autumn of 1989. Article one of that labour agreement broke rather new ground. In effect both parties to it – the union and the management – committed themselves to work towards a new, less adversarial and more co-operative relationship. What is more there is an explicit acknowledgement in the text of the article that 'changes in attitudes cannot come about by written words but result from action and deeds'.

The article went on to lay down a framework within which these new relationships could be developed; and to commit the two parties to the joint appointment of one or more consultants to help the whole process along. It was foreseen that the new framework and new process would, in the words of the agreement, 'provide for employee involvement and an increased sphere of input and responsibility for all employees, enabling them to perform with limited or, in some cases, no supervision'. It is worth quoting two further passages from the opening article of this new agreement. First, there is an explicit affirmation in favour of 'a co-operative and non-autocratic style of management'. Second, the article looks forward more specifically to the development of a 'program designed to provide continuing improvement in all aspects of the business as well as substantial improvement in relationships'.

Against this background, it is reasonable to claim that an impressive start was made, through a series of supply side measures,

in implementing the commitments contained in article one of the
new labour agreement in the period which followed it. The new
labour agreement of autumn 1989 provided that it would itself
run for three and a half years; and would then be succeeded by a
second agreement, reached if necessary by compulsory arbitration,
and running for the same length of time. As already noted, a second
labour agreement was signed in August 1993.

The most important of the early successes were, no doubt, the
cost reductions which we have already noted: achieved without any
blue collar redundancies and quite largely as a result of changes in
working practices. Possible cost savings were first identified, then
implemented. An initial target of $50m of cost savings was set
towards the end of 1990. Later the target was increased to $80
million. By the end of 1992 the actual savings achieved totalled
somewhat over $40m.

A key individual, at least in the earlier stages of this cost reduction process, was a consultant, Dr Walton Sharp, appointed jointly
by the union and the management. Such an appointment had been
foreshadowed in article one of the 1989 labour agreement. It was
made in 1990. Dr Sharp had been well known to the head office of
USWA for a number of years. The focus of his work at RESI was as
much to do with quality as with cost reduction.

The success of the cost reduction and quality improvement
programmes, through which RESI managed to survive the recession, can be sensibly linked to two rather different sets of structural
changes which date from 1990. The more conventional was the
reorganisation of the undertaking into four separate and financially
responsible businesses. The changes were reported in *American
Metal Market*, the US steel industry's newspaper, on 21 February
1990:

> Under the restructuring . . . there will be four divisions respon-
> sible for their own financial performance: the steel division
> which will melt and produce semi-finished products; the Roll-
> ing division, which will produce hot rolled bars; the cold
> finished division, which will produce cold rolled bars and the
> Specialty Steel Group, which will produce all stainless, alloy,
> tool steels and vacuum remelt grades.

Those who follow employee ownership closely will know that

reorganisations of this kind have featured elsewhere on both sides of the Atlantic – at the Polaroid Corporation for example and at the Baxi Partnership. Wherever they occur, they seem to have the same essentially two-pronged objective: to spread and sharpen financial responsibility or, in the words of the epigraph, '[to] get "ownership" of profitability by everyone in our organisation'; and second to focus the attention of the different parts of the whole organisation on their own particular customers. The 'customers', in this sense, may be inside or outside the larger organisation. For example, in this case the customers of the new steel division are almost all inside. About restructurings of this kind I should only add that they are not peculiar to employee-owned businesses.

The second restructuring at RESI which facilitated the cost saving and quality improvement programmes is certainly less common in conventional businesses. In a general way it is probably best understood as an effort to introduce arrangements of 'co-determination' at all levels in the organisation. We noted at the outset that the board of directors in the new post-buy-out business is co-determinational in character; with a group of independents holding the balance between equal numbers of union and management appointees. The aim of this second restructuring was to introduce similarly co-determinational arrangements, but without the independents, at all the levels of the organisation down to the work crew and its foreman at the bottom. It is this second restructuring which best reflects the aims of article one in the 1989 labour agreement. It may well also have been the most important precondition of the cost savings and quality improvements that had been achieved to the end of 1993.

What was developed was an integrated system of co-determinational meetings. At the top, more precisely at the top level below the board of directors, was a monthly corporate meeting of senior management on one side, and the elected presidents of the various union 'locals' on the other side. At the next level down, in RESI's individual plants, these joint management and union meetings took place more frequently, either weekly or fortnightly. Finally, at the level of actual production, where work is organised on the basis of crews, weekly meetings were instituted. The system allowed for, and to some extent ensured, a two-way flow of information. A downward flow was made possible by the requirement that management must present comprehensive reports at these meetings: reports covering past performance, current problems, and prospects. It seems that there was no real doubt in its early years about the reality of this new information-sharing with the union.

In the opposite direction the new system also facilitated the flow of information – from the bottom up. This second flow was what enabled 'continuous improvement' to happen. Proposals for changes in practice – to cut costs and/or to improve quality – flowed upwards from the crew meetings, and were given fast-lane treatment from the decision-making bodies higher up. There were two linked hypotheses behind these arrangements. The first is that there is almost unlimited scope for improving performance, above all at the level of the work place where actual production happens. The second and linked hypothesis is that the knowledge which will unlock the potential improvements is mainly in the heads of the production work crews. One of the key functions of the new weekly crew meetings was to provide a forum in which ideas for improvement could surface.

The final supply side response at RESI to a combination of the recession and its employee ownership was in fact specific to the latter. With some financial help from the Ohio State Government the company commissioned the preparation of a mass programme of 'tutorials', devoted to employee ownership in general and its own employee-owned business activities in particular. Initially the programme had a life span of two and a half years. That was later extended.

The body commissioned to prepare the subject matter for these tutorials was the North East Ohio Centre for Employee Ownership, a body affiliated to Kent State University. Sessions were planned to last for an hour and take place in company time. For most of its first three years attendance was compulsory. That rule was relaxed early in 1993.

An indication of the subject matter is given by the content of some of the earlier sessions. After an overview of the whole project in session one, the programme went on to cover RESI's two distinct Employee Stock Ownership Plans – its common stock plan and its preferred stock plan in sessions two and three. The aim of the fourth session was to put over an understanding of what Americans call the company's 'income statement': what in Britain is the 'profit and loss account'. Subsequent sessions typically focused on business issues which RESI had currently been facing. The frequency of the sessions declined somewhat at the beginning of 1992. (They were, of course, among the casualties of the snap back in 1996/7 of the relationship between union and management into their old adversarial mode.)

But it is still worth pinpointing what was perhaps the most radical feature of this exemplary even if non-permanent programme. Though people at the North East Ohio Centre for Employee Ownership were responsible for proposing the content of sessions to a joint top management and union group at RESI; and though they were also responsible for preparing the material, and indeed for much else besides, people from the centre did not themselves undertake the teaching work. The actual teachers were drawn from the ranks of RESI's employee owners. Individual sessions were handled by teams of two. When they peaked there were twenty-five of these teams; and so far as possible each was composed of one blue collar and one white collar employee owner. One of the centre's most important responsibilities, under its contract, was to train these pairs of teachers over a rather long induction course at the beginning and later in advance of each session.

In many ways this was a heroic undertaking, both in its concept and in its execution. The challenge was to impart to a student body made up largely of blue collar employees a measure of business literacy in general and of employee ownership literacy in particular. Even though it has not survived, it may well offer a valuable model to other employee-owned companies in the future. No doubt it would be wrong to expect a really high capacity for developing a good understanding of business and finance in the blue collar workforce of a steel company in today's America. On the other hand what can be said with a fair degree of certainty is that, in the absence of employee ownership, the task of imparting a measure of business literacy would be immeasurably more difficult.

Such then were the main components of RESI's supply side response to a combination of its new ownership arrangements on the one hand and the recession of the three years starting 1990 on the other. An informed judgement, if made in 1993, would probably have concluded that as between the RESI management and the union's international and regional leadership the traditional mistrust had been significantly reduced, though no more than that. As for the relationships between management and the local union leadership, changes for the better were probably not all that great.

As subsequent events made clear, it was all too easy in 1993 to exaggerate the extent to which mistrust at RESI had been reduced and, conversely, the extent to which all – that is management, the union and the shop floor – had come to be working on the same side within the framework of the new employee-ownership arrangements. Even before the big snap back in the relationships in 1996 and 1997 there was recurrent evidence of enduring mistrust. The mistrust was between top management and all other parties – top union, local union and shop floor – and between the workforce and the union leadership.

There was a striking episode in the autumn of 1991 which illustrates the last point. With the support of the union's national leadership, the presidents of the union locals at RESI recommended acceptance by the membership of a provisional agreement with the management about the linked issues of employment security and flexible working. On offer from the management side was a deal under which medium-term employment security would be traded for an undertaking to work flexibly by the union membership. Despite the fact that the proposal enjoyed their union's backing at both local and national levels, it was given the thumbs down by a significant margin in a membership vote. Moreover, though, as we shall see, a conditional deal involving greater employment security on one side and flexible working practice on the other was one of the most consequential and innovative provisions of the new labour agreement signed in August 1993, the conditions for implementing it were never in fact satisfied.

There were, it is true, some notable examples of co-operation. There were also notable examples of the opposite. Among the former my own favourite is a rather specific agreement between one of the union locals and the management reached in the summer of 1991. It was to the effect that every single job in the business, management as well as shop floor jobs, should be studied by pairs of assessors, one each chosen by the management and the union. The task of the assessors was to distinguish between those jobs which clearly added value and those which did not. The agreement is eye-catching for a number of reasons, not least because it shows a readiness by management to open up management jobs to the scrutiny of the union. It may also be regarded as a kind of trailer for a set of most significant 'functional analysis' provisions which figured in the second labour agreement of August 1993.

If we stand back for a moment and reflect about the state of industrial relations at RESI from the buy-out onwards, the sensible reaction is not to be surprised by it. Given the mix of the past history and the new ownership arrangements, the relationships were bound to be problematic. The achievement of those striking cost savings in 1992 tells us, to be sure, that there was some progress towards the goal of shop floor and management working together. Yet no one in either union or management would ever have claimed that the attainment of that goal was other than a long way off. To remind ourselves of what is at least theoretically possible in that direction, it is worth quoting some remarks of an ordinary worker in one of the surviving employee-owned plywood co-operatives in the US. The date is the early 1980s. The speaker is contrasting his position in the co-operative with what it was when he was working for a conventional capitalist business:

> It is altogether different. It took me a good time to get used to this because when I worked over there, there was a union and you did your job and you didn't go out and do something else. Here you get in and do anything to help . . . Everyone pitches in and helps. . . . The people stick together, that's the reason that we've gone so far and production is so high, 'cause everybody works together. [*Worker Co-operatives in America,* edited by Robert Jackal and Henry M. Levin.]

It is not a criticism, it is simply factual reporting, to say that the feelings which the typical RESI employee has for his or her company are profoundly different from those for his plywood co-operative of the man just quoted. Yet the so-called 'bottom line realities' are surely more or less identical. For in both cases people are working for themselves in the precise sense that they, and not outsiders, are the beneficiaries of any extra effort which is successfully put in. The difference between RESI and the co-operative is not the result of differences in their respective financial workings. It lies mainly in the different class character of their respective leaderships and in the enduring survival of class conflict. This particular source of difficulty and conflict was most persuasively delineated by the late Mr James Smith shortly before his most untimely death early in 1995. Before retiring at the end of 1993 he had been an assistant to successive international presidents of the steelworkers' union and the chief player in the evolution of its employee ownership policies. We shall quote from his writing at the end of the discussion of the second labour agreement of August 1993. He also figures prominently in the study of employee ownership and unions.

But here I must return to the fundamental point. It is that the evidence of enduring conflict at RESI, between union, management and shop floor, should occasion no surprise. Nor is it a criticism of what happened at RESI from the time of the buy-out onwards. The same is true in many, even most, employee-owned companies where there are also strong union traditions, and it is true on both sides of the Atlantic.

We will come on in a moment to 1993, the fourth employee-ownership year at RESI. But here, if only to provide a statistical foundation for RESI's early employee ownership record, it makes sense to put some of the main numbers side by side.

RESI: 28 November 1989 to 30 September 1993

	89/90[1]	90/91[2]	91/92[2]	92/93[2]	93 3rd Qtr
Sales ($000)	379,061	581,665	566,141	646,162	174,010
Tons shipped	534,054	807,473	795,374	935,792	254,990
Profit (loss) ($000)	4,002	(33,004)	(8,389)	(7,368)	(12,386)
Cash flow ($000)	n.a.	30,300	7,500	56,000	4,100

1 Period from buy-out (28 November 89) to 30 June 1990
2 Years to June 30

It is worth highlighting from the above statistical table that notwithstanding the fact that the business was showing losses from the years to end June 1991 onwards, its cash flow was positive throughout this period. That, as we have seen, was made possible partly by non-cash expenditures that figured in the profit and loss account – depreciation, non-cash ESOP expenditures and post-retirement benefit expenditures – and partly, at least during the two years to end June 1992, by a run-down of stocks.

It is also worth highlighting the figure of tons shipped in the third quarter of 1993: over a quarter of a million. In other words by the end of 1993 the business was operating at an annual rate of around one million tons – or roughly at its pre-recession and capacity levels. Given the cost reduction and quality improvements achieved since the buy-out, RESI was therefore well placed to take advantage of this upturn. Those favourable conditions supply the background to two events of 1993 which we have already flagged: the raising of new finance and the new labour agreement. But before turning to each of those in turn, a brief word is in order about the business objectives being set for the RESI by its top management in early 1994; that is in the wake of the successful new financing exercise and of the new labour agreement.

For a business in which the main activity is the production of SBQ – that is special bar quality – hot-rolled and cold-finished steel, and which also produces speciality steels, the central objectives set for RESI by its top managers at the end of 1993 are obvious enough. As set out in the prospectus associated with the raising of new finance in December 1993, the aim is clear: 'Republic's strategic objective is to be the leading domestic innovator and producer of SBQ steel and specialty steels.' The prospectus goes on to spell out the means: 'To achieve this objective Republic concentrates its resources on improving its steel production processes and metallurgical expertise, while continuing to reduce manufacturing costs.'

Both RESI's top management in early 1994 and the prospectus document of December 1993 confidently claimed that significant results towards the objectives had already been achieved in the early post-buy-out years, especially in relation to productivity and quality improvements. Top management made the further claim that by virtue of having significantly increased its market share during the recession, RESI was in fact already America's leading producer of hot-rolled SBQ steel, and that it was not far from being the top producer of cold-finished bars. In the first of those activities its precise objective, therefore, was to hold onto its top position; in the second it was to move to the top. As for its position in relation to the production of speciality steels, top management acknowledged in early 1994 that RESI was some way behind the product leaders. It was examining ways of catching up.

The 1993 Labour Agreement Both when it was concluded and for some time afterwards – at least down to the early autumn of 1995

– the new 1993 labour agreement between RESI and the United Steelworkers was widely acclaimed both for its good sense and for a number of strikingly innovative features. That needs to be remembered notwithstanding the very different judgements which were being expressed about it when I visited the business in the autumn of 1997. For example it was then forcefully criticised by Mr Russell Maier, the chief executive, president, and company chairman, as having given too much away to the union's members. More telling than this verbal judgement was an action taken by the company some months before, on 19 May. RESI had then filed an appeal in the Northern Ohio District Court challenging a decision reached by a process of mandatory arbitration which had itself been provided for in the original 1993 labour agreement. The details of the challenge need not concern us. Its grounds were that the arbitrator's rulings had ignored criteria which they had been required to follow. For our purposes here it is enough to assert that the action of the company in mounting this challenge was manifest evidence that its relationship with the steelworkers' union had broken down. I shall touch on this point once again briefly at the end.

But despite what happened later, and even if its most innovative provisions never reached the point of serious application, this 1993 labour agreement is well worth an extended discussion. Apart from anything else, future employee-owned companies may well find it makes sense to negotiate similar agreements with labour.

What seemed, even if quite wrongly, at the time likely to become the most consequential of this new labour agreement's provisions – as they were unquestionably the most innovative – were given the somewhat opaque heading of 'The Functional Analysis Provisions'. That phrase was then clarified and made more specific as 'work restructuring by local agreement'. In the text of the agreement, the relevant background – in the shape of 'understandings between the management and the union in the run up to the buy-out' – is first rehearsed:

When we launched our company in 1989, the Company and the Union agreed that RESI would need to reduce its work force by attrition to survive and thrive over our first seven years. Specifically we predicted that approximately 4% of the bargaining unit would leave our ranks each year, we

forecasted that our first seven years would see a 28%
workforce reduction, and we vowed to make every reasonable
effort to avoid new hiring over the seven year period – to
translate attrition into steady productivity gain. By a substantial margin, RESI Steelworkers in 1989 supported this approach. Since then, our numerical estimates of workforce
changes have proven roughly accurate: in the first three years
of Company operations, for example, our forces did in fact
reduce by approximately 12% (or 4% per year).

Essentially, the functional analysis provisions of the 1993 labour
agreement grew out of, and built upon, that earlier experience.
What they establish, and call functional analysis, is, to quote again
from the text of the agreement, 'a process by which the Company
and the Union will look carefully at work processes and practices to
find opportunities for reducing costs'.

It may be helpful to recall some further important pieces of background. To begin with, we need to remind ourselves of the cost
saving programme entitled 'Target 80' to which the company and
the union committed themselves in 1990. As we have seen, that
eventually resulted in annual savings not of the targeted $80m, but
of over $40m. Second, we need to remind ourselves of the attempt
made by management in 1991, and supported by the elected union
officials, to persuade RESI's blue collar workforce to agree to 'work
flexibly', in exchange for employment security, over the life of the
labour agreement. As we have seen, that proposal was rejected by
the union membership in a referendum.

Against that background, the functional analysis provisions of
the 1993 labour agreement can best be understood as an agreed
method of extending the earlier cost saving programme into the
future. Moreover these provisions were linked to a prospective flexible working and employment security deal of the kind rejected by
the workforce in the earlier referendum. Fundamentally, the deal
negotiated in the 1993 labour agreement was that, once a first phase
of functional analysis had been successfully completed and implemented in RESI's main plant in Canton, and the resulting costs
savings achieved, the blue collar workforce would enjoy virtually
complete employment security for the balance of the agreement's
duration. In return for that employment security the union member was committed, under the new agreement, to working very

flexibly indeed, including, for example, the undertaking of 'community work' if nothing else was available.

All this, it may be acknowledged, looked most striking on paper. But the hard facts are that a first phase of functional analysis was never in fact completed and implemented in Canton's steel-making plant. So what was supposed to follow never actually happened.

Nevertheless, there were further important features in the 1993 labour agreement which deserve to be put on record. For the union side, the one of which its leaders were probably proudest was an arrangement under which their members enjoyed what amounted to a systematic prepayment on the projected cost savings – before ever the latter have been achieved. Thus the agreement included an extra $1 per hour precisely in the shape of such a prepayment or advance. On the other hand, in an elegant piece of bargaining counterpoint, pending the achievement of the necessary cost savings, this extra $1 was paid only for hours actually worked: it was not 'consolidated' into the basic wage and so there was no change in the associated overtime, holiday pay, or pay for the purposes of calculating pension entitlements.

The hourly $1 prepayment on anticipated savings was linked, in the 1993 labour agreement, to annual cost reductions of $20m. The arithmetic suggests that the benefits of the savings, when achieved, would be split roughly 50:50 between labour and the company. We should also note that this same arrangement, with a prepayment and with the prospective savings' benefits split roughly 50:50, was extended under the agreement to cover a total new target of $60m of cost reductions. There was no more than a marginal adjustment of detail in the later stages. After the savings of $20m associated with the first $1 prepayment had been achieved, subsequent steps were to be in smaller units: viz 25 cents of prepayment and $5m of cost reductions. In fact by the autumn of 1997 the total of the cost savings that had been achieved, though more than $20m, was not that much more.

The cost reduction programme was to be mainly achieved, to repeat, by the functional analysis process which we will come on to look at in a moment. There was, too, the conditional link with an employment guarantee.

The guarantee was defined as 'the opportunity to work a full 40-hour week (including hours paid but not worked)'. Always given the condition that the first Canton plant phase of the functional analysis had been actually applied, the guarantee extended for the entire prospective six-year life of the relevant parts of the guarantee and were then subject to only minimal exceptions. Essentially it would cease to apply if either there was a union/management agreement to that effect or in the event of a pre-specified 'disaster'.

Like the no-layoff guarantee, the provisions relating to flexible working may well be treated as models of their kind even if they have never come into effect. At least in part they are worth quoting from the text:

> ... at a time when an employee would otherwise be laid off, he or she will be assigned to an Employment Security 'Pool' for alternative job assignment. Based on seniority and consistent with employee skills and capabilities, assignments from the Pool may be to *traditional* assignments ... or *non-traditional* assignments such as:
> Quality Teams
> Statistical Process Quality Control
> Training and Retraining
> Customer Service Agents
> Community Work Assignments
> Functional Analysis Teams

We now come on to the functional analysis process itself, the process at the heart of the cost reduction project; indeed, it may be plausibly argued, of the new labour agreement. Having posed and answered the question of what this functional analysis *is*, the new 1993 labour agreement goes on to say that it involves the following:

> As each department participates in it, Company and Union representatives (aided by the employees from the units involved) assemble a joint Functional Analysis Team. That team will look closely at all phases of department activities, that is, what the department does, what it is supposed to do, who does what, when and where and how work might be performed more efficiently. With no preconceived notions, and aided by the variety of inducements and protections described below, the Functional Analysis Team takes an honest and exacting look at such things as materials handling and usage; work flow and processes; job duties; manning levels; trade and craft lines etc.

As the process unfolds, Company and Union representatives must agree on any changes in order for them to take effect. The goal of the process is *to wring waste, duplication and unnecessary effort out of operations* [emphasis added]. To accomplish this, the local parties may agree upon changes that involve the following: the usage of materials; equipment revisions; changes in work flow; scheduling; changes in the numbers or requirements of jobs (including, if Functional Analysis shows it is needed, the addition of a job); craft combinations; self-directed work-teams; pay for knowledge systems; job combinations etc.

Early in 1994 work preparing the ground for the effective launching of functional analysis teams on RESI's big steel-making site in Canton was well under way. Already 'seven steps of functional analysis' had been identified and these too deserve to put on record.
They relate to particular units of activity in the work place and they are:
– Develop Process Map Flow Chart
– Identify Process Functions
– Identify Waste in the Process
– Brainstorm for Process Improvements
– [Bring Forward] Problem Solving Ideas and Evaluate
  Solutions
– Review for 'Fitness' (i.e. 'Beware! Proceed with Caution')
  and Develop . . . Action Plan
– Implement Solution and Monitor Process for Results
To conclude this discussion of the functional analysis process which is described in the 1993 labour agreement as 'entirely unique to our employee-owned company' and which is unquestionably the agreement's most innovative feature, the employment protection offered to union members deserves to be stressed once more. In a sense there was a double-lock protection. One lock is the no-layoff provision. A second is provided in the rules of the process itself, under which no actual job would be either eliminated or combined without the express agreement of the union. As we now know and at least down to my visit in the autumn of 1997, there was not a single case in which either job elimination or combination was agreed to by the union. Management jobs were indeed combined and/or eliminated, but not blue collar ones.

This is not the place for a detailed discussion of why nothing, in all this exceptionally sophisticated deal about sustaining employment through cutting costs and working flexibly, was ever actually implemented. But two points stand out. The first is the market environment from 1994 onwards. Contrary to more optimistic expectations which had been widely current in 1993, it remained ferociously tough. Competition in effect intensified. As we shall see there was considerable success at RESI in cutting costs. But it is not too much to say that these cost reductions were simply swallowed up by more or less concurrent reductions in product prices. One of the strikingly innovative features of the 1993 labour agreement was, as we have seen, a deal in advance about how the prospective benefits of cost cutting should be shared. On the other hand it contained no similar deal in advance about how to cope with the consequences of offsetting price reductions in the market place.

The second point to be made about the non-implementation of the provisions of the 1993 labour agreement can be extended: to help explain what I called at the outset the 'snap back' in the relationship between the blue collar workforce and the steelworkers' union on the one side and the management on the other. It was a 'snap back' from what seemed, at least tentatively, like a more co-operative relationship to one in the traditionally adversarial mode. It should almost go without saying that the snap back reflects a high level of underlying mistrust between management and labour.

A man who understood this mistrust better than most was the late James Smith. He was mentioned earlier as one of the two men in the steelworkers' union most responsible for the change in its policy towards employee ownership. He was also closely involved in the buy-out at RESI. He spoke with unusual eloquence about the problems of mistrust between management and unions in the American steel industry at a conference in Bucharest in the autumn of 1993. His main point can be simply stated and grasped. It is that at least in the old American steel industry, managers and union officials have substantially built their identities on their adversarial relationships. Those are hard to change.

Let me quote in conclusion some extracts from what the late James Smith said about these crucial matters in his presentation at the Bucharest Conference on 27 October 1993:

To sustain a permanent improvement in the productivity of a group of employees, the USWA experience indicates that *the sociology of the workplace itself must change* [emphasis original].

The traditional 'master-servant' relationship of managers and workers in productive processes must give way to a partnership – in which all workers, and managers, are enabled to earn respect for their individual contributions of knowledge, skill, and mental and physical effort! All employees must begin to perform mental work, even though some also perform physical work.

In effect, a worker does not seem to give more of himself to his job than he (or she) would otherwise give, just because there are now some shares in the company's stock in the worker's ESOP account. Rather, the buy-out creates the conditions under which managers and workers may each begin to think more about their common interests, and think less about their respective social status as superior or inferior.

If top management and the union act decisively, immediately after the buy-out, to create joint decision-making structures within which workers and managers can focus on their common interests in safety, product quality, the work environment, and efficient operations – workers and managers may begin to form partnerships in the workplace. If the top managers and the union encourage such partnerships, a permanent change towards higher productivity can occur.

In practice, the change is easy to talk about, but difficult to bring about. Many managers have built their self-image on their skills at coercing, intimidating, or manipulating workers. To become partners with 'inferiors' may destroy many of the status symbols they have struggled to acquire. Such persons are comfortable in the traditional relationships, and feel real pain if forced to abandon them.

Similarly many union leaders in the United States have built their self-image on their skills at non-violent class struggle. Their sense of self worth is related to their ability to defend abused workers from exploitation by greedy masters. Like status-conscious managers, these traditional unionists are comfortable with things as they are, and uncertain of any advantages of any change towards a partnership with their habitual adversaries.

Because of this conflict with their perceived psychic self-image, either managers or union leaders may sabotage efforts to introduce partnership systems – either by conscious actions or by habitual subconscious behaviour.

The partnership concept will be supported enthusiastically, however, by most individual workers who have an opportunity to participate in it. With their help a committed top union leadership and top management have a chance to bring about the change. Under the best conditions, they will make mistakes. Therefore they need to learn to be patient with one another – while engaging in honest, objective discussion of their own, and their partners', mistakes.

From the 1993 Labour Contract to the Autumn of 1997 Visitors to RESI's headquarters in the twin towns of Canton and Massillon between the middle of 1993 and at least the end of 1995 were likely to come away with a sense of at least cautious optimism both about the business itself and its employee ownership: the recession was increasingly a thing of the past. Management liked to argue that thanks to the vigorous and imaginative supply side response to it undertaken in a series of joint projects and programmes with the union, employee-owned RESI was significantly stronger than it had been under a succession of conventional capitalist owners in the past. A new labour contract had been signed with the United Steelworkers of America (USWA) in the middle of 1993, and work was underway to make a reality of its most striking provisions: in effect a scheme for cutting costs and introducing more flexible work practices in return for a conditional employment guarantee.

New finance was raised by RESI, in December 1993, in two different ways. First, on behalf of the company, Citicorp and Salomon Brothers, acting as underwriters, offered for sale what were called '$9\frac{7}{8}$% First Mortgage Notes due 2001'. Second, the company signed with its bankers a new credit agreement. The total amount of the First Mortgage Notes offered for sale and fully underwritten was $200m. Under the new credit agreement the company was provided with a 'four year facility of up to $90m'.

After deducting the underwriters' discount of 2.5% (or of $5m) and other transaction costs, the proceeds of the sale of the First Mortgage Notes which passed to the company was $194m.

Top management at RESI argued strongly at the time that the interest and other conditions associated with the successful offering of the First Mortgage Notes, and indeed with the new credit agreement, were in all the circumstances as good as, or perhaps rather better than, might reasonably have been expected. Depending on linguistic preference, the notes may be described as either 'high yielding' or 'junk' bonds. According to RESI's top managers, in discussions in early 1994, the rate of 9 7/8%, was just below what they had been led to expect on the basis of the offering of similar bonds in the months before.

Essentially, the company used the $194m proceeds of the December 1993 offering to repay its existing debts and at the same time to roll back the maturity date of its main indebtedness. A proforma capitalisation table, contained in the prospectus associated with the offering, depicts the company's long-term debt following its receipt of the proceeds of the sale. There is only one item: $200m of 'First Mortgage Notes offered hereby'. As compared with the position before the offering, bank indebtedness of $110m and other 'subordinated debentures' amounting to close on $56m have been eliminated.

In connection with this new finance raised, we have already mentioned more than once the big capital investment project – of a new continuous caster and direct rolling billet mill – which the company started to implement early in 1994. And we have also mentioned its projected cost of $165m. Here we need to underline what is implicit in the account just given of how the proceeds of the $200m offering were to be used. The implication is that the caster was to be otherwise financed. In the prospectus there is a sentence about where the estimated $165m will come from: 'The company intends to finance this expenditure with cash on hand, borrowings under the credit agreement and cash flow from operations.' To be fair to the authors of the prospectus, it immediately goes on to make a proper cautionary point, that there 'can be no assurance that . . . the company will have the ability to borrow the funds necessary to complete the Project under the Credit Agreement'.

Here I simply wish to make an obvious point about the new finance raised at the end of 1993: both by the First Mortgage

Notes and under the new credit agreement. The point is that in relation to the big RESI capital investment project, the two are probably best seen together. The notes, as we have seen, essentially roll back the maturity date of the company's main indebtedness. The new credit agreement fits, as it were, into the 'space' thus created, and is earmarked as the main source of finance for the big project.

Turning back finally to the prospectus associated with the $200m of First Mortgage Notes, the tone of the document is properly cautionary throughout. Indeed there are four pages explicitly headed 'Risk Factors'. Part of the impression left by reading the document is similar to what you get from reading a health warning on a cigarette packet. But the prospectus also notes the improvements in RESI's performance since the buy-out, and especially the linked cost reductions and higher productivity levels on the one hand, and the improvements in quality on the other. It also refers to the new labour agreement of August 1993, and draws out one of its key points:

> The company has been able to incorporate in its recently concluded collective bargaining agreement ... additional incentives to reduce manufacturing costs and improve productivity, such as the provision that certain of the additional wage increases will occur only if specified cost savings are achieved.

This was also a time of acquisitions. In 1993 the assets of the former Western Steel Group were acquired for $4.5m, resulting in a 22% increase in RESI's capacity for producing cold finished bar. Then in 1994 the company acquired additional stainless steel production equipment by buying the assets of Baltimore Specialty Steels, the Aramco subsidiary.

Perhaps most importantly, this period marked the commissioning of a new, state of the art, cast-roll facility and the start to the long process of its installation. The total investment, spread over a number of years but with spending concentrated in 1994/95, amounted to some $165m. Here is how the cast-rolling capability was described in the Annual Report for 1994/95:

> The company's Cast-Roll facility is the only one of its kind in North America and the largest and most sophisticated in the world. [It] links five proven technologies in a continuous

process, which will result in significant cost savings and enable the company to substantially improve bar quality. When fully operational [it] is anticipated to provide a further direct cost reduction in excess of $50 per processed ton as a result of improvements in product yields, labor, energy and inventory efficiencies . . . [it] will also provide indirect savings . . . to cold-finished facilities.. and may increase . . . hot rolled bar shipping capacity.

Though it is clearly to anticipate and falls within the period following the big 'change in the weather' at RESI, a postscript to the story of the cast-roll facility, in the form of a few sentences from the 1996/97 Annual Report, are worth quoting:

> . . . the performance of Republic's technologically advanced cast-roll facility has been steadily increasing. In the fourth 1997 fiscal quarter [that is the second calendar quarter], we ran 53% of our total production through the cast-roll operation, as compared to 42% a year ago. When all customer approvals are received, the cast-roll production level is planned to reach 70% of Republic's total production.

Finally, from the 'fair weather' period of cautious optimism at employee-owned RESI – running from say the start of 1993 to the end of 1995 – one further development and milestone should be pinpointed: the successful floating of $50m worth of shares in RESI's common stock, on America's NASDAQ market in June 1995. I quoted as one of my epigraphs a notably 'fair weather' view about industrial relations at RESI which figured in the prospectus to that offer. It is worth repeating: 'The company's unique partnership with its employees and the USWA has greatly facilitated the company's ability to achieve cost savings and improve quality.'

At this point it makes sense to put on record the main statistics of RESI's performance not only from 1993 to the time of writing but for the whole of its life: from the buy-out in December 1989 to the end of the company's fiscal year 1996/97, that is in mid-summer of 1997. The figures for 1989/90 cover just over seven months, from the date of the buy-out (28 November 1989), to June 30 1990. All the others cover the company's full fiscal years of twelve months to the end of June.

RESI: 28 November *1989 to end-June 1997*

	89/90	90/1	91/2	92/3	93/4	94/5	95/6	96/7
Shipped tons ooos	534	808	795	936	1,057	1,042	897	1,010
Sales $m	379	582	566	646	745	805	746	754
Ave price per ton $	710	720	712	691	705	773	832	746
Ave manufacturing Cost per ton $	603	653	645	613	630	677	768	685
Gross margin/ton $	107	67	67	78	75	96	64	61
Profit (loss) $m	4.0	(33.0)	(8.4)	(7.4)	(23.4)	(4.8)	(33.4)	(34.3)
Cash flow $m	n.a.	30.3	7.5	55.7	30.6	57.8	6.3	20.4

As a measure of its *relative* prosperity – or, less buoyantly, of its survival prospects – RESI's cash flow 'bottom line' is probably the least objectionable indicator. If we look not at the individual numbers, but at averages, a most striking contrast is apparent. For the five years down to 30 June 1995, cash flow showed an average positive annual number of a little over $36m. By contrast for the two subsequent years it averaged less than half that, or around $13.5m, having dived to a post-buy-out all-time low of $6.3m. in 1995/96.

The other two numbers to highlight from the table are those also associated with what must have been a real *annus horribilis*, namely the twelve months to end-June 1996. At 897,000, tons shipped were over 10% down on the previous year and the lowest since the depth of the recession at the start of the 1990s. Partly as a result, average manufacturing costs per ton rocketed to a post-buy-out all-time high of $768.

A specific but mainly temporary source of the high manufacturing costs incurred in 1995/96 is pinpointed in RESI's annual report for the following year (1996/97) which mentions 'added costs resulting from operating three steel processing routes instead of two . . . while customer approvals were being obtained for the use of products from the cast-roll facility to replace the then idled vertical caster. . . .'

Of longer term consequence for RESI's future prosperity is a factor which shows up most clearly in the table's numbers not for 1996/97 but for the following year. Compared with the previous twelve months, average selling prices per ton fell by just over 10% from $832 to $746. Understandably this was highlighted by Russell

Maier, in his letter to stockholders introducing the annual report for 1996/97: 'The single largest contributing factor to Republic's financial performance is that bar steel prices have been forced down by foreign and domestic competition, as well as intense customer pressure.'

About the domestic competition faced by RESI in the American market two points are worth bringing out. The first and more general is that there is increasing competitive pressure from America's mini-mills and that bar products from this source are moving up-market to start threatening RESI's position in some of its higher-value added lines. Because they are mostly non-unionised and are thus mainly free of the legacy of traditional 'work practices', because their plant and equipment tends to be more or less state of the art, and because they are able to rely on steel scrap to the extent of 100% for their raw material, these mini-mills enjoy and will continue to enjoy huge cost advantages as against RESI in all those markets in which they can compete on quality.

The second point about the domestic competition faced by RESI since 1996 is more specific. The voluntary liquidation in the early 1990s of the bar division of Bethlehem Steel was noted much earlier in this case study. It had been unable to adjust sufficiently to the recession. The RESI management believed at the time that the liquidation represented the permanent closedown of an important competitive facility in the bar market. They were wrong. With new owners and a big infusion of new capital, the old plant and facilities were reopened for business in 1996. What is more many of those taken on were ex-employees of Bethlehem Steel, and of those a large proportion were people already receiving a pension. They were hired at rates of pay way below those prevailing at RESI. What can hardly have been other than especially galling for the RESI management was that these much lower rates were accepted by the steelworkers' union. Nor can USWA's rejoinder – to the effect that without its involvement the rates would have been that much lower still – have supplied more than limited comfort.

And that brings us back to the apparent snap back to a traditional adversarial mode in the relationship between the RESI management on the one hand, and the union and the blue collar workforce on the other. Of course such changes are continuous as well as discontinuous. But my guess is that the calendar year of 1996 was probably when most of the change back took place. As we have seen from the numbers, this was the *annus horribilis* from the viewpoint of RESI's finances, with its positive cash flow squeezed to its lowest ever since the buy-out. It was also the year when what had been the bar division of Bethlehem Steel came back into play as a 'returned competitor', and one with what must have been seen by RESI's management as enjoying, to repeat, an unfair advantage.

It seems too that 1996 was the year in which it became apparent that in one of their chief goals – the introduction of more flexible working in return for a conditional employment guarantee (the key 'functional analysis' provisions of the 1993 labour agreement) were going to prove a dead letter. There had not been a single instance when the union had agreed to a significant manning change. It must have seemed highly improbable that a different outcome was on the cards, at least in the short term.

Finally, it was early in 1996 that, under the terms of the 1993 labour contract, management and the steelworkers' union were to start negotiating about the rates and conditions which would apply in the three years from mid-1996. Under the 1993 contract it was further provided that in the event of a failure to reach agreement binding arbitration would be accepted by both parties.

The detailed bargaining positions of the two sides need not concern us. It is sufficient to say that the gap was large. The union's final demand was for a substantial wage increase. As against that what the management offered was a reduction in basic rates with some possible offset through profit sharing. The union also sought a move in RESI's pension arrangement from the existing so-called defined 'contribution plan' to a defined 'benefit plan'. The latter was also unacceptable to management but that is a detail which we cannot pursue here.

Compulsory arbitration followed. Ignoring the pension question, on the main wage rate issue the arbitrator supported neither the union's final demand nor the final (negative) offer from the management. Instead he ruled that the existing rates should run on.

As we already know, the management challenged the arbitrator's ruling by lodging an appeal against it in the Ohio distict court in the summer of 1997. No official statement was issued at the time but, to repeat, the essential ground for the appeal was that the arbitrator had failed to take account of criteria that were specifically laid down in the 1993 contract. Management has kindly clarified the point for me. In its view the arbitrator was required to 'consider the

Company's ability to carry out its modernization program, and the wage and benefit levels enjoyed by Union-represented employees at competitive firms'.

As we know, management's appeal was still pending when this was finally revised. But it is hard not to believe that the reopening of the former Bethlehem Steel bar division with a union-represented workforce but much lower pay rates is a development which should tell at least formally in its favour. As for modernisation, a persuasive case, according to management, can be made for the view that the construction of a new bar mill is essential if the business is to have a serious future in the next century. But management further argues that, given the state of RESI's balance sheet, it would not be possible to finance the new mill by further borrowing.

When I visited RESI in October of 1997, the good news was that the union has accepted that a new bar mill was essential to future survival. The question was how best it might be financed.

Failing agreement on that issue between management and union it may just be possible, as it was in some sense and for some of the time at Weirton, for management to press on with its plans with no more than minimum union co-operation.

Whatever may happen in the future, policy makers should note from this experience that employee ownership is a formula which had by late 1997 secured several thousands of jobs in RESI for nearly eight years. As for employee-ownership 'professionals', they should be able to learn much from the quite exceptional supply side response with which management and the union at RESI confronted the recession in the early 1990s. It is a real pity that the most important parts of the later functional analysis project were still born. But there is much to be learnt from that experience too.

Sales to Blackstone Group, September 1998 By a deal which was completed, following a positive vote by USWA members, in September 1998, RESI was acquired as a going concern by the Blackstone Group, a big American conglomerate, containing various steel industry undertakings among its wide range of subsidiaries.

The deal was struck at a price which enabled RESI's employee stockholders to be paid $7.25 for each share held. USWA members received a pay increase, an employment guarantee running for three years, and a new early retirement scheme was promised by the Blackstone Group. Finally the Group undertook to build and commission the new bar mill which had been seen for a number of years as essential for the long-term future of steel making in Canton and Massillon. The successful introduction of the new bar mill will eventually reduce total numbers employed by about 20% or perhaps rather more.

The deal was publicly welcomed by the leadership of the United Steelworkers of America at both national and local level.

22

The Trade Union Story

Employee ownership is a powerful tool to help workers get a better deal. *Lynn Williams, lately International President, United Steelworkers of America (USWA)*

20 Ways the United Steelworkers of America Makes a Difference in ESOPs. *Heading of a USWA hand-out, 1994*

We believe that our plan will catapult the company light-years ahead of its competitors by enabling it to serve the global community more flexibly and efficiently than any other major American carrier ... *Joint letter to United Airlines from the Airline Pilots Association (ALPA) and International Association of Machinists (IAM) in the US about their proposed buy-out of the business. Quoted by the 'Wall Street Journal', 27 December 1993*

... worker ownership isn't just a way to save jobs, as important as that is. It means the workers have a major say in who buys the plant, who doesn't buy it, and how it operates. *Lynn Williams. From his keynote speech at the union's Constitutional Convention, Las Vegas, 1988*

Union Hostility to Employee Ownership Historically, trade unions in the English speaking world on both sides of the Atlantic have shown almost unqualified hostility to employee ownership and all its works. But starting in the 1980s there has been a remarkable shift in their attitudes, at least in some cases. The change has been much more striking in America, where it has been endorsed by officials elected to the highest positions, especially in the United Steelworkers of America (USWA).

To appreciate the extent of the change we need to highlight the earlier hostility. There is a wide choice of material to choose from. For America one of my favourites is from a speech made by Mr James Smith, then a high USWA official, at a Yale seminar in 1981, a date already seven years after the enactment by the US Congress of its first ESOP legislation. Towards the end of his speech, Mr

Mr Smith somewhat modified his hostility. But in the early part it could scarcely have been expressed more sharply:

> During the 1970s a new weapon was added to the armoury of anti-union managements – the ESOP, or Employee Stock Ownership Plan. While there are as many kinds of ESOPs as can be imagined, the predominant form of the ESOP ... [is] ... an anti-union scam.

My British illustration has a more specific focus, having been provoked by an actual employee buy-out proposal, that of what was to become NFC. The speaker was Mr Alex Kitson, then Assistant General Secretary of Britain's Transport and General Workers' Union (TGWU), which represented a large majority of the business's blue collar workforce. Mr Kitson left no room for doubt about his attitude:

> The shares which are going to be on offer are going to be cheques that can only be cashed by redundancies ... meal tickets on the way to the dole queue.
>
> The TGWU's Finance and General Purposes Committee Meeting today held detailed discussions about the proposed selling-off of the National Freight Corporation, and expressed its total opposition to this act of asset stripping against the public sector of the road haulage industry.
>
> The TGWU is also very concerned about the prospect that workers in the industry could be offered small shareholdings under one of the possible sell-off schemes.
>
> In the TGWU's view share purchases for the workers are aimed at undermining opposition to the asset stripping of the public sector, and would result in worker shareholders subsequently being involved in further selling off of their own assets and jobs when private capital has a clearer picture of the choice of assets which it wants to extract from the vast NFC operation.
>
> What could be on offer is a phoney element of control adding up to a political con-trick staged by Transport Minister, Norman Fowler, who is desperate to put Trojan horses into the trade union camp. This aim is to confuse the stand which the trade union and labour movement must take against the destruction of public enterprise ... [Lynch, *TG&WU Handbook*].

Part of Mr Kitson's all-out hostility no doubt reflected the fact that the National Freight buy-out was an act of privatisation. It may be argued that faced with an employee buy-out of a conventional private capitalist undertaking his own and his union's line might have been different. I would be inclined to answer 'Yes perhaps; but not *very* different.' I would also point out that the union's advice to its members in this case – to practise total self-denial when it came to the offer of shares – has since been widely criticised by those unfortunate enough to act on it. Readers need only refer back to the National Freight case study to see why.

But that is by the way. My aim is to show the prevailing climate of fierce union hostility to employee ownership in the early 1980s when it started to surface as a real issue in the US and the UK. My three epigraphs demonstrate the extent of the change of attitude since then, at least in the US. The second, from an USWA presentation to potential new members, shows that by 1993 the union reckoned that its ESOP expertise was worth highlighting as a sales pitch. That must count as a profound shift compared with what James Smith was saying in 1981.

As for the airline pilots and the machinists, we now know that their bid for a majority shareholding in United Airlines was a triumphant success. Indeed the bid, its background and what happened thereafter form a separate case study towards the end of this book.

Top union officials on the European side of the Atlantic have never expressed themselves as positively as those I have quoted from the USA. Statements about employee ownership from top union brass in the UK were rather few in the early 1990s. When they were made they tended to be either delphic or grudging – often to the effect that, in certain extreme cases, an employee-owned business may be the 'least worst solution'. A good example of the latter appears in a foreword from the pen of Mr Ron Todd, then General Secretary of the T&GWU, to the handbook from which I quoted earlier. Two sentences will give a sufficient indication of what was then his attitude:

The plain fact of the matter is that the better of these [employee share ownership] schemes have provided the only way for many TGWU members to retain some sort of union control over their jobs against the ravages of deregulation and privatisation.

Nowhere has this been more true than in the passenger industry, where many TGWU bus workers have become involved in taking a stake in their firms to keep out the worst of the pirates and profiteers.

And yet in others ways, the employee ownership running on the labour side has been made in the UK rather than the US. I mentioned Unity Trust Bank earlier, a banking business in which Britain's leading trade unions are the majority shareholders. It has been the pioneer of ESOP lending in the UK and is attracting increasing attention from trade unions elsewhere. Another interesting British initiative has been the organisation set up in 1993 to service the needs of rank-and-file employee owners in employee-owned businesses. Rather oddly for a rank-and-file organisation, it has taken the name of the *Centre* for Employee Ownership and Participation (CEOP). One of its key promoters and its first chairman was Mr David Wheatcroft. He is the elected employee director in the local bus company in Chesterfield. As we saw in an earlier case study, that bus company became 100% employee owned following a successful employee buy-out in 1989 and remained so owned until sold on to the large, quoted company, Stage Coach, in 1995. CEOP is an expression not only of support by rank-and-file union members for employee ownership but also of widespread support among local, as opposed to national, trade union officials.

It will not be surprising if the future progress of employee ownership is determined more by its effects on the attitudes and behaviour of rank-and-file union members than by the winged words of union leaders. In that respect the anecdotal evidence from employee-owned undertakings in Britain, or anyway from the best of them, suggests that the attitudes of UK employee owners are not significantly behind their US counterparts.

Most of the rest of this review of the trade unions' position is devoted to the evolution of employee ownership policies of the United Steelworkers of America (USWA). This is because by the early 1990s that evolution had almost certainly gone further in USWA than in any other union. Moreover it was for The United Steelworkers that James Smith worked for many years before, and indeed after, his retirement in 1993 and effectively up to his most untimely death in 1995. On the union side he is the person who has given most thought to the issue.

CHANGING POLICY AT THE UNITED STEELWORKERS
OF AMERICA

The Steelworkers Organising Committee [predecessor of the United Steel-workers of America], as a progressive union, stands for a policy of security and plenty for all. In order that all our people, wage earners, farmers and other useful people may have more, we need to produce and distribute more, not less. *From 'Production Problems, A Handbook for Committee-men and Local Lodges of the Steelworkers Organising Committee' (1938)*

We used to think of employee ownership defensively, as an alternative to a company going under. But we are now going in that direction much more aggressively. *Lynn Williams, lately President of the USWA, Noble, 1993*

Among North American union leaders [Lynn] Williams, a Canadian, is considered a visionary who has embraced power sharing and employee participation as salvation for his and other ailing unions. *Steve Franklin in the 'Chicago Tribune', 8 August 1993*

. . . worker ownership isn't just a way to save jobs, as important as that is. It means workers have a major voice in who buys the plant, who doesn't buy it and how it operates. *Lynn Williams: from his keynote speech at the union's Constitutional Convention, Las Vegas, 1988*

I make no apology for repeating from the first part of this review of trade union policies and attitudes the final epigraph from Lynn Williams's Las Vegas speech in 1988. When he sat down at the end of it, he is reported to have received 'thunderous acclamation'. Both his sentiments and the reported response of his union's membership were remarkable developments in the late 1980s. Moreover, even if with qualifications, they were essentially new developments. One qualification is about the American labour movement's substantial innings with workers' co-ops towards the end of the last century. Another, reflected in the publication from which the first of my epigraphs is taken, is about the sustained interest of organised American steelworkers in projects to increase and improve production. We shall look at each of these two qualifications, but especially the second, in a moment.

The economic context in which this apparent shift in the union's outlook took place was the calamitous downturn in the American steel industry's fortunes in the early 1980s. The country's total steel output fell from over 90m tons in 1981 to just 62m tons in 1982.

According to USWA's estimates the industry's losses in just one year, 1982, were $3.4bn. Between 1982 and 1992, years when Republicans were in the White House, the cumulative loss was $14.4bn. Altogether during Ronald Reagan's eight years in the White House 'more than half the jobs in American steel mills simply disappeared'. My source for that last estimate of cumulative job losses is the late James Smith.

In fact as early as 1980 James Smith was the author of a key report on these issues: submitted to the then USWA president, Lloyd McBride. This is how Mr Smith recalled the main thrust of what he wrote:

> I reported ... that the steel companies, although barely profitable, were not generating enough capital to modernise, and therefore falling behind the international competition.
>
> Our pattern of wage increases had made our members the highest paid workers in any major American industry, whilst return on invested capital was one of the lowest in any major American industry.
>
> It was not, in my opinion, politically wise to reduce the level of our wage increases. Neither would it have been good for the economy of the U.S. to set a pattern of lower levels of consumption. However, I believed that a majority of our members would accept the concept of investing some of their future wage increases into ESOPs, the investment could be mandated for capital expenditures, and that we could help in this way to solve the modernisation problem.

We will see later how Mr Smith's recommendations were to be embodied in various agreements between USWA and America's steel-making companies. But before turning to those important 'investment bargaining' developments – as they have sometimes been called – we need to take a look at the main other ingredient in what eventually became USWA's employee ownership policy. I mean the union's long-standing advocacy of employee 'participation' in a non-financial sense: its support for arrangements designed to give employees a voice in enterprise policy making and government

James Smith used to trace these policies back to:

> the early leaders of the ... unions ... in the 1930s [who]

generally believed that workers must participate in correcting the errors, mistakes and failures of management of the major industries.

This was particularly true of Philip Murray and Clinton Golden of the United Steelworkers and Walter Reuther of the United Auto Workers ... Murray lent his name to a book on the subject, which was primarily written by Morris L Cooke and is entitled *Organised Labour and Production, Next Steps in Industrial Democracy*.

It would go beyond the scope of this discussion to follow in any detail this strand in USWA policy. But we may note without surprise that, in Mr Smith's words,

... as soon as World War II ended managements rejected any help from USWA and insisted on their unalloyed management rights. This phase continued until W. Edward Deming's quality programmes with Japanese industry forced America's steel industry managers to recognise the need for change.

An important landmark in what became an evolutionary process was registered in 1980, in the shape of so-called 'Labour Management Participation Team' provisions in contracts signed in that year between USWA and a number of undertakings. According to Mr Smith:

These ... provisions essentially called upon each company and the union to jointly select one plant ... to begin experiments in joint problem solving teams, to work on quality of work life, productivity, waste, product quality, and similar problems in the plants. US Steel, Bethlehem, National, and Jones and Laughlin moved rather promptly to do so, and later the smaller companies followed along. In almost every case the experiments proved successful beyond expectation.

A further landmark was the labour contract signed in 1986 between USWA and National Steel which included a 'gain sharing bonus system'. According to Mr Smith this 'motivated managers and local unions to broaden and deepen their participative activities'. The same year, 1986, was also something of a landmark for USWA's 'investment bargaining' policy. In this case the pattern setting agreement was between the union and the LTV Steel

Company, signed in April of that year. Employee shares and bonuses were traded off against labour cost reductions of $3.65 per hour. Union members were compensated for what they sacrificed in wages by the allocation of up to 20% of pre-tax profits in the form of cash bonuses. We may recall in parenthesis that ex-LTV employees involved in the 1989 buy-out by Republic Engineering Steels used the employee shares in LTV as a source of funding for the buy-out.

Other American trade unions, particularly in the airline and road haulage industries, have become involved in employee ownership and participation in the twenty years since the first ESOP legislation in the early 1970s. But the USWA's has been substantially deeper and more sustained than that of any other, as is borne out by the table which comes at the end of this second part of our trade union story.

Whether we look at Weirton Steel and the Independent Steelworkers' Union and/or at USWA and the rest of America's steel industry, the main reasons for the initial steel union involvement in employee ownership during the 1980s are identical and unambiguous: the threat of either closure or of a sale to the kind of third parties, typically anti-union ones, that were judged to be worse even than employee ownership. Growing union hostility to threats of this second kind, together with accumulating evidence that employee ownership can operate in union members' interests, explains some of the later buy-outs with which the USWA has been involved but not the early ones. Adversity was the chief midwife of the marked change during the 1980s in the USWA's policy towards ESOPS, and towards both partial and majority employee ownership. For the union, the keenest measure of that adversity was the decline in its own membership numbers – from a figure of of some 1.2m in 1980 to no more than 560,000 in 1993. The total had climbed back to around 600,000 in 1997.

The change in policy occurred in the mid-1980s. For his 1981 speech at Yale Mr Smith had taken as his title 'The Labour Movement and Worker Ownership'. Already by that date the original ESOP legislation in the U.S. was seven years old. Moreover, the USWA was in fact already engaged in a controversy with management in a union-organised business, South Bend Lathe, where the ESOP dated back to 1975. (The controversy about that particular ESOP rumbled on for many years; indeed until South Bend Lathe

was more or less restructured out of existence in the early 1990s.)
Yet the first part of Mr Smith's presentation to that Yale Conference is a series of unqualified negative messages about worker or
employee ownership:

> In its earlier form, of production co-ops started by the Knights
> of Labour, America's earliest unions, in the 1870s and 1880s,
> worker ownership failed to muster even one single enduring
> success . . .
>
> Among the chief reasons for this failure was the fierce hos-
> tility of conventional corporate business; and it would be ab-
> surdly naive to suppose that the same would not happen in the
> 1980s . . .
>
> Worker ownership, therefore, is most unlikely to happen in
> the U.S., anyway on any considerable scale, for the foreseeable
> future . . .
>
> As for the new ESOPs, their appearances are deceptive. They
> should be seen for what they are: new weapons in the struggle
> against the labour movement of anti-union management . . .
>
> If evidence of this last point is required, an excellent ex-
> ample is the ESOP at the company South Bend Lathe where
> the blue collar workforce are members of the USWA.

Mr Smith had three specific criticisms of what he implied was the
typical ESOP of 1981. In the USWA's later policy statements they
came to be known as 'the three fatal flaws' of the standard ESOP, as
indroduced by management. The first had to do with workers' pensions. Mr Smith argued:

> Workers are persuaded, by owners, managers, and/or ESOP
> promoters, that they don't need funded pensions. Instead they
> are led to believe that their retirement income needs can be
> met solely by holding stock in the employer-company. Once
> workers abandon the concept of a funded pension plan, of
> course, the money which would have been paid to pension
> funding is saved, and the employer's profits increase, or losses
> decrease, by that amount. In steel, for example, pension fund-
> ing currently exceeds 11% of wages.

Mr Smith went on to allege that the employee stock in the typical
ESOP is disenfranchised:

Workers are told that they are now part owners of the company, but by one device or another, they are deprived of any effective voting control, under the stock plan designed by managers, ESOP promoters etc.

His third specific criticism related to the money values of the shares:

Stock is not publicly marketed, so that each worker's shares have no value except by management's decision. Thus an employee's retirement income ultimately depends not only on the success of the particular employer firm – but also on the arbitrary judgement of management at the time an employee retires, as to what price shall be set on the stock shares.

The subsequent development of the USWA policy towards ESOPs can in part be quite simply understood: as a successful search for ways to design these plans so that they are *not* open to any one of these three specific criticisms. For example, they can be and have been designed so as to be entirely distinct from any pension plans, to have their shares valued independently, and to be structured so that employees may vote their shares. But at the time of Mr Smith's Yale speech all that lay in the future.

To understand where the union policy has come from, we need to convey the flavour of Mr Smith's full-blooded condemnation of ESOPs when he spoke at Yale and to take on board his conviction at that time that to believe in the possibility of genuine worker ownership was to be deluded.

I have already quoted his general condemnation of ESOPs as an anti-union scam. He grounded this in a historical analysis of why production co-ops had failed towards the end of the last century:

In most cases worker-owned co-operatives were driven out of business by organised capital, although many undoubtedly died from natural causes. Discriminatory freight rates, cancelled rail service, discriminatory credit arrangements, refusals to supply raw materials, and refusal to retail the goods were all used to choke off competition from worker owned enterprises.

Then, a few sentences later:

To now advocate worker ownership, as a means of improving the condition of workers, one would have to believe that some characteristics of the business world have changed since the 1880s. Is modern management less jealous of its prerogatives? Has it lost some of its power to freeze out competition? I am not aware of any such changes. I don't believe such changes have occurred.

Given that premise, his conclusion is the logical one:

I therefore conclude that worker *ownership*, in the sense of enterprises totally owned by workers, is not likely to happen here on any large scale, in the foreseeable future. It could happen in small businesses, but only to the extent that organised capital is willing to permit it.

Mr Smith dwelt on the South Bend Lathe ESOP at some length in his Yale speech and it seems that its ESOP was open to all three of his specific criticisms. It was partly financed by pension fund money, while its employee shares had no voting rights and their value was determined by management. As a result of changes in federal law in the late 1980s the valuation by management of employee shares is no longer legal. But the South Bend Lathe ESOP remained open to the other two criticisms as long as the business survived.

However, by the middle 1990s the number of majority employee buy-outs in which the USWA itself had played a leading role was already well into double figures and extended across the 39th Parallel into Canada. Even when we acknowledge that some of these were quite small operations and that some involved majority employee ownership rather than a 100% stake, it can hardly be denied that Mr Smith's prediction at Yale about total employee ownership turned out to be spectacularly wrong.

If we go back to the main thrust of that speech, we find that in its second part the tone becomes much more positive. There is still no concession on complete employee ownership, with Mr Smith reiterating the view that it would only happen in small businesses and then only on the sufferance of big business. But part ownership could be a different matter. He noted that: 'Ownership of minority, but significant stockholdings by employees in larger firms exists frequently today, and is strongly encouraged by current tax law.'

He went on to pay a qualified tribute to Senator Russell Long, the political architect of successive ESOP measures in the US Congress. He then proceeded to lay out three advantages which, subject to various conditions, partial or minority employee ownership might well have to offer. By owning minority shares, workers, he said,

> can, first, assist their employer to have the needed capital to keep their tools and equipment modern. In industries engaged in world competition that can be critically important.
>
> Second, workers could accumulate some investment to add a few luxuries or conveniences to their retirement income, or greater security in periods of lay-off, major illness, and the like.
>
> Third, like any other investors in common shares workers should gain a voice in selecting managers, and thereby exercise some influence over managerial policies.

In his concluding remarks about partial or minority employee ownership, Mr Smith chose to sustain this distinctly positive approach to them. Of course he insisted that any minority ESOP plans would have to be so designed as to avoid the three fatal flaws. He insisted too that in a world of such ESOPs, the union would still have all its old work to do. But, with those provisos, he ventured to point out that such ESOPs would offer management 'a very inexpensive source of capital . . . for their investments'; and he allowed himself an undeniably positive speculation:

> Where such arrangements are entered into sincerely, there could be a significant reduction in management-labour hostility and tension. This in turn may lead to a freer flow of communication between workers and managers and some consequent increase in productivity.

His three closing sentences were, if anything, even more positive:

> . . . these experiments may be very worthwhile. From them we may learn much that we need to know to improve our structures of capital, management, and labour. I therefore look forward to them and I think many others in the trade union movement do also.

At that point in his thinking Mr Smith distinguished sharply between what he called 'total' employee ownership on the one hand and employee ownership of a 'partial' or 'minority' character on the other. In later speeches and writings by officials of the USWA, the main distinction is drawn slightly differently and more simply: between majority and minority employee ownership. Moreover this distinction has since been seen by the union as being one of use and function as well as of degree. A 1991 paper by two officials from the union's research department, Steve Newman and Mike Yoffee, explains these differences of use. After emphasising that 'the impetus for most of these [ESOP] plans has been job retention', they go on:

> The major uses of employee ownership fall into two categories. The first use involves companies that are not for sale, but are experiencing temporary cash flow problems. In these situations USWA has engaged in 'investment bargaining' resulting in the establishment of 'minority ownership' ESOPs. These plans help employers recover and preserve member jobs. The second use occurs in situations when a company or facility is up for sale or would otherwise close if not purchased by an employee group. In this case USWA helps . . . employees purchase a controlling stake in their companies through a 'majority ESOP'.

Taking these two uses together, Newman and Yoffee reported that towards the end of 1990 50,000 USWA members were participating in 23 employee-ownership plans. The table at the end of the chapter was compiled by the same two USWA researchers, but some years after their journal article. They then estimated that in early 1994 close on 70,000 of their union's members were participants in ESOP plans of one kind and another. Later in the autumn of 1997, when this was finally revised, Mr Yoffee explained to me that there had been no significant additions since then. Essentially he attributed the standstill to the robust good health of the American economy over those intervening years.

In their 1991 article, Newman and Yoffee explained that the union first started to get seriously involved in minority ESOPs as a result of investment bargaining in the wages round of 1985/86. The background against which the negotiations took place was exceptionally tough:

> Employment in the steel industry had dropped 56% between 1977 and 1985 – from 452,000 to 200,000. Battered by foreign imports and the worst economic recession since World War II,

the major integrated steel companies lost a total of more than $4.2bn in operating profits in 1985 and 1986.

In response to these dire circumstances the union, in its 1986 wage policy statement, 'recognised', in Newman and Yoffee's words, 'that *some* of the major steel companies required temporary short term financial relief'. They described what happened in the union's negotiations with LTV, the major integrated steelworks from which Republic Engineered Steels was later bought out.

In April 1986 USWA and LTV Steel Corporation reached a three year labour agreement that became a model for negotiations in the rest of the steel industry. The new LTV agreement established a unique 'Employee Investment Program' enabling dollar-for-dollar repayment of employee sacrifices through a combination of annual cash profit sharing and stock ownership through a non-leveraged ESOP.

Similar agreements, also involving minority ESOPs, were later negotiated by the USWA with other large companies in the steel industry – for example with Bethlehem Steel Corporation and with Wheeling-Pittsburgh. Indeed between 1986 and the end of the decade they came to affect quite large numbers of USWA's members. They also seem to have worked as intended. The authors report that, with the industry's financial recovery in the later 1980s, 'the wage and benefit sacrifices made in 1985 and 1986 were restored at many of the big steel companies'.

Because majority employee ownership is so much more eye-catching and radical, there is perhaps a danger of devoting less than the attention it deserves to this investment bargaining pioneered by the USWA, and to the minority employee ownership resulting from it. Yet on the face of it, this is a most valuable extra device for enabling businesses to get through difficult times with a lower incidence of redundancies and lay-offs. If the alternative on offer to the workforce is a straight wage cut, then it is easy to see that a trade off of shares for pay reductions must be a preferable alternative for employees. It also scores more highly on the scale of fairness. Perhaps what is remarkable is not that investment bargaining was pioneered by the USWA in the 1980s, but that it has been so little tried at other times and elsewhere. Presumably it will at least remain a feature of the steel industry in the US, and an especially valuable one during periods of recession in the business cycle.

In its policy of investment bargaining and of support for minority ESOPs, the USWA deserves high marks for correctly identifying the thrust of its members' enlightened self-interest, and then persuading them to move in accordance with it. And the same is true, and arguably even more so, when we move to its record in relation to 'majority ESOPs'.

In this case the statistics tell much of the story. The starting point is the table at the end of the case study which includes eighteen businesses in which USWA played the leading role in a buy-out and the ESOP purchased a majority of the corporation. Among those majority buy-outs there had been just two failures by the autumn of 1997. One was a small roofing business, Chester Roofing, in West Virginia. The second was another quite small undertaking, Pittsburgh Forgings. It is true and it is made clear in the table that not all of the 'majority buy-outs' have remained so owned. For example, Northwestern Steel and Wire and the titanium business Oremet in Oregon moved from being majority to minority employee-owned following needed injections of new capital. The Copper Range Mine in Michigan also moved from being a majority to a minority ESOP, but in rather different circumstances. There the change is essentially explained by success. The subject of a majority employee buy-out in 1985, the business was so successful that the mine's employee shareholders attracted an offer from a German company which they felt unable to refuse. According to Newman and Yoffee, 'as a result of the sale the typical USWA member received approximately $50,000'. They round off the story by telling their readers:

> The German buyer also agreed to a new labour agreement with wage and benefit improvements as well as establishing a new ESOP that can acquire up to 20% of the successor company; and agreed to continued union representation on the successor company's board of directors.

The resale of the Copper Range Mine is one of the most significant events in the whole of USWA's majority ESOP experience to date. But in terms of achievement, it is the overall record – of successes well into double figures and only two failures – for which the union deserves the highest praise. There are very few venture capital undertakings which can match this success rate.

The union rightly attributes this success rate to the thoroughness of the studies which it insists must be carried out before it will consider recommending a buy-out. In some cases as many as three studies have been undertaken: first a relatively low cost pre-feasibility study; and then full feasibility studies, by consultants and investment bankers, including a business plan. Well over 80 companies have been the subject of these preparatory studies, of which the union eventually supported a buy-out in 15 to 20 cases. In other words, as Newman and Yoffee point out, 'approximately 80% of these studies indicated that an employee buy-out was *not* feasible'.

We have seen that adversity was what first impelled the USWA to look at employee ownership, whether partial or majority, as a possible way of saving its members' jobs. But its experience of success in both versions extended its range of interest. It became prepared to consider supporting employee buy-outs in cases where the jobs of its members were not immediately at risk. It did so when it judged that an employee buy-out of a reasonably healthy business, or part of a business, would better serve its members' interests than purchase by a particular third party.

Standing back we can now see that the USWA has an unusually developed and sophisticated policy about employee ownership of both the minority and the majority variety. Its chief features are really twofold: first an insistence that any ESOP which the union backs must be free of the 'three fatal flaws' identified by Mr Smith in his Yale speech; second, an insistence that no decision to support an ESOP may be taken without a most thorough antecedent study.

As we approach the end of this discussion, it is worth recalling the final epigraph at the start of this case study of the USWA's employee ownership record. When USWA's international president, Lynn Williams, finished his keynote speech on employee ownership at the union's 1988 Congress, he was greeted with 'thunderous acclamation'. Subsequently the union's head office was asked to prepare proposals for the setting up of a new independent agency to look after its members' interests in majority employee-owned companies.

In what was perhaps the final notable event of Mr Lynn Williams's notable presidency, the USWA executive, at the end of January 1994, approved the funding necessary to establish the

Worker Ownership Institute. The step was taken after the AFL-CIO, America's equivalent of Britain's TUC, had found itself unable – through lack of sufficient support from other unions – to set up a similar body with a broader base. Initially membership was restricted to those working in USWA-organised companies which are majority or minority employee-owned. Later it was opened up to other employee-owned companies so long as they satisfy a union membership, but not necessarily an USWA condition.

Even with the initial restriction, people working in Canada as well as the US were eligible for membership. For as the table shows, Algoma Steel in Ontario, Canada's third largest steel business, became employee-owned as a result of an USWA-led employee buy-out in 1992. It is as certain as anything can be that in the absence of USWA and the employee ownership policy developed by it, that buy-out would not have taken place and Algoma Steel would not have survived. But there is not the space to tell the Algoma story here.

Steelworker ESOPs (Worker Ownership Plans)

Company	State/Province	Date	USWA-led	%ESOP	Nos
Alabaster Inds	Alabama	1992	No	50	176
Algoma Steel	Ontario	1992	Yes	60	6,500
American Alloys	W.Virginia	1985	Yes	30	150
Ansonia Copper	Connecticut	1990	Yes	50	250
Badger Northland	Wisconsin	1987	No	50.9	190
Bethlehem Steel	Pennsylvania	1985	Yes	10	20,000
Bliss-Salem	Ohio	1986	Yes	100	150
Channellock	Pennsylvania	1978	No	40	400
*Chester Roofing	W.Virgina	1988	Yes	–	40
Colorado Fuel	Colorado	1986	Yes	38	1,000
Continental Steel	Indiana	1983	No	9	1,400
Copper Range	*Michigan	1985	Yes	Changed	750
CXT	Washington	1990	No	38	54
Dow Chemical	Michigan	1986	No	1	2,200
Erie Forge/Steel	Pennsylvania	1990	Yes	85	280
Indiana Steel	Indiana	1993	Yes	84	265
Johnstown Corp	Pennsylvania	1984	No	20	500
Kaiser Aluminum	Alabama etc	1985	No	N/A	4,000
Kemp Mfg Co	Minnesota	1993	Yes	60	43
Karostest M.C.	Pennsylvania	1983	No	100	300

LTV Steel	Illinois etc	1986	Yes	N/A	14,000
Market Forge Ind	Minnesota	1993	Yes	100	100
Maryland Brush	Maryland	1990	Yes	80	120
Mclouth Steel	Michigan	1983	Yes	87	1,800
Northwestern Steel	Illinois	1988	Yes	Changed	2,500
Oremet	Oregon	1987	Yes	Changed	270
*Pittsburgh Forge	Pennsylvania	1988	Yes	80	200
Rep/lic Container	W. Virginia	1985	Yes	100	55
RESI	Ohio etc	1989	Yes	100	5,000
Rep/lic Storage	Ohio	1986	Yes	100	400
Sharpville Qlty	Pennsylvania	1993	Yes	53	100
Vither Mfg Corp	Wisconsin	1987	No	N/A	125
Wheeling Pittsburgh	Pennsylvania	1982	Yes	3	5,500

* Closed

Source: Adapted slightly from data supplied Steve Newman and Mike Yoffee of the USWA research staff.

23
Mondragon – One of a Kind

INTRODUCTORY OVERVIEW

Co-operatism is not an ideology at Mondragon. It is a business strategy. *Mondragon Corporacion Cooperativa, 1995*

The enlightened goodwill of men acting in an individual capacity is the only possible principle of social progress. *Simone Weil, 1977*

From 1976 to 1986 we have been able to create 4,200 jobs when in Euskadi [the Basque Country] more than 150,000 jobs were *lost* [emphasis added] in the same period ... As you see it is not a brilliant result, but only a process of adjustment carefully calculated, reflecting the spirit of solidarity and audacity, has made it possible to avoid having any co-operative member unemployed. *José Maria Ormaechea, former chief executive of Caja Laboral (formerly the Caja Laboral Popular), 1986*

Late in 1995 the leadership of the Mondragon Co-operatives was summoned to a ceremony in New York to receive one of fifty awards worldwide which were handed out for an outstanding contribution, awards issued to celebrate the fiftieth anniversary of the United Nations. And indeed, the Mondragon Group is one of a kind among these case studies of employee-owned businesses. During forty years well over 100 co-operative enterprises were created, providing more than 30,000 jobs by the mid-1990s. It is true that the Mondragon Group is still smaller than either Britain's John Lewis Partnership (JLP), for example, or the group of German businesses associated with Germany's Carl-Zeiss-Stiftung. But it had grown from a standing and employee-owned start. By contrast, John Lewis and Zeiss have 60 and 100 years respectively of employee ownership behind them and each was the offspring of previously successful and long-established capitalist undertakings dating back to the mid-nineteenth century. If average annual rates of growth are the best measure of socio-economic business success, then the Mondragon Group is probably the star performer of all those studied in this book. By the mid-1990s the Mondragon cooperatives affiliated to Mondragon Corporacion Co-operativa (MCC) – the umbrella organisation for most of them – were in aggregate the ninth largest business in Spain by turnover, generating profits of pesetas 30–40bn.

As for Mondragon, which is pronounced with the stress on the final syllable, it is the Spanish name of a small town in Guipuzcoa, one of the country's three Basque provinces. The town's Basque name is Arrasate. Even in the mid-1990s a large minority of the group's total activity was still concentrated in Mondragon itself or in its immediate neighbourhood.

Apart from geography, the other cornerstone of the group – almost from its inception – has been the co-operative membership arrangements. These were based on three main principles: first, employees have to buy their way into a job by making a down-payment before they start employment; second, employees must be members of the co-operative where they work (and thus indirectly of bodies like MCC); and third, each employee has an equal vote. These arrangements are discussed in the last section of this study.

The group includes a wider range of activities than any other of the businesses or groups of businesses among these case studies. For it extends from manufacturing to banking and from farming to retail distribution. It also includes schools and housing co-ops and an array of specialised institutions ranging from a research centre to its own social insurance and welfare agency. However, despite this astonishing diversity, it is the group's manufacturing co-operatives which have been historically at its heart. Until the last decade they accounted for easily the largest share of both employment and value added. The service sector became mainly responsible for the continued growth of the group from the later 1980s; but even in the late 1990s the industrial co-operatives still accounted for well over half of group employment.

Moreover, within the industrial or manufacturing sector there is a wide span of activity. Domestic appliances, or so called 'white' goods and their components, were traditionally the most important product lines, but there are others, including car components, machine tools, building materials, castings and dies.

Apart from membership of the group and a set of common co-operative arrangements and rules, most of these ventures share a common geography and a Basque national identity. This comes from their location in one of the three provinces of Spain which are officially Basque – Alava, Vizcaya and Guipuzcoa – or in neighbouring Navarra.

However, changes started to happen from the mid-1980s onwards. Geographically there were the beginnings of an expansion in Spain outside the Basque heartland and even abroad, especially in retailing (Eroski) and banking (Caja Laboral, formerly Caja Laboral Popular), but also increasingly in manufacturing too. Second, new business structures began to be permitted diluting the co-operative 'purity' of the earlier years. Whether this dilution indicates a failure of the co-operative model in the face of growing competitive pressures – or whether it is a case of peripheral adaptation which ensures survival and future success is one of the debates surrounding Mondragon as it looks to the future.

Mondragon was conceived with the arrival in the town in 1941 of a Basque catholic priest, Fr José Maria Arizmendiarrieta. Under his leadership a modest apprentice school was opened for local boys. It was five of the original graduates from that apprentice school – who later studied part time to achieve engineering degrees at Zaragoza University – who were the founders of the first co-operative, ULGOR. At the apprentice school and other youth clubs and associations organised by Arizmendiarrieta, they had listened to lectures by Fr Arizmendiarrieta on Catholic social teaching. He was later their adviser when it came to the starting of ULGOR and the establishment of the first co-operative structure; and he remained the key adviser and inspiration for the rapidly expanding group down to his death in 1976.

ULGOR's five founders were not only professionally qualified engineers. They had gained management experience by working in Mondragon's largest business of the conventional capitalist kind – the Union Cerrajera, which was mainly engaged in steel fabrication. Very rarely in the history of the last 150 years have the founding fathers of a new start-up co-operative had this combination of professional qualifications and managerial experience – otherwise the typical life story of those ventures would have been notably more successful.

After making full allowance for the drive of Fr Arizmendiarrieta, it is clear that ULGOR's founders, or at least the four of them that remained in the group, were entrepreneurially talented. ULGOR started in 1956 with a workforce of just over twenty people, and a modest oil stove as its only product. Particularly after the founding of the group's bank, the Caja Laboral Popular (CLP) in 1959, growth was explosive:

	Number of Co-ops	Number of Members
1956	1	23
1960	4	395
1964	32	2,620
1968	49	5,981
1972	57	10,436
1976	69	15,417
1980	92	18,733

*Note: numbers include the bank, the group's retail network and its agricultural co-ops, but not educational establishments and housing co-ops.
Source: Wiener(1987)

Growth was qualitative as well as quantitative. This earlier period was marked by an almost uninterrupted increase in the output of 'white goods' and in the size of ULGOR, the business in which this production was concentrated. At its largest, in 1979, employment in ULGOR reached close to 4,000 people.

As implied in the third epigraph, it is arguable that the golden years of growth ended in the mid-1970s. When he wrote the article from which the epigraph was taken, José Maria Ormaechea, one of ULGOR's founders and later chief executive of the CLP, was contrasting the ten years' experience down to 1986 – when the group had to struggle to avoid the consequences of recession – with the easier conditions which had prevailed before. In an earlier period, he noted, employment in the group had been growing 'at the rate of about 15% annually, in a national market that was growing at the rate of 6 to 7% of gross national product'.

There may be differences of opinion about exactly when the slowdown of growth should be dated. But the main point is not in doubt. It is that the the group outperformed Spain's conventional capitalist competition both in the long expansionary phase of the economy's business cycle; and in the subsequent years of recession. It grew faster in the former period; and it withstood the recession much more effectively, even managing a significant amount of real growth during those difficult years. One of the most interesting success stories in the group's whole history is how the effects of that recession on group employment were contained – a story which repeated itself in the early 1990s.

What then of the period since Mr Ormaechea wrote his article in 1986?

Among the manufacturing businesses these years have been marked by an almost continuous process of restructuring which indeed started earlier. Symbolic of this restructuring is what has happened to ULGOR. Numbers employed there fell dramatically from their earlier peak. They did so as the output of 'white goods' was restructured and as the earlier mass production systems were largely replaced by more flexible ones. By the early 1990s employment in what used to be ULGOR, but was renamed Fagor Electricodomesticos in 1989, was not much more than half the peak level of 1979, though by 1997 it had jumped back to 3,500..

On the other hand, as a partial offset to the employment consequences of the continuous restructuring of its 'white goods ' production, the group succeeded in the second half of the 1980s and mid-1990s in establishing itself in a major new market – for motor industry components. By the early 1990s, car components accounted for as much as 20% of group manufacturing sales. In the industrial sector the successful penetration of this new market has been a most notable achievement of the group's later years. Furthermore the quality of the group's motor car components has been widely praised – for example in 1992 it received from General Motors Europe its 'Best Supplier of the Year' award.

These successes notwithstanding, most of the growth since the mid-1980s has come either in the service sector or from acquisitions and joint ventures. Two early notable acquisitions were of Fabrelec and Luzuriaga. Each employing over 1,000 people, these were simply acquired by purchase after a change of group policy in the late 1980s. Fabrelec makes 'white goods' in the neighbourhood of Bilbao; and Luzuriaga is a foundry operation spread over a number of sites which produces castings mainly for the motor industry. In both cases their acquisition was designed to strengthen the position in their respective markets of important existing group businesses. On the other hand those working in these two undertakings, Luzuriaga and Fabrelec, chose to settle for different corporate identities over the long term. The former is to remain a conventional wholly-owned subsidiary of the group as a whole. At Fabrelec, by contrast, the workforce voted in 1997 to become a cooperative and for a name change to EDESA. What's more that is not the only example of workers in a newly acquired business voting themselves into a cooperative future. MAPSA when acquired was a bankrupt capitalist undertaking which made components for the motor industry. Like their counterparts at Fabrelec a majority of its workforce voted to adopt a cooperative structure with the associated capital contributions by its members.

But to refer to the question of growth: if the effect of these acquisitions is excluded, then the numbers employed in the group's manufacturing businesses fell. Again, if acquisitions are excluded, employment growth in the group as a whole has mainly been attributable to expansion by the group's retail network, Eroski, its bank, the Caja Laboral Popular, and other smaller service activities.

About the present (late 1990s) and future levels of employment in the group's manufacturing businesses two rather different points seem worth making. The first is that over the middle years of the 1990s manufacturing employment, measured as a percentage of the total, appeared at about 55% to hold up rather well. But second and over the long term the proportion of total group employment engaged in manufacture seems bound to decline, a trend common to all the developed countries of the West. It is also almost a necessary consequence of the continuing success of the group's manufacturing businesses at improving the productivity of their labour. To highlight just one statistic: in the four years down to 1989/90 labour productivity in the consumer durables businesses within the group's manufacturing activity – that is in its mainly 'white goods' undertakings – increased by an annual average of 8.5%. With one qualification, it seems out of the question that the group could manage to increase its market share of these essentially 'mature' goods at the same pace. So, subject to that qualification, employment in those businesses seems bound to decline.

The qualification is, of course, about exports, which fluctuated around 25% of total industrial sales during the 1980s and early 1990s. But they had rocketed up to 46% by 1997 and it looked as if they might well be on target to achieve the goal of 50% which had been set for the year 2000.

It is a plausible hypothesis that the removal of Spain's tariff barriers associated with its EU membership was, to begin with, more a source of new problems than of new opportunities for the group. On the other hand the huge increase in the export percentage in the middle and later 1990s suggest that the balance of advantage from Spain's EU membership later moved in the group's favour. It had needed to become more market-orientated and that was clearly a key factor behind the decision to expand, in joint ventures and otherwise, outside the geographical limits of the Basque country and indeed of Spain itself. But what the export figures of the later 1990s seem to show is that the group had by then substantially achieved a shift to greater market orientation.

With the benefit of hindsight, the need for greater market orientation may turn out to be a key shift of emphasis. The first two major acquisitions were driven by a market rather than a co-operative group logic and others have followed. Joint ventures have been established which are not structured as co-operatives. And the whole relationship of the co-operatives with each other has been formalised and centralised around the Mondragon Corporacion Co-operativa (MCC), founded in two stages in 1990 and 1992.

Like much else in Mondragon, the structure of the group started evolving rapidly from the mid-1980s onwards. In effect, from the early 1960s to the mid-1980s what bound these businesses together was their set of formal ties, embodied in a contract of association with the bank (the CLP). During that period the CLP, quite apart from its banking and banking-related functions, performed a leadership role. But at the end of 1984 that was all changed. An elected Co-operative Congress was established and held its first meeting on 19 December of that year. Subsequent to that, the CLP dropped much of its 'special' relationship with the Mondragon co-operatives and its management consultancy role was spun off into a separate co-operative or into MCC headquarters control department. Now, for most of the co-operatives, MCC performs a federal government role, particularly in strategic planning – although a few refuse to participate in these new arrangements.

Finally, a point of history. With one exception, the founders of ULGOR had all gone into retirement by the end of the 1980s. In effect the group's leadership was passed to a new generation. Inescapably the prestige of the new leaders is less than that of the founders. What is perhaps striking is that the group has managed to weather this once-and-for-all transition without any marked conflict or instability.

Early History down to 1959 In 1956 five young engineers set up a small new manufacturing business, in a factory built for the purpose, in their home town of Mondragon in Spain's Basque province of Guipuzcoa. Their family names were Usatorre, Larrañaga, Gorroñogoitia, Ormaechea and Ortubay: which they rolled into the acronym ULGOR, to supply the new venture with its name. At the start there was just one product line, unsophisticated oil stoves for cooking, and a workforce which is reported to have numbered twenty-three. In its early days the business was incorporated as a conventional private company limited by shares.

Earlier, in 1955, these same five young engineers had tried to establish their own new business in a less direct way: by the purchase of a bankrupt one in nearby Vitoria. That attempt was not a marked success. But Mondragon had the great advantage of being their home town and one in which they were already quite well known as 'local boys who had made good'. Above all they had the support in Mondragon of the local Catholic priest, Fr Arizmendiarrieta, a man who had already shown outstanding ability as a catalyst of local community initiatives. A convivial institution in the life of young men in the Basque country of those days was the so-called *chiquiteo* – a kind of peer group drinking club and entity for mutual support. It seems that the five relied partly on the friends and contemporaries in their *chiquiteo*, and very much on the support of Fr Arizemediarreta, when it came to raising the capital of ptas 11m needed for the company to open for business.

ULGOR evidently got off to flying start. An early observer, Desroches, reports that it was already employing a workforce of 143 by end-1958, less than three years from start-up. The potential of the business was greatly strengthened when, in the same year, butane gas having reached Mondragon for the first time, the production of gas cookers was added to that of the original oil stoves.

For a British reader Mondragon may perhaps usefully be compared with one of the small towns in the valleys of South Wales. Even if the mountains of South Wales are scarcely a match in height or cragginess for their Basque country counterparts, in the early postwar years the economic and social landscape was not dissimilar. The characteristic settlements of both regions at that time were small industrial towns and/or large industrial villages.

Within the category of small Basque industrial towns, Mondragon might have claimed, before it became world famous for its co-operative group, several special features. One was the antiquity of its metal-working tradition. According to *Encyclopaedia Britannica*, the swords of Mondragon became famous well before those of Toledo. In the early 1940s, when the five engineers who started ULGOR were in their early teens, that metal-working tradition was chiefly represented in Mondragon by a steel-fabricating business of a substantial size and a conventional capitalist character: the Union Cerrajera.

A second feature which distinguished Mondragon from other small Basque industrial towns was the radicalism of its political tradition: a radicalism which embraced both the politics of labour versus capital and the politics of Basque nationalism. Evidence of the former includes an apparently ferocious strike mounted by its labour against the managers and owners at the Union Cerrajera in 1916. The stoppage is reported to have lasted several months before the strike eventually folded. Other evidence comes from the Asturias rebellion in 1934: when the Asturias miners raised the flag of workers' revolution at Oviedo in 1934, the only armed contingent which marched to their support from outside the region came from Mondragon. Then again, in the Spanish Civil War three Mondragon battalions fought on the side of the Republic against the forces of General Franco: one socialist, one nationalist and one made up of less directly affiliated volunteers.

It seems too that Mondragon's Basque nationalism was strengthened by its geographical position. It was never of course the region's capital and it did not have the singular associations with Basque history enjoyed by Guernica. But it was in a central position roughly equidistant from the three main centres of Basque population – Bilbao, San Sebastian and Vitoria.

The Basques, and not just the citizens of Mondragon, were solidly against General Franco in the Civil War. And that was true almost as much of the region's Catholic priests and hierarchy as of its Catholic laity. In February 1941 Arizmendiarrieta arrived in Mondragon with a special mission enjoined upon him by his bishop: to pay special attention to the needs of youth. In 1941 he had behind him not only his years of study at the seminary in Vitoria. He had also been in uniform, on the Republican side, in the Civil War. In fact, he had quite narrowly avoided execution after being captured by Franco's soldiers. His rather unusual army job was editing a trade union newspaper for his fellows in the Republican army to read.

When Fr Arizmendiarrieta arrived in Mondragon, the Civil War had ended less than two years before. Franco's soldiers and police were quartered in the town and evidently behaved like an army of occupation. It was forbidden to speak the Basque language in public. It goes without saying that there was a complete interdiction on political or trade union activity, except within the Government's Fascist framework.

In his mission to the youth, Fr Arizmendiarrieta's first initiative, in these rather unpromising conditions, was an approach to the top management of the Union Cerrajera. The company operated a small apprentice school for boys, the only facility of its kind in the town and neighbourhood of Mondragon. Fr Arizmendiarrieta's request to its top management was that the size of their apprentice school should be modestly increased. The request was coupled with an offer that, with the help of the local church and local parents, he would find the necessary extra cash. The company refused. What happened next was described in my earlier book as follows:

> Fr Arizmendiarrieta then set about achieving his ends in a different way: he would promote a new and separate technical school. Support from the community was mobilised by techniques which were both ingenious and daring. Ballot-box type objects, 'urns', were placed at street corners; members of the local community were invited to drop pieces of paper inside, indicating whether they would support a new technical school with cash or in kind. It is said that 600 positive responses were found when the 'urns' were emptied. Since Mondragon's population was then about 8,000, the response represented support from roughly 25% of the town's families.

In any case, though both the local authority and the Union Cerrajera chose not to contribute, the support promised in the 'urns' was judged sufficient to go ahead. A small new school, with an initial enrolment of twenty students, was opened in October 1943. Equally important, the involvement of the local community was strongly maintained. Those who contributed elected the school's management committee. Moreover, because of recurrent costs fund raising continued. The students themselves, we are told, played a large part in organising the activities which brought in the money. Their link with the local community was thus put on a more or less permanent basis – and they had gained some first experience of organising themselves and others to get things done.

There are no prizes for guessing that the first intake into the new school included those five young men who later became the founders of ULGOR. There are no prizes either for guessing that the school's curriculum included, as well as technical subjects, lectures by Fr Arizmendiarrieta on Catholic social teaching.

The upper limit of the technical teaching at the new school was quite modest. It could equip people for junior technician posts and even to be foremen. But it was in no position to offer courses leading to professional degrees. To overcome that limitation Fr Arizmendiarrieta performed another invaluable service. He persuaded the authorities of the engineering institute in Zaragoza to accept eleven of the new Mondragon apprentice school's graduates as part-time students. The arrangement was that these young men would combine working for their living with part-time study. And so it came about that these same eleven successfully passed the professional engineering examinations at Zaragoza in 1952. There are no prizes for guessing that ULGOR's five founders were among this group as well.

Before leaving what were in effect a series of educational initiatives which predate the setting up of the first Mondragon business, one further development must be chronicled. As early as 1948 Fr Arizmendiarrieta was instrumental in the creation of an umbrella organisation to have responsibility for education and training development in the town. It was called the League for Education and Culture. Its most famous subsequent offspring was Mondragon's exceptional polytechnic-type institution, the Escuela Profesional Politecnica.

The remaining parts of the intervening story can be quickly told. Before launching out on their own – first, as we have seen, in Vitoria with limited success, and then in Mondragon itself – four of these five young qualified engineers took junior management posts with the Union Cerrajera. There they apparently sought to persuade its top management to reform the structures of the business in ways suggested by Fr Arizmendiarrieta's lectures. It was only when this effort at persuasion ended predictably in failure that they decided to try to start a business of their own.

The successful start-up of a new business from scratch is often, and rightly, presented as one of the most challenging tasks of the twentieth century. What is striking about this case of ULGOR is how quickly its founders seem to have had the time to devote to additional activity of an entrepreneurial character. As early as the second year after start-up, in 1958, ULGOR took over two previously capitalist foundries in the neighbouring village of Escoriaza; thereby, among other things, securing a supply of one of its main needed materials.

In the case of those foundries the entrepreneurship of ULGOR's promoters was directly involved. But their example also seems to have been of great importance in these early years. For by the end of the 1950s five other 'confederate' manufacturing businesses had been started, either in Mondragon itself or nearby. They can be described as confederate because in 1959, following ULGOR's example, they transformed themselves from share companies into cooperatives; and because, when the group was later formed, they joined it.

The 'Confederate' Five

Name	Where	Main Product
Arrasate	Mondragon	Machine tools
Construcciones San José	Hernani	Grinding machines
Funcor	Elorrio	Foundry products
Talleres Ochandiano	Ochandiano	Food-handling equipment
Tolsan	Amorebieta	Forgings

The establishment of the first consumer co-operative, also in Mondragon itself, dates from this same period. From the small beginning of a single store can be traced the development of today's rapidly expanding retail network: Eroski. Eroski is notable not only for its size and its rapid expansion in the late 1980s and 1990s. What is perhaps most striking about it is the sophisticated ownership and control structure which it developed in its early days: in which the interests of the consumers and of those who work in the retail network are finely balanced.

The real key to future development in these early days was the legal registration of a credit co-operative in 1959, a step formally acknowledged by a notice in Spain's official gazette in July of that year. Before the end of 1959 two branches were in business: one in Mondragon and one in Elorrio, across the provincial boundary in neighbouring Vizcaya. The rightly famous Mondragon Bank, the Caja Laboral Popular (CLP), was under way. This was the brainchild not of ULGOR's founders but of Fr Arizmendiarrieta. It is not too much to claim that the subsequent development of the group would have been impossible without the local savings which the bank mobilised and then invested in co-operative ventures. From the early 1960s to the mid-1980s it was the set of links between the bank and the individual co-ops which constituted the Mondragon group structure. Those links took the form of a set of contracts of association. The two top posts in the CLP were held for many years by two of ULGOR's founders: the chief executive was José Maria Ormaechea and the chairman Alfonso Gorroñogoitia.

The change in corporate status from companies to co-operatives was effected both by ULGOR and by the other new start-up businesses in 1959. Again, the head and the hand of Fr Arizmendiarrieta was behind them.

Some will divine the hand of providence behind the growth of the co-operatives in Mondragon after Fr Arizmendiarrieta first arrived. But two other ways of looking at what happened seem worth suggesting. One is to point to a kind of dialectic: between the interdiction by the Franco regime of any genuinely free political or trade union activity; and the channelling of creative energy into rather different fields – technical education and Catholic social teaching. We may then pose the question: could the second, and today's quite exceptional co-operative grouping which is its fruit, have happened without the first?

But perhaps the whole story is best presented as yet another example of the importance of the contingent in human affairs. If we look at what happened in this way, we will be inclined to emphasise the absence of any necessity in the sequence of developments. There was nothing necessary about Fr Arizmendiarrieta's arrival in Mondragon in 1941; nothing necessary about his bishop's injunction that he should specially concern himself with the problems of the youth; nothing necessary about the community's response to the initiative he proposed after having been rebuffed by the Union Cerrajera. And this line could clearly be extended indefinitely. In other words, what we have here may be no more, but also no less, than a case of one good thing happening to lead on to another.

From the Early 1960s to 1980s: The Golden Years of Rapid Growth
In the article from which I quoted in the epigraph, José Maria Ormaechea suggested that the Group passed over something like a watershed in the mid-1970s, after which economic conditions were never really the same again. (In fact the statistics seem to suggest that the discontinuity occurred rather later.)

If we include the Caja Laboral Popular (CLP) and the retail store, eight of these Mondragon businesses – by then all co-ops – were trading in 1960. Total numbers employed at that date seem to have been just short of 400.

For the twenty years down to 1979 the numbers of co-ops and the numbers employed are set out in the table.

Year	Numbers Employed	Numbers of Co-ops
1960	395	8
1961	520	12
1962	801	18
1963	1,780	29
1964	2,620	32
1965	3,441	36
1966	4,202	39
1967	5,082	48
1968	5,981	49
1969	7,945	47
1970	8,543	52
1971	9,416	55
1972	10,436	57
1973	11,417	58
1974	12,915	63
1975	13,808	65
1976	15,417	69
1977	16,504	73
1978	17,022	78
1979	18,295	87

The striking feature of these figures is the consistency of the speed of expansion, at least after the slower build-up of numbers employed in the earlier years. Between the start of 1961 and the end of 1969 a total of 39 extra co-operative businesses were added. Between the start of 1970 and the end of 1979 the corresponding figure was a total of 40 new businesses. Over the 20-year period the group was growing by an average of just less than 4 new co-ops each year: 79 new ones over 20 years.

Two further points are worth underlining. First, very nearly all the additional businesses added to the group during these years – over 70 out of the 79 – were brand new undertakings started from scratch. Very few were the result of the conversion into co-ops of businesses which had previously existed as conventional capitalist companies. The extra numbers due to the splitting off as separate entities of parts of an earlier integrated business were also very few. And so were the numbers of previously independent co-ops which successfully applied to join the group. In fact I know of only one in this category: a leading manufacturer of machine tools, Danobat. Thus far the greatest part of this expansion consisted of the 'organic' growth of new co-operative ventures. So far as I know there has been nothing to compare with it in previous co-operative history.

Second, in this twenty years of new business start-ups there were almost no failures. Once again there is nothing to compare with this in the history of co-operative business. And the proportion of survivors is far higher than would be expected by, for example, a successful venture capitalist.

The rate of employment expansion was also remarkably steady. That emerges particularly clearly if we divide the twenty years into five sequential periods of four years.

Growth of Numbers Employed: 4-Year Periods 1960–1979

Years	Extra Numbers
1960–63	1,385
1964–67	3,300
1968–71	4,334
1972–75	4,397
1976–79	4,487

This steadiness is partly explained by the fact that over this period the responsibilities of a particular division of the bank, the

Caja Laboral Popular (CLP), covered the promotion of new jobs in existing co-operatives as well as in new ventures started from scratch.

A final set of statistics traces the growth of group sales:

Group Sales: (Billions of Pesetas) 1965–85
Constant 1985 prices

1965	17.2	1972	65.1	1979	114.2
1966	25.1	1973	72.6	1980	119.5
1967	29.3	1974	83.9	1981	126.0
1968	32.3	1975	80.1	1982	124.8
1969	48.4	1976	85.6	1983	128.9
1970	50.8	1977	94.5	1984	131.0
1971	54.1	1978	101.3	1985	141.0

Any explanation of this phenomenal growth should take full account of the propitious features of the Spanish economy during the 1960s and early 1970s. These were very much, to use the cliché of the time, the years of Spain's economic miracle. There was a strong and sustained growth in domestic demand and it took place within a heavily protected market. It was not only the group of Mondragon co-operatives which achieved high levels of growth of manufacturing output and manufacturing employment during this period.

And yet, as we saw earlier, during this whole period the employment growth of the Mondragon co-ops easily outperformed that of the Spanish economy as a whole. So it looks as if there *is* something extra to be explained. During the 1960s that extra is probably best accounted for by the example of ULGOR and its early associates; and by the fact that from its very beginnings the CLP was in principle prepared to make loans to help new co-operative ventures to get off the ground.

But from 1969 onwards there is a more specific extra factor which helps us to explain this extraordinary phenomenon of successful new business start-ups and subsequent growth. In that year a decision was taken to set up, within the bank, a new and specialised agency. The agency was to have special responsibilities for the future growth of the group and for overseeing the quality of business performance. It was given the Basque name of Lankide Sustaketa (LKS) which is how it has been known since it was spun off from the CLP in 1991. But during the years which it spent inside the CLP it was most generally known by its Spanish name, the 'Empresarial' Division. The best English translation would be the 'Entrepreneurial Division'. For some reason most of those who have written about it in English have favoured a more insipid translation and called it the Management Services Division. In what follows I shall use the Spanish word 'Empresarial'.

From its inception, the most specific responsibilities of the Empresarial Division concerned the provision of specialist assistance to the existing co-ops and help with the process of getting new ones started. An equal priority seems to have been assigned to each of these tasks. Specialists in the division's professional staff, which was built up quite rapidly until it numbered just over 100, worked with the existing co-ops or with prospective new ones, depending on the balance of need at any particular time. The work with the potential new start-up businesses was no doubt more eye-catching and original, and commentators have understandably devoted more attention to it. But it seems probable that more of the time of the division's professional staff was in fact spent working with the existing businesses: whether helping them to expand or simply to stay out of trouble. There is no need to describe that work. Its character is obvious enough. Evidence of its success is the almost complete absence of business failure in the group over many years. In effect this branch of the division's work can perhaps best be seen as a kind of 'hands on' version of the superintendence exercised by German and Japanese banks over the businesses in which they are important shareholders.

On the other hand, if only because of its originality, there is a case for offering a brief account of the work of the Empresarial Division in relation to new start ups. What perhaps can best be called a selective and stage-by-stage midwifing process was invented by the division and is described at some length in my earlier book. I summarise it here.

The midwifing process evidently came into existence in response to local demand. We may imagine would-be co-operative entrepreneurs approaching the new division and asking for help in the task of going forward to the establishment of a successful new business. At the stage of this first approach, the business would already have had a specific product and market focus. The would-be co-operative entrepreneur might be an individual alone or a group. The division was a natural choice as an appropriate body to approach with such a request. For it was part of a co-operative bank which was already in the business of making loans to co-operative ventures. The bank could thus be expected to offer similar borrowing facilities to such newly starting businesses – provided that its own lending conditions could be satisfied.

It needs to be stressed that in all cases the first approach, and the associated product and market ideas, came from the would-be co-operative entrepreneur. From its inception, the staff of the Empresarial Division insisted on that as a matter of rule. Any other policy would have called into question the ultimate responsibility for the success or failure of the potential project. It was essential, in the Division's view, that this responsibility should rest from the outset with the would-be entrepreneur; or rather with the would-be entrepreneur and his or her associates. The qualification is necessary because the division further insisted from the start that it would not offer its services to would-be co-operative entrepreneurs on their own. The potential other members, or at least some of them, the potential employees of the prospective co-operative business, had also to be involved from the start of the midwifing process.

The 'high summer' of this co-operative midwifing activity by the CLP's Empresarial Division was the 1970s and early 1980s. Thereafter policy changed and new ventures were promoted, if at all, marsupially – inside existing co-operatives – and only later split off as separate entities. During the high summer period an average of three of four new ventures were successfully midwifed annually. It is this record which has frequently been presented as the single most remarkable business achievement in the Mondragon group's whole history.

As compared with this annual average of three or four new start ups, it seems that the division was typically approached by perhaps ten would-be co-operative entrepreneurs each year. The rest evidently failed to satisfy the sequential conditions which the division imposed during the midwifing process. Only those who satisfied all the earlier conditions were permitted to go forward to the final stage. This was an approach to the CLP's banking division to provide, in the form of loans, whatever finance was judged to be necessary for the venture and which could not be raised by the co-op's prospective members. Typically, a capital contribution per prospective co-operative member equivalent to around one year's salary was required under CLP rules.

What conditions were required for success and how did the midwifing process work? In a fair proportion of cases the product around which they were centred was judged inappropriate within the framework of the group's existing businesses and objectives. Products, and therefore approaches, were turned down because their capital needs per member of the prospective co-op were judged to be beyond the resources of a combination of those members and the bank. As frequently, they were turned down for something like the opposite reason: because the product was judged to fall below a minimum level of technology and sophistication which the division insisted upon. The logic of that was a clear policy objective that the group should seek to raise the quality of the goods and services produced in the Basque country.

Given the satisfaction of this first pair of conditions, a lengthy process, lasting in many cases for well over twelve months, got under way. The key first step was the requirement to choose a prospective manager. If the first approach had been made by an individual would-be entrepreneur, then that person might be chosen as prospective manager. That was not compulsory, how-ever, and a prospective manager could even be chosen from outside. The important point was the suitability and commitment of the potential manager to do the job not his or her provenance.

What happened after that was perhaps the most original feature of the whole process: the prospective manager was taken into the division, and given a salary and an office to work on the project. That happened under a set of arrangements which continued, anyway in principle, until either the new venture got under way or it failed to satisfy one of the subsequent conditions in the series. Meanwhile, a senior member of the division's professional staff was assigned to work jointly with the prospective manager on the project, and to assume a role of 'godfather' to it. Where the project went forward to actual implementation, this 'godfather' was required to stay with it for at least the first twelve months after the start of trading.

With the help of the 'godfather', and with access to the whole range of the division's specialist departments, the prospective manager was essentially required to produce successive drafts of an ever more detailed feasibility study and business plan for the proposed venture. Throughout this pre-investment period, he or she was also required to keep in regular contact with the other members of the prospective co-op and to keep them fully informed. In relation to the prospective membership, he or she had the further task of offering them a full account of what their obligations and rights would be in the event of actual start up: and in particular their obligations to make significant capital contributions to it.

In other words, the process was designed around two main objectives. First it had the objective of making sure that when the bank itself eventually came to decide whether or not it should lend the money necessary to allow the business to get under way, that decision would be reached with the benefit of the best possible information. The second objective of the process was to maximise the commitment to it, and indeed to the group as a whole, of its prospective members, including its prospective manager.

Since it was largely discontinued in the mid-1980s, this exceptional business midwifing process has been the subject of some criticism inside the group. It has been suggested that the process itself was not sufficiently entrepreneurial; too 'bookish' perhaps, and not sufficiently market-orientated. It is also pointed out that the claim of a nearly 100% success rate, through strictly correct, is subject to an important qualification. The qualification is that the success of a fair number of the businesses started by this process, at least in its later years, was achieved only at a high cost in financial support by the bank, over significantly longer periods than was originally foreseen.

No doubt the fact that it has been largely discontinued – or retained only in highly modified form – may be taken as evidence that this method of new business midwifing will not always work. Indeed in a really competitive business environment, like those which have prevailed in Spain since it was discontinued, it may work only rarely if at all. All the same it seems to me quite wrong, as well as churlish, not to concede that it had real success in the times for which it was invented. It also seems to me probable that in similar conditions a similar method would also have been likely to produce good results. Indeed I would be inclined to go further and agree with those who have argued that this method and the results achieved by it were the single greatest achievement of the group during the years of its golden growth. The charge that the costs were excessive, in the sense of imposing an unacceptable drain on the financial resources of the bank, will scarcely stand up in the light of the actual record of the CLP.

So far we have discussed mainly the statistics and the processes of the group's growth in the 1960s and 1970s. In the final part of this section we look at the range of activities spanned by the co-operative businesses which made up the group during this period, and at a small number of particular co-ops.

We begin by excluding – for separate and later discussion – those of the group's businesses which produced services and not actual goods: most notably the bank itself, the social welfare organisation (Lagun-Aro) and the retail stores. We are concerned here only with its manufacturing businesses.

In 1963 ULGOR added to its range of cookers a further product line in the same general category of domestic appliances – refrigerators. By the mid-1970s ULGOR produced a full range of domestic appliances: gas and electric cookers, refrigerators, washing machines and dishwashers. In the 1980s this family of products came to be widely described as 'white goods'. For the country's suppliers of these 'white goods' the Spanish Government proposed a restructuring programme in the mid-1980s, that they should be slimmed down to just three groups. Two of these were to be foreign-owned: by Philips and Electrolux. The third was ULGOR.

The Spanish Government restructuring programme tells us that in the case of ULGOR we are dealing with a business which managed to develop from small beginnings to compete with the top multinationals in Europe-wide markets. It also highlights the supreme importance of ULGOR in the history and results of the group as a whole.

By coincidence, ULGOR's employment and membership numbers peaked in 1979 at a figure of 3,855. That was just over 20% of total group employment and membership at that date. But it was closer to 25% of the employment and membership in the group's manufacturing co-ops. Moreover, if we add in the numbers of those employed by co-ops mainly engaged in supplying components or capital equipment to ULGOR, or in making the castings and forgings which it bought in for incorporation into its domestic appliances, then its weight in the economy of the whole group throughout this period would be shown as that much greater: up to 40% and quite possibly more. A Mondragon resident of some years standing cites what he claims used to be a frequent comment: 'If ULGOR sneezes the whole group will catch a cold.'

Though there have been subsequent changes of classification, the original breakdown by the CLP of the group's manufacturing businesses was into five categories. For the mid-1970s, when the number of manufacturing co-ops was between 50 and 60 and when they employed together between 13,000 and 14,000 people, the approximate distribution of employment between the CLP's five sectors was:

Manufacturing Employment/Mid-1970s Percentages

Foundries & forges	13%
Capital goods (including machine tools)	20%
Building materials & construction	9%
Consumer durables & furniture	32%
Intermediate goods & components	26%

What about the other product lines? Furniture-making has been an important activity in the group since quite early days. At least six furniture-making co-ops were started before the end of the 1960s. In his 1987 study Dr Hans Wiener noted that one of them, the co-operative Citamare in Bilbao, had been in the process of closure in 1986. Export markets are perhaps especially difficult to penetrate if your product is furniture. It seems likely that these businesses found it exceptionally difficult to survive the recession of the 1980s.

Much the same general comments may be applied to the co-ops in the building materials and construction sector. In this case too we are dealing with businesses which have been a feature of the group since the early days. The 1960s saw the start up of five co-ops in this sector. All five were still in business in the early 1990s. Yet it must be imagined that they had a hard struggle to survive.

If export performance is a good measure of quality then we find metal-working is pre-eminent. In Dr Wiener's study the sectors are ranked by the percentage of their total sales accounted for by export sales in 1984: foundries and forges head the table by a significant margin. The capital goods sector is broken into two subsectors: industrial plant and machine tools.

Export Sales as a % of Total Sales by Sector 1984

Foundries and forges	42.4
Components	36.9
Industrial plant	31.3
Machine tools	26.1
Consumer goods	25.3
Building materials etc	11.5

Group exports had climbed to 23% of overall production by 1984

The manufacture of machine tools and industrial plant has figured in the group from early days. There were as many as ten machine-tool co-ops in the group in the middle 1980s. The largest at that time was Danobat. According to Dr Wiener: 'The main product lines have always been grinding machines and lathes, which now appear in their modern guise as numerically controlled machines. Later automatic handling equipment was added to the range and quite recently robots.'

The 1991 accounts of the group's bank, the CLP, identify for the first time a new category of manufactured products: components for the motor industry. The motor components sector is spread over three provinces. One of its oldest, Dr Wiener tells us, was 'making moulds and dies, primarily the dies used in pressing steel sheets into motor car body sections'.

The name of this co-operative, which has since left the group, was Matrici. Dr Wiener, writing in 1987, supplies a thumbnail history:

[It] started in 1963 with twenty-nine members and is still expanding; it is one of the world's leaders in the development of the technology, and it already has the full computer-aided design and manufacturing capability, though most car makers do not yet supply the design in numerical form. Its customers already include General Motors, Mercedes and Volvo, and it is currently attempting to enter both the British and the Japanese market.

Thus, notwithstanding the weight of 'white goods' and their components in the group's manufacturing, there were also other important product lines – especially, perhaps, castings and forgings, machine tools and motor industry components. Given the maturity of Europe's markets for 'white goods' it may well be that these other products will make the greater contribution to employment and value added in the future.

The fundamental fact is that there is no similar co-operative manufacturing group anywhere in the world. There is certainly none with this combination of product range, typically small-scale production units, and export success. There are, of course, clusters of highly successful and relatively small manufacturing businesses in Italy; and they are frequently major exporters. But these small Italian manufacturing businesses cannot match the product range of the Mondragon group. Typically their manufacturing activities are confined to textiles, clothing, footwear and building materials.

Restructuring and Continued Growth in the 1980s and 1990s. With the odd exception, for example 1982, the 1980s and early 1990s were years of continuing output growth in the Mondragon Group, despite the steep recession of 1992/93. Though the growth rate was lower than it had been in the earlier golden years, it was still positive and significant after taking rising prices into account. For the first half of the 1980s Dr Wiener has supplied a series in 1985 prices. For the years 1986 to 1991 I have used the annual reports of the CLP to calculate a similar series, expressed in 1991 prices. In each case we are talking about the turnover of the group's service operations, of the bank and the retail network, as well as of its manufacturing businesses.

Turnover at Mondragon

Ptas bn, 1985 prices until 1986, thereafter in 1991 prices

1980	119.5	1986	211.6
1981	126.0	1987	230.0
1982	124.8	1988	251.5
1983	128.9	1989	285.8
1984	131.0	1990	306.6
1985	141.0	1991	315.2

Following the establishment of MCC in 1990, not all co-operatives remained members of the group. Four healthy manufacturing co-ops chose to leave MCC in 1992. There is at least one earlier precedent for such withdrawals. But so far as I know, they have not happened before in such numbers in a single year. The four, with their main products are: RPK, springs; Gaiko, valves; Ampo, foundry products; Guizpar, reproduction sporting guns and farm spraying equipment.

They were followed by others (notably ULMA in 1993). The later numbers in the statistical series are therefore no longer continuous. From 1991 to 1995, the statistics recorded by MCC for co-ops which are members of the group are as follows:

Manufacturing Co-ops

Year	Sales (bn. psetas, current prices)	Employment nos.
1991	204	16,907
1992	204	16,193
1993	198	15,101
1994	227	14,793
1995	252	15,826

Distribution and Other Service Co-ops

1991	152	6,878
1992	193	7,408
1993	226	8,229
1994	269	9,111
1995	307	10,500

Source: MCC Annual Reports

The overall group numbers give us an indication of the rather differing fortunes over these dozen years of the group's service as against its manufacturing activities. For the decade from the mid-1980s it is only by including acquisitions that the manufacturing sector can be represented as growing. For example, the acquisition of Luzuriaga in 1990 brought in just over 1,300 manufacturing jobs, though growth began again in the middle and late 1990s.. Both in sales and numbers employed, the non-manufacturing sectors – chiefly the activities of the bank (the CLP) and the retail network (Eroski, 'distribution' in the table above) – enjoyed much faster organic growth. For example sales by Eroski accounted for just 22.7% of total group sales in 1985. Its corresponding percentage in 1991 was 29.3. Put differently, but again in constant prices, manufacturing sales increased by just under 48.5% between 1985 and 1991. The corresponding increase in the output of the group's main service activities was just under 62%. By 1997 over half of the MCC sales were accounted for by the retail distribution group (excluding the financial group).

Given the economic conditions, to have managed a nearly 50% increase in manufacturing output over the period 1985 to end-1991 is no modest achievement. On the other hand, competitive pressures forced onto the group's manufacturing co-ops a relentless pursuit of productivity improvement through more or less continuous processes of restructuring. 1989 was also marked by an event in the group's history which has occurred only rarely: a medium sized co-operative called Zertan, which made switches and had a 1989 workforce of nearly 400 people, left the group.

The 1989 accounts of the CLP are notable for the disapearance of the proud name of ULGOR. That did not mean that the 'white goods' production of the group was suddenly discontinued. Essentially, some parts of ULGOR were put into a large white goods specialist manufacturing operation: Fagor Electrodomesticos. And other parts were put into a second white goods specialist which concentrated on smaller objects like microwave ovens and toasters: Fagor Minidomesticos.

The experience of ULGOR may be taken as an example of the intensive restructuring which was experienced during the 1980s by many of the group's manufacturing businesses. After peaking at 3,855 in 1979, ULGOR's workforce fell to 2,256 in 1985. When ULGOR finally disappeared in 1989, and its workforce re-emerged in Fagor Electrodomesticos and Fagor Minidomesticos, the total had come down below 2,000. But then again, by 1997 the total had bounced back to over 3,000.

The continuous restructuring of ULGOR went well beyond any de-manning exercise. There was a general switch to more flexible from mass production systems. With the collaboration of Hitachi from Japan there was investment in new technology. For the mid-1980s Dr Wiener (1987) recorded that the annual production capacities for each of the four main 'white goods' lines which resulted from this restructuring were as follows:

Cookers and ovens	500,000
Refrigerators	400,000
Washing machines	350,000
Washing up machines	150,000

The de-mannning exercise was achieved in two main ways. A minority of the workforce was persuaded to become self-employed: '. . . the workforce was brought down by . . . 466 by persuading the after-sales service people to exchange their membership of the co-operative for contracts as self-employed operators, with the option to rejoin within a stipulated period if this did not work' (Wiener, 1987).

But most of those who were de-manned found jobs elsewhere in the group under a scheme which was used to ease the effects of the recession throughout the group as a whole. For the restructuring was achieved with virtually no compulsory redundancies. Indeed, as José Maria Ormaechea reminded his readers in the article quoted in the third epigraph, the group managed to go on increasing its employment all through these more difficult years. I suggested earlier that the successful midwifing of new start-up co-operative ventures was perhaps the single most important business achievement of the years of golden growth. The success of not only avoiding redundancy but of actually managing to add to total employment during times of recession and restructuring was perhaps the most important business achievement of the 1980s.

The measures taken to avoid redundancy are another original 'social invention' of the group. They are centred on the activities of Lagun-Aro, the Mondragon group's social welfare institution. This was first developed early in the group's history as part of the CLP; and later split off as a separate entity.

The formal need for the group to establish its own social welfare operation arose after 1958 when, by order of the Ministry of Labour, members of co-operatives were excluded from the State social security system. For certain purposes Spanish law treats worker members of production co-ops as if they were self-employed. Early in the 1980s, when the severity of the recession was becoming increasingly intense, Lagun-Aro devised and introduced a scheme whose central aim was to prevent redundancies. By this time the whole group was divided into sub-groups partly sectoral and partly geographical in character. And it was already standard practice for transfers to be made from one co-op to another within these sub-groups, following changes in the demand for labour. At the heart of the 'anti-redundancy' scheme introduced by Lagun-Aro in the early 1980s was a set of measures to facilitate transfers between sub-groups:

For transfers to a co-operative in a different sub-group Lagun-Aro provides quite handsome relocation benefits such as travel expenses in the case of temporary transfers, cheap loans to help with housing if the transfer is permanent, and contributions towards the maintenance of earnings if the transfer is to a lower grade job. For people whose old co-operative has lost some or all of their capital Lagun-Aro makes up what is needed for the capital stake in the new co-operative – often the most important benefit. *But the conditions that have to be met to qualify for these benefits are very stiff* [emphasis added] [Wiener, 1987].

Basically, the co-operative wishing to transfer people out

. . . has to prove that it needs to cut back at least forty people or a fifth of its workforce; it must stop distributing profits, if any, to its members and paying out the interest on their individual shareholdings; and it must cut its members wages to bring them down, grade for grade, to 85% of those on the Caja Laboral's scale [Wiener, 1987].

In other words if a co-operative wants to 'de-man' part of its workforce by transferring them to work in a different sub-group, then those who are going to remain employed by it are required to make considerable sacrifices.

Between 1982 and 1985 these transfers aggregated nearly 2,000 people. More than 10% of the group's workforce was thus covered by these arrangements. It is scarcely too much to claim that, given a willingness to accept the sacrifices which such a scheme requires, then it should be possible for a group in which activities are as diverse as those of the Mondragon co-operatives to come through a recessionary downturn in the business cycle without significant numbers of compulsory redundancies or early retirements.

Assisted Transfers between Co-operatives 1982–1985

Year	Permanent	Temporary	Total
1982	109	314	423
1983	62	428	490
1984	99	322	421
1985	109	416	525

476 *Restructuring and Growth in the 1980s and 1990s*

Over the first half of the 1980s the group's main achievement was therefore restructuring without significant numbers of forced redundancies and *with* some continuing growth in real turnover. The key to this success was a combination of acceptance by some co-op members of real financial sacrifices and a readiness to move to different jobs within the group: whether on a temporary or a permanent basis.

José Maria Ormaechea has contrasted a loss of 150,000 jobs in the Basque region of Spain between 1976 and 1986 with an increase of 4,200 in the number of jobs in the co-operative group. He conceded that that was not a brilliant result. But he observed that it had not come about automatically. On the contrary, he wrote that . . . only a process of adjustment carefully calculated, reflecting the spirit of solidarity and audacity has made it possible to avoid having any co-op member unemployed.'

Dr Wiener reports that the policy of seeking to prevent the recession from causing significant unemployment was not universally welcomed by the co-operative membership. Critics pointed out that the distribution of financial sacrifice was not always fair and reasonable. Some argued less equivocally: that 'the sacrifices needed to avoid redundancies are stretching solidarity a bit far'.

This may be one factor behind the greater flexibility in employment practices which became characteristic of the Mondragon group in the subsequent decade.

It is not altogether clear how far the arrangements designed to contain redundancy pressures in the 1980s continued to be used in the 1990s. The 1991 annual report of the CLP, for example, records a 'loss' of 650 industrial jobs; it has nothing to say about transfers to alternative employment within the group. Certainly, arrangements for coping with recession by transferring co-op members to other jobs were still kept formally in place. In the summer of 1993, a senior official of MCC insisted in a conversation with me that, in some sense, the employment guarantee implicit in Lagun-Aro's job transfer system still stood. But whether because of an unwillingness by individuals to accept conditions of transfer or for other reasons, it seems that from the early 1990s the system became less effective in its delivery of that employment guarantee.

At any rate from the early 1990s, it is clear that some co-op members began to be made redundant. The change was said to have been allowed with great reluctance. Generous redundancy terms included the possibility of eventual reinstatement. Through Lagun-Aro, the redundant worker was guaranteed 80% of full pay: half coming from Lagun-Aro and half from the member's co-op, and thus his or her former colleagues. In cases where whole co-ops had to be closed, any of its members who could not be relocated within the group were paid the whole of the 80% by Lagun-Aro. It was hoped that re-employment could be achieved before the system became unaffordable. And by the mid-1990s this hope seemed to be justified. The trend of employment aid paid out by Lagun-Aro, which had continued to increase in 1993, turned in 1994 and fell sharply in 1995. In 1994, Employment Aid accounted for 43% of total unfunded payments, but was down to 27% in 1995.

However, the extent of any change from an earlier solidarity should not be over-estimated. In *MCC: an Investor Profile*, which was prepared in connection with the possible sale of non-voting equity stakes in a proposed new investment company, MCC comments that 'In the dark days of the 1993 Spanish recession, the worker-owners of some co-operatives within MCC's industrial division reduced their wages in order to restore competitiveness. The event is noteworthy as much for its rarity in labour relations as it is for the strength of co-operation as a business strategy'.

The other way in which the co-ops sought to cope with the ups and downs of the economic cycle was to make a higher proportion of their employees 'temporary', and for longer periods. In the mid-1990s this was a delicate issue in Mondragon. It was one thing to set up joint ventures which were not co-operatives, especially outside Spain; but quite another to break the link between employment and co-operative membership in the heartland of the group in the long-established co-ops in Mondragon itself. Individual cases were 'monitored', and it seems that guidelines on the limits of 'acceptable' temporary employment arrangements were drawn up. As this book went to press, it emerged that a new form of 'temporary' co-op membership was being introduced, offering similar rights to temporary employees as to permanent employees with the one exception of job security.

At bottom, these changes reflect the greater exposure of the Mondragon group to market pressures, especially as a result of Spain's membership of the EEC/EU. Before EU membership, and especially before the Single Market, many of Mondragon's products had enjoyed higher tariff barriers protecting their markets in Spain than they had encountered in selling abroad. The removal of this protection was a serious threat, which could have been fatal. Thus in the late 1980s and early 1990s the group moved somewhat away from the high solidarity of its earlier years and in the direction of more market-orientated policies.

Another example of this greater market-orientation was a further shift in the rules governing maximum pay differentials. The original rules set a 3:1 maximum ratio between the remuneration of top management and that of the lowest paid. The limit was raised to 4.5:1 in the 1970s and then to 5:1 in the early 1980s. Thereafter a number of exceptions were permitted, essentially where these were necessary either to secure or to retain the services of needed managers and other professionals. In 1992 the rules were changed again. From 1993 onwards top management could be paid up to 70% of the market rate for their jobs. That is apparently expected to coincide with a maximum payment differential limit of around 8:1.

The executives on Mondragon offer a plausible defence of these changes. First, the original 3:1 ratio was put in place when the co-ops were much smaller and easier to manage. Now that some individual co-ops are much larger and the group as a whole employs some 34,000 people, there is a great deal more managing to be done. It is also true that Spanish income tax has changed dramatically since the 1950s when there was none: now it rises to a maximum of 50%. So after tax the apparent increase in maximum differentials is lessened.

The policy shift of the late 1980s which allowed corporate acquisitions for the first time, can also be seen as a move away from the original co-operative principles. The acquisitions have been driven by a market rather than a co-operative logic. Moreover the group has not sought to impose on those employed in these recently acquired businesses the same terms and conditions as apply to those in the co-operatives. Indeed the corporate character of these businesses remains unchanged. But the emphasis here should be on the absence of any policy which sought to impose a co-operative struture on newly acquired businesses. As noted much earlier there have been a number of cases where the employees in an acquired undertaking have voted by comfortable majorities to adopt the legal form of a co-operative and have agreed to make capital contributions into these new ventures accordingly. The two businesses mentioned earlier, Fabrelec and the previously bankrupt firm which took the name of MAPSA when it became a co-operative, are both in the manufacturing sector. But there have also been examples in the retail sector where those working in new ventures developed by EROSKI in the 1990s have chosen to take the co-operative road.

The other big change in the last decade of the twentieth century is the group's move abroad, both by the retail organisation and by various of the industrial co-ops. Orona, for example, which manufactures lifts, has subsidiary companies in Toulouse, Paris, Milan, Oporto, Lisbon and Andorra.

In 1995 it looked as though the strategy for further expansion would rest partly on bringing in capital via what Sr Ormaechaea called the new 'Holding Company'. The mission of the group, agreed by a group-wide Congress in the mid-1990s, had been summarised as follows:

> The scenario has changed because the market is larger, competitiveness is sharper and the size of the companies has taken on other proportions, precisely to tackle the effects of a new situation. We need action, based on the hypothesis of a financial grouping, corporation or holding company, which will result in a reduction in unit costs, an increase in competitiveness, access to greater market share, capacity for investment in new technology, in an audacious effort to increase profitability, keeping external threats at bay and consolidating the future. [MCC, 1995.]

According to Sr Ormaechea this was to be achieved by creating a new holding company:

> The plan is to create a holding company which will carry out these initiatives, constituting an appropriate tool to back the financial investment necessary to launch or control companies in accordance with the strategic decisions of the group.
> The purpose of the Group in the future is to respect the basic principles which inspired its creation, and to search for the best way to adapt to changing circumstance.

By 1996 this proposal seemed to have been put on hold. But the decision in principle by the Mondragon Group to sell equity in its heartland enterprises to financial investors (including foreign investors) raises two related issues. First, how can it sell equity without giving up employee ownership? Second, if the biggest star in the employee-owned firmament worldwide cannot find resources, except by giving up its employee ownership status, does this not indicate that employee ownership has distinct limits as a system for ownership of a business?

The basic answer given by MCC to the first question is that employee ownership would not be surrendered. Investors in the holding company would have no more than a financial interest – the privilege of sharing in the annual profits and capital growth of one of the most successful businesses in the Western world but no votes and no control of management. This would be underpinned by two other aspects of the arrangements. First, investments by the holding company would be mainly and unconditionally in new ventures; any investments in existing co-ops would be subject to their approval. Second, they would be restricted to a small minority: not more than 20%.

The answer to the second question is best seen as a balance. On the one side is the imperative: 'adapt or die'. On the other, there is no intention of risking the central tenets of the co-operative system. As for more directly business objectives, the conclusion of a booklet issued by MCC in 1996, to celebrate the fortieth anniversary of the foundation of the Mondragon co-operative system, sets an aim of doubling both overall sales to ptas 1,000bn and the volume of international business by the turn of the century, and quadrupling the number of production plants outside Spain. More qualitatively, it describes the future as follows:

> We do not mean to say that we have fully achieved our aims, nor that our experimental co-operative cycle is complete. What we wish to convey is that we are in a constant process of development and adaptation of our social aims and our capacity to compete in ever more demanding international markets where nobody, as the purists would say, is going to look at our 'social credentials', but at the efficiency and performance of our co-operatives.

However, the same document re-enunciates the ten basic principles approved at the first co-operative congress in 1987:
– Open membership – equal employment opportunities for all

– Democratic organisation – one member, one vote
– Worker sovereignty
– Instrumental and subordinate nature of capital
– Management participation by members
– Wage solidarity
– Co-operation between co-operatives
– Social transformation via majority reinvestment of profits
– 'Universal sharing' objectives: of peace, justice and development
– A commitment to education

THE MONDRAGON SYSTEM

Ownership The Mondragon Group differs in a number of ways from the other businesses and groups of businesses which we are reviewing in this book. Of these one of the most eye-catching is the size of the capital stake which new recruits are required to contribute as one condition of permanent employment and co-op membership. The figures in pesetas have been constantly adjusted for inflation. For those who joined existing co-operatives, the typical sum from the early 1960s to the early 1990s was the equivalent of six months' salary. By the mid-1990s, it was roughly equivalent to one year's salary in the lowest rung of employment. For those involved in the start-up of new ventures from scratch – something which admittedly more or less ceased to happen from the mid-1980s onwards – the capital sum required has typically been twice as much.

Moreover, the financial commitment required of new recruits is, in a sense, even more substantial than these figures imply. Of the capital sum contributed by the new recruit, 25% is immediately deflected to collectively-owned reserve funds. Whatever the fortunes of the co-operative business over the period during which the new recruit works for it, he or she will never see that 25% again.

On the other hand, if we leave on one side those working in businesses which have been acquired by the group as wholly-owned subsidiaries from the late 1980s onwards, these arrangements seem to have been accepted by new recruits as entirely reasonable ever since they were first instituted. Indeed there has typically been an over-supply of potential new recruits, ready to accept these conditions of permanent employment, compared with the number of places on offer. There is little or no evidence that the capital contribution requirement has acted as a deterrent to those whose cash resources are limited. New recruits have been required to find a part of what they must contribute in a cash down payment. But they have normally been permitted to subscribe the balance out of their earnings over a period of up to three years.

The capital contribution of the new recruit, reduced by what is deflected to collective reserve funds, then becomes the starting balance of his or her individual capital account, as it has come to be called. This balance is adjusted annually in line with the economic performance of the business and the strength of the balance sheet – upwards if there has been a profit and downwards if there has been a loss. The share of profits or losses so allocated is proportionate to the sum of the individual member's earnings during the year in question, plus the interest due on the balance of his or her capital account. In the early years 70% of annual profits and losses were normally allocated to individual capital accounts in this way, with the remainder being passed into collective reserves. However in the more difficult economic conditions of the 1980s this proportion was lowered to 45%.

It is important to be clear that profit shares allocated to the individual capital accounts of co-operative members in this way remain locked in. They cannot be turned into cash until the member in question stops working for the business, either through retirement or on some other grounds. Then, and only then, does his or her final capital account balance become payable. On the way it will have been subject to an annual valuation adjustment in line with changes in the cost of living. Those retiring from the co-operatives in the early years of the 1990s, after thirty years of service, have turned capital accounts into cash which amount to the equivalent of about two years of their final salary. Because profits were harder to achieve after 1980 than in the earlier years, those retiring at the same time with shorter periods of service behind them have taken out rather less.

All those working in the Mondragon co-operatives are bound by these ownership arrangements. Moreover the rules do not allow ownership by outsiders. So the arrangements may be said to include an identity rule: that there must be an identity between those who work in a co-operative business and those who own it.

At least from the viewpoint of the group these arrangements seem to have worked well. The capital contributions of new recruits have contributed significantly to the accumulation of capital. The lock-in rules have worked to increase the ability of the co-operatives to invest. It seems, too, that the requirement of having to make a significant capital contribution has had an effect on the prevailing culture. Visitors have often been struck by evidence of 'peer group monitoring'.

On the other hand, in any particular co-operative the deflections to collectively-owned reserves involve some sacrifice by present to future co-op members. Whether that will seem reasonable to particular individuals will no doubt much depend on their family situations; and especially on whether there is a son or daughter who is hoping to find work in the group.

This began to become a significant issue in the 1990s as an increasing proportion of the original co-operative members reached retirement age. The larger numbers of retirements threatened the capital resources of the co-operatives. One solution – whether officially or unofficially – has apparently been for relatives of retiring co-operative members to be offered a job in return for allowing the money to stay invested in the co-operative.

Control Just as ownership is governed by an identity rule in the Mondragon group, so is control. Only those who work in the group can have a voice in its top policy-making bodies; and all those who are so working must have one. As is normal in almost all corporate bodies, top policy-making power is vested in a general assembly of all members. It is the character of the members that is unusual. They are workers and holders of capital accounts – worker shareholders, if I may simplify a little. In the early years, when income differentials were limited to a maximum of 3:1, voting in these general assemblies was proportionate to rates of pay. But since the early 1960s the voting rules have been democratic: one worker one vote.

The General Assemblies elect the boards of directors and the latter appoint top management: usually just the chief executive who may then choose his or her top team. The elected directors cannot be part of the top management team. To that extent the position is perhaps closer to that in Germany – with its two-tier management and supervisory board system – than to the unified boards of the US and the UK. On the other hand the powers of Mondragon's elected boards are significantly greater than those of supervisory boards in the Federal Republic of Germany. They frequently include a significant proportion of middle managers and professionals. The prediction that blue-collar majorities tend to elect blue-collar boards of directors is confounded by this Mondragon experience, as indeed it is elsewhere.

Those who wish to may see these control arrangements as reflecting a sensible separation between the powers of business *government* and those of business *management*. Within reasonable limits, the managers are left free to do the professional job of managers. Three further points of detail are worth noting. The first is that the chief executive normally attends and may speak at board meetings, but has no vote. Second, his or her position will normally be to some extent protected by a service contract against the consequences of sudden dismissal. Third, in all or most of the co-operatives the top management and the board of directors have regular joint meetings. Apart from anything else these are designed to prevent the two bodies from going their separate ways.

Such are the ownership and control arrangements of the individual co-operative businesses of the Mondragon group; or rather they are what applies in the case of so-called first degree co-operatives: that is, of all the manufacturing businesses and all those others which do not – as for example does the bank and the social welfare organisation Lagun-Aro – supply group-wide services. The latter are essentially owned and controlled by the co-operatives of first degree. Those who work in them are required to make capital contributions to them and are allowed a voice, albeit a minority one, in their governing councils.

The ownership and control arrangements of the first degree co-operatives have been subject to various modifications of detail as a result of their having been brought together in a successive series of sub-groups starting from the late 1960s. For example, the sub-groups have normally involved a degree of profit and loss-sharing. And much the same applies in relation to the umbrella group, Mondragon Corporacion Co-operativa. However, such modifications did not fundamentally alter the basic arrangements.

A description of the formal position may not describe what actually happens in practice. A plausible characterisation of these arrangements is that they amount to passive democracy. That does not mean that votes by the membership of the co-operatives are not taken, or that they can be ignored when they have been. But it does mean that in normal circumstances regular managerial decision-

making is not significantly affected by the democratic arrangements. It is also true, as we shall see later, that managerial control
at the centre began to be sharply strengthened in the early 1990s.

Industrial Relations Neither the group nor the individual co-ops
recognise any trade unions for wage bargaining, or any other collective purpose. The origin of this state of affairs is historical: independent trade unions were outlawed by the Franco regime and
remained so down to the mid-1970s. But it is also true that there has
been no move by the co-operatives to recognise the trade unions
since then. Moreover, though individual co-op members are entirely free to join any trade union of their choice, it appears that
only a small minority have done so. Nor, so far as I know, has there
ever been any substantial movement of opinion in favour of official
recognition.

Given that neither the blue-collar workforce nor the management has favoured recognition, it is scarcely surprising that that has
not happened. The existing arrangements have stood the test of
time, and to change them would be to take an unnecessary risk. But
there is also some specific evidence of more positive attitudes to the
existing arrangements. In the early 1980s a survey found that only
25% of those working in the group favoured a change in the arrangements in order to give a strong role to trade unions. For comparison with the sample of those working in the co-operatives, the
survey authors also questioned a second group working in conventional capitalist firms. One of the questions put to the latter asked
them to express a 'preference between co-operative structure [*sic*]
and trade unionism as vehicles for the advancement of labour'.
More than half (52%) gave their preference as the former (Bradley
and Gelb, 1983).

Special institutions in the industrial relations of the co-ops were
introduced at an early stage and survived into the 1990s, having
acquired greater prestige and authority on the way. These are the
social councils which are a feature of every co-operative. Their
basic logic is threefold. First, the need for a channel of communication between top management and the rank-and-file membership. Second, the need for a forum in which non-top-manage-
ment opinions can be aired. And third, the need for a body to
process complaints, grievances and questions of discipline at the
lower levels of the rank and file. Neither the meetings of the general

assembly of all members nor the meetings of boards of elected directors could, it was felt, properly fulfil these important and necessary functions. Hence the need for social councils, which became essentially elected non-management bodies from about the mid-1980s.

On the other hand, during the earlier years these social councils were at least partially controlled by top management, which enjoyed the right to appoint one of their nominees to take the chair, William Foote Whyte and his wife Kathleen King Whyte describe an extended process which ended when the right to take the chair at social council meetings passed from a management nominee to one of their elected members. At least since that change took place, the social councils can partly be seen as 'in house' unions; and thus as exhibiting some similarities with 'company unions' in Japan.

It need scarcely be said that no system of institutions, cultures, and worker *mentalité* can deliver entirely trouble-free industrial relations. We need to remind ourselves too of the strike at ULGOR in the early 1970s. On the other hand, it would be a complete mistake not to acknowledge that the whole 'Mondragon system' confers on the co-operatives a significant and substantial industrial relations advantage. On successive visits, I have almost invariably had the reply from management that the industrial relations in the group are for the most part quite unproblematic.

Social Welfare At least for certain key purposes – like absence from work through sickness, and unemployment – worker members of co-operatives are treated by Spanish law as if they were self-employed. There are semi-Government institutions which co-operatives are free to use and which can provide the necessary cover. There are also some cases in which co-operatives are required to make use of these semi-Government institutions, at least to some specified extent, for example for pensions.

Early in the 1960s a decision was taken that, so far as the law allowed, the group would provide a full range of social services for those co-operatives which chose to take advantage of them. Until the early 1970s these functions were carried out by a specialist division of the CLP. Later they were were spun off and came under what was essentially a free-standing and not-for-profit provider of a range of welfare benefits called Lagun-Aro. The English phrase 'social welfare' may give an inadequate view of the range of functions and services supplied by it. In a sense it is better seen as a mini, non-Government, provider of many of the services which in Britain, for example, are supplied by the welfare state. The services it provides are wide-ranging and efficient:

– It was substantially as a result of an ingenious and tough scheme introduced by Lagun-Aro that the group was able to negotiate the 1980s recession with virtually no redundancies at all.

– It seems to have been notably successful at keeping down the overhead costs of its services. Both on pensions and sickness benefits Lagun-Aro appears to provide better value for money than the state competition.

– Lagun-Aro has devised an original system of rewards and punishments for discouraging extravagant use of non-essential medical services. Those covered by it are divided into groups and the groups are set target annual budgets. Subject to a non-penalised overshoot of 10% compared with these budgets, any further overspending results in a surcharge on members of the group in the following year. Conversely there are rewards, in the shape of discounted charges, for members of groups which underspend.

– On the evidence of Lagun-Aro, small may well be cost effective when it comes to the provision of these 'welfare state' type services. However it seems improbable, in the short and medium term, that political conditions will be such that this example will be widely followed. (For further details of Lagun-Aro, see *Job Ownership*, 1982.)

The Bank Of all the employee ownership success stories in today's world, that of the Mondragon bank, the Caja Laboral Popular, is in some ways the most appealing. There is a wonderful contrast between the genesis of the project and what has become of it. Who would have thought that in little more than a third of a century a new start-up credit co-operative, initiated by a few obscure young engineers on the advice of a priest, would have grown to be one of the largest and most profitable banks in a large Western economy? It is a story to confound the textbooks of the schools of business administration.

For the first twenty-five years, from 1959 until the mid-1980s, the development of the bank was linked so closely to that of the Mondragon Group as a whole that it has seldom been presented as a success story on its own. There was real symbiosis. The bank needed the growing and multiplying co-operative businesses as entities to lend money to; and those businesses in turn needed the bank as a source of loans. The Empresarial Division invented the method of midwifing new co-ops as described earlier. The essence of the bank's achievement was mobilising *local* resources for *local* investment; and this was not necessarily dependent on its own co-operative status.

By the early 1980s the growth of the bank had run well ahead of that of the Group. In 1964, 77% of the bank's total resources were invested in the group. The proportion fell to 49% in 1979, 25% in 1985, less than 10% in the early 1990s, and by 1997 was under 5%.

When the bank started in 1959, there were two branches. One was in Mondragon itself, which is in the province of Guipuzcoa and the other in a small town across the provincial boundary in Alava. The logic behind this was that the provincial authorities in either of the two provinces might move in and frustrate the initiative – but were unlikely to do so simultaneously in both. When the idea was first proposed by Fr Arizmendiarrieta, the initial response of the 'simple engineers' who had founded ULGOR was consternation. But those same engineers frequently remarked later that success comes more easily in banking than in manufacturing. In the first twenty years alone, the bank grew a hundredfold.

Total CLP Resources

Ptas bn, constant 1985 prices

1963	1.3
1968	13.0
1982	129.1
1985	187.0

Source: Wiener(1987)

Ptas bn, constant 1991 prices

1985	277
1988	316
1991	429

Source: CLP Annual Reports

CLP Deposits and Equity

Current prices

	Deposits, Ptas bn	Equity, Ptas m
1991	355	43
1992	408	50
1993	439	56
1994	457	64
1995	586	74

Source: MCC Annual Reports

From the two branches when the project first started in 1959, the bank grew to 201 in 1991, and 230 in 1995. Employment rose, but more slowly.

Numbers Employed

1975	587
1984	1,226
1991	1,279
1995	1,384

In 1991 the former Empresarial Division became a free-standing consultancy. With the launch of two new financial services companies, one specialising in insurance and the other in leasing, the bank moved to offer the same range of services as those available from other major banks. It has also divided its functions between wholesale (business) customers and retail (individual) customers, and moved out beyond the Basque heartland.

The Retail Network The group's retail network was set up as 'Comerco' in 1969. In the next year it adopted the Basque name EROSKI. It was based on the merger of five local consumer co-ops. Until the 1980s it received little attention from the admirers of the Mondragon phenomenon. This is partly because consumer co-ops are common in many countries. Moreover, the growth of EROSKI was slow by comparison with the more glamorous manufacturing co-ops. It is also probable that many observers failed to notice the most interesting feature of Modragon's retail co-ops: their hybrid ownership and control arrangements in which the interests of the stores' workforce is finely balanced with those of its customers. Dr Wiener called this balance 'a beautiful compromise'.

Dr Wiener argues that given the character of the Mondragon Group as a whole, the natural structure for a Mondragon retail business should have been as a workers' rather than a consumers' co-operative. He then goes on:

> But it would have been too much of a break with tradition simply to abandon the consumer interest. For this reason there are also (as well as worker members) consumer members and for them there are centrally organised activities and events. To ensure a proper balance between the two interests, the board of directors (of Eroski) consists of six members elected by the employees, and six elected by the consumers. The chairman is always from the consumer side.

The 1990s witnessed an important new development. Eroski merged with the Valencian co-operative Consum to form the Eroski Group. These two companies also operate a number of subsidiary companies, including Erosmer, a holding company created in 1992 to promote large hypermarkets in Spain. Numbers employed at Eroski grew from 744 in 1979 to over 1,000 in 1981, and nearly 2,000 in 1989. In 1990, Eroski abandoned its old self-imposed geographical restriction of confining its activities to its home Basque territory. In these new shopping developments, Eroski also dropped the co-operative form and promoted what were at least to begin with straight capitalist ventures. Eroski the co-operative became owner or part-owner of developments which were not structured either as classic consumer co-ops, or in its own image of mixed consumer and employee co-operative ownership. On the other hand, and as noted much earlier, employees in those new ventures were later enabled and indeed encouraged to become part owners.

Already, by the early 1980s, the relative growth rates of the manufacturing and consumer co-ops in Mondragon had switched places. By 1992 Eroski's sales accounted for more than half the group's total.

Eroski: Sales and Numbers Employed 1991-95

Current prices

	Sales Ptas bn	Workforce
1991	153	6,878
1992	193	7,408
1993	226	8,229
1994	270	9,111
1995	307	10,500

Source: MCC Annual Reports

The Group and the Subgroups From its earliest beginnings the leaders and thinkers in the Mondragon Group have emphasised its experimental character. It is true that the Spanish phrase most commonly used to describe the whole project has been the Experiencia Co-operativa. But the Spanish word *experiencia* seems to have more of an 'experimental flavour' than the English word 'experience'. When they use the phrase *Experiencia Co-operativa* spokesmen for the group seem to want to tell us that it has been, and will go on being, a continuously evolving experience.

In the later 1980s and the early 1990s that was especially true of the arrangements covering not the individual co-operative businesses but those of the group as a whole; and those of the continuously evolving subgroups which occupy the space in between.

From the mid-1980s these arrangements were in almost continuous change and flux. The group as a whole was initially embodied in links between the individual co-operative businesses and the group's bank, the Caja Laboral Popular, and *not* in a group structure properly so called. Those links, as we saw earlier, took the form of more or less identical contracts of association between the individual businesses and the bank. In effect the contracts imposed on the businesses the common set of arrangements – about ownership, control, industrial relations and so on. At least by implication, these contracts also conferred on the bank the role of group leader.

In the mid-1980s, while the old contracts of association remained in place, the bank gave up its leadership role. There were a number of reasons for that major change. Perhaps the single most important one had to do with the quite outstanding growth performance achieved on its own account by the bank. As a result the co-operative businesses accounted for an ever smaller proportion of its loan book. Its obligations to its clients outside the co-operative group were judged to be incompatible with a continuing group leadership role.

The group-wide arrangements which have come into existence since the bank gave up its leadership role have various distinguishable elements. The first and largest which confers legitimacy is a democratically elected body called a 'Co-operative Congress' which meets formally about every two years and informally in between and may be thought of as a group-wide general assembly. The central task of the congress is to debate and set general policy for the corporation as a whole. The second element of the new arrangements is the so-called Standing Congress Committee (SCC). The designation is perhaps best taken to be a form of shorthand. The committee is perhaps best understood as a co-operative of third degree, for its members are one or more of the elected directors from each of the sectoral subgroups. Given that these subgroups are best understood as second degree co-operatives – with their directors in turn elected by and from the boards of the co-operatives of first degree, the characterisation of the SCC as a third degree co-operative is logical even if a little cumbersome. Its (the SCC's) members elect from their number a president who presides over meetings of both the SCC and the congress. The SCC president and its members serve for four-year terms and may be re-elected.

At the apex of the new arrangements is a new corporate entity: the Mondragon Corporation Co-operative (MCC). The SCC appoints its chief executive and must approve his or her selections for the fifteen senior posts which make up its 'management council'. That council in turn selects the top management staff who form the secretariat of this new apex entity. If it is helpful, the SCC can perhaps be seen as an internal board of directors for the MCC, with the twin main tasks of implementing congressional policy and monitoring the performance of senior MCC management.

In the mid-1990s these new group-wide institutions were still evolving. They were formally agreed at a meeting of the 'Congress' in early 1991, when they replaced an earlier set of more interim arrangements. It must be more likely than not that they will continue to evolve.

And the same is likely to be true about the set of subgroup

arrangements which were also agreed at the 1991 Congress. Here the main background can be summarised in just three points. The first is that the earliest subgroup dates from as far back as 1964: when ULGOR came together with three of its supplying co-operatives to form ULARCO. Then, second, in the 1970s the entire population of individual co-operatives was formed into subgroups with either a geographical or a sectoral character, or both. The third is that a part of the profits of the individual co-ops was normally pooled as also, in some cases, were various management, sales and financial functions. And labour could also be pooled, in the sense of being temporarily transferred from one co-operative business to another, in response to fluctuations in demand.

The main feature of the new subgroup arrangements agreed at the 1991 Congress was to replace mixed – regional and sectoral – subgroupings with exclusively sectoral ones. And the main reason behind the change was that sectoral subgroupings were seen to be more market-orientated than regional ones.

What all this amounts to is a substantial strengthening of the central co-ordination among the Mondragon co-ops. This is embodied in a huge new central office building which would not disgrace a big multinational. The formula for the continuing reality of 'co-operation' is two-way communication between MCC at the Centre and the lowest-paid employee, in the smallest individual co-op, at the periphery. On the one hand, the corporate government of MCC gives control of it to representatives of the co-ops. On the other, major new developments for the group as a whole – for example the proposal to set up a holding company – have to be discussed at general assemblies of the members of individual co-ops. In this way the group seeks to retain the best of co-operation whilst meeting the challenges of the global markets of the 1990s.

24

The ESOP Phenomenon in the United States

Today 1,000 public corporations that are traded on stock exchanges – the Employee Ownership 1,000 – have significant employee stock ownership. The average holding is over 12%, while employees are the top shareholder in almost half of these companies. Significant employee ownership now encompasses a third of the *Fortune* 500 industrials and a fifth of the *Fortune* 500 Service Corporations. By the year 2000, a quarter of *all* public corporations will be more than 15% owned by their employees and a quarter of private sector employees will be in such companies. *From the blurb on the dust jacket. 'The New Owners: The Mass Emergence of Employee Ownership in Public Companies and What It Means to American Busines', by Joseph Blasi and Douglas Kruse, 1991*

Table 4 shows ... how the Employee Ownership 1,000 compares to the employee-ownership sector in the US economy, which has about 10,000 firms with more than 4% employee ownership. Only 10%, or 1,000, of these firms, are publicly traded corporations, but they account for about 40% of employee holders, while 9,000, or 90% of these companies are closely held ....

The startling news is that 12.5% of the private-sector workforce, or 10.8m American workers, own stock in companies in which employee ownership exceeds 4% of total company market value. *Ibid.*

Perhaps because of a combination of the relative youth of their country and the relative influence of marketing men in it, American academics, more so than their UK counterparts, have an engaging fondness for hyperbole. I suspect that most readers of what follows will take away a more qualified picture of employee ownership in today's America than that conveyed by the two epigraphs above. Nevertheless, they do have the great merit of conveying a real and valid impression of the scale of the broadly-based employee ownership that spread across the USA in the period of rather more than twenty years from the passing by the Congress in 1974 of the country's first legislation on employee stock ownership plans (ESOPs) down to the time of writing. Its scale dwarfs that of all other phenomena of this kind at any time and in any other country. True, there was a fashion for employee stock purchase plans in the corporate America of the 1920s, and the number of US employee-stockholders is reported to have been proportionately much higher then than seventy years later. But this earlier movement was not strong enough to survive the sequence of the Wall Street Crash and the Great Depression. In any case, that stock purchase movement happened without legal or fiscal support. By contrast, what we started to have in 1974 was something rooted and underpinned in laws and tax reliefs. What is more, it is the American ESOP legislation that has put broadly-based employee ownership on the international business map. Without this American experience – both the ESOP legislation and its take-up – what has happened elsewhere could at most have attracted the interest of a small band of specialists and enthusiasts.

There is no real doubt about the drivers behind this broadly-based employee ownership. In research at Baltimore University, Michael Conte and Helen Lawrence argued convincingly in the early 1990s that 'the significant growth of ESOPs during the 1980s may have been caused by two factors: a philosophy that workers are more productive when they own employer stock, and special tax benefits accorded to employers to establish these plans'.

To US readers the story of how these special tax benefits were first introduced is no doubt well-known. For readers outside the USA, however, it is important to emphasise that the origins of the ESOP are in right-of-centre American populism rather than left-of-centre social liberalism. The driving political value has been about the importance of spreading wealth rather than about shifting power at the place of work from the agents of capital to the shop floor. There is apparently also some evidence from the record of votes in the Congress that the issue has been somewhat more popular with Republicans than Democrats, although the ESOP movement's original and outstanding political champion was a southern Democrat, Russell Long, a Louisiana senator from 1948 until 1986. Russell Long's father, Huey Long, was elected to the Senate, also as a southern Democrat, in 1932 – and assassinated three years later. Before his election, during several terms as

Governor of Louisiana he had been responsible for various public works and similar measures which in some important respects prefigured the New Deal.

Huey was widely criticised by his contemporaries for his propensity to behave like an elected dictator and that may well explain his assassination. But for our purposes, what is chiefly of interest is his strong advocacy, during the last years of his life in Washington, of government measures to transfer property from richer to poorer citizens. His central idea seems to have been simple – to confiscate the 'excess' wealth of the rich and pass it to the poor. For example, had Huey Long's 'Share Our Wealth' project ever been implemented, those with two houses or two motor cars would have been liable to have one of them confiscated.

His son Russell Long later elegantly distinguished between his father's policies on wealth spreading and his own. He called his own ESOP measures an example of 'populism without Robin Hood'. And he tirelessly pointed to a key distinction: between a set of measures designed to spread *existing* wealth, which could scarcely avoid compulsory transfer; and another set designed to rearrange the ownership of *future* wealth so that its distribution would be different. He saw the latter, as is of course the case with the whole body of America's ESOP legislation, as being entirely voluntary. The intellectual foundations for this approach had been laid by Louis Kelso, who also invented the ESOP concept.

Judged by its take-up at least down to the middle 1980s, the American ESOP legislation was a first-class success. As we have seen, it has been taken up in special situations and it has been taken up more widely, if also more on the margin, across great swathes of corporate America. Have the hoped-for effects on business performance been realised?

There is growing evidence that, if linked up with appropriate schemes and policies of non-financial employee involvement, significant employee ownership can be followed by measurable improvements in performance. The word 'significant' is used here in two senses:

– for the individual employee his or her ownership stake needs to be significant: worth a good deal more than the value of a few days' wages;

– for the workforce as a whole the aggregate of employee ownership needs to be significant: such as to make their voice an important and even perhaps the dominant one in setting the long-term policies and objectives of the business.

For America, the most authoritative evidence for these benefits is probably that collected in a sample study undertaken by the American Government's General Accounting Office in the late 1980s. Its findings have been widely confirmed by academic sample studies in the USA. (British evidence has so far been confined to monograph studies of individual firms. But it points in precisely the same direction.)

The National Center for Employee Ownership (NCEO) summarises the US evidence as follows:

ESOPs and Corporate Growth: a 1987 NCEO study of 45 ESOP and 225 non-ESOP companies found that companies that combine employee ownership with participative management style grow 8% to 11% per year faster than they would otherwise have been expected to grow based on how they had performed before these plans. Subsequent studies by the General Accounting Office and by academics in Washington State and New York found the same relationship. Studies in participative management alone find a small positive impact on performance, but not nearly enough to explain the synergy between ownership and participation these other studies have found.

ESOPs and Stock Price Performance: Data compiled between 1992 and 1995 as part of an ongoing study by Joseph Blasi, Douglas Kruse, Michael Conte and, after 1993, American Capital Strategies, found that an investment of equal amounts in a basket of securities in public companies with more than 10% broad employee ownership would see a return of 80.19% compared to 48.69% for the Dow and 44.87% for the S&P 500s. The researchers point out that this does not establish a causal linkage between employee ownership and stock performance because companies that set up these plans may also have certain other consistent features that make them perform better.

ESOPs and Bankruptcy: A 1995 study by Michael Conte at the University of Baltimore found that during the 1980s fewer than one out of 100 ESOPs were terminated because of the bankruptcy of the plan sponsor. (NCEO Web Page, March 1996.)

Before coming on to the vexed question of what actually constitutes employee ownership, readers may need to be reminded of an important distinction: between, as the Americans say, leveraged and unleveraged ESOPs. Both are tax-privileged mechanisms by which shares in the companies they work for can be transferred into the ownership of their employees. In the case of unleveraged ESOPs (which are very similar to what are known as 'stock bonus plans'), the cost of the shares transferred to employees is normally financed directly, with help from significant tax reliefs'. In the leveraged cases, the money is borrowed; and what the company pays for, again normally out of tax-relieved profits, is the subsequent stream of interest on those borrowings, and their repayment. Clearly if the aim is a rapid shift of large chunks of ownership – and, in the limiting case, of the *entire* ownership of a business – then what you need to do the job is an ESOP of the leveraged type. According to the Conte/Lawrence numbers, in the late 1980s about a third of ESOPs were leveraged – slightly more in 1990:

	All Plans	Leveraged	Unleveraged
1988	8,543	2,591	5,952
1989	7,618	2,534	5,084
1990	7,560	2,711	4,849

Conte/Lawrence supply an annual series for the total number of ESOPs going back to 1980 and forward to 1990, though with a gap in 1981. The series shows a peak in 1986:

Esop Numbers: All Plans 1980–90

1980	4,925	1986	10,834
1981	na	1987	9,358
1982	8,405	1988	8,543
1983	8,470	1989	7,618
1984	8,618	1990	7,560
1985	9,878		

A similar trend line, though with a suggestion of some pick-up in 1990 and an earlier peak, is apparent if we take the Conte/Lawrence statistical series not for the number of ESOP plans but for the number of employee participants.

ESOP Participants: 1980 to 1990 in 000s

1980	5,342	1986	10,828
1981	n.a.	1987	10,816
1982	6,906	1988	7,925
1983	9,680	1989	6,672
1984	10,573	1990	7,017
1985	10,944		

Conte later managed to unearth a statistical series for a subset of larger ESOP companies, those which file form 5500 with the US tax authorities. This confirms the trend of the earlier Conte/Lawrence research. It also extends to 1991 and shows that in the final year there was some recovery in the numbers. There were 2,657 'form 5500 companies' at end 1991 compared with 2,404 at end 1990.

So how do we reconcile these statistics with the figures of 10,000 firms and 10.8m employee shareholders cited from *The New Owners* in the epigraphs? The main answer is that Blasi and Kruse have cast their net wider than Conte and Lawrence. The latter focus narrowly on companies with actual ESOP plans. The estimate offered by Blasi and Kruse embraces, in addition to ESOPs, employee ownership which has come about in other ways as well: for example through what they call deferred profit-sharing plans, employee stock-purchase plans and stock-bonus plans.

There are two further points. First Blasi and Kruse fix their threshold of significance at only 4% of the equity capital of a business being held by its employees. The top management team alone could, in many cases, own that percentage of a firm's equity between them. Nothing wrong in that; but it is clearly rather different from what most people understand by 'employee ownership'. Second, at least so far as I can understand, Blasi and Kruse's overall totals are informed *estimates*, no more than that, though equally no less.

We still have to ask both how to understand and how to interpret the declining numbers in the two Conte/Lawrence series after they had peaked in the middle 1980s. The authors themselves offer three suggestions. First they note the elimination by the Congress in 1986 of the earlier tax-credit ESOP provisions. These had produced rather meagre amounts of employee ownership at rather high tax cost. So the Congress was quite easily persuaded to revoke them. The two further explanations arise from changes in the economic rather than the tax climate in the second half of the 1980s. The stock market crash of Black Monday happened in the autumn of 1987; and it is suggested that for some time thereafter companies may have felt reluctant to pass what managers would have seen as undervalued shares to their employees. Moreover, as economic conditions became tougher towards the end of the 1980s, companies may have become less willing to use profits, even pre-tax profits, to reward their employees with shares.

That brings me to a key question: not what caused the declining numbers in the two Conte/Lawrence series but how the reductions were typically effected. According to Dr Conte all, or almost all, plans confer a buy-back right on the business and these buy-back rights have been almost invariably exercised when terminations have taken place. It may well be that in some cases fears of not being able to cope with ever-increasing buy-back liabilities in the future have prompted private companies to go for 'buy-back terminations' of their existing ESOP plans.

I have discussed the overall statistics of employee ownership in the USA at some length partly because of the apparent conflict of evidence between Blasi and Kruse on the one hand and Conte and Lawrence on the other. For the most up-to-date information, perhaps the best source is the NCEO. It estimates that in 1995 there were 9,500 ESOPs and stock bonus plans in the USA with assets of $225bn and covering 10m employees. The NCEO series shows a fall-off in the numbers of ESOPs since 1990, and the organisation regrets in a 1996 newsletter the apparent fall in political support for them in the 1990s.

But the relative stagnation of the ESOP numbers in the years between the late 1980s and when this was written should not obscure the main point: that the phenomenon of the American ESOP dwarfs, to repeat, all experience at other times and in other places. By comparison with the American numbers, Mr Malcolm Hurleston of London's ESOP Centre estimated that in 1994 there were perhaps sixty so-called 'case law' ESOPs in the UK and less than ten of the so-called statutory variety.

So much for the overall scale of America's employee ownership experience. But no introductory discussion to my American case studies would be complete without looking at the rather different purposes to which that most versatile American social invention – the leveraged ESOP – may be applied. For all the American case studies in this book have involved a leveraged ESOP. The changes of ownership resulting from leveraged ESOPs tend to be both more radical and more interesting.

However, before we move on to the uses of leveraging, a critically important qualitative and analytic distinction must be introduced. It goes without saying that the entire body of ESOP companies are attracted by the tax reliefs that employee ownership can offer. But our understanding of this whole ESOP phenomenon will be greatly sharpened if we separate off a subset from the aggregates. The subset consists of those ESOP companies which are attracted not only by those tax reliefs but by the opportunities of sharing power with their non-management employees – of transforming them from wage labour into real business partners – which employee ownership also offers. Of course, this distinction should be seen in practice as a spectrum. Of course, too, a business may be first attracted to employee ownership by the tax reliefs – or for example by its 'defensive potential' – and then later wake up to what we may call its human opportunities. Nevertheless, much that may otherwise be puzzling when we come to examine actual ESOP experience will be made clearer if we keep this distinction in mind. And it has its complement on the union side: between those that do and do not welcome the 'partnership potential' of employee ownership.

Turning back now to leveraged ESOPs, their general purpose is to buy big blocks of shares, with a view to the gradual allocation of those shares to employees, and in many cases indeed to acquire 100% of the equity capital. One of the three American case studies which follow in these final chapters, Allied Plywood, is in effect a 100% ESOP. A second, United Airlines (UAL)), is majority (55%) employee-owned. In the other case, Polaroid Corporation, a leveraged ESOP was indeed used to acquire no more than a minority shareholding. Like UAL, Polaroid is also unusual in that it was a quoted rather than a private company when its ESOP was introduced, and indeed has remained that way.

That brings me to a more general point. According to the NCEO, about 15% of all ESOPs are in public firms. They are much more frequent among private companies, and, to judge from Conte's data, this is even more true for the narrower category of leveraged ESOPs.

Leveraged ESOPs
Breakdown between Public & Private Companies

	Total Leveraged	Public	Private
1988	2,591	346	2,245
1989	2,534	377	2,157
1990	2,711	446	2,265

The imbalance in the use of leveraged ESOPs as between private and publicly quoted companies is even more marked among small businesses than large ones. Leveraged ESOPs are roughly *twenty* times more likely to be used by small private companies than by their publicly quoted counterparts:

Leveraged ESOPs
Breakdown among Smaller Companies: 1988-90

	Total Leveraged	Public	Private
1988	1,530	70	1,460
1989	1,368	62	1,306
1990	1,490	66	1,424

It is often argued that the most important and frequent purpose for which American private companies use leveraged ESOPs is as a mechanism for buying out the shares of a main shareholder or shareholders – especially in the case of family businesses. The case study of Allied Plywood is an example of precisely that. There is a fair expectation that this will also turn out to be the principal use of the much more recent statutory ESOPs in the UK. Ownership succession in private companies and especially in family businesses is a growing problem to which ESOPs offer an attractive solution, and that is one reason why the Allied Plywood case study is included at the end of this book among others which look forward to the future of employee ownership. The other reason is that – exceptionally for a US ESOP-owned company – Allied Plywood has so structured its arrangements that its employee ownership may perhaps be sustained almost indefinitely.

As we saw in the steel industry case studies, more rare but also more dramatic use of the leveraged ESOP in today's America is as a mechanism which can save businesses, or parts of businesses, and thus jobs and incomes, which would otherwise almost certainly be lost. There can be no certainty that if the ESOP mechanism *is* used for this more dramatic purpose, the result will be success. It is also true that these dramatic and potentially job-saving ESOPs are no more than a small minority in the whole population of America's ESOPs. In the highly competitive national and international markets for steel and other manufactured goods, there are situations where it is almost impossible to save these jobs in Western countries unless the workers concerned either accept a pay cut or notch up significant and rapid improvements in productivity, or both. A cut in wages will almost always deliver an improvement of competitive edge more rapidly than any scheme of productivity improvement. On the other hand, if workers are to accept restraint in relation to wages they will clearly prefer to do so when they will themselves be the main beneficiaries of any resulting improvements in profits. That as we have seen, was the logic behind each of the two dramatic employee buy-outs – at Weirton and at Republic Engineered Steels Inc – included among my case studies. We should not hesitate about insisting to politicians that the jobs saved are real jobs and that the source of saving them was ESOP legislation.

The reasons for the establishment of ESOPs in American steel companies were, to repeat, especially to save jobs. At Polaroid Corporation, the world famous manufacturer of instant cameras, instant film and all kinds of instant images. the logic of the ESOP was essentially defensive: the ESOP was established by Polaroid's directors and then used to acquire a big block of shares as a key move in defending the business against a hostile takeover bid. On the other hand, the high court in Delaware later ruled that there was nothing illegal about what Polaroid had done, basing its judgment on the argument that, as well as being a defence against the takeover bid, the ESOP was also in line with Polaroid's long-established policies of enlightened employee relations.

We noticed earlier that relative to their use in private companies the use of leveraged ESOPs in American businesses which are publicly traded was quite modest. But the numbers are not negligible – between 400 and 500, or perhaps between 2% and 3% of all quoted US businesses. One hypothesis is that where they have been used by quoted American companies, a motive has been as a preventive defence against precisely the kind of hostile takeover bid with which Polaroid was confronted. As an extension of that preventive use, leveraged ESOPs have been used to take public companies private – and so remove them beyond the reach of hostile takeovers. Probably the most famous example of this was at the car hire company, Avis, in 1988. And the Avis experience remains important notwithsdtanding the fact that the company was the subject of a conventional capitalist offer in 1997, and gave up its employee ownership when the offer was accepted.

This discussion has concentrated mainly on leveraged ESOPs. As I have said, they tend to be more interesting. But there is also a more general reason for this focus: the subject matter of this book is not employee ownership on the margin but total or at least substantial employee ownership. More precisely, the book is about employee ownership which is so substantial as to demand a new status for a business's employee shareholders and new systems of involvement such that they can make their influence properly felt.

By fixing their cut-off point at 4% ownership by employees, the authors of *The New Owners* that I quoted in the epigraph are effectively telling their readers that they are interested in employee ownership of *all* kinds. That is fine, but readers of that book should probably be advised to keep the distinction clearly and continuously in mind. The differences between employee ownership of 4% and 100% are so great that it is improbable that they share any significant non-formal characteristics. Of course, there is a whole spectrum of incremental ownership percentages stretching from 4% to 100%. It may be arguable that (a) in most of the cases of minority employee ownership, the employee-owned percentage is growing year by year; and (b) many of the companies which end up being substantially or wholly employee-owned have started with a lower percentage. But this still leaves a very large and potentially growing number of US businesses in which the employee ownership is maintained at a steady but quite small percentage – whether at the 4% base level taken by the authors of *The New Owners*, or at their 12% average, or even somewhat higher. Although employees own shares in these companies, both the current and prospective level of ownership is so low that it can surely add little if anything to employees' sense of involvement or influence in the business.

At the heart of my interest are those American companies which are majority employee-owned. I know of no very reliable estimate of their total number but it probably falls somewhere around 1,000. It is the quality of these businesses and the effect of their ownership arrangements on those who work in them which seems to me to be at least as interesting and important as their number.

For the future, perhaps the most critical question to emerge from these case studies is whether majority employee ownership is likely to be sustainable without changes in the present US law. The earlier evidence of the two big steel companies tells forcefully against sustainability. And in the absence of some quite exceptional developments, the same is projected to be true of United Airlines.

And that brings me back to the contrast between the American and British employee ownership experience. In terms of relative size in the middle 1990s, there is no comparison. But there is one respect in which employee ownership in Britain may be said to be ahead of that in the USA. It is that the leading British businesses which are majority or wholly employee-owned have structured their employee ownership in such a way that it should even be possible for it to be sustained indefinitely. That is surely important though the numbers involved are only tiny. What is surprising is that the issue of sustainability seems to have been largely ignored, as one of only minor importance, in the USA. It may indeed seem odd, to readers as well as to the writer, to spend huge amounts of time and effort adapting the corporate culture of a business so as to be in line with employee ownership – only to be forced to abandon that ownership after what is unlikely to be much more than a decade.

25

Polaroid: Using an ESOP
as a Takeover Defence

INTRODUCTORY OVERVIEW

Excellence . . . We employ excellent people and we expect excellent performance.

Ownership . . . Each of us is responsible for knowing what our business goals are and each of us is responsible for doing all we can to achieve them. Each of us expects to be informed on matters that affect our business and to have an opportunity to influence the decision making process. Each of us expects to share in the Company's fortunes – both good and bad.

Respect . . . We believe in the dignity of every individual in the Company. *From a statement of Polaroid's Company Values, February 1987*

Employee Owners . . . have a longer perspective. While they also have an interest in quarterly results, they have an even greater concern about the very long-term success of their company and the stability of their jobs. Far from abating, the *current* move toward employee ownership of company stock is likely to increase, perhaps dramatically. Like institutional investors they will demand – and deserve – to be heard.

Employee ownership is not a fad . . . not an anti-takeover ploy. It's a global phenomenon . . . it's important . . . and I'm all for it. *Taken from 'Some Thoughts on Corporate Ownership in the 1990s'. Remarks by I. M. Booth, then President and CEO of Polaroid Corporation, delivered before the Cornell Club of Boston. 4 April 1990*

In the fashionable industrial relations language of the late 1980s and early 1990s, the use of the words 'own' and 'ownership' have been extended beyond their older conventional limits. For example, it has become normal to talk about 'owning' and 'ownership' not only in relation to pieces of property but also in relation, say, to a problem. In this extended usage 'owning a problem' means taking responsibility for finding a solution to it. As can be seen in the first of the two epigraphs, Polaroid was using the word 'ownership' in this extended sense in a statement of its company values as early as February 1987, eighteen months before the employees started to become 'real' employee owners in July 1988.

Whatever judgement may be made about the 'real' employee ownership, at least from July 1988 to the completion of the repayment in December 1997 of the company's original ESOP loan, employees certainly had to 'own' their share of the problems of Polaroid. For in 1995, for the second time in less than ten years, Polaroid embarked on a big restructuring operation with job losses on a large scale. The redundancies were virtually all voluntary – indeed some argue that redundancy was made very attractive. Nonetheless, in this second instance the restructuring, when completed, will have reduced Polaroid's workforce in the mainland USA by 20%.

The 1995 restructuring came two years before the maturity, in December 1997, of the company's ESOP, which was set up in connection with the earlier restructuring exercise in 1988. Alongside that earlier restructuring, just under 10 million of newly issued shares, amounting to 14% of its common stock, were bought on behalf of Polaroid's employees. The buyer was an ESOP trust set up earlier in the same month.

In fact, as the management is understandably keen to emphasise, discussions about a possible ESOP had begun inside Polaroid at least as early as 1985. The necessary authority had been given at a board of directors' meeting in May 1988, that is two months before it was formally used for establishing the ESOP in July.

Some months later, in March 1989, the company bought in and cancelled 16 million of its common stock shares. Following these two transactions (July 1988 and March 1989), Polaroid's employees were, through the mechanism of the ESOP trust, the owners of just under 20% of its common stock, a figure which later reached a high of 22%. Collectively, they had in fact become the largest single stockholder on the morrow of the ESOP trust purchase of July 1988.

But it was not so much any corporate philosophy about the metaphysical importance of ownership which precipitated the ESOP share purchase. Rather it was self-defence – more precisely it was anticipatory or preventative self-defence in what became a hard fought takeover battle. Through an informal telephone call, management apparently became aware of a take-over threat in late

June 1988. In the form of an unsolicited letter written by a California-based financial conglomerate, Shamrock Holdings, and dated 19 July, the threat rapidly materialised. A formal bid followed in September 1988.

After an intense battle and a crucial court judgment, the bid was formally withdrawn in April 1989, when Shamrock also undertook to refrain from any further takeover attempt for at least ten years. In this case, the ESOP turned out to be the decisive factor in the takeover defence. That alone gives this case history a particular interest.

For readers whose interest extends beyond the study of takeover battles within the framework of conventional Anglo-Saxon capitalism, the Polaroid ESOP, its largest even if still minority shareholder for more than nine years from 1988, raises a number of other questions:
– What effect did it have on industrial relations?
– What effect did it have on business performance?
– To what extent did its employee owners start to behave like real owners?
– Given a choice, would Polaroid's employee owners seek to sustain that ownership when the ESOP came to an end in 1997?

As we shall see, the answer to the fourth question, when it came up in 1997, was apparently more 'yes' than 'no'. But that is to anticipate.

The Company and Its Record in Outline Because of its instant cameras, Polaroid is a household name all over the world. Its head office is built around Technology Square in Cambridge, Massachusetts, a town with a notable concentration of what President de Gaulle used to call *'la matière grise'*. Its headquarters building is scarcely a stone's throw from the Massachusetts Institute of Technology (MIT) and not much further from Harvard Yard. From this base, Polaroid in 1995
– made sales of $2.2bn, of which just over half were outside the USA;
– employed 11,662 people worldwide, sharply down on 1994, and scheduled to fall further after the latest restructuring;
– made profits from 'operations' of $89m, down from $200m in 1994.

In 1990 Polaroid was no. 218 in the list of America's largest companies compiled by *Fortune* magazine; but measured by the popular recognition of the Polaroid name its position was much higher: no. 42 in the USA according to Landor Associates' *Image Power Survey* of the world's most powerful brands. It came no. 65 even in Europe according to a Landor measure of 'familiarity and esteem'. (By 1996 Polaroid had slipped out of the *Fortune* 500, but its brand image was still way up on its size.)

Polaroid's founder, Dr Edwin Land, was born in Bridgeport, Connecticut, in 1909, began studying at Harvard in the late 1920s but left to work as an inventor on his own account before completing his undergraduate degree. In 1932, jointly with George Wheelwright III, who had taught him physics at Harvard, he founded the Land-Wheelwright Laboratories. The Polaroid Corporation was founded by him in 1937. In 1947 he made public the most famous of his many inventions, the Polaroid one-step camera.

From the early 1950s to the late 1970s, Polaroid was essentially a single-product business. Employment peaked at just under 21,000 in 1978. At just over $72.50, the 1978 year-end share price was also higher than ever before or since.

The story of Polaroid during the 1980s, if we exclude the Shamrock bid and the company's response to it, is mainly one of consolidation and diversification. In a foreword to a booklet which summarises the statistical record of the business between 1980 and 1990, Ian MacAllister Booth, Polaroid's chairman, president and CEO until 1995 – from whose remarks to the Boston Cornell Club I quoted in the second epigraph – wrote of the 1980s as being a decade of transition: 'During the past decade, Polaroid Corporation managed a significant transition from a pioneering company which invented and developed instant photography to a broad-based imaging company offering instant, conventional and electronic imaging products.'

It was towards the end of this process of restructuring that the company became exposed to the bid from the financial conglomerate Shamrock Holdings, which had little or no experience of photography or of what Polaroid likes to call the 'instant imaging' business.

The conditions which prompted the bid were typical enough. The Polaroid share price had been steadily falling from its peak in 1978. There had been progress in achieving Mr MacAllister Booth's 'significant transition' – away from being a one-product company.

Workforce numbers were sharply down and profits, after actually turning negative in 1985 (following a notably high tax charge) had shown a respectable recovery in 1986 and 1987.

The aftermath of the Shamrock bid and the restructuring was a sharp improvement in profits. Indeed, the highest operating profit ever achieved was in 1989, and the results for each of the subsequent five years were also good.

Profits from Operations: 1985-1995, $m

	Operating Profits	Special Costs*	Profit from Operations
1985	33.6	nil	33.6
1986	135.7	nil	135.7
1987	153.8	nil	153.8
1988	173.8	151.9	21.9
1989	304.2	40.5	263.7
1990	284.3	nil	284.3
1991	246.6	nil	246.6
1992	213.8	nil	213.8
1993	185.4	44.0	141.4
1994	200.3	nil	200.3
1995	89.2	247.0	-157.8

*Mainly restructuring costs

Up to the end of 1997 there were no further attempts to take over the company – indeed, so long as the original ESOP continued, it was probably takeover-proof. The consensus, in relation to the arrangements which followed, was that they would probably provide adequate protection.

I conclude this introductory overview with three rather different points. The first is commercial: the tension between technical and market orientation in relation to the company's profitability. Until 1995, Polaroid essentially remained a technology-driven company. However, new products introduced in the first half of the 1990s did not fare as well, or at any rate did not take off as fast as management had hoped. Moreover, the Polaroid range of products is technically wide, as well as broad-ranging in its target markets. At one end is the simplest modern version of its original 'single-product', one step camera. Sales of this product were forging ahead in the mid-1990s but the most promising new markets were uncertain – countries like Russia and China. The Captiva (or 'Joshua') line, by contrast, a compact and more sophisticated version of a one-step camera introduced in 1992, 'has not met sales and profit targets, and been restructured to reduce production while still meeting consumer demand', to quote from the 1995 annual report.

At the other end of the spectrum, Polaroid introduced sophisticated medical scanning equipment called Helios. Announced in 1992, this was still making substantial though declining losses in 1995. Finally, there are the graphics imaging products – mainly intended for use in offices – which was still too new to be judged at the time of writing (1997). The commercial skill and new product judgement of Polaroid's ESOP period top management was called into question by the sales record of these new products. The new CEO, Gary T. DiCamillo, who took over in 1995, sharply changed the focus of the company from technological development to market orientation.

But future success will not depend only on whether this change of emphasis proves to be right or wrong. The fact that between the two big restructurings in 1988 and 1995 the employees were the single largest body of shareholders was important not only for defence against possible takeovers but also for the internal functioning of the company. Was employee ownership and motivation significant in the relatively trouble-free achievement of the massive job cuts? And would the commercial effect of mistakes in relation to new products have been compounded without it? In the case study which follows we look carefully at the so-called 'Total Quality Ownership' and 'Ownership Stretch Objective' programmes which were introduced in the early 1990s. Did these programmes 'change the culture' at Polaroid to the point where processes of 'continuous improvement' got under way and can now be sustained? And how do these interrelate in this non-union company with what some have seen as an accident-prone record of labour relations, as symbolised by the benchmark case brought against Polaroid in 1995 by the US National Labor Relations Board?

Finally, it is appropriate to record the death, in 1991, of Polaroid's founder, the inventor of genius, Dr Edwin Land. Dr Land had stepped down from the posts of Polaroid's president and CEO as long ago as 1975. And in 1982 he had given up the chairmanship and resigned his place as a director. Of course it is as an inventor that he will be chiefly remembered. But he may also be credited with responsibility for having created a rather unusual combination of industrial relations policies: non-union, but whether despite or because of that, with a humanistic centre. He was also something of an inspirational leader. In the annual report for 1990 which records his death, his successors quoted the following passage from his letter to shareholders in 1980, ten years before:

> Do not undertake the program unless the goal is manifestly important and its achievement nearly impossible. Do not do anything that anyone else can do readily; industry should be the intersection of science and art; the second great product of industry should be the fully rewarding working life for every person; the most intelligent use of a science requires understanding that comes only from increasing the knowledge in that science; it is relatively easy to organise a company with a homogenous set of good minds; but the ultimate greatness of a company depends on the variety of good minds within it.

Before the Takeover Bid: The First Phase – Down to 1978 The Polaroid story begins with the birth of Edwin Herbert Land in Bridgeport, Connecticut, on 7 May 1909. *Encyclopaedia Britannica* (1974 edition) highlights his invention of a 'one step process for developing and printing photographs [which] culminated in a revolution in photography unparalleled since the advent of roll film' and goes on to sketch in the background to his invention:

> While a student at Harvard ... Land became interested in polarized light, light in which all rays are aligned in the same plane. He took leave of absence, and, after intensive study and experimentation, succeeded (1932) in aligning submicroscopic crystals of iodoquinine sulphate and embedding them in a sheet of plastic. The resulting polarizer, for which he envisioned numerous uses and which he dubbed Polaroid J sheet, was a tremendous advance. It allowed the use of almost any size of polarizer and significantly reduced costs.
>
> He developed and, in 1936, began to use numerous types of Polaroid material in sun-glasses and other optical devices. Polaroid was later used in camera filters and other optical equipment...

Land began work on an instantaneous developing film after the war. In 1947 he demonstrated a camera (known as the Polaroid Land Camera) that produced a finished print in 60 seconds. The Land photographic process soon found numerous commercial, military and scientific applications. Many innovations were made in the following years, including the development of a colour process.

I have a dim memory of special dark glasses, called Polaroids, being on sale in British shops in my childhood – during the war and immediately after it. There is a sentence in the *Encyclopaedia Britannica* article about the work of Land and his Polaroid Corporation during that conflict: 'During World War II he applied the polarizing principle to military hardware, including infrared filters, lightweight range finders, sights for anti-aircraft guns and other weapons, and night adaptation goggles.'

It is not clear how far Polaroid continued to work on defence contracts after the war, probably not very much. For the period from the invention of the instant camera in 1947 onwards we have the judgement of Mr MacAllister Booth quoted earlier for the view that down to about 1980, the Corporation was 'a pioneering company which invented and developed instant photography.'

In other words, for over thirty years after 1947, Polaroid was essentially a one-product business. But it needs to be emphasised at once that its chief characteristic was its almost unfaltering sales growth, reflecting rapid growth in the demand for Polaroid cameras, in the United States and worldwide.

Both Polaroid's employment numbers and its share price reached a peak in 1978 of 20,884 and $72.5 respectively. The company's sales and employment growth during the final years of its 'pioneering . . . instant photography' phase were as follows:

Sales ($m) & Employment 1973 to 1978

	US	Other	Total	Employees
1973	493.1	192.4	685.5	14,277
1974	487.3	270.0	757.3	13,019
1975	495.6	317.1	812.7	13,387
1976	586.7	363.3	950.0	14,506
1977	645.8	416.1	1,061.9	16,394
1978	817.4	559.2	1,376.6	20,884

The year 1978 was in fact an *annus mirabilis* for Polaroid by a third measure: return on stockholders' equity. That reached a figure of 13.8%, which was not exceeded until 1989.

What seems to have driven the growth of employment during the decade down to 1978 was a combination of two factors: first, the continuous increase in the sales of instant cameras and, second, a policy of bringing inside the business the manufacture of components previously made outside. By the end of 1978 the second process was all but complete. It seems clear too that by then the growth in the sales of instant cameras had started to slow down. In any event, Polaroid's employment began to fall in 1979.

A Transitional Decade: 1979 to the Eve of the Shamrock Bid A way to measure Polaroid's performance between the 'high peak' year of 1978 and the unwelcome receipt of the unsolicited letter from Shamrock holding in July 1988 is to trace the year-by-year evolution in the percentage return on stockholders' equity. After its peak of 13.8% in 1978, and if we exclude a rebound to 9% in 1980, the pattern is one of almost continuous decline to 1985 – when a negative figure of minus 0.3% was registered – followed by a strong recovery in 1986 and 1987.

Return on Stockholders' Equity: % 1978–87

1978	13.8	1983	5.4
1979	4.0	1984	2.8
1980	9.1	1985	(0.3)
1981	3.2	1986	11.7
1982	2.5	1987	12.5

For sales, there is much the same pattern. But because of falls in the numbers employed, output per employee over this same eight-year period was held steady at around $85,000 in constant prices from 1978 to 1985. But that run of six almost flat years was then followed, as in the case of the other measures, by a sharp improvement to $94,000 in 1986 and $104,000 in 1987, nearly 20% above the 1981 figure.

Sales and Employment 1981–87

	Current Price ($m)	Constant (1981) Prices ($m)	Employees
1981	1,420	1,420	16,784
1982	1,294	1,247	14,540
1983	1,255	1,164	13,871
1984	1,272	1,136	13,402
1985	1,295	1,115	12,932
1986	1,629	1,387	14,785
1987	1,764	1,426	13,662

To complete this statistical summary of the period down to 1987, two other series are worth putting on the record :

	R&D	Capital Spending
	$m, constant (1981) prices	
1981	121.4	42.5
1982	114.0	30.3
1983	114.2	46.5
1984	120.5	73.9
1985	102.1	89.9
1986	107.7	70.5
1987	115.1	94.3

Compared with total sales varying between $1.1bn and $1.4bn in constant prices, R&D expenditures were fluctuating between a low of about 8% and a high of just over 10% of turnover. On the other hand the movement of the capital spending figures show a radically different trend. After falling sharply between 1981 and 1982 there was a sustained recovery. Presumably it was this investment which funded the transition from a single-product company to Mr MacAllister Booth's 'broad-based imaging company offering instant, conventional and electronic imaging products'.

On the other hand, given the long decline down to 1985 in the return on stockholders' equity, this was no time to be overgenerous with dividends. Between 1981 and 1985 the annual payout to stockholders was held steady at 50 cents in nominal terms – and thus declined in real terms. Stockholders had to wait till 1987 for their reward: an increase to 60 cents on the dividend. Moreover this was payable on each of two new shares into which the old shares had been split.

In fact, between the 'low' of 1985 and the high of 1987 – the stock split year – shareholders saw a more than threefold rise in the value of their shares. The price went from a low of $12.19 in 1985 to $42.63 in 1987. Allowing for the stock split these figures imply a sixfold rise in the value of a retained shareholding. On the other hand, even in 1987 the price of Polaroid's shares exemplified the rule that what goes up may come down: the shares traded down to a 'low' of $16.75 in the fourth quarter.

In summary, this ten-year period from the 'high peak' year of 1978 to July 1988 contains both positive and negative elements. On the positive side, the management had succeeded by 1986 and 1987 in turning round the direction in which profits were moving and propelling them sharply upwards. There was also a big improvement in labour productivity. But on the other hand, when faced with the Shamrock challenge, management showed itself capable of improving the company's profit performance at an altogether faster pace. At least in theory it might surely have been possible to achieve an acceleration in the pace of improvement without the Shamrock challenge.

In any event those behind the bid from Shamrock evidently felt that Polaroid was well positioned to deliver substantial further improvements: more precisely at the price they offered of $34.50 per share, later increased to $42.00, and under their management they reckoned that that there was a fair chance of that happening.

What of the 'culture' of Polaroid during this period? Before his retirement early in 1993, Owen Gaffney was a group vice-president. He had been with Polaroid for thirty years – with responsibility for overseeing manufacturing operations and then for human resources. His view is that in the headlong expansion of the mid-1970s the company somewhat lost its way; and in particular that it partly lost touch with the humanistic values of its founder, Dr Land. On the other hand, and as a result of sustained remedial efforts by management during this period, he also believes that by 1987 both the morale of the workforce and the values of the company were back in fairly good shape. As evidence for this, he cites first the statement of values, promulgated in 1987 (see epigraph). He also cites the fact that already, before there was any threat of a takeover bid, the management had started discussing an ESOP, and eventually set one up, at least partly because of its apparent congruence with company philosophy.

Whatever the state of workforce morale in late 1987 and early 1988, that was due to be sharply tested by the conditions associated with the purchase of shares by the ESOP in July 1988; and more generally by the conflict with Shamrock and what may be called the costs of victory.

THE ESOP AND THE SHAMROCK BID
JULY 1988 TO APRIL 1989

Polaroid publishes a fortnightly in-house magazine *Polaroid Update*. The front page of the issue dated 3 April 1989 carries a simple headline across two columns: WE WON. What this referred to was the withdrawal of the Shamrock takeover bid coupled with an undertaking that it would make no further attempt to take over Polaroid for at least ten years.

When a substantial company is subjected to a takeover battle, even when it wins and as in this case sees off the challenger, it will normally emerge somewhat changed. At Polaroid, the main changes were two: a massive 'restructuring plan'; and a purchase of company stock by the ESOP Trust which the company had set up in March 1988, but which was only wheeled into action in July. Strictly, the events associated with the ESOP were a part of the restructuring plan – that is how the two were presented by management at the time. However, for clarity, the ESOP and the restructuring exercise are treated separately for the purposes of this study.

Restructuring and Job Cuts Management announced its restructuring plan on 12 July 1988. This was a week before the receipt of the formal letter from Shamrock Holdings, but roughly a month after the first intimation by telephone that a bid was in the offing. There is no reason to doubt the link between the intimation of the bid and the plan to restructure.

Top management set a precise goal for the restructuring plan: to reduce costs by $70m annually – or by just less than 4% compared with total costs in the previous year. Looking back in the light of the 1995 restructuring proposals, the job cuts of 1988 look quite modest. But they were easily the largest and the toughest components of that earlier cost-cutting exercise. There were two parallel programmes of voluntary early retirement and voluntary redundancy. Here too a numerical target was set: that 1,500 jobs should go. In fact the figures show that employment fell by just over 2,000 between 1987 and 1988, from 13,662 to 11,613.

The *Polaroid Update* of 1 September 1988 reported that as many as seven of the company's corporate 'officers' – its top-line managers – would be taking early retirement. These included a senior vice-president for finance and a group vice-president for worldwide marketing. Although redundancies were generally voluntary, one can only imagine that these were painful decisions. Polaroid's CEO, Mr MacAllister Booth, was quoted in the *Polaroid Update* as describing the seven early retiring officers as 'valued, colleagues, dear friends, builders of this Company and, in many cases, personal mentors of mine'.

The total workforce reduction in 1988 was 18%. That was followed by a ballooning of payroll and related costs in the latter year because of special redundancy and early retirement payments. It was not till 1989 that the benefits of the manpower reductions began to show up in Polaroid's cost base. Total payroll and benefit costs in 1989 were $547m – down from $585m two years before.

It would be wrong to imply that this massive restructuring programme consisted exclusively of manpower reductions. Quite apart from the ESOP, it included, as reported by the *Polaroid Update* on 1 August 1988:

– [the] worldwide marketing of conventional films to increase revenues, and

– an internal reorganisation to strengthen the focus on instant imaging and accelerate the development of new products.

The effects of these two other changes cannot be quantified directly. One possible measure of the overall success of the restructuring was the increase in operating profits from $154m in 1987, the last full year before it, to $264m in 1989, the first full year after it.

This improvement suggests two general reflections for a business the size of Polaroid. The first is that even where a striking improvement in performance has been achieved – as was the case at Polaroid between 1986 and 1987 – there is probably always room for substantial further improvement. Second, such is the force of inertia that in some circumstances an outside challenge may be a necessary condition for securing that extra improvement.

However plausible or otherwise those reflections may be, there can be little doubt that the Shamrock challenge had a notable influence on the Polaroid ESOP: namely on the timing and the size of the stock purchase, to which we now turn.

The ESOP and Shareholder Neutrality Like many other American quoted companies, Polaroid introduced a special kind of ESOP called a 'tax credit ESOP' in the early 1980s, soon after the relevant tax credit was voted by the Congress. The company continued to make contributions to it until those credits were withdrawn in 1986. While the relevant credit lasted, the company received a dollar off its tax liability for every dollar – up to a maximum of 1% of payroll – it contributed to the plan. It would have been perverse not to have taken advantage of these provisions. On the other hand, it was surely unrealistic to think that the Congress would allow such 'free benefits' to continue indefinitely.

It was not until March 1988 that Polaroid took steps to set up an approved ESOP, although the management had begun to discuss the possibility at least as early as 1985. The ESOP was conditionally approved by the board of directors in May 1988. The condition was that the plan should be 'shareholder neutral' – in other words, not inimical to their interests. As the ESOP came to an end in 1997, the way Polaroid had handled the issue of maintaining neutrality, *vis-à-vis* non-employee shareholders, was beginning to look like a precedent for all quoted companies which want to channel profits into an ESOP. In this respect Polaroid may reasonably claim that its ESOP was something of a pioneer.

I simply do not know to what extent the possibility was foreseen in March 1988 that the ESOP might come in handy should Polaroid be subject to a takeover challenge. But it is hard to believe that all of the top managers were wholly unaware of the possibility.

In any event, when the company announced its massive restructuring programme on 12 July, the ESOP was swung into action as part of it. A total of 9.7m new Polaroid shares were issued and bought by the ESOP at a price per share of $30.875. The new stockholding gave the ESOP around 14% of the total Polaroid equity.

But what must have struck the employees with the greatest force was the set of management decisions about how the purchase of the ESOP's stockholding was to be financed. It was to happen through reductions in pay and the suspension of some other benefits, for management and non-management alike. There was a 10% cut in total 'compensation expenditures' for all staff. A further cut of 5% was imposed on top managers – the eighteen corporate officers. These reductions, calculated to cover the $300m loan repayments and associated interest over the ten-year life of the ESOP, would not be restored at least until after the conclusion of the loan repayments. In this way, or so the management argued, the ESOP could be judged 'neutral', or 'fair', to Polaroid's existing shareholders.

The 10% reduction in total compensation payments can be broken down into three components: (i) 5% was a straight wage cut; (ii) a further 3% took the form of a reduction in the annual cost of living pay adjustment that would otherwise have become due in full in the month following the restructuring exercise; (iii) the third component, 2%, took the form of a suspension of various non-cash benefits in Polaroid's employment contracts. From then on the management kept track of the resulting savings and claimed throughout that they had matched the principal and interest payments on the ESOP loan. A question-and-answer sequence in *Polaroid Update* (1 August 1988) set out the principle behind this technique for achieving 'stockholder neutrality':

> *Question*. Why can't the company pay for the Stock Equity Plan, instead of the employees doing it?
> *Answer*. The Company *is* [emphasis original] paying for the Stock Equity Plan. As part of the overall restructuring of the Company's compensation and benefits plan, corporate funds that would have been allocated to payroll will instead be used to fund the ESOP.

The logic of the answer, as explained to me by management, has two parts. First, the reduction of 10% in 'compensation' can be seen as amounting to a switch from one form of compensation to another – the prospective ESOP benefits. Second, the company is the provider in both cases. Readers must judge this logic for themselves.

However satisfactory or otherwise this answer, the question and answer taken together suggest that the most sensible way of looking at the ESOP from the employees' point of view is as a scheme of compulsory saving of a rather special kind. It was of a rather special kind because (a) it was a significant gamble, but also (b) because those who were forced to do the saving could have some influence on the likely outcome of the gamble. For the record we should also note that, since the dividends on the ESOP shares were used to to help pay off the ESOP loan, these were forced savings which were to yield no income for up to ten years.

Allocations of shares into the individual accounts of employees took place every six months. Given the ten-year maturity of the loan taken out to finance the ESOP stock purchase, it was calculated that roughly 5% of 9.7 million shares – or just less than 500,000 – would be allocated out (pro rata with earnings) every six months. Favourable subsequent developments outweighed unfavourable ones. In particular, lower than projected interest rates outweighed the impact of lower than projected payroll savings – which arose because there were fewer staff on the payroll. So the original repayment timetable might have been brought forward. In practice, the company reduced the cost to employees by starting to pay dividends (originally earmarked to help pay off the loan *throughout* its life) about three years before the loan's maturity date.

A useful calculation of 'who gets what' was circulated to employees by the company for the first sixth-month period of 1990. The total number of shares to be allocated was shown to be 483,000. The total relevant payroll aggregate for the six-month period was then shown to be $165.6m. Dividing the latter by the total number of shares to be allocated yielded the calculation that each eligible employee would receive roughly 2.9 shares for each $1,000 of annual earnings. Thus someone earning $20,000 annually would receive a share allocation of 58 shares, and someone on twice that would get 116.

This circular went on to provide estimates of the likely number of shares which would be built up by employees when the loan repayments had been completed in 1997. For someone paid an annual $30,000 in 1990, it was estimated that his or her package of accumulated shares would number 920 at the end of 1997. The circular concluded by showing the value of such a share package, on different assumptions about the share price. At a price of no more than $20 the value of 920 shares would be $18,400; at $30 per share the value would be $27,600; and at $42 per share, the value would be between $38,000 and $39,000. If the price per share at end-1997 was $100 then the value of 920 shares would be $92,000. The figure that the circular does not give is the accumulated value of benefits foregone. However, in May 1996 Ralph Norwood, vice president and treasurer, estimated that the break-even share value for employees would be about $40 per share – after making allowance for interest they might have earned if they had saved this money in a more conventional way. For the record, the final price was comfortably above the break-even figure, approximately $45.

When Mr Norwood gave that estimate, Polaroid (and its employees) were considering whether to continue with an ESOP after the completion in late 1997 of the final interest and loan repayments in the original plan. The decision which was later taken may well surprise critics of Polaroid's whole long-running employee-ownership project, both inside and outside the company. Though there was no actual voting, the management judged that a big majority of the workforce favoured a second infusion of employee ownership, albeit at a reduced level. Moreoever management was sufficiently confident about this to introduce a new set of employee ownership and related employee savings and make them a condition of employment from 1998 onwards and to present them to new recruits as benefit of working at Polaroid. The full details need not concern us. But the essential numbers are a 5% reduction in wages compared with what these would otherwise have been, split between:

– 3% to buy shares for employees;
– 2% as an enhanced pension contribution.

The management is prepared to offer two rather consequential judgements about these developments and they seem worth having on the record:

– The main reason for the strong employee support behind a second infusion of employee ownership was a widespread recognition of the value of the forced savings which had beeen accumulated through the original ESOP.

– Although, following the end of the original ESOP, there will be no chunk of employee-owned equity held as a block, there are likely for at least a number of years to be enough shares in friendly hands to see off a hostile takeover bid.

Legal Challenges Over the first few months of 1989 Polaroid managed to survive a series of Shamrock challenges brought against it in the courts of the State of Delaware where Polaroid is registered. What is mainly of interest here is the ground on which the

Delaware courts rejected Shamrock's challenge to the ESOP. Essentially the court accepted the 'good faith' of the Polaroid ESOP and ruled that that 'good faith' was not seriously undermined by the fact that it had also operated as a valuable defence mechanism in a takeover battle.

In January 1989 the challenger had increased the price it had earlier offered to pay for Polaroid's shares from $42.00 a share in September 1988 to $45.00. However, with hindsight, January 1989 was the month that marked the turning point against Shamrock. For it was on 6 January that the vice-chancellor of the Delaware Chancery Court, Carolyn Berger, gave the thumbs down to its submission that Polaroid's 1988 ESOP was 'invalid'. The vice-chancellor's judgment ran to 53 pages. A few key sentences from it were published by *Polaroid Update* on 18 January:

> 'I am satisfied', she wrote, 'that the Polaroid ESOP is fundamentally fair. I do not find either the timing of its implementation or its possible anti-takeover effect objectionable under the facts of the case.
>
> 'The fact that the ESOP was partly defensive ... does not make it unfair. This is a defensive device – assuming that it is one – that is designed to and appears likely to add value to the company and all of its stock holders. It does not prevent the stock holders from receiving or considering alternatives. In sum, the plan adopted by the directors is fair and should not be invalidated.'

In making her judgment, Carolyn Berger was apparently influenced by two specific points. The first was the humanistic tradition of industrial relations at Polaroid. And the second was the so-called 'neutrality' of the ESOP *vis-à-vis* the interests of Polaroid's existing shareholders. Commentators were quick to point out that if one or other of those two conditions had not been satisfied, the vice-chancellor's ruling might well have gone the other way.

Shamrock Holdings appealed against this ruling but without success. In a second and later legal move, in March 1989, it launched a court challenge to Polaroid's $50 a share buy-back plan which had been announced in February. But in this case too Shamrock failed. Before the end of March, the Shamrock directors showed the white flag by offering up all its Polaroid shares for buy-back treatment.

The buy-back offer may be seen as having clinched the issue 'game, set and match' against Shamrock Holdings after the latter's challenge had already been decisively weakened by the vice-chancellor's ruling in the Delaware Chancery Court. It effectively secured the loyalty of the majority of Polaroid's existing shareholders. It was made possible by the support of an investment fund called Corporate Partners, headed by two partners, Lester Pollack and Ali Wombold, of Lazard Frères in New York. Given the Delaware Court ruling and the support of Lazard Frères, it was only a question of time before Shamrock caved in.

Finally we turn to litigation between Polaroid and its employees. This arose from the decision taken in February and March 1989 not to offer the ESOP shares for re-purchase when Polaroid launched a $1.25bn stock buy-back plan. The buy-back plan was in fact announced on 21 February 1989 with a price per share of $50 – well above the figure at which the shares were then trading. Not surprisingly, the offer was a success. What then became the subject of a legal challenge was the fact that not all of the ESOP shares were offered back for re-purchase. The result was that at the conclusion of the re-purchase exercise the ESOP's stockholding amounted not to the original 14% of Polaroid's equity, but close on 20%.

The Business Record 1989–96 Measured by operating profits, the performance of Polaroid during 1989–91 was well ahead of anything that had gone before. However, this progress was not sustained and in 1995 the company launched its second massive restructuring plan which involved the loss of a further 2,500 jobs or 20% of the workforce.

What happened? All began well. The results of the 1988 restructuring programme started to work through to the bottom line in 1989. The costs of payroll and related benefits were almost $40m lower in 1989 than they had been in 1987. In round figures average operating profits ran at $265m for the three years to end-1991, compared with no more than $108m for the three years to end-1987.

Moreover, Polaroid, though not its operating profits, benefited from a huge out-of-court settlement with Eastman Kodak. Net of money distributed to employees, that settlement strengthened the balance sheet by the equivalent of more than three years' net profits at the new post-restructuring average annual rate of $265m. The case arose out of a long-standing claim for patent infringement by Polaroid against Eastman Kodak. After a series of court judgments in 1990 and 1991, an out-of-court agreement was finally announced on 15 July 1991. Under it, Kodak paid Polaroid a total of $924.5m in a combination of cash and what the accountants call 'short-term instruments'. Of this total the management allocated $50m pre-tax to Polaroid employees in the form of cash bonuses while a net figure of $871.6m was brought into the 1991 accounts as a 'litigation settlement'.

It is worth setting out the wide difference in the value of the company implied by the different prices put by different people on the Polaroid shares from 1988 onwards: the price paid for its new shares by the ESOP trust in July 1988 was $30.875; eight months later, in March 1989, $50 a share was paid in the buy-back transaction; in between, in September 1988, Shamrock Holdings made a formal offer at a price of $42.50 a share, having suggested $34.50 per share in the 19 July letter announcing its bid. Looking forward and by way of comparison, the *New York Herald Tribune* of 10 December 1997 showed Polaroid stock trading at $46.03, with a high and low of $60 and $30 over the previous twelve months.

Wall Street was not notably impressed by the 1988–91 turn-around. Indeed almost continually from the end of the Shamrock bid in April 1989 until the end of 1997, the price movement of the company's shares underperformed that of the market average by a significant margin. At $28.50 in mid-January 1989 the price was not much more than half the $50 a share which the company had paid for the 22% of its equity which it had bought back in early 1989. And it was also well below the final price of $42 which had been offered by Shamrock. On the face of it, Polaroid shareholders would have been better off if Shamrock had won in 1989 and they had pocketed the $40 a share which had then been on offer.

No doubt the 'Wall Street Community' was disappointed by the decision, taken by Polaroid's directors early in 1992, not to pass on to the shareholders any of the money received from Kodak in the out-of-court settlement. Instead, the board had decided simply to maintain the dividend at the level of 60 cents a share which had been paid without interruption since 1987.

More fundamentally, Wall Street investors may also have been disappointed by the company's performance. Indeed, already by the end of 1994 the company itself was disappointed by the performance of the key product launched in 1992, the 'Joshua' camera (sold under the name 'Captiva' in the USA).

The story as told by the company in 1996 was that market research, including 15,000 focus interviews, had identified a niche market for a small sleek version of Polaroid's traditional one-step camera; but the investment needed to develop the product was much greater than could be justifed by a small niche market. The company went ahead all the same – and the product did not sell as well as had been hoped. Production was discontinued in 1996.

The new medical imaging equipment called Helios, launched in 1992, also opened up more slowly than expected; but by 1996 prospects were improving – for example a deal had been signed with the Japanese company Konica for it to market Helios in Japan.

One thing which kept Polaroid going was burgeoning sales of its long-standing one-step camera in emerging economies – in 1995, Russia was Polaroid's second largest market, with nearly $200m in sales (a success attributed by some to reluctance on the part of the Russian man-in-the-street to hand over film to third parties to be developed – and perhaps to be inspected by the Russian authorities). In 1993, 54% of sales were in the USA; by 1995, this had fallen to 46%.

Despite the company's marked successes in overseas sales, the commercial story of Polaroid in the first half of the 1990s was stagnation or worse. The decline in profits was set out in the introductory overview. Other key data, taken back to 1986 for ease of comparison, are as follows:

Polaroid 1986–95 (current prices)

	Employees	Net Sales ($bn)	% Return on Stockholders' Equity	Shares Outstanding
1986	14,765	1.63	11.7	61.9m
1987	13,662	1.76	12.5	61.9m
1988	11,613	1.86	(2.2)	71.6m
1989	11,441	1.90	33.5	52.1m
1990	11,768	1.97	63.3	50.1m
1991	12,003	2.07	148.6	48.9m
1992	12,359	2.15	12.7	46.7m
1993	12,048	2.24	9.3	46.8m
1994	12,104	2.31	14.7	46.0m
1995	11,662	2.24	(17.8)	45.5m

Notes: The 149% return on stockholders' equity in 1991 reflects the settlement with Eastman Kodak. The number of shares outstanding for 1986 have been restated to reflect the 1987 two-for-one stock split.
Source: 1995 Annual Report

This was the background to the 1995-6 restructuring programme of which the first wave, launched in the first quarter of 1995, proved inadequate. Further job cuts followed late in the year. As in 1988, seven corporate officers were among those who went. There was also a freeze on pay during 1996 (with some flexibility for 'exceptional' performance-linked rises). The focus of the company was shifted from technical research to marketing, and it launched a new promotional effort to recoup its position in US markets. In 1995, too, Mr MacAllister Booth, the long-serving chairman, president and CEO, reached retirement age. His successor, Gary DiCamillo, formerly the number two at Black and Decker, brought with him a marketing background. The 1995 developments were summarised in Mr DiCamillo's first annual statement, published in the 1995 annual report:

> Combined with the February 1995 severance programme, the December 1995 restructuring will reduce our workforce by about 2,500 positions, or roughly 20 percent, and will reduce our expenses by more than $150m on an annualized basis. We expect to complete the plan by mid-1997 . . .

On the company's shift from technical to market orientation, he commented:

> We curtailed several major research and engineering programs, shifting more research dollars toward those projects with the greatest potential for commercialization. In so doing, we continue to maintain our strong research focus, but are concentrating resources on those projects that are closer to the commercialization stage.
>
> We are refocusing our high-resolution business for medical and graphic arts markets, and also our electronic imaging business so that their infrastructures are aligned more closely with their near-term revenue potential.

Whether all this will cost Polaroid its technical edge in the medium and long term, only time will tell. However, the first fruits of the change of tack were positive: the first quarter figures for 1996 included a 13% sales increase over the first quarter of 1995, including a 10% rise in flagging US retail sales of integral film. This was said to reflect 'the ongoing impact of the company's more aggressive promotional efforts'. International sales rose 9%, with a decline in Russia being offset by growth in other developing markets like China and Latin America. 'Western Europe saw improved sales of integral film both at dealer and retail levels'. Helios was going well, while the company's new graphics imaging business had sales orders 'in line with estimates'. Before allowance for restructuring, which cost $247m in 1995 and a further $110m in the first quarter of 1996, operating profit was $4.5m. This compared with an operating loss of $31.6m in the 1995 first quarter.

Trying to Change the Culture Advocates of employee ownership will weaken their case if they fail to recognise at least three key caveats. The first is almost a point of logic: that employee ownership is only one among an enormous range of variables which influence business performance. It follows that in any particular case its influence – for better performance or otherwise – may well be swamped by the influence of other variables. The results of employee ownership at Polaroid should be at least partly understood in that light. Proof is not possible in cases of this kind. But it is plausible to suppose the effects on the business of the problems associated with its new product development were such over the eight years down to mid-1996 as to swamp any benefits which could have flowed from its employee ownership during this period.

The second caveat surfaces in a number of other case studies in this book but can scarcely be too often reiterated. It is that the benefits of employee ownership do not materialise spontaneously, they have to be intensively worked for. Any expectation that, given a significant level of employee ownership, then continuous improvement will follow automatically, is certain to be confounded. There is a growing accumulated body of empirical evidence to that effect in the USA. The most reliable research study is probably one carried out in the 1980s for the Congress by the American Government's General Accounting Office (1987). This looked at the performance over a five-year period of a matched sample of companies with significant levels of employee ownership (EOBs) on the one hand, and their conventionally owned counterparts on the other. It showed that by itself the effect of the employee ownership on the relative performance of the companies that had introduced significant amounts of it was zero, but that when associated with effective systems of non-financial participation and involvement by employees then the picture was very different. EOBs which also satisfied that second condition were shown to outperform both their conventionally-owned counterparts and their own pre-employee ownership performance. A combination of profit and employment growth were used to measure performance.

Top management at Polaroid probably became aware of this second caveat only rather gradually. That is not to charge them with having entertained a naive expectation that their ESOP would, of itself and automatically, deliver improvements in performance. But in the early days after the introduction of the ESOP in 1988, their priorities were doubtless somewhat different: with managing the restructuring exercise as smoothly as possible. But there was later a strong and public commitment by top management to the introduction of effective employee involvement systems. The programme around which the desired changes started to be introduced was called Total Quality Ownership (TQO). It was described in a letter to shareholders jointly written by Mr MacAllister Booth and Mr Sheldon Buckler, the board's vice-chairman, and published in the Annual Report of 1991:

> This initiative, involving all 11,000 Polaroid workers world-wide, coaches employees on how to increase the value of our products while reducing significantly the time between product design and delivery in the market place. The central principles of TQO are designed to bring employees closer to customers, to meet, then exceed, customer requirements, and to continually improve, innovate and participate *as owners* [emphasis added].

By mid-1992, according to a pamphlet called *Our Growing Ownership Culture:* 'More than 1,500 Polaroid employees, including most officers ... have gone through what is known as the Participation Workshop.'

Where continuous improvement is achieved at all, it takes place typically in the actual work places and work units where people engage in their productive activities. According to Owen Gaffney, there were some failures as well as some successes in its first couple of years. On a visit to Polaroid in December 1992 I was introduced to one group that had taken over real responsibility for seeing that they all pulled their weight. Measurable benefits had already started to appear. I was given to understand that it was not the only one.

Perhaps, too, the company achieved some improvements in performance from a series of organisational changes, in 1991 and then again in 1992 and 1995. Out of the 1991 reorganisation emerged three separate, semi-autonomous and customer-focused divisions; together with a fourth unit which had more of a support function. The three semi-autonomous divisions were focused on instant imaging products for family, for business, and for technical and scientific markets respectively. The fourth had responsibility across the whole field of electronic instant imaging products and development. Then, at the end of 1992, further changes were superimposed on this earlier re-organisation, with the aim of achieving still faster responses to developments in the market. A third stage came in 1995 when the division of responsibility between electronic products and all others had come to seem unhelpful: in particular those engaged in making film based products had an interest in preventing customers from making a switch to electronic imaging and vice versa. The new organisational breakdown introduced in 1995 was based on three core areas of focus – established business customers, the retail consumer, and new lines of business. According to Mr DiCamillo, each of these three new divisions '. . . has global operating responsibility for setting strategy, developing products, and marketing those products to its customers. Each will be accountable for its own sales, profits, and asset management.'

Each of this pair of new departures, the TQO programme and the successive changes of organisation, is very similar to what has been tried, since they became employee owned, at, for example, Republic Steel in the USA and the Baxi Partnership in the UK – and also in many conventionally-owned undertakings. The extent of their success is always hard to measure – quite apart from the fact that it may always be swamped by the consequences of more powerful variables. On the other hand it may well be, in the case of both this TQO programme and this series of reorganisations, that they have been successful in the sense and to the extent that performance would have been worse without them.

At the outset of this discussion about cultural change at Polaroid I made the general point that employee ownership advocates should recognise three caveats. Having now dealt with the first two of these, we now move on to the third.

The third caveat may be put most simply by saying that, in businesses above a microscopic size, employee ownership probably needs a legitimised representative institution of one kind or another. The aspirations and potential of the rank and file employee owners are unlikely to be fully realised if their voice can only find expression through a combination of appeals to management on the one hand and speeches in general assemblies of employee shareholders on the other. The needed representative institution may take the form of a trade union, as it has frequently done in the American steel industry. But it does not have to take that form. Indeed there is one example in this case study series, though admittedly only in a subsidiary undertaking, of a union going into 'voluntary liquidation' following the successful introduction of employee ownership (a Tullis Russell Group subsidiary, Brittains). That experience may or may not tell us something about what is likely to happen when employee ownership is successfully introduced and the union chooses to ignore it. But then a company may have a long-established non-union representative institution: the paradigm example is the John Lewis Partnership.

It is true that the Polaroid board of directors always includes a Director selected from the rank and file of employees – a notable feature of the company even though such a director must by law represent all shareholders. The selection process starts with self-nomination and the finally successful appointee is selected by a committee of the board.

Nonetheless, it is probably not too much to say that problems relating to the need for a legitimised representative institution for rank and file employees have been an important source, possibly by themselves but probably alongside widespread management scepticism, of employee ownership difficulties at Polaroid. It seems probable, though this cannot of course be proved, that they have had an independently negative effect on any performance benefits which may or may not have been delivered for the company by its employee ownership.

A Legal Drama First, the background. To begin with and down to its dissolution by top management in August 1992, there existed at Polaroid – and had existed since anyone then working there could remember – an elected Employees Committee (EC). It was not a union, not even, as in the case of the Independent Steelworkers at Weirton, a single-company union. It was not a union because it was financed not by the rank and file employees who voted to elect its members, but by the company. It was summarily closed down by Polaroid's top management in August 1992 because a case, challenging its legality under America's New Deal trade union laws of the 1930s, was pending in the courts. Presumably management believed, rightly or wrongly, that the challenge might succeed.

The New Deal trade union legislation of the 1930s was embodied in the Wagner Act, named after the sometime mayor of New York. It aimed among other things at inhibiting the establishment by managements of sweetheart unions. The main provisions of the act include the denial of its protection to representative employee bodies which are financed by the company and at the same time have dealings with the management. The provisions of the act may also be breached when, as in the case of Polaroid's former EC, the top officers of the representative institution are elected not directly, by the rank-and-file employees, but by a pre-elected body of committee members.

The 1992 court challenge to the legitimacy of the EC was in fact launched by one of its own recently elected members, Charla Scivally, a secretary. After three years of employment with Polaroid, she had successfully stood for election to the committee in February 1992, on a platform calling for change. Apart from bringing the challenge which led to the EC's dissolution, Ms Scivally later showed notable energy organising a campaign aimed at achieving the recognition by Polaroid of an authentic and legitimate union. For that to happen the law requires a vote by not less than 30% of rank-and-file employees. In this case she needed 2,700 signatures. According to her own count she managed to muster 1,200.

Later Ms Scivally was dismissed by Polaroid. The alleged ground was that she had disclosed a confidential company document to a third party. She apparently had a different story. According to Polaroid, the National Labor Relations Board conducted an investigation but dismissed her 'unfair labor practice charge' against the company.

On the other hand, what seemed *possible*, at the time of writing in late 1997, was that, as it were by proxy, Ms Scivally had at least an outside chance of winning another, quite different, challenge to Polaroid in the courts. This is a challenge to a new thirty-member body which was set up by the company some time after the dissolution of the EC, and on the basis of fairly extensive research and discussion. It is called the Employee Owners Influence Council (EOIC). Its constitutional arrangements were carefully designed, under the leadership of Ann Leibowitz, the company's in-house labour counsel at the time, to avoid falling foul of the provisions of the Wagner Act. The chances that they would survive the court challenge were presumably strengthened when America's House of Representatives passed new legislation in September 1995 aimed at protecting the right of employers to establish organisations for sounding out employee opinion along the lines of the EOIC. From the company's viewpoint, its key relevant characteristics are that it is a selected cross-sectional group of employees rather than an elected one, and that it will not negotiate with management. Rather, its members simply express their individual opinions and responses to questions.

But there is a danger in the opposite direction: of massaging the character of the new EOIC institution so far that it loses all legitimacy among large numbers of rank and file employees. Doubts about the likely perceived legitimacy of the EOIC were also expressed to me privately in Cambridge in December 1992 by Vin Tognarelli and Nick Pasquarosa, both then with management posts but both previously having held top positions in the EC.

In that same conversation with me in December 1992, Mr Tognarelli and Mr Pasquarosa were also critical of the Polaroid top management's insensitivity to the interests of rank-and-file employees. They cited specifically the way that the bonus paid out of the Kodak settlement had been split between management and non-management personnel. And they claimed that at least once in recent times managers had received bonus payments that had been linked to performance targets which had not been met.

Whatever the truth may be in any particular instance, it seems probable that the balance of public opinion among Polaroid's rank-and-file employees will have interpreted the dissolution of the EC and its replacement by the EOIC as going against their interests and against the spirit of employee ownership. On the other hand, the strength of that shift of opinion, assuming that there was one, should not be overstated. Otherwise Ms Scivally would surely have attracted more signatures in her campaign for union recognition.

The New CEO As for the views of the new chairman and chief executive, Mr DiCamillo, on Polaroid's employee share ownership, their balance was starting to become clear towards the end of 1997. On the one hand there is no doubt at all about his support for the second infusion of employee ownership decided on in 1997. On the other hand there is some doubt about whether his commitment to employee ownership it total. The importance he attaches to a new scheme of performance-linked cash profit sharing, announced in May 1996, and his apparent downgrading (at least relative to other aspects of management) of the priority given earlier to the TQO programme are good evidence of his conventional capitalist thinking. But then, with a few individual exceptions, it seems doubtful whether there was ever a strong commitment to employee ownership by Polaroid's top managers, similar to that of, say, Tullis Russell in the UK. Given that the majority of Polaroid's shares have remained in the ownership of outside non-employee shareholders, it is perhaps inescapable that the level of commitment of its managers should be less.

None of which means that the ESOP at Polaroid has been a failure. And that is true even if it is also true that the company's then shareholders would have been financially better off if Shamrock had won the takeover battle in 1988/89 and they had walked away in early 1989 with a price of $42.50 a share. The point is that the value of a company to its employees, and to the national and local economy, may be very different from its immediate money value to absentee shareholders.

Moreover, from the employees' viewpoint it seems reasonable to claim that the employee ownership has been a success at least in the weak sense that in its absence their experience might well have been worse. In relation to Polaroid's second major restructuring exercise launched at the end of 1995, this point was put with force by Mr Ralph Norwood, vice president and treasurer, in a conversation with Mary Campbell in May 1996:

In the USA, some 2,000 people have been involved in job losses. Numbers have gone down from 8,000 to 6,000. We have done that overwhelmingly on a voluntary basis, and with minimum disruption in terms of angry people. Without an ESOP people could say, you're doing that just for the interests of absentee shareholders . . . wealthy New York people .

Who knows? In Margaret Thatcher's splendid phrase it's a rum old world'. Who would have guessed that there would be sufficient rank-and-file support in 1997 behind a second infusion of employee ownership for management to introduce a new scheme? And who would have guessed the apparent reason behind it: a recognition of the value of forced saving?

26

Allied Plywood: A Paradigm Case of a 'Neat Exit'

'How many houses have you got now, Jonah?'

'Well, there you are, Mr Sanders, it is still just the two.'

'And how many motor cars, Jonah?'

'Two again, Mr Sanders, yeah, just the two again.'

'And what's your ESOP account standing on, after the latest valuation, Jonah?'

''Bout $80,000 if I remember rightly, Mr Sanders. But then there's still a good few years before I reach fifty-nine and a half; and as you know there would be all that tax on the final sum if I were to cash him in before that. By then, most likely the 'count will be well into six figures.'

Jonah was not a high-flying executive in a financial services company, who benefited from a subsidised house mortgage, a company car, and a top management share option scheme. He was middle-aged and semi-skilled. At Allied Plywood Corporation's main warehouse in Alexandria, Virginia, just south of the Potomac River from Washington DC, he sometimes drove a forklift truck. Sometimes he was 'on deliveries'. And sometimes he did other jobs again.

I was lucky enough, early in 1988, to listen to that exchange between Jonah and Mr Ed Sanders, the former joint owner of Allied Plywood, a wholesale distributor of plywood and other building materials. Using an ESOP, and over a period of years starting in 1977, the business was sold to its workforce by Mr Sanders and his wife Phyllis, who had together built it up in the first place. They retired in 1982.

INTRODUCTORY OVERVIEW

When the ESOP was first introduced, Allied Plywood operated from the one Alexandria site and employed twenty people. Fifteen years later it had seven sites as far apart as Maryland, Georgia and South Carolina and employed 124. During the ten years to 1991 its turnover increased by nearly five times: from $6.2m in 1982 to $30.2m in 1992. By 1996 turnover had doubled again, employment was 180 and it operated from fourteen sites in five states.

So Allied Plywood has been a notable success; and part of the point of this case study is to illustrate the way that an employee-owned company can adjust itself to growth without losing the identification of interest between the individual employee and the whole. For readers in countries like Britain and France, it is also interesting for the reason I have given in the heading: as a 'Paradigm Case of a "Neat Exit"' – or *'une belle sortie'*. This French phrase was first used to me by a young Frenchman who had taken over as Président Directeur Général when the business he worked for in France was sold to its employees by its former *patron*. They had formed a co-op to buy it. (For the English translation, I am indebted to a headline in the *Financial Times*.)

Since the American ESOP legislation was introduced in the early 1970s, or more precisely since the 1980s when rollover relief was granted to those who sold to an ESOP trust, there have been hundreds of these 'neat exit' transactions. Ed and Phyllis Sanders sold without the benefit of rollover relief which was enacted only later. In fact the relevant provisions of the subsequent law became known as the 'Sanders amendment' because their example was used to persuade the Senate to be more generous in its encouragement of similar deals. Perhaps the single most important success of employee ownership advocates in Britain came in March 1994 when, with the removal of two previously crippling restrictions, the relevant UK rollover relief provisions became as good as or better than those in the USA.

Allied Plywood is also interesting for two further reasons. The first is that it operates, and has done for decades, the most spectacular scheme of profit-related pay that I have ever come across. It may be argued that this is irrelevant because the scheme predates majority employee ownership. But that is to miss the key point – the congruence between the two.

The case of Allied Plywood also highlights two alternative approaches to the valuation of shares in non-quoted and majority employee-owned businesses: the difference between a net asset based approach and one which calculates value mainly on the basis of market place data.

From the Beginnings in Akron, Ohio, to the Retirement of Mr and Mrs Sanders in 1982 Allied Plywood was incorporated in Akron, Ohio, in August 1951. That area of Ohio, also the home ground of Republic Engineered Steels, is classically part of what has been called America's 'rust belt'. Even in the faraway 1950s, when times were still good for industries like steel, the local economy was not all that buoyant. After four years of uphill, even if just profitable, struggle, Mr Sanders came across a study which ranked different American districts by their current and forecast levels of building activity. Akron came close to the bottom; the neighbourhood of Washington DC, and especially its southward spillover into Virginia, came close to the top. With true American spirit Mr and Mrs Sanders upped sticks and moved to Alexandria. That was in 1956. They rented some warehouse space and started by employing no one except themselves. Later they hired one other person.

In its new home, the business began to prosper. Eventually the Sanders built their own warehouse and associated offices and moved out of the earlier rented premises. The workforce too started to expand – posing the challenge of employee motivation. The Sanderses' solution was essentially the radical scheme of profit-related pay which I describe later.

The first Allied ESOP, introduced in 1977, was a non-leveraged one. Mr and Mrs Sanders, who have no children, were beginning to think about what would happen to the business when the time came for them to retire. A part of Allied's profits was passed each year to the ESOP's trust; and the trustees used that money to buy Sanders' shares. A block of shares, about 12% of the equity, was also sold to Mr Robert Shaw, the man who became chief executive when Ed Sanders retired in 1982.

As a result of these sales, the Sanderses' shareholding was already, in 1981, below 50% of Allied's equity. In that year the ESOP trust was the largest single shareholder, with just five shares short of 50% of the issued total or 2,090 out of 4,190. Then, in 1982, to coincide with the Sanderses' retirement, the ESOP trustees took a bank loan, and used the money to buy out the balance of the Sanderses' shares.

The year 1982 was one of sharp recession in the US economy. For the first time since Mr and Mrs Sanders moved to Alexandria, Allied's total sales fell below what they had been the year before. We get a more balanced picture of their achievement in the building up of the business if we take the statistics for 1981. Sales in that year came to $7.8m and the net asset value of the business was $1.3m. It was on the basis of that asset valuation that the remaining Sanders shares were bought out. However we should notice that the Alexandria warehouse and office accommodation were not included either in the net assets valuation or in the sale and purchase agreement by which Mr and Mrs Sanders were bought out.

Majority Employee Ownership 1981 to 1995 Total sales increased nearly tenfold between 1982 and 1995 and the workforce over seven times:

Allied Plywood: Sales and Employment 1982 to 1995

Year	Sales $m	Employment
81/82	6.2	22
82/83	9.9	28
83/84	12.0	31
84/85	16.1	35
85/86	21.1	50
86/87	25.5	65
87/88	30.9	82
88/89	35.2	91
89/90	32.6	88
90/91	30.4	113
91/92	64.3*	124
92/93	45.8	132
93/94	56.3	149
94/95	58.7	166

* Includes a company which was bought and then resold
Note: Years are to end-September

We will leave on one side the effects of the recession between 1989 and 1991 and the impressive rebound since then. The first eight years of majority employee ownership saw sustained growth. Total sales increased by more than five times between 1981/2 and 1988/9. 1981/2 was a year of recession, but still using 1980/1, when sales were $7.8m, as a base year there is a more than fourfold increase in dollar sales between that year and 1988/9. Even after allowing for inflation, which was some 50% between 1980 and 1989, sales increased nearly three times between those same dates. It is a record of which a conventional capitalist business would be proud.

What drove the expansion of Allied in those years, as again from 1991, was acquisition, mainly of new warehouses and sales outlets. But in one case a small hardwood manufacturing operation, Austin Hardwoods in Lorton, Virginia, which had previously been a supplier, was also acquired. The major early phase of acquisitions was between 1985 and 1988. Apart from Austin Hardwoods, Allied acquired new warehouses and sales outlets in places as far apart as Atlanta, Georgia, and Frederick, Maryland. In 1996 the company's fourteen sites were in Virginia, Maryland, Georgia, North Carolina, and Tennessee. Though it does not sell direct to retail customers, the products filling its sales outlets were spread over six states: they ranged from kitchen units (including laminated worktops which it manufactures itself) through to 'lap siding' (with or without plasticised coating) – the wooden boards used horizontally as the cladding on the outside walls in so many homes in the USA.

A policy of growth by acquisition became possible in the middle 1980s partly because by that time, ahead of schedule, the money borrowed to buy out the final Sanders shareholding had been completely paid off. Another positive factor, which has continued, was Allied's strong cash flow. Given that acquisitions were thus possible, market opportunities determined whether they were actually made. For example, it seems to have been a special market opportunity which explains the decision to acquire a substantial new warehouse and sales outlet in Charlotte, North Carolina. That happened in 1991, as the US economy started to pull itself out of recession.

The architects of this policy of growth by acquisition were the two members of the team which took over from Ed Sanders in 1982: Mr Robert Shaw as chief executive and Mr Gene Scales as secretary/treasurer. In the early days of the expansion, Mr Shaw is emphatic that the objective of expansion was not set in advance. However, looking back in 1996, he commented that the policy would have been unavoidable if success was to continue because the big suppliers have increasingly required their distributors to cover a lot of ground. Allied's suppliers include companies like Georgia Pacific Lumber Company, Weyerhaeuser, Boise Cascade and, for hardwood, Columbia Products. 'If you can't deliver multiple markets, they're not interested,' says Robert Shaw. For this reason alone, Allied's expansion in future is also likely to be geographical, and especially in the southern states. Vertical integration, say into more manufacture, is not on its current agenda.

Allied has also enjoyed the confidence which has come from its success in operating its own particular version of employee ownership, including its profit-related pay scheme. This success has encouraged a belief that if the Allied formula is applied to the businesses which it acquires, their performance will improve. However, while Allied has retained the original principles of its employee-ownership and profit-related pay, expansion has meant changes in the way these are implemented.

Profit-Related Pay Allied introduced its radical scheme of profit-related pay (PRP) in response to the challenge of getting a growing workforce motivated. Its two eyecatching features are a basic wage somewhat below market rates coupled with an equal share of 30% of operating profits, paid monthly in arrears. It seems designed to promote not only individual employee motivation but also solidarity within the workforce, including solidarity between management and blue collar workers.

The most important condition for the acceptability of this trade off to the blue collar employees whom it was chiefly designed to motivate was higher levels of monthly financial rewards than would be available under the conventional alternative of a market-determined rate of pay, and/or one negotiated by a union. Except for special cases (e.g. for staff in newly opened branches) the scheme yielded more than market rates in all but about half a dozen months between when it was first introduced in the mid-1960s and the late 1990s – more than thirty years later.

Still, the outcome of such a trade off cannot be known for certain in advance. So there remains an obvious problem of how to introduce so radical a scheme in the first place. Ed Sanders's solution was to make it initially voluntary. Those employed by Allied when the scheme was first introduced were given the choice: to soldier on with their existing rates of pay; or to accept a cut of what was apparently some 20%, in return for that 30% equal profit share. Eventually, nearly all those employed at the time the scheme was introduced decided to switch into it. After 1977, when ownership of Allied started to move to the ESOP, all those who participated in the ESOP arrangements were required to accept the radical scheme of PRP. On the other hand, new recruits normally have to wait up to twelve months before they become ESOP participants. During that period they are paid conventionally at prevailing market rates.

The motivational impact of the scheme is backed by up-to-the-minute reporting of the score. Performance, measured by financial results, is recorded daily as it happens. There is an announcement each month to mark the achievement of the break even point. Thereafter profits are continuously reported as they occur, in units of $500 'goals'. Since every one in the scheme qualifies for an equal share in 30% of these, i.e. an equal share in $150, he or she needed only to know the total numbers in the scheme to calculate his or her share.

There is more to the PRP scheme at Allied than this equal monthly share. There is also an annual cash profit distribution, going back all the way to the far-off beginnings of the business in Akron, Ohio. But unlike its monthly counterpart, this annual distribution does not go in equal parts to participants. It takes place on the basis of a weighted points system. The number of days worked during the year, the importance of the job, and the employee's length of service have the main weight in determining the points score. But so also does an assessment which each employee is given by his or her peers: a rule which extends to the company's president, Mr Robert Shaw, whose performance is assessed by the other members of the top management team.

There have been specially good years when, taken together, the monthly and year-end cash bonus has exceeded annual basic pay. And that, of course, is not counting the value of shares allocated to employees under the ESOP. In more typical years the two bonuses together have comfortably exceeded 50% of basic pay. For example, in both 1988 and 1989 they amounted to 58% and were still equivalent to 40% in the recession year of 1990. Later, increasing market-place uncertainty brought into question the proportion of profits distributed; but aggregate bonuses in 1995 were still big.

From the early 1990s onwards, issues arising from the company's expansion have caused the profit-sharing system to be somewhat changed. As the company expanded, the relationship between the individual's productivity and the company's profitability was at risk of being diluted. The central problem was that different branches made different levels of profit. The monthly profit share received by each employee was changed to become based on the profits of the particular site where the employee works. Moreover, central administrative staff who serve all the branches ceased to get monthly profit shares: instead, their share of the 30% of profit is paid to them quarterly in arrears and based on the overall performance of all the branches over this longer period.

As the company expanded, it also took on board some other characteristics of more traditional capitalist undertakings. For example, healthcare insurance became part of the standard remuneration package. On the other hand, Allied's pension arrangements remained similar to most majority ESOP companies in the USA. Only in the final years before retirement may an employee-owner shift his or her ESOP nest-egg outside Allied into other investments, and at no stage can they be converted into cash without a swingeing loss of tax advantages.

In one notable respect the company has resisted the luxury often associated with growth and success. Once the head office could no longer be on the same site as one of the branches without risking charges of favouritism from the others, it was moved into a six-room condominium in a cul-de-sac. The latter is so obscure that even local taxi drivers do not know where it is.

Two key characteristics of capitalist owners are their attention to profits and the closeness of the link between those profits and their personal rewards. There are examples of profit-related pay in all or almost all of the case studies brought together in this book. That at Allied Plywood stands out as the one which most closely ties the fortunes of the individual to those of the firm.

The ESOP, the Shares and their Valuation Already, well before the introduction of the ESOP, and before they even knew about the existence of ESOPs, Mr and Mrs Sanders had become concerned about how to turn their shares in Allied into cash to provide a capital sum for their retirement. The question was how and to whom should the business be sold. Explaining what was eventually decided, Ed Sanders is fond of saying that he and his wife felt that, at the very least, the workers should have the 'first crack' at buying it, because they, after all, 'had made it grow'. When pressed, Ed Sanders does not deny that he and his wife might well have got a higher price by selling to a third party. His reasons for favouring a sale to the workforce were 'a sense of fairness and gratitude'.

As a way of starting down that road, before he had any knowledge of ESOPs, Mr Sanders sold a few shares to some employees at book values in the early 1970s. These included Robert Shaw and Gene Scales. But it soon became clear that individual employees did not have the personal savings or access to credit to buy out the Sanderses' shareholding.

Not to be easily frustrated, Mr Sanders next explored a rather different possibility: that Allied Plywood should itself start to buy his shareholding at its book value. There would have been nothing remotely illegal or improper about such a transaction. It might have been an American counterpart to the main ownership transfer transaction at what became the Baxi Partnership in Britain. But, though it would not have been illegal, Mr and Mrs Sanders soon discovered that it would have had seriously adverse consequences for their personal tax liability. It was established that America's Internal Revenue Service would treat the proceeds of such a sale as a 'distribution', meaning that first corporate and then personal income tax would be payable.

When Mr and Mrs Sanders became aware of the possibilities opened up by America's ESOP legislation, they quickly recognised that it offered a solution: and one which, if not ideal from a tax view point, was practicable and at least just acceptable. So a simple ESOP was introduced at Allied Plywood. It was simple in the technical sense that it was not 'leveraged' (i.e. not associated with any borrowing).

When this ESOP was introduced in 1977, the Sanderses' shareholding amounted to 83% of Allied Plywood's equity. In each of the next five years, taking advantage of the then available tax reliefs, a percentage of the company's pre-tax profits was passed to the ESOP's trustees. It was next applied to buy shares from Mr and Mrs Sanders at net book values. As a result, the Sanderses' shareholding had fallen to 36.5% of the equity by 1981. By the same year the ESOP's shareholding had reached just below 50% of the total.

After the Sanderses retired in 1982 the ESOP borrowed the money necessary to buy out the balance of their shareholding, again on the basis of net asset values. They had now achieved their twin objectives of turning their ownership of Allied Plywood into cash and turning the employees of the business into its new owners. The sale proceeds did *not* enjoy the important tax advantage which is called rollover relief on both sides of the Atlantic. If they had chosen to sell to a quoted third party, by what is technically known as a 'merger' or an 'exchange of stock', the proceeds of the sale would have qualified for rollover relief: no capital gains tax would have been payable unless and until the shares acquired in the initial transaction were themselves sold.

The loans taken out to buy the shares had been fully paid off, ahead of schedule, by the end of 1985. Up to that point the numbers of Allied Plywood shares in issue remained essentially unchanged. The annual contribution to the ESOP was made in cash so as to pay off those loans. The result was not the issuing of new shares; but a shift of existing ones – out of what amounted to an ESOP suspense account, and into the accounts of individual Allied employees.

On the other hand, once the repayment of the loans was completed, that changed. From then on, the annual contribution to the ESOP was largely made by issuing new shares with the obvious advantage of freeing up financial resources for investment. Cash was provided to meet the liability to buy back the shares of those employees who left Allied on reaching the retirement age of fifty-nine years and a half. But, given the age structure of the workforce during this period those numbers were small. Consequently, the number of Allied's issued shares more than doubled between 1981 and 1989 and then nearly doubled again in the subsequent six years.

Issued Shares & Ownership Breakdown

	1981	1989	1995
Mr and Mrs Sanders	1,528	–	–
Robert Shaw	520	456	230
Gene Scales	4	4	4
Others	48	30	30
ESOP	2,090	8,742	17,240
Total	4,190	9,232	17,504

For a better understanding of how the employee shareholdings evolved at Allied after the Sanderses' retirement, we need two further sets of statistics – the total value of the stockholders' equity and the the value of the shares:

Allied Plywood: Stockholders' Equity & Share Values

	Stockholders' Equity $m	Share Values $
1981	1.3	313
1982	0.9	241
1983	1.2	298
1984	1.6	369
1985	1.9	400
1986	2.3	403
1987	2.8	416
1988	3.3	414
1989*	3.9	417
1990	4.1	278
1991	4.3	224
1992	4.8	351
1993	5.7	463
1994	6.5	496
1995	7.4	503

*Professional evaluation from 1989 onwards

A few general points can be made about these rather striking statistics. To begin with, we may notice that the nominal value of the business's stockholders' equity, what in Britain would perhaps more normally be called its net asset value, increased between five and six times in the fourteen years from 1981 to 1995. Allowing for inflation, we can say that its value more than trebled. On the other hand, over the same period of a dozen years the nominal value of Allied's shares increased much more modestly: by about 60%. If we allow for inflation in this second case, the share values hardly increased at all.

What explains the very different movement? An important part of the answer is apparent from the earlier table, showing that numbers of issued shares more than quadrupled – from 4,190 to over 17,000 – between 1981 and 1995. Another was a change in 1987 in the official rules which govern the annual valuation of ESOP businesses in the USA. We shall come to that in a moment.

As can be seen from the table, both net asset value and the share price fell sharply in 1982, the year of the Sanderses' retirement, from $1.3m to $0.9m and from $313 to $241 respectively. These falls were essentially happenings in the world of accountancy rather than in that of real business experience. They reflect the sale of the outstanding balance of the Sanderses' shares to the ESOP, and the fact that since the borrowings associated with that transaction had not then started to be paid off, an appropriate debit was required by the accountants to figure in the balance sheet.

That is perhaps a specialist's point. Of more general interest and importance is the logic and the mechanics of the ESOP at Allied. Because new shares are continually issued annually to the ESOP and thus indirectly to the individual accounts of each person employed there, the employee ownership does not apply only to those who happened to be working at Allied at the time of the Sanderses' retirement, nor, for example, does it apply only to the people who worked there during the period of the repayment of the loans which made possible the final stages of the buy-out. On the contrary, this employee ownership in principle applies to future as well as current members of the workforce. It is solidaristic, one might say, as between successive incoming cohorts to the workforce; and has been designed, again at least in principle, to continue in this way indefinitely.

We should recall the difference in the source of ESOP shares allocated to Allied's employees as between what happened when the Sanderses' shareholding was being bought out, and what happened after the transaction had been finished. In the earlier phase it was the Sanderses' shares which were allocated to Allied's employee shareholders. Thereafter the allocation came mainly from newly issued shares.

The mechanics of issuing these new shares may be seen as a two-step 'loop' process. At the end of its financial year the company makes a cash contribution to the ESOP. The contribution is made out of pre-tax profits though limited to a maximum of 25% of the company's payroll. That cash contribution is step one. Step two is the purchase of newly issued shares from the company by the ESOP, using the money contributed by the company to it. All the money so used to make the purchase, which is not subject to tax, then goes to increase the stockholders' equity or net asset value of the business and is available for investment.

A by-product of this distribution system is that taxable profits are kept low. As in some other employee-owned companies cited in this book – the Carl-Zeiss-Stiftung for example – the key indicator watched by management is not so much profits as cash flow. After their share of operating profits had been distributed to employees, and 25% of the payroll had been given to the ESOP to buy shares, the results for 1988 actually showed small losses. But the main point is that for all or almost all of its history, Allied's taxable profits have traditonally been little more than negligible, both in actual numbers and in comparison to cash flow.

What about the value of the company? How is that arrived at? Before the Congress enacted a change in the relevant regulations in 1987, it was open to the managers of Allied, as to those of other private ESOP companies in the USA, to make their own valuation. After the 1987 change, which came into force in 1988, an independent valuation was required to be done by a firm of valuation specialists.

This change of responsibility for the valuation work was accompanied at Allied Plywood by a change of valuation method. Allied's own managers had made their valuation on the basis of the 'stockholders' equity' or net asset value in the annual balance sheet. They had taken the dollar number of the stockholders' equity as the dollar value of the business. The approach adopted by the external and independent valuers is more complex. It takes into account not only data about Allied, but also data about other supposedly comparable undertakings.

For the years down to 1987, when Allied's management was responsible for the valuation, the results of its net asset value approach come forward quite straightforwardly in the record. (The increase in share value was less than the increase in value of the business because new shares were issued each year – priced at the value of the year before.) Moreover, to ensure the maximum tax benefit, Allied's management sought to maximise the annual contribution from the business to the ESOP up to the legal limit of 25% of the payroll. This policy of issuing new shares had the further important result that new shares were available to newcomers who joined the scheme.

It is true that the policies of issuing new shares and of maximising the company's annual contribution to the ESOP continued to be applied, notwithstanding the new valuation rules and procedures, after 1988. On the other hand we can see from the table that for the five years 1988 to 1992 there is no longer an invariable identity of direction between the movement of Allied's 'stockholders' equity', or net asset value, and the movement in the value of its shares. The former continues the upward movement which dates back to 1982. The latter goes down as well as up. There is a notable drop between 1989 and 1990.

We know that Allied's 1990 valuation was significantly based – to the extent of 50% – on data about comparable businesses over the previous twelve months. The sharp fall in the value of Allied's shares in that year is explained to a large extent by the fact that the performance of the businesses with which it was being compared was worse, during the then prevailing conditions of recession, than its own. It is not altogether surprising that managers and non-managers at Allied Plywood have expressed dissatisfaction, and indeed more than that, over the imposed change in the valuation approach. Ed Sanders's comment on the 1990 valuation exercise was:

> To me the [evaluation] report is a good example of how the damn lawyers take you on a trip to a Never Never Land of pure guess work. Allied Plywood does what it does and who should care about competitors or the rest of the world if the stock is not publicly traded. I got dizzy reading it. All I could think about was the cost of making these 'evaluations'.

Ed Sanders's criticisms are cogent and persuasive. On the other hand it is clear that at the time of the change there was a widespread belief that the old system gave too much latitude to management and was subject to quite serious abuse. It is impossible to make an informed judgement on the extent to which these criticisms were justified. But there were certainly influential voices outside as well as inside the Congress which called for change and especially for the change to independent valuation. Among those voices was the United Steelworkers of America.

Ed Sanders himself acknowledges that there is a problem – which has grown significantly since the early 1980s: companies and their lawyers constantly find loopholes in the ESOP legislation, which just as constantly attract Congressional action to stop them up. According to Allied, this means there is a lot of work just keeping up with legislative and regulatory change. Companies' ESOP plans may now have to be rewritten every couple of years: Robert Shaw bemoans the increasing costs of running an ESOP – now $10,000 or $15,000 a year. Some of those who have long been involved with the company question whether the ESOP could have been set up at all if costs in 1977–82 had been as high as they are now – and whether any small company can any longer afford to establish an ESOP.

Fundamental as these points may be to the future growth of the US ESOP movement, they are something of a digression in the context of Allied Plywood. It remains for us to track the effect of the change in the valuation rules from the point of view of a sample employee. Let us take as our example the value of Jonah's shareholding – the Jonah we met in the opening snapshot and whose ESOP shareholding was then (in 1987) valued at about $80,000. From the table we can see that the share value in that year was near its peak, at $416. So in round numbers we can see that in that year Jonah held 190 shares. Five years later, as a result of annual allocations of new ESOP shares, there were a total of 367 shares in his account. At the provisional 1992 valuation of $351, Jonah's parcel of ESOP shares was then therefore worth between $125,000 and $130,000. However, my calculations suggest that in the previous year the value of his shareholding was significantly below what it had been in 1987. Of course he had more shares in 1991 – approximately 300 shares. But the increase in the number of shares which he held was insufficient to offset the reduction in the price: from $416 in 1987 to $224 in 1991. His shareholding which had been worth $80,000 in 1987 was thus probably not worth much more than $67,000 in 1991. Had Jonah's retirement fallen in that year and had he therefore been obliged to turn his shareholding into cash on the basis of the 1991 valuation, he might reasonably have felt that the change of approach by the new outside valuers had worked unfairly to his disadvantage. Under the then rules of the Allied Plywood ESOP, a retiring employee was immediately paid out on his shares in cash. Because of the zigzag pattern of valuations in the early 1990s, the Board of Trustees allowed employees the option to phase their withdrawals from the ESOP over five years.

Any change in the valuation rules is bound to disturb past patterns and may to that extent cause temporary unfairness. But Ed Sanders' criticism is different. He is challenging the entire logic of a large part of the independent valuers' work and arguing that data about what has been happening to the valuations of comparable and competitor companies is simply not relevant in the case of a near 100% ESOP-owned business, none of whose shares are traded on a stock market.

It seems to me that so long as those two conditions apply, Ed Sanders's criticisms have undoubted force. In cases where those conditions apply it seems to me that annual share valuations should aim to meet just four criteria. First, they must be affordable, in the longer as well as the short term. That is to say that the valuation must be such that, on any reasonable assumptions of what the future is going to hold, the ESOP-owned business should be able to meet its buy-back liabilities. Second, though there is clearly some overlap between this and my first point, the valuation should be fair both to the employee shareholders who are leaving and to those who are staying on. Third, so far as possible, the valuation formula should include some link with profits, or in this particular case with cash flow, as a way of sharpening employee motivation. And fourth, the valuation approach should aim to reduce and smooth over the sharper fluctuations of stock market prices.

This is not the place to defend these proposals in any detail. But for what it's worth they would meet Ed Sanders's criticism of the new outside valuers' approach because the criteria they involve are essentially internal to the business. Moreover if fluctuations can be somewhat smoothed out, that would go some way to avoiding the 'unfairness' with which Jonah might have claimed to have been treated if he had retired in 1991.

But my own and Ed Sanders's criticisms should not be misunderstood. Neither of us would want, for a moment, to be associated with those who wring their hands at any suggestion that blue collar workers should ever be exposed to risk. On the contrary, one of the most important single lessons of Allied is that the degree of its financial success has been closely linked to the readiness of its workforce, blue collar as well as other, to take risks. Let us remember too that Jonah's ESOP shareholding is something which his counterpart in a conventional capitalist business simply does not have. Even in what the Americans call a 'worst case scenario', in which the value of Jonah's ESOP shareholding fell to zero, he would still be no worse off than his counterpart in a conventional capitalist business. In fact he would probably still be better off: for he would still enjoy what appear to be benefits which have resulted from his participation in Allied's radical scheme of profit related pay: his second house, for example.

To me the main conclusion from Allied Plywood's experience is that if we want improved business performance then we need to move away from both conventional systems of capitalist ownership and conventional systems of wage payment: no more than that, but equally no less.

Ownership and Control Finally, I need to say a brief word about how the ESOP ownership at Allied Plywood is reflected in its system of control. To begin with, under a combination of a company's own by-laws and the rules of its ESOP, the business is controlled, for the purposes of all normal decisions, by a five-member board of directors. Moreover, this board of directors doubles up as the trustees of Allied Plywood's ESOP and so, given that it is empowered to vote the ESOP shares in all but defined exceptional cases, it determines all normal issues of business policy. The composition of these two-in-one boards – of directors and trustees – is essentially paritarian. There is equal representation of shop floor and management; and there is an agreed independent to hold the balance between those two groups. Since the retirement of Mr Sanders in 1982, the two management representatives on these boards have been Mr Robert Shaw and Mr Gene Scales. There have been periodic changes in the identity of the board members elected by the shopfloor. There is also a management advisory committee which meets from time to time. Taking these various arrangements together, it seems reasonable to claim that the employees have a real voice, as well as far and away the largest financial stake, in the business.

In practice, on the other hand, it is probable that even the big decisions have been in effect taken by the management: because those lower down the company have been more satisfied than dissatisfied with the way the company is being run.

27
Co-operative Home Care Associates

INTRODUCTORY OVERVIEW

The emancipation of women and co-operative production are, I fully believe, the two great changes which will regenerate society. *John Stuart Mill*

After several months of successful employment, each individual has the option of becoming a worker-owner in her enterprise. Currently over 250 home health aides have chosen to become owners within their co-operative – receiving a yearly dividend and voting to elect their board of directors. *Peggy Powell, Home Care Associates Training Institute, The Bronx, New York*

Co-operative Home Care Associates (CHCA) supplies care to mainly elderly clients in the south Bronx and north Harlem neighbourhood of New York City. By mid-1996 it had completed its ninth successive year of profitable operations, and the eleventh year of its remarkable life. Including management and other support staff, it employed over 300 people. Its annual sales were around £6m.

In other words CHCA was established as a business success. But in at least two other important respects, it is notably different from the other successful businesses which appear in these pages. First, its direct labour force of home care aides, or health service 'paraprofessionals' as they tend to be called in CHCA, is overwhelmingly female, and very largely black and Hispanic. Second, they can be classified as belonging to the 'working poor'. In his writing about co-operative production John Stuart Mill frequently used the phrase 'associations of labourers': it is not fanciful to suppose the working poor is what he had in mind. Probably he saw co-operative production as offering special benefits to non-management employees. Where the latter are predominately women, as at CHCA, then, on the basis of the belief expressed by Mill, we may anticipate a double 'regeneration'.

CHCA's achievements have not come easily. Quite the contrary. In its first two years, it ran up big losses. During that period the top management position was held by three people who each failed in turn. More than once its backers were within an ace of pulling the plug. Moreover, there were major struggles even after the business had started to show a profit during its third year: for example, a struggle to persuade the relevant New York authorities to increase what they pay for work of this kind.

Still, the figures in the table leave no doubt about the fact of success:

CHCA 1985–1995 Key Statistics

Year*	Care Staff Nos	Sales $m	profit/Loss $000
1985	60	0.2	(187)
1986	116	0.6	(78)
1987	125	1.5	98
1988	160	2.0	95
1989	160	2.3	236
1990	200	2.7	170
1991	250	3.5	102
1992	260	4.1	128
1993	295	4.7	155
1994	303	5.7	208
1995	291	5.9	154
1996	320	5.9	139
1997†	380	6.5	180

* Years are to 30 September up to 1989; calendar years thereafter. There were separate accounts for the three months October/December 1989.
† Estimated

To make a fine judgement of CHCA's performance on the basis of these crude statistics would be a mistake. There have been considerable subsidies from charitable sources. By 1996 CHCA's notable enrolment training and education programmes had been separated from the main business and were charitably funded. On the other side the management has achieved at least some success in persuading the New York public authorities to increase the rates it pays for care work in people's homes. CHCA may have had help from various sources but conversely it has secured benefits which have spread out across the community.

Even with those qualifications the crude statistical record is impressive, considering that this was a new start-up undertaking. In fact the authors of a 1992 study claim that CHCA has the best growth performance of any new start-up American employee-owned business ever (Dawson and Kreiner 1992).

The still sceptical reader may be offered two independent pieces of evidence of success. The first is the continuing support of New York's Visiting Nursing Service (VNS). VNS is well known among the agencies which put out care work contracts in New York on two related grounds. It values quality of service and is prepared to pay slightly higher rates for it. VNS has in fact awarded contracts to CHCA since 1987. Towards the end of 1991, impressed by the quality of CHCA's work, it offered a substantially increased contract. By 1996 the Detroit equivalent of New York's VNS was considering setting up a joint operation with a local clone of CHCA.

The plan for a Mid-West cloning followed replications of CHCA in Philadelphia in February 1993 and in Boston the subsequent year – the second piece of independent evidence of CHCA's success. Each of these is now profitable. Two prominent American charities, the Mott and the Ford Foundations, had made available the finance necessary for this replication programme.

Thus, since 1987 the management team at CHCA headed by Rick Surpin has built a successful employee-owned business and provided jobs for many who at first glance might be classified as rather unpromising human material. Moreover, they have built a business, it seems to me, which has gradually begun to attract the loyalty of most of its home care staff, of whom a substantial majority are now its co-owners. It offers real opportunities to do worthwhile jobs and to enjoy feelings of self-respect when doing them. The statistical evidence for these assertions is to be found in the high proportion of the home care staff who are now paid-up employee owners, or are in the process of so becoming, for the not insignificant sum of $1,000 a head. It can also be seen in its low level of employee turnover – about 20% in 1995. This is understood to compare with an industry average of 30% to 40%. Those lucky enough to visit the business in the South Bronx are aware that CHCA's success is more than just statistical.

ORIGIN AND START UP

Because of a combination of generally higher costs in institutions and the ageing of populations, public authorities have long been looking to switch the delivery of health and care services from hospitals and nursing homes into clients' own homes. In New York State this trend had perhaps gone further by the mid-1980s than elsewhere in the USA. The state's nursing homes were the subject of a major scandal in the 1970s, with widespread convictions of nursing home owners for fraud. As a result the authorities put a moratorium on new nursing home construction. A minority of far-sighted local doctors had also been speaking up for many years about the benefits to patients of home care – as long ago as the late 1940s Dr E. M. Bluestone at the Montefiore Hospital in the Bronx had argued that patients should be treated in hospital only in situations of defined and exceptional emergency. It was with this same Montefiore Hospital that CHCA negotiated its first contract. That may be no more than a coincidence but the views of Dr Bluestone serve to remind us that there are medical as well as cost arguments for switching patients' care to their homes.

To supervise this home care, hospitals like Montefiore have built up major departments. The work itself is contracted out to the private sector. The supervising departments are known as the hospitals' certified home health agencies. When CHCA signed its first contract, it was with the Montefiore Hospital's certified home health agency rather than with the hospital itself. The public money to pay for the contract came from the two programmes on which Americans without private medical insurance depend: Medicare and Medicaid.

Already in the 1980s the US Department of Labour was classifying home care as a 'growth industry'. That was one of the features which made it attractive to Rick Surpin, CHCA's promoter, and to the New York charity, the Community Service Society (CSS), which was his principal backer. Another was the fact that the home care industry, in which the overwhelming majority of the undertakings are private, profit-seeking companies, was characterised in the mid-1980s by low wages, low status, and almost zero employment benefits. Those who did the actual work were almost all women and almost all black or Hispanic. Typically they were lone parent mothers and heads of families. As such they were eligible to receive state welfare cheques and Medicaid health cover for themselves and their children. The starting wage for home care work in New York in the middle 1980s was often as low as the statutory minimum rate of \$3.35 per hour, the jobs on offer were typically part time, and health insurance was almost never part of the contract. So the incentive for these women to move from public welfare into this employment was rather limited. Dawson and Kreiner tell us that '. . . the norm in the industry was for women to float back and forth between part-time . . . work and public assistance.'

For Rick Surpin and his CSS backers, home care provided the attraction of rising demand and thus an opportunity to create jobs. It also offered a further challenge: to make the new jobs good ones – with decent wages and other benefits, with full-time work for those who wanted it; and with appropriate training arrangements and promotion possibilities. And as if those challenges were not enough, it was decided that the jobs should be created within a business which, after an initial 'trusteeship' period, would be majority-owned by its employees and controlled by them on a democratic basis.

Mr Surpin had been operating as a kind of social entrepreneur in New York for some years before CHCA was ever conceived. While working with a community development organisation called the Mutual Aid Project, he had become attracted by the ideas of employee ownership and researched the possibility of promoting employee-owned cafés and restaurants. Nothing came of those particular studies but they seem to have strengthened Surpin's belief in employee ownership. His work with the Mutual Aid Project also brought him into contact with Peggy Powell, whose contribution to CHCA has probably been second only to his own.

In the early 1980s Mr Surpin became director of the Centre for Community Economic Development, one of the main operational agencies of New York's Community Service Society (CSS). This is a widely respected charitable organisation which can trace its origins back to 1848 and commands considerable resources. It had, for example, an income from all sources – endowment, donations and government grants – of nearly \$10m in 1986/7. CSS accepted his proposal that he should promote new jobs within the framework of employee-owned, or potentially employee-owned, businesses.

The first venture of this kind to which he was midwife, in association with two other local community groups, was a small carpentry operation. It failed – but Mr Surpin learnt important lessons. One was the need to make a really thorough study of any project of this kind before deciding to go for it. A second was the need to recruit an effective manager. He turned now to home care and produced a combination of a feasibility study and business plan.

Mr Surpin's plan attracted a sympathetic response from the Bronx's Montefiore Hospital. In particular, the staff of the hospital's certified home health agency approved his aim of improving on the industry's wages, conditions and status, including his linked objective of achieving a majority of full-time jobs. But the agency's staff made clear that in any contract they signed the hourly rate of pay specified could be no higher than for any other contractor. If Mr Surpin was going to pay more than the competition, the difference would have to come out of the allowance in the contract for profits and overheads – typically around 25% of the total – or else from donations made by the CSS or other well-wishers.

An important contribution to Mr Surpin's business plan was also made by Janet Saglio, the vice-president for business services of an employee ownership and co-operative promoting agency in Boston – the Industrial Co-operative Association, or the ICA Group as it later became.

The key features of the business plan which was duly approved by the CSS, and the project's other outside backers, were as follows:

–The goal of improving the conditions and status of the actual homecare workers would be reflected from the beginning in a starting hourly rate of pay which, at $4.25, was some 75 cents higher than the industry average; and in an annual uniform allowance of $100.

– The goal of achieving full-time work for 70% of the workforce was affirmed as a major commitment; but one to be achieved only by stages.

– Because of the need for a continuous reduction in overhead costs per unit of home care supplied, there would be a corresponding increase in workforce numbers up to an initial target of 200.

– The budget would allow for losses in the first year; but a break-even result moving on to a small profit would be projected for the second.

– So as to bring forward the receipt of the first income, the starting workforce would consist of people already trained for care work. Thereafter the project would train all its recruits itself and devise its own training programme.

– The project would be managed by a professional with experience of the industry.

– The initial board of directors would be chaired by Mr Surpin and would represent the CSS and other financial backers. But these would be transitional arrangements during which the outside directors would behave as 'trustees' for the project's prospective employee owners.

– At an appropriate stage, members of the workforce would be urged to become members of CHCA, and its employee owners, by subscribing for one share each. The shares would be priced at $1,000, but could be paid for by instalments.

– These employee owners would progressively elect directors who would progressively replace the original 'trustee' directors.

– The project would be endowed with its start-up equity by the CSS with further contributions from other well-wishers if possible.

About the time that Mr Surpin was completing this work, there was good news from the Montefiore Hospital: a firm offer of a contract if it proved possible to meet the various conditions for starting up, including the necessary finance. The financial needs were considerable. Working capital had to be high because of the long delay – 90 or 120 days – between the performance of services and the receipt of payment for them.

However, the support from the CSS sent a strong signal to progressively minded charitable funds. The involvement of the ICA Group did the same to funds with money to lend to co-operative and other employee-owned type ventures. A starting capital of $420,000 was, in fact, fairly quickly put together – with a little over 25% of that in donated equity ($115,000) and the balance in debt. Easily the biggest source of these funds was the CSS, which donated $50,000 in equity and lent a further $75,000 at 6% over five years. Other charitable backers included Christian sources – the Adrian Dominican Sisters, the Sisters of Charity in Ohio and the US Catholic Conference of Bishops' Campaign for Human Development. Among the co-operative backers was the Development Corporation of the National Co-operative Bank. With one exception, all the loan money came in at well below market rates. The exception was the loan from the revolving fund of the ICA Group:

$50,000 at 11% over 3.5 years. But the Group took over the essentially 'monitoring' responsibilities of lead lender, a far from costless function.

His experience with the failed carpentry venture had impressed on Mr Surpin the key importance of high quality professional management. But high credentials do not always correlate with actual business success, perhaps especially when managers move from a conventional to an employee-owned business. In the case of the man originally chosen to be the prospective CHCA's first chief executive we shall never know. As the former branch director of a national home care agency he had good credentials and the right experience. But two weeks before the completion of the start-up financial package he jumped ship and took a job in a major hospital: later it emerged that he had been mugged in the South Bronx some years before and was nervous in that neighbourhood. The replacement recruit, also with appropriate homecare industry experience, came from the Mid-West.

THE CHEQUERED ROAD TO PROFIT

As we saw at the outset, CHCA made significant losses in each of its first two financial years. But the amount of the loss was more than halved in the second year and both workforce and sales rose substantially.

The losses actually incurred were substantially higher than forecast. Essentially, it took longer than expected to build up work, and so the overhead burden was reduced more slowly. It was only in the financial year 1985/6 that the business secured a second contract – with New York City's Visiting Nurse Service (VNS). This was important because of VNS's special concern for the quality of care.

There was also what might be called a 'learning curve component' in the bigger than expected initial losses. Moreover there were repeated changes in top management. It is doubtful whether the second CEO ever felt comfortable with the employee ownership framework and he was asked to leave. He was followed by an experiment with a kind of collegiate top management which lasted for roughly ten months and was also judged to have failed – or anyway not to have worked well enough to justify going on. Finally, in August 1986, Mr Surpin himself took over the reins. Quite soon after that, CHCA began to prosper and has continued doing so.

The first two years of losses were a close-run thing. CHCA

would not have survived without the invaluable backing of the CSS. By August 1986, when Mr Surpin took over, CSS had increased its equity in the project from its initial $50,000 to $200,000; and its loan support from $75,000 to $125,000. In effect CSS injected new capital to offset the initial losses and a little more. Not only that. It also undertook to pay Mr Surpin's salary and those of two other senior staff, including Peggy Powell.

The first lesson of the story up to this point is: find a sympathetic charitable backer with a long purse. Dawson and Kreiner also suggest that the CHCA experience challenges conventional wisdom about what to look for in the top manager of a participative and employee-owned business. Someone with top management experience in a conventional capitalist business in the same industry may not necessarily be right in this sort of environment. Dawson and Kreiner point to CHCA's failure under the CEO from the Mid-West who had industry experience compared to the success under Mr Surpin, who had no such experience and who had never before managed a business employing over 100 people. There is obviously something in this contention: the experience of employee-owned businesses elsewhere certainly confirms that some managers whose experience has been confined to conventional businesses never succeed in adjusting to the different environment of employee ownership.

When Mr Surpin took over as CEO in August 1986, he found the office administration in poor shape, and he hired Kathleen Perez to take it over. She was an old colleague from Mutual Aid Project days both of himself and Peggy Powell, and thus there was a good chance that she would fit in.

On the other hand, though more contracts were still needed, the work load was by this time substantially larger than early on. Also important, the pattern of the contracts was such that around 50% of CHCA's care staff could work full-time. This was still below the business plan's target of 70%, but a big improvement on anything that had gone before. That perhaps partly explains another feature of the business at that time: divided morale among the care staff. Those with longer service felt critical of the project's failure to meet its own target of 70% full-time jobs; the more recent recruits tended to compare their wage rates and indeed other aspects of their work situation with what they had experienced elsewhere – to the advantage of CHCA.

A further feature of the scene when Mr Surpin took over was its training programme. Over the previous nine months, in conjunction with a local community college, CHCA had developed its own training programme for new recruits. The main architect of this was Peggy Powell. It was later to become, in conjunction with CHCA's sophisticated selection programme, one of the foundations of the venture's success.

Following Mr Surpin's takeover, CHCA grew fast. After little more than twelve months sales were up by 110% to $1.5m, and care staff by around 8%. He had achieved this virtuous pair of outcomes by pushing up the number of full-time jobs to the original target figure of 70% of the total. An annual loss of just under $80,000 had been turned into a profit of almost $100,000.

Morale also began to improve. Labour turnover started to fall sharply and already in early 1987 CHCA passed two important landmarks. In March, 40 of its workforce applied for membership and started to subscribe the $1,000 needed to buy the required single share. Shortly afterwards there were elections for a new board of directors on which elected 'worker directors' were to be in a majority. The end of the period of the project's 'trustee board' pre-dated by a few months the confirmation that it had become profitable.

SINCE 1988

At the time of writing, CHCA had been continuously profitable for nine years. However, while total sales increased about four times between 1987 and 1995, the *rate* of profit fell: expressed as a percentage of total sales the profit rate in 1995 was little more than a third of what it had been in 1987. We shall see why later.

Apart from survival and profitability, the main achievements of CHCA since 1987 have been:

– More than doubling the numbers employed from 125 to over 300, combined with real improvements in pay and working conditions;

– A steady improvement in the quality of the service provided.

– The replication programme.

– The establishment of the training system as a separate entity.

– The development of an agenda and organisational structure on the political field.

The slower growth rate in numbers employed, as compared with sales, reflects a shift to full-time working and some progress by CHCA in improving rates of pay. The original plan seems, at least in some sense, to have set a target wage at an annual rate of $15,000. Moreover, the project had showed its commitment to higher rates of pay for its staff by offering, as we saw earlier, a starting rate of $4.25 per hour to those who joined at the beginning in 1985, a premium of some 50 cents an hour over the industry norm.

Annual pay of $15,000 for a full-timer equates with an hourly rate of about $7.50. In July 1992 CHCA raised its hourly rate for new recruits to $6.00. Even after allowing for inflation since the business plan was written in 1984, Mr Surpin and his colleagues could claim real progress in improving basic wage rates. By 1995, CHCA claimed that the package it offered employees was 'among the best in the industry' – wages averaged over $7 per hour, with around $2.50 more in benefits including health insurance, paid vacation and sick time. An employee can also reckon on average hours of 35 per week – compared to an industry norm of 25-30 hours.

That progress can be seen as partly political – the result of pressure on the relevant New York State authorities to lift the rates paid by them for work under the Medicare and Medicaid programmes. Mr Surpin took the lead in the formation of a body which called itself the New York City Home Care Work Group and which represented a coalition of interested parties including 'unions, elderly and disabled consumer organisations, public policy advocates, provider agencies and academic researchers' (Dawson and Kreiner).

Late in 1988, the Work Group succeeded in persuading the authorities to raise pay rates by a modest amount. When that eventually came through in late 1989, the starting wage at CHCA was lifted above $5.50 for the first time.

As with wages, so with conditions. From the beginning new recruits were paid an annual uniform allowance of $100. Some paid holidays were first introduced in 1988. Soon afterwards the care staff and their children became covered by health insurance. In 1992, when cash was unusually tight, a decision was reached democratically to drop the health insurance for children.

A final point about wages and conditions concerns VNS which gave CHCA a second contract in 1991. This notable agency has developed a policy of rewarding higher quality work with higher volume. When VNS proposed its second contract to CHCA, so Dawson and Kreiner tell us, it 'offered to substantially re-direct its case load' towards the business. They explain what was clearly a most welcome offer by telling their readers that 'VNS had concluded that CHCA's quality of care was superior to all its other subcontractors'.

Judgements about the quality of work of this kind can be based on the numbers and intensity of patient complaints. CHCA keeps careful records of complaints against its care staff. They are evidently few compared to other companies. Co-ordinators at head office keep in daily touch with clients by telephone. By 1996, CHCA was handling about 250 cases at any one time, each of which might last six and nine weeks. Not least because of its careful initial screening programme of job applicants, it reckons to have five or less cases a year of theft.

It is also possible to quantify some less direct indicators of quality, especially when we remember the importance of continuity of service by the same provider, which partly depends on the labour turnover rate at the business which is supplying the service. By this measure the record of CHCA is notably superior to the average for the competition. Dawson and Kreiner link this with the growing number and percentage of the business's care staff who decided to become worker owners and either 'bought themselves in', by subscribing for a $1,000 share, or started to do so.

Sherman Kreiner, joint author of the study to which I have constantly referred, was hired by Mr Surpin in early 1990 'to design and lead a major strategic planning process', with finance from the Ford Foundation. He drew up a progamme of planned growth.

The substantial growth since Mr Surpin had taken over in 1986 had already called for extra finance. This had been provided by one of the venture's original backers, The National Co-operative Development Bank, in the form of a $250,000 line of credit to finance receivables. Growth was also shortly to require extra office space.

Mr Kreiner tells us that his first task was to help CHCA's 'senior managers to overcome their resistance to growth':

> If the co-operative was to meet its long-term hopes for higher quality jobs, it simply had to become more cost effective. The

company was indeed stable and profitable, but higher revenues were essential to attain further improvements such as better wages, guaranteed salaries, and better health benefits. However, in such tight margin, labour intensive, business, only growth seemed to offer a significant answer – by providing an improved economy of scale [Dawson and Kreiner, 1992].

Accordingly, Mr Kreiner recommended that CHCA's care staff should increase at a rate of not less than 30 each year until the total had reached 500. Geographically, it was recommended that the co-operative should extend its reach beyond the South Bronx into northern Manhattan where a branch office would be opened in Harlem at an appropriate stage. In fact, 40 new care staff jobs were added during 1992. As a further detail for the New York expansion, the plan recommended that two specialised care services be developed for those suffering from Alzheimer's Disease and Aids.

Finally, outside New York, the plan recommended that expansion would take the form of a 'replication programme', and specifically that ventures designed on the CHCA model should be mid-wifed by the South Bronx prototype. This would also act as trustee for their prospective employee owners during the early stage. The plan went on to suggest that the first two of these might be launched in Philadelphia and Boston.

The formal developer of the cloning operation was the Home Care Associates Training Institute. Founded in 1991, 40% of its $2m annual budget came from the Charles Stewart Mott and Ford Foundations and other charities, with the remaining third provided by state and local governments. One of its functions was to organise homecare co-operatives modelled on CHCA. The premise of the replication programme was that the most effective way to influence a highly regulated industry was to demonstrate that changes were possible from within the industry – rather than trying to influence practice and regulations purely as an outside advocate. Apart from cloning, this Institute has now taken financial responsibility for the professional training of the home care workers, so that the accounts of the co-operatives providing the care reflect the activities of that business alone. Training at CHCA is a four-month process, starting with one month of classes, followed by three further months' 'on-the-job' training.

Founded in 1993, the Philadelphia clone employed over 75 care staff by 1995, of whom nearly half – virtually all of those who had reached the length-of-service eligibility criterion – were in the process of buying a $500 share in the $1.6m business; over 90% of them had previously been on public assistance. The most recent clone in Boston started with 14 staff in spring 1994, was running profitably within eight months and recorded 'sales' worth over $800,000 in 1995. There were over 70 staff by mid-1996: about 70% of the 65 home health aides were former benefit claimants being paid $7 per hour or more, plus differentials, and averaging close to 35 hours a week. The replication programme was being extended, with two in the Mid-West next on the list.

However, even if one priority is change from within the industry, the movement started by CHCA is not neglecting the political dimension. Another of the original functions of the Institute was to be an 'advocate for employment and service delivery reforms within the home health care industry'. Until the mid-1990s, the (non-party) political work of Rick Surpin and the rest of the movement had been concentrated at state or local level. By 1996 developing a political presence at the national level was an overt aim. A series of 'concept papers' were already in print.

The support from the Mott and Ford Foundations for the CHCA model and the work of the Institute do much to lay at rest the doubts about the adequacy of the co-operative's profits. And that seems to be a reasonable judgement despite the fact that, at the margin, income which might have made them larger has been applied to improving the pay and conditions of the care staff. The Foundation support suggests that this priority of the business from the start has been kept within the limits of proper prudence.

But the point on which to close this section is rather different. It is that by endorsing the replication programme the Ford and Mott Foundations have also passed a favourable verdict on other aspects of the CHCA formula: its co-operative, democratic, ownership and related arrangements. It is to these that we now turn.

CO-OPERATIVE AND RELATED ARRANGEMENTS

In the absence of specific co-operative legislation such as exists in Britain and some countries in Europe, the corporate form of CHCA is that of a company limited by its shares. But it is also formally organised under worker co-operative incorporation laws in the state of New York. Its share capital is divided into two categories:

class A common stock and class B common stock. Voting rights are restricted to the class A common stock which may be owned only by employees. The ownership of the class B stock is also restricted. It was owned at first exclusively by the project's parent and midwife – the Community Service Society of New York. It has since been given to the company, not to be allocated to individual employees, but to remain as collective capital.

To begin the discussion in this way is not, I hope, to assign undue weight or importance to CHCA's legal form and structure. On the whole I share the increasingly fashionable view that an organisation is shaped, and its culture – what the French call its *mentalité* – is coloured, as much by its informal arrangements and relationships as by its legal framework. I suspect that that applies quite strongly in this case.

All the same, the legal framework is important in itself because it provides an anchorage in law for the position of CHCA's employee owners in relation to the project as a whole and to the management. The rights and powers of CHCA's employee owners are grounded in law; they are not enjoyed simply by virtue of the grace and favour of the project's management or that of the CSS. To borrow a thought from Mr Surpin, CHCA's legal structure and employee ownership arrangements offer a guarantee against any backsliding by the management.

Across much of Europe and the USA in the late twentieth century the word 'co-operative' carries negative as well as positive connotations. Given its actual legal structure, CHCA would almost certainly not be permitted under British law to use the word in its name. But here we may emphasise a positive aspect of the word co-operative. It does carry with it the implication that, as between the co-operative's members, or more exactly in this case between CHCA's employee shareholders, democratic relationships will prevail. In the general meeting of the holders of its Class A common stock, which is CHCA's sovereign body, each employee owner has one and only one vote.

By 1992, 175 staff members had subscribed $1,000 to purchase one share, or were in the process of doing so; 75% of those who were eligible. The only qualification for eligibility is the successful completion of a three-month probationary period. Given the prevailing incomes of the workforce and their low savings, it is entirely understandable that the acquisition of an employee share has not been made compulsory. The figures for worker owners in subsequent years were as follows:

1992	1993	1994	1995
197	182	243	256

The democracy in CHCA is, by all accounts, lively and active, though not to the point of destabilising the management. We saw earlier how in 1987 a majority of the project's board of directors came to be elected by its employee shareholders. Dawson and Kreiner report that there is vigorous competition for seats on the board of directors when the elections come round.

There is a reality too about the financial as well as the control dimension of the project's employee ownership. Cash bonuses of $500 – more strictly dividends – were paid to CHCA's employee shareholders for each of the two years preceding 1991 – a persuasive rate of return on a $1,000 share. Because of lower profits the dividend for 1991 was cut to $200. The consequences of that reduction were probably not all bad: the lessons that dividends are linked to profits, and that the latter can go down as well as up, are useful as well as painful. Moreover, in order to avoid any possible doubt, I should underline the fact that these payments are genuine dividends: they are not paid to those who are not employee shareholders.

Let us turn, finally, to some key features of the informal culture, spirit, or *mentalité*, at CHCA. Clearly the behaviour and openness of the management is of great importance. It does not seem too much to claim that Mr Surpin and the CHCA management team are perceived by the care staff as being on the same side as themselves and not as the enemy. The success of the project in reaching some of its original workforce goals – and in making progress towards others – must surely too be an important factor in keeping morale at a high level.

All of this seems to me to be underpinned by the project's training and education programmes; and especially by its training of new recruits and the associated screening of applicants. This is the province of Peggy Powell who was director of education and training until mid-1996, when she became full-time executive director of the Training Institute. Dawson and Kreiner place great emphasis on the care and attention which is put into the screening of applicants. They cited a remarkable pair of statistics about the success of this whole process: on average 80% of those who entered the enrolment training programme in the early 1990s came to it from being on public assistance; and of these 80% completed the programme successfully. This picture remains basically unchanged: in a joint mid-1996 brochure, *The Co-operative Homecare Network,* the three care co-ops in New York, Philadelphia and Boston claimed that of the 200 participants enrolled in training that year, 150 would begin employment within five weeks from the day they enrolled, 120 would remain fully employed three months after placement and 100 would still be employed six months after placement: 'This retention rate – 50% of those entering the training program still employed after six months – is exceptional among welfare-to-work programs,' it says. The brochure goes on to list five key elements which contribute to this success:

– Clear selection standards which owe little to academic or professional achievement and much to character qualities like caring, and problem solving and communication potential.

– Supportive counselling to help resolve work and home-related problems including negotiating the maze of regulations on public financial assistance.

– Individual responsibility – 'candidates must demonstrate their commitment to employment, both before acceptance and throughout the program', which includes punctuality and completing homework assignments.

– Skill building and individualised attention, with special concentration on problem-solving and communication skills.

– Worker ownership – see epigraph.

Important initiatives of the late 1980s and early 1990s sought to provide personal development 'ladders' for those of the care staff who want higher qualifications, improved education, and more responsibility or any combination of these. The first was a programme to enable care staff to become, after an extended period of education and training, fully qualified professional nurses. It has been only a partial success for one main reason: the low educational starting points of a number of those who have attempted it. Because of the only moderate results it was decided in late 1992 to phase out that particular programme and provide opportunities for generalised educational upgrading instead. Two further initiatives were launched in 1992 with the same aim of providing opportunities for personal development and advancement – a pilot project to train Senior Home Care Aides, and a team leader training programme.

Common sense must insist that this remarkable training and education programme has an important, and positive, effect on the culture, morale, and *mentalité* of the CHCA project. It is not surprising that the CSS and others continued to finance large parts of it into the late 1990s.

28

United Airlines

INTRODUCTORY OUTLINE

We believe that our plan will catapult the Company light years ahead of its competitors by enabling it to serve the global community more flexibly than any other major American carrier and to compete head to head with 'low cost carriers' in the shorthaul domestic market place. *Letter to members of pilots' and machinists' unions at United Airlines introducing the proposed buy-out deal, December 1993*

Companies which operate in growth markets but find themselves becoming uncompetitive because of their rates of pay and benefits, face a clear choice. They can cut either jobs or their pay and benefits by the required adjustment percentage. If they choose the latter then, given the ESOP tax reliefs in both the US and UK, those who give up wages can be compensated by shares and the profits of the business can benefit from the tax reliefs. To overcome the crisis of the early 1990s, United Airlines chose to cut wages and benefits. By contrast, two of its main competitors, Delta Airlines and American Airlines (AMR), chose to cut jobs even if it is also true that the reduction was achieved on a largely voluntary basis at AMR. Readers must judge for themselves which of the two main alternatives they would prefer to go for. Investors scarcely need to make a judgement. At least in the summer of 1997, the arithmetic would have done the job for for them. Between the date of the deal and the end of June 1997, shares in the common stock of United outperformed those of Delta and AMR by a substantial margin.

I need also to emphasise at the outset that the deal that was completed in July 1994 was not merely the response to a crisis. For the Association of Airline Pilots of America (ALPA) at United it was indeed the culmination of a ten-year dream. On three previous occasions specific buy-out plans had been prepared, only to founder.

The deal has been variously described as an 'employee buy-out' and as a 'capital restructuring'. I shall argue that it was a bit of both. But whatever its essential character there can be no arguing about its main results: trustees acting on behalf of over 50,000 of United's then 69,000-strong America-based employees, members of ALPA and of the International Association of Machinists (IAM) and the entire non-unionised workforce, became the owners of 55% of its voting capital. What is more, those covered by the deal gained almost total employment security over the roughly six-year life of its main provisions as well as voices at the top table for a much longer period. At least as much as the new majority employee shareholding, these latter should be seen as the defining characteristics of a potentially historic bargain between capital and labour. On the labour side, only the cabin staff, organised as the Association of Flight Attendants (AFA), stayed out.

The former shareholders were compensated for what they gave up by an ingeniously mixed package which cannot easily be characterised by a one-word description, but of which a cash payment of $84.81 and a half share in the stock of a recapitalised United were the main ingredients. On their side, the majority employee shareholders gave up wages and made other concessions which were reckoned to have a so-called net present value (NPV) of $4.886bn. Measured both by that number and by the numbers of resulting employee shareholders, this was the largest ever transaction of an even remotely similar kind.

Readers will be immediately anxious to learn whether the glittering predictions made for it by Captain Roger Hall and Mr Ken Thiede (authors of the opening epigraph) were validated by United's subsequent performance. The best short answer must be 'yes and no'.

To begin with there can be no serious dispute about the surface quality of United's financial results following the deal's completion. For each of the two calendar years, 1995 and 1996, the company turned in results which were glitteringly good. Moreover, it was a good bet, when this was written in the summer of 1997, that a flow of apparently top class financial results would continue at least to the end of the century.

What is more, these results were unquestionably seen as good on Wall Street. The company's share price was among the top performers in the quoted airline sector over the period of thirty-six months from the completion of the deal to June 1997.

The non-employee shareholders, who retained a 45% stake after the deal was done, had no obvious cause for complaint at least over the deal's first three years. They were entirely free either to hold on or to say 'Thank you' for an attractive capital gain and move on. But in that last respect the position of the employee shareholders was different. Under the rules governing ESOP shareholding at United, they are in effect only free to sell when they stop being employed by the airline. However, and for what it is worth, with the price of United's shares above $70, as it was in June 1997, the employee shareholders had comfortably recouped on paper at least the cash component of what they had forgone in wages and other concessions up to then. In a notice to members dated 2 May 1997 – when the share price was around $75 – Mr Ken Thiede spelt out the value of shares already allocated to a 'lead' mechanic and contrasted that with 'his' investment: the numbers were $41,100 v. $17,400.

There is, however, still more compelling evidence as to whether the early union predictions were validated by the company's subsequent performance. A flow of friendly incoming telephone calls were received by the ALPA union office at United over much of 1996. They came from banks and other 'investment community' institutions. Their gist was that if the pilots got wind of any deals similar to that completed by them with United in 1994, they – the bankers and other 'investment community' people – would greatly welcome a tip-off.

This particular flow of friendly incoming telephone calls to United's ALPA office was interrupted in early January 1997. What had happened just before was that the members of the 'ESOP unions', first the pilots and later the more highly paid among the machinists, had voted to reject an offer of a 'mid-term wage adjustment' which had been provisionally negotiated by their leaders with the company.

This is not the place to go into details about either the offer or its rejection. But three key points have to be made. The first is that the union leaders accused the management of refusing to develop the kind of 'ESOP relationship' which they had expected and thought reasonable. Second, the management moved quickly to contain the damage, by making a new offer which included a real sweetener as well as improved pay increases. Third, it is possible that this whole episode may turn out in retrospect to have been a case of 'all's well that ends well'. In any event, following recommendations by their leaders, union members quickly voted to accept the new offer.

Nevertheless the episode shows that the management and the two 'ESOP unions' did not succeed in developing a trouble free relationship over the first two and a half years following the deal's completion. Despite the financial successes in 1995 and 1996, we cannot say without qualification that the prediction in the epigraph was validated by what then happened.

Arguably too, the results might have been better. On the face of it the numbers are first class. But a closer look is needed. It can tell us what were the sources of the main improvements and their relative weights. Well over 95% of the clearly demonstrable improvements can be attributed to four sources:

– Savings associated with the main wage reductions and other concessions agreed in the 1994 deal.

– ESOP tax reliefs, partly linked to United's share price, which had started to exceed projections by 1996.

– Improvements in demand, evident most concretely in improved 'load factors' (seat occupancy rates).

Improvements and savings resulting from the special deal associated with the so-called 'United Shuttle'.

The third of these four sources of improvement had not much to do with the deal. Its competitors were in principle as well placed as United to take advantage of it, though United did in fact succeed in increasing its share of 'premium' passengers.

As for the first two and the last, it is open to a discerning critic – or anyway a devil's advocate – to argue that the resulting improvements were no more than the 'mechanical and automatic' consequences of the 1994 transaction.

Sceptics may also argue that the size of the improvements which can be persuasively attributed to more ownership congruent behaviour were rather modest. Let it be clear at once that they are not negligible. But they are quite modest both in absolute numbers and relative to what has been achieved in some other of America's majority employee-owned companies. On the other hand it is open to those at United to argue that the scope for 'process improvement' savings is probably that much less in a service business, like theirs, than in a manufacturing business, like a steelworks. These are issues that can be easily discussed but not at all easily settled.

But it remains a common misconception that a switch to majority employee ownership will of itself result in a change of culture, towards attitudes which are conducive to continuous and significant productivity improvements. Both management and the unions at United must know that that is not the case. It is also true that a number of important steps were taken in the two years following the deal to promote a culture more oriented towards productivity improvement. But the evidence is that, for one reason or another, those efforts were not sufficient to change attitudes very much.

The 1994 deal was a transaction notable not only for the numbers. It was even more notable for the pilots' union initiative that was the prime mover behind it. And it was notable too for the fact that though the unions were worried about employment security and the management about profits, it cannot reasonably be characterised as a 'crisis transaction'. More about this later.

Here we may note that their majority shareholding gave United's new employee owners a strong voice in the strategic decisions of the business. In that connection one specific point needs to be emphasised at once. The deal included changes at the apex of United's management team. Mr Stephen Wolf, the former CEO, stepped down together with his number two, Mr Jack Pope. Mr Gerald Greenwald and Mr John Edwardson came in as CEO and chief operating officer. Mr Greenwald was, and had indeed already been for a number of years, ALPA's favoured candidate for the top job. His status as a union-chosen CEO is both a detail and not a detail.

For America's airlines the years 1990 to 1993 were ferociously tough. With one exception, all the larger companies lost money and by the end of 1993 had chalked up total losses close to $13bn. One of the country's most famous carriers, Pan American, went bankrupt just before the fighting started in the Gulf War. Because of its effects on fuel prices and its tendency to discourage the fainthearted from flying at all, that conflict was a part of the problem. But overcapacity and intensifying competition were the big factors behind the losses. Only Southwest Airlines, the no frills short haul operator, with routes mainly in the Texas-California triangle, avoided them.

Pan Am was not the only airline to go bust, simply the most famous. Eastern and Midway suffered similar fates. Others, TWA, Northwest and Continental, filed for protection under Chapter 11 of the bankruptcy code. All took steps to cut costs within their control, to move out of unprofitable routes and to reduce both labour expenditures and labour itself.

United, alongside American Airlines one of the country's 'big four' since before the war, and normally either the first or second airline in the US, was no exception. It made its then biggest loss ever, of $332m, in 1991 and in 1992 went much further into the red, with a figure nearly three times that.

In fact all its competitors except Southwest faced the same crisis in the early 1990s. But United was in a class of one in relation to the way out of the crisis which it chose. In the language of headlines, the instrument chosen to overcome the crisis was a massive employee buy-out. In the more prosy language of investment bankers, what happened was a massive 'capital restructuring exercise'.

In fact an enlightened bargain was struck, centred round pay cuts. Led by the pilots, over 50,000 of United's then 69,000-odd American-based workforce agreed to significant wage cuts and made various other concessions – including most importantly the acceptance by the pilots for a twelve-year period of a two-tier wage system. The concessions were estimated to have a net present value (NPV) of $4.886bn. In return those employees obtained, as well as their 55% shareholding, near total employment security for up to six years, an important voice at the high table and the choice of their two favoured top executives.

We shall have to look later at the details of this buy-out bargain and capital restructuring exercise. As so often in transactions of this kind, the deal could not have been done without the details. But some further general points about it are worth bringing out already at this stage.

Subject to a conditional qualification which in the event did not apply, both the percentage of the equity (55%) and the associated number of shares in the common stock (precisely 17,675,345) were fixed at the outset. On the other hand, not common stock but preferred shares were to be allocated to qualifying employees and were only to be changed into the former when employment came to an end. The eventual exchange, of preferred shares for shares in the common stock, was to take place on a one for one basis, regardless of the market value of the latter at the time the exchange took place. So United's employee shareholders stand either to gain or to lose depending on the actual share price levels when they come to sell. At the end of June 1997 that price, after allowing for a four to one split, was between two and three times what it had been when the deal was completed.

For a period roughly twice as long as the duration of its members' main wage reductions – 12 years against 5.75 – ALPA accepted what amounted to a two-tier wages and benefits arrangement: with pilots flying what was named the 'United Shuttle' or the 'U2' – up and down the north-south corridor on America's West Coast – receiving lower pay rates and flying longer hours than on the company's other routes. This was not an entirely new departure in the history of collective bargaining between ALPA and United. The agreement which followed ALPA's successful strike in 1985 offered a kind of precedent. But the duration of that earlier 'two-tier' agreement was far less extended: two years against twelve.

Notwithstanding the near total employment security provisions of the deal, the IAM agreed that up to 20% of United's aero-engine and airframe maintenance work might be outsourced for the same twelve years. It further agreed to specified changes in work rules – including an end to the paid half hour lunch break – over the twelve-year period.

ALPA's acceptance of a 'two-tier' wages-and-hours arrangement over a time span of twelve years is an especially important feature of what was agreed. Academic economists have been frequently listened to with respect when they have asserted that unions would never accept any such thing. That was one main reason why the deal at United was widely seen, at least until the turbulence over the mid-term wage increases, as one of special and path-breaking importance. It is true that by 1994 two-tier wage arrangements had been accepted by unions quite widely across America's airline industry, in other US industries and also in the UK. But something of a spotlight was switched on when that arrangement formed a key part of the deal at United.

The deal was partly seen as important because of the numbers, both of dollars and of employees. But it was mainly seen as special because of the union initiative behind it, and the fact that the initiative was not born of impending disaster or prospective close down. It was substantially born out of a decided preference for greater employment security over higher financial rewards in the medium term. But that is not a disaster indicator. And the same applies to the mounting losses which the airline had been accumulating. They were serious but not desperate. For both by its balance sheet and its market position United remained relatively strong.

No, the key point about the deal is that though partly born out of labour's concerns for employment security and management's for profits, it was also partly born out of a belief on the part of some of the key actors – and especially of the pilots and the new CEO – that majority employee ownership would make United both a more successful business and a more attractive one in which to work. As we shall see, it also happened because the pilots threatened to strike if the management chose to cut jobs and not pay, a threat which was evidently credible.

What then of the rejection by the pilots and the higher-paid machinists of mid-term wage deal as first proposed? I suggest that it should be seen as resulting from success rather than failure. More exactly it resulted from what was perceived by a majority of the 'ESOP Unions'' membership as an inequity in the distribution of 'extra' benefits that had flown from the deal. As we noted earlier, 1995 and 1996 were by various measures financially the best in United's history. What's more and to repeat for emphasis, from the deal's completion to the middle of 1997, the United share price had comfortably outperformed most of its airline competitors.

There is some evidence too of higher social morale and a better atmosphere at work during at least the first two years which followed the mid-1994 buy-out. Moreover, evidence from the length of applicants' waiting lists continued to show, throughout this period, that there were plenty of qualified pilots and qualified machinists who were quite ready to work for United at its new and lower than previous rates. Presumably they saw attractions in its enhanced employment security, employee shares, and the labour voices at the top table.

In the end we should probably see the rejection by the pilots and the higher-paid machinists of the mid-term pay adjustment, as originally proposed, as a protest – a protest against what they judged to be an unfair distribution of the big gains that had substantially flowed from their sacrifices. The pilots had given up over 15% of their salaries. For the machinists, when account is taken of an increase agreed earlier, the sacrifice was not much less. Against those numbers it is not surprising that offers of two 3% annual increases followed by two at 2% may have seemed less than generous when the company was proudly reporting record profits. Moreover, the first offer may have seemed galling as much for what it failed to contain as for what was in it. In the jargon it gave no guarantee of an automatic 'snap back' after the duration of the main wage cuts, no promise of wages being restored, to their pre-1994 levels.

As we all know, feelings of unfairness can 'well up', whatever may be laid down in a formal contract. The big increase in the share price over the two and a half years following the buy-out deal may indeed well have contributed to the feelings of unfairness. For this upward movement is bound to have been widely seen as driven by the employee sacrifices. Thus, even though the employee shareholders have been major beneficiaries, there could well be resentment against the gains of the outside shareholders in what will be seen as an essentially 'free ride'. We can imagine that there was some resentment too among the pilots and machinists when, following the successful achievement of profit and other targets in 1995, the company's 600 top managers received significant cash bonuses early in 1996. The fact that these bonuses and the logic behind them were widely known and understood before they came to be paid out, may well not have reduced the resentment by that much.

Similarly it seems reasonable to suppose that there was resentment among the unionised staff, as reported in the press, that the deal allowed some upward flexibility in rates of pay for those newly recruited into managerial posts, and some tolerance of accelerated management staff promotion. Such a flexibility is almost a necessary feature in situations of this kind if an employee-owned business is going to hire and hold on to the management people it needs. United is not the first example either of this asymmetry in the way unionised and management employees are treated during an agreed wage freeze, or of the potential resentment which that can cause. It was one of the factors which contributed to bankruptcy at the employee-owned Hyatt Clark in the early 1980s and it was a big factor in the breakdown of relations between the management and the Independent Steelworkers' Union at Weirton in the middle 1990s.

Against that background and United's ballooning share price and profits, the votes against the initial offer in the mid-term wage adjustment process can perhaps best be understood as conveying a clear double message: first, we are not getting our fair share of the extra wealth creation; second, it is unfair not to promise to restore to us our old wage rates when the period of the main deal comes to an end in the year 2000.

The truth is that over the first period of its employee ownership United suffered from the inflexibility of the initial deal in a way similar to what happened at Weirton Steel in its early employee owned years. But there is also a key difference. At Weirton the benefits of the initial inflexibility went substantially to labour. Indeed the union members had eventually to be persuaded to modify what had been the agreed rules and do so against their own short-term money interests. At United, by contrast, at least in the unions' eyes, the benefits of what almost everyone saw as the larger-than-expected improvements went to outside capital and top managers.

We have now reviewed at some length the main causes of the discontent which led to the rejection of what was first offered in the mid-term wage adjustment process. Here, for the benefit of those who believe that employee ownership can offer a better way than conventional capitalism, I make three main final points. First, to repeat for emphasis, the problems encountered in the first phase of employee ownership at United were at least partly the problems of success. Second, despite the apparent quality of the financial results in 1995 and 1996, the management, the ESOP unions, and the rank-and-file employees had made only fair progress in securing the improvements made possible by its majority employee owner- ship. There had been only limited progress in the vital task of squeezing inefficiencies out of the system. Limited progress in the early years gives scope for improvement later.

My final point is that we should see this labour capital bargain at United not only as a success in itself, but also, and indeed even more so, as compared with what was the most obvious alternative available under conventional capitalism: to cut costs by cutting jobs. That was the solution chosen, for example, both at Delta and at American Airlines (AMR), the two closest of United's com- petitors. At Delta, instead of an agreement to cut wages by up to 15%, there were imposed redundancies of the same order of mag- nitude. At AMR the reduction in jobs was of the same order of magnitude, though it was achieved, to be fair, on a largely volun- tary basis.

The lucky ones at Delta who kept their jobs were not required to take any reduction in their wages. Clearly the savings directly achieved by similar percentage reductions in employment numbers on the one hand, and in wages and benefits on the other, are themselves likely to be similar. But, as we shall see in some detail later, America's ESOP tax reliefs mean that the choice between the two solutions is not simply a matter of a higher or lower preference for employment security. The choice of cutting wages instead of cutting people carries with it important tax advantages. That is why the solution chosen at United could in principle be a 'win' for both capital and labour. At the time of writing, in the summer of 1997, that is how it should perhaps best be seen. Moreover, it can be seen in that way without prejudging the question of whether the majority employee ownership at United will turn out to be of longer or shorter duration. It is enough that it offered the best solution to an acute set of problems of transition.

As a highly specific footnote for highly specialist readers, it is just worth having on the record, the respective 'provisions' made for their employment reduction programmes by Delta and AMR. The numbers were approximately $775m at AMR and $115m at Delta.

THE BACKGROUND UP TO 1987

The origins of the deal completed at United in July 1994 go back a long way. I quote from Thomas Petzinger, Jr's *Hard Landing* (1995):

> As . . . Dubinsky saw it, buying United was the only way for the pilots to take control of their destiny – the only way to get the company out of the hotel business and the rental car business and to start rebuilding the *airline* again. United was once a premier carrier, he thought; under Ferris it was fast becoming an also-ran. The only strategy that made sense for the pilots was to bid for control of the entire airline; the Eastern unions, among others, had provided a painfully instructive example when they traded away hard fought wages for a minority interest and a few board seats, which proved meaningless. At other places the unions gave up concessions simply to keep their jobs. 'We will not buy our jobs,' Dubinsky declared. Buying jobs was indentured servitude. Instead, he said, 'we will buy the company'.

In the summer of 1985 the then chief executive of UAL, Dick Ferris, a graduate to the airline business from a hotel and catering background, took on ALPA in a full-dress strike and lost. About a

year earlier – though this became public knowledge only long afterwards – Ferris had himself proposed to the board that the business
be taken private, using what would have been essentially a management buy-out led by him. It was a proposal which, in the light of a
hostile response from the directors, he hastily withdrew.

Roughly two years after losing to the pilots in the strike, Ferris
resigned his top post. The ALPA leadership at United had just had a
first crack at achieving a buy-out. That first attempt did not come
off. But the response to the pilots' proposal from those to whom
they then spoke in America's financial community was sufficiently
positive to inspire them to try again.

It was at their fourth attempt – and the first to be backed by
the members of the International Association of Machinists (IAM)
working at United – that they succeeded in pulling it off. There is
evidence that a buy-out project was in fact originally mooted in pilot
discussions during the 1985 strike. In other words nearly ten years
separated the first surfacing of the idea and its eventual implementation. We are not dealing here with an impulsive gambler's throw,
or something which took everyone by surprise by just happening to
come off. With the benefit of hindsight we can almost say that the
transaction completed in July 1994 was an event waiting to happen.

Where did these developments come from?

More precisely the questions are:

– Why did the first deal of its kind in the US – a union led buy-out
which aimed to use majority employee ownership to achieve co-
determination in a big, succeessful and fundamentally strong company – take place in the airline industry rather than elsewehere in
corporate America?

– Why, within the airline industry, did it take place at United?

– Why was the lead taken by ALPA, the pilots' union and not say
the IAM, the machinists' union, which had much larger membership at United?

There are three key factors which offer partial answers to the
first and the last questions. One is the high percentage of wage and
salary expenditures, and especially the high percentage of pilots'
pay, in the total costs of the airline industry. The second is the
rather unusual culture of the pilots' union. Third, there is the
character of the airline industry as essentially a top quality service
operation and thus one in which success is supremely dependent on
the efforts of individual employees, on what each of them puts in

and on what they achieve by working effectively in teams. Neither by themselves nor taken together do the three come near to being a sufficient condition of what happened. But they seem, at minimum, to have predisposed the stars towards it.

In 1993, the last full year before the transaction, United's total operating costs were $13bn. Within that total two items are worth highlighting, in dollars and as percentages:

1 Total salary and related costs: $4.75bn (36.5%)
2 Subtotal for pilots within above: $1.38bn (10.5%)

By themselves those numbers do no more than quantify what every regular airline user knows: that this is a business which employs lots of people and is to that extent labour intensive.

Both the pilots and the skilled personnel among the machinists are highly paid, the pilots of course very much so. A Harvard Business School Study in 1995 says that the pilots take home pay (after pension contributions and taxes) 'averaged over $100,000' and 'topped out at $180,000-$200,000'. It also says that just under 27,000 IAM members employed at UAL when the deal was completed had 'salary and related costs' of about $1.45bn. That suggests average take home pay of at least $45,000. The highly paid group of IAM members who actually maintain and repair frames and engines probably took home around $55,000; the less skilled group of baggage handlers and others, sometimes known collectively as 'ramp staff', about $35,000. Readers don't need reminding that a 15% – or any – pay cut is painful, however high a person's discretionary income. However, a 15% pay cut is easier to cope with if you take home $100,000 or $55,000 a year and not just, say, $25,000.

In the three years which preceded the 1994 deal, United's accounts show average annual losses of some $450m. The 'opportunity for doing a deal' may well have looked that much more promising in the light of the relationship between the total of salary and related expenditures, and those losses. For it will have suggested that a cut of 10% in salaries could have been sufficient to turn the results into modest profits. In the event the flight attendants, an important and then roughly 17,500-strong sub-group of the unionised workforce, decided to stay outside the deal. On the other hand any deal would also offer substantial ESOP tax reliefs.

The key business numbers in United's antecedent situation were conducive to – or at least did not seriously inhibit – the 1994 deal.

Because of the large numbers employed and the relatively high salaries of a significant percentage of the total, United may be said to be a 'labour intensive' undertaking. On the other hand, because of the hugely expensive equipment which it uses, it is also capital intensive. As against approximately $1.2bn of shareholders equity, UAL's 1993 accounts show non-current liabilities of close to $6.75bn.

United's dependence on debt must have strengthened the bargaining position of its unions, especially ALPA's which had triumphed in its full-dress strike against Dick Ferris in 1985. In his *Hard Landing,* Thomas Petzinger, Jr has a vivid account of what impelled Ferris to give in to the striking pilots:

> But ultimately there arose the issue of cash, which can make even the sturdiest CEO weak in the knees. This affliction hit Dick Ferris on about the seventh day of the strike. Watching cash fly out of the window at a dizzying pace, he called his senior managers together and said he was going to settle on the terms last agreed by the union.

The high level of debt was not the only reason cash had started to 'fly out the window at a dizzying pace'. But it was an important contributory factor. To the extent that it thus strengthened ALPA's bargaining position, it will also have strengthened its confidence in relation to a possible buy-out.

Finally it was not only the numbers themselves but the reaction to them of certain individuals and institutions that help us to explain the 1994 deal. As early as the ALPA buy-out bid which preceded the Ferris resignation in 1987 the pilots 'had conferred with [T.] Boone Pickens. They had consultants on the payroll. They knew what they were doing.'

The fact that the 1994 deal was ALPA's fourth attempt should not obscure the attractions to America's 'financial community' in the 1980s and 1990s of 'leveraged buy-outs', particuarly those involving strong businesses, like United. Four points are worth making:

– So long as the operations of the business to be bought out are sufficiently profitable to cover interest charges and debt repayments, the 'arithmetic' will do a nice job for the holders of the equity – by shifting the price of their shares progressively higher.

– The banks and other financial institutions which provide the 'leverage' are likely to be more than content with the relationship between the interest rate they can charge and real level of risk.

– In cases where the new equity holders are substantially the employees of the business being leveraged, there are the extra attractions of the ESOP tax reliefs.

– Whatever may have been the case in earlier times, by the 1980s and 1990s, cash flow projections had probably become the single most important consideration which determined corporate bank lending decisions at least in the worlds of US and UK business. Airlines that can cover their costs are almost bound to have positive cash flows.

Striking evidence in support of these considerations was made available to inquiring visitors at ALPA's headquarters office for United pilots outside Chicago in the autumn of 1996. Evidently the office had received a fair number of friendly incoming phone calls from financial institutions, including the highly prestigious bankers J. P. Morgan. The gist of the message was, to repeat, the same in all cases: if you know of any further deals of the kind which you led in 1994 with United, we would be greatly interested to hear about them.

In the jargon of financiers we might say that the 1994 United deal provided a favourable opportunity for 'securitisation': to offer capital in return for an assured income. In this case, the markets were prepared to offer significant capital in return for payments from the cash flow linked to the salary reductions accepted by a majority of the workforce. We might imagine a senior banker at, say, J. P. Morgan, remarking to a group of pilots: 'Cut us in on the top slice of your income and we will lend you what you need to buy control of the airline.'

The Pilots' Union What then of my second key factor in the background to the 1994 deal? I have called it the 'culture' of the pilots' union, ALPA. The average pay of ALPA pilots must be among the highest of any trade union members anywhere in the world. What is more, up to the 1994 deal United's pilots were certainly among the highest paid of any airline in the US. After taking account of differences in hours flown, they cost in the early 1990s roughly 50% more than those of Southwest Airlines. Pilots also command high social status, both within the industry and in the wider world.

Undoubtedly the ALPA culture contains conservative elements.

Many of the unionised pilots have backgrounds in the armed services. There is also a strong link between pay and seniority, which is measured in years of employment and not normally transferable when a pilot switches between airlines. But it would be a great mistake to expect ALPA to bend over backwards to 'see management's point of view', or be less than wholly committed to the pursuit of normal 'labor union' objectives and the use of normal weapons, including strikes, to achieve them. ALPA's historian, George Hopkins, in his *Flying the Line*, leaves his readers in no doubt about this: 'Skill, courage, and devotion to duty have less to do with why modern professional airline pilots have the best salaried jobs in the world than do history and the Airline Pilots Association. ALPA is first and foremost a labor union, an AFL-CIO affiliate.'

ALPA, a union with a long and self-confident history, was the creation of one man, David Behncke. This remarkable if not altogether appealing man came from a poor farming backgound and had no higher – and not that much lower – formal education. By sheer force of personality he persuaded the military authorities to let him learn to fly in the First World War. His preferred career choice is said to have been as a commissioned pilot in the armed services. But his lack of education made that difficult if not impossible.

Towards the end of the 1920s Behncke was working for Boeing Air Transport – one of the original constituents of United Airlines – as a commercial pilot. Not later than 1929, in the face of concerted efforts by airline companies to cut back on wages following the Wall Street crash, he started spending much of his time as a freelance organiser for a full-blooded labour union of commercial airline pilots. Once set on that course, his behaviour became that of a man driven by a mission. ALPA was formally established in July 1931 and its affiliation to the AFL-CIO – America's equivalent of Britain's TUC – came in the same month.

David Behncke was a man with a truly Goliath-sized ego. Eventually, in what was partly a real tragedy and partly a piece of melodrama, it proved to be his undoing. His staff turned against him and even tried to form their own independent union. In the end he had to be removed from his top post by ALPA's top representative body.

More important for our purposes here is what we may call his cultural legacy to the union he created. I believe that that has two conceptually quite separate elements which in turn reflected two quite separate 'drives' which impelled Behncke's work for ALPA. One was the straightforward 'class interest' of 'labour' against 'capital' (or 'labour' against top management as the agents of capital). His poor farm home background and lack of education may help to explain the intensity of this drive. The second drive was quite different: its aim was to secure recognition for ALPA as a body that was much more than just a labour union and deserved to be treated as an equal with government and top management in the controlling organs of the industry.

In his drive towards this second goal of ALPA as a co-leader in the industry, David Behncke developed something of a special relationship for the union with President Roosevelt. It was one that persisted under President Truman and has recurred in ALPA's relations with some of the Democratic party administrations since then. At least twice in its history the union has been saved from probable defeat in industrial disputes by Democratic administrations in the White House: by Roosevelt's in the 1930s, and prospectively by Harry Truman's in 1948.

A good illustration of this relationship is what happened in the wake of Harry Truman's victory in 1948. ALPA had chosen to go on strike against National Airlines and in the run-up to the early November vote of that year – in which Truman was pitted against Governor Thomas Dewey of New York – appeared to be losing. National, under its autocratic boss George (Ted) Baker, had evidently managed to replace many of the striking pilots with 'scab labor' and had also benefited from extra airmail subsidies passed on by the Civil Aeronautics Board. By late October ALPA's members had already been on strike for many months and the resources to sustain the action were rapidly running out.

Then, and since then, the informed consensus has been that if Dewey won, the company would have continued the fight and would have seen off ALPA in fairly quick time. But Truman's surprise victory and the resulting prospect of an ALPA-friendly government intervention changed all that. It also produced a classic *volte face*, or, more precisely, what Americans apparently call a 'foxhole conversion' on the part of National's chief executive, George (Ted) Baker (another man incidentally with a Goliath-sized ego):

> Baker suddenly announced that, owing to a deep religious conversion that had put Christian love in his heart and

forgiveness in his soul, he wished to settle. He became a devoted admirer of Dr Frank Buchman's Moral Re-Armament, a religious movement then much in vogue among corporate executives. Immediately after the presidential election, when Baker realised that he had backed the wrong horse, he departed for Dr. Buchman's headquarters on Mackinac Island, Michigan [Hopkins, *Flying the Line*].

Both this 1948 strike against National and the essentially political character of what determined its outcome are helpful to an understanding of ALPA's culture. One of the elements of that culture is clearly a readiness to embark on out-and-out strike action – what the French call 'les grèves à l'outrance'. A second is the assumption of a friendly relationship when a Democratic President is sitting in the White House.

Politically the relationship found its most consequential expression in two key pieces of legislation. One, which permits Government intervention in disputes between management and labour in the airline industry, was still in force when this was written and was indeed invoked by President Clinton, when he intervened in a dispute between American Airlines and its pilots, unionised in their own union, in February 1997. The second piece of law was the Civil Aeronautics Act of 1938. Its importance from ALPA's viewpoint was essentially threefold:

– It set maximum limits on pilots' flying hours.

– It gave legal protection to a formula which linked pilots' pay rates to miles flown. It thus gave them a built-in cut into productivity improvements associated with higher aircraft speeds.

– By giving the unionised pilots independent representation on the industry's safety watchdog, it went some way towards recognising ALPA as the third member, alongside top managements and Government itself, of an industry-wide ruling *troika*.

It is true that the provisions of this 1938 Act relating to pay and conditions were swept away by President Carter's deregulation measures of the late 1970s. On the other hand ALPA's independent representation on the industry's safety watchdog has survived. In my view this should be seen as an example of the way that ALPA both sees itself, and is seen by the public, as having something of a second personality in addition to that of a labour union: a second personality as something of an airline industry 'statesman'.

What is indisputable is that America's professional pilots were held in astonishingly high regard by sections of the public in the 1930s. George Hopkins quotes a telling passage from a speech made by Representative John Martin of Colorado in 1938:

> In my opinion the piloting of these great airplanes is the most responsible, the most skilful, occupation mankind has ever engaged in. It is a profession to which many are called but few are chosen. These men ought to be as free from worry about their economic condition or future as it is humanly and legislatively possible to achieve. If there is anything we can put in the legislation that will keep worry from the airline pilots, it ought to be done.

That such sentiments should have been expressed in the Congress is a remarkable tribute to the political skills of David Behncke and above all to his success at playing the 'safety card' in the interests of his members.

The Background at United We must next ask why it was at United, rather than at another of America's top airlines, that the first deal of its kind happened to take place. The analysis so far is of some help. The pay and allowances of United's pilots were above the average for the industry. Taken together with the company's strong balance sheet that tended to mean that the opportunity for a deal was probably more favourable at United than at most of the other US airlines.

A second strand of explanation arises from the evolution of relationships over the years between ALPA and UAL's top management and from the business philosophy and backgrounds of its successive chief executives. There were just four holders of the top post between the early 1930s – when United took on more or less its present form and became an airline rather than an airmail carrier – and 1987:

UAL's Top Managers: 1934 to 1987

Name	Dates	Industry Background	Orientation
W. A. Patterson	1934-66	Banking	Humanistic
George Keck	1966-70	Internal appointment	Unclear
Edward Carlson	1970-74	Hotels	Profit
Richard Ferris	1974-87	Hotels & catering	To own the world

There is evidence that before the first Roosevelt presidency and the New Deal which went with it, **Patterson** was unenthusiastic about unionised labour in general and a pilots' union in particular. But there is no doubt at all that he later came to accept ALPA, and even to see virtue in its role. Frank Taylor leaves no doubt on this point. After asserting (*High Horizons,* pp. 167–89) that 'unions have played an important role in Patterson's scheme of things' he goes on to quote the man's own words: 'When all the ideas are contributed from one side, it is impossible for an employer to know if he is doing everything he can for his people. Unions call your attention to things you will never notice.'

Given that United was able to achieve adequate profits, Patterson was a 'people oriented' businessman. In the 1950s, way before their time had come, he introduced a company-assisted employee share scheme. Though its active life seems to have lasted for hardly more than six years, it is clear evidence of the direction of his thinking. The same is true of his company pension plan, the first in the industry. He made his business philosophy quite explicit in what he wrote and said: 'The balance sheet of United Airlines places no dollar and cents value on our employees, but in my opinion they represent the most important asset the company has on its books.'

Evidently he had a habit of speaking about the company as if it were a responsible moral person rather than just a corporate entity. My second quote is if anything even more striking: 'I keep asking myself what kind of *person* is United Airlines.'

Patterson goes on to offer as his answer what he thinks it *ought* to be: 'A man who devotes the best years of his life to United is entitled to the assurance that the company, next to his family, is his best friend in time of need.'

And yet it would be a great mistake to think of Patterson as soft. Indeed he stood up to a pilots' strike and won. The contrast in this respect with Dick Ferris, his successor but two in the top post, could scarcely be sharper.

George Keck was hand-picked by Patterson from United's more youthful senior managers to succeed him. He was unlucky in the timing of his appointment. It coincided with the coming into service of the big new jumbo jets, which brought altogether new levels of overcapacity. Most of the country's top airlines started losing money. Keck was also unlucky in that during his innings United lost its near-monopoly position for flights between the West Coast and Hawaii.

For our puposes here, the Keck years are important for two reasons. The first is the losses sustained during them – which partly explain the degree of priority assigned by his successor to making profits. The second is that his final year marked the first step in a new policy of diversification into non-airline tourist businesses. In 1970, using the mechanism of a complex exchange of shares, the airline effectively took over Western International Hotels. What is more, when they sacked George Keck the board of directors offered the post to the man who was the hotel chain's chief executive, Edward Carlson.

By eliminating unprofitable routes and 'downsizing' manpower, **Carlson** succeeded in returning the business to profit in fairly quick time. The airline had run up losses of roughly $50m. in Keck's final year, 1970. The next three years saw a turnaround. 1971 . . . $5m loss; 1972 . . . $20m profit; 1973 . . . $51m profit.

Carlson's main goal was 'to make United the industry leader in effective profit ratios and the leader in earnings' (Johnson, *Airway One,* p. 182). Fair enough. Businessmen like the UK's Lord Hanson have adopted much the same goals with some success. But Patterson's stated goal – to make United the *best* airline – was rather different. Moreover it is hard to believe that Carlson's 'downsizing' exercise endeared him to the United unions.

But perhaps the biggest single factor in this analysis of why what happened happened at United, rather than elsewhere the pilots' pride in their profession. It is impossible not to believe that the pilots resented having a hotel man in the top position. From the thinking of the influential United pilot and successful ALPA strike leader, Rick Dubinsky, we know that there was strong pilot hostility to the policy of non-airline investments which had been started by George Keck and was continued by his two successors. What I am now suggesting is that the pilots may well also have resented the passing of the airline's leadership to a man from the hotel trade. It is true that much later their candidate for the top position, Jerry Greenwald, came from Chrysler, and not from the industry. But Greenwald's well-known sympathy with labour was sufficient to outweigh the negative factor of his non-industry background.

At Western International Hotels, Carlson had reached the top entirely through his own efforts. **Dick Ferris,** by contrast, was essentially a Carlson creation. As a young hotel manager he had caught Carlson's eye. Moreover it was Carlson, when he took over the top post at United, who invited Ferris to join him at the airline and become the manager of its kitchens and in-flight catering services. Finally, it was on Carlson's recommendation that United's board of directors accepted Ferris as Carlson's successor. He was then less than forty.

Two trends stand out in Dick Ferris's thirteen-year reign from 1974 to 1987. Each culminated in dramatic events. The first was the ever-increasing competition which followed President Carter's deregulation of the domestic American airline industry at the end of the 1970s. That was the key factor behind the dramatic pilots' strike which was courted by Ferris in 1985 and then lost by him. The second was an extension by Ferris of the policy of diversifying into non-airline tourist industry businesses which had been started by George Keck in 1970 and then continued by Carlson. The extension of that policy precipitated two dramatic events in quick succession: the first ALPA attempt at a buy-out of the business in 1987, and then, no more than weeks later, successful pressure by 'investors' to remove Ferris from his top post and to unwind all, or almost all, of the diversification which had taken place.

Partly because they had a big influence on the 1994 deal, the key specifics of the 1985 strike are worth spelling out. The airline had come to be faced by increasingly ferocious competition on its short haul routes especially in California and the south west, where Southwest Airlines was its main competitor. Though it was in fact at that time more, rather than less, unionised than UAL, Southwest had substantially lower pilot costs. So too, on its shorthaul flights, had American Airlines. Here Robert Crandall, Ferris's counterpart as CEO and arch-rival, had achieved a breakthrough deal some years before with his unionised, though non-ALPA, pilots: a two tier wage system such that pilots flying short haul services were paid significantly less than what had previously been the going rate for the job. What precipitated the 1985 strike at United was an attempt by Richard Ferris to impose on its pilots a long term two-tier wage scheme on lines similar to those negotiated by Robert Crandall. He failed. But it is also true that United's pilots had accepted such an arrangement, on a short term basis, even before they came out on strike. What is more, that arrangement was in fact incorporated into the final strike settlement.

The pilots' success in their 1985 strike can have left them in no doubt of their power at United when they chose to play in their labour union role. It is a fair bet that Dick Ferris was a poor loser: 'Dick Ferris displayed all the caveman aggression that gripped Bob Crandall – the impatience for victory, the compulsion for control, the desire to dominate.' (Petzinger, p. 64.)

Ferris's subsequent sortie into major new acquisitions should be seen at least in part as a 'rebound response' to having lost the strike of 1985. In quick succession in late 1985 and in early 1986, he bought first Hertz, the car rental business, and then the Hilton hotel chain. United paid just under $600m for Hertz and approximately $1bn for the Hilton hotels. Huge sums of money were borrowed to finance these deals. On the other hand, given the prices at which they were later sold on, Dick Ferris is entitled to claim that they were bargain buys. Nevertheless these acquisitions were made at the expense of new investments in the actual airline businesses. This was the light in which they were fundamentally seen by Rick Dubinsky, the highly influential ALPA member at United who had been a key figure in the leadership of its great strike.

By Dick Ferris they were evidently seen as the major building blocks of a vast tripodic travel empire which would circle the world with its international airline routes and spread out all over it with hotels and hire cars. Every kind of wonderful 'synergy' was foreseen, and with advice from appropriate consultants the new 'vision' was even given a new name: the Allegis Corporation. Ferris was apparently 'thinking less and less about airplanes. He still had the number one airline, and on top of that the number one car rental outfit and the number one hotel chain in the world. As he later put it, "We were ready to own the world."'

It was not to be. Here indeed we may reasonably suggest that, as with David Behncke in the early 1950s, so with Dick Ferris in the middle 1980s, his Goliath-sized ego caused his downfall.

First it blinded him into a making a grave misjudgement about his own and ALPA's relative staying power in a trial of strength. He provoked ALPA, the labour union, into a strike which he lost. Second, his vision of 'empire' and the non-airline businesses which he acquired in pursuit of it, brought ALPA back on to the stage. But this time, in 1987, ALPA was playing its other role – as an airline industry statesman; and it was bidding to buy the business in order to save it from Ferris's imperial dreams.

That bid was not itself a success. Nevertheless it was a key stage in a process which led to a revolt by United's leading shareholders. They insisted that Ferris resign, that Hertz and the hotels be sold, and that a big part of the proceeds of sale be returned to shareholders.

THE WOLF YEARS: 1987–94

After an interregnum of a few months, and a search on both sides of the Atlantic, Stephen Wolf was brought in to the top executive position in the autumn of 1987. He was the third man to be offered the post, after Sir Colin Marshall at British Airways and Robert Crandall at American Airlines. Nevertheless, he is understood to have had the strong backing of the United director who became responsible in its later stages for leading the search for a successor: none other than the celebrated and moon-landing astronaut, Neil Armstrong. The deal agreed between the two men included options for Wolf over 250,000 UAL shares.

At the time of his appointment it was his industry experience rather than those options which were important. His instructions were to sell the non-airline travel businesses – the hotel chains and the Hertz car rental operation – which had been acquired under his three predecessors, and then concentrate all his energies on the airline itself.

Stephen Wolf was in fact a top industry professional having served a fifteen-year apprenticeship in senior positions at American Airlines. He had also built up something of a reputation for toughness: for having successfully carried through a number of wage and manpower reduction exercises. It was on these episodes that the pilots at United chose particularly to focus. The ALPA organisation at United was hostile to him from the start, partly because of his toughness and partly because many of them remained strongly committed to a pilot-led buy-out and saw the new top executive as an obstacle in the way of realising that goal. There was probably at least an undertow of pilot hostility to him throughout his seven years at United, and that notwithstanding the fact that in 1989 he joined ALPA in a failed buy-out attempt which he had been persuaded to lead.

At the low point of its fortunes in the ALPA strike year of 1985, the business made a loss of just under $50m on a turnover of some $5.25bn. By the end of 1988, the first full year of Wolf's watch, the results showed a dramatic turnaround to record profits of over $1.1bn. In between, the new chief executive had successfully sold off Hertz, the Hilton chain and the other hotels. The accounts for 1988 include a second dramatic number as well as the best ever profits. They show shareholders equity at just $1,226m, down from $2,922m in 1987. The non-airline businesses had been sold well and substantial capital gains had been returned to shareholders.

The 1989 Buy-Out Attempt: Stephen Wolf Joins ALPA At least as early as the 1985 strike, United's pilots had started to argue that investment in the airline was being starved to free up finance for the purchase of non-airline businesses. The return to shareholders of substantial capital gains resulting from the sale of Hertz and the hotels must surely have strengthened the position of those in the union who argued for a buy-out. For they became entitled to assert that unless and until ALPA had a main voice at the top table, the long-term interests of the airline were liable to be put behind those of financial 'investors'.

ALPA's determination to acquire a big say in strategic decision making was one factor behind the buy-out attempt of 1989. The other was an unsolicited $5.4bn bid for United which surfaced from a Californian 'investor', Marvin Davis, in the summer of 1989. It had the effect, if nothing else, of concentrating minds at United's headquarters outside Chicago: Stephen Wolf was persuaded to join forces with ALPA in an attempted 'internal' buy-out of the business which, if successful, would have taken the airline private under his leadership.

With an infusion of $750m. provisionally promised by Sir Colin Marshall at British Airways, Wolf and United's pilots put together a prospective offer of just under $7bn. It exceeded Davis's earlier bid by a comfortable margin and was indeed provisionally approved and accepted by the board of directors. On the other hand, it was to be massively financed by debt: by borrowings from banks scattered across the world, but with disproportionate involvement by banks in Japan.

On Friday 13 October 1989 the Japanese banks withdrew from the deal. The provisional bid put forward by United's ALPA members and Wolf instantly unwound. United's pilots tried yet again to mount a bid in the autumn of 1990 – this time on their own. Partly because of the nervousness which had followed Iraq's invasion of Kuwait, it proved impossible to raise the necessary finance. However, this third buy-out attempt by the pilots had one important legacy. They approached Gerald Greenwald and made him a conditional offer of the post of chief executive – conditional on the implementation of a pilot-led buy-out, then or later.

Increasing Competitive Pressures: 1989 to the Buy-Out Deal From their high point of $1,124m at the end of Wolf's first year, United's profits (net earnings) fell in each of the four years to 1992. There was something of a rebound in 1993, but not enough to return the airline to profit.

Results: Profits & Losses over Six Years to 1993. $m.

1988	Profit 1,124	1991	Loss 331
1989	Profit 324	1992	Loss 957
1990	Profit 94	1993	Loss 50

During the very difficult years of the early 1990s, United's performance was slightly less bad than the average. Nevertheless its huge 1992 losses of nearly $1 billion made the need for radical change inescapable.

Apart from general overcapacity and the effects of the Iraqi invasion of Kuwait, United faced a particular threat from Southwest Airlines, especially in California. Southwest had just a 2% share of the California market in 1988. That had grown to 47% by 1993. United's share of that market also increased but much less dramatically – from 14% in 1988 to 26% in 1993. Moreover, whereas United showed a loss on its West Coast operations at least from 1991 to 1993, its main rival in the region was continuously profitable. In competition with Southwest, the United cost base, at least down to the 1994 buy-out, was well out of line.

The biggest single element in United's higher costs was almost certainly that associated with paying its pilots. After adjusting for the longer hours flown by the latter, its pilots in California are understood to have been roughly 50% more expensive than Southwest's.

Wolf and his top management team made as their first proposal a $400m cost reduction plan. It included job reductions in the low thousands but did not touch the pilots.

It soon became clear that those measures would not be sufficient. At this point, in the early months of 1993, Wolf opened discussions about tougher measures with all the unions at United and especially with ALPA. The pilots reacted sharply:

'Downsizing', Roger Hall of ALPA told Wolf, 'means war'. It would be one of the most cataclysmic wars ever, Hall vowed. It would make the pilots' strike of 1985 look like a warm-up act. Hall warned Wolf that he had no idea how bad it could get: 'You've never been involved in one of those and I have.' [Petzinger.]

Given ALPA's victory in 1985, we must assume that the threat was not lightly dismissed. In any case soon afterwards the management switched from an active role in the resolution of the crisis to a more reactive one. In June 1993 it agreed to discuss with ALPA and the other unions the pilots' old scheme for an employee buy-out of the business. In putting forward this scheme once again, ALPA's leaders evidently indicated to Wolf that the sacrifices he was looking for might just be acceptable if enough stock could be offered in return and if there could be appropriate guarantees of employment security.

And that – as we know – was more or less the bargain which was eventually struck. Moreover, given the magnitude of the issues and the unprecedentedly high numbers, the negotiations between the parties which made the bargain possible seem, with just two main qualifications, to have been rather smooth. The only other main characteristic of the bargaining process will scarcely surprise many readers: the early offers to the United's existing shareholders had to be substantially raised.

There were two significant hitches. First, in the early autumn the cabin staff, organised in the Association of Flight Attendants (AFA), decided to withdraw. For one thing the AFA membership already had two pre-agreed annual wage increases of 4% in the pipeline. Those would have to have been forgone, as part of an agreed reduction, had the union remained within the deal. The AFA was also in dispute with United's management on at least two specific issues. The first was the recruitment of non-US attendants at a number of overseas centres to service selected international routes, and the second a set of weight restriction rules which were later lifted.

Mr Kevin Lum was the AFA's President at the time, and still held that position when this was written. He argues that the first of these issues was a specially serious problem for the union and its members because it had 'resulted in real job losses and greatly diminished earning power for flight attendants who have been long time United employees'. As for the weight restrictions which were later lifted, Lum sees them as a 'classic example of disparity between how flight attendants were treated at work versus the rest of them'. He argues that they were not the only example of relative discrimination against flight attendants.

Third, though the influence of this has been more inferred than demonstrated, the relatively low wages of the flight attendants are thought to have made wage reductions that much less acceptable to their members than was the case for members of ALPA and the IAM. For the record, the AFA fully accepts that the pay of many United employees in the non-union group is substantially lower than that of its own members.

Lum also criticises the two other unions. He claims that there was an understanding from the outset that the possible buy-out was a 'union coalition' project and that therefore if any one of the three unions felt obliged to withdraw, the other two would follow suit. Neither ALPA nor the IAM accept this claim.

The second hitch should perhaps be better described as a crisis. It involved not the AFA but the machinists, and it came close to derailing the whole negotiating process in November 1993 – only weeks before the approval of the provisional deal in December. Management announced a unilateral and non-negotiable decision to sell the airline's flight kitchens. An enormous number of IAM members, just over 5,000, were affected, and in consequence the whole buy-out project seemed to be briefly at risk. But as it was, the negotiations survived the crisis. It should also be put on the record that when the final deal was eventually signed it included higher redundancy payments for the luckless former kitchen staff.

Especially perhaps for the benefit of union readers in Britain, it is worth commenting briefly on the involvement of the IAM in this whole employee ownership project at United. It need hardly be emphasised that despite the very high skill levels of its aircraft maintenance membership, the IAM is a much more 'normal' union than ALPA. What is more, on each of the three earlier ALPA attempts at a buy-out of United, the IAM had said a firm and unequivocal 'No, thank you' when invited by the pilots to take part. If we ask why their leaders agreed to be involved on this occasion, the answer is both important and in no serious doubt. They judged that a combination of the prospective employment security and a voice in the top decision-making body would justify a deal if the right terms could be agreed. Evidently, if only by a small margin, this judgement survived the sacrifice of IAM members' jobs in United's former kitchens.

So much for the IAM. What of the bargaining process itself? In the formal document which went to existing shareholders and which is called in America a 'Proxy Statement/Joint Prospectus', there are brief references to the main stages of the process. What they show is that the 'coalition' of United's unions had to increase its earlier offers very substantially before agreement was eventually reached. At the start this applied to all three, but after the AFA's withdrawal, only to ALPA and the IAM. For example, on 11 November, a proposal presented by ALPA and the IAM is reported as having had a nominal value of \$3.496bn and a so-called net present value (at a 9% discount rate) of \$2.874bn. By contrast, as we know in the deal which was finally completed, the net present value of what was put on the table by the two unions and the non-union group together was \$4.886bn. That was on the basis of a 10% rather than a 9% discount rate. In pushing for that higher figure, those who represented the interests of the existing shareholders insisted, according to the prospectus-type document, on a 'key requirement in any transaction involving the transfer of control: to deliver an appropriate premium over market to the holders of old shares in a transaction that was fair to such stockholders'.

It only remains to be noted that in the final and critical stages of the bargaining process a key contribution was evidently made by Felix Rohatyn, a senior partner in the New York investment bank of Lazard Frères. As some readers will know, Mr Rohatyn is probably the most distinguished member of America's top financial community to have come out publicly and forcefully in favour of the widespread promotion of employee ownership and profit sharing. His bank has also had a hand in a number of the most important employee ownership deals in America since the early 1980s.

Rohatyn's involvement in the final stages of the bargaining

process is a detail. But it was clearly important at the time. From a public relations and political viewpoint, it will continue to be so. But in any event a provisional buy-out deal was approved by the United board of directors on 21 December 1993. Effectively it offered over 50% of the corporation's voting equity, embodied in special voting preference shares, to a combination of members of the two unions which had stayed in the negotiations – ALPA and the IAM – and the airline's non-union staff. The share capital was offered in return for wages and other concessions estimated to have a prospective 'net present value' of about $4.886bn. The prospective employee owners were also offered solid employment guarantees through the approximately six-year lifespan of the main deal, and voices at the top table for a much longer time.

Between the provisional deal approved by the board of directors in December 1993 and the one completed in July 1994 there was perhaps one significant change, though it was evidently not too problematic. The percentage of the United stock to be acquired unconditionally by its employees was increased on the margin: from 53% to 55%. There were also some small changes in what was almost up to the last minute a package of money and securities offered to the existing owners in return for the reduction of their equity stake from 100% to 45%. But these latter are understood to have been essentially technical adjustments. For the record we should note that in the deal that was actually completed the existing shareholders, apart from their shares in the 'recapitalised' business, received just cash rather than the combination of cash and loan notes originally proposed.

We will set out the main details of the transaction in the next section. But here it is worth offering a comment or two on what might be called its ideology. The first is that it was evidently not popular with sections of what might be called the conventional capitalist establishment – for example with editorial writers on the *Wall Street Journal* and the London *Economist*. Conversely it was most popular with the ALPA pilots' organisation at United and its members. This is scarcely surprising given that an ALPA led buy-out had been a semi-explicit goal of the pilots for nearly ten years and that they were the prime movers behind the whole process.

We should note finally that in the case of ALPA the deal was approved by a comfortable majority of its so-called Master Executive Council at United. The ALPA leadership was evidently sufficiently confident of its members' support not to go for a members' vote. On the other hand, in the case of the IAM a vote was taken among the members. The total numbers in favour were in a majority but by only a small margin. The result was indeed later challenged and the challenge only seen off with some difficulty.

THE DEAL

Within a close [emphasis added] range, what are the employees going to be paying for this stock which should have a street value of approximately $85 per share?

... While it is our view that the employees in the aggregate are paying more than $1.00 of investment for $1.00 of stock (based on the Company's going-in projection of $85.00 per share of stock), there are a number of non-pecuniary benefits received by the employees, such as job security and governance provisions, the value of which it is impossible to quantify.

The above was one of a series of questions and part of the answer included with the information circulated to ALPA and IAM members with the letter of 22 December 1993, signed by Captain Hall and Mr Thiede, and quoted in this case study's epigraph.

Whether we call the transaction an 'employee buy-out' or a 'plan of recapitalisation', or indeed a hybrid, its logic and its arithmetic will only be understood if readers keep three key considerations in the front of their minds:

– When a business is basically strong, then, compared with the going price of its shares in public markets, the purchaser of a controlling interest must expect to pay a premium.

– Other things being equal, the premium will be that much higher if the original initiative for the transaction comes from the prospective buyer.

– Existing holders of what will become a minority interest, may favour the application of a part of the value put up by the buyers to a strengthening of the capital base of the ongoing business – rather than to an increase in the cash price they receive for the shares due to be sold by them under the deal.

The key to understanding this unusually complex hybrid deal – part buy-out and part recapitalisation – is, I think, in the last of those three points. Looked at from the viewpoint of the employee buyers, there is the $4.886bn of net present value which they eventually put on the bargaining table and which persuaded the existing shareholders to approve the deal.

On the other hand only a part of that $4.886bn was in fact transferred directly to the existing shareholders in a package which, for each of their old shares, combined a cash payment with a half share in the stock of the recapitalised business. The balance of the $4.886bn of value brought to the table by the employee shareholder buyers was not transferred to the sellers but is being – or will be – reinvested in the business for the benefit of both the business and the whole shareholder body. Using this breakdown, we might reasonably characterise that part of the value transfer that went to existing shareholders as a 'buy out', and the balance as a recapitalisation exercise.

It is an essentially linguistic and therefore trivial point whether we say that what the employee shareholders 'paid' for their shares was the whole of that $4.886bn of net present value which they brought to the table, or alternatively only that part of it which was of direct benefit to the existing shareholders and of benefit to them alone. What is more important is the breakdown of the $4.886bn into those two analytically separate components.

Against this background, we can now go on to look at some of the main numbers associated with the transaction.

Some 28.9m of United's old shares were outstanding when the deal was completed. As against that number the deal provided that trustees acting for the new employee shareholders would acquire a total of 17,675,345 new shares in the recapitalised business, representing 55% of its voting capital. That actual number of new shares was arrived at essentially by arithmetic. If half of the old 28.9m shares are to account for 45% of the shares in the recapitalised business, then the number of shares which corresponds to 55% is 17,675,345.

It remains to put a value on the package of cash and a half share in the recapitalised business for which the existing shareholders exchanged each of their old shares. In round figures and on the basis of the opening price at which the new shares were traded in July of 1994, the value was $130 per old share, of which roughly two thirds was the cash component.

For the record and for what it is worth we are now in a position to offer two alternative answers to the epigraph's question: 'What are employees going to be paying for this stock which should have a street value of approximately $85 per share?'

We get one answer to that question if we take the view that what the employees 'paid' for their 55% stakeholding in the recapitalised business was the whole of the $4.886bn of net present value which they eventually brought to the table. In that case, by dividing the $4.886bn number by those 17,675,345 shares we come out with a figure of roughly $277 per share.

On the other hand, if we take the view that what the employees paid was only that part of the $4.886bn needed to provide for the $130 of value with which, for each of their old shares, the existing shareholders emerged from the deal, then, of course, what the employees 'paid' for their shares was that much lower – something like $3.7bn in total and something over $200 per share.

If we have to choose between the two answers, there is a further specific argument which favours the second and lower pair of numbers. The deal provides that all the employee shares will be allocated to individuals by the end of the year 2000. But some key concessions in the make up of the $4.886bn will still at that date have a further six years to run.

Before going further we need a better understanding of the concept of 'net present value' (NPV). In the technical language of accountants the $4.886bn figure represents the *discounted* NPV, on the date of the transaction's completion, of the agreed employees 'investment'. The latter is a combination of the wage reductions accepted by them and of the other 'concessions' that they agreed to offer.

For those not fully at home with accountants' language, I hope a brief word of further explanation will suffice. The same table in the prospectus document which is the source of the $4.886bn estimate of the NPV, also offers a second big number: viz. the sum of all the money values year by year which are to be given up by the employees over the duration of the deal. That second number is not $4.886bn but $8.190bn. With minor qualifications the second number is reduced to the first by applying a progressive discount of 10% to the annual totals after year one. The amount of the discount was settled by negotiation but was also taken to reflect the weighted average cost to the business of the capital employed by it. Readers with a taste for detail may like to know that the then weighted average capital cost at United reflected a relatively small percentage of high cost equity and a much larger percentage of lower cost debt. This is the standard method of valuing 'future money' for the purposes of a transaction completed on a particular date. There can be arguments about whether the 10% discount rate was fair. Indeed the unions predictably argued for 9%. That would have increased the NPV of their wage cuts and other concessions. On the opposite side, others predictably argued for 11%. There can be reasonable disagreement about which discount rate most closely reflected the relevant realities. But no one could reasonably quarrel with the method used to make the valuation.

We will turn back just once more to the question about what the employees are paying for their stock raised in the epigraph. As we have seen, the two union leaders conceded in their letter that 'it is our view that the employees in the aggregate are paying more than $1.00 of investment for $1.00 of stock (based on the company's going in number of $85 of stock).'

But Captain Hall and Mr Thiede are careful in their subsequent discussion not to offer a numerical answer to the question at all. Instead the discussion introduces an array of qualifications, with the implicit aim of persuading the reader that the answer should not simply – and crudely – be found by setting the NPV of the employee concessions against the total number of shares acquired, and then reaching a price per share by long division. The qualifications were:

– That the number of shares to be purchased was not yet known.

– That valuing the employee concessions was an inexact exercise.

– That it was hard to be sure what alternative might have been on offer if the proposed transaction had fallen through.

– That in addition to the actual shares they were 'buying' with their wage reductions and other concessions, the employees also stood to benefit from 'a number of non-pecuniary benefits . . . such as (i) security and (ii) governance provisions'.

It makes sense to look at these briefly in turn.

About the first we are now in a position to take into account what actually happened within a range of possibilities set out in a formula contained in the July 1994 agreement. The range reflected different views, as between the company and the unions, about the evolution of the price of the new shares which would be traded on Wall Street after the deal.

Predictably the unions expressed their belief in a higher, and the

company in a lower price trajectory. What was agreed in negotiation was that if, in the twelve months after the deal's completion, the average price of the new shares exceeded $136, then the
$4.886bn of NPV committed to the transaction would buy more
than just 55% of the shares in the new stock. A sliding scale was in
fact agreed such that in the limiting case – reached if the average
share price over the first twelve months was to exceed $149.10 – the
55% would jump to 63%. However, as it turned out, and though
the price of the new shares later climbed rapidly higher, the condition of exceeding the average price threshold of $136 agreed for the
first twelve months was not met. And so, retrospectively, the first
qualification fell away.

The second and third qualifications are about two separate difficulties: of putting a precise value on the employee concessions;
and of comparing what is proposed with any alternative. In both,
the concern again is to persuade the questioner that the employees
are not being required to pay too much for their shares. One possible rejoinder in the first case is that the qualifications may cut
either way. The estimated value put on the employee concessions
may be too low as well as too high.

The qualification about the problem of comparing what is
proposed with whatever might be the most likely 'non-deal'
alternative is harder to evaluate convincingly. It is true that any
alternative would almost certainly have involved compulsory
redundancies. For example, at Delta Airlines, as we know, redundancies were imposed on between 10% and 15% of the total
workforce. To that extent what we may in part be dealing with here
is the security of employment offered by the deal to which we move
on next. For the rest the reference to an alternative 'base case', and
to the difficulty of assessing it, may in part reflect no more than the
strong commitment of the ALPA leadership to the proposed deal.

Pursuing the qualifications, the sceptical commentator might
even offer a 'could cut either way' rejoinder to the penultimate one:
namely the extra employment security which will be enjoyed by the
participants as a result of the deal. My point is that given the
resulting reduction in the sources of possible management/labour
disagreement, the 'bottom line' of the business, as well as the
individual employee shareholders, may benefit from the new levels
of employment security.

We are left with the final qualification in the response in the union leaders' letter to the key question: 'What price are the employees being asked to pay for the shares?'

This last is about what are called – perhaps a little quaintly – the 'governance provisions' in the deal: that is the provisions under which each of the two unions, and the non-union employee group, are to be represented on the board of directors and to have considerable other influence at board level as well. The provisions were flagged in the introduction. They are set out alongside other details at the end.

Put more robustly, this last qualification about the price paid by the employees for their shares, has to do with a 'control premium' which must be assumed to figure in a price which has to be paid for a shareholding in an essentially strong business, which confers control. In a business of the kind that United was in 1994, this premium would be significant as well as positive. We may remember too an important passage in the prospectus document where it reviews the bargaining process which led up to the deal, which was quoted earlier. This passage explicitly points up the requirement of a control premium. Prospectus readers are told of 'a key requirement in any transaction involving the transfer of control: to deliver an appropriate premium over market to the holders of old shares in a transaction that was fair to such stockholders'.

Given the earlier breakdown of the NPV of the employee concessions – into what was needed to cover the compensation to the existing shareholders and a reinvested balance – it seems to me impossible to make any persuasive estimate of the size of whatever was the control premium in this case.

In any event, it is clearly not possible to be sure that the existing shareholders could have been persuaded to do a deal in return for substantially less in the way of concessions than what was actually given up. Moreover, once the deal was agreed it became in a sense true by definition that the premium embedded in it – whatever that was – was simply what the 'market', essentially the existing shareholders, had demanded.

We may conclude this discussion about what the employees 'paid' for their shares by allowing for the possibility that there is likely to be a different emphasis in the answer offered to different groups. For a financial community audience, it must make obvious sense to put the emphasis on just how much was being paid, on *how reasonable* from the viewpoint of the sellers was the offer from the buyers, and *not* to subject the headline number of $4.886bn to a host of qualifications.

On the other hand, when the question is being answered for an audience of the buyers – of ALPA and IAM members and of the non-union employee group – the emphasis is likely to be different. To the buyers the deal needs to be defended against the charge that they are paying too much. So there will be an inevitable tendency to stress the qualifications to the headline number.

I come on next to three further and more or less general aspects of the deal. The small print details, to repeat, are spelt out at the end of this chapter.

The first was already flagged in the introduction and is reasonably straightforward. In shorthand it is referred to as the 'snap back' question: whether the deal provides for the wage reductions, and other concessions contributed by the employees, to be restored at the end of the deal's duration – that is at the end of either five years and nine months or six years in the case of the major sacrifices, and of twelve years in the case of the subsidiary ones.

As readers already know in a general way, the original answer to the 'snap back' question was radically changed in the agreement which eventually emerged from the 'mid-term wage adjustment process'; and was then ratified in a vote by the membership of the company's two ESOP unions, the pilots and machinists. Under that agreement the company became committed to restore the pre-ESOP wage rates once the duration of the main deal finishes in the year 2000. There will then, at minimum, be an automatic 'snap back' of the main wage cuts.

Up to the time of that 'mid-term' agreement there was no such commitment on the part of the company and thus no guarantee of a 'snap back'. But the change, which is certainly seen by the ALPA leadership as being of great psychological and political importance, is not quite the end of the story. For our purposes here it is enough to say that the automatic 'snap back' agreed in March 1997 does not apply to the set of subsidiary concessions which figured in the 1994 deal and which extend in time to 2006. For the pilots those concessions include the rates paid and hours flown on the 'Shuttle'. In the absence of further negotiated changes, these will remain below the fully 'snapped back' rates by the same percentage margin as provided in the original deal. For the machinists these longer term concessions include the continued giving up of their pre-1994 paid lunch break and an important concession about outsourcing: up to a 20% maximum of maintenance work out-sourced until 2006.

Second, it is necessary to say a word about mechanics: how shares in the business reach the participating employees. What are initially allocated to employees are not shares in UAL's common stock but preferred shares which, however, also carry a vote. Normally preferred shares enjoy votes only in narrowly defined circumstances. On the other hand, in line with common practice, these preferred shares in United attract dividends year by year, but dividends in this case not in money but in the form of additional preferred shares. Dividend shares are allocated annually after the first year to the value of 8.89% of the accumulated balance of an employees' shareholding. For the rest only when an employee shareholder retires or leaves for other reasons are his or her preferred shares converted into shares in UAL's common stock. One main reason for this cumbersome process is tax efficiency.

But we should also acknowledge that these arrangements offer a quite unambiguous link between the ownership interest of United's employee shareholders and the value of the shares in the com-pany's common stock on the date when the conversion from their preferred stock takes place. The total numbers of the preferred which may be distributed under the deal in a combination of straight allocations and dividends is, as we know, fixed at the figure of 17,675,345 already identified several times.

Up to the time of writing the price of the shares in the cor-responding United common stock had easily outperformed those in other competing airlines. Moreover, in May 1996 each of the original shares had been split into four. In the absence of a major future price fall, the employee shareholders will convert their preferred shares at a dollar price way above the notional value of the preferred shares when the deal was completed. Those prospec-tive gains, provided they remain secure, will do much to mitigate criticism of the 1994 deal to the effect that the 'price' paid by the employees was too high.

But we still have to raise one more big question: who has benefited from the ESOP tax reliefs associated with the 1994 transaction? Given that those reliefs over the period of the main employee concessions are estimated to apply to accounting charges of some $4bn, the way that the tax reliefs have been treated in the deal is clearly not a marginal issue.

Here again a word of explanation may be helpful for lay readers. What is involved is the company receiving a tax relief relating to an 'approved accounting charge' which is not a cash payment. In this case United is able to claim a tax relief for 'payments' which it makes each year to the ESOP trustees to enable them to buy shares for employees. These, however, are then immediately returned by the trustees in exchange for shares purchased. So what is involved here is simply a set of book entries or 'accounting charges' with no actual cash payments at all. However, in cases of approved payments of this kind to ESOP trustees, American tax law allows companies to treat these 'charges' as if they were actual cash payments.

It may also be helpful to spell out how exactly the tax relief works and what it amounts to. There are three key points to grasp. The first is that the accounting charges are not themselves the same as the tax reliefs. The reliefs are just 40% of the charges – namely the amount of extra corporation tax which would have had to be paid in their absence. The second is that the accounting charges theoretically finance the purchase for employees of those preferred shares which we identified earlier. Third, the size of the charges from which United is permitted to benefit will vary in part with its share price: the higher the share price, then the higher the 'accounting charges' from which the company may benefit, although under the country's ESOP laws there is a maximum 'accounting' charge for which a business may claim benefit.

The Harvard 1995 study projects what then seemed to be the likely amounts of these accounting charges over the six-year life of the deal's main provisions. The assumptions on which the projected numbers were based have partly been overtaken since then. Nevertheless they will help readers to understand the orders of magnitude of what is involved.

Non-Cash ESOP Accounting Charges: Projections Years 1 to 6

Year 1	Year 2	Year 3	Year 4	Year 5	Year 6
619	630	642	662	689	532

The projections enable us to have a useful order of magnitude estimate of the value of the associated ESOP tax reliefs over the six-year period. Added together, the six-year total of these projected charges comes to $3,774m. The corresponding tax relief, at 40% of that number, comes to just over $1,500m.

We are now in a position to understand rather more clearly the answer to the question posed earlier: who benefits from these substantial, $1,500m-odd, ESOP tax reliefs?

The short answer is that both the employee shareholders *and* the business benefit from these reliefs.

The letter from Captain Hall and Mr Thiede to union members from which I have already quoted more than once, is reassuring on this point. It tells its readers that the 'ESOP tax savings' are 'implicitly' recognised in the method used to value the employee investment. What they wrote is worth quoting:

> Q How was the $4 billion of ESOP tax savings factored into the value of our participation?
> A The ESOP tax savings are implicitly recognised in the method used to value the employee investment. Pre-tax, rather than after tax, cash flows were used to calculate the value of the employee investment. The employees were thus given credit for their concession as though those concessions did not represent taxable income to the company. If the ESOP tax shield was not available, the employee investments would be worth approximately 40% less to the company than the pre-tax cash flows.

To understand how that is so, we need to remind ourselves of three related points. If wages are cut by a fixed amount and all other variables are held constant, then profits will increase by the same amount; so the profit tax liability will go up correspondingly; and so the after tax savings will be less than the pre-tax values of the wage reductions.

On the other hand in this case the projected ESOP tax reliefs are roughly the same as the increase in the profit tax liability which is the crude 'first time round result' of the main wage reductions.

Here now, for the record, are the employee investment savings projected in the same Harvard Business school study over the period of the deal's first six years. All have been estimated on a pre-tax basis.

Projected Value of Employee 'Investment Savings'

Year 1	Year 2	Year 3	Year 4	Year 5	Year 6
564	673	774	813	838	793

In the absence any offsetting ESOP tax reliefs, the after tax value of these savings to United would be reduced by 40%. As it is the value of the projected ESOP tax reliefs roughly equals the extra tax due on the projected values of the employee concessions. That is what lies behind the assurance offered to union members in the December 1993 letter from Captain Hall and Mr Thiede: 'The ESOP tax savings are implicitly recognised in the method used to value the employee savings.'

MAJORITY EMPLOYEE OWNERSHIP: THE FIRST TWO AND A HALF YEARS

For the second consecutive year, UAL posted record full-year earnings, with 1996 fully distributed net earnings surpassing the $1 billion mark. *United Airlines 'Fact Sheet', 28 January 1997*

Readers will be looking for provisional answers to a number of questions from this final section:

– Given that the financial results were apparently the best ever, how have they compared with reasonable expectations before the deal's completion?

– What were the main sources of the improved financial performance and were the benefits fairly distributed among those who contributed to success?

– How significant, especially for the prospects of continued majority employee ownership, was the January 1997 rejection of the mid-term wage adjustment as originally proposed?

– Following the rejection of those proposals, how reasonable were union criticisms about management's failure to 'change the culture'?

– After nearly three years, should majority employee ownership be counted a success? Or was the London *Economist* right to imply in early January of 1997 that the sooner this experiment can be phased out, the better for everyone?

– Has United sustained its commitment to near total employment security over the life of the main deal? More generally, how does its recent employment record compare with the experience at other airlines?

At least up to the end of 1996, the cost savings associated with both the main labour concessions and with the ESOP reliefs were reasonably close to pre-deal projections, though the reliefs were lower than projected in 1994 and 1995 and higher in 1996. Largely because the new services were introduced more slowly than planned, the savings associated with the 'shuttle' were well below the projections. On the other hand there was an important bonus in the shape of higher 'load factors' – that is fewer empty seats – which had a disproportionately positive effect on profits. By contrast, the value of improvements which can be persuasively attributed to more ownership orientated attitudes, though far from negligible, seemed rather modest. That can of course be seen as an opportunity and challenge for the future as well as a criticism.

As important – or indeed perhaps more so – than any of the foregoing was United's employment record over the three years following the deal. According to its own figures, its US-based employment increased by more than 16% and its total numbers by even a bit more:

Employment at United Pre-ESOP and June 1997

	At Home	Abroad	Total
Pre-ESOP	68,862	6,462	75,324
June 1997	80,139	8,359	88,498

It is true that for the different period from end 1993 to end 1996, US Department of Transport figures show a not much better than marginal increase in the numbers of 'full time employment equivalents' at United: from 78,105 to 79,205. No doubt part of the difference is explained by the fact that United's figures count part timers as full units. It is also plausible to argue that the official numbers for end 1993 include those luckless 5,000 members of the machinists' union who were working in the kitchens when they were spun off. However, in another important respect these numbers are most striking. Those at United are in marked contrast to those at Delta and AMR, the two airlines in the US which are most closely comparable with United.

	End 1993	End 1996	Growth/ (Decline)
United	78,105	79,205	1,100
Delta	69,5375	58,839	(10,698)
AMR	91,773	78,902	(12,871)

* Full time equivalents.

The eloquence of the numbers makes comment superfluous.

Savings in Labour Costs The table summarises operating results from 1993 to 1996 and also includes employment costs. Our focus here is on the lower costs associated with the wage cuts in the 1994 deal. For the years 1993 to 1996, spending on 'salaries and related costs' show a gentle fall and then a sharper rebound, though the 1996 figure remains below that for 1993.

All in $m	1996	1995	1994	1993
Operating revenues	16,632	14,943	13,950	13,325
Operating expenses	15,239	14,114	13,429	13,062
Earnings*	1,123	829	521	263
Salaries etc	4,719	4,524	4,679	4,760

*From operations

How can we best arrive at a reasonable estimate of the cost savings which are embodied in these actual figures? My own preferred answer involves estimating what the labour costs would have been if their ratio to a combination of sales and capacity had remained unchanged at 1993 levels, and then comparing those estimates with the actual salaries and related costs shown above.

For the volume of sales, I take the best measure to be what the airlines call 'revenue passenger miles', roughly the number of miles travelled by ticket buying passengers. For capacity I take the best measure to be so called 'available seat miles'.

In 1993 every dollar of labour cost yielded 21.3 revenue passengers miles and 31.65 miles of seat capacity. The table applies these rates to the actual miles flown in each of the subsequent years and then compares the resulting notional labour cost figures with the actual ones recorded above.

	1996	1995	1994	1993
Actual salaries & related costs ($m):	4,719	4,524	4,679	4,760
Revenue passenger miles (bn):	116.7	111.4	108.3	101.3
Labour costs ($m), 21.3 miles per $:	5,479	5,230	5,084	4,760
Estimated savings ($m):	760	706	405	n/a
Available seat miles (bn):	162.8	158.4	152.2	150.7
Labour costs ($m), 31.65 miles per $:	5,152	5,013	4,187	4,760
Estimated savings ($m):	433	489	138	n/a

We may make an estimate therefore of United's aggregate savings on labour costs, between 1994 and 1996. This would fall between $1.06bn, arrived at using the available capacity approach, and the $1.87bn yielded by the alternative revenue seat mile approach. The savings estimate linked to seat capacity takes no account of the load factor improvements which are captured by the alternative revenue seat mile approach.

In the operation of an airline, the link between labour costs and seat capacity is, no doubt, much closer than the links between those same costs and the numbers of seats filled by paying passengers. At most, it is probably reasonable to raise the lower of the two figures by 10% to arrive at what might be called a 'best guesstimate' of the savings actually achieved. That 'best guesstimate' figure would then be around $1.2bn.

I must acknowledge that this whole 'constant ratio' approach to the question of labour cost savings is inescapably rough and ready. There are no precisely constant ratios in fields of this kind. Moreover the changes in the percentage of labour costs not only reflect changes in those costs themselves but also changes in other costs. For example a rise in fuel costs, as in 1996, cannot leave the labour cost percentage unchanged.

How does my 'best guesstimate' of $1.2bn of labour cost savings compare with earlier projections of what they were going to be? The most authoritative projections are in the prospectus document:

Labour Savings Projected in the Prospectus. $m

1994	231
1995	511
1996	591
Total	1,333

I am almost inclined to claim that the two numbers are elegantly close. But that should not perhaps be the source of excessive surprise. After all, these savings in labour costs flowed in a sense 'automatically' from the deal. We know too, as a matter of fact from the testimony of the finance department, that the actual wage reductions embodied in the deal, and forming the largest part of the 'labour savings' total, have been scrupulously followed. There is thus almost a sense in which, at least up to the onset of the mid-term wage adjustment increases, we should in fact *expect* those projections in the prospectus to be more or less echoed by the actual numbers. As for the proviso about the mid-term wage adjustment, it is no more than a footnote. It is apparently the case that the labour savings projections in the prospectus assume a rather smaller wage increase in the mid-term adjustment than what was actually agreed. But that discrepancy will show up in the relationship between the projections and reality only from mid-1997 onwards.

The ESOP Tax Reliefs For the three years 1994 to 1996, the table reproduces the so-called 'ESOP Accounting Charges' shown in United's annual accounts together with my estimates of the associated tax reliefs, taken as being just 40% of the charges.

Actual ESOP Charges & Associated Tax Reliefs. $m

1994	182	73
1995	504	202
1996	685	274
Totals	$1371	$549

The ESOP accounting charges projected in the Harvard study totalled $1.57bn – for the first three years. So for the first two and a half years there is a reasonable correspondence. But there are important differences in the year by year numbers. The key point of explanation is the link between United's share price and the maximum ESOP charges it is allowed to claim. The Harvard study's projections were too high in 1994 and 1995, and too low in 1996.

In summary, two and a half years into the life of the deal, the delivery of its two single most important financial results – its lower wage costs and its ESOP tax reliefs – was pretty well on track. As a bonus there were extra financial improvements, probably worth a much as $400m over the same two and a half year period. These which resulted from higher levels of demand, were precisely reflected in higher load factors.

What about the 'Shuttle' and the savings expected to flow from it? The prospectus document specifies a target of achieving this new service with a total of 130 aircraft by year five. It also specifies a target cost of 7.4 cents per available seat mile. As for the resulting savings, the prospectus projects that they will have reached a cumulative total of $275m after two and a half years.

The latest progress reports that had been made public by management when this was written in early July 1997 were to the effect that there were 56 aircraft in the new service and that costs per available seat mile were down to 8 cents. Management had no doubt that the results had been positive and that real savings had been achieved. But it was unwilling or unable to quantify these – or both. Given the difficulties of comparing the new service with what went before, it is easy to sympathise with management in this case.

Indirect Cost Savings and Mid-Term Blues I turn now to savings and improvements which in no sense flowed automatically from the 1994 deal, but which can plausibly be seen as being among its indirect results. In the autumn of 1996, that is before the rejection by a majority of the two unions of the originally proposed mid-term wage adjustment, the management claimed cumulative cost improvements worth a little over $60m in this general category:

Savings from reduced sick pay	$22m
Savings in lost time due to injuries	$10m
Value of work team improvements	$30m
Total	$62m

The savings from lower sick pay and injury time may be characterised without too much hyperbole as being among the exemplary indirect benefits which should flow from majority employee ownership if it is working at all well. So, though in a different way, are the improvements attributable to work teams. The former reflect a greater readiness on the part of employee owners to refrain from anti-social behaviour at least on the margin. The latter reflect, again at least on the margin, a greater employee readiness to apply their specialised knowledge and experience to improving their own productivity and service quality, and to reducing unnecessary cost.

On the other hand, in discussions at United's international head-quarters office outside Chicago in the autumn of 1996, it was freely acknowledged that the quite sharp reductions in sickness and injury costs which characterised the first year or eighteen months after the deal of July 1994 had later started to fall away. For what it is worth, an initial 'honeymoon' followed by a 'cool-off' is a frequent pattern in businesses which have become majority employee owned. The same pattern indeed frequently occurs in the wake of other innovations at the workplace.

A second qualification which may limit any surge of enthusiasm about these improvements is their size. Put bluntly they *seem* modest, amounting as they do in total to less than half of one percent of United's annual cost base. True, we are talking about the achievements of not much more than a two-year period. Nevertheless there are a number of majority employee-owned businesses in the US and the UK which have set themselves significantly higher targets for cost savings of this kind and then gone on to achieve them or at least come close.

But the rather modest total of the savings linked to 'voluntary' improvements, if indeed they are modest given the whole environment at United, may surely also be explained by a deterioration in relations between top management and the two ESOP unions once the post-deal honeymoon period was over. Certainly the rejection by pilots and the machinists of the first mid-term wage adjustment points in that direction. Without much doubt the key factor behind that rejection was an inequity, or more exactly a perceived inequity, in the distribution of the benefits that had flowed from the deal.

Assuming a starting value for the new shares in the recapitalised airline of $85 – the price taken for the purpose of the deal's calculations and roughly the price at which trading in them started in July 1994 – then it is plain that the outside or public shareholders had already enjoyed considerable capital gains between July 1994 and the end of December 1996. They were entirely free to cash these in. If we allow for the 4:1 share split, we can say that the share price increased by between two and three times by December of 1996.

It is true that over the same period the notional value of the shares allocated to employees under the deal went up by the same percentage figure. But while the public and outside shareholders are free to sell at any time, the employee shareholders may only do so when they leave. Moreover, at least among the pilots, there is a direct link between salaries and length of service. So the number who leave before reaching retirement age is small.

On this analysis it may well have seemed in December 1996 that the benefits of the savings achieved under the deal had gone disproportionately to the outside public shareholders. And that seems to be a fair and valid conclusion, even if it is also true that if we take the value on paper of the employee shareholdings, by the end of 1996 that already exceeded, by a fair margin, the sum of net wages which had been given up over the same thirty months. Rather later, in May 1997, Ken Thiede, the IAM leader, cited in a notice to his members a rather striking calculation about the value of the shares then held by a 'lead mechanic' and the amount of the associated investment saving up to that time. On the basis of a then share price of $75, the share value was calculated at just over $41,000 against total investment saving of some $17,500. For others among United's employee shareholders the actual numbers in May 1997 will have been different, but the relationship between share value and investment savings will have been similar.

In this discussion of the chief beneficiaries of the 1994 deal, a number of further points are worth making. The first is that the outside public shareholders are perhaps better seen as beneficiaries – not to the full extent of the capital gains enjoyed by them between July 1994 and end December 1996, but to the extent that these gains exceeded the average for the industry's shares between those two dates. If we switch to that second measurement formula, the size of their gains is reduced.

Second, it seems reasonable to include among the beneficiaries of the 1994 deal the additional employees taken on by United between July 1994 and June 1997. According to United's own statistics, that increase in American-based jobs alone was astonishingly high – over 11,000. The actual numbers have already been cited – 68,862 and 80,139. Perhaps, as we also saw earlier, that increase should be qualified by the rather different official numbers of the US Department of Transport. But a qualification on those lines must not be allowed to obscure what is the main and most important fact: that over its first three years, the deal was highly positive for jobs at United. It was highly positive in itself, and that much more so, as we have seen, when compared with what happened at Delta Airlines and AMR.

In this discussion of how the benefits of the 1994 deal were distributed or, more exactly, how at the end of 1996 they were perceived by union members to have been distributed, my final point is rather different. It seems to me reasonable for members of the two ESOP unions to argue that over its early life, the deal offered disproportionate benefits to United's top managers. That is because of the substantial bonus component in the 'compensation packages' of its 600 most senior managers. Once profits started to come through in line with the projections on which the deal had been based, big bonuses became payable to these top managers. I am not for a moment claiming that there was anything unethical in the way the bonuses were paid. On the contrary, they are a long-established feature of top people's pay at United. Nevertheless it seems clear that there was quite widespread resentment when they came to be paid. The feeling was that the profits had been largely driven by the sacrifices of the non-management staff. It was thus seen as inequitable that big 'extra' rewards should go to top managers.

For management staff below the top levels, union members apparently believe that there has been a tolerance of some upward flexibility, through promotion and the upward adjustment of management posts. They also believe that the deal's freeze of salaries was not therefore fully effective over its first two and a half years. In permitting such a flexibility, assuming it has done so, the top management at United may reasonably claim to have been constrained by economic necessity. Without it, the airline might easily have found itself unable to hold on to the services of key people and/or to hire in new recruits. Management may also point to the precedents of similar tolerances in other majority employee-owned companies. And yet, however reasonable the management case, it is unlikely to have been sufficiently so to overcome feelings of resentment.

Based on feelings of inequity, resentments among rank-and-file union members were, I think, an important part of the background music when the first mid-term wage adjustment proposal was rejected. The actual facts of what happened at the end of 1996 and in early 1997 are not themselves in dispute:

– After some months of negotiation with the elected ALPA leadership, management announced at the end of November that the two parties had reached provisional agreement about the wage rises to be recommended under the provisions of the mid-term 'wage adjustment process' in the 1994 deal.

– After similar negotiations with the IAM leadership, management announced in early December that a similar provisional agreement had been reached with the IAM.

Though there were some differences over non-wage points which figured in each of the two provisional agreements, the wage numbers were the same in both: an increase of 3% in each of the two years 1997 and 1998, followed by further increases of 2% in 1999 and in 2000. All increases to run from early July, that is from the anniversary of the deal's completion in 1994.

In mid-January United's ALPA members voted decisively, by a margin of 4 to 1, to reject what had been provisionally agreed by their leaders.

Less than a week later the IAM members voted. In line with their established practice they voted in two separate groups: the real mechanics – the people who actually maintain and repair the airframes and the aero-engines – in one group; the others, sometimes colloquially known as 'ramp staff', in a second. The first and more highly paid group voted to reject the proposal by a margin of about two to one. The second group voted to accept it. Though much lower paid than the first group, their rates, even after the cuts, evidently enjoyed a valuable margin over the competition.

Before the votes of the pilots had actually been counted, but when it must have become clear which way they were going to go, the elected ALPA leader at United, Captain Michael Glawe, announced in effect that his union would no longer co-operate with management.

The weeks that followed were marked by something approaching a war of words between the ALPA and the management. After contacts in early March between the leadership of the two unions and United's top management, the latter made a new offer. The two principal new features were:

– a lift to 5% from 3% in the annual wage adjustments offered to run from July 1997 and 1998;

– an undertaking by management that following the end of the main deal's duration in the year 2000, the wage rates applying before July 1994 would be restored.

Following the recommendations of their leaders the members of the two unions voted by comfortable majorities to approve the new deal.

In the conventional 'two sides' language of labour relations, we can say that those two new features represented significant management concessions. Indeed the fact that there was a second offer at all represented a concession by management. For the terms of the original deal specified a binding arbitration process if no agreement could be reached in negotiation. Management would have been entirely within the contract if it had chosen to invoke that arbitration clause. Moreover the odds are thought to be that an arbitrator's ruling would have cost less than the management's second offer.

Critics are entitled to argue that if the second offer was at least in some sense affordable, it would have been wiser to have made it first time round. But it also makes sense to commend management's decision, after its initial mistake, to move fast to limit the damage.

The initial mistake, if it was one, seems to have reflected a major disagreement between management and the unions about how the basic logic of the provisions in the 1994 deal relating to the mid-term wage adjustment process should be interpreted. The language of the key opening clause of these provisions is the same for both ALPA's and the IAM's members:

> At the end of the second year of the agreement, the parties will meet to establish increases, if any, in both the book rates of pay and the actual rates of pay for the Wage Adjustment Period. If the parties do not reach agreement by the end of the thirtieth month of the agreement, the increases, if any, in such rates of pay will be determined by expedited arbitration before a neutral arbitrator (it being understood that the company will retain the right to contend that no increase of any type should be granted).

There is also an identity of language in the final clause of these provisions in the agreements with the two unions:

> In no event will the arbitrator establish i) any pay rate that is less favourable to [union-]represented employees than the pay rates in effect when wage rates for the adjustment period are submitted to interest arbitration under this wage adjustment process; or ii) any pay rate in either the fourth or the fifth year

that is more than five (5) percent above the actual rate in effect in the previous year.

What was in dispute at the time of the rejection of management's initial offer was whether the apparent open-endedness of the first clause, which does not itself limit the amount of the adjustment that the parties may agree, is restricted in fact – if not in law – by the limits laid down in the final clause. Clearly it was always open to each side either a) not to reach agreement in their discussions under the first clause, or b) to reach an agreement that the union member-ships were almost bound to reject, and so c) to shift the decision to binding arbitration under terms that clearly are subject in law to tight numerical limits. In that sense, or so it seems to me, the final clause cast its shadow over the whole bargaining process. On the other hand it would not be easy for management to rebut a fairly simple argument which may well have been advanced by the unions in relation to what they took to be a real and genuine open-ended-ness in law of the first clause: namely that if the intention had been that the clause should limit what might be agreed under it, then that could without too much difficulty have been made explicit.

If we stand back a moment from the details of the language, the combination of the first and last clause together appeared to offer management a decisive advantage if its main aim in the negotiations was to restrict any wage adjustment to 5%. In the first discussions which preceded the negative union votes on a package which was freely negotiated below the two-year 10% target, management declined to forgo that advantage. The sub-sequent protests of the ALPA leadership at United amounted to the claim that, given the new majority employee ownership and against the background of higher than projected cost savings and other financial improvements, it was unreasonable by management to press the advantage offered to them by the language of the two key clauses.

In the event, as we know, management's second offer also remained within the 5% limit. But as well as the increase to 5% from 3% compared with what had originally been proposed, it contained a second sweetener: the undertaking that the pre-ESOP wage rates would be restored in the year 2000. For Captain Glawe, it was the new 'guaranteed snap back' provision which was the key to his members' acceptance of the second offer.

Following the acceptance of the second offer, management seemed anxious to put the whole episode behind it. It signalled this intention by a change at the apex of its bargaining team, bringing in a top labour relations lawyer, Bill Hobgood, with long experience in the mediation field. A good test of his skills in that respect came quickly. Negotiations on a new labour contract with the Association of Flight Attendants (the AFA) – the one union which remains outside the United ESOP – got under way in late April, and appeared to reach a successful conclusion in July. The AFA leadership later recommended that its members accept a new labour contract to run for ten whole years. Albeit by a narrow margin, the membership vote in the autumn was to accept.

But, following his apparent success with the AFA, Hobgood faces a wider challenge; or rather there is a challenge which will have to be faced both by the entire top management team at United and by the leadership of the two ESOP unions. The challenge is to develop a new 'culture' of management/union relationships which is more congruent with majority employee ownership. The goal to be aimed at is easy to identify but much harder to achieve. Within a framework of shared and reliable information – including agreed projections of what is likely to happen – the goal is to reach rational and agreed decisions about (a) how 'extra profits' if any, should be shared as between higher wages and investment, and (b), in the painful eventuality of reduced available resources, to reach agreed decisions in advance about what should be cut back.

That is all in the future. What we need to acknowledge about the past and present is that the whole ESOP project at United was breaking new ground from the day the deal was completed in July 1994. Indeed it was moving the company into a world for which the rule books have not yet been written.

What also needs to be said is that the record of United over the first thirty months following the deal was on the surface stunningly successful. Quite apart from the financial results, it increased total employment according to its own figures by, to repeat, an astonishing 11,000 jobs. What is more, it did so over a period when employment numbers at Delta and American Airlines, its two closest competitors, were cut by roughly the same amount.

In the long run a combination of greater employment security and greater employment buoyancy may well come to be seen as the real potential blessing of majority employee ownership. In that respect United did wonderfully well in the first two and a half years after the 1994 deal.

Given this success in relation to jobs, many readers will be surprised by the relative performance of the United share price over the first phase of its ESOP deal. A share which is a top relative performer over one period may always do that much less well in the next. Nevertheless the stock market performance of United, relative to that of its main competitors, between the end of April 1994 and May 1997 is so striking – and in some ways, to repeat, so surprising – that it demands to be put on the record. What is measured is what the Americans call the 'Cumulative Total Return on Equity' (CTRE).

Three Airlines, an Airline Index and the Dow Jones
Industrial Average: CTRE April 1994 to May 1997

April 1994 equals 100. Values for May 1997

United	362.620
Delta	207.847
AMR	179.864
S & P Airlines*	163.158
Dow Jones IA	209.929

* 9 Airlines in S & P 1500. United not included
Source: American Capital Strategies in Maryland

But to return to management union relationships at United. By highlighting the turbulence associated with the mid-term wage adjustment I have intentionally left the impression that much needs to be changed if United is to benefit from the full potential of its employee ownership. However, it is also right to argue that during the first phase of that ownership relationships began to change and that more voices, including union and other employee representative voices, were heard round the tables at which the top decisions are made. The headline example is well worth some emphasis: the decision *not* to attempt a takeover of US Air. I suggest that it should be seen positively as reflecting a proper bias of majority employee-owned companies towards employment security. For what it is worth, it is also apparently true that top management eventually came round to the unions' view that a bid would be a mistake. Nevertheless, the fact of the union and other employee-representative involvement in that decision is what marks a really dramatic change with, and departure from, the past.

In the end it will not be easy for ideological critics to argue convincingly that the disadvantages of this majority employee ownership at United, at least over its first two and a half years, have outweighed its advantages. For the outside shareholders the benefits are unquestionable. But both financially and otherwise, the company's employee shareholders have also gained. So long as the share price can be sustained at about its level in early 1997, the employee shareholders will do that much better than they could reasonably have expected when they voted for the deal in 1994. More precisely, if we see the wage reductions which they voted to accept as self-imposed savings, then, with the same proviso about the future level of the share price, we can say that the financial return that they may expect to enjoy on those savings looks as if it will be rather attractive.

Of course we must not fudge the proviso about the future level of the share price. It may not stay at even roughly its early 1997 level. And yes, it may come down and perhaps do so rather sharply. But that is the logic of employee ownership. Those who are averse to the risks should not vote for the arrangement.

As for the national economy, research does not yet permit a balanced conclusion. Of course we know about the 'first round' costs to the American budget of the ESOP tax reliefs. But the overall and 'net' tax costs are a different matter. Without the buy-out would profits have risen so much? If not, the higher taxation liability arising from United's higher profits would not have existed anyway. Would employment have risen? If not, there would have been no extra taxes paid by United's newly recruited employees. And what about the additional future welfare which, given the now familiar proviso about the share price, will eventually be enjoyed by UAL's employee shareholders and their families?

This raises what seems to me to be one key challenge for America's 'ESOP Community': to come up with a persuasive balance sheet of what has been achieved from the viewpoint of the national budget and the welfare of America's citizens.

There is also a second and final challenge: how to make majority employee ownership indefinitely sustainable.

We know that there are significant players in the financial

community, for example J. P. Morgan, who have expressed a readiness in principle to get involved. Friendly and patient finance would be a necessary condition of success. A second necessary condition is that management, the unions and the rank-and-file employees should want to keep their present majority employee ownership, and want it enough to be willing to make new sacrifices for it. If those two conditions were satisfied then it seems to me that there would be a fair chance of securing a third: some necessary changes in the present ESOP laws.

On the other hand, if those conditions cannot be satisfied, this United Airlines experience will end up being just another example of successful but temporary majority employee ownership in America. It should not at all be dismissed for that reason. It is indeed a splendid vindication of the good sense, where that is possible, of choosing to cut employment costs rather than employment. But it will be a matter of regret to some that the life of this bold and path-breaking experiment in employee ownership will have been necessarily limited.

But I cannot leave this United Airlines experience without repeating a general observation about it. It is a conclusion that may be specially commended in a Europe where jobs have become the overriding political and economic issue. It should be of interest to stock market investors as well as to those concerned about employment security. My observation is that companies which operate in growth markets, but which find themselves becoming uncompetitive because of their rates of pay and benefits, face a clear choice. They can cut either jobs, or pay and benefits by the required percentage. If they choose the latter then, given the ESOP tax reliefs in both the US and the UK, those who give up wages can be compensated by shares, and the profits of the business can benefit from tax reliefs. To overcome the crisis of the early 1990s, United chose to cut wages and benefits. By contrast, two of its main competitors, Delta Airlines and American Airlines (AMR), chose to cut jobs – even if it is also true that the reduction was achieved on a largely voluntary basis at AMR. Readers must judge for themselves which of the two main alternatives they would prefer to go for. Investors scarcely need to make a judgement. The arithmetic will do the job for them. Between the date of the deal and the end of May 1997, shares in the common stock of United outperformed those of Delta and AMR by a substantial margin.

APPENDIX: DETAILS OF THE 1994 DEAL

Employee Shares Subject to a conditional qualification which in the event did not apply, both the employee-owned percentage of the equity (55%) and the associated number of shares in the common stock (precisely 17,675,345) were fixed at the outset. The agreed mechanics are that qualifying employees are allocated preferred shares: to be converted into ordinary ones only when employment ends, whether through retirement or otherwise. The eventual exchange of preferred shares for shares in the common stock takes place on a one for one basis regardless of the market value of the common stock at the time the exchange happens. So when they come to cash their shares in, the employee shareholders stand either to gain or to lose depending on the actual price level when they sell. At the end of the first quarter of 1997, that price, after allowing for a 4:1 split, was between two and three times what it had been when the deal was completed. As between the three employee shareholder groups – ALPA and IAM members and the non-union group – the distribution of what may be called 'investment-related' shares is proportionate to the total value of wages and benefits given up in each case. The actual percentage share going to each of the three main groups is: pilots, 46.23%; machinists, 37.13%; and the non-union group, 16.64%. Within each group, the distribution is proportionate to pay. There are also dividend shares (see below).

Non-Employee Shareholders The existing shareholders were paid $84.81 in cash for each of their shares in the old common stock, and issued with one share in the new common stock for every two they had held in the old. The money payments were funded by a combination of running down cash reserves and borrowing on the security of the employees' agreement to wage cuts and other concessions.

Wage Cuts The pilots (ALPA) took a 15.7% cut in wages over a period of 5.75 years, the machinists (IAM) took a 14.7% wage cut (which included the forgoing of a previously agreed increase due to have taken effect in May 1994) for a six-year period, and the non-union group took a cut of 8.25% over 5.75 years. For ALPA members, company pension contributions were cut from 9% of old wage levels to 1% of the new (lower) ones.

Other Concessions For a period lasting twelve years, ALPA accepted a two-tier wages and benefits arrangement whereby pilots assigned to flying the 'United Shuttle' up and down the north-south corridor on America's West Coast, do so at lower pay rates and longer hours than when flying the 'non- shuttle routes'. The IAM agreed that up to 20% of United's aero-engine and airframe maintenance work might be outsourced for twelve years. They also agreed to specified changes in work rules, including an end for twelve years to the paid half-hour lunch break. For the same twelve-year period the non-union staff accepted a two-tier wage arrangement for non-management grade people, with new recruits to be paid at 'market rates'. By virtue of the latter, maximum compensation rates for newly recruited non-management and non-union staff come down to about 50% of their former levels. These new recruits are also required to make a 25% contribution to their medical costs.

Employment Security Almost total job security for all those ALPA and IAM employees and those in the non-union employee group for the periods of the main wage cuts – 5.75 years for the pilots and non-union people and six years for the machinists.

No Strike Clauses The new labour contracts with ALPA and the IAM included no strike clauses for the duration of the main wage cuts and the associated periods of employment security.

Corporate Goverment ALPA, the IAM, and the non-union employee group each appoints one member of the twelve-person board of directors. Of the remaining nine members, two are United's top executives, three are elected by the non-employee shareholders, and the remaining four are independents, initially selected jointly by ALPA, the IAM, and the CEO, and later to be approved by at least one of the union directors. Among the first group of independents to be chosen was Paul Volcker, previously chairman of the country's Federal Reserve. The three employee appointees to the board enjoy rights of veto in certain sensitive areas: mergers and substantial non-airline investments and asset sales worth over £200m.

Sunset Arrangements These provisions will continue for so long as the employee shareholding exceeds 20%, actuarially estimated to last until about the year 2016.

Mechanics of 'Investment Related' Share and Dividend Share Allocations The deal provided that the total of 17,675 345 shares – four times that number after the May 1996 stock split – will be allocated out in tranches. In each of the five full years between 1994 and 1999 a total of 3,073,973 shares will be allocated. For the months covered by the main deal in 1994 and 2000, the numbers are 1,448,384 and 857,096 respectively. From the 1995 allocation onwards, the employee shareholders receive dividend shares as well as their so-called investment related ones. The dividend shares are calculated on the basis that employee shareholders should enjoy an 8.89% return on the value of their outstanding balance of preference shares. The latter are the subject of independent valuation. The number of dividend shares that the 8.89% return will 'buy' depends ultimately on the market price of shares in the common stock. The value of the preference shares is linked to this by a prespecified formula. The allocation of 'investment related' shares takes place, from the 1995 allocation onwards, only after the numbers needed for dividend shares have been calculated and deducted from the pre-set tranche total.

29

Tullis Russell

INTRODUCTORY OVERVIEW

In a letter dated 17 June 1994, the family shareholders in Tullis Russell, a long-established family paper mill business in Scotland's county of Fife, were made an offer. By the time it closed less than a month later, they had all accepted. Already by the summer of 1995 a majority (52%) of Tullis Russell's shares had come to be held either by its employees as individuals, or on their behalf by one or more employee trusts. A charitable foundation, the Russell Trust, held the balance of 48%, having had voting control for some twenty years before.

The business is sizeable as well as profitable. For the 55% of the share capital which they were holding in the summer of 1994, the family shareholders received the equivalent, essentially in loan stock, of £19m, in an offer which valued the company at £36.9m. The company proudly claims that it is the third largest private paper-making business to remain independent in the whole of Western Europe (after two in Germany). Despite two significant employment cutbacks in the 1980s and early 1990s and a productivity explosion in 1994/5, the workforce at Tullis Russell's pair of neighbouring paper mills, the Auchmuty mill and the Rothes mill, still numbered over 850 in late 1995. In the twelve months to end-March 1995 those employed in Fife had broken all their previous production records by a large margin, achieving a total output of 106,000 tonnes of paper. Subsidiaries elsewhere were also flourishing.

Before the ownership changes of 1994, Tullis Russell had been an almost quintessentially family business for nearly 200 years. The Tullis family and then the Russells were in control one after the other, with an overlap period when a controlling interest was shared between the two families during the fifty years from 1874 to

1924. The most recent family chairman, David Erdal, who took over in 1985 and stood down to become simply a non-executive director, was in fact the fourth generation of that family to lead the business: his late mother was born Sheila Russell.

Tullis Russell: Some Production Milestones: Tons & Tonnes

Year	Milestone
1900	5,000 tons exceeded
1916	10,000 ” ”
1928	15,000 ” ”
1938	20,000 ” ”
1950	25,000 ” ”
1971	50,000 ” ”
1993/4	80,000 tonnes ”
1994/5	106,000 ” ”
1995/6	108,000 ” ”

Calculations on the basis of the much higher figures of the mid-1990s show that Tullis Russell's paper output was then roughly the same, in proportion to domestic UK consumption, as it had been in the 1860s. The key achievements of the company over nearly 200 years – or perhaps more exactly of the two families which have successfully guided its destinies – seem therefore to have been three. First, to have grown with Britain's market; second, to have adapted to a continuing flow of changes; and third, to have declined to sell out to a competitor. This has happened over a period when the domestic industry's share of the home market has fallen to 50%.

The acceptance of the buy-out offer by the family shareholders was an act of enlightened self-interest. Had the sale been made to a competitor the prices would almost certainly have been fixed at a level higher than the 80p per voting share and the 72p per non-voting share which were accepted. But that would have been possible only if the payment for the Tullis Russell shares had been made in the shares of the buyer. The non-diversified consequences for the family shareholders of that would have been notably inferior to what they actually accepted.

The ownership outcome of the process set in motion by the acceptance of the June 1994 offer – with a majority of the share capital already split a year later between the employees as individuals and an employee trust or trusts – has been designed to be sustainable over an indefinite future. The French have a phrase for this, '*la perennité de l'entreprise*' – the potential everlastingness of the business. As for the current process of ownership transition, projections indicate that it will be completed some time between 2002 and 2009, when the shareholding of the Russell Trust will have been reduced to about 25%. Having been founded in 1809, the year 2009 will mark the start of the company's third century.

The team which designed the offer and the eventual ownership outcome was led by David Erdal, the company's non-executive chairman who is also a family shareholder. In his own and the team's view the scheme had three main attractions:

– For the family shareholders, the unlocking of capital at a price which, taken together with the tax reliefs, was certainly acceptable and perhaps attractive.

– For the future employee-owned business, the opportunity to remain independent indefinitely, perhaps for ever.

– For current employees, a good chance that, if they remain so employed till the process of ownership transformation is complete, they will have built up a nest egg of capital worth at least one year's wages.

This combination is widely seen as a winner by advocates of employee ownership. It was made possible by key changes in Britain's employee-ownership law, changes which were accepted by the Government only in late March 1994, barely three months before the offer to Tullis Russell's shareholders was made.

Three earlier case studies cover what I have called 'employee ownership by benefaction': John Lewis and Baxi in the UK and the Carl-Zeiss-Stiftung in Germany. In all those cases, and in a number of other similar examples in Britain and elsewhere in Europe, the ownership arrangements are indeed, as at Tullis Russell, intended to be indefinitely sustainable. On the other hand, the former owners of those three businesses transferred their ownership rights either as complete gifts or at deep discounts. This was a price that their former owners were in effect prepared to pay, because by doing so they gave maximum protection to the independence of the successor employee-owned businesses. Because of the 1994 changes in the UK's relevant ESOP laws, the family shareholders of Tullis Russell were not required to make a similar sacrifice.

Even after the 1994 changes, Britain's ESOP legislation is of course far from perfect. Nevertheless, the example of Tullis Russell shows what may well be widely possible for the owners of family businesses who face problems of ownership succession. But only time will show the extent to which this exemplary ownership change is going to be followed.

The Two Families and the Business: 1809–1994 It may come as some surprise that there are still four separate paper-making businesses within the Scottish county of Fife, north-east of Edinburgh. Two of them, Tullis Russell and the much smaller Smith Anderson, are still privately owned. The county's high level of pre-industrial prosperity is perhaps a factor. This can be traced back at least to the 1400s and the establishment at St Andrews of Britain's third – and Scotland's first – university. But the main explanation seems to lie in Fife's swollen and fast-flowing rivers. The chief attraction was probably water power. Water is also a vital ingredient of the paper-making process: a rule of thumb among paper-makers is that 100 tons of water is needed for every ton of paper produced, though the net figure is less after recycling.

Tradition has it that when Robert Tullis converted a grain mill at Auchmuty in 1809, it was because Napoleon's blockade threatened paper supplies for his existing business. This combined printing and publishing with the sale of books and stationery in the market town of Cupar ten miles away. Robert never seems to have shifted his main interest to paper making – indeed, in the 1820s he founded a local newspaper, the *Fife Herald*.

After his death, the Cupar businesses were taken on by his eldest son, George. It was left to the two younger sons, William and Robert, to make a go of paper making. Robert died young but not before a second mill had been acquired in 1836, at Rothes, less than a mile downstream from Auchmuty. To this day, the key processes of Tullis Russell's paper making continue at these two mills.

The year 1836 is a good starting point for a more detailed look at the history of the business. For with the acquisition of the Rothes mill and its so-called Fourdrinier machine, the undertaking ceased to be essentially a dependent supplier of paper to the founder's mini-conglomerate in Cupar, and struck out on a path and destiny of its own. I will first trace the family thread of the story, running as we have seen from Tullis to Russell, with a kind of condominium of the two families in between. I will then move to the business record.

Leaving Robert the founder behind us, the key figure in the

paper-making business for the first phase of this 150-year period was his son William. It is true that the eldest brother George, who had taken over the family interests in Cupar, remained a partner in the paper business for many years. But his partnership was of the financial, and essentially sleeping, kind. So, after the third son Robert's untimely death in 1839, William carried the main paper-making responsibility alone.

In addition to paper making, in 1846 William acquired a small bleaching business on the banks of the Leven close by. In those days it was sometimes necessary for some of the material used in paper making to go through a preliminary bleaching process. The significance of the acquisition was that it formed part of the final settlement between the Tullis and the Russell families in the 1920s.

The Russells made their first appearance in this family story when Agnes Russell married William Tullis in 1846. The couple had no children. When William handed over the main reins of the business in the 1870s, they passed in effect jointly to his nephew Robert Tullis, the son of his elder brother George, and to his brother-in-law David Russell (senior), a brother of his wife Agnes. The former became a partner in the business in 1872 and the latter in 1874. What I have called the 'two-family condominium' then continued till 1924. Following the death of the 'senior' David Russell in 1906, his position in the joint leadership was taken over by his son, another David (knighted in 1946).

Just before he died, David (senior) had masterminded a change in the corporate status of the business – from a partnership to a private limited company.

The rest of the family story can be quickly told. In 1924 the second David Russell negotiated a deal which in effect bought out Robert Tullis mainly for cash. This settlement also involved the passing to the Tullis family of the bleaching business. At this point members of the Tullis family make their exit from this story, though it is pleasant to record that old Robert soldiered on for a dozen more years and that, having first become a working partner in 1872, he is said to have enjoyed what was surely a well-deserved retirement in his eighties and nineties, 'as a gentleman'. Perhaps what is surprising is that the condominium lasted as long as it did and that the business not only survived but was apparently stronger at its end than when it began.

For most of the period from 1874 to 1924, the Russell voice, first that of the father and then that of the son, seems to have been the dominant one. That is speculation: what is certain is that, other than their place in the name of the business, the Tullis family played no further part in this story after 1924.

When eventually, ten years after his knighthood, and fifty years after his father's death, Sir David Russell died in 1956, it was his eldest son, Dr David Russell, who took over the leadership of the business.

Sir David's second son, Patrick, had died of wounds during the Second World War, serving with the Artillery in the Italian campaign. The death of this younger brother explains the origin of the charitable foundation, the Russell Trust. The original Russell Trust was set up by Sir David Russell as early as 1947. He gave it a 25% stake in the equity capital of the business, seen as Patrick's inheritance had he lived.

Then, in 1969, Dr David set up a second trust, which he named the David and Catherine Russell Trust, after himself and his wife. He passed over to it some 30% of the then voting shares in the business, himself at that time retaining control in his own hands. Then, in 1975, he handed over a further block of voting shares, thereby passing voting control to the two trusts together. Finally, in 1985, these two trusts were amalgamated. From 1985 onwards they exercised voting control as a single entity.

That new unified trust was given a new trust deed. However, both in terms of its beneficiaries and its control arrangements, it is very similar to those of the two antecedent Russell Trusts. The beneficiaries are essentially charitable entities to which the Trust passes its dividend income. Control is shared by Tullis Russell's top management and members of the family. As a final point of clarification, from 1975 down to the 1994 employee buy-out, the ordinary share capital of Tullis Russell had been split 30:70% between voting and non-voting shares. That explains how it came about that at the time of the 1994 buy-out, it was possible at the same time for (a) the Russell Trust to enjoy control, and (b) the family to hold 55% of the shares.

We shall look later at the motives behind those benefactions. Here we may simply note that, as a result, the family had created a starting point which made an eventual transition to majority employee ownership much less problematic than it might otherwise have been.

The Business Record: 1836–1924 According to Coleman's history of Britain's paper industry, it was in the 1820s that the output of the country's machine-made paper first exceeded that made by hand. And yet it was only when they acquired the second mill at Rothes, in 1836, that the Tullis brothers, William and Robert, started to include machine production in their total output. One of the new so-called Fourdrinier machines had been installed there by the previous owner, evidently at some time between the mid-1820s and the early 1830s. There has been speculation that the machine may have been the source of difficulties, and we know that the disposal of the Rothes mill was a post-bankruptcy sale. We know too that the Fourdrinier at Rothes was one of the earliest in Scotland, perhaps even the second, following an installation by Lewis Smith in Aberdeen in the first decade of the century. In any event it seems that machine production at the original Tullis Auchmuty mill began not earlier than the 1840s and perhaps the early 1850s. Given the speculation about the difficulties at Rothes which lay behind its sale, there may have been an understandable nervousness on William Tullis's part about introducing too much machine production too soon.

The switch from hand to machine production in the textile industry during Britain's industrial revolution is well known: who has not heard of the handloom weavers and their sorry plight as the new machines spread through the industry over the fifty-odd years to 1840? The same applies to the names of the main textile industry inventors and of their new machines: Hargreaves's jenny, Arkwright's frame and Crompton's mule. On the other hand, the similar switch in the paper industry, if my own ignorance is at all typical, is hardly known outside the ranks of those actually working in paper. Hands up those who have heard of the Fourdrinier machine. Its basic design has barely changed – though there have been massive changes in size and speed – since the first working model was installed in England. This first machine, stemming from an original French invention, was installed in the first decade of the nineteenth century. Since this was the first serious technical problem encountered by the fledgling paper business at Rothes and Auchmuty, it seems worth describing the main features of the Fourdrinier machine and what was involved in the change:

The Fourdrinier machine represents a straightforward mechanisation of what was formerly done by hand . . .

The basic principle of Robert's [the French inventor of the Fourdrinier's precursor] machine was to form paper upon an endless belt of woven wire, instead of upon the separate moulds of the hand made process. This principle remained equally true when the invention was developed by Donkin and the Fourdriniers, and remains true of the modern Fourdrinier machines and the largest newsprint machines. The latter turn out newsprint at over 2,000 feet per minute.

Two vital elements in the making process – the 'shake' which the vatman gave to the mould whilst forming the sheet, and the 'couching' of the wet sheets on to a felt – were incorporated in the machine. The former was carried out by imparting a side-to-side motion to the 'wire', the latter by running the newly-formed sheet of paper on to a felt-covered roller [Coleman, 1958].

Coleman quotes various more or less contemporary estimates of the savings in costs and labour which could be achieved by switching to machine production from production by hand in the middle years of the nineteenth century. For example, it was estimated that where a machine replaced seven vats, the savings in money might be as much as 72% (down to £734 from £2,604). The corresponding workforce reduction would be from forty-one persons to just nine. It would be well beyond the limits of this case study to explore these details any further. But two points are relevant to the early pioneering days at the Auchmuty and Rothes Mills. The first is that once a Fourdrinier machine had been properly established and bedded down, there were sharp reductions in costs, and thus potentially big increases of profit. The second is that if those mills had continued to produce mainly by hand after, say, the early 1850s, they would probably never have passed the milestone output of over 1,000 tons annually. Moreover, having fallen at that fence, they would surely not long have survived.

Though output records are not available, we may imagine that the next thirty-five years, from 1860 to the middle 1890s, were characterised by gently increasing annual production. The company's historian, Miss C. D. M. Ketelbey, suggests that there were neither major successes nor major disasters over these years. The tasks were those of maintaining output and profitability, and of pushing the latter gradually higher in the face of continually tough conditions both in the market and in securing raw material supply.

Higher output seems to have been achieved partly by adding new machines of the same specifications, and partly by replacing existing ones with larger and faster versions of the same basic Fourdrinier model. In any event, when some continuous records start to become available in the second half of the 1890s, annual output had increased by about four times, to approximately 4,500 tons, compared with that earlier peak of 1,133 tons quoted by Miss Ketelbey for 1858/9.

Annual Output: Five-Year Averages 1896 to 1925 in Tons

1896–1900	4,410
1901–1905	6,260
1906–1910	6,530
1911–1915	9,800
1916–1920	8,648
1920–1925	9,523

The second, and perhaps most remarkable of the hat trick of David Russells, took over the reins alone when he bought out the business from Robert Tullis – and thus ended the condominium – in 1924. Given his energy and his quite exceptional range of talents, and the fact that today's Tullis Russell still very much bears his stamp, it is perhaps inevitable that the Tullis family's contribution has been substantially overshadowed. Still, it is almost always harder to start successful businesses than to sustain them. The founder, and more especially his second son, William, deserve to be remembered for having established what later became a first-class business. It is to the particular credit of William that he successfully negotiated the tricky switch from hand-made to machine-made paper, and then went on to lay the foundations for substantial levels of machine-made output which were later achieved. As for the founder's grandson, William's nephew Robert Tullis, he must surely be given credit for the fact that the firm survived the fifty years of his condominium with two successive David Russells, and achieved much higher output. Finally, he must be given credit for accepting the buy-out offer from the second David Russell in 1924.

Thirty Years' Growth of Output and Sales: 1924–55 The period from the buy-out of the Tullis family interest in 1924 to the assumption of the chairmanship by David Erdal in 1985 is divided into two almost equal halves by the death in 1956 of the second of that remarkable trio of David Russells. Apart from half a century of outstanding business leadership, Sir David, as we will from now on for convenience call him, was a great benefactor of two of Scotland's most notable institutions: St Andrews University and the revived religious community on the island of Iona. He jointly started the Iona project with the Revd George Macleod and was one of those whose financial and other support enabled Macleod to bring the project to fulfilment.

In business, a typical indication of Sir David's values was an arrangement during the Second World War under which all Tullis Russell's employees serving in the forces continued to be paid by the company at the rate of ten shillings a week. Ten shillings in the money of the early 1940s is probably equivalent to about £15 today. Moreover, though paper making during the Second War conferred 'reserved occupation' status on those who worked in the industry, as many as 200 of the company's employees were beneficiaries of this unusually generous arrangement.

Sir David's contribution to the making of the modern Tullis Russell is a useful reminder that culture may be the single most important ingredient in determining the success of a business. The culture which Sir David stamped on Tullis Russell was in part, no doubt, no more than a reinforcement of what he inherited from its past. It combined family business paternalism with business leadership, treated essentially as a duty of service, almost in a sense of *noblesse oblige*. Some features of those values and of that culture may well be out of place in the rather different setting of employee ownership in the Tullis Russell of the 1990s. But this should not be allowed to call into question the contribution of paternalism to earlier phases of Tullis Russell's success – however politically unpalatable it may be in some quarters.

Telling evidence of both the impact of those values on the rank and file of the company's employees, and of the fact that they significantly predated Sir David's assumption of what the French call the *pouvoir* in 1924, comes from Tullis Russell's experience during the General Strike of 1926. Though there were complicating factors, as we shall see in a moment, the company historian is in no serious doubt about what underlay the behaviour of the company's workforce: 'Many mills in Scotland came out, as in England, but in the Tullis Russell Mills *the balance of conditions and sympathies was in favour of no action and not a man went on strike* [emphasis added]'.

The main complicating factor was that in the paper industry of those days two unions recruited members: the National Union of Printing, Bookbinding and Paper Workers (NUPB & PW) and the Amalgamated Society of Paper Makers (ASPM). As was already the norm, the former was affiliated to the TUC, the body which actually called workers out in the General Strike. On the other hand, for reasons which are not immediately clear, the ASPM had disaffiliated from the TUC not long before. To some extent, the response of the paper industry men to the strike call may have varied in line with the balance of the membership between the two unions.

However, Sir David did not always get it right – as was shown by an experiment in what might be called the cultural life of Tullis Russell during the Second World War. According to his biographer:

> In 1940 the Reverend George Macleod, founder of the Iona Community, had had the idea of a 'factory-community' with a minister having a room in a factory and sharing the experiences of the workforce. It was not a novel concept, since there were factory chaplains in the south. It was agreed that the Scottish experiment would begin at Tullis Russell, with the Reverend Ian Fraser taking up appointment in the mills as a minister in industry under the aegis of the Iona Community, from September 1942, for two years [Macintyre 1994].

The experiment led to quite sharp differences of opinion, and in October 1944 the Revd Ian Fraser's appointment was not extended but simply 'terminated'. Sir David's view had been, according to his biographer, that an industrial chaplain had to be 'part of management – in other words one whose sphere of activity would be the spiritual, mental and physical welfare of the people'. On the other hand Fraser, with the support of Macleod behind him, interpreted his duties to include those of challenging the status quo where he deemed it justified. In the case of the seating arrangements in the canteen he evidently took the view that a challenge was necessary and put a written warning on the record: 'Though not serious at the moment, this may be the beginning of a policy which will have serious consequences in the division of the mill into separated groups who squabble.'

Sir David's biographer goes on:

> The canteen dispute was compounded by an advertisement in the *Scotsman* for a lecture in Edinburgh on 'Common Wealth: Piety and Politics', given by the Reverend Alex Miller of the Iona Community. David Russell complained to Macleod:
> 'This has brought a shower of criticisms about my head. Is the Iona Community a Communistic organisation? etc, etc; and all this has been accentuated by one of the staff bringing in a copy of *World Digest* with an article, "A Parson in a Factory", in which this is said: "Unless the Church is prepared to stand for some form of communal control and ownership in business etc."'

This is perhaps already in danger of becoming an over-extended digression. But I cannot resist quoting the first sentence of of Macleod's reply to Sir David: 'Providence got us together on this first chaplaincy experiment and now honours us with difficulties, which is proof that something is really happening.'

Nor can I resist, finally, quoting from the jacket of the biography that Sir David was a 'pioneer of New Age thinking' and a close friend of Tudor Pole, who was in his turn almost certainly more gifted with psychic powers than any of his British contemporaries. There seems to be no serious doubt that, like Pole, Sir David believed in some sense in a life after death. As he looks down from his cloud on the employee ownership being pioneered by his grandson, one cannot help wondering what he is thinking.

To return to the record of Tullis Russell as a business. Among Sir David's earlier contributions, Miss Ketelbey rightly singles out his appointment before the First World War of an industrial chemist rather than an industrial chaplain. In making this appointment he was evidently well ahead of his times: it was the first step towards a research and development department.

Moreover, the historian of the family business leaves her readers in no doubt about the grand scale and comprehensiveness of Sir David's overall contribution:

He was a supreme organiser, and his reorganisation of all branches of the firm's business amounted almost to a refoundation. He overhauled production policy and methods; he revolutionised sales policy; he revised the costing and accounting system; he brought a welfare programme into the Mills; he enlarged the whole scale of the firm's operations, changed the character of its products and modernised its techniques, and he put the company into the front rank of Papermakers [*sic*].

At Auchmuty Mill he reduced the diversity of production and concentrated on high-grade twin-wire papers for printers, the now well-known Ivorex Boards, Mellotex offset Cartridge, Artine (an imitation art since discontinued) and cheque and security papers. He studied and met the needs of the printer. Twin wet ends were installed on the machines to give a uniformity of printing surface to both sides of the sheet. Esparto papers were for the first time mill-conditioned, ready for immediate use on the printing presses, and the printers' confidence was sought and won by strict attention to control of quality, shade and finish.

Rothes Mill was even more drastically reorganised. All the old wrappings, browns, long elephants of assorted sizes and colours were in time replaced by speciality papers for technical and industrial purposes, a relatively new field in which the firm has since achieved and maintained a leading position. Production there was gradually turned over to papers of this kind – insulating papers for power cables and telephones, base papers for plastics and electrical purposes and spool papers for photography. This exceptions to this were two lines, Sorbex blotting and Duplex envelope papers, which were, and still are, kept on the current list.

We will come back in a moment to the key technical concept of 'twin wire' papers. But here is the place for a brief look at production levels between Sir David's accession in 1924 and his death, thirty-two years later, in 1956.

Output of Paper in Tons: Five-Year Averages 1921–5 and 1951–5

1921–25	9,523
1926–30	16,224
1931–35	15,648
1936–40	19,418
1941–45	17,533
1946–50	23,434
1951–55	26,335

Partly because of the particular five-year periods they fall into and partly because they are five-year averages, those numbers understate the impact on Tullis Russell of the 1929 stock markets' collapse and of the resulting depression of the early 1930s. The annual output figures which reached a then all-time high of nearly 18,500 tons in 1929 fell some 20% to a low of just over 14,750 in 1933. Curiously enough the maximum impact of these external shocks on the Tullis Russell workforce seem to have preceded the low point in production: 'Auchmuty was on short time for eighteen months between July 1930 and December 1931, and Rothes for nine months from February to November 1931.'

Perhaps the lag is explained by the movement of stocks. But however that may be, the main comment on this whole experience should be rather different. It is that compared with many in other industries and perhaps in other paper-making companies, the Tullis Russell workforce came through the great depression of the 1930s relatively lightly. Though they suffered from extended periods of short-time working, they seem to have managed to escape actual unemployment. The same was certainly not true in the nearby coal pits of West Fife: good evidence for that was the victory of the Communist Party candidate, William Gallacher, in the Parliamentary constituency of West Fife at the general election in 1935. In fact he held on to that seat until the general election of 1950, a unique achievement in Britain's politics.

No doubt, if there had been no depression and no Second World War, Tullis Russell's rate of growth during Sir David's leadership years would have been greater than it was. Output more than doubled between 1925, the first year for which he was alone responsible, and 1955, the last year over which he can have had real influence. It reached a tonnage of 27,378 from 12,789. The average annual increase over this thirty-year period was around 2.5%.

It would be wrong to suggest that a verdict on Sir David's stewardship at Tullis Russell should be based merely on that record of production growth. During his time there was clearly a huge improvement in the quality of Tullis Russell's commercial activity. And though it happened in 1923, a year before Robert Tullis finally bowed out, Sir David should presumably be given the main credit for a particular innovation: Tullis Russell was one of the first – perhaps *the* first – of Britain's paper makers to install a special kind of 'twin wire or double machine', with the second wire reversed. The 'ordinary' twin wire machine produces a kind of two-ply paper with an acceptable quality surface for printing top and bottom. Those of the special kind installed at Tullis Russell have an extra competitive quality advantage because the flow along the wire of each of the two plies is so arranged that their two 'bad sides' come together in the middle. This apparently gives an ususual advantage when paper is of the heavier weights – above 180 grams per square metre – which are sometimes called 'boards' in the paper trade and of which Tullis Russell is evidently one of Britain's master suppliers. The 1923 installation of this machine was judged sufficiently important to merit a mention by the British industry's latest historian, Dr Richard Hills. He tells his readers that Tullis Russell's 'latest and largest [twin wire] machine, which started operating in 1979, has a capacity of 20,000 tonnes per annum'.

That is to anticipate. Here, for the final verdict on the years of Sir David's stewardship, I return to the issues of values and culture with which I started. In some respects Sir David was well ahead of his time. As an expression of the importance of continuous improvement and of his firm's commitment to it, you can scarcely do better than a sentence written by Sir David as long ago as 1930:

> The position we hold as a firm, commercially technically and socially, has been won through years of persistent effort. Such an effort has been stimulated always by the desire each day to see some improvement upon past records, some new ideas for the improvement of methods and conditions, some step forward to make each today an advance upon yesterday [Ketelbey].

But perhaps as important as Sir David's commitment to the value of continuous improvement was a commitment of a quite different kind. I can put that most simply by calling it an idea of family business leadership as a stewardship in which the interests of the business itself, had they clashed with those of the family during his years of control, would almost certainly have prevailed. Of course, which way a decision would have gone in the event of a 'one way or the other' clash can only be a matter of speculation. But Sir David's decision to pass to the Russell Trust the shares that his second son would have inherited had he survived must be a pointer towards that direction. And it was in the same direction that we must interpret the decisions of his son to set up and endow an additional Russell Trust, and to pass a further substantial shareholding to it, and to merge the two trusts into one. This continuing concept of business leadership as stewardship is elegantly congruent with the idea of an employee-owned future for Tullis Russell, which began to evolve under the third of the David Russells, Dr David.

More Growth in Output and Sales: 1955–1985 Sir David Russell's act must have been difficult to follow. All the more reason for a positive verdict on the thirty years which followed his death. These years of his son's *pouvoir* and stewardship were a most notable success. I begin with the company's performance.

Under the leadership of the man who became Dr David Russell when he was awarded an honorary doctorate by St Andrews University in the 1970s, the growth rate of the business, measured by the average annual increase in the weight of the company's physical output, continued to fluctuate around 2.5% a year, and to double, more or less, over thirty years. But whereas 'doubling production' meant adding a total of about 13,000 tons of additional paper in Sir David's time, it meant adding roughly twice that under his son. In 1956, the year of his father's death, Tullis Russell's output totalled just over 28,000 tons of paper. Thirty years later, when Dr David retired, the corresponding figure was just over 56,000 tons.

One explanation for the continuing increase between those two generations is the size and speed of the paper-making machinery: the extra production came in much larger chunks in Dr David's time than in his father's. We have seen that the new twin-wire machine installed in 1979 was capable on its own of producing paper at an annual rate of 20,000 tons. Arguably Dr David's replication of his father's growth rate was not just 'more of the same' but a new achievement in its own right. This is because when you reach the really high numbers attained during Dr David's stewardship you are entering quite new territory.

Where Dr David was undeniably innovative compared to his father was in adopting a policy of growth by acquisition. Three businesses were acquired as going concerns – Coated Papers in the Manchester region, Brittains in the Potteries, and Watson Grange outside Glasgow. Perhaps especially in the case of Brittains, these businesses commended themselves as prospective buyers of Tullis Russell's paper. But they were also attractive as potential sources of group profits during the characteristically sharp down-turns in a paper-maker's business cycle.

In the case of Coated Papers the name describes the product. As for Brittains, it has since achieved a commanding position in an international niche market – making special transfer papers for application in the quality porcelain and other businesses (see Appendix A). The main products manufactured by Watson Grange are book covers for hardbacks. In the mid-1980s, around the time of Dr Russell's retirement, they employed together just less than 350 people – or roughly a quarter of what was then the group's 1,400-odd workforce. By 1994/5 they employed fewer people but accounted for a higher proportion of group employment:

Tullis Russell Subsidiaries: Workforce Numbers 94/95

Brittains	110
Coated Papers	130
Watson Grange	70

Dr David was also more innovative than his father in his promotion of technical collaboration with Scottish universities. Examples include a battery separator papers project undertaken jointly with Heriot Watt; and special papers for cheque books and projects with St Andrews. In all cases the results of this collaborative work were eventually brought to the market.

But in other important respects Dr David followed his father. For example, towards the end of the Second War Sir David had broken quite sharply with what had previously been family tradition. He started appointing the top executives of the business – the top sales manager for example and the top production manager – to the board of directors. This practice was continued by Dr David. Moreover, as his father had done in 1947, so in 1969 Dr David set up a charitable trust, the David and Catherine Russell Trust, and transferred to it a significant block of shares.

In 1975 the two charitable trusts were merged into one. By a rearrangement of the equity into voting and non-voting shares, Dr David ensured that the merged charitable trust should enjoy voting control, though having no more than a minority of all the issued ordinary shares. What is more, at the same time he brought in the top managers of Tullis Russell as co-trustees with members of the family of the merged trust and gave them a right of veto over trust decisions. The result was an important distinction – between the beneficiaries of the newly merged trust (the charities enjoying its support), and its control. Over the latter the top management at the Tullis Russell business has the final say.

In a general way these arrangements may be seen as a logical culmination of what I suggested earlier was Sir David Russell's idea of stewardship in relation to the destinies of a substantial family business. If the interests of the family shareholders and of the business itself should ever conflict, then those of the latter should prevail. Almost precisely the same bias is reflected in the ownership arrangements of those employee-owned firms where control is vested not in the individual employee owners for the time being, but in a permanent employee trust. And behind that same bias is the same thinking.

But there is also evidence that when he thought about the future of the business after his own retirement, Dr David initially gave serious consideration to a more or less explicit arrangement of employee ownership. Under such an arrangement all the company's share capital would eventually have come to be owned by a trust of a kind similar to that of the John Lewis Partnership. According to family tradition he was argued out of that by a quick-talking financial adviser from Edinburgh. The adviser's key point was about the different social environment of a shopping business based in the south of England and a manufacturing one in Fife. What worked well in the former would involve unacceptable risks if transposed to the strongly unionised environment of East Fife.

There is another family tradition about Dr David's thinking on the question of ownership succession which his nephew David Erdal tells, partly as a joke against himself and his siblings and cousins. Having fought in the Second World War, so the story goes, Dr David was very much aware of the differences in values and climate between his own generation and the generation who came of age in the swinging sixties and early seventies. David Erdal interprets in *that* light his uncle's decision to vest final control with the merged trust, and thus indirectly with the company's top management. In other words, Dr David felt he could not risk leaving the business in the hands of a generation of anarchists and dangerous free thinkers. Perhaps this is understandable: David Erdal's political odyssey in the 1970s included spells in Britain's Workers' Revolutionary Party (WRP) and Mao's China, as well as at Harvard Business School.

Dr David initially opposed his nephew's insistence that he must spend two years at Harvard Business School if he was to take over the chairmanship. Yet, notwithstanding those spells with the WRP and in Mao's China, he chose David Erdal to succeed him. He and his wife had four daughters but no sons. Women were at that time scarcely eligible, because of prevailing industry opinion, for top positions of leadership. He had several nephews and David Erdal was only one of them. We know that Dr David, who lived on after his retirement for a few years, approved his nephew's first cautious steps towards employee ownership.

1985–1995: Rising Output and Declining Employment The main employee buy-out – 'sale by family shareholders' would be a more precise term – happened only in 1994, after changes in the law made it acceptable to the family shareholders. However, direct employee involvement started in 1985 with cash profit-sharing and a tax-assisted scheme whereby profits were used to buy shares for employees. In 1987 the process was taken one step further, when an Employee Benefit Trust was set up to borrow money to buy shares for employees. By 1994 employees owned 20%, either directly or collectively, through the trust. Detailed discussion of the whole employee buy-out process is left to the next section. However, the business performance of Tullis Russell in the intervening ten years must be viewed against the backdrop of increasing employee ownership and the expectation that it would accelerate.

To those outside it, the apparent ferocity of the business cycle in that part of the paper industry in which Tullis Russell's products are mainly concentrated is almost bound to cause surprise. And that remains true even though:

– The down-swings from the peaks to the troughs have been

getting progressively less severe, whether measured in tonnes or percentages, over the last twenty-odd years.

– The company's two latest output peaks, in 1990 and then in 1994-5, were both way above anything which had been achieved earlier. (The figures for the following year showed a small further improvement.)

Over the last twenty years the largest fall, from a peak to the subsequent trough, was in the mid-1970s and associated presumably with the combined effects of the first oil price shock and the near runaway inflation at the start of the last Wilson Government in 1974. Measured in tonnes, the paper output of Tullis Russell fell over 30% from a high of 63,455 to a low of 43,572 just two years later. Next time round, between a 1980 peak and a 1983 trough, tonnage declined by 23%, or just under 14,000. The most recent fall was of 11% – 8,500 tonnes – between 1990 and 1992.

Further research would probably show that this softening in the ferocity of the business cycle down-turns for Tullis Russell is partly to be explained by the growth in the company's exports. In 1995 exports were some 40% by value of output compared with less than 10% twenty years before. But that is a detail. The eye-catching numbers of the Company's most recent output peaks compared as follows with earlier ones:

Production Peaks over the Last Fifteen Years in Tonnes

1980/81	59,107
1989/90	79,185
1994/95	106,000
1995/96	108,000

(Financial years to end-March)

There is a special supply side explanation for much of the 'great leap forward' in output from the 1993/4 figure of 83,575 tonnes to the 1994/5 peak number. This was associated with a major change in working arrangements – a move from discontinuous to continuous production achieved by a change from a three-shift to a five-shift system. Similar moves have been made in recent times by paper manufacturers elsewhere. But Tullis Russell believes that it was on its own in the time needed to discuss and implement the changes: just five months compared with an industry average of two years. It attributes its success in part to the relationships of higher trust which have been made possible by its employee owner-ship.

The strongly rising trend of production, notwithstanding the down-turns of the business cycle, was in marked contrast to a continuous fall in employment. When Mr Erdal took over the top position in the New Year of 1985, the total number employed in paper making was 1,160. Production that year was just under 52,000 tons. Ten years later, although production had doubled, employment was down 27% to 844. Thus annual output per employee rose from about 45 tonnes of paper to nearly 130 tonnes. That ten-year improvement in labour productivity corresponds to an annual rate of close on 9%. It is best seen as the company's response to the competitive pressures of the market.

The odds must be that the same competitive pressures will force a similar response in the years ahead which in turn will make further manpower reductions inescapable. Even in a growing market and with an increasing market share, the company will be unable to increase its sales at the same pace as its labour productivity improvement.

It is often felt, and sometimes argued, that conditions of continuing manpower reductions are inimical to the success of employee-owned firms. No doubt it is always easier to achieve business success in conditions where demand is rising so fast that employment is also rising. Such conditions are also good for employee morale. On the other hand, those conditions will be satisfied rarely, if at all, in the mature industries of developed countries. So if employee ownership has to confine itself to those rare cases, it is unlikely to become at all widespread.

Mr Erdal and some others are inclined to turn this argument on its head. Their main point is that under a regime of employee ownership any necessary manpower reductions are likely to be managed in ways which minimise the pain and are thus likely to be more acceptable and, in the long term, less costly. This analysis is strongly endorsed by America's two large and substantially employee-owned steel companies – Republic Engineered Steels and Weirton – which faced similar market conditions for years. The argument is attractive and in many ways persuasive. But only time will tell whether employee ownership has given Tullis Russell a cost advantage over its competitors.

Manpower reductions tend to be associated in the public mind with the blue collar sections of a workforce. But in the early years of employee ownership there is often a tendency to move towards a flatter organisation and fewer management layers. It seems that at Tullis Russell, in the ten years following Mr Erdal's appointment as chairman, the manpower reductions were proportionately as big or bigger among the management staff as among the rank and file.

Changes of management personnel have also resulted from an inability on the part of a significant minority of the management staff to adjust to the new world of employee ownership and the changed relationships which it ushers in. Those managers unable to make the necessary adjustments have had to leave.

On the other side of what evidently used to be quite a high adversarial fence, there have been those among the elected shop stewards on the work site who have found the adjustment hard to make, or anyway hard to accept. The elected convenor of shop stewards is said to have lamented more than once the loss of his power base, a loss which he attributes to the company's employee ownership. That, or so he is alleged to have observed, effectively eviscerated his authority, by removing the credibility of a strike threat. Once again only time will tell whether that change, if a change indeed it is, will turn out to be permanent.

Mainly because of sharp fluctuations in the price of the pulp which the company buys in, there seems to be no very consistent relationship between higher output and higher operating profits:

Paper Output in Tonnes and Operating Profits (Losses)
1985 to 1996 (Years to End-March)

Output	Tonnes	Operating Profits £000
1985	56,476	(19)
1986	59,318	4,118
1987	70,853	5,484
1988	77,733	5,576
1989	79,083	4,791
1990	79,185	3,432
1991	77,729	289
1992	70,514	801
1993	71,200	(1,242)
1994	83,575	1,649
1995	106,000	3,727
1996	108,000	4,700

This twelve-year record of the company's paper-making activities offers no evidence of consistently improved performance, whether related to employee ownership or otherwise. But it points us towards an important result of the earlier business acquisitions by Mr Erdal's uncle and predecessor, Dr David Russell. For the profits of these acquired subsidiaries were sufficient to change 1993's operating loss of £1,242 into a group operating profit of £2.7m, to increase the 1994 figures to nearly £3m, and those for the twelve months to end March 1995 to just over £6m. The star performer among the subsidiaries was Brittains, the specialist manufacturer of transfer papers. Those acquisitions by Dr David Russell have therefore served the whole business rather well. For they have enabled the profitability of the whole undertaking to be maintained through the cyclical down-turn in Tullis Russell's paper-making activities. This has made it possible for shares to go on being distributed to employees out of profits, even if at a reduced level.

Efforts to Create an Ownership Culture The 'ownership culture' at Tullis Russell has not yet had time to get bedded down, not least because typical shareholdings of individual employees have not yet reached a significant size. Some believe that employee ownership will make no significant impact on productivity before the value of those individual shareholdings reaches at least five figures. Bryan Greene, a friend of the whole project and until 1996, when he acepted a managerial post, one of the company's most senior elected share councillors, is on record that the necessary cultural change may be forty years away. In fact, evidence elsewhere suggests that with the right policies, appropriate leadership, and effective involvement and communications systems, changes of attitude and behaviour can happen quite quickly.

It is already clear that significant numbers of the company's managers were unable to adjust to the new relationships implicit in a set-up involving employee ownership. To repeat, they had to leave. The phrase 'participative management' is widely used to describe what employee ownership requires even if it is still somewhat elusive to pin down. What is clear is what employee ownership excludes – namely styles of management which are authoritarian, militaristic and/or, though perhaps to a lesser extent, paternalistic. It clearly involves some relinquishment of control by management and conversely a readiness to enable rank-and-file employees to contribute more to decisions and to have more say. Mr Erdal offered a compressed account of these matters at a workshop in Cape Town in August 1995. Having told his audience that the chief purpose of sharing ownership with employees is to improve performance, he went on:

> There is now considerable evidence that this enhancement of performance does not take place unless the managers move to a participative style. *For most managers, who like to control things, this is a major change which takes time* [emphasis added]. It involves a massive amount of communication and consultation, of training and team working, and of quality improvement groups. There are many ways to skin this particular cat, but it is clear that participative management is necessary.

We can conclude this discussion of efforts at Tullis Russell to promote an 'ownership culture' with a look at changes and developments in the linked areas of 'the two Cs – Communication and Consultation'.

In the area of communication, or more accurately of company journalism, Tullis Russell's most eye-catching innovation has been borrowed with full acknowledgement from John Lewis. A new company magazine is distributed to all employees. At least a part of it is believed to be almost universally read: the magazine's letters column. Following the radical tradition pioneered by John Lewis, employees are strongly encouraged to write in, whether in their own names or anonymously. Called *Points of View*, there is an undertaking by the magazine's editor to publish virtually anything and everything sent in. The only exceptions have to do with material which is commercially sensitive or where references to individuals would be likely to cause unacceptable pain. But in the latter case the letter will not normally be censored. The reference to a particular individual or individuals will simply be edited out. Here again, in relation to these details, Tullis Russell is following the John Lewis model. And it follows that model too in the magazine's rule that if letters are of the kind which call for a management answer, that will be provided with a minimum of delay.

Mr Erdal had to use all his chairman's authority to launch *Points of View*, which was fiercely opposed before the event by a large majority of managers. On the other hand most of those who were originally opposed now concede that they were quite wrong. So far from mainly undermining its authority, the anonymous letters make management's task that much easier – by acting as an early warning about sources of shop-floor complaints. And there is a second major benefit. The replies by managers to complaints and criticisms are widely read.

Moreover, *Points of View*, including its anonymous letters column and rules for management reply, has since been copied at the Baxi Partnership, of which Mr Erdal was appointed non-executive chairman in 1994. There is no greater praise than to be copied. It is surely a fair bet that the company journalism pioneered by John Lewis in the *Partnership Gazette* will be increasingly followed by employee-owned businesses elsewhere.

Finally, consultation. The need for some elected representative body of employee shareholders was identified early on in the process of moving towards employee ownership. Since 1992 the resulting institution has been called the Share Council. Members are elected to it by geographical constituencies and have regular, rule-established, meetings with Tullis Russell's top executive bodies. The council also appoints half of the trustee members of each of two employee trusts.

In the summer of 1996, these arrangements at Tullis Russell were being re-examined by an *ad hoc* committee of 'wise persons' drawn from both the share council and the group management board.

First Steps towards Employee Ownership and the 1994 Buy-Out On the eve of the 1994 buy-out, the ownership of Tullis Russell business divided four ways. The family shareholders accounted for the largest block, with 55% of the equity. On the other hand, control lay with the Russell Trust, by virtue of its 51% holding of voting shares: of the combined voting and non-voting shares together its holding was just 25%. Employees held the remaining 20% either directly as individuals (7%) or via the Employee Benefit Trust (13%).

Both types of employee shareholding had been built up since David Erdal took over in 1985, when he also introduced cash profit sharing, perhaps the classic first step for those heading in an employee-ownership direction. The cash scheme is notable in two respects. It provides that an unusually large fixed percentage of pre-tax profits – 15.7% – be allocated annually to employees in proportion to their basic rates of pay. Second, so that the link with individual efforts may be as close as possible, the relevant profits are not those of Tullis Russell and its subsidiaries taken together, but those of the individual businesses for which the employees are working.

The Inland Revenue approved employee share scheme introduced in that same year is linked with the profits of Tullis Russell as a whole. Here again the scheme provided for a fixed percentage of profits – in this case 7.5% – to be allocated annually to buy shares for employees. As with the cash scheme, allocation was proportionate to basic rates of pay, at least initially. Later, as a result of perhaps predictable pressure from the subsequently formed Share Council, that formula was modified in a more egalitarian direction. Under the new formula only 70% of the pool is allocated pro-rata with pay, the balance being distributed equally. The issue was still the subject of lively debate when this case study was being finally revised.

Unlike the arrangements for cash profit sharing by employees, the share scheme had the extra advantage of providing a mechanism to enable the family shareholders to find a buyer, at least for small parcels of their shares. For the annual 7.5% of profits was deliberately used to buy from existing family shareholders rather than, as the law also permits, to subscribe for new shares.

But though these two processes could go forward hand in hand, it is easy to see that they could do so only at a painfully slow pace. If the business were valued at ten times its pre-tax profits, over 130 years would be needed to complete the transfer of the ownership at an annual rate of transfer of just 7.5% of those pre-tax profits. In fact, the price agreed for the 1994 buy-out reflected a multiple of pre-tax profits slightly higher than ten.

To speed up the purchase of shares from family members, a third step was taken in 1987. By establishing a special kind of employee benefit trust (EBT), the company was able to operate what has come to be known in the jargon as a 'case law ESOP'. Given careful attention to legal technicalities, the EBT could borrow money to buy shares from existing shareholders and could hold those shares on behalf of the employees. Above all – and thanks to the precedent of a series of case law judgments that have gone against the Inland Revenue – the company was and is permitted to pass money from *pre-tax* profits to the EBT. This enabled the latter to pay back its borrowings, including the principal as well as interest charges.

Approximately £5m was borrowed from two banks, the Royal Bank of Scotland, and the trade-union-controlled Unity Trust Bank. This was used to buy the 13% shareholding owned by the EBT on the eve of the 1994 buy-out. In this one transaction the family shareholders were able to sell almost twice as many of their shares as via the employee share scheme mechanism which had started in 1987.

So the EBT sharply speeded up the rate at which the family shareholders were enabled to sell. But even after this improvement, family shareholders were anxious, given the company's objective of buying them out completely, to secure a further acceleration. This was not unreasonable. For in the absence of anything new, they faced the prospect that even if the EBT and the employee share scheme were used jointly and separately to best effect, it could well be twenty-five years before they could unlock the last of their capital from Tullis Russell. Moreover, on the basis of past experience, they could scarcely expect a very generous flow of dividend income during the intervening years. And they had to face the prospect that, except for quite modest annual reliefs, they would have to accept full capital gains tax liability on the proceeds of their continuing sales of Tullis Russell shares.

It is not therefore surprising that new ways were sought to speed up, and make more tax-efficient, the process of transferring ownership from the family shareholders to the individual employee shareholders and the EBT. After the Government had given its blessing to so-called statutory ESOPs in 1989, and more especially after it had approved in 1990 a conditional rollover relief from capital gains tax on the proceeds of sales of shares to them, the company and its advisors, spearheaded by its chairman, combed through the new legislation to see whether any seriously practicable new opportunities had been opened up.

But as readers with a taste for detail in matters of this kind may remember, the Government had attached to its new statutory ESOPs two conditions which had such a deterrent effect on possible users that for the five years after 1989 the take-up was virtually zero. One of these deterrent conditions provided that a majority of the trustees of the statutory ESOP had to be elected by a majority of the whole workforce. Because of the control of voting shares held by the Russell Trust, that was something which Tullis Russell might have lived with. But after extended research and the projection of a range of possible 'scenarios' the company decided that the other condition was unacceptable: namely that all the shares acquired by the statutory ESOP must be distributed to individual employees over a maximum period of about seven years – on pain of a claw back of all earlier tax reliefs. After extensively 'modelling the future' the company decided that, partly because of the severity of the business cycle in the paper industry, that was a risk it could not reasonably take.

At the end of March 1994, the Government announced significant relaxations in those two deterrent conditions. In particular, the period allowed for the distribution to individual employees of shares in the statutory ESOP trust, was extended from seven years to twenty years. Tullis Russell embarked on a new round of 'modelling the future'. The conclusion was that it would now be safe to use a statutory ESOP as the key new mechanism for achieving both the desired speed up and an enhancement in the tax efficiency of the ownership transfer.

It must be acknowledged that what we are dealing with here is a fairly complex set of transactions. For employee ownership fans at least, there is a certain elegance about this complexity and it does not immediately give rise to thoughts about lawyers' fees. However, now that Tullis Russell has shown how to negotiate the legal and tax pitfalls, any other family-owned companies who wish to sell to their employees should find it much easier. (For details of the 1994 buy-out deal, see Appendix B.)

What Tullis Russell has achieved is a winning combination: it has been judged by Mr Erdal to be a 'win, win, win buy-out'.

– A win for the family shareholders because it unlocked their capital at an acceptable price.

– A win for the company, because it is enabled to retain its independence on a sustainable basis.

– A win for the employee shareholders because, with any luck, they can look forward to shareholdings worth not less than the equivalent of one year's salary in the not *too* distant future, say by the time of Tullis Russell's bicentenary in 2009.

– It seems reasonable to suggest that the local community at Glenrothes, and those in the neighbourhoods of Tullis Russell's three subsidiaries, are also winners. For there can be a fair certainty that the new group will not be taken over by a competitor and that therefore the security of future employment will be higher than it otherwise would have been.

Is the country also a winner? If we set aside for a moment the narrow calculations of a cost accountant the answer must surely be yes. For, unless the buy-out has *adverse* effects on performance, the country must benefit from the greater spread of wealth which the deal has made possible. And there are also prospective intangible benefits. One of these comes in the form of a workforce with an understanding of business which, according to Mr Erdal, is being transformed by the employee ownership experience. Who knows, this might even turn out to be one of those rare cases where extra tax revenue arising from improved performance more than compensates for any taxes forgone as a result of the employee ownership reliefs. But it will be some time before it becomes possible to make the necessary calculations, if indeed it happens at all.

APPENDIX A: BRITTAINS (TR)

In January 1980, Brittains (TR) – with the TR standing for Tullis Russell – was formed to buy from the receivers the assets of what had previously been Brittains converters, whose parent company had gone bankrupt. Largely because of special factors in its first four months, trading showed a significant loss – of £142,000 on a turnover of just over £1.2m, in its first year. For the sixteen subsequent years, it was consistently and increasingly profitable. Trading profits reached new records in each of the four years down to 1994/5 when they were just over £2.25m on a turnover of just over £12.3m. The later results were achieved by a workforce of scarcely over 100. Basically because of higher paper prices, there was some decline in profits to £1.8m in 1995/6.

In fact, by the end of the 1980s Brittains' contribution to overall group profits, if measured against the size of its workforce, was way ahead of any other part of the business. As elsewhere in Tullis Russell, the new profit-sharing and employee-ownership incentives started around the mid-1980s. Especially through the profit-sharing scheme, Brittains' workforce participated handsomely in the outstanding results of the early 1990s.

As in all Tullis Russell businesses, a cash scheme allocates to the employees 15.7% of profits. This is at the generous end of any spectrum. Still, if profits are modest and have to be shared between large numbers, the cash per employee may not be more than the equivalent of two or three weeks' pay. At Brittains in the two years down to the end of March 1995, the money per employee was equivalent, after taking into account the available tax reliefs, to over 30% on top of annual basic pay. When a forklift driver earning £12,000 a year (taxable) in basic pay receives an after-tax £3,000 as a cash profit share, he must, you would think, feel that things are changing somewhat in his world.

Brittains (TR) has just one product. It is made by applying special coatings to paper supplied by its sister company, Tullis Russell Papermakers, in Scotland. It is known by a wide range of technical names including, apparently, decalcomania paper. I expect that the one best known to the public is 'transfer paper', which can also be understood as a functional description. Readers of middle age will be familiar with 'transfers' from childhood: typically rather dark small postage-stamp-size pictures which go through a brightening up process of transformation when pressed off from their original backing onto a bright field of clean white paper. Brittains makes what can be simply understood as transfer backing paper for grown-up uses: for pressing brilliantly coloured decorations onto porcelain or enamel for example. Among its most important customers are the specialist printers who supply the up-market porcelain manufacturers, businesses like Wedgwood and Royal Doulton in the UK. Each of those two are close neighbours of Brittains in Stoke-on-Trent.

Turning from production to sales, it is not too much to claim that in the fifteen years since it came to be owned by Tullis Russell, Brittains has become one of two world leaders in a quintessentially niche market that is growing fast. Believing that the information would be helpful to its chief (German) competitor, the company does not publish a geographical breakdown of its sales. But it does acknowledge that well over three-quarters of its output is exported, and that at least since the start of the nineties sales growth has been especially buoyant in the Far East. The big question about further sales, according to the managing director, Mr Downes, is whether the porcelain manufacturers on mainland China are going to move significantly to a decoration technique based on waterslide transfer paper. Up to the time of writing they had only just started to take a very first step down that road.

A key feature in the detail of the Brittains experience in the fifteen-odd years since its acquisition by Tullis Russell has a striking similarity with that of its Scottish parent: after marking time for a bit, output went up sharply but employment came almost continually down. Here are the two series:

	Area of Paper Sold	Numbers Employed
1980/81	113,000	n.a.
1981/82	109,000	188
1982/83	108,000	171
1983/84	115,000	153
1984/85	123,000	161
1985/86	117,000	158
1986/87	120,000	136
1987/88	129,000	134
1988/89	133,000	132
1989/90	167,000	120
1990/91	190,000	123
1991/92	177,000	108
1992/93	188,000	107
1993/94	221,000	108
1994/95	232,000	107

As a technical footnote for the specialist reader, it is worth putting on record the units in which the area of output is measured. They are so called 'medium reams' containing 500 sheets of transfer paper in the dimensions 18" x 23".

Of more general interest in relation to the statistics of output and employment is the proud claim of Brittains' management that the 'downsizing' of its workforce has been achieved without anyone becoming unemployed. Attrition and early retirement have been used as extensively as possible. When, in any year, they have not gone far enough, great and largely successful efforts have been made to help those affected by the restructuring to find acceptable alternative jobs in the Stoke-on-Trent area. Apparently there has been only one employee over the whole period covered by the table whose job had to go and for whom it has not been possible to find alternative work elsewhere. She has been kept on to do simple odd tasks as they come up.

The management is also keen to emphasise that the reason why the restructuring has been relatively painless is that since the computerisation of the production process in the mid-1980s, Brittains' employees have accepted what amounts to almost total job flexibility. Unusually for a managing director, Mr Downes is prepared to commit himself explicitly to the proposition that the acceptance of near-total 'work flexibility' by the employees is linked, at least psychologically, to their situation as cash profit sharers and shareholders in the business.

In the absence of any convincing alternative explanation, Mr Downes also attributes to Brittains' ownership and cash profit sharing arrangements a rather startling *événement* which took place shortly before he took over the top job in 1992. One Monday morning, and without prior warning, a deputation of all Brittains' shop stewards 'waited on' Mr Downes outside his office. When the knock came at his door he was, he reports, quite at a loss about what to expect. But what they proposed was, he further reports, well beyond anything he had anticipated or even dreamed of. Their proposal was simple: that they and the whole union arrangement in the company should disband – as having finished its useful shelf life. Faced with this bombshell, Mr Downes's response was surely the right one. He suggested that no decision be taken until the unions and company had jointly sought advice from the statutory Arbitration and Conciliation Service (ACAS). To shorten a potentially longer story, ACAS duly advised that the functions previously performed by the unions should be taken over by an elected works council. That has since happened and the arrangements are said to be working well.

It is no doubt too early to say that an 'ownership culture' is properly, let alone irreversibly, 'bedded down' at Brittains any more than it is anywhere else in the Tullis Russell group. But Mr Downes and his colleagues are ready to talk about the conditions which might make that happen. The main condition that they specify is that the value of an employee's shareholding should reach five figures, or, even better, come to equal one year's pay. As elsewhere in the group that goal is still some way off. But with one proviso it is not entirely out of reach. The proviso is essentially, of course, that the company should continue to be commercially successful and to make at least reasonable profits.

The great increase in Brittains' output over the eight years starting

1988 was partly a matter of an expanding world market and partly of the company's successful efforts to secure a larger share of it. The latter was essentially made possible by changes in the company. An important change was what amounted to the computerisation of most of the manufacturing process, coupled, as we have seen, with an acceptance by employees of almost completely flexible working.

Since its acquisition by Tullis Russell in 1979, Brittains has probably enjoyed, at least against its main German competitor, one specific supply side advantage: the fact that it is a one product business, and that all the efforts of both its production and sales staff are concentrated on transfer paper and nothing else. No doubt that makes it vulnerable in the very long run. But there is little doubt that it confers a real advantage over the short and medium term.

As a footnote to that contention, it is worth noting that the bankruptcy of the antecedent Brittains was widely attributed at the time to a rash of ill-considered 'diversification' in the 1960s and 1970s. From its original core activities of paper making and coating, the earlier Brittains had diversified by the middle of the 1970s into such non-contiguous fields as civil engineering, road haulage and insurance.

And that brings me to a final point which is unashamedly historical. Paper making and coating at the Brittains Ivy Mill site in Stoke-on-Trent did not start quite as early as 1809, when, as we know, what became known as Tullis Russell opened for business in Glenrothes. But the activities on the Stoke site do go back to the 1820s. There have been no bankruptcy discontinuities at Glenrothes; but on the Ivy Mill site in Stoke-on-Trent there have been not just one but two – the first in the 1830s. What then was the name of the original owners and paper makers who went bankrupt? It is a name as illustrious as any in the history of paper making and we ran into it in the main section of this case study. It is the name Fourdrinier.

APPENDIX B: THE BUY-OUT DETAILS

The buy-out deal was effected within the framework of an offer from a new company set up for the purpose. The new company was the Tullis Russell Group Ltd, and its offer was to buy the entire share capital of the existing business, Tullis Russell & Co. Ltd.

With minor exceptions, the shareholders in the existing business were offered a choice between two alternatives:

– To accept loan stock in return for their shares at a specified price and on specified interest rate terms and with a pre-specified exit at various dates in the future.

– To accept a shareholding in the new 'group' company which would be the same in all important respects as their shareholding in the existing one, in effect exchanging their old shares for new shares on a one-for-one basis.

As may be inferred, the first of these two alternatives was essentially aimed at the family shareholders and was designed to offer them a deferred exit. Conversely, the offer of shares in the new group was essentially aimed at the Russell Trust and the EBT. In fact, the two trusts' acceptance of the share alternative was recorded in the offer document.

As for the individual employee shareholders, the management's view was that an acceptance by them of either alternative was entirely reasonable even if a choice of the second would be seen as showing a higher level of commitment to Tullis Russell's employee-owned future.

When the offer closed, just three clear weeks after it had opened, family members had opted to exchange all their shares for loan stock. At the same time over 90% of the employee shareholders (representing over 90% of employee-owned shares) had chosen the share alternative.

It goes without saying that the pricing and other arrangements had to be acceptable both to the family shareholders and to the company. The two parties were separately advised. What appeared in the offer document was the result, essentially, of a negotiation between these two sets of advisers.

The background to the key negotiation about the share price was a series of annual valuations. As required by law, these had had to be agreed each year since 1986 with the Inland Revenue, as an essential component of Tullis Russell's tax-assisted employee share scheme. More precisely there were two series of annual share valuations, one series for the voting and a second for the non-voting shares. However, by custom and agreement the valuation of the latter was not fixed independently but set at 90% of the value of the former. For the five years down to 1993, the actual valuations in pence per share were:

	Voting Shares	Non-Voting
1989	81.5	73.3
1990	58.8	52.9
1991	57.9	52.1
1992	43.8	39.5
1993	45.3	40.8

Given these valuations in the years running up to the buy-out, the 72p price which was agreed for the non-voting shares – the category which accounted for almost all of the family members' shareholdings – may seem rather generous. On the other hand, it seems that it was already clear when the negotiation took place that the business was heading for far and away its best year of paper production and that, despite the high pulp price, profits were rising with the upturn in the business cycle.

There is also at least hearsay evidence that a higher price could have been negotiated if the buyer had been a quoted company competitor of Tullis Russell. A competitor will often offer the highest price for the business – so the hearsay evidence is persuasive. But so is the rejoinder to any suggestion that the family shareholders should therefore have been advised to approach such a buyer. Capital Gains Tax (CGT) rollover relief applied in both cases – to sale to the ESOP or to a competitor, with the competitor paying for Tullis Russell in its own shares. But the value of these two rollover reliefs – and this is the key point – is not the same. For in the first case – a sale to a statutory ESOP trust – the relief applies to what are in principle diversified portfolios of shares and other assets and financial instruments into which the proceeds of the sale to the ESOP trust might legitimately be reinvested. In the second case it is retsricted to a totally non-diversified shareholding in the paper of the quoted competitor. The professional advisers to the family shareholders evidently formed the view that the lower level of risk exposure involved in accepting the offer from the Tullis Russell group was at least adequate compensation for any higher price that could realistically have been expected from a competitor.

As for the rate of 7.5% interest on the loan stock, the offer document points out that compared with their dividend income over the recent past, this meant an increase of well over 200% for the family shareholders. The offer document further specifies that the interest rate payable would be hoisted to 9.5% if there was any slippage in the loan stock redemption timetable it lays down: namely redemption (at par) in three equal instalments, in 1996, 1999 and 2002. For the record, the date of the first of these instalments was in fact brought forward, and half of the first instalment was paid to the family shareholders in the summer of 1995.

I need to explain how these arrangements are linked in to the sale of the family members' shares to the statutory ESOP trust, and how therefore the eligibility for CGT rollover relief is secured. The answer is that immediately before the effective redemption and the pay-out of actual money, the loan stock is converted back into ordinary shares which are then bought by the statutory ESOP trust. What that trust pays for those shares is then paid out to the family shareholders. In this way they 'make a sale of their shares to the statutory ESOP trust' and so qualify for CGT relief on the assets into which the proceeds of the sale are reinvested.

Readers with a memory for detail in matters of this kind will realise that the shares so acquired by the statutory ESOP trust cannot, at least as the law stood in the autumn of 1995, hang about in there indefinitely. They must be 'got out' to individual employees within twenty years – on pain of a retrospective claw back of all the tax reliefs associated with the statutory ESOP. To make that 'getting out' out process tax effective in its turn, it will be achieved through the conduit of Tullis Russell's pre-existing employee profit share scheme. Furthermore, and in order that that process does not take for ever, the company will lift substantially from the present figure of 7.5 the percentage of pre-tax profits which it applies to finance that scheme.

There is one further point which needs to be taken into account and which is in fact a precondition for the achievement of ownership stability at Tullis Russell. If the 55% of the equity bought from family shareholders were to be held indefinitely by individual employees, the employee-ownership arrangements would simply not be sustainable. What we are dealing with here, if the phrase is permitted, is an example of a *sequential* Scylla and Charybdis. Tullis Russell's prospective employee-ownership path must first avoid the Scylla of the clawback. But having done so it must still, subsequently, avoid the Charybdis of unsustainability. It will avoid the second by taking steps to enable its long-established EBT, and the associated 'case law ESOP', to buy shares from individual employee shareholders to the extent needed if a sustainable equilibrium is to be achieved. The best estimate by Tullis Russell's top management is that sustainability requires that not more than 35% of the shares be held by individual employee shareholders at any one time.

Soon after the buy-out offer had been accepted, the company granted share options to approximately fifty top managers at a price of 69p per share. As provided in the offer document, these options were granted at 85% of the price of the shares in the buy-out transaction. The document also laid down limits on the total value of the options that any individual could be granted: not more than the equivalent of three times annual salary or (if greater) £100,000.

As the loan stock is converted back into shares at the point of its redemption, the number of shares in issue will steadily increase and more than double between the date when the options were granted and when the last redemption instalment is paid. Thus the business will have to achieve substantial success if these options are going to be worth very much. And, of course, if that success is achieved all the employee shareholders – not just those who have been granted options – will benefit from the higher share price. These points are worth making because the options, even if a detail, are an intrinsically important one. Also, this issue provoked lively debate in the Share Council and vigorous letters to *Points of View*.

30
Concluding Remarks

A · THE CASE

In the middling and inferior stations of life, the road to virtue and that to fortune, to such fortune, at least, as men in such stations can reasonably expect to acquire, are, happily in most cases, very nearly the same. *Adam Smith, 'The Theory of Moral Sentiments'*

The starting point of this book is the still widespread, and in my view largely justified, discontent among ordinary people with the system of conventional private capitalism, especially as it is practised in the US and Britain. The fact is that however optimal it may look from the eagle's nest occupied by the editor of the *Economist* or from the trading floors where men – and 'superwomen' – could earn, with bonuses, well over £1m a year in the mid-1990s, the system's main features seem a good deal less than optimal to many; and almost certainly to a majority of those in Adam Smith's 'middling and inferior stations'. Among the system's particulars most subject to criticism are income differentials which offend against any reasonable idea of shared citizenship and barely acceptable levels of employment security. In more general terms, what is seen as the top downwards oppressiveness of the system is widely resented, as is the way in which it serves to perpetuate the subordination of one class to another.

From that starting point I go on to emphasise that these discontents are substantially non-existent in Japan, despite the fact that in law the Japanese system of corporate capitalism is very similar to what it is in the Anglo-Saxon world. Following Professor Ronald Dore, I then suggest that because of a Confucian component in Japanese culture, the living realities of its capitalism, even though not encompassed by its corporate law, have been modified and softened with immense benefits to the country's economy. Always following Professor Dore, the argument is that because of this softening the typical Japanese business is seen as a more or less acceptably fair and reasonable organisation by the majority of those working in it. In consequence the country's businesses attract high levels of employee commitment. As a further consequence Japan's trade unions behave for most of the time as if their members' interests are very closely linked to the success of the businesses for which they work. And that link is objectively reinforced by a typically high variable component in employee remuneration which moves up or down with financial results.

Given the obvious potential benefits if similar levels of employee commitment, and similarly union attitudes conducive to business success, could be achieved in the US and the UK, there is an obvious question: whether any effective method exists for injecting the desired Confucian component into other cultures. But if, as seems on the face of it more likely, there is no such method, then it makes sense to see whether there are any other means of achieving, in the Anglo-Saxon world and elsewhere, levels of employee commitment and pro-business trade union attitudes similar to those in Japan. The central hypothesis of this book is, of course, that employee ownership offers the most promising way forward.

Here as earlier, and in anticipation of wrongly targeted objections, I must again flag up some of the ways in which my own recommendation of the 'employee ownership alternative' needs to be qualified. Though myself committed to its promotion, I am still more fundamentally committed to a pluralism of corporate institutions and to voluntarism, assisted by tax reliefs where appropriate, as the only way to achieve changes that will endure. Employee ownership is not for everyone or every business and it should never, or anyway almost never, be imposed. For what it is worth, I think it is true that most, though certainly not all, of the employee ownership enthusiasts in my acquaintance are, like me, paid up members of the open, broad and pluralist 'church of tolerance'. Many have come to it through the writings of Karl Popper and of Isaiah Berlin.

My prior commitments to pluralism and voluntarism also partly explain why I do not favour the kind of full-blooded, and exclusive legal and moral endorsement of the democratic and employee owned firm advocated by some enthusiasts and most eloquently by Professor David Ellerman. I agree with Ellerman that there are *some* parallels between renting another person's labour and owning it. I think too that his intellectual contribution to the thinking through of ownership and corporate government issues has been outstanding. Especially notable in my view has been his discussion of the asymmetry in the way in which employment law deals with questions of personal responsibility: essentially the law assigns full control in the driving seat to the employer and only assigns any real responsibilty to the employees when there is an accident. More generally I accept as persuasive, though not overriding, his arguments for the primacy of labour and for the democratic accountability of management if what we want are more truly just business structures. I also remember being delighted years ago by his discovery that ex-slaves who failed to 'make it' in Liberia and/or Sierra Leone in the 1840s and 1850s, and then returned to the southern states of the US, were liable to have to seek the permission of a court if they wished to 'resume the state of slavery'. I am fairly sure that the name of the ex-slave in the case to which he referred was Emile.

As against David Ellerman's 'whole hog' approach to employee ownership and democratic corporate government, I earlier characterised my own as pragmatic. For one thing I believe it would take at least 100 years – if indeed it could ever be done – to persuade a mature electorate that the employment contract is sufficiently like a contract of self-enslavement for it to be outlawed. I also believe that even in the relatively affluent welfare states of today's world, employment may be so important that it in any particular case it may make sense for employee shareholders to sell out if, for example, greater employment security can thereby be achieved. Had I been a bus driver in Fareham or Chesterfield in 1995, I would have voted to sell. And the same might well have been true had I been an employee shareholder in the Michigan copper mine which sold out to German buyers in the early 1990s. Who knows, I might also have been one of those who voted to sell the venerable co-operative glass works in Albi when it became apparent, again in the early 1990s, that that was the only way – in the absence of truly heroic sacrifices – in which a significant number of its jobs could be saved.

As well as being pragmatic my own approach is also incremental and incremental in two senses. First, I can see some virtue or at least potential virtue in the co-determination laws in Germany and those which prescribe profit sharing in France. Each can be seen as a halfway house to employee ownership, the former along the dimension of corporate government, the latter along that of financial participation. Second, I can also see some virtue or at least potential virtue in employee ownership which is less than 100%, whether no more than a significant minority stake as at Polaroid, or over 50% as at United Airlines.

The reference to *potential* virtue should serve to remind readers that the benefits of employee ownership are never, or at least only very rarely, automatic. Rather specific steps will normally have to be taken if ordinary employee owners are to be both motivated and enabled to improve the performance of the business in which they work. All or at least almost all of my case studies point to that truth. Naive employee ownership zealots who believe that by itself it will work to raise levels of 'x' efficiency are flying in the face of almost all the empirical evidence. There are striking parallels between the faith of these zealots in employee ownership and that of the orthodox Christian opponents of the Pelagian heretics in the early Church. The former believed that the grace of the holy spirit would do the job of making believers into genuine Christians. Against that the Pelagians argued that a good deal of personal effort was also required.

Given this approach, my case is not confounded by examples of failure. As we have seen, most American studies show that employee ownership by itself, without a supporting buttress of appropriate employee involvement in corporate government, makes no difference to business performance one way or the other. In the limiting case, ownership alone may even have negative consequences if it gives rise to expectations of a bigger say in corporate government which are then confounded.

But it would be absurd to go over all the empirical evidence once again. The question is whether what has been brought together in this book is sufficiently persuasive to justify further Government support on public interest grounds and a shift to more positive attitudes by the key players: by top management, by the trade unions, and by financial institutions.

Aside from the evidence of my own individual case studies and what they say about the quality of working life as well as about performance, it may just be worth reminding readers of the semi-aggregate evidence from sample studies in America. To repeat, the single most important piece was published by the American Government's General Accounting Office in 1987. Comparing a sample of 'significantly employee-owned firms' with a matched sample of conventionally owned ones, the study showed that those among the former which had also introduced schemes of effective employee participation in decision making were the clear winners. By measures of both employment and profitability growth they were shown to outperform the conventionally owned competition. They were also shown to outperform themselves, in the period before their employee ownership started. What is more, not quite all but the great majority of a growing bookshelf of similar but academic American sample studies of matched ESOP and non-ESOP firms have come up with the same conclusion. Finally, and this only came to my attention early in 1997 when I had just started to think about this last chapter, an important new piece of evidence surfaced from reasearch work in Washington State in 1994. Again we are dealing with a matched sample study. But in this case a number of firms which were significantly employee owned and significantly participatory were set for comparison against a matching sample of firms which, though conventionally owned, had also introduced advanced schemes of employee participation. Those in the first group emerged as the winners in the study, strongly reinforcing the commonsense view that ownersip is an important independent variable which, when added on to participation, can produce extra benefits. (The title of this study is *Comparing Growth Rates in Employee Ownership Companies to their Participatory Competitors: A Supplement to Employment and Sales Growth in Washington State Employee Ownership Companies: A Comparative Analysis*. It is written by Peter Kardas, Ph.D. of the Washington State Employee Ownership Programme.)

With one possible qualification, my own view is that fair-minded readers, having absorbed and reflected upon the evidence, will see it as sufficiently positive to justify further steps of promotion. The qualification I will highlight at the conclusion of this chapter. It has to do with the performance of economies as a whole rather than that of individual firms or groups of firms. But in relation to the latter, I have no serious doubt that fair-minded readers will see the evidence as positive, notwithstanding the acknowledged examples of failure and notwithstanding the acknowledgement of special reasons for failure by employee-owned businesses. For it is true that those businesses, as I have shown with examples, may face difficulties linked to their ownership and corporate government structures as well as all the difficulties faced by any business in a competitive market economy.

The empirical evidence about the potential benefits to actual businesses of a combination of employee ownership and employee involvement in corporate government must be the primary and necessary condition for urging further steps in the same direction. Without that we should collapse the whole project like a tent and try something else. On the other hand, if that condition is satisfied, then it is reasonable to take account of changes which might be expected to follow outside the actual businesses: beneficial changes in the economy as a whole and perhaps also in the health and well-being of the communities in which these businesses are located.

I have space for no more than a really brief discussion of these likely consequential changes. In terms of the political priorities of the 1990s, the most important would be lower levels of unemployment. The case studies have shown this result in relation to particular businesses and business groups. Whole steel plants, as we have seen, can be saved from closure by employee ownership, and thus so can the communities which depend on the associated incomes. We have seen too, for example in the case of the Mondragon group, that these firms may deliver hugely more new jobs when the business cycle is in an expanding phase, and be hugely more successful at preserving jobs when it is contracting. Nearer home we have seen that partly because of the high but variable bonus component in the package of benefits enjoyed by its partners, the John Lewis Partnership has been more successful than its top British competitors in sustaining employment levels during recessions.

In relation to particular businesses I should also mention, for a fuller discussion shortly, the significant employment loss which results from the failure of private companies to solve problems of ownership succession. The potential of employee ownership for saving those jobs is obvious enough.

Standing aside from the employment generated and sustained and indeed lost by particular businesses, it can be plausibly argued that the more widespread the incidence of employee ownership and profit sharing in a market economy the higher will be the 'safe' level of economic growth which the authorities may target. Here we are referring to growth rates which will be compatible with non-accelerating rates of inflation. The hypothesis that that will be so is explained by the judgement that, other variables being equal, there will be lower pressure for big wage increases in employee-owned and/or profit-sharing firms. On the basis of these arguments a well-known Wall Street investment banker, Felix Rohatyn, was in fact prepared to go on the public record in 1996 with a bold prediction: to the effect that if employee ownership and profit sharing were to become really significant features in the American economy, then it would become safe for the authorities to increase by a full percentage point their target rate of growth for the country's economy.

I would like to make one more point about the potential benefits 'outside the factory gates' that employee ownership, and the employee involvement which needs to go with it, might be expected to bring with them if sustained in a community, a region, or indeed a country, for any considerable period of time. My point here is in fact an old hypothesis which goes back at least as far as John Stuart Mill. But it is one which, so far as I know, only began to be seriously researched in early 1997. Put crudely, the hypothesis is that the two together, employee ownership and employee involvement, can result in measurably higher levels in the quality of a community's life – for example in the quality of its parenting, in the educational achievement of its children, in improved health, in reduced crime, in greater rates of citizen participation in civil society, perhaps even in less time spent watching the television. As some readers will know, apart from its intuitive appeal, the hypothesis appears to enjoy some tangential support from the work of scholars like Richard Wilkinson and Robert Putnam. I have no space for a proper discussion of their work here. But in summary Putnam's work seems to show a link between democratic participation and the quality of a community's life. The link which Wilkinson's work suggests is one between narrower income differentials and higher scores on some standard measures of public health and well being – for example, life expectancy and levels of crime. Putnam's data comes from Italy. Wilkinson's comes from a number of countries. The location of the new research is the small Italian town of Imola with which, from two of my case studies, readers will already be familiar.

B · MAIN OPPORTUNITIES

Those readers who are at least half persuaded of the case for promoting the gradual and voluntary spread across British business of employee ownership, and of its complementary employee participation in corporate government, may welcome a brief discussion here of the situations which offer the greatest promise for these changes. Having reviewed those situations we can then go on to ask whether, always within a framework of voluntarism, some additional measures of encouragement by the authorities would be appropriate.

The most common business problems to which employee ownership can offer attractive solutions are, as has already been argued, those of ownership succession in private companies, perhaps especially when those are family businesses. (By private I mean 'non-quoted', with their shares not listed on a stock exchange.) Listed companies do not have to face up to ownership succession problems, at least not in the same way as private companies. As their shares are bought and sold, ownership simply rolls over. In that process the employees are no more and no less than 'part of the furniture' of the business in which shares are being continuously bought and sold.

But it is not only argument which points to the ownership succession problems of unlisted companies as the most promising source for changes to employee ownership. The American evidence demonstrates that once employee ownership becomes reasonably well known and once hostilities to it (of one kind and another) have been at least partly damped down, that is what actually happens. In the the first half of the 1990s, as in the 1980s, the wish of main shareholders in private companies to be bought out was the starting point for the largest single cluster of moves in America to employee ownership. We are talking of annual US numbers in the middle hundreds of businesses. So we might reasonably look forward, once employee ownership becomes better known and more accepted in Britain, to annual numbers of between 50 and 100 in the UK.

Next I want to highlight a converse point: the cost measured by job losses and thus reduced employment if employee ownership is not seen, and therefore not used, as one solution to these problems. I know of no studies which have estimated the scale of the employment numbers lost in Britain for this reason. But a semi-official French study in the 1980s estimated that 10% of the country's combined annual total of bankruptcies and voluntary liquidations – perhaps an average annual total as high as 2,000 cases – result from a failure to cope with ownership succession problems. (Reported in brochure on *Loi sur le Développement de l'Initiative Economique, Ministère de l'Economie, des Finances, et du Budget,* 1984.) Since then the European Commission has come up with estimates running into the high tens of thousands, for the annual job losses from this source in the countries of the European Union as a whole. Yet the Commission's enthusiasm for recommending employee ownership to member countries as one means for reducing the numbers has been at best limp and watery, and for most of the time virtually zero.

After the ownership succession problems of private companies, the available evidence suggests that at least in the UK the spinning off of non-core activities by conglomerates – whether the latter are private or listed – is potentially the next most important starting point for changes to employee ownership. Indeed, with only minor and probably revenue neutral changes in the law, the numbers of businesses moving into employee ownership in the wake of corporate spin-off decisions could come in Britain to exceed those from all other sources and do so by a comfortable margin. That is because of the consistently high numbers of management buy-outs (MBOs) – and more recently also of management buy-ins (MBIs) – which have featured in Britain's business life at least since the early 1970s. According to the well-established Centre for Management Buy-out Research at Nottingham University, the annual number of these transactions averaged between 500 and 600 over the seven years down to 1996 and roughly two thirds were in the MBO category. The proportion that have subsequently failed has varied from year to year around 10%. Typically most of the survivors either go public, that is float their shares successfully on a stock exchange, after between five and ten years or are the subject of a trade sale. The resulting capital gains for those involved in the original transaction typically reach seven figures and often more.

To repeat, with relatively modest and probably revenue neutral changes in the law, many of these MBOs and MBIs could be replaced by what are now normally known as management-led employee buy-outs or MEBOs. Indeed the main obstacle which prevents that from starting to happen, as I shall come on to explain shortly, is not so much the law, let alone the availability of finance, but the typically hostile attitudes of both managers and trade union officials.

As exemplified by my two case studies from America's steel industry a third starting point for a move to employee ownership is the impending, and sometimes actual, close down of a more conventionally owned business. Of course, in the absence of a widespread readiness by employees to make truly heroic sacrifices, many 'impending closures' will have become inescapable by the eve of the closure happening, or indeed well before. On the other hand the best available evidence suggests that in an important minority of cases that calamity can be averted. Maybe all the jobs will not be saved but a worthwhile number can be. The United Steelworkers of America (USWA) must be given enormous credit for its role as the prime mover behind processes which successfully used employee ownership in the late 1980s, and then in the 1990s, to avert closures. Tens of thousands of jobs have been saved in this way through its advocacy and good offices. The union's experience in the late 1980s and the first half of the 1990s suggests that in 20% of all cases in which its help was sought, the threatened jobs, or at least a substantial percentage of them, were saved. Thereafter the success rate was over 90%.

My two British local bus company case studies and that of Britain's NFC point to privatisation as a further starting point for changes to employee ownership. So does the study of Hungary's Herend Porcelain Manufactory, a most exemplary MEBO privatisation, if ever there was one. As we know, the resulting employee ownership in my three British privatisation cases lasted no more than a few years. Sill it was not without its benefits nor indeed without its rank-and-file employee beneficiaries. But there is no need to go over that ground again. It makes more sense to point to another privatisation MEBO in Britain's local bus industry where its employee ownership, like that at Herend, was still very much alive and well when this was written in the spring of 1997. That other example is Preston Bus which operates in and around the Lancashire town from which it takes its name. With roughly 300 employees it is similar in size to each of the two local bus companies studied earlier in this book. Like Chesterfield Transport it was previously owned by the local authority. Its actual buy-out in 1993 has other points in common with Chesterfield's: for example it was very much a joint management and trade union effort.

In many ways Preston Bus deserves a full-length case study. Among other things its 100% post-privatisation employee ownership seems certain to survive into the next century. But I would risk presenting an unbalanced picture if I pursued it here. For the main point about the Thatcher and Major privatisation programmes in

Britain is that for employee ownership, except on the margin, they were missed opportunities on an unprecedented and probably never to be repeated scale. As for the similar opportunities thrown up by privatisation programmes in former Communist countries from 1989 onwards, I explained in the preface why, Herend always excepted, I have chosen to leave them out of this book.

What about the opportunities that could be thrown up by programmes of privatisation which might be enacted by the Blair Government? I keep an open mind about whether any new privatisation will in fact be enacted by Mr. Blair's Government. After all, given what was removed from the public sector by the successive Thatcher and Major programmes between the early 1980s and the spring of 1997, there was not much left for Mr Blair to privatise, at least not unless schools and hospitals are to be included as possible targets.

But two positive points are perhaps worth making. The first is that given their character as service undertakings, two of the largest still unprivatised businesses after the May 1997 election, the Post Office and the London Underground, look like rather promising candidates for employee ownership. Even more promising candidates, or so it seems to me – and this is my second point – are the residential care homes owned by the local authorities. Of course there are some formal and some real financial differences between residential care and care delivered in people's homes. All the same they are sufficiently similar for the now well established successes of employee ownership in home care to create a reasonable expectation that the same would happen in residential care. Readers can refresh their memories about the evidence for the former by turning back to the case study of Co-operative Home Care in New York. Or, nearer home, they might visit Sunderland Home Care Associates in the North East.

The wish of principal shareholders in private companies to be bought out when faced with problems of ownership succession, the decisions by conglomerates to spin off non-core activities, the privatisation programmes of Governments and local authorities, and lastly impending closures where a successful rescue is still possible, these will surely be the main starting points for the spread of significant employee ownership in the future. I say 'significant' advisedly. Readers may remember that in my view employee ownership, if it is to qualify as significant, must satisfy two tests.

First, taken together, the shareholdings of all the employees must
exceed the threshold necessary to give them a defined collective
voice in the corporate government of the business. Second, taken
individually, the average employee ownership stake – or average
annual bonus where that constitutes the main ownership reward –
must be sufficient to have a real chance of influencing individual
behaviour. An average bonus with the value of Christmas dinner
won't do. Nor will an employee shareholding worth a few weeks'
wages.

There may be other starting points for particular employee-
ownership projects. Readers will remember the examples of
Polaroid and of United Airlines from my case studies. At Polaroid,
its employee ownership was introduced as a defence against a
threat of take-over. At United Airlines the prime mover behind the
project was the pilots' union, namely ALPA. The reasons which led
ALPA to go for employee ownership, which it had tried three times
to achieve before its eventual success in 1994, were fully discussed
in the case study. But were other unions to follow the example of
the ALPA pilots at United, and decide that employee ownership
offers a better framework in which to exercise their calling, or at
least that it is worth a try, then we might begin to see quite
appreciable shifts in the prevailing corporate ownership furniture.

What is more, it can hardly be emphasised too much that
the ESOP mechanism invented by the late Louis Kelso is almost
protean in its range of possible applications. There will be new
particular starting points, to add to take over defences and pioneering union initiatives. There will be a few cases too where the ESOP
mechanism is used to help start up new businesses from scratch.
Nevertheless it is not cases of those kinds, but ones that fall into the
four main categories that we have just reviewed, which will best
justify a public interest argument for new Government assistance.
We must turn next to discuss what forms such assistance might
most sensibly take. I will focus first on possible measures to
encourage employee ownership to be used more frequently as the
solution to problems of ownership succession in private companies.

The good news is that the most helpful new measure would be
revenue neutral except in so far as it encouraged a bigger take up of
existing reliefs. It can be easily and briefly specified, even if the
language is inescapably technical and cumbersome. What is needed is
that a key existing condition, relating to the tax reliefs available

when shares are sold to a statutory ESOP trust, be modified. The relevant condition specifies that all shares which are sold to such a trust with the benefit of a rollover relief for capital gains tax, must eventually be got out to individual employees. The condition needs to be modified in such a way that the relief will also be available when an appropriate percentage of the share capital of the employee owned business is not got out to individual employees at all, but is held indefinitely on their behalf in a permanent employee trust.

The logic of what lies behind the need for a substantial percentage of employee shares to be held indefinitely on their behalf in an employee trust if the employee ownership is to be sustainable, was spelt out in some detail in the Tullis Russell case study. There is no need to go to such lengths again here. But three points are worth making.

Without a substantial holding of employee shares in a permanent trust, it will simply be impossible both a) to buy back shares from individuals who leave and b) to make the investments necessary to remain competitive.

What we are dealing with is a matter not of law but of business logic. So it applies to employee ownership in America – or indeed Hungary or indeed anywhere else – with precisely the same force as it does in the UK. The case studies of, for example, Weirton and Republic Engineered Steels provide unchallengeable evidence to that effect.

Some argue that there is no need for or virtue in sustainability and/or that it is at variance with America's more mobile culture and/or that the thinking behind it may be either unacceptably paternalistic or possibly unacceptably impious – by virtue of seeking to go on 'for ever'. There are three common-sense rejoinders. One is that people working in employee-owned firms are as free to leave them as people who work in more conventional ones. The second is that if employee ownership can deliver the benefits which the case studies of the best ones suggest is possible, then it is absurd to settle for a framework which makes that ownership necessarily unsustainable. And third, as a counter to the possible charge of impiety, it is worth pointing out that conventional companies are free under company law to plan corporate lives co-terminus with that of the planet.

What, next, about changes in the law to encourage a switch from MBOs or MBIs to MEBOs when conglomerates decide to spin off subsidiary businesses that are deemed to fall outside their inner core? In this case, to repeat, the main obstacles to change are almost certainly the reluctance of managers to share the potential capital gains with a wider group and the reluctance of union leaders and officials to push reasonable demands for their members to take part. The managers should be more enlightened and generous. The union leaders should show more courage and be prepared to bargain for defined employee 'MEBO rights' when corporate spin-offs take place. But of course it is much easier to offer prescriptions than to change attitudes .The latter will remain the biggest obstacles. They are at the heart of the wider problem of successful employee ownership promotion.

But to return to the legal issues. The company lawyers say that there is one rather specific and revenue neutral change which might be helpful in promoting a switch to wider employee involvement in spin-off deals. The point is almost unacceptably technical but perhaps just worth spelling out. Currently a subsidiary company may not form a statutory ESOP. Given that the value of such a company's shares is liable to manipulation, the case for a general prohibition is reasonable. However, an unintended consequence of what is otherwise sensible is that when a large company is selling a non-core subsidiary, the subsidiary cannot itself set up a statutory ESOP. Consequently it is that much more difficult, and may be relatively less tax effective, to include the rank-and-file employees in any associated buy-out. The consensus among lawyers, or at least among the small minority who are reasonably sympathetic to employee ownership, is that it should be possible to frame the desired exceptions to the general prohibition without any seriously adverse consequences.

What finally about extra encouragement by Government for employee ownership when businesses are threatened with closure – or have actually been closed – and when they are privatised? In relation to the first I don't think I can do more than commend and draw to the attention of a larger audience a rather specific measure of support which relates to situations following actual closures and which was enacted by the Italian Parliament in the 1980s. This is the so-called Marcora law, named after the senator who was the prime mover behind it but who has since died. Under it and so long as a number of well-designed conditions are satisfied, those made unemployed when a business is closed down are free to take a part of their prospective unemployment benefit in a lump sum. An obvious proviso is that the lump sum must be invested within the framework of a plan to get the defunct business, or part of it, started again.

No doubt there will always be a vocal minority of ideological Schumpeterians who posit long-term benefits if the 'creative destruction' of capitalism is simply allowed to get on with doing its stuff without serious contrary interventions. There is obviously something in that view so long as it is taken to do no more than a recommendation of caution: in stopping the close down of businesses heading in that direction and in encouraging those which have already closed to re-open. Nevertheless both the experience and the procedures of the United Steelworkers of America (USWA) seem to provide us with excellent guidelines to follow. In relation to policy and procedures, as readers may remember, USWA will only be prepared to seek help for a failing or failed business if the chances of success have been shown to be reasonable or better on the basis of top quality feasibility studies and business plans. As noted earlier, USWA has supported efforts to get help in some 20% of the cases that have been brought to it. On the other hand, when help has been forthcoming there has then been a success rate of over 90%.

As for changes in the law to encourage more employee ownership outcomes of privatisation, the politicians face an extended spectrum of choice even if we confine ourselves, as we should, to a framework of voluntarism. No one in their senses would seek to *impose* an employee ownership outcome on a process of privatisation. Even in a country like Slovenia, where the main privatisation law is as employee ownership friendly as any that I know, the rank-and-file employees and their managers are free *not* to take advantage of what is on offer. Moreover they are required to put in either 'citizens vouchers' or money or both, if they are to take maximum advantage of the employee ownership opportunities available to them. For the record, in the case of most of the businesses in Slovenia's main privatisation programme, that maximum is such that the employees and ex-employees together can acquire up to 60% of the share capital of the business on a privileged basis.

At the other end of the spectrum is what was typical of the main privatisation projects under the successive Thatcher and Major administrations between the early 1980s and the election of 1997. If we exclude the local bus industry, NFC and few other one-off cases of MEBO privatisation, those responsible for selling off the state's industries offered no more than gestures to their employees. The gestures took the form of 'sweetener packages', typically consisting of a few giveaway shares worth the equivalent of say ten days' wages – offers to buy rather more at a discounted price, and the privilege of queue jumping over the general public's 'Sid and Doris' in the subscription for shares at the full issue price. In no case, so far as I know, did the acquisition of employee shares in this way satisfy the first of my two tests of significance and exceed in aggregate the number needed for a defined voice in corporate government. Of course some employees, especially among the higher paid, bought blocks of shares of undoubted financial significance to them as individuals. Many will indeed have made substantial killings. I sometimes think that an important unstated aim of the Tory privatisation strategy was to allow a small minority of the already well-off to become even richer. Certainly that seems like a plausible inference from the high numbers of management buy-outs which were waved through, especially in the local bus industry. Fair enough, or so some will say. But others may detect unacceptable class bias and wonder whether what happened is really compatible with the reasonable aim of moving in the direction of a less class-ridden society. Is it a sensible objective of public policy that the already well off should stand to be far and away the main beneficiaries of what are essentially *political* acts, namely privatisation programmes?

Moreover, it is not really plausible to argue that those responsible for the Thatcher and Major privatisations, the politicians, the civil servants and their advisers, acted as they did because there was no knowledge of any realistic alternatives. NFC, as was made clear in the case study, was one of the very first of the post-1979 privatisation projects. It happened in the life of the first Thatcher Government and had indeed been targeted for privatisation in the party's manifesto for the 1979 election.

As a commentary on all this I can do no better than remind readers of what the late Philip Mayo had to say about it. Philip's were the legal brains which enabled NFC's pioneering buy-out to happen. In politics he had started as a member of the Liberal Party but by the time of the buy-out in the early 1980s he had already for many years been prominent in his local Conservative party and as a

Conservative councillor in his home town of Hemel Hempstead. At the end of the NFC case study I shared with readers his commentary – part critique and part lament – on the Conservative Party's privatisation record down to the early 1990s. Given a combination of its force and his credentials for making it, it is well worth citing again. It figured in a letter written to me shortly before his most untimely death in early 1993:

> It is a sad expression of the dysfunctioning nature of capitalism in this country that the later privatisations took on board our experience in reaching out to ordinary people as investors; but only to use it to create a new sort of gambling chip for 'Sid' to play with. Not, as we hoped, a new sort of ownership for industry.

C · BIG CHALLENGES, DESPITE SOME REAL PROGRESS

I would speculate that the majority of the top Tory politicians of those years had no serious wish to see a 'new sort of ownership for industry'. In part, no doubt, that had to do with the close links between the party and the almost all powerful financial community in the City of London. It is true that Barclays Merchant Bank – as it then was – made a killing on its holding of NFC shares between the buy-out and the float. But my guess is that the overwhelming majority of top City people, like their top Tory counterparts, and indeed the top civil servants, had no serious wish then and still had no serious wish in early 1997, to see a 'new sort of ownership for industry'. To be fair, I have no real doubt that the same was true at that time of least a large majority of the country's top trade union leaders and top industrialists. And I suspect it was still true when Mr Major lost the election of 1 May 1997.

The fact is that despite quite a flow of rhetoric in favour of employee ownership and participation from managers and trade union leaders alike, there is a huge reluctance on both sides to make any really courageous moves to promote significant deals of any ESOP kind. Those close to the early stages of the railway privatisation deals in 1996 reported numerous examples of a proclaimed management interest in the involvement of rank-and-file employees in the deals they were hoping to clinch. At least one of the railway unions also made some supportive noises in favour of securing some employee ownership when the undertakings were privatised. But when real decision time came, the managers typically preferred to keep any prospective capital gains to themselves. On the other side the union leaders felt that they would be more comfortable if their familiar role was not exposed to any possibility of modification as a result of their members becoming significant employee shareholders.

The pity of it is that even when employee ownership has come about and has succeeded either in saving jobs or perhaps securing worthwhile capital gains for rank and file employees, or even both, there seems to be a very widespread propensity on both sides, by management and union people, to slip back into the old adversarial relationship and even to express satisfaction about having done so. Among the case studies Weirton Steel offers the most glaring example and Republic Engineering Steels is not far behind. But David Wheatcroft, the long-serving employee director on Chesterfield's buses and someone who has already made a number of appearances in this book, tells me that there are plenty of examples in the bus industry: of both managers and trade union leaders who have 'gone back' to the old adversarial relationships with relief and even with enthusiasm.

It is those attitudes rather than any deficiencies in the law, or any prospective financing difficulties, which will inhibit the spread of employee ownership in Britain – and indeed elsewhere – over the remaining years of this century and into the next one. I sometimes think that one day it may be possible to *shame* British managers and union leaders, by confronting them with the contradiction between their rhetoric and their actions, to make a serious commitment to a major employee-ownership project. I sometimes think too that the growing body of positive empirical evidence will eventually provoke a quite widespread change of mind.

And yet, it is also reasonable to point out that by comparison with anything of this kind which has ever happened before, the progress of employee ownership over the period of roughly twenty-five years, since Louis Kelso persuaded Russell Long to become the political champion of employee ownership in the US has been of a new kind. We need not go over the numbers again, nor the empirical evidence for success. But let me remind readers, with a a series of quick flash ups, of developments which would surely have been beyond anyone's dreams before the 'new era' started.

In 1996 one of the most famous of New York's investment banks, J. P. Morgan, makes a telephone call to a trade union office and asks to be kept informed if the union officials get advance information of any buy-out deal similar to the one which they completed roughly two years before. Admittedly the union was not an altogether normal one but the Airline Pilots' Association (ALPA). And admittedly the company was a little bit special too – one of the foremost airlines in the US. But the point is that the deal had not been an affair measured in peanuts but in billions of dollars (from rather over $2bn to just less than $5bn depending on how measured).

After more that seven years' experience of 'employee ownership lending', Britain's Unity Trust Bank, in which the country's leading trade unions are the majority shareholders, reported in 1996 that its bad debts from that lending were sharply less than for its lending to more conventional businesses.

Over the twenty-five years to the middle 1990s those working in two of Britain's most long-established, but otherwise very different, employee-owned businesses – The John Lewis Partnership and Equity Shoes – enjoyed average annual bonuses, on top of fully competitive wages and salaries, of over 15%.

In Italy, the country with easily the largest population of industrial co-ops in today's Western Europe, a top manager in one of the most successful of them launched, in the autumn of 1996, a strong initiative aimed at introducing 'Anglo-Saxon style' employee ownership law in his country.

Contrary to the still overwhelming orthodoxy of the professional economists in the classical liberal tradition, a few brave voices started to ask important questions in the 1990s. Perhaps the key one was this. Is it likely that optimum performance will be achieved by systems of corporate government which put the interests of passive outside shareholders in the driving seat and exclude the vast majority of those whose task it is to deliver the desired performance?

Perhaps after all something has started to change. Perhaps if it goes on, well just perhaps, those who can be classified in Adam Smith's 'middling and inferior stations in life' will eventually find themselves among the beneficiaries. Perhaps, just perhaps, as a spin-off from these changes there will be both more jobs and more fairness, and even conceivably better parenting, less crime, and less sitting in front of the television. But don't count on it and don't for a moment expect the action to speed up of its own accord. The vested interests and class prejudices against that happening are far too strong. Even to prevent the process from sliding back is likely to require unusual efforts.

It may not be too much to claim that starting from about 1995 the near consensus of mainstream intellectual, political and business support for the Reagan and Thatcherite economic policies of the 1980s and early 1990s began to show some cracks. In relation to America, I remember an important article by Simon Head which was published by the *New York Review of Books* in the spring of 1996 and given a striking title: 'The New Ruthless Capitalism'. Its theme, later to be re-echoed all over America and elsewhere, was that despite the continued growth of the country's productivity, the real wages of blue collar America were no higher in the early 1990s than they had been in the early 1970s. Virtually all the gains of a twenty-year period had gone, either in the form of higher salaries or higher dividends, to the better off and the biggest gains to those at the top. The article, in short, offered a most serious critique of contemporary American capitalism but not one which started from socialist premises or that wished to abandon the free enterprise system.

But the article itself was perhaps less significant than the way its themes were taken up across the American political spectrum. Its themes were taken up by the luckless Robert Dole, then campaigning in the primaries for the Republican nomination.

Then, early in 1996, the consensus in America behind the Reagan and Thatcherite orthodoxy was again challenged – this time by a voice even, perhaps, more unexpected that of then leading candidate for the Republican Party's presidential nomination. This was the multi-billionaire Hungarian financier and philanthropist, George Soros. His uneasiness about what I may crudely call the 'excesses' of contemporary capitalism was voiced in an article published in *Atlantic Monthly* early in 1997 and reproduced around the world. This is not the place for even the briefest summary of his arguments. But I can't resist noting that they were immediately subjected to the most dismissive criticism in a short and maddeningly know-all piece in the *Economist*. Equally predictable was the editorial hostility of *Forbes Magazine* which ran an article headed 'Beware of Billionaires Bringing Gifts.' But Mr Soros stuck to his guns and rapidly expanded his article into a book, *The Crisis of Global Capitalsim* (1998).

The ground swell of a similar non-socialist critique of the same Reagan and Thatcherite orthodoxy was also increasingly in evidence in Britain in the early 1990s. Here the running was brilliantly made by the economic journalist Will Hutton whose book, *The State We're In*, was an instant bestseller and who was appointed to be editor of the *Observer* in 1996.

It is true that Hutton's critique was widely condemned as 'populist' and or 'unhelpful' and 'simplistic' by commentators in the mainstream of Britain's economic orthodoxy. But at least some of his criticisms were later echoed, even if in modified form, by for example the widely respected business journalist who contributes frequently to the *Financial Times*, John Plender.

Two overlapping anxieties about the consequences of the Reagan and Thatcherite orthodoxy are perhaps common to all these critics. One is about the hugely inequitable redistribution of the fruits of economic success which has come in with them. The second is about how it is characteristic of the new-style capitalism to be exclusive rather than inclusive in its embrace, and to be so both inside and outside actual businesses themselves. These anxieties prompt the question whether a more human, and thus almost certainly more labour-orientated, capitalism needs to be sought if the system is not to become so unpopular as to call into question its own survival.

And that at last brings me to the possible qualification about the persuasiveness of my evidence for the advantages of employee ownership which I signalled earlier in this final chapter but deferred for discussion to this final stage. It seems to me that at the level of the individual firm, and at that of groups of firms, we are now entitled to be sure that if best practice is followed performance will be at least as good as under conventional capitalism and more often better. There is also I think a strong presumption – to be validated or otherwise by the research just getting under way in Imola – that these businesses when they become reasonably well established will produce quality of life benefits for those in their local communities.

But there is still perhaps an important unknown. What might be the consequences if a largely employee-owned capitalism was to replace the conventional variety not only in a firm or a group of firms but quite widely across a national economy. No doubt, if nothing else, we can predict that a dramatic move in that direction – as opposed to a slow incremental process – would precipitate a flight of mobile capital.

However it is not that, but the likely comparative performance of a substantially employee-owned economy which needs to be examined. Moreover I have a rejoinder to the obvious objection that no such substantially employee-owned economy exists and thus cannot be examined. There are possible proxies given that what we are really wanting to find out about is the comparative performance of a more human, more people-orientated and indeed more labour-orientated system always within a free enterprise framework.

It seems to me that the German economy offers one proxy for what we want to know more about. I would also argue that Japan offers another. In the case of Germany, and in comparison with both Britain on the one hand and Europe's three main Latin countries on the other, a Dutch economist, Dr de Jong, has already done some important preliminary work. For what it is worth, his research seems to suggest that the greater labour orientation of the German economy has stood it in good stead, at least for most of the last forty-odd years. On the other hand, there are important recent studies of the effective use of capital by German businesses on one side and by their US counterparts on the other. These apparently suggest that by this measure the less labour-orientated 'Anglo-Saxon' capitalism achieves hugely better results.

The starting point of this book was the widespread surviving discontents with conventional capitalism and my sympathies with them. Those who share those sympathies should also share my view that we need a better understanding of the comparative performance of capitalisms which are more or less orientated towards labour. That for me is the big unknown which now cries out to be examined. Employee ownership is only one form, if perhaps the most radical one, which a more labour-orientated capitalism can take. But we now know that it can work, and work well, at the level of individual firms or groups of firms. I think we can also be confident that it offers undoubted benefits to those at the middle and lower levels of enterprise wage scales. Surely the records over many years of the John Lewis Partnership and Equity Shoes tell us that. I hope that people so placed on those wage scales won't mind if I equate them with those in Adam Smith's 'middling and inferior stations' and suggest a) that employee ownership could modestly increase their share in the returns to their work and b) that their local communities as well as themselves should benefit as a result.

Let me close by attempting to dispose of an obvious but ill-founded objection – that a more labour-orientated economy, like that of Germany, has been experiencing, by virtue of that orientation, much higher levels of unemployment in recent years than its Anglo-Saxon counterparts. I would argue that it is not the sort of labour orientation that goes with employee ownership which is responsible for Germany's high unemployment levels but something very different: a labour orientation which finds its expression in a whole tangle of unhelpful government restrictions – especially those relating to employee dismissals. As my case studies show, the kind of labour orientation embodied in employee ownership need not suffer from any such handicaps at all.

Postscript

Numbers are given in chapter 3 for the total of private and public companies which had introduced all-employee schemes in 1994:

With all-employee profit sharing/share schemes, 1,100

With all-employee SAYE schemes, 1,250

In December 1998 the Treasury published a pamphlet entitled *Consultation on Employee Share Ownership*. It included a table with the 1998 totals for those same two schemes:

With all-employee profit sharing/share schemes, 869

With all-employee SAYE Schemes, 1,201

In the case of the US, the latest data comes from an academic rather than an official source. Professor Richard Freeman of Harvard University chose employee ownership as the subject of his Lionel Robbins Memorial Lecture, with the title *The Road to Shared Capitalism and Economic Justice*. It will have been noticed that in the discussion of the numbers in the US in chapter 24 there is a superficially bewildering array of statistics. The main explanation is that different sources measure different aggregates. The following numbers are taken from Exhibit 3a in Professor Freeman's lecture:

Shared Capitalist Institutions in US and Multinationals

Millions in 401 K plans	23.1
With some employer stock	6.9
Largely in own firm	2.0
Millions in ESOPs	7.7
Millions in stock ownership	7.0
Millions with all-employee stock options (AESOPs)	5.0
Millions on employee improvement (EI) committees	22.0
Percentage of multinationals with AESOPS/share purchase	27%

In Exhibit 5b of the same lecture, Professor Robbins brings together the results, in relation to employee ownership, of:

Meta-Analyzes and Large Studies of Productivity Effects

ESOPs

All studies	3.3%
Cross-section study	6.2%
Longitudinal study	4.4%

(Cash) Profit Sharing

All studies	5.0%
Longitudinal study	7.4%

Worker Participation in Decisions

All studies	6.0%

Select Bibliography

Adams, Frank, Gordon, Fred and Shirey, Richard, *Co-operative Home Care Associates: From Working Poor to Working Class through Job Ownership*, Boston, ICA Group, 1991.

Andrewes, Professor Anthony, *The Greeks*, London, Hutchinson and Co, 1967.

Auerbach, Felix (translated by Paul Siegfried and Frederic Cheshire), *The Zeiss Works and the Carl-Zeiss-Stiftung in Jena: Their Scientific Technical and Sociological Development and Importance Described*, London, Marshall Brookes and Chalkley, 1904.

Batt, Francis, *The Law of Master and Servant*, 5th edition, London, Sir I. Pitman and Sons, 1967.

Baxi Partnership, *From Participation to Partnership*, Baxi Partnership, 1983.

Belloc, Hilaire, *The Servile State*, London, Constable and Co, 3rd edition, 1927

Berlin, Isaiah, Interview with Nathan Gardal, 'Two Concepts of Nationalism', *New York Review of Books*, 21 November 1991.

Bernstein, Aaron, 'Why ESOP Deals Have Slowed to a Crawl: Few Executives Seem Comfortable Sharing Power with Employees', *Business Week*, 19 March 1996.

Blasi, Joseph and Kruse, Douglas, *The New Owners: The Mass Emergence of Employee Ownership in Public Companies, and What It Means to American Business*, New York, HarperCollins, 1991.

Bradley, Keith and Estrin, Saul, *The Success Story of the John Lewis Partnership: A Study of Comparative Performance*, London, Partnership Research, 1986.

Bradley, Keith and Estrin, Saul, *Does Employee Ownership Improve Company Performance?*, London, Partnership Research, 1988.

Bradley, Keith and Gelb, Alan, *Co-operation at Work: The Mondragon Experience*, London, Heinemann Educational Books, 1983.

Bradley, Keith and Taylor, Simon, *Business Performance in the Retail Sector: The Experience of the John Lewis Partnership*, Oxford, Clarendon Press, 1992.

694   *Select Bibliography*

Brecher, Jeremy, 'Canst Thou Draw Out Leviathan with a Fishhook? A Community-Based Response to an Out-of-Control Economy', Connecticut, Grassroots Policy Project, 1992.

Brierley, Ian and Dolan, Patrick, *A Tale of Two Bus Companies*, London, Partnership Research, 1992.

Brown, Wilfred and Jacques, Eliot, *Changing Culture of a Factory*, London, Tavistock Publications, 1951.

Bullock, Alan, *Report of Committee of Inquiry on Industrial Democracy*, London, HMSO, Cmd. 6706, 1977.

Burke, Edmund, *Reflections on the Revolution in France*, Harmondsworth, Penguin edition, 1982.

Chesterton, G. K., *The Outline of Sanity*, London, Methuen and Co, 1926.

Cole, G. D. H., *A Century of Co-operation*, London, Allen & Unwin for the Co-operative Union, 1947.

Coleman, D. C. *The British Paper Industry 1495–1860*, Oxford University Press, 1958.

Conte, Michael and Lawrence, Helen, *Trends in ESOPs: in Trends in Pensions*, U.S. Department of Labor, Pension and Welfare Benefits, 1992.

Cott, Jeremy and Gilson, Professor Stuart C., *UAL Corporation*, Harvard Business School, 1995.

Darling, Malcolm, 'The Zeiss Works or What a Factory Should Be', in the *Irish Economist*, July 1923.

De Jong, Dr, in *Review of Industrial Organisations*, vol. 10, 1995.

Desroche, H. in Garcia, Q, *Les Co-operatives Industrielles de Mondragon*, Paris, Les Editions Ouvrières, Editions Economie et Humanisme, 1970.

Dore, Ronald, *Taking Japan Seriously*, London, Athlone Press, 1987.

Earle John, *The Italian Co-operative Movement: A Portrait of the Lega Nazionale delle Co-operative e Mutue*, London, Allen & Unwin, 1986.

Eccles, Tony, *Under New Management*, London, Pan Books, 1981.

Ellerman, David, *The Democratic Worker Owned Firm*, Boston, Unwin Hyman, 1990.

Estrin, Saul and Jones, Derek, 'Workers' Participation, Employee Ownership and Productivity: Results from French Producer Cooperatives': in Jones, Derek and Svejnar, J. (edd), *Advances in the Economic Analysis of Participatory and Labour-Managed firms*, vol. 5, Greenwich Conn, JAI Press, 1995.

Flandars, Allan, Pomeranz, Ruth and Woodward, Joan, *Experiment in Industrial Democracy*, London, Faber, 1968.

Fowler, Norman, *The Right Track: A Paper on Conservative Transport Policy*, London, Conservative Political Centre, 1977.

Fruhan, W. E. Jnr, 'Management, Labour and the Golden Goose': in *Harvard Business Review*, Autumn 1985.

Garcia, Q., *Les Co-operatives Industrielles de Mondragon*, Paris, Les Editions Ouvrières, Editions Economie et Humanisme, 1970.

Gates, Jeff, *The Ownership Solution: Towards a Shared Capitalism for the Twenty-First Century*, Harmondsworth, Penguin Books, 1998.

General Accounting Office of the US Govt., *Employee Stock Ownership Plans: Little Evidence of Effects on Corporate Performance*, Washington, DC, 1988. [Ref. GAO/PEMD-88-1, 1988.]

Goyder, George, *The Future of Private Enterprise*, Oxford, Basil Blackwell, 1951.

Goyder, George, *The Just Enterprise*, London, André Deutsch, 1987.

Goyder, George, *The Responsible Company*, Oxford, Basil Blackwell, 1961.

Hardy, Thomas, *Tess of the D'Urbevilles*, Wordsworth Classics, 1995.

Hills, Richard, *Paper Making in Britain 1488–1988*, London, Athlone Press, 1988.

Hoe, Susanna, *The Man Who Gave His Company Away*, Wollaston, Northants, Scott Bader, 1978 and 1995.

Hopkins, George, *Flying the Line*, Washington DC Airline Pilots Association (ALPA), 1982.

Hutton, Will, *The State We're In*, London, Vintage, 1986.

Jackal, Robert and Levin, Henry, *Worker Co-operatives in America*, University of California Press, 1984.

Job Ownership Ltd, *Lagun-Aro: A Report on the Non-Profit-Making Welfare Mutuality at Mondragon*, London, 1982.

John Paul II, Pope, *Laborem Exercens*, Papal Encyclical, Vatican, 1983.

Jones, Ben, *Co-operative Production*, Oxford, Clarendon Press, 1894.

Kardas, Peter, *Comparing Growth Rates in Employee Ownership Companies to their Participatory Competitors*, Washington State Employee Ownership Programme, 1994.

Kelso, Louis O. and Adler, Mortimer J., *The Capitalist Manifesto*, New York, Random House, 1958; reprinted, Westport, Connecticut, Greenwood Press, 1975.

Ketelbey, C. D. M., *Tullis Russell 1809 to 1909*, Fife, Tullis Russell & Co, 1967.

Keynes, John Maynard, *Essays in Persuasion*, London, Macmillan, 1931.

Kirkham, Mavis, 'Industrial Producer Co-operation in Great Britain', unpublished MA thesis, Sheffield University, 1973.

Kornai, Janos, *Growth, Shortage and Efficiency, A Macrodynamic Model of the Socialist Economy*, University of California Press, 1983.

Lamas, Andy, 'Pace of Philadelphia, the Enduring Legacy of Franklin and the Striking Carpenters': in Len Krimerman and Frank Lindenfield (edd), *When Workers Decide: Work Place Democracy Takes Root in America*, Philadelphia, New Society Publishers, 1992.

Leo XII, Pope, *Rerum Novarum*, Papal Encyclical, Vatican, 1881.

Lewis, John Spedan, *Fairer Shares,* London, Staple Press, 1954.

Lewis, John Spedan, *Partnership for All,* London, Kerr-Cross, 1948.

Liberal Party, *Britain s Industrial Future* ('The Yellow Book'), London, Ernest Benn, 1928.

Liebenstein, Harvey, 'Allocative Efficiency versus X-Efficiency', *American Economic Review,* June 1966.

Liebenstein, Harvey, *Beyond Economic Man,* Harvard, 1980.

Lindenfield, Frank, 'The O and O Supermarkets: Achievements and Lessons': in Krimerman, Len and Lindenfield, Frank (edd.), *When Workers Decide: Work Place Democracy Takes Root in America,* Philadelphia, New Society Publishers, 1992.

Locke, John, *Two Treatises on Government,* new edition, Baldwin Printer, 1824.

Loi sur le Développement de L'Iniative Economique, Ministère, de L Economie, des Finances, et du Budget, Paris, 1984.

Lynch, Malcolm, *ESOPs, ECOPs, and Employee Ownership, A Guide for Trade Unionists,* London, Transport and General Workers Union, 1990.

Maclntyre, Loin, *Sir David Russell: A Biography,* Edinburgh, Canongate, 1994.

Mackin, Christopher, 'Employee Ownership and Industrial Relations': in *Perspectives on Work,* Madison, Wisconsin, Industrial Relations Research Association, vol. 1, no 1, April 1997.

Mackin, Christopher, 'Ownership Theory: Rights and Responsibilities': in *Foundation for Enterprise Development (FED) Annual Journal,* La Jolla California, FED, 1996.

McLachlan, Sandy, *The National Freight Buy-Out: The Inside Story,* Macmillan, 1983.

Maslow, Abraham, *Motivation and Personality,* 2nd ed., New York, Harper and Row, 1987.

Meade, James, *Agathatopia, The Economics of Partnership,* Aberdeen University Press, 1989.

Mill, J.S., *Principles of Political Economy,* London, Longmans, 1909.

Morais, Richard, 'Beware of Billionaires Bringing Gifts': in *Forbes Magazine,* 7 April 1997.

National Center for Employee Ownership (NCEO), *The ESOP Reader,* Oakland, California, NCEO, 1998.

Nejad, Aaron, *The Employee Buy-out of the National Freight Consortium,* London, Partnership Research, 1986.

Newman, Steve and Yoffee, Mike, 'Steelworkers and Employee Ownership': *Journal of Employee Ownership and Finance,* 1991.

Oakeshott Michael, 'The Tower of Babel': in *Cambridge Journal* 1 (1948–9); reprinted in *Rationalism in Politics and Other Essays,* London, Methuen 1952.

Oakeshott, Robert, *The Case for Workers Co-ops*, Routledge and Kegan Paul, 1978; 2nd ed., Macmillan, 1990.

Oakeshott, Robert, 'A Neat Exit': in *Financial Times*, 15 April 1986.

O'Boyle, Thomas, article on the then two Zeisses: in West Germany(at Oberkochen), in the G.D.R. (at Jena): in *Wall Street Journal*, 12 January 1989.

Panichas, G. A. (ed.), *The Simone Weil Reader*, Wakefield, Rhode Island, and London, Moyer Bell, 1977.

Partnership Research Ltd (PRL) Case Studies commissioned and published by PRL, London: *Employee Stock Ownership Plans in the United States: An Introductory Study with Material from Two Major Buy-Outs*, 1987.
- *Workers as Entrepreneurs: Two Striking Success Stories from Italy*, 1990
- *The Carl-Zeiss-Stiftung: Its First Hundred Years of Impersonal Ownership*, 1990.
- *Struggling to Be on the Same Side: The Experience of Republic Engineered Steels Inc (RESI), after a Union-led Employee Buy-Out*, 1991.
- *World Leaders in Low Voltage Cables and Luncheon Vouchers: A Study of Two Outstanding Industrial Co-operatives in France*, 1992.
- *The Winding Road to 'X' Efficiency: The First Ten Partnership Years at Baxi*, 1993.
- *Using an ESOP to Save and Sustain Jobs: The First Ten Years of Employee Ownership at Weirton Steel*, 1994.
- *Progress Towards Getting on the Same Side: The First Four Years of Employee Ownership at RESI*, 1994.
- *The United Steelworkers of America and Employee Ownership: An Exemplary Contribution to the Preservation of Jobs and the Improvement of Business Performance*, 1994

Pepper, S. W., *100 Years of Equity*, Equity Shoes, Leicester, 1986.

Petzinger, Thomas, Jnr, *Hard Landing*, Times Business (Random House), New York, 1995.

Pigou, A. C. (ed.), *Memorials of Alfred Marshall*, London, Macmillan, 1925.

Porter, Michael, *The Competitive Advantage of Nations*, London, Macmillan, 1990.

Putnam, Robert, *Making Democracy Work*, Macmillan, London, 1990.

Rodgers, Loren and Freundlich, Fred, 'Nothing Measured, Nothing Gained': in *Employee Ownership Report*, Oakland, California, NCEO, January/February 1998.

Rosen, Corey, Klein, Katherine and Young, Karen, *Employee Ownership in America*, Lexington, Mass., D.C.C. Heath, 1986.

Schumacher, E. F., *Small Is Beautiful, A Study of Economics as if People Mattered,* London, Vintage, 1983.

Sloan, Rachel, *Co-operatives in Community Care: A Multiple Case Study,* London, Partnership Research, 1996.

Sloan, Rachel, 'NPS Shoes', Unpublished Research Note, London, Partnership Research, 1992.

Smith Adam, *The Theory of Moral Sentiments,* D. D. Raphael and A. L. MacFie, edd., Oxford, Clarendon Press, 1976.

Soros, George, 'The Capitalist Threat', in *Atlantic Monthly,* February 1997.

Tawney, R. H., *The Acquisitive Society,* London, George Bell, 1921; republished, Wheatsheaf Books, 1982.

Temple, William, *Christianity and Social Order,* Shepheard-Walwyn for SPCK, London, 1942; new edition, 1976.

Uvalic, Dr Milicia, *The 'Pepper Report', the Promotion of Employee Participation in Profits and Enterprise Results in the Member States of the European Community,* European University Institute, 1 - 50016 San Domenico, Florence, Italy, 1980.

Vanek, Jaroslav, *The General Theory of Labour Managed Market Economies,* Cornell University Press, 1970.

Vienney, Claude, L'Economie du Secteur Co-opératif Français, Paris, Editions Cujas, 1966.

Webb, Beatrice and Sidney, *A Constitution for the Socialist Commonwealth of Great Britain,* published privately by the authors, London, 1921.

Wedderburn, Lord, *The Worker and the Law,* London, Penguin Books, 1965.

Weil Simone, translated by A.F. Wills, *The Need for Roots,* London, Routledge and Kegan Paul, 1952, reprinted 1995.

Weiner, Dr Hans (ed.), *Bismarck to Bullock,* London, Anglo-German Foundation, 1983.

Weiner, Dr Hans, *Mondragon Revisited,* London, Anglo-German Foundation, 1987.

Weitzman, Martin, *The Share Economy,* Harvard, 1990.

Wright, Mike, Dobson, Paul, Thompson, Steve, and Robbie, Ken, Occasional Paper 38: *Buy-Outs in the Local Bus Industry,* Centre for Management Buy-Out Research (CMBOR), University of Nottinghham. 1992.

Whyte, W. F. and K. K., *Making Mondragon,* Cornell, 1988.

Wiles Peter, *Schumpeter's Vision,* London, Praeger, 1981.

Wolff, Edward N., *Top Heavy: A Study of the Increasing Inequality of Wealth in America,* New York, 20th Century Fund Press, 1995.

Index